PLANET
MEDICINE

PLANET MEDICINE

Origins

RICHARD GROSSINGER

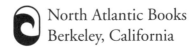

North Atlantic Books
Berkeley, California

Planet Medicine

Published by
North Atlantic Books
P.O. Box 12327
Berkeley, California 94712

Cover art by Sergei Ponomarov
Cover and book design by Paula Morrison
Typeset by Catherine E. Campaigne

Printed in the United States of America

Planet Medicine is sponsored by the Society for the Study of Native Arts and Sciences, a nonprofit educational corporation whose goals are to develop an educational and crosscultural perspective linking various scientific, social, and artistic fields; to nurture a holistic view of arts, sciences, humanities, and healing; and to publish and distribute literature on the relationship of mind, body, and nature.

Library of Congress Cataloging-in-Publication Data
Grossinger, Richard. 1944–
    Planet medicine / Richard Grossinger.—6th ed.
    v. <   >. cm.
    Includes major revisions.
    Includes bibliographical references and indexes.
    Contents: v. 1. Origins— v. 2. Modalities
    ISBN 1-55643-179-1 (paper)
    1. Holistic medicine.   2. Alternative medicine.   I. Title.
R733.G76   1995
610—dc20   95-22428
                                                   CIP

1 2 3 4 5 6 7 8 9 / 98 97 96 95

I dedicate this book to those whose vision, compassion, and acts of healing made it possible:

Paul Pitchford

Randy Cherner

Amini Peller

Elizabeth Beringer

Richard Strozzi Heckler

Ron Sieh

Cybèle Tomlinson

ACKNOWLEDGMENTS

T HE PEOPLE WHO helped me the most with the material in this book are noted in the dedication and throughout the book. Here I would like to acknowledge those colleagues who contributed directly to the preparation of the text.

I acknowledge and thank Amy Champ for her research on the "Practical Ethnomedicine" chapter of *Origins;* Don Hanlon Johnson for his thorough reading and comments on the entire manuscript; Michael Salveson, Elizabeth Beringer, John Upledger, Bonnie Bainbridge Cohen, Judyth Weaver, Fritz Smith, and Dana Ullman for their reading and comments on particular sections of the text; Kathy Glass for her thoughtful and patient editing; Victoria Baker for her exceptional index; Paula Morrison for her elegant and spirited design; Catherine Campaigne for her technical work in the preparation of the finished book; Janna Israel for her updating of the bibliography; Jay Kinney and Richard Smoley of *Gnosis* for their assistance in finding artwork; and Sergei Ponomarov, Spain, Kathy Park, Alex Grey, and Kathy Maguire for drawing images specifically to fit in the text.

We come from an unknown place and go to an unknown place. These do not concern me. But the trajectory of my life, which I share with this body, does.

I want us all to participate in reconstructing the temple, to heal the planet, which is a masterpiece in danger.

—Jean Louis Barrault (the mime in *Les Enfants de Paradis*)

TABLE OF CONTENTS

*Table of
Contents*

TABLE OF ILLUSTRATIONS

Many of the illustrations in this book are used in clip-art style from a wide variety of sources. They include rock art, cave paintings, indigenous graffiti, codex glyphs, Buddhist woodcuts, amulet insignias, pottery motifs, old European alchemical and scientific books, contemporary scientific texts, Asian medical books, and traditional totemic designs from the different regions of the Earth. Because some of this material was collected from secondary and tertiary sources, including torn pages from old books sold separately at used bookstores, complete citations are not always possible.

Table of Illustrations

Table of
Illustrations

ORIGINS

WHEN RICHARD GROSSINGER invited me to write a preface to his Sixth Edition of *Planet Medicine,* I felt simultaneously complimented, privileged, and overwhelmed. Richard then eased my anxiety during a conversation in which he told me that a "preface essay" would be fine. So, a "preface essay" it is.

Planet Medicine is truly a classic work. The author has done an excellent and thorough job of placing "medicine," as most of us in this hemisphere currently know it, in perspective. He shows us where it came from, he discusses quite effectively many of the influences that our modern medicine has received along the way, and he lets us know where we are at the moment. It seems strange that with all of our modern technology and scientific genius we have created something as obsolete as a "medical dinosaur." It just doesn't work, and if it doesn't evolve into a more adaptable and functional form, it will collapse and pass out of existence, as will the species that practices it and possibly the planet upon which it is practiced.

In our present American health-care system, we do not really offer health care—we offer disease curing, and whether or not we really cure disease is debatable. I'm not sure that we define disease at all correctly. If curing means fixing the cause of the disease, we seldom do that in our present "health-care" system. More correctly we are in the business, underline business, of symptom suppression and cause obscuring. We have trouble defining "health"—so how can we "care" for it?

In my own experience of interaction with patients since 1963 as an osteopathic physician and surgeon, I have come to define health quite simply as the organism's ability to adapt to and accept the challenges of the milieu in which it lives. The adapting organism must have the freedom of motion, the mobility to change. Therefore, to me health becomes synonymous with motion. Similarly, disease is stasis. The ability to adapt requires that freedom of motion. By motion I mean motion way down on the ionic, atomic, molecular, and cellular levels. I mean that fluids must be free to move and interchange with other fluids and to transport the tiniest particles in and out of the various real and virtual compartments of the organism's body. All of the movement must be effective and in response to the grand commands from whatever commanders govern that body as well as its psyche. By "psyche" I mean to include all aspects of the mind, the emotions, and the soul or spirit. In this sense health must then include one's ability to evolve, and to survive while evolving.

In our present system of "health care" a disease is not really diagnosable until it presents categorizable symptoms. By the time that the symptoms and signs fit into one of the diagnostic categories, the disease has usually reached a level of significant advancement. Hans Selye in his book *In Vivo* describes one of his early experiences as a medical student in which a professor presented a patient to the class for diagnosis. When finally the class came to the realization that the patient was undiagnosable, he explained that the patient was sick. He then explained that the disease only becomes diagnosable after the sickness (or disease) has advanced to an identifiable level. In our present system we are often required by regulations to diagnose before we can officially treat. Therefore, the patient must be sick enough to be diagnosed before help can be given, except in the form of supportive care and rest. Or the patient can turn to one of the branches of non-reimbursable alternative medicine which makes diagnosis and prescribes treatment on a very different level than conventional American medicine.

Certainly, our present "health-care" system does not recognize the possibility that a deep, hidden conflict within the patient is making him or her dysfunctional, or uncomfortable, or anxious, or just plain sick. Nor does it recognize that a symptom may be the patient's inner voice trying to gain attention for some meaningful lesson that this patient must learn before he or she can progress along their evolutionary pathway. The pathways to self-discovery, enhanced levels of health and higher levels of evolution are seldom traveled without some pain and anguish. Our present "health-care" system focuses on removing the pain with analgesics and quieting the anguish with mind altering drugs. This approach seems counterproductive if the goal is to assist the patient along an evolutionary pathway.

Over the years, my observations of people and patients suggest that as human beings we are seldom able to learn significant lessons in comfort. We seem to require challenges with varying levels of pain and discomfort in order to learn our life's deep lessons. We seldom go quietly with life's guides. More often we have to be dragged kicking and screaming to a mirror, and forced then to look at ourselves for as long as it takes to realize "what fools we mortals be."

In our modern "health-care" system I agree with Grossinger that a majority of allopathic physicians and some of the others have become warriors. They fight the disease. There is a confusion in this system between defeating disease and facilitating healing. When the physician does battle with the disease and "wins," the patient usually loses for at least a couple of reasons. First and foremost, the patient has been deprived of the experience of self-healing. The self-healing process promotes self-love and spiritual growth. Second, and just as important, the patient may very well have been deprived of the lesson that the disease was trying to present. Thus the lesson has been suppressed for the time being, and the inner or higher self of the patient must then find another way to gain attention and represent the lesson. The next presentation may be in the form of a more serious disease than the last. If the suppressions of the diseases continue and the lesson is not learned, it seems inevitable that ultimately a non-suppressable ("incurable") disease will be presented. Then the patient must die and begin again.

On the other hand, if the physician warrior loses the battle with the disease, he or she may become angry at the patient. One of the favorite words which this type of physician applies to such a patient is "non-compliant." Many ego-inflated physician warriors create scenarios wherein when the patient gets superficially well, the physician gets the credit. When the patient does not get superficially well, the patient gets the blame. They didn't do it as they were instructed or advised to do it. So the physician warrior maintains the "hero" status.

Healing and curing need clear definition. It is my own belief that healing can only occur when one heals within his or her self. Unpopular though it may be, I have a strong feeling deep in my gut that when a proclaimed healer does his/her healing work on a patient it should be called "curing." I view healing as something that must come from within the patient. It requires a resolution or a learning within the patient's core which likely originates from that patient's higher self. The so-called "healer" who imposes his/her "healing" by working with supposed energetic or even spiritual levels may possibly be considered an "allopathic healer." This "healer" is not using scalpels and pharmaceuticals; rather, he or she may be using rituals, recruited energies, and the like. If the reason, purpose, or lesson for the disease is not first realized and moved towards acceptance and resolution, then this form of "healing" may also be disease suppression. This poses the same kind of problem as surgical intervention.

I am not convinced that every disease or symptom has a deep underlying lesson or reason for its existence. I do still believe in accidents and chance. But, I believe that every symptom or disease should be explored for deep meaning and given the chance to speak and teach before it is suppressed or eradicated. And I do largely equate suppression and eradication with cure as we use the word in modern scientific medical circles. On this basis I am cautious when in the presence of self-proclaimed "healers." I suspect that the self-proclaimed healer may be a physician warrior in disguise.

It does little good to criticize a system without offering a way to improve it. I have worn the moccasins of those I criticize and so have no

guilt or shame in taking the position from which I speak my critical words. In the beginning of my career as a "health-care" professional, I was a *doctor*. I fixed people, I cured people, I cut out diseased parts of their bodies, and I did this for over a decade. A few experiences began to show me that there was a time to die. I saw that perhaps some degree of suffering and pain might be beneficial. I became a *physician*. <u>In my view, physicians do more teaching and less fixing or curing.</u> I began to realize that to some degree the patient must accept responsibility. In order to accept responsibility, the patient needs to be educated. I began to offer this education as best I could.

The next step along my own evolution as a "health-care" professional was when I began to see myself more as a *therapist*, which to me signified less curing and fixing than I did as a physician. I also talked less about my own views of the problem to the patient. I offered softer treatment and tried to elicit more of the patient's views. I soft-pedaled my own opinions. Over the past ten to fifteen years (I have been seeing patients for more than thirty years at this writing in 1994), I have ~~Since 1964~~ watched myself become a *facilitator* and a *mirror*. I am happy with how I do things now. I give my total effort to the facilitation of the patient's own self-healing process. I rely heavily upon my ability to mirror back to the patient what they are doing with and to themselves. In order to be a facilitator and a mirror, you have to get your own "baggage" out of the therapeutic-facilitative setting. You have to suspend your own judgment. You have to elicit the patient's judgment of themselves. You have to negotiate between the parts of each patient that are in conflict and so on and so on. Each patient is a teacher. Each patient ultimately becomes my therapeutic-facilitator as I am theirs. Sometimes the depth at which we communicate is awesome and sacred. Each patient is a privilege.

The methods I use in my practice are mostly CranioSacral Therapy, SomatoEmotional Release, and Therapeutic Imagery and Dialogue. I still do some manual medicine, some acupuncture, some pharmacological medicine, some exercise treatment, and some nutritional therapy. But, most of my work centers on the first three methods. Encompassed in them are concepts of the power of intention, intentioned and loving touch, tissue memory, energy cysts, respect for any patient's belief system, and stasis is disease/motion is health.

As an example of the kind of method I now follow as my first choice, let me present to you the following interesting and unique case. Fortunately for us, Joyce has given me permission to write this for your information. Even though we have permission, I am not going to use Joyce's last name here.

Joyce has been a student of CranioSacral Therapy since April 1991. She continued to study through the Advanced level course, which she completed in April 1993. Joyce practices as a massage therapist.

In August 1993 she discovered some suspicious lumps in her right breast. On August 31, 1993, a lumpectomy was done. The laboratory report, a copy of which is reproduced and included as Appendix A, indicated a highly malignant form of breast cancer. The pathological report named this cancer as a "moderately differentiated, infiltrating duct adenocarcinoma." There were also a large number of lumps in her armpit, which presented suspicious evidence that the cancer had spread. These lumps were not biopsied at the time of the breast lumpectomy. Joyce was scheduled for a modified radical mastectomy.

Shortly after Joyce received the news of the cancer diagnosis, she called me and asked if we could do some sessions. She came to Florida and we did two sessions together, September 20 and September 21, 1993. During these sessions Joyce was able to discern the reason for her cancer through the use of SomatoEmotional Release with Therapeutic Imagery and Dialogue. Once the underlying reason for the cancer was acknowledged and understood, Joyce was able to negotiate with her Higher Self to turn the malignant cells back into normal cells. Nothing was said about the tumors disappearing; it was only agreed that they would no longer be malignant.

After two sessions Joyce felt confident and ready to return home. She was sure that her cancer had turned non-malignant.

Upon her return, both her husband and her surgeon prevailed upon her to have the breast removed surgically along with the lymph nodes in the armpit. After much discussion and argument, Joyce agreed to the surgery. The operation was performed on September 30, 1993. It was essentially uneventful and Joyce healed normally.

What is so unique about Joyce's case is that none of the tissues removed at the time of the surgery showed any signs of the cancer. This includes the whole breast and twenty-nine lymph nodes from the armpit. The breast tissue showed that some fatty tissue was degenerated (fatty necrosis) and that there were many giant cells present. These cells clean up debris. The pathology report is included as Appendix B.

What happened to the cancer? It is possible that Joyce prevailed upon the cancer control system to reverse its activity in view of the fact that she now understood the reasons for the cancer and promised to change her lifestyle, her behavior, and her life philosophy as directed by her Higher Self.

This approach requires faith and deep trust, but I have seen it work on more than one occasion.

I advise Joyce never to even think about breaking her promises to her self and her Higher Self. If those parts of her that began the cancer in the first place and then took it away should feel any sense of betrayal, I'm sure that they can bring the cancer back again.

Richard Grossinger, thank you for a wonderful book and thank you for the privilege of contributing a "preface essay." I hope with all my heart and all my being that people will read your words of wisdom and truth. I hope that they will see the balance between criticism and optimism. I hope that we can break the chains of the present "health-care" power structure and the territorial and monopolistic hold that it has upon us. I hope that we can learn to heal ourselves with the help of caring and open-minded facilitators and mirrors.

John E. Upledger, D.O., O.M.M.
Palm Beach Gardens, Florida

Preface

INTRODUCTION TO THE SIXTH EDITION

THE BULK OF *Planet Medicine* was written between 1976 and 1978 and published by Doubleday/Anchor Books in 1980. It was republished by Shambhala/Random House in 1982, at which time I revised the chapter on Wilhelm Reich and wrote an epilogue ("How to Choose a Healer"). Three subsequent editions have appeared from North Atlantic Books. The 1985 edition was substantially the same as the final Shambhala edition. For the 1987 edition I made further revisions in the chapter on Wilhelm Reich and added a foreword on "the epistemology of cure." In the 1990 edition I added a long suffix ("Planetary Healing") that in essence rewrote the entire book in miniature.

Unlike those predecessors, this 1995 edition in two volumes is an entirely different book.

THE SIXTH EDITION OF *Planet Medicine* had its beginnings in the fall of 1992 as my draft of another book, one exploring somatics, Buddhism, shamanic initiation, and their points of connection. Most people write new books rather than rewrite published ones, and such was my intention. Yet, no matter where I searched for clear ground, I found *Planet Medicine* in the way.

By 1992 I had not read my own book in over ten years and did not remember its exact contents. Nonetheless I intuited that many of the new ideas I was trying to articulate had their origin in that book's unfinished themes. When I finally reread *Planet Medicine* from start to finish, I was appalled at its sloppiness and lack of boundaries. It was filled with errors, gaps, repetitions, and diatribes, and the mere attachment of new writing to old without integration had made the book even more amorphous. In addition, much of its contents no longer applied, either for me personally or in the culture at large.

Yet some aspect of *Planet Medicine* overcame these flaws. The heart of the text was compelling and poignant; its propositions remained timely and fresh; and more than anything, it cried out to be finished. Its holistic sections needed updated material, and its critique of the medical establishment needed to be redefined in terms of a spreading crisis of commodization. The bankruptcy of the mainline system, alluded to as a metaphor in 1976, was now a fact. The emergence of a whole new paradigm of medicine, also barely more than a counter-cultural metaphor (and wishful thinking) in 1976, was now a fact as well. So I decided not so much to abandon my new book as to begin it anew in what had become the debris of my earlier assemblage.

T HE 1976–78 EDITION OF *Planet Medicine* was my first expository book. Prior to it I had written only experimental prose in an avant-garde mode or formal academic papers. In *Planet Medicine* I instinctively tried to blend the two styles, to please both my editor at Doubleday and myself. This was successful to the degree that the book took on simultaneously an authority and a sense of freedom and honesty, and unsuccessful to the degree that in some places it read like projective verse, in others like a thesis. There was no way for a reader to distinguish between authentically factual information (ethnography) and, to use the poet Charles Olson's phrase, "causal mythology."

The copy editor at Doubleday/Anchor compounded the problem. Having worked on expository, semi-academic books her entire professional life, she was stuck with this as her farewell project before retirement. She chose to push me into a less poetic, less intuitive-sounding style. In the process I learned a great deal. In fact, her copy-editing taught me how to edit the work of others and was a bridge to my own future expository books. However, in *Planet Medicine,* she left "appearances" throughout the text (i.e., rhetorical constructions covering my tracks to make the best out of what she viewed as a bad situation), thus further blurring the distinction between research and mythology. The result is that the voice in the original *Planet Medicine* tries to posture itself out of its own equivocations and sound authoritative in a way that it is not, exaggerating claims of authenticity and presenting associative ellipses as if discovered truths.

Additionally, under a deadline, I stuck to material already familiar to me or accessible in the culture at large, emphasizing ethnomedicine, homeopathy, and psychoanalysis. My blithe omission of osteopathy, Feldenkrais work, *Chi Gung,* and innumerable other disciplines, along with my superficial portrayals of Chinese and Ayurvedic medicine, polarity therapy, and paraphysical medicines in off-the-cuff riffs, attest to the work's being more a "poem" in the genre of my *Book of the Earth and Sky* than a comprehensive account of medicine. It is also true that the marketplace of alternative medicine has blossomed since 1977: much is accessible now that was a glimmer then. One would have not have been able to find *Chi Gung Tui Na,* Breema, or craniosacral therapy virtually anywhere in 1977.

My decision to rewrite *Planet Medicine* was a result not only of wanting to complete its ethnography and correct its errors but also of having gotten back into its narrative and unresolved arguments, many of which centered on the epistemology of somatic and energetic systems. I could not begin a new somatics book any more effectively than by reopening my unfinished narrative on this subject. Thus, this sixth edition has come to envelop and include so much of my prospective somatics writing that I no longer plan a sequel.

Two residual issues also encouraged a thorough rewriting. First, a Japanese publisher purchased the rights to translate *Planet Medicine,* and I wanted to give them a current version. Second, the continued publication of the book without first-generation pasteup or film ensured difficult-to-read broken typography. No boards or film were ever recoverable from Doubleday, so it was a matter of "shooting the book" and reusing the film. What was in print in 1992 was not only an accumulation of diverse, disorganized material with independent essays at its beginning and end, but a hard-to-read reproduction that was also physically unattractive on the page.

In addition, I had selfish reasons for not wanting to let the book go out of print. *Planet Medicine* has been the most read and influential of my works. It has continued to be used as a text in a growing number of medical anthropology, history-of-medicine, ethics, and related courses in both universities and naturopathic colleges. Over the years I have met at least a hundred practitioners in different holistic fields who credited the book in one or another of its editions with having played a major role in their professional career. *Planet Medicine* was required reading at, of all places, the Food and Drug Administration (FDA) for a period during the 1980s. If, flawed as it was, the original text could accomplish such things, I did not want to lose it as a public statement. I also did not want to continue publishing it or have it translated into more languages in its existing form.

M Y PROCESS OF MAKING a sixth edition began with photocopy-enlarged 1990 pages, rearranged with the help of a pair of scissors and rubber cement. At the initial stage, I chose to eliminate whole sections, including the four entire and two partial chapters on homeopathy, which I updated, enlarged, and turned into an entirely separate book (*Homeopathy: An Introduction for Skeptics and Beginners,* North Atlantic Books, 1993). This established a procedure of revision I used for the rest of the material.

After finishing with the homeopathy, I further edited the repasted *Planet Medicine,* crossing out no longer relevant material at the sentence and phrase level and squeezing corrections into its still-tiny margins with a very sharp pencil. Then, when it was too dense and messy to work with in that form, I had the entire edited text rekeyed. From there I treated it as a first-draft manuscript, changing language freely, taking out sections, and writing whole new ones.

IN REMAKING *Planet Medicine* I have tried, where possible, to preserve the core book with its language. However, there were at least five distinct styles and narrative lines in the edited fifth edition: the original text, the epilogue, the foreword, the suffix, and my 1992–93 writing. These were separate voices, functioning sometimes on quite different and contradictory levels of irony, intellect, and meaning. The current book attempts to blend them into one narrative flow based on subject matter rather than tone. But they don't always blend. I have decided to leave the disjunctions as they are, at a few points putting sections in parentheses, brackets, or sub-sections if they clash too strongly with the flow for my ear. They stand as alternative voices on the same subject matter.

The diatribe against technological medicine, predominantly in the first two chapters, seems dated and shrill to me now. However, it was an important part of the 1977 book. To remove it would make a quite different statement. I suggest that readers think of much of these first two chapters as a journey back into the more dogmatic 1970s. Chapters Seven, Ten, and Eleven in Volume One, and Chapter Seven in Volume Two also contain substantial sections that reflect a 1970s perspective. Although my patchwork more or less holds, at times I find this text to be like a city—new highrises and well-designed neighborhoods in some areas, and renovated slums and old though still habitable apartment buildings in others. Nothing is unlivable, but some parts definitely show the wear and tear.

THE MOST MAJOR REVISION in the sixth edition involved writing through the excision of a hundred or so pages on homeopathy. Taking them out created a gigantic hole. The original book was, in fact, assembled around these four and a half chapters, initially my first draft of an entire book on homeopathy (encouraged by an editor at Harper and Row). When she couldn't sell the project to her superiors in 1976, I offered the chapters to an editor at Doubleday. She read them and came back with a proposal that instead I incorporate them in a gen-

Introduction

eral book on the history and philosophy of medicine. Thus in 1977, I wrote chapters leading up to homeopathy and chapters leading away from it.

To a certain degree, my most substantial objection to the 1976–1990 version of *Planet Medicine* is that it was artificially based on a preexisting analysis of homeopathy. Not only did this distort the larger discussion and lead me to downplay other systems, but it even put homeopathy out of scale and context. Such was the price I paid for not wanting to abandon a piece of successfully finished writing.

The new *Planet Medicine* doesn't drop its story-line to engage "Homeopathy: The Great Riddle," as the earlier version did. It continues building from ethnomedicine and ancient medicine into contemporary alternative systems of healing. This radically alters the meaning and message of the book.

Planet Medicine (versions one through five) invoked as its central theme: how do energy medicines deliver invisible cures? Beneath that was a series of subtexts concerning the meaning and commodization of those cures and the social ramifications and archetypal expression of medicine itself.

Planet Medicine (version six) takes the subtexts of version one as its central theme and then builds toward a demonstration that medicine and disease are crossculturally and epistemologically indistinguishable and that "planet medicine" serves as a vehicle of both entrenchment and transformation in a modern crisis of identity and well-being.

Whereas homeopathy (a magical Jedi sword) was quite rightly the star of version one (at the crest of the counterculture and "May the Force be with you!"), somatics provides a shifting cast of front-line players for version six. These better serve as a medicine for an era of physical devastation and redemption, of both entertainment and politics by sex and violence.

Another task was finding a way to blend the distinct endings emerging from the different voices within the text. The book now ends at least three times: after the "Somatics" chapters, after the last numbered chapter, and after the Suffix. This isn't an elegant solution, but it is a representative one. The plot itself has no single termination.

L ET ME AFFIRM at the outset: I do not consider this book an explication of medical resolutions nor myself an entitled critic of the medical industry. I am writing through gaps and contradictions in all paradigms—mainstream and alternative—toward a new cultural and ontological context for the act of healing. Yet text has a way of forging its own authority; printed words take on an absolutism not indicative of the crises and doubts that underlie their assemblage in sentences. While this text rather seamlessly attacks the superstructures of technological medicine, I myself stand willing to be refuted and sent journeying to an even deeper dialectic. The attack is the only means I have of shattering the seal of silence around a hegemony that is beginning to terrify even its advocates—not the seal that is routinely and ideologically shattered to great hurrahs by medicinal and political radicals but the seal of which neither they nor their foils are aware.

My own personal relationship to all matters herein remains one of ambivalence and irresolution. I write not because I am the spokesperson for an apostate belief system or because I have wonderful new answers to the dilemma of diagnosis and cure. Mainstream medicine in its most conventional guise is still our avowed protector against the Black Plague and other deadly invasions of the human genome. It is our one militia of "good guys." The "doctor" archetype has been an active force all my life, from shadowy figures who came in childhood—some wise and magical, others fumbling and foreboding—to kind professionals who cared for my children when they were young and various M.D.s and healers who extended only patience and compassion to me. I hold no grievance against them or their profession. Likewise, I am not advocating rampant "quackery" over medicine, as some more ideological allopaths might presume. I am not an unquestioning ally of the "New Age" alternative. If anything, I continue to blame myself for a lack of faith in the existing order. It is not that mainstream medicine

Introduction

has earned undying faith from any of us, but I would not recommend either vacuous nihilism or spiritual affirmation as livable alternatives.

I am far more troubled by the specter of a deteriorating planet and a suffering and grief that seem unfathomable and inconsolable than I am triumphant over an exposé of the malefic physician. Would that he could do half the things his advocacy promises and that we could trust him with our lives and deaths. But medicine is merely one song from the abyss. And the overall soundings from the present pandemonium come to us as shrieks beyond nightmares. I am only a little ashamed to say I write this text in flight from such turmoil while turning ever so slightly to face it. Yes, I am afraid. This text is my magical act to turn away goblins who seem to acknowledge no present secular power.

I am searching for another "doctor"— beyond individual roles and cultures—in hopes of exposing and liberating both the mythical devourer of bodies and souls and the healer who stands at the apex of all spiritual systems (as well as at the crossroads of science and religion). I am saying that all doctors share in his twin shadow and epiphany. Because it is not yet clear in our time which of those who come to us bearing the tools of medicine is the healer, which the destroyer, I offer this text as their battleground.

Finally, I am most compelled by the fact that all text—whether published or not—is perishable. All text is revised, if not in actual rewriting, by subsequent unrecorded changes in the mind of the author, where it originated, and by the changing perceptions and cultural perspectives of readers. All text is made up of layers of subtexts and, as the years pass, we go back to them to read, with astonishment, the many hidden layers and unexamined edicts and prejudices of ourselves. Language in that sense is both fresh and prefabricated, and those prefabricated aspects of it that any of us inattentively promulgate get to have their say too, much like the multiple versions of a myth or interpretations of a dream. This edition must suffer the same fate. As has been pointed out *ad nauseam* in the late twentieth century, unconscious agendas of racism, sexism, "speciesism," and other vanities scream out from the writings of authors no longer in a position to quell or camouflage them. Many other, quite different voices scream out also, but they are not yet in vogue, so no one hears them still.

T HE ORIGINAL EDITION OF *Planet Medicine* began a nine-year project of research and writing for me that led to two subsequent works as well: *The Night Sky: The Science and Anthropology of the Stars and Planets* and *Embryogenesis: From Cosmos to Creature—The Origins of Human Biology.* This trilogy as a whole explored the reciprocal syntaxes of atoms, stars, cells, tissues, animals, and symbols, and the moral and epistemological dilemmas of science—which is, after all, the language by which the twentieth century addresses itself.

This sixth edition curiously takes *Planet Medicine* from the beginning of the trilogy to its present position as the terminus. In such an open-ended quest, beginnings become conclusions anyway. The circles of the universe itself, enforced by a new cosmology of light defining relativity of time (or by the old Buddhist doctrine of karma and rebirth), promise that all such adventures return to their beginning to begin again until their arguments are resolved, which they never are. Disease and its "alter ego" cure speak this logos perfectly.

Richard Grossinger
Berkeley, California, 1995

Introduction

PART I

SHAMANS

CHAPTER ONE

Medical Traditions: Lineages and Dichotomies

Alternative Medicines and Their Subtexts

THIS IS A BOOK about healing: its origin in primary and ancient systems of knowledge, its basis as a social category, and its diverse meanings and values, from culture to culture and through human history. Our starting point is the oldest medical images and activities. Though we cannot know these exactly, we imagine them in comparison with our own modes of perception and idea formation, we reconstruct them from Ice Age remnants, and we find their equivalents practiced by tribal peoples in Africa, Australia, Asia, and the Americas. Literacy and civilization bring with them new medical philosophies and models for the behavior of the doctor. This book examines prior hermetic and elemental medicine, medicine of the vital force, and medicine reconciling mind and body. Contemporary thought holds two vying images of the evolution of medicine. From the perspective of progressive technology and global culture, we have finally arrived at a universal industrial medicine. But, from the perspective of the unknown quanta of disease and cure, we must return to primary processes and reinvent a working medicine we no longer have.

During the 1970s our culture used the terms "alternative medicine," "new medicine," and "holistic medicine" almost interchangeably. There are, however, some differences of connotation. "Alternative medicine" describes the general and continuous emergence of systems of treatment in opposition to a universal technological medicine. It includes various ancient and folk medicines that reassert themselves from era to era, as well as idiosyncratic medicines that may derive, at least in part, from aspects of the scientific model. When I speak of the "new medicine," I mean particularly the present constellation of alternative practices that emerged during the last half of the twentieth century in the United States. Although many of these practices are quite old and originate from divergent sources, they share a fresh political and ideological thrust as well as often unstated social and economic alliances. I use "holistic medicine" to suggest the significant similarity between the "new medicine" and traditional medicine as it was practiced in prehistoric and ancient times. In both Stone Age tribes and countercultural clinics, medicine is simultaneously an art, a philosophy, a science, and a craft; it treats the human being as an entity of mind and body in a biological and cultural circumstance from which he or she cannot be extricated.

The danger of accepting the new alternative medicine movement in the innovative and modern terms in which it often tends to view itself is that it engenders a false and shallow sense of invention and breakthrough. There *is* a momentum of creative redefinition different from anything else we have seen lately that represents a break with certain aspects of Euro-American tradition, but its roots still lie deep in Western thought and even deeper in a pre-Western arcanum. How we inherit certain methods and choose them from among the vastness of possibilities is a fundamental issue of this book.

It is important to realize that archetypally medicine is a limitless unplowed field. The diverse paradigms harvested thus far by the human race (including medicines known historically and ethnographically and even those proposed in myths and science-fiction tales) are but a fraction of the actual possibilities. There is thus no medical "encyclopedia" from which cultures sequentially select and reject methods. The true medical encyclopedia contains at least an equal number of unfamiliar paradigms yet to be tried (if the human race survives). These will not

4

be mere refinements or reformulations of existing medicines. They will be utter novelties. Medicine is still—and likely forever—an unfinished work.

However, medical practices come to us in a clear lineage because paradoxically (and in contradiction to the above) all new medicines must arise from old medicines unless they come from other planets or manifest spontaneously from archetypes. What can be declared truly "new" is much more prescribed when we see how each system combines ancient practices and new phenomenologies. In order to understand radical medicines in contemporary terms, we must perceive them initially as seeds, as primal reimaginations of body and mind; only later as systems of practice. Yet there are problems in defining the sources and boundaries of hybridized medicines, especially in distinguishing their pure ideologies from their ranges of effectiveness.

New holistic medicines often promote the same kinds of wishful simplifications that technological medicines do; for instance, whole complex systems get reduced to a prescription of a potentized herb or acupressure on the foot. I was recently visited by a German practitioner of an innovative system of energetics. He had a machine that combined the diagnostic aspects of Chinese acupuncture, the circumstantial "proof" of Kirlian photography, and the curative scope of Reich's orgone therapy. It was a very provocative and optimistic machine, and probably a useful one. What was intolerable, though, was its bearer's insistence that it healed absolutely everything and that other methods of bodywork, polarity, acupuncture, herbs, etc., were now obsolete. When I tried to offer a more subdued assessment, he told me, kindly but patronizingly, that I was simply not informed and thus ignorant of the implications of the breakthrough.

Such claims leave no room for individuality and creative doubt; they are orthodoxies equal to that of allopathy. Human beings are not robots that can be spontaneously vitalized, medicinalized, *chi*-ed, or shamanized into their own higher beings. They are extremely conservative organisms, and their mere contact with a medium, or their reading a book about reincarnation or chanting, or doing a weekend's shamanic or EST exercises, is not going to transform their lives, or even affect each person in the same way. Very concrete, almost miraculous things are possible, but only in gradual ways and with attention to details and idiosyncrasies. There is not yet a universal cure-all or even a metaphor for one.

In fact, we have very limited access to both the fields of disturbance and the fields of treatment. Insofar as we take disease "personally," we overendow the personalities of not only ourselves, doctors, and pharmacists but *Chi Gung* masters, medical dowsers, and directors of biotechnology firms. Even when we know better, we conceive of our ailments as indecencies; thus, depending on our loyalties, we seek a purveyor of magic or miracle drugs to make us well. However, disease is not only self/other and mind/body; it is individual/society, organism/cosmos, and all of these things in relation to one another (cure likewise).

While practitioners of holistic systems go about attempting to cure people and challenging the medical establishment, they inevitably raise other, basic questions concerning laws of nature and the meanings and goals of human life. When we explain these systems to ourselves in terms of "positive thinking" rationales and methodologies, and their anomalous elements are resolved forcibly and only in terms of one mythology or another, validation becomes a mere matter of faith.

It is not enough to assert or even to project energy; one has to direct it, modulate it, and free it from the traps of language. The word "energy" is one of the greatest hindrances to the actual practice of energy medicine. To bypass both the medical and academic authorities and to pretend to resolve our now global crisis by making its redemption spiritual, "holistic"—or both—is a naive overvaluation of our ability to redefine and thereby alter our condition. This overvaluation is a credo of the "holistic health" movement as a New Age religion and the reason why this is not a "holistic health" book.

I am in sympathy with many of the alternative systems, but I have

trouble with their tendencies to present themselves as if coming from a higher authority and as adjudicating all intervening issues of level and meaning. Alternative medicine is no different from existential philosophy, Marxist theory, or urban sociology. It must swim in real lakes and encounter those perennial problems of the human condition every other system encounters.

For some enthusiasts, it is as though, by definition, a vitalistic medicine like homeopathy or *Chi Gung* encounters and activates the palpable life force of the organism, which then distributes its "elixir" to every region of body, mind, and spirit. I do not think this is generally true (if true at all). I also do not think its "lie" negates the often almost-miraculous effects of certain so-defined treatments; it does, however, entail reexamination of their often shrill liturgies.

Many current books advocating forms of alternative healing plunge the reader into the dilemma of post-"new physics" romanticism. "We are not only bodies," we are invariably told. "We are fields of energy, processes, radiant matter. Nothing has reality separate from mind. Our thoughts influence the production of cells in our bodies and transmit primal messages which become diseases and then, under the right circumstances, their spontaneous modes of cure."

The objection to this—I repeat—is clearly not that it is "wrong." On the contrary, it is almost certainly true. However, it is sterile and truistic and by-passes the complications of life as lived. There is a tendency among its advocates to fall back on derivative concepts from theosophy, quantum physics, and parapsychology in place of a precise and hard-won logic or even vision. The real objection is that if this must be the answer, what is the question? What would knowing this about ourselves, or pretending to have such images for our innermost life, tell us about who we are, why we get sick, and how we get better?

It is also true that this Pollyannaism (matter is energy, energy is matter, etc.) disguises a wide range of impasses that differ historically,

*Medical
Traditions:
Lineages and
Dichotomies*

crossculturally, and epistemologically. Fritjof Capra, Larry Dossey, Deepak Chopra, et al., have provided helpful paradigms for viewing this territory, but what is needed now is an opening of the territory itself through something other than an energy-matter paradigm. After all, people still get sick for no discernible reason, and the explanations supplied by pop cosmology often end up in a moralism that mirrors the nihilism of technological medicine.

In our optimism, we are often inclined to accept the holistic cure (because it is, by name, entire) without knowing what it is we want to have cured and whether it is holistic by the same definition.

Moralism and Shamanic Idealism

OUR CONTEMPORARY CONDITION may well be the fulfillment of the archetypal medicine man's dreams, especially of power (at least until he could look more closely). This is not coincidental or accidental, for we are our ancestors' realization, physically and magically (the continua of DNA and totems ensure that). We have taken the medicine bundle which was passed to us and have sought to fulfill our parents' and their ancestors' grail quests and dreams.

The same "medicine man" is real, and he is also a character, cast by "aboriginophiles" in the West to offer a fundamental self-criticism. Decadent and destructive modern civilization is a myth, too. Obviously, in our obsession with the externalization of power, we have suffered a loss in ability to internalize power. Yet any culture gives up things to gain others. Any culture operates within limitations, unexamined imperatives, cruelnesses, and alienations. Just as the "Africans" and "American Indians" were no more backward than nineteenth-century Europe in any absolute sense, so they were no more enlightened than the inhabitants of twentieth-century America by any universal yardstick. Both are part of a planetary process that seems, if not inevitable, at least beyond our power to judge or meaningfully reverse.

Our romanticization of the native and his technologically primitive society heralds the epochal spiritual and material crisis of modern civilization and our troubled quest for a sacred voice, for a morality and rationale in our time. Clarifying that matter (or failing to clarify it) is the background to every expository notion I will engage.

While this book certainly assumes that the West has lost the key to something, all people have lost it, in some way or another. I would rather unravel a few of the many levels of this paradox than go toward any ideological resolution of it. I am interested in disjunction, in finding meaning at the moment of losing it again. I take it that we do not have the answer—not that we have it and do not live it. If we had it, we would live it. There would be no other way. All the combative chatter on this point merely provides grist for various apocalyptic and harmonic-convergence myths that balance each other in our psyches.

The Serbs and Rwandans did not kill their own people because they were stupid or evil. They did so because they were in a trance. Pornography and genocide are not vacuities but diseases, cures in protean form. All these things, hopeless and bankrupt as they are, represent our best attempts—the attempts of the living to heal a primal rift. They are ripples in a horrifying darkness that would devour us all if not for ripples. The rest of "enlightened" mankind do not know how they would behave if they were tossed into the heart of these crises and to what degree pandemonium would take them over. Anything, after all, is potentially lethal, anything potentially curative. As deep as we sink into pathology, that deeply (by definition) are we mobilizing a defense response.

Thus, opinions about degrees of enlightenment, uncorrupted justice, and cultural aesthetics remain cheap, and are inevitably transitory and misleading. "Good guys" and "bad guys" among whole societies is a game that leaves everyone out.

This book suffers from the initial paradox that, while it describes the loss of healing power in the West, it is itself a product of that civilization, the civilization it is attempting to set outside its new, optimistically derived boundary. This cannot finally be possible. If the book says anything hopeful about non-Western healing, it must also be saying an identical thing about Western healing on another level. So my inveterate romanticism must be challenged and then reclaimed if I am to avoid my own traps and leave behind any basis for actual hope and revival.

On the one hand, it is essential that we see the vacuity behind modern arrogance and chauvinism, that we understand the rightness as well as the profundity of non-Western and prehistoric cultures. On the other hand, our glorification of primitive peoples is always an attempt to say something else about ourselves and, by proxy, to enlarge our scope and grandeur. In that sense, it is disingenuous. By criticizing our own racism, sexism, and cultural elitism, we are also boasting about our essential goodness and the range and flexibility of our intellectual hegemony, as if we truly change by changing our documentation and professional ideologies. The Comanche and Cree knew better than to sign papers we called laws. We should also know better than to pretend to sign them ourselves and go over to the other side. At the distance of Chiapas or Sierra Leone our cultural and political correctnesses must look mainly like new means of excusing our academicization of the right to knowledge.

The present humanitarian justification for this monocultural dominion of the Earth is that mankind is one, and our salvation lies eventually in a mutual sharing of all knowledge. Though representatives of Third World peoples have come to share some of this perspective and have participated in our globalism, we still should have no illusions we speak for objective humanity first; we speak for science, modernism, our own utopian fantasies, and the security of the status quo—exactly the kinds of dialectics and diplomacy in which I too am indulging. It is an intellectual and corporate "United Nationalities," not a shamanic one.

Also, we should remember, most so-called "noble aborigines" are not trying to heal us or head us off from disaster. Most of all, they would like to see the wound we have gashed into the Earth swallow us and our entire civilization and then sew itself back together. It is not that reconciliation is no longer possible, but it cannot be on our limp peace-and-love terms.

Sources of Medical Knowledge

INDIGENOUS TRIBES INVITED spirits regularly to their ceremonies, a pact broken by the transition to civilization. We are now in a position of having to recover the ceremony which is also a medicine. Current forms of experimental theater and contact improvisation are working toward this original authenticity, perhaps on an even more profound level than many alternative medicines. Some choreographers use the dance itself to recover lost or unconscious forms of human movement. Their movements are far more disjunctive and elliptical than those in conventional ballet or modern dance, and they also conjure a different level of mind/body. Joanne Kelly, Carolee Schneeman, and Yvonne Rainer are healing dancers, each in her own way. Nancy Stark Smith has made Contact Improvisation a formal therapeutic ritual. Ruth Zaporah has developed a shamanic Buddhist theater. Bonnie Bainbridge Cohen has turned her "dance" into a journey of attention into the mind and expressions of individual organs. Meredith Monk has integrated voices of the American Indian Southwest into her performances; these may not invoke the same things among her audience that they do in the native rite, but they are clues to new curative modes. It is through "crazy wisdom," to use the Tibetans' American translation of their own ancient name for it, that we change as a culture; it is through improvisation that suffocating modes are replaced by dangerous new styles of being, breathing, and moving.

Attraction to images and iconography can mislead. It would be difficult to cure many Euro-Americans by Navaho sand painting and chanting because they would not be attuned to the levels of mythology internalized in the ceremony: they might absorb the exoticism rather than the dynamics. But this does not mean it is impossible. In a familiar healing paradox, an American who does not know a word of Navaho experiences remission of a tumor after such a ceremony, but another Westerner who has studied Navaho for years is unaffected. This is not only because we do not know the active properties of the medicine and the forces involved, but because we do not begin to understand the nature and source of our own resistances to treatment and cure or what attracts us to a pathology in the first place. We do not know on a biochemical level, and we certainly do not know on psychological and parapsychological levels. The individuality of lives outweighs the commonality of the species. The modern allergist practices a pale replica of this protean medicine. The polarity therapist, reaching into the thousands of years of Ayurvedic provings, touches a deeper chord.

OUR MYTHS OF ancient non-Western medicines have arisen in the same context as our novel and alternative medicines *per se.* Although these events are separated by millennia, as is traditional shamanism from Rolfing, the forms of knowing them are contemporaneous. There is no actual account of the various peoples, past and present, of this planet. Our perception of who we are, genetically, socially, historically, is an academically based and kitsch diorama of events that have taken place over millions of years. Our images of alien cultures are reforged continuously of present needs and biases. We have only a series of changing images, politically and economically manipulated, for any period of history—this applies to the origins of healing as much as to the construction of the Egyptian pyramids or the causes of the First World War. The Middle Ages become in our imagination a castle-studded, feudal landscape of Christendom (or some more sophisticated version of the same) despite the actual lives of individual people who lived then. We must drop our standard chronology of medical origins and be open to a less linear and progressive web of lineages.

Shamans and medicine men seem to stand near the beginning of this book. The elemental doctors of the early Eurasian world must have been their unwitting followers and apprentices. By other names, their torch was passed through the European Renaissance, surviving the birth of industrialism, into the modern world. Thus, primitive medicine has no center or limits and exists forever in a vast and undifferentiated field. It originates in the skills of the shaman and the apothecary, whose cures likewise recoil to the beginning of time. Science must literally fold back on itself, millennia later, to discover that it has indispensable roots in prehistoric ceremonies and crafts. We recover this text—i.e., that such forms existed at all—artificially in our archaeology and ethnography, as our formal documentation of "mute peoples." These races and tribes are also a well-disguised fiction which is meant to support us in time from underneath, to justify to us who we are and where we came from. The actual peoples of the past, despite their evocative tombs and bones, are quite incidental now, as they keep "changing" even their own ancestries, genotypes, and Ice Age routes of migration.

Our futurism has always been inextricably linked to our classicism. In many cases, new medicines are launched, consciously or unconsciously, from actual documents or oral accounts of ancient or remote practices. The new thing is the old thing reborn, a variant uniquely suited to our present situation and needs. Ancient Chinese medicine is now Western holistic medicine, but a substantial transmutation lies between the two because neither the practitioners nor their patients, nor even the diseases, exist in the same cultural situation. Anthropological reconstructions of native Peruvian medicine, to take one random example, are "fictions" of exactly the same order. They retain some element of authenticity, but their real meaning to us is in our ongoing transformation of them. For convenience, we will overlook this proviso in many parts of this book, but it is still the framework in which we should approach all non-Western systems, even those fully reclaimed and integrated in holistic circles.

Religion and mythology recreate origins in the hope that our sheer depth as beings will correct for the loss of information and thinning out of creative intensity over time. Certainly philosophy looks inward for basic laws of nature, and science and mathematics are as much reflections of the mammalian mind as they are replicas of some outer world. "The interior is anterior,"[1] proposed theosophist Owen Barfield. That is, the primal complexity of the earliest systems (whether of matter itself, or of thought, or of language), as well as the specific transformations and evolutions of their fabrics over thousands and millions of years, are contained entirely in the present system in some other form, even as gaps left by absences. The ineluctable continuities—of matter and energy, of DNA, of cultural tradition—ensure that ancient modes are locked into current modes. They are contained there not at the surface or by simple parallel. They are contained in depth. Looking inside ourselves, into the flux of mind and matter that we are, we can perceive the sum of remote influences of which we are the result. As they are anterior to us in time and space, they become interior to our physical and psychic recomposition. From here alone we continue to refresh and revive institutions. Technology notwithstanding, salvation from outside is not a possibility.

Yet virtually a fanaticism of this century and its professional life is omission of the inside of things. I take this as a political event. People have staked their reputations and occupational integrity on the fields of inquiry as they are presently constellated. To bring in materials that cannot be exteriorized, objectified, and categorically assigned by the academic mind is to threaten the corporate security of the individual disciplines. But I do not take that security to be any more deep, in most circles, than the fact of a continuity of employment and a paycheck.

Few academics and scientists fully live out the vision they present professionally (if it is vision at all), and it is exactly that difference between the vision—the actual lives—and the argument presented in academic terms that concerns us. For it is in the lives of people that issues of life and death, disease and health, are established. Just because academicians and bureaucrats were unaware of the ecological viewpoint for so long does not mean that important ecological issues were not being decided by them in the absence of conscious imperatives.

There is no true history, either of self or of cosmos. The stars shining in the heavens are those whose light reaches us now, as this wind blows through oak leaves. The thoughts we are having now contain the lone referents that will enable us to understand who we are and how we became this. Our bodies are their sole locus. The healing of which we are now capable is the only nexus potentiating Chinese herbs or Yaqui vision quests.

My narrative begins in the place that indigenous medicine holds in our contemporary mythology. I gradually go from there to the place that alternative medicine has in the same myths. As we have just seen, these myths are not of course separated by millions, or even thousands, of years; they are parallel designs, aspects within the same design. It is a convention of chronology that places native medicine at the beginning of a sequence concluding with contemporary holistic medicines. The book could as easily begin with the contemporary revolution in healing and medicine and then work back, through its celebratory image of holism, to such forerunners as we can discover (including our messianic images of them). Let us then neither overestimate nor underestimate the kinship of primitive medicine to holistic health. It is genealogized in at least two antithetical ways—first, by the fact of actual (though mostly unknown) lineages, and second, by the ideological affinity we have adopted for these in our stubborn quest for meanings.

"Planet medicine" is the name I have given to the medicine of most of the people on the Earth through most of human history. "Planet medicine" comprises systems that ask basic and original questions about the human condition while treating disease as a fundamental disorder of meaning and spirit. This would include not only shamanism, voodoo, and faith healing, but also homeopathy, acupuncture, and herbalism. "Planet medicine" is both prehistoric and contemporary; it has been with man and woman during the whole of their incarnation on the Earth and has evolved beside them. I do not deny that academic medicine is a branch of "planet medicine"—it is, but only in its exact techniques for curing the sick, not in its claim to a universally applicable system of health in homage to progressive science.

We can summarily say here that the thing which is wrong with orthodox medicine is not the system itself, but the way in which it presents itself as the only or most effective way to treat sickness.

Professional medicine is a singular Western deviation, begun with the occupational stratification of society and hastened by a one-note technological revolution. It has since spread globally, giving the impression that all less "scientific" forerunners bear merely a trial-and-error relationship to the corrected Western system. Yet, as unlikely as it sounds, we still do not know what this medicine is, i.e., what the real meaning of its present orthodoxy is—what its treatments say to the system all the time they are doing their famed Nobel Prize chemical and surgical numbers. This problem lies at the heart of any attempt to universalize health care.

When this book does not deal explicitly with new medicines, it deals with the quest for primary structures and the roots of healing itself. By analyzing the nature of ethnomedical thought instead of further reifying individual extant systems, it works toward explaining what orthodox medicine actually is and provides a context for understanding not only present medical practices but also the "possible structures of forms of healing which have yet to be invented." — EFT ?

Science and Its Shadows

EVEN IF WE are to support nontechnological modalities of healing, we must acknowledge the importance of machines in our collective psyche. Since the Industrial Revolution, marvelous humanitarian inventions have changed our living conditions; washing machines, gas-driven plows, combine harvesters, power vehicles, video recorders, space satellites, telephones, chain saws, and the like have made for longer and easier lives. Within medicine itself new diagnostic and curative techniques are being invented almost daily, and our society has even begun a mapping of the genome in search of rectifications of genetic disorders.

Modern technology is a great riddle, and a dismissal of its modalities would be an evasion of many of our most profound discoveries about the universe and ourselves. These revelations, ranging from the explosive environment of galaxy formation to chromosomes determining heredity, may prove one day to be no more than a mythology of skewed and partial truths, but they will never be proved "wrong." Furthermore, there is an enlightened and holistic aspect to technology (why else have we promoted progress so devotedly these last few centuries?). Unless our destiny as a species (and a planet) points to an ecological "stone age" following a cataclysm instead of journeys to the stars, we should not reject progressive science in its birth throes. In fact, as will be noted throughout this book, we are inseparable from its crisis and have long ago passed the failsafe point. We are the children of industrialism, and, as Gregory Bateson has pointed out, renunciation, at this stage of the game, is not only difficult but impossible.[2] Even our anti-materialist dreams are the products of post-industrial upbringing and education.

But something else has not changed at all. We have all these tools and more, yet we do not really know how to use them in a healthy, beneficial manner. That is, we do not know when we are improving conditions and when we are making them worse. More horrifying is, of course, the possibility that all this technology will ultimately destroy life itself.

If we accept this heritage and remain optimistic about science and, at the same time, decry the present scientific-technological reductionism, we must admit a split in the scientific tradition. What we claim presently as science is only one aspect of its larger truth. We can then postpone our declaration of universal objective knowledge by proposing that an imposter now rules in the name of science and enlightenment. It is certainly clear by now that science is no longer—if it ever was—the neutral observer it pretends to be. It has been usurped by a cult of quantification, a religion as fanatically observed as any during the Middle Ages.

This may seem like a capricious point of view, especially in the face of the technological advances of this century. Medicine and science are not supposed to be biased and limited. They are universal objective systems, not only open to criticism but requiring self-critical, selfless experiments for their very existence. Without a belief in cumulative scientific progress and the hope for equivalent advances in the future, the late half of the twentieth century becomes a mighty lonely place to hang out. What else do we have to show as the civilization spawned by the Enlightenment? What other justification do we have for the destruction of native cultures and ecosystems?

Psychologist Charles Tart distinguishes between the current fad of scientism and true science: "Scientism ... [is] the psychological dominance of a materialistic philosophy hardened into dogma and masquerading as an authentic science to draw on the latter's prestige."[3]

How, most scientists would counter, under the elaborate and neutral scrutiny of the world community, could fundamental errors have contaminated our collective experiment? Is not the cry for "another" science just a last gasp of superstition and romanticism? Yet I hold that the priests of modern science are not unlike the church officials who denied the existence of sunspots, moons circling Jupiter, and Saturn's rings because these phenomena were blasphemous. Scientists have reportedly closed their eyes in defiance when shown a Kirlian photograph of the etheric field or a picture of the mesa on Mars which resembles a human face. Most modern scientists will not even discuss *psi* phenomena or *chi* energy or participate in an inquiry into the causative agents of acupuncture and homeopathy. In a documentary, the much admired Stephen Hawking, incapacitated by Parkinson's Disease, types out a denial of any such forces on his keyboard, which then echoes his words in an ironically metallic voice, "There is no God!" We assume we have the map if not the territory. Yet the present human perspective is but one interpretation of the universe among billions that may arise and come and go among sentient species, all of them as fervently "universal" and real during their reigns as this one. Our extraordinarily complex mathematics and measuring systems are but stepladders through a fraction of a fraction of infinity.

Science is at the very least not truly objective unless it operates from an ecological perspective taking into account the ultimate scope of consequences of all its propositions and discoveries. This does not only mean the obvious technological consequences of scientific application (like weapons, pollutants, economies based on nonrenewable resources, etc.); it means the human and "consciousness" implications of every pure law and theory (nonspecificity of subatomic particles, expanding universe, materialism, random numbers, evolution by mutation, propulsion by reaction, transmission of electrical signals, and so on). How does it change humanity internally to work on these concepts and adapt them by mass industry on assembly lines? What is the yet undelivered meaning of a technology on whose streets and in whose props and vehicles we carry out much of our lives?

Science presumes that the standard way of knowing—a culturally trained, objective mind—is the only verifiable source of knowledge. The knowledge of other minds—the somatic mind, the "big" mind achieved in meditation, the mind tuned to other dimensions by hallucinogens, the dream mind, etc.—constitutes lesser, fragmented, or purely imaginary realms: no verifiability possible. Hence, medical knowledge gained from visions or internal scanning or <u>energetic touch</u> is scorned and discarded by the orthodox establishment. Even if it produces cures—or their functional equivalents—it is viewed as quackery and fraud. As we shall see, <u>"unscientific" cures don't count as cures</u> in a society in which a certain limited, dogmatic science operates as the ruling authority.

Even if one denies the possibility of a universal meaning (for anything, science included), we must choose from among hierarchies of relativism. Every law and every application comes with a unique cognitive frame in a specific society in space and time. Unless laws and their applications are "corrected" for this provincialism, they will always be ethnocentric and, in some way, self-serving.

Dilemmas and puzzles represented by such diverse putative phenomena as wave/particle quanta, telekinesis, and biological transmutation may themselves be another face of the distortion caused by the misapplication of technology to society. Polluted atmosphere and seas denote the parallel error of mistaking content for context.

More and more, knowledge itself is becoming meaningless. Our plunge into black holes, quasars, and gigantic cosmological events has context only in relation to aesthetics and moral law. Presently it is a cosmic metaphor for destruction of rivers and forests, genocide, drugs, and street gangs, though astrophysicists would be the last to recognize their projections. Just remember that a Peruvian shaman or Tibetan lama educated in the same academic departments would see entirely different things in the universe and would provide us with divergent collective images of creation and cosmogony.

Technological Medicine and the Art of Healing

THERE ARE KEY AREAS in which technological medicine is unmatched by any system which has appeared on the planet. It reverses deteriorative physiological processes quickly, antidoting the effects of life-threatening injury and shock. It prolongs life also by neutralizing pathological toxins, removing diseased tissue, and poisoning body-destroying microbes and parasites. It foresees diseases in often invisible symptoms. It applies incredibly complex and powerful machines to the body's also complex attempt to restore its tissues. These machines use the same lenses and lasers that scour the insides of atoms, grind the shapes of distant galaxies, project holograms, and program missiles onto single buildings on city blocks. Surely they can wreak havoc upon germs and tumors. And they do. As a result of generations of cumulative experiments, we have a means of saving lives consonant with our means of taking lives.

Doctors practicing industrial medicine are able to regulate large concentrated populations and establish parameters of collective hygiene and public health, from genetic and contagious disease to protection from environmental and industrial poisons. For instance, they are able to determine, on a statistical basis, the likelihood of certain diseases arising from exposures to particular chemicals, organisms, or matings between genotypes carrying particular chromosomes. Whole other disease classes have been eliminated by the destruction of pathogenic agents such as smallpox.

Standard medicine also serves a collective cultural function by training masses of people in groups in one objective and accountable system. Adequate medical personnel matriculate cyclically from courses and research laboratories. This professional corps is immediately needed to treat an expanding global populace. Large numbers of doctors must be recruited along with lawyers, engineers, policemen, etc., because the response to the crisis of disease is crucial to the cohesion or disruption of society. We discuss the prehistorical basis of this in Chapter Three.

Over the centuries, Western culture has developed a system which handles wounds, shock, poisoning, pathology, and contagion in a humane and accountable manner, which is confidently transmitted, and which reaps the benefits of a central evolving technology. Nothing else would be reasonable. Certainly nothing else would be politically acceptable.

FOR GENERATIONS NOW, this mainstream medicine has also existed as theoretical schools of anatomy, pharmacology, and surgery. The abstract and collective need of these to identify themselves as technical science dooms them to the little bit of science they have mastered. While physics has a Newtonian core which carries it through most of the complex operations of urbanized society (the buildings finally stand and the planes take off), medicine suffers, all through its structure, a vagueness of relationship among actual disease, specific organ, quality of being sick, and appropriate cure. Its own solution seems to have been a division of itself into a core area, where most operations are simple, and various outlying districts, or specializations, where individual physicians are responsible for only one aspect of a complicated situation. A specialist makes repairs in his own territory, but he often does so without particular regard for the whole system. This may work in engineering, for a bridge across a river, however complex its technology, must finally link two points on a simple surface; it has no other required relevance. For medicine, the equivalent is not true. If it links two points in its own sense of what it is doing, it links many points on other levels of being.

Because of this fragmentation, the overall development of medicine may transform a specialty in a decade, so that when a patient returns, a totally different but equally "scientific" solution is now offered. It is not that the first operation or medicine was wrong; both the first and the second are right, but the second "right" treatment is the one in present use. Most physicians regard this as a temporary crisis while cleaning house. The nature of the house may be, however, that it can never be cleaned.

In the meantime, a large number of ailments remain incurable. These include both serious life-threatening diseases and a great variety of chronic illnesses that fence-sit between mental and physical. Scientific medicine works to "conquer" both "incurables," perhaps the former more heroically, but both in the sense that they are violations of its completeness. Psychiatry and internal medicine continue to assign thorny and persistent chronic diseases to rational categories so that cures can be developed.

A second difficulty is the large number of conditions that "heal themselves" or are healed for inexplicable reasons. Sometimes a patient will use an unsanctioned medicine, such as a radionics device, an aroma essence, or a formula chosen homeopathically. Generally, orthodox medicine holds that these things could not have caused the improvement, so the cure must have been a psychological response to the method of treatment, or a change in the person's life that made him or her get better. The placebo effect has not only been trivialized but misnamed from a failure to understand the complexity of active factors.

(Incurable ailments and mysterious cures are not fatal cracks in the armor of technological medicine. Spontaneous cure, after all, has a number of possible orthodox explanations, one of which is the unusual self-repair ability of DNA molecules, though we might still question what activates it.)

If any kind of standard doctor is unable to help his patient, neither partner is necessarily outraged by the situation. The patient accepts that <u>his bad luck</u> may have brought him an incurable ailment, either minor or serious. The doctor accepts that all things cannot be done with the present tools and knowledge. Both are Western businessmen and Enlightenment figures, looking to the progress of the future to solve the present lapse in ingenuity. Cryonics is probably the most extreme case of belief in technological progress. Bodies are frozen, to be thawed in future years when solutions may have been found to their presently incurable ailments. In many ways, this is the *reductio ad absurdum* of treating disease as an isolated mechanical problem. Even if the freezer is kept going and the eventual thawing awakens the patient— a large stretch of imagination in itself—he will have given up the social context of his life in his desperate quest for sheer survival. He may live, but he will be no one nowhere.

Orthodox Western medicine is concerned with the organic causes of diseases. Its various medicinal, surgical, and psychological treatments are mechanical responses to demonstrated disease paths. Although a successful treatment may often be continued without clear reason for its success, the overriding tendency of orthodoxy is to <u>reject inexplicable cures</u> and to search for categories of cause that will generate classes and subsets of treatment. The isolated cures of the individual practitioner are meaningless if they cannot be generalized into a universal law of cure, adaptable by other physicians. The laetrile controversy and others like it illustrate this point well. No matter how many "successful" treatments of cancer occurred with this drug, they were meaningless without a generalized explanation for chemical viability. Without this, a doctor cannot be legally and ethically responsible for his own practice.

Seen from one perspective, even orthodox medicine is a patchwork of myriad inconsistent techniques and magical cures. But this patchwork is under ongoing mainstream scientific review and criticism. Knowledge of the body represents centuries of anatomical research. A map of the subvisual world of genes, viruses, and living cells comes from decades of intense microscopic investigation; the behavior of entities in this undisclosed arena continues to be viewed every day by thousands of well-equipped observers. Blood and hormonal chemistry, miniscule tissue changes, and specific drug activity are also under continuous rigorous observation.

No legal treatment exists outside this network. The doctor sees each patient as a living example of collected laws and ongoing experiments. He can track the person's chemistry, the functioning properties of his or her organs, the statistical likelihood of certain sorts of pathology, the visible and laboratory signs of such pathology, and the most efficient methods of countering a disease, either by chemical change or surgical intervention. From the standpoint of modern medicine we are mere catastrophic diseases in temporary remission.

In the most extreme challenge to this world-view, the disciples of the new medicine see sickness as a symptom or by-product of the lifelong movement of an organism toward integration through self-exploration. We contain the seeds of disease potentiation at birth. They shape us, limit us, expand us; they make change inevitable. Even as we neutralize the symptoms of specific illnesses, we cannot eliminate illness itself, for it is an integral part of who we are and a nucleus of our very personalities.

Insofar as we are self-maintaining organisms in interaction with an environment, clearly, no illness of ours will ever be totally cured, i.e., excised from our living system. Disease is our metabolic interface with the universe, so indelibly it is the signature of our responsiveness and individuality. It maintains our necessary separateness from the unity of substance at the same time that it is the revolt of nature against our exclusivity—an unrelenting attempt to return our body-minds to the anonymous flow. It is our education, unto death.

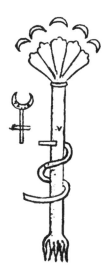

The moment we start treating health and disease as concrete identifiable entities subject to linear, technical remediation, we have lost the meaning of an integrated system.

We can synthesize and summarize many of the foregoing arguments with the following simple propositions: From the origin of our species, there have been two distinct traditions of the practice of medicine. One is the art of healing, which is exactly that: an art, practiced through sympathy and intuition, cultivating its own training and techniques and requirements of skill and education. The other tradition is the academic one giving rise to technological-scientific medicine (allopathy). It includes the ancient and primitive skills of surgery and pharmacy as well as all the sophisticated forms into which they have evolved.

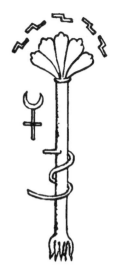

Throughout history, these two traditions have interacted; each has catalyzed the other and supplied it with elements that it lacked. In some situations their identities have merged in one system or individual; mostly they are in active opposition. Sometimes their identities are so confused that one actually passes for the other. At all times, though, information from the systems passes back and forth between them, and they necessarily develop in relation to each other.

X-ray machines, microscopes, and computers add a depth and scope to diagnosis and treatment that is awesome in terms of the equipment with which most medicines throughout history have worked. If the early practitioners of acupuncture, homeopathy, or, for that matter, Navaho sand painting had had access to these devices, they would have been able to use them well (certainly homeopaths have incorporated modern laboratory techniques and computer programs, and traditional medicine has been merged with Western medicine in China).

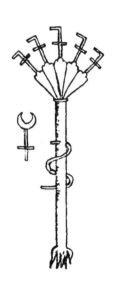

There is nothing, *per se*, about the repertoire of modern medical tools and skills that stands against "other" medicines. These innovations may be overspecialized or unneeded in individual circumstances, but they are mere robots at our service and the service of our projections; *they* do not require an alternative. What requires an alternative is our rigid pattern of application and use.

Medical Traditions: Lineages and Dichotomies

27

Unfortunately, technology and the art of healing each pretend to be the exemplar of universal medicine. The art of healing views technology as a shallow modernist imposter, and the mainstream of technology views the art of healing as an archaic, superstitious troublemaker.

Yet the creative relationship between these traditions is a major topic of this book. That is why my point of view seeks the actual place of technological medicine in an eventual "planet medicine" rather than its exclusion.

[The rise of scientific medicine against the background of ancient healing has also produced multiple hybrid systems, systems which reflect some of the profundity and empiricism of original shamanic and divine medicine yet are the products of the tools and concepts of academicism. For instance, it would seem that both homeopathy and psychotherapy draw many of their strengths from their retention and/or recovery of early Indo-European magic. Their empirical innovations and their potential for incorporating the complexities of modern life are equally significant. Primitivity is not enough for them, and parapsychic futurism is not enough either. The virtue of all medicines of the middle ground (between healing and science) is the ongoing process they track and embody, whatever their origin or philosophy.]

WHEN WE SPEAK of modern medicine to which an alternative is proposed, we mean a set of beliefs about what an organism is and what disease is; we also mean a medical system that is a reflection of social, economic, and political goals (and under attack for the same reasons many of these are). In the latter instance, doctors put financial gain before the needs of their patients; neglect the poor; try to hide their mistakes, even at the risk of a patient's welfare; and, often, are puppets of the pharmaceutical companies from which they cull favors. If not all doctors are guilty of these lapses, most doctors implicitly condone a system in which these things must happen. Yet these are not the major issues.

Our dilemma is hardly as simple as the unchecked profitability of surgery and drugs. It is that the medical establishment is invisibly regulated by cultural beliefs and taboos. The persona of the doctor standing within his system is usually more important than his or her curing of disease. This abandonment of objectivity is so complete and at the same time so subtle that few doctors understand it.

There is a naive tendency among doctors to assume that if they are enlightened and humane they will be medically sound. But there is no reason to assume either this or its inverse for either holistic or technological medicine.

The technological style of treatment, based on the allopathic philosophy of disease and cure, is enthusiastically made available by "our best and brightest" to those who can't afford it. Liberal physicians and social workers become involved in rural health clinics with sliding fee scales and aggressive "outreach programs," and they initiate facsimiles of these in undeveloped countries. For most of the left-wing critics of medicine, this represents an admirable social outreach. Insofar as universal health care is viewed as a birthright and an eventual panacea, its export is a form of justice and philanthropy.

But this is being ideological in the most narrow sense. People blithely overlook the relationship between the institutional methodology itself and the politics of medicine. From a holistic point of view, universal technological medicine administered by governments and insurance bureaucracies is simply a beachhead of the bankrupt establishment—enlarging its constituency while pretending to cover its social debts. Global medicine portends the same ultimate catastrophe as global agriculture (with its pesticides) and the petroleum economy. They are expensive, simplistic, and non-renewable. It is foolhardy to short-circuit a complicated and interconnected system of suffering, meaning, and redemption for, at best, temporary luxuries.

Medical Traditions: Lineages and Dichotomies

Definitions of Self and Disease

THIS BOOK IS a statement of the cultural and metaphysical status of all medicine and an attempt to revise assumptions, both academic and popular, about the cycle of disease and cure. It is a guide not to systems of holistic medicine as such but to the ethical and epistemological issues that are externalized as we encounter the inner turmoil of disease and apply contemporary logic and technology to its resolution. In its collectivity, the new medicine is beginning to parallel the major political and philosophical epistemologies of our time. The incredibly complex and interrelated dynamics of "disease and cure" replicate our equally complex dynamics of semantic analysis and cosmological inquiry. At the same time that medicine treats specific complaints—actual diseases—it examines the overall aesthetic and social framework in which human beings exist. But medicine is different from philosophy and politics in one key way. Whether its interpretation is existential, semantic, nihilistic, or phenomenological, all of these, or none of these, it proves each case each time by cure alone. The response of the disease to the application of a remedy is a medical system's harshest and only critic. (I myself finally prefer the rugged exercises of Wilhelm Reich to the much more exquisitely reasoned diagnoses of Jacques Lacan et al., if only because the former submerge the body in the somatic criteria of its survival whereas the latter are always subject to the clever manipulations and evasions of the professional persona.)

After all, it is not that we don't understand. We have virtually exhausted ourselves watching every action twice and three times over. It is that we understand and cannot change things. So action speaks louder than words. (And healing speaks louder than understanding.) It does not matter that action limits complexity, for it generates another kind of complexity.

THE PRESENT CRISIS of medicine and health care is initially a crisis of definition. For we encounter complex systems of medicine and healing operating at different levels of concreteness and contradicting one another's definitions of the same processes and terms—while at the same time each proposing universal holism. It is no wonder we often degenerate into rival cults whose *actual* processes are identical or complementary though proclaimed in different xenophobic dialects. The wars of therapeutic ideologies distract us from the quite unique and complementary usefulnesses of entirely different practices and systems.

We unconsciously suffer such a profound ambivalence vis-à-vis disease categories and their treatment it is as though we had experienced a kind of cultural amnesia in which antitheses are now ready to replace one another seemingly at will. Recommendations change from month to month as to the things which harm and the things which help. In effect, we are in collective psychoanalysis, and the terminology of medicine serves as both the static crust of our resistance and the active medium of our transference. Holism provides a new theater for this drama.

Each person's "struggle" with his or her biological being is recorded in health. A state of relative health or disease has a priority that ideas and attitudes, which merely emerge from it, cannot. That is, there are deep and urgent collective hungers, both personal and cultural, which cannot be expressed except as variations and distresses of health. Their "philosophical" meaning is akin to that of the genes themselves, which also carry a biological message into the world.

(Healing is a desperate act, and all cures are miracles. Disease embraces life and is its close ally from the beginning when the fertilizing sperm is little more than a virus to which the egg accedes. Throughout the wondrous transformation that follows, disease is the basis of all the defense mechanisms and immunities that keep this creature alive. The final disease is the *nigredo* of the original infection. Life is not a process of freeing oneself of complexes; it is a process of transfusion through them.)

Sigmund Freud defined this *modus* of sublimation and transformation as a virtual "first law of life," but he seemed to mean psychological process only. By now we recognize that in his "psychology," he wrote the laws of all medicine, and that the body is likely the reservoir of the invisible unconscious mind, thus an equal arena for symbolic transmutation. This is why his dynamics of unconscious process and ritual unwinding remain so important to practitioners of holistic health and phenomenological philosophy: both of these are based on a recovery of mind/body unity and, with it, experience of the whole.

People rarely notice the real profundity and intricate variability of origin of the health and disease that they experience. They may sense, at times, that all is not well, that they have a sickness, that they are confused, that "there must be a way out"; at other times, that a sickness has dissipated, that something else is wrong, that they feel "good," that they do not know whether anything is wrong.

Suddenly or gradually we are sick. We may not even recognize a change at first, but ultimately the illness disrupts our plans and takes on priority. That is how we seem to experience it. However, long before an identifiable symptomology penetrates awareness, the same disease is also present, making those very plans, working as an inextricable part of the overall personality. The body bubbles with contradictions and the mind chatters ceaselessly, agreeing and disagreeing: I am strong. I am weak. I like my job. I hate every day of it. I love him. I can't stand being with him. I'm creative. I'm stuck. Why don't I feel more? It's all finally coming together for me. When did that wonderful feeling of clarity leave me?

Most of this conflict appears on a mental level, but if that were its whole genealogy, a resolution might present itself. The mind is only the top of the pyramid. The body "thinks" these things too, in its own quite different way. Because people do not understand that their mental and social conflicts are fundamental and biological, they either pretend to dismiss them or think to change them too easily by changing their "mind" about them.

As Charles Olson put it: "We live out, until there isn't any, the argument of our lives."[4]

Perfect health is actually a chimera. We have no idea how we would feel without illness. What we feel, as mind/body, is a blur made up of health, illness, external impingement, and internal consciousness, into which we project our egos, our hopes and fears and plans, our sense of being; it is from this cauldron that we derive our "experience."

There is a common misunderstanding of health as not feeling anything at all. That is, if we do not feel our bodies, everything is okay; if we begin to feel something, it must be sickness.

The tragedy of this unexplored stasis is that we tend to block out sensations and body wisdom as well as the seeds of disease. So we misread warning signals because we experience them, often for years, only as vague irritation or numbness. And when we experience disquieting emotional sensations as somatic shifting, we block them also, making our lives and relationships thin and sentimental. We choose to feel as little as we can so that we can have our "health" as we understand it. It is no wonder that the "twentieth century" was ushered in by the psychological sciences and that it has since been visited by a great variety of self-proclaimed psychosomatic and religious therapies. In our obsession with psychological causation, we are not any more able to distinguish between the so-called mental and physical (or to keep our "souls" and bodies in balance) than our "unpsychological" forebears.

T HE GREAT ARCHETYPAL THERAPIST, homeopath, and M.D. Edward Whitmont writes:

Healing at its fundamental level might well be a rebalancing of constituent parts of the whole organism, and a reconciliation with the appropriate superordinate pattern—with Self, world, Tao, God or whatever we choose to call it. In view of the reciprocal relationship between part and whole, our own state of being might actually be significant to the health of the whole cosmic order, even in its material bodily aspect. If we take such a perspective seriously, it might lead us to approach illness differently. We could consider it instead of a disturbing calamity as a meaningful dramatic crisis in an individual's life, as his or her way of being in the world and reciprocally interacting with the world. Healing would then require discovering the inherent 'intent' of the crisis.

This perspective does not limit us to a psychological approach to illness. Neither does it imply that all illness can be explained in terms of psychological inadequacy. Each person's ability to integrate new growth possibilities sooner or later meets its limits. We exist not only as psyches but also as physical bodies. We embody; we somaticize. Hence, we also depend on the remediation of what we call material substance.[5]

Whatever we tell ourselves about psyche and spirit, the biophysical aspect of this existence will terminate. We are involved in an esoteric process that transcends ideology and purity of intent. The major religions of both the East and West teach this same doctrine as revelation through suffering.

Disease, in that sense, is a collective or even cosmic neurosis written into our boddhisattva bodies in the hope that we can heal not only ourselves but the collectivity. According to some spiritual systems, that alone is why we are incarnate.

The writing of this book is a small act of coming to awareness, like turning within sleep to an unvisited level of dream. We cannot skip the struggle of awareness or we will forever "cure" the wrong things. On this planet, in our haste, we have cured many wrong things. And it has left us with nations and economies out of touch with both history and the esoteric basis of disease.

The hope is that a primal knowledge from our being—from our flesh and bones, nerves and meridians—can enter

into our science and philosophy and change

34

them, and society with them. This cannot happen as long as we talk about "therapy" and "holistic health" and an "alternative medicine" rather than the thing they are: a revolution of those who lie deeper and more oppressed than the workers or refugees or homeless—those actual beings whom previous decades got away with naming "peasants" and "workers," thus consigning them to "the revolution"—to *that* revolution, which now crumbles toward the hinter edge of its century, just as unaligned, the dispossessed just as exploited as before.

Notes

1. Owen Barfield, *Unancestral Voice* (Middletown, Connecticut: Wesleyan University Press, 1965). Indirect quote from page 81.

2. Gregory Bateson, "Restructuring the Ecology of a Great City," *Io #14, Earth Geography Booklet No. 3, Imago Mundi* (Cape Elizabeth, Maine: 1972), p. 141.

3. "Science vs. Scientism," newsletter article, no author given, *Brain/Mind,* Vol. 18, No. 5, Los Angeles, p. 1.

4. My source for this is the tape of Charles Olson's reading/talk before the University of California (Berkeley) Poetry Conference, in Wheeler Hall, July 23, 1965.

5. Edward C. Whitmont, *The Alchemy of Healing: Psyche and Soma* (Berkeley, California: North Atlantic Books, 1993), pp. 34–35.

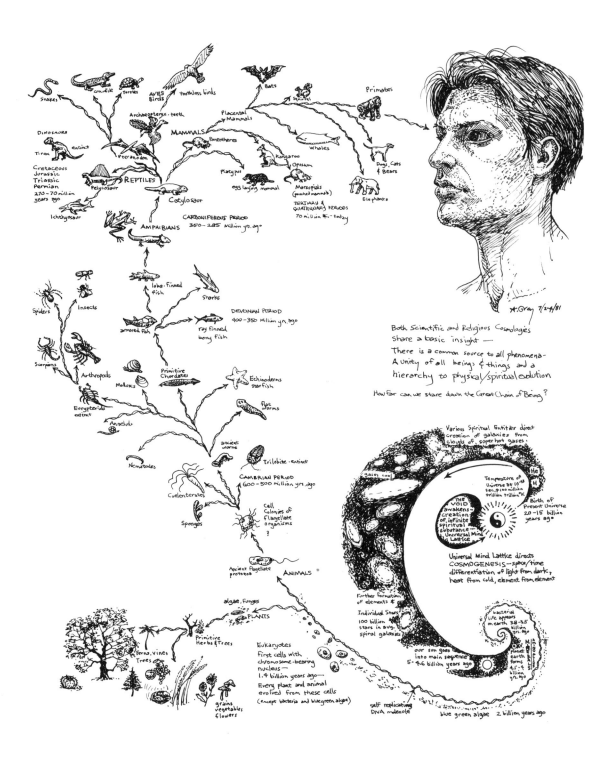

CHAPTER TWO

Disease and Cure:
Image and Process in Medicine

Us

WE LIVE ON a planet of seas and vapors, mud, fire, and dust. We are suspended in a field of attractions cast by heavy objects which go on eternally, nesting in each other so that the smallest things we know are under continual touch and influence from the largest things and from things beyond visibility. We have no simple beginning, no precedent, no explanation.

We live too in a sea of light pouring from a sun-star many thousands of times the size of our world. This light is so full and rich that we are bathed in it at all times. It has penetrated the planet so long that our bodies are wired of its deposits. It has become the oils of buttercup and volcanic embers; it is rain, and it is also snow. The heat of the ground, of every breath and organism, comes from it. Our very thought and civilization are by-products of sun.

In the daytime sky we see the absolute condition of our atmosphere like a painting—temperatures and relations of winds strung out in clouds. Each clump of trees breathing carbon dioxide, each lake evaporating, each electrified city, each mountain deflecting currents of air, every yarn of density in the cloud matter itself registers again in the sky as mottles, streaks, and whips within the prism blue.

At night, when sunlight is bent out of the prism, we see a universe. There is no sense of where it is, only that it is held together by lines and attractions. There are stars where matter and gravity have built them; blackness elsewhere. Each deliquescent object is a world of some sort, composed as this one is. If creatures inhabit any of them, they live outside our entire reality and history, outside even our biology; yet we silently share the creation. From any one world, all other worlds appear as points of light, each the relative size and brilliance of its makeup and remoteness. There is no self-apparent reason for distance and angularity, but things are distributed in this way, and we come into being as spatial creatures, from the minute geometries of genes to the topology of our flesh and the birth canal to the holography of the senses and the brain. All known space is arranged, as it were, in a river of time which enfolds the creation.

We see fiery, watery, and empty conditions where they are: the Milky Way where primal hydrogen is thickest, twenty miles of dandelions in a field in Maine, a clump of purple phlox in a backyard, giant rocks glaciers have rolled into Quebec. Billions of ant eggs spawn; bird nests appear in trees. Villages emerge along Indian trails that were once buffalo migration routes.

We are inside this condition. We are, in fact, the inside of this condition—the only inside we know. As big and dense and distributed as the universe is, our senses give it to us as normal and inhabitable, even cozy. We do not question our presence here. We assume we are natives. The amount of everything does not overwhelm and destroy us because we experience it as ourselves. We know it within us and not out there where it is.

When the surf crashes from the horizon, its whorls echo in similar ratios inside our flesh. The ocean and sky are vast; we know this and name it so because our awareness of them is vast in a whole other way. Their raw infinity could not touch us without destroying us, so we will never know *it*.

Matter itself does not challenge us or intend our defeat. It is the cutting edge of our being, and it keeps processing us, as perception and mass, through the thing of which we are made.

We have solid-seeming bodies; yet our actual being is a shimmering, multidimensional thing, embodying in its ongoing cellular life and continuum of perception the first cell and the beginning of thought.

We swim in a mountain pool. Sun-warmed currents blend with rivulets of ice; these waves pass through our nervous system, changing our feelings, reviving memories. Our nerves and tissues alternately record light sparkling on the surface.

We live within such a pool, a pool so sensitive that these words and images, as they pass through consciousness, change my present chemistry as I write them, yours as you read them.

We are charged quanta of tissue, energy, trauma, scars, immunity, aura; every trace of everything radiates through zones of our wholeness, forever.

Yet all the time, that thing we are, which does this feeling, seeing, knowing, imagining what it is, is water, mud, dust, and fire. Even if we were predestined to arise from matter—a common religious interpretation of science—we have done so only by the chemical properties of that matter, without shortcuts, without disjunctions, and in full accord with the laws of nature. We are extraordinarily complicated and hierarchicalized, but our bloods and hormones are fundamentally seawater and volcanic ash, congealed and refined. Our skin is

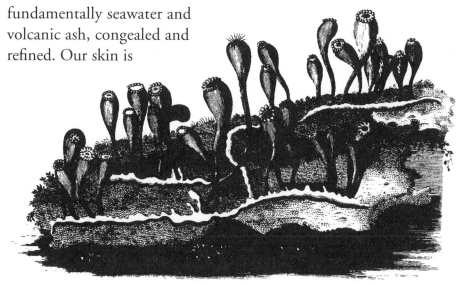

molecularly a maple leaf and a moth wing. The currents our bodies regulate share molecules with the solar wind. Nerve synapses and flashes of lightning are related events at different levels. (If aliens cloned our species from their own "protoplasm," as others claim, we have since become so interwoven in the molecular and viral fabric of the Earth we are now inextricable.)

We are a particular form in a larger pattern, shaped within it, hewed to it, held there by an invisible contour of being. Our consciousness and even our textualization are natural features of creation. We cannot exceed it or evade it; we cannot duck it or be driven outside it. (There is but one creation, and even so-called supernatural events must occur within it.)

Mind and Body

 TRADITIONALLY, MIND INCLUDES such epiphenomena as thoughts, ideas, intentions, visualizations, images, fantasies, and neuroses. Body includes organs, fascia, skeletal structure, systems of circulating fluids, kinesthesia, physical movement, and coordination. However, proprioceptively, organs merge with images, feelings with hormones, intentions with movements in such a way that the realms are interdependent and indistinguishable.

But for centuries now, we have trained ourselves to honor the external components of phenomena only and derive their characteristics objectively, separate of being. We thus come to think of ourselves as dead matter with a phantom life kindled in it or as carbon flesh activated and maintained by a genetic code. We neglect a whole category of information that floods us from the entity that is both mind and body. Yet that information forms the background of our lives, our existence. We focus instead on a foreground of thoughts and actions and pretend that our minds give us intentions which our bodies carry out. Modern definitions of pleasure emerge in this way, so it is no wonder that definitions of health have the same etiology. The majority treat their body like a date picked up at the singles bar. They hustle it, punish it, and try to make it give them things they want. These bodies do our work, have our pleasure, and keep healthy for us (or fail). Note the current popularity of gym workouts and jogging. In a sense, we live a life which is abstracted from the actual life that lives us. We have no language for the mind/body pool that we are, so we borrow language from either mind or body to explain systemic changes.

When the day-to-day functioning is viewed in terms of a static machine, we picture ourselves as unchanging algorithms—our organs as separately functioning sites in an assembly line. A workout becomes a tune-up. It is hard to envision where the "mind" originates in such a schema. To the doctor it is probably a troublesome by-product, the alias of systemic activity in the patient; in himself, it is mostly an unexamined projection of his professional ego. To the patient the self is an innocent observer trapped in a sophisticated vehicle of meat. No amount of ideological "holism" can overcome this experiential prejudice.

We declare, "Get rid of this disease!" as though the locus of its interaction with us could be concretized, isolated, and severed. Then (we tell ourselves) we will feel better. Often we simply feel less, thus feel less disease. Often, too, the disease is an externalized aspect of the healing process, and without it we are sicker.

Disease is our intrinsic response to an invasion rather than the invasion itself; it delineates our degree of susceptibility rather than our possession by an outside entity. Disease may be reflected in pathology and tissue damage, but it is also the most intimate writing of the turbulence and changes of life on the single bodies and collective body of the biosphere. Nothing else, except maybe dreams or visions, forces the organism to reconcile itself instantaneously with the pagan powers of which it is made.

Because medicine treats personal experience directly, and because it embodies the most powerful metaphor for transformation we have, healing is also potentially redemption and reclaiming of our own depths; hence, it becomes a paradigm for both social revolution and self-development.

I return to this theme in earnest in the closing chapters of Volume Two of this book.

New Western holistic models strive toward doing away with mechanism and duality, but their proposed unity is insufficient. What we have already assigned to mind and to body, most notably in the distinction between psychology and physiology, are expressions of such a trenchant cultural polarity that no synthesis can be proposed that does not inherit the dichotomy. Thus, many holistic models merely delegate phenomena among their own prior hierarchies. At first glance, this makes sense. Some things (drugs and herbs, for instance) change us by our assimilation of them in our chemistry; other things (prayers or mandalas) change us by our senses, i.e., how we experience them and experience ourselves in their context. Conventionally, the latter are mental, the former are physical; but the organism is an integrated whole and does not really distinguish between these. Our minds may, intellectually, but our bodies do not. If our bodies do not, diseases certainly do not.

Psychosomatic medicines, as well as holistic-health exercises, often reify the division they pretend to resolve. That is, the fashion of psychosomatic medicine tends to focus on specific episodes of mental/physical feedback rather than the prior simultaneity of all things mental and physical. I continue this discussion at the beginning of Chapter Six.

Self-Healing and Other Healing

IF WE DO NOT RESIST, our life itself will carry us through most crises; we will die with the scars of diseases we cured that we did not even know we had. The most fundamental medicine is our own metabolism. Day by day, through our movements, our thoughts, our breath—and by night, as an autonomous by-product of our sleep and dreaming—we are healing ourselves in a process intrinsic to the individuation of our organism. Even the most heroic medicine merely stimulates and supports that and cannot add to its "meaning." More than ninety-nine percent of all medicine is such self-healing. In fact, healing originates in the synthesis of an entire organism from two seed cells. No physician comes close to such a "cure."

A doctor stands always outside a body, outside its universe. He is but one point of contact in the environment. The sick person experiences the disease directly and can change it with each internal gesture—the deeper and less impeded the gesture, the deeper the change. Whatever a doctor does, he cannot convince the body—the uneducated intelligence of the body—that he means well or ill, that he means, in fact, anything. Stated otherwise, medicine is granted no cognitive priority for having developed a therapeutic language. In this I indict its nonverbal "language" of actual treatment as well as its rehearsed cause-and-effect semantics of diagnosis and cure. I mean specifically that both the physical and syntactic aspects of simple drugs, chemotherapies, and the like attain no special priority in the body or immune system by dint of their curatively defined roles and trajectories. They take on priority only when they break into a self-healing loop. Drugs are thus merely a chimera of the fantasy of solving a "wrong thing" spontaneously.

Likewise, a psychiatrist certainly cannot convince the body by convincing the mind. So he cannot convince the mind, either. (Meditation may change mental states, but it does so by tapping the neurophysiological basis of thought; it trains consciousness, but does not attempt to convince consciousness.)

Personal chemistry, dreams, feelings, daily relationships with other people, weather, food, and air all permeate the plane on which the doctor is working. These autonomous events do not cease in order to listen to a medicine. They are either enhanced or obstructed by a "cure" and also continue right through it. There is no medicine that obviates all other conditions, and there is no medical treatment that breaks the continuity of organism and environment without creating worse disease or destroying life itself. Medicine deflects and catalyzes. It does not create.

Disease and Cure: Image and Process in Medicine

The doctor who works to change illness by definition simultaneously works to invent illness. That is, he changes the body and all things that are in it, even when he has no consistent effect on his designated target. Most of his residual changes may be random and trivial; some may not be trivial—they may ultimately be more important than the intended "cure." (For an enlarged discussion of this topic, see "The Pathogenic Healer" in the second volume, Chapter Two.)

Categories of Disease

TAXONOMIES OF DISEASES and the medicines that ostensibly cure them grow up in conspiracy with each other in a larger and more complex field of meanings and references than is generally admitted.

The conviction of supposed "real" diseases is a mutual folly in which patient, doctor, medical school, and custom have collaborated over the ages.

We assume that we know disease by the feel of the internal organs of our body. But this is not true. With the exception of obvious injuries and hurts, pain is undifferentiated, and the perception and cognition of one's self are not only dim and globally diffused but evolve and change over a long period of time. The tissues of our sensorium and brain are not actually arranged to transmit localized sensations from deep organs. These "sensations" must first be brought to the surface, as concepts, as dialogue with one's self, and finally, as discourse with society and its "doctors."

It is extremely difficult to match subtle organ changes with visible internal geometries, and both of these with the perception of internal change and the language categories of either sick people or physicians. Subjective choices are imposed all the way down the line: for the doctor, which organs and geometries to emphasize; for the patient, which inward discomfort to dignify and act out and in which way; for the diagnostic manual, which action to relate to which geometry, and at which scale. No wonder there are unexplained remissions, miracle cures, and voodoo deaths. Yet these may also be no more than our baffled names for simple processes of life. Endocrinologist Deepak Chopra writes:

> We might casually think that everyday life is too commonplace and simple for science to bother with. In truth, it is far too complex. Although a molecule of hemoglobin is structured out of 10,000 separate atoms, it can be isolated and mapped—a feat that has led to several Nobel prizes. However, to trace what hemoglobin is doing when you take in a single breath would be impossible, because each red blood cell contains 280 million molecules of hemoglobin, each of which picks up 8 atoms of oxygen. Considering that the lungs expose about one quart of blood to the air per breath, containing 5 trillion red cells, the total number of chemical exchanges is astronomical. The whole process quickly disintegrates into a swirling chaos of activity.
>
> When you open the human body during surgery, what confronts you is not the well-defined map of textbook anatomy, with the nerves in blue, blood vessels in red, and a green liver neatly set off from a yellow gallbladder. Instead, an uneducated eye sees a jumble of tissue that is mostly undifferentiated—almost all of it is pink and moist; one organ slides imperceptibly into another. The great wonder is that scientific medicine has learned as much as it has about this pulsating chaos. But in return for its knowledge, science has paid a high price by having to abandon ordinary experience.[1]

Thus, medicine always mediates between a cover story on the one hand—a classificatory reality—and on the other whatever actually happens.

The French philosopher and historian Michel Foucault has written:

> The exact superposition of the "body" of the disease and the body of the sick man is no more than a historical, temporary datum ... For us, the human body defines, by natural right, the space of origin and of distribution of disease: a space whose lines, volumes, surfaces, and routes are laid down, in accordance with a now familiar

geometry, by the anatomical atlas. But this order of the solid, visible body is only one way—in all likelihood neither the first, nor the most fundamental—in which one spatializes disease. There have been, and will be, other distributions of illness.[2]

Medicine, for that reason, often behaves more like popular philosophy than physical science. The unpredictable and boundlessly creative lexicon of personal pathology outduels any fixed categories of science. Even concrete words slip: "blood," "virus," "cancer," "schizophrenia," "tonsil," "brain" have different meanings and connotations today than a decade ago and give no indication of stopping here. Disease becomes anything which a group considers deviant, including ways of behaving, menstruation, or aging itself. When societies do not distinguish between biological disruption and social taboo, their systems of medicine do not either, with the result that every society, including our own, has a difficult time defining what disease is and assigning legal or supernatural responsibility, as the case may be. Individual doctors or institutions may also respond politically in the absence of a concrete disease image and decide it is social behavior which must be cured. There have been some brutal techniques historically for that.

OFTEN, AS WE SHALL SEE, the unconscious tenets of the physician hold more sway over his or her treatments than anything consciously intended or delivered as health care. The unconscious tenets and unexamined beliefs of the patient are equally procedural to treatment. The practice of medicine institutionalizes an interaction of cultural categories and remote belief systems so powerful as to be able to catalyze or negate a physical-mechanical cure, yet so deep-seated they are invisible beneath other cultural categories and belief systems. Cures both happen and fail to happen for "no discernible reason." We may intuit cultural and psychosomatic interferences and cooptions, but we rarely even pretend to be able to identify them or their degree of intrusion.

(Healing has always worked in an overwhelming din of static, so must enlist powerful allies.)

Tibetan illustration of internal organs

A wild and ineffable quality in disease and the language of anatomy will continue to evade a universal system. Where ancient plagues have disappeared into historical ledgers, new maladies bud. As medical treatment becomes more complex and profound, diseases appear to toughen and take on unsuspected dimensions. Are these successive conditions even biochemically the same? Are lab panels sufficient evidence of their sameness?

Disease and Cure: Image and Process in Medicine

Edward Schieffelin, working in the 1970s among native peoples of New Guinea, found that a new disease category, "Evil Spirit Sickness," had arrived with the missionaries. Local people began to explain all sorts of different chronic ailments by this suddenly popular illness. Social, psychological, and physiological factors were now combined in a dynamic set of meanings, which could be presented to the missionaries for their resolution. As a disease, "Evil Spirit Sickness" elicited a sort of sympathetic attention that a rebellion would not have, and it brought the natives and newcomers together in a single diagnosis. Clearly, though, most of the manifestations of this illness had existed before and were explained then in other ways.[3] Likely we too confuse "missionaries" and viruses with each other.

POTENTIALLY ONE OF the most scandalous frauds in the history of science is the identification of the HIV retrovirus as the sole direct cause of AIDS. Unquestionably a serious immunity-based illness has spread globally, but the explanation that its symptoms are the result of the so-called Human Immunodeficiency Virus is quite possibly as much a myth as anything of which a materialist might accuse an astrologer. The major advantage that pure HIV causation confers is the sustenance of a research empire based on this virus and overseen by the ostensible discoverer (even this "fake" discovery has been challenged as theft by the French government protecting the patents of its own scientists). But if the accused virus is only a late scavenger of a diseased immune system (or an innocent scapegoat), then the whole wild goose chase becomes one more symptom of our preference for images and ideologies over realities.

University of California microbiologist Peter Duesberg points out that there is no reference *anywhere* in the medical literature to the "smoking gun" experiment proving that HIV is the cause of AIDS. In its "place" stands a suitably Orwellian declaration in 1984 by the Center for Disease Control in Atlanta: HIV is the sole cause of AIDS; hence, there will be no further funding for any other kind of research. The micro-hunters got their reprieve big-time—an annual six-billion-dollar-plus wild goose chase after an obscure retrovirus sure to carry their budget into the next century.[4] Yet ten years of this has done more to promote a conservative social agenda than even to hint at a possible cure.[5] If HIV is not the cause of AIDS, in truth no cure will ever be found in this manner.

"AIDS does not fit any definition of an infectious disease," declares Duesberg. HIV is "typically an extremely rare and inactive [virus] and frequently not even present" in AIDS victims.[6] By contrast, there are more than twelve million HIV-positive individuals with no disease. Duesberg asks a number of related questions:

How is AIDS in Africa different from pneumonia or malaria (or malnutrition) when its victims are mainly added to the body count undiagnosed because they so fear the "wasting disease" they shun the Western doctor? Additionally, what does it mean epidemiologically when victims of malaria die because they suspect they have AIDS and would likely be diagnosed on the spot as having AIDS (if they went to one or another clinic unlikely to waste precious funds on expensive testing)? In what manner does AIDS even exist (lacking an explanation of how HIV damages immune systems) apart from a variety of other category-floating conditions such as Chronic Fatigue Syndrome, drug- and antibiotic-based immune deficiencies, and congenital syphilis?

AIDS is actually at least thirty-seven different types of conditions, says Duesberg. If the person with one of those conditions has HIV, then AIDS is said to be the cause of death. If not, the cause is listed as malaria, pneumonia, cancer, hemophilia, a drug overdose, etc. His explanation for the present epidemic of immune-deficiency diseases ranges from overuse of party drugs and antibiotics (mostly in First World and sex-industry Third World countries) to starvation and poor hygiene in Africa, and the consumption of AZT and other immune suppressants everywhere. It is a self-fulfilling trap if a person diagnosed as HIV-positive is then prescribed an immune depressant as a cure. The drug all but guarantees that the person will contract some disease; then the disease will be called AIDS. (Chronic diarrhea, prolonged fever, a persistent cough, and ten percent body weight loss in two months are sufficient for a diagnosis of AIDS in most of Africa.)*

On the other hand, if an underground contact sensitizer (dinitrochlorobenzene, or DNCB) developed by a dermatologist can boost cell-mediated immune response and prolong the lives of AIDS victims indefinitely, the simple viral model collapses. Not only is the research empire put in jeopardy by a different etiology of AIDS, but rampant immune-deficiency conditions in Africa, South America, and Asia can be treated by cheap, easily available drugs (the estimated cost of DNCB is about $70 per 3,000 patients[7]).

Of course, none of these renegade propositions is yet proven (nor for that matter is the HIV thesis), but a hypothetical objective observer of our civilization might be left with the suspicion that even negative concepts (like an explicit AIDS virus) are more easily (and hysterically) marketed than the complicated realities they disguise.

Once upon a time the Soviet Empire existed as a real entity despite our images; that entity was also engaged with our images at various levels of collective consciousness and unconsciousness, whatever "it" actually was. A whole nuclear arsenal was developed in response to that "reality." Yet the "Soviet Empire" was many other things too—since revealed in layers. By 1994 Mikhail Gorbachev was already an ikon, and there had been many "Boris Yeltsins" plus a Vladimir Zhirinovsky. All of these manifestations of just the surface layer of the national government were present in some other form even within the "Empire," and there would have been still other manifestations through the Cold War era if we in the West had been more observant. Whenever we

---

*Among the subtexts of HIV causation are: the legitimizing of anti-gay programs under the guise of disease control (see the Cuban quarantine for the most draconian institutionalization of a homophobic "health policy"), a moralistic attack upon the sexual revolution along with media control of sexual practices, and an excuse not to feed Africa based on the argument that the money would be better spent on expensive corporate science to find a cure for AIDS.

engage the image of the enemy—be it tooth decay or the Red menace—we define the enemy, and ourselves as well.

We create transient concrete images of diseases that exist as names. Their images are real and the sick person is also real, but in a different way. The images and their diseases then continue to interact and produce further varieties of cultural categories. By this stage of textualization (in the twentieth century) we are as deeply in the forest of symbols as in any true disease epistemology.

Orthodox medicine freezes a sanctioned set of disease images and proceeds to work on those, while other images, other "diseases," continue to exist in nonexistence. Though aware of these discrepancies, most professional doctors have no leisure in which to examine them. They are satisfied to be technicians and reify what they can. Even if we leave the deep metaphysics of disease out of this discussion for the moment, we are left with a phenomenon that probably more than half of the problems people bring to doctors are human and social malaises expressed in aches, discomforts, and even tissue damage. Most doctors do not feel comfortable with these dimensions nor are most able to work with them. Some doctors do not even feel they should treat them. In any case, the average physician is hopelessly overmatched.

The remedy (or cure) is caught on the horns of the same dilemma. We have forgotten what cure is. We have forgotten not because we have forgotten the word "cure," but because the word has lost concrete applicable meaning. It can be the substance, activity, or event which helps restore biological functioning and harmony (or intends to), but it can equally be the substance or process which leads to culturally desired behavior. In some cases, it is the agent which helps promote a change of which disease is an aspect. Throughout this book, we will consider two degrees of cure: one which has a limited and predetermined goal in relation to a particular ailment, and one which works through palpable symptoms in an attempt to bring an overall state of health to the organism.

Finally, there is no universal methodology. How one treats disease depends on what one considers the nature of man and woman and the universe to be. Different cultures express unique aspects of the human condition and, although skills can always be translated, definitions often cannot. For a person born into an industrialized Western nation, a disease complexity begins to organize itself at birth, and from the manner of birth, and is thoroughly integrated by the age of consciousness. All of us who have been raised in this system already have the system as an intimate environment by the time we start to choose our doctors and report our symptoms. Even when we adopt new medicines we retain our cultural context.

The patient is never completely cured; nevertheless, he or she is changed by a disease and its treatment and must proceed on a new course. How that change is integrated into future lifestyles, whether it prevents or spawns new illnesses, is a function of how the particular culture or style of treatment educates or indoctrinates the patient. And this has much more to do with the ethics and cosmology of the group than with the absolute nature of either the disease or the cure. This is as true in our own civilization as it is in the most primitive hunting band: a doctor alleviates the immediate distress as best as he can; then both he and the society prescribe the appropriate course for the patient's life. There is no final court of right or wrong except the populace which allows itself to be treated in this manner. In a certain sense, medical treatment expresses how a society distinguishes itself from raw, totemic nature (or, in many cases, how it identifies itself with aspects of nature).

Disease as Epochal Cycles

A DISEASE IS REQUIRED because of an individual's genetic destiny, relationship of susceptibility to other organisms, or psychological and social failure of adjustment. In this sense, a disease cannot be accidental or random, even when it seems to be. As an old Roman proverb states, *Fata volentem ducunt, trahunt nolentem* (Whoever is willing the Fates will lead, the unwilling they will drag along). So too *morbi.*

Modern civilization is surrounded by a flagrancy that resembles collective disease: industrial waste, nuclear bombs, addictive drugs, forced-growth economies, left- and right-wing dictatorships, the political applications of torture, pornography, sadomasochism, and crime—from urban alleys to African and Thai villages to corporate board rooms and shadow governments. As we discussed earlier, these are profound crises on the edge of an utter void. They are diseases. An aspect of all of them recurs again in our individual bodies. We respond to their existence in the only way we can—by our existence. As we evade responsibility for them consciously, we are still unconsciously and somatically implicated in their overall matrix. Diseases truly arise from social and environmental imbalances, but then these broader conditions and individual illnesses share an even deeper origin in the rhythm of our civilization. Concentration camps and genocidal armies are cancers and immune disorders expressing themselves at a collective level. Likewise their effects are individually and psychosomatically pathological. By the same order, the environmental consequences of the Gulf War and Chernobyl are precisely equivalent to a Black Plague or smallpox epidemic. Conditions flow like waves from the molecular and cellular to the cultural, demographic, and ecological, and back. We are nowhere close to a science able to treat this reality.

The current fad of horror movies and violent video games reflects our immune response to a civilization that has embalmed its bodies in synthetic food and high-fashion personae and merchandized alienation at every level. Look at the extent to which modern pornographers have to go to excite a response (sodomy, bondage, femicide) and you will see the sheer deadness of our collective sensorium. Violent images meant to titillate are "psychic immune-system" projections of disease states as "ugly" as anthrax or leprosy. Photographs of a prone woman being penetrated by a large pig and a detached breast with fruits in a dessert bowl posing as erotica reveal as serious a pathology as any tumor or bright-colored pox in a medical textbook.

It is of course not only the direct effects of technology (radiation leaks, toxic industrial wastes, ozone depletion, antibiotics breeding

exotic new germs, etc.) that make us sick, and then keep us from getting well; it is the degree of our mesmerization with the concept of
technology that prevents us from accepting our lives in an intrinsic
way. We need only consider the effects of automobiles on habitation
and land use and of nuclear weapons on general political life to realize that we invariably prefer a powerful, energy-consuming device to
bind the status quo. The collective residue of all our displacements and
postponements of responsibility shows up in our health—automobiles
and nuclear weapons internalized along with everything else—so of
course (paradoxically) we want to enact their same machine "magic"
on our bodies. Scientific medicine cannot alter this basic condition; it
can add only its own complexity of drugs and interpretations to the
jumble already corporealized.

It is no accident that the largest expanding category of lethal diseases in the West includes those that directly attack our immune
response, that dampen or eliminate the power of self-cure in our bodies. Cancer, lupus, arthritis, diabetes, asthma, allergies, AIDS—even
pornography and prostitution—alert us to turn away from externally
imposed energy technologies and artificial adrenalization and hedonism, which are mere postponements—treatments often more toxic
than their diseases—and toward vital and immune-oriented systems.

Dehumanization and the Health Establishment

In 1994 President William and Hillary Rodham Clinton faced a
medical and legal system so complex, prejudicial, and out of touch
with actuarial reality that it will surely, unchecked, send the national
debt to the next galaxy. They recognized this. Yet despite their well-
meaning agenda of reform, the corruption was beyond any simple
adjustment. Even the goal of universal therapeutic justice is impossible through a medicare system which treats imaginary diseases with
expensive fictional cures and sets its own economic growth and abstract

knowledge-gathering ahead of real scientific truth.

The cumulative effect of such latent beliefs in a profit-oriented society is disastrous. Hospitals have come to view patients as investments. A sick individual is not only a mechanism like a clock; he or she is a commodity, a product on an assembly line. If too much "care" and time are put into the product, the hospital's profit-margin is reduced. The fewer the resources put into a product, the blacker is the bottom line. So, the goal of treating patients humanely is not only one step removed by the mechanization of biology, it is removed a second step by commodization. If a sick person's insurance profile does not match the disease prognosis, i.e., does not guarantee that there will be money available to pay for the full treatment, bureaucrats are advised if at all possible not even to admit the patient. A good doctor, by some present definitions, is one who knows how to process as many patients in as short a time as possible, and also how to spot unprofitable ones for rejection. Only those patients whose disease conditions fit the model of expensive high-technology diagnosis and remediation are desirable, and then only if either they or their insurance account can afford them. If such medicine is extended with liberty and justice for all, no amount of thrift or bottom-line maintenance will be able to keep the costs from expanding exponentially.

The cures that take place under such a regime are not only symptomatic and mechanical, they're the cheapest symptomatic and mechanical solutions that can be legally perpetrated and, even at that, so expensive that the difference between a hundred and a thousand dollars is literally a matter of a zero here or there. (It is an irony that Andy Warhol, who turned the assembly-line image into art, was killed by such assembly-line health care.) It is not impossible to get adequate and compassionate treatment in this situation, but such treatment would be entirely incidental to its institutional goals—and a growing indigent percentage of the population would always be denied even this skimpy and shoddy mode of care.

Although it borders on incendiary to compare the medical system to the practices of the Nazis (even metaphorically), I feel that one of the most distinctive horrors of our century is an unfortunate living-out of the semeiological discovery that bodies can be made into signs and objects and used for purposes other than lives. People are converted to statistics hundreds of times over, as if this were the natural consequence of existence. Genocide is inertial if not declared government policy the world over. A planeload of innocent people can be exploded to make a statement about a whole other thing (admittedly, the passengers are in some way implicated or they wouldn't be there, but then everything is implicated in everything else, and that proves nothing).

From birth in the hospital to death in the morgue, our bodies are potential victims and guinea pigs of a science that ostensibly seeks to grant them longevity while gaining knowledge about itself. Dozens of diagnostic exams provide each individual with "significant" information about his or her own being: the biological computer has replaced the Oracle at Delphi, and it speaks a stochastic language exiled from a universe of either life energy or gods.

There is literally "no way out," and the 1989 movie of that title provides a series of images for the dilemma: not only are we trapped like the hero by a computer that will reconstruct us from a single cell (and likewise destroy us through the secrets of our genetic material), but we are tracked even after our death like the heroine by the actual molecules extracted from our digestive system. Our biology may outlive us in labs. People become *only* their diseases.

In an age of gene-mapping and splicing we are mesmerized by the illusion that we are by-products of our own existence. We hardly know which self to identify with. Any way you look at it, the goal is to make us into products and to replace our freedoms with service to the most conventional images of the state machine—all under the guise of health care (or other "well-fare"). We may intuit the degree to which we are sexually manipulated by the media (as well as by the perfumers and food-and-drink merchants), but we do not always realize that this is just a minor chord in the overall biological manipulation. Our body/minds are spies who *cannot* come in from the cold.

[The fierceness of the Tibetan Siamukha figurines, devouring infants and skulls and bearing flayed humans on their backs, is precisely the clarity available when we adopt their demeanor in confronting the real enemies (who generally come with smiling visages these days). We face so many genial assassins that compassion requires a fierce internalization, a wrathful embodiment from the spectrum of energy, devouring obscurity to the dharma and serving as a manifestation of enlightened mind. We have no other way of confronting the false priests and physicians, the real cannibalizers of souls.]

People are finally led to fear becoming sick almost to the degree they fear being arrested. Either way freedom is coopted by the establishment; the body is turned over to the authorities for their disposition, and the treatment may well make the person far sicker (or terminally depressed). What is most askew with the health establishment is that it is operating more and more invasively on the physical by-products of our existence and less and less on the mystery and spirit of life itself.

But this "invasiveness" is not a requirement of science, only of a society superstitiously attached to a form of materialist fundamentalism in the name of science.

Psychiatry

MAINSTREAM PSYCHOANALYSIS HAS fallen into the same morass that gene-mapping and fictive viruses portend in the somatic side of the realm. A whole rainbow of possible mind-body medicines is ignored, as the psychosomatic model becomes a somatic engine driving a mere ghost. Aberrant behavior, neurosis, and psychosis are interpreted biomechanically from the obvious connection of brain, nervous system, hormones, and organs. Psychological illness is conceived as a derivative of physical illness. Psychiatrists may *behave* as though they believe in dialogue and insight, but when the chips are down, scientifically, most of them adopt a conventional reductionist model of biological function.

In fact, the chips have been quite down recently, for the profession has had to explain its poor record of insight therapy. The collective response has been to adopt even more mechanical solutions to illness, i.e., to drift from a psychodynamic interpretation of a chemical model of consciousness to a purely chemicodynamic model.

In recent years psychiatrists have gradually abandoned the mental or insight-trauma-abreaction approach and replaced it with drug-based therapies on the assumption that the complex chemistry of the body generates and controls all thoughts and behavior. This simplification has been played to the hilt by our drug-oriented culture. Many psychiatrists argue that depression, anxiety, and schizophrenia, insofar as they are chemical disorders, *cannot* be cured by insight. Individuals may learn to live with them, but their imbalances themselves do not improve. A new generation of psychiatric experimenters hopes to locate the precise chemical and genetic loci of mental diseases in the context of a burgeoning psychotropic pharmacy, which will then provide the precise antidotes in drugs like Lithium, Prozac, et al. One editorial commentator notes, "Unfortunately, Prozac and its ilk (Paxil, Zoloft, and many others to come—SSUIs: selective serotonin uptake inhibitors) are already a very significant and pernicious player in America's neurochemistry, and have been successful in buttressing the idiocy of the psychopharmacological golden rule: that emotional distress should almost always be medicated (and can be done so safely and effectively) because it is a symptom of faulty neurotransmission."[8]

When symptoms suggesting incipient schizophrenia or panic reactions are noted in children now, for instance, a regimen of medication is routinely adopted to "manage" the disease. These treatments are popular enough that continued "successful" experimentation, even if delusional and punitive, may lead to the supplantation of the whole class of insight practitioners and humanistic psychologists.

Animals growing up in a world of chemical dependency, genocide, recreational murder, private armies, ethnic and religious wars, nations armed with nuclear weapons, ozone-layer depletion, and portending drought *should* suffer anxiety. Does it really serve the planet—or even our species—to drug and addict people to expensive psychoreductive substances? And what happens if the guinea pigs break free of their medications? What will they confront then in the form of personality deterioration and panic? And how hard will it be for them to distinguish between the original conflicts in their souls and the dark moods they associate addictively with the alleviation of the drugs?

If we routinely take to prescribing medication for fear of the shadow world, we will have no Faulkner, or Kierkegaard, or Doris Lessing, or R.D. Laing, but long before that we will have no world at all.

No doubt the strength of the drug pushers within psychiatry has come about from the failure of traditional psychoanalytic methods to provide the seemingly promised "cure." The insight methodology itself may have intrinsic lacks, but certainly one of its growing residual problems is a large number of individuals already too disconnected from deeper societal structures of shared meaning to be helped by a system based on verbal application of those structures. In this environment insight therapists come to care less about breakthrough and recovery and more about whether a patient can be enticed into their ritualized dialogue. That leaves them with a mere binary decision: the patient is cooperative or not. The doctor becomes more skilled at inventing and "naming" psychosis than in treating it.

It would be quite a surprise if a society losing millions of acres of farmland a year and dumping radioactive materials into its offshore waters were willing to invest in long, complex episodes of insight therapy with its citizens. I see no place for the dialogue between therapist and patient, even in its most stereotyped and watered-down Oedipal version, in a nation satisfied by TV sitcoms and tabloid shows, Trump palaces, media presidencies, and multi-million-dollar sports contracts. In 1969 we could go to the Moon with *esprit;* little more than a decade later we barely cared enough to put viable O-rings on a space shuttle or, failing that, to hold off the launch at least till the icicles melted. So why would an analyst sit for hours and years with his patient trying to track down the unknowable origins of trauma? Why bother with such creative fictions when one can simply prescribe an anti-anxiety or anti-depression drug?

The sheer volume and enormity of problems discourage creative therapeutics and seem to reward mere "processing" or fraud. In fact, the temptation to medical fraud may arise from the impossibility of diagnosis and cure (anyway) under these conditions.

In the course of this book we will discuss a great diversity of psychological therapies—ones arising from native shamanism, Chinese medicine, osteopathy, and a variety of naturopathic and radical psychoanalytic sources—all of which demonstrate to one degree or another that "mental" cure is possible without drugs and that the mind profoundly affects the body right to the cellular and neurotransmitter level. Chemical reductionism is not the only game in town; in fact, psychotropics may actually antidote many potential self-healing processes and addict a patient to his or her disease. At least insight therapy avoided that fate.

Medical Propaganda

DESPITE ALL ITS PROBLEMS, orthodox medicine means to give people the illusion it is handling everything and that other methods for curing disease are primitive, untested, exotic, unscientific, or un-American. The entire range of alternative healing systems from every culture on Earth is ignored, patronized, plundered, or vehemently opposed as quackery. The longstanding empirical traditions behind most of these medicines are belittled, while the empiricism and scientific rectitude of orthodox medicine are exaggerated and put on a pedestal.

Doctors may curse the high malpractice insurance rates, but they have brought them on themselves in part by their disingenuous stance of objectivity. While traditionally the American Medical Association has wielded the legal threat ensuing from malpractice as a tactic to keep other medicines from competing with it, it lacks any legally consistent set of rules and procedures of its own. Even long-sanctioned treatments become suspect when doctors routinely contradict one another and reverse their own opinions about disease etiologies from year to year.

MRIs are read these days by experts in different areas with almost as much variation as tarot cards; pathologies "appear" and "disappear" from office to office. A medicine preaching accountability with no means for implementing it with consistency must fall into the precise legal snares it has set for its competitors.

Most patients do not require truth anyway, even in the face of disablement and death. It is still, apparently, less terrifying to die within the auspices of science than, perhaps, to live by the grace of an alien witchcraft.* A person cured or not by his local physician remains an American in good standing, a citizen of the century that gave him life. A person cured exotically is by definition converted to paganism, for the body cannot deny the reason for its new health and develops traits in recognition of the treatment.

The AMA promulgates a standard and legitimate humanitarian argument: a patient bewitched in a maze of alternative and fantastic treatments may delay getting competent professional help for a condition that then becomes incurable. What makes this argument so difficult to challenge is that while sometimes it may be provincial and self-serving, at others it is a sincere caveat against the criminal grandiosity of some alternative practitioners. A classic case of the latter was published in a San Francisco magazine in the fall of 1978. A woman from South Africa (with degrees in mathematics and chemistry) attempted to heal an ostensible eye disease of hers with a combination of iridology, acupuncture, and meditation. By her own interpretation, she was positively transformed by the healing experiences, which included learning how to make her own poultices and herbal medicines and calling up her own positive "cosmic energy" to fight the disorder. But the disease turned out to be a melanoma which had spread to such a degree during the holistic treatments that even chemotherapy and laser treatment were impossible.[9]

---

*In *L'Amour Médecin* Molière had a self-important physician proclaim, "It is better to die according to the rules than to recover against the rules."

Cases like these make it far too easy for members of the establishment to remain smug in their trade guild. Yet much of science, as we have noted, is itself cleverly disguised and sophisticatedly funded quackery—academic semantics without an object. Yes, a chiropractor may well miss diabetes—and even worse—attempt instead to treat his own mythological version of the disease. But a urologist might, in noting increased urination, likewise miss the basis of a thirst introducing excessive liquid. Errors of diagnosis and cure are simply human and finally transcend ideological boundaries. They confirm the complexity of the relationship between symptomology and pathology rather than the guaranteed dire results of relying on an alternative practitioner. An Ayurvedic doctor may well be more observant and use more precisely compounded remedies than an internist. After all, he is working in a different vocabulary of disease and cure.

Some conditions may be truly incurable, for either psychological or organic reasons; some people may not want to get well. Even where holistic modalities turn out, in retrospect, to have been ill advised, there is no surety that a standard allopathic doctor would have been able to cure the same disease, or that the holistic treatment did not have a secondary beneficial effect on the patient.

Many people risk the path of illness—perhaps dreadful illness—in order to attain inner goals deeper than life or death. Mythical heroes knew this and thanked the gods for such opportunities, but we are rarely even aware of the invitation to take the journey.

Ethical practitioners of all persuasions fortunately acknowledge what they can handle and what is outside the realm of their practice. If a practitioner is unwilling to acknowledge his limitations and his treatments do not bring improvement, the client is under no obligation to remain in his care. A side-effect of our modern health regime is many a patient's unexamined assumption that the doctor is both all-knowing and doing her a favor, that his time is more valuable than hers. In truth, she has hired the doctor, and can fire him. She may be wrong, but she has to know that is her right and to consider it as a legitimate option.

Part of taking responsibility for one's own health is learning _how_ to communicate with doctors and healers, i.e., to approach them and their practices in ways that elicit contact and accountability, to assess their promises critically, and, by all means, to avoid asking them to carry out a miracle which someone else has failed to produce. Uncritical, passive reverence can be a dangerous guise in which to seek treatment.

For every patient like the woman with the melanoma, there are countless others who have wasted time and money under an almost lifelong superstition of diseases and irreversible conditions, attempting to track down the "ghost in the machine." At some level the price we all pay for our professional medicine establishment is a paralyzing fear of esoteric maladies and insidious unknown bugs and viruses; the very process of obsession with exogenous pathology leads one to imagine alien organisms everywhere. Some people can afford to keep an absurdly prophylactic guard against these fictive invaders; even many who cannot afford it do. Their whole lives are built on medical nihilism. Meanwhile, no real disease is ever found. Even where real diseases abound, the nihilism that underlies allopathy reduces people to regarding themselves as victims in a shooting gallery. They are so busy dodging germs and other personalized misfortunes that they forget to live or to contribute to the world. Our planet shows the scars of this solipsism.

And now we face an epidemic of iatrogenic (physician-caused) diseases, diseases that are the side-effects of treatments for previous diseases and are usually more serious than the conditions whose treatment engendered them. Psychiatric disorders caused by medical treatment of both physical and mental diseases make up rapidly growing chapters of the current pathological atlas.

So when we grant the medical establishment its recognition as the planetary first-aid center, present as well as future too, we must note also that it is a mirage, a source of pathology, abandoned hope, and the manipulation of people's illnesses, fictional and real, for profit and self-esteem. Much that passes for illness is a message that should lead into a world filled with lights, colors, sounds, pleasures, tingling, unconstricted breathing, personal growth, and awakening vision, to which the panorama of sterile chemicals and operating tables is a cruel reversal and wasteful joke.

Notes

1. Deepak Chopra, *Quantum Healing: Exploring the Frontiers of Mind/Body Medicine* (New York: Bantam Books, 1989), pp. 139–40.

2. Michel Foucault, *The Birth of the Clinic,* translated from the French by A. M. Sheridan Smith (New York: Pantheon, 1973) (originally published in France in 1963), p. 3.

3. Edward Schieffelin, research associate in medical anthropology, University of California, Berkeley; personal communication, 1977.

4. Peter Duesberg, personal communication, 1994. Material is summarized in his forthcoming book *Infectious AIDS: Stretching the Germ Theory Beyond Its Limits* (Berkeley, California: North Atlantic Books, 1995).

5. David Perlman, "Controversial AIDS Theories Debated at Forum in S. F. ," *San Francisco Chronicle* (June 22, 1994), p. A7.

6. Duesberg, *Infectious AIDS: Stretching the Germ Theory Beyond Its Limits.*

7. Charles R. Caufield with Billi Goldberg, *The Anarchist AIDS Medical Formulary: A Guide to Guerrilla Immunology* (Berkeley, California: North Atlantic Books, 1994), pp. 43–46.

8. Jeremy Ginzberg, "Pharmaco-Hell Calling," *East Bay Express* (Berkeley, January 21, 1994), p. 3.

9. Kathleen Goodwin, "Alternative Medicine: A Note of Caution," *City Miner,* Vol. 3, No. 3, 1978.

CHAPTER THREE

The Cultural Basis of the Cure

The Social Definition of Medicine

IN ANY CULTURE, the medical establishment "establishes" customs of belief even as the political establishment imposes laws and an economic establishment determines the basis of exchange. Through the medical establishment, disease and death are brought into collective cultural security. People are born into the same "world," are threatened by the same germs or spirits, and aspire to the same *mens sana in corpore sano.*

Sharing definitions of reality holds a culture together. If political experiences were not commensurate, there would be no parameters of justice and conflicts would escalate. If economic categories were not mutual, it would be impossible to exchange goods or to tell the difference between rightful ownership and theft. Sanity and health are, likewise, legalities and accreditations.

Medicine is a near impossible category to apply cross-culturally. The very name "medicine man" challenges any similitude. In primitive and tribal societies, the most common on this planet throughout history, there is no medicine in Western terms, but then there is no economics, politics, or religion either in terms of Western conceptions of these things.

A people exists not in categories of professions anyway but in a pantheon of customs, ideas, and artifacts. Medical

events were originally integrated with other aspects of life; medicine overlapped with prayer, farming, marriage, war, behavioral sanctions and taboos, etc. Although our own professional medicine is culturally imbedded in the same way, we have gradually, in the evolution of stratified society, abstracted occupations from primary social structures and institutionalized them as formal systems with their own professional rules.

By contrast, the native doctor never leaves or enters an office; he is always there, and he is never there. In tribal societies, medical language is social and mythological language addressed to specific healing rituals.

Our own medical mythology has replaced these safeguards with other ikons: academic authority, religious materialism, antigen theory, technological progress, and the like. We trust remedies whose names and constituents we rarely understand and which are as esoteric as any diagnosis by rat entrails. We have confidence in the dark bottle from the industrial hospital because we accept its general system of manufacture and commodization. In swallowing the medicine, we confirm a chain of meanings: how the ambiance of the medicine feels and how we are supposed to feel subsequently is how the society feels to us. We assume that this is also the objective meaning of the medicine, just as we assume that the presenting ailment and succeeding health have objective loci. Often they do. But we are fooled by these instances into the illusion that we are free of mythological and internalizing ramifications and that we ingest the medicine and the therapeutics clean.

(Some substances and treatments *are* universal remedies, particularly in the realm of botanicals, and we should acknowledge this category without letting it confuse the cultural issues behind institutionalized medical treatment. When Jacques Cartier and his men arrived in Quebec in 1535 with scurvy, it did not require an Algonquian ceremony for them to be cured by

68

white cedar bark from the local apothecary. Algonquian medicine as a whole, though, is not located in this transcultural event.)

Societies spin their webs by disguising institutions and professions in one another. By the time a person in our culture decides to be a doctor, he has been initiated into the same system of meaning as an electrician, a corporate executive, and an academic philosopher. He treats his patients by the same order of logic and is rewarded in the same abstract currency quantifying social exchange. The hospital in which he works is also a jail, a school, a factory, a resort hotel. From outside the culture, these complexes of buildings may not even look that different from one another. They are contiguous institutional complexes that impose different confinements based on distinct moral and developmental premises; they are sustained by the same general sense of what kinds of things go wrong, what must be done to remediate them, and (parenthetically) what activities are pleasurable. It is no wonder that people may fear the hospital as if under a life (or death) sentence and seek jail, unconsciously, by committing sequential crimes when they are sick. The culture sets the definitions, but the acts are prior or subliminal to definition. The penal psychiatrist might as well draw straws as try to distinguish the criminally insane in any consistent fashion from the punishable. Tests of legal sanity are acts of cultural desperation. In the end, criminals and mad persons are both punishable, are both treatable. (We will reevaluate this paradox from a totally different perspective in the Epilogue in Volume Two.)

A luxurious room in a hotel fronting the beach

The Cultural Basis of the Cure

may be more pleasurable than either a hospital room or a jail cell, but its occupant may be just as miserable and trapped. One would prefer not to be in prison, but—from the perspective of life and death—numbness, illness, lack of freedom, and synthetic pleasure overlap, no matter how they are culturally defined.

The Origin of Social Categories

THE SIMPLEST SURVIVING human societies are organized as hunting bands and do not differ much, in functional ecological terms, from higher primate bands. In present-day Africa baboon troops form with anywhere from nine to 185 members. Otherwise separate troops often mingle at waterholes. The diet of these creatures is mostly vegetarian, but they have been observed capturing young hares, small deer, nestling birds, and insects. Each troop operates in an area of three to fifteen square miles, with a more tightly defended core. The troop itself is organized in a strict dominance hierarchy such that at least its males stand in an order of precedence to one another. Animals not only know their status in relationship to each other, but maintain it in space as they move and feed, their leaders in the center. Apparently hierarchical organization was the key to survival for onetime tree dwellers outside the protections of the forest.

One should not imagine insectlike rigidity and sexual-biological destiny. A baboon troop is held together by social principle, not blind instinct. We recognize this because we remain loosely in such a troop. It little matters if one believes in a linear evolution of mankind from Pliocene apes. Either we remain them or have become them in our image of protean society globalized. Bushmen bands in Africa continue to mirror these primate troops. We find them contemporaneously organized in shifting territories around waterholes with a defended core and sharing hunting-and-gathering space with other groups. The head male's position is passed on patrilineally (along a male line of males). His power is restricted and situational. Although he ostensibly owns all the resources, he cannot deny access to them to any member of the troop.

Our observations of such groups provide images that have become clichés for the origination of social contracts: a nuclear family is built around two adults in an economic and sexual unit. The men hunt (a boy's first large kill is qualification for marriage). Women gather small animals, nuts, beans, and wild plants; they also cook and take primary responsibility for the children. Incest taboo necessitates a flow of genes and customs between groups. Since marriage is not permissible within the nuclear family (and one band could hardly breed enough families to prevent incest), two or more groups must always be bound in inter-marrying chains. Society is thus continually regenerated and transposed geophysically. Any member has uncles, nephews, and in-laws in sur-rounding groups.

As these bands move by season through different territories (based picturesquely on the ripening of mangetti nuts and tsi beans and nomadic game), goods are shared, gifts exchanged. The migratory pattern works against major material accumulation. The men carry only weapons and meat; the women load ostrich eggs with water and food and sling on the youngest children. This is our idyllic, tyrannical paradigm of our own ancestry.

Plains living frees primates' arms to make tools, the use of which then frees their jaws, which (over generations) molds the skull allo-metrically to encase a larger brain, a brain which provides more synapses and cells to invent new tools and organize more complex social life. Tools allow the strategic killing of larger animals, which produces meat to share and goods for storage and transport. The very old and sick can now be nurtured while contributing in unique ways to the larger group. Simple survival becomes a web of responsibility based on reciprocal rights and obligations.

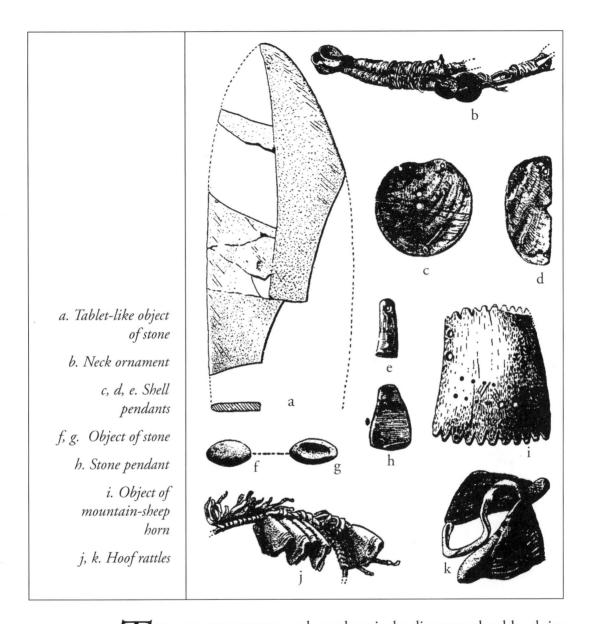

a. *Tablet-like object of stone*

b. *Neck ornament*

c, d, e. *Shell pendants*

f, g. *Object of stone*

h. *Stone pendant*

i. *Object of mountain-sheep horn*

j, k. *Hoof rattles*

T HE BASIS OF MODERN anthropology is the discovery that blood ties map a social and symbolic configuration in space and time ... even beyond space and time. This figure—the society itself—is supported by complex structural terminology and bounded by legend and cosmology. Kinship did not originate full-blown as a practical and

ORIGINS

72

deductive system of organization. It was born in the desperation of chaos out of the riddles of night. All culturally recognized relationships hang not on universal logic but a phenomenological array of natural objects, relationships, and spontaneous symbols. These elements were primordially fused because their fusion kept chaos at bay. Animistic explanations of cause and effect (gods throwing boulders to make thunder and turkeys giving birth to clans) did not satisfy some "primitive" need for explanation and security; they satisfied a desire to escape the void itself—the "nothing" between animal and human. The alternative to naturalistic logic is not just no explanation for the mysteries of nature but no rationale for society either. Humanity was thrust forward into language and taboo in order to avoid falling backward into Babel. Science, medicine, and religion all began as strictly enforced totems and segments of social structure. They were not luxuries; they were necessities.[1]

The coherence of any group is maintained by its segments alone, there being no outside systems or higher authorities (except those cosmologically invented). Members of different families ultimately trace descent from a common ancestor; a number of these lineages then converge at an even more remote ancestor, until, at the highest and most widespread level of alliance, they share not a real ancestor but a totem being or animal.

These lineages, with their in-law members, become clans, and the clans form communities. There is no formal church and no elected government. Power is earned charismatically, or it is passed down in clubs (sodalities, guilds). Temporary chieftainship often evaporates when a particular military crisis or ceremony ends.

The segments are the polity, the marketplace, the army, the church, the corporate ownership, the maintenance crew, the masters and initiates of the ceremonies, and the source of all ethical and political sanction. They form the outer wall.

The segments also generate a profound internal geometry such that no one even comes close to the wall, and—where the forest of symbols is thickest—poetry, art, and mythology sprout. From this pre-conscious intersection between the segments of society and the forms of nature arises a system of categorization that underlies all human speculation; in its widest application, it is called totemism: "Totemic classifications have a doubly objective basis. There really are natural species, and they do indeed form a discontinuous series; and social segments for their part also exist. Totemism, or so-called totemism, confines itself to conceiving a homology of structure between the two series. . . ."[2]

The homology of structure is a crutch enabling consciousness to leap from undifferentiated sensation into a full-fledged human realm with replicas of stars on bison hides and bodies of the dead decorated with amulets in shallow tombs. It is a world of fire-lit cave paintings and choreographed ostrich dances in place of rigid claw tracks in bark and mating rituals. These glyphs and ceremonies are the raw materials of primordial totems. The totems themselves are hybrid categories of natural objects and modes of thought. Nascent social interaction cannot sustain all its own subtleties and transformations, so it blends them with acts of dream, geomancy, and shamanic vision. Totemism defines society before society can define either itself or totemism because myth alone can name the dread and nameless artifacts that arise between dream and waking, in the hiatus between animal and human thought. Some argue compellingly that wild hallucinogens spontaneously impelled the primate brain into these first worlds of magic and science; thus, rational thought was provided its primal lexicon of images by—of all benefactors—mushrooms, berries, and vines, or the spirits within them.[3] Where *those* images originated, either within or without the luminosity of DNA, will always be our mystery. (See the first chapter in Volume Two for further speculation on this.)

The origin of the universe merges into the origin of the web itself, which marks the limits of society (and being). The singular creations of all exterior things—sun, moon, plants, stars, animals, diseases—are inseparable from the emergence of social segments, so each derives its reality, respectively, from the other and they come to share an identity in daily social life. After all, since the societal boundaries cannot be transcended, thought becomes cosmological precisely as it becomes remote, but it does not stop being social in the sense that "social" is the ongoing regime of men and women in durable groups. Tools, methods of farming, boatbuilding, healing, and other activities express the primordial segmental realities of which they are extensions. This may be as simple as the Sun inventing a medicine stick at the same time that he is the founder and father of the Hopi Sun Clan, or it may come more ambiguously and mysteriously from within the properties of the web and its symbols, as a jaguar emerging from the forest speaking semi-intelligible syllables in a moment neither waking nor dream. (Etiology is our obsession with the temporal quality of timelessness.)

> The jaguar and the man are polar opposites, and the contrast between them is doubly formulated in ordinary language: one eats raw meat, the other cooked meat; in particular, the jaguar eats man, but man does not eat the jaguar. The contrast is not merely absolute: it implies that between the two opposite poles there exists a relation based on a total absence of reciprocity.[4]

Yet the jaguar is the discoverer and guardian of fire. The jaguar clan, composed of human "jaguars" as well as feline ancestral ones, is the primary source of marriage partners for those of the adjacent clans. Add to this the fact that fire—the primary artifact of the Sun—is a marriage gift of wild jaguars, a gift which is crucial in cooking and in making men *not* jaguars. All the while, wild jaguars still precede, totemically, every instance of a jaguar clan. The absence of perfect reciprocity is the very basis of indigenous insight into the totemic aspects of both nature and society.

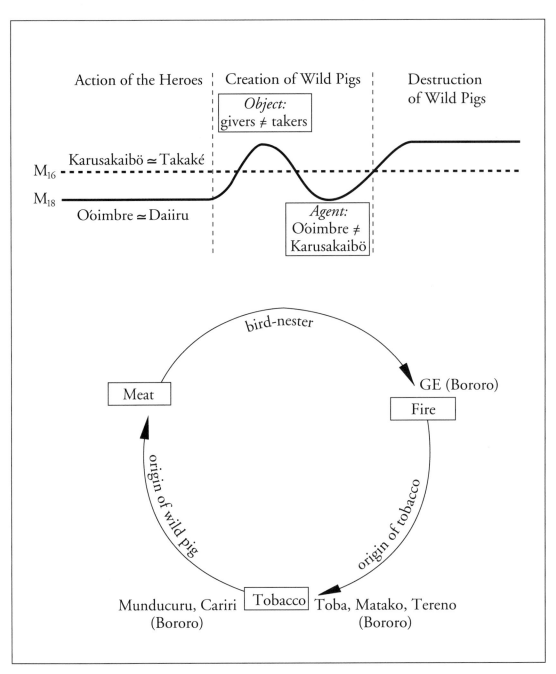

Action of the Heroes | Creation of Wild Pigs | Destruction of Wild Pigs

$$\boxed{\begin{array}{c}\textit{Object:}\\ \text{givers} \neq \text{takers}\end{array}}$$

Karusakaibö ≃ Takaké

M_{16}

M_{18}

Oóimbre ≃ Daiiru

$$\boxed{\begin{array}{c}\textit{Agent:}\\ \text{Oóimbre} \neq\\ \text{Karusakaibö}\end{array}}$$

bird-nester

Meat

GE (Bororo)

Fire

origin of wild pig

origin of tobacco

Tobacco

Munducuru, Cariri
(Bororo)

Toba, Matako, Tereno
(Bororo)

Mappings of totemic categories after Claude Lévi-Strauss,
The Raw and the Cooked.

In order that all man's present possessions (which the jaguar has now lost) may come to him from the jaguar (who employed them formerly when man was without them), there must be some agent capable of establishing a relation between them: this is where the jaguar's human wife fits in.[5]

Two not merely opposing but utterly disjunctive systems suddenly lock into place and make nature and society a seamless machine.

[The reader should not mistake this discussion as making the more familiar assumption that magic, primitive science, and religion are mere opiates, the purpose of which is to facilitate sociopolitical functioning. My argument here (borrowed in large part from Lévi-Strauss) is that the mythological and philosophical elaborations of individual epistemologies—even those that arise from ritual consumption of hallucinogens—emerge into communal language as totems, that is, as segmental adjuncts to family and clan differentiation. Magic, science, and religion all have their own discrete archetypal existences—even hypothetically in ape society—but they are unverbalized, hence nonexistent, until they are framed in totemic terms. Lévi-Strauss writes: "Mythical thought . . . is imprisoned in . . . events and experiences which it never tires of ordering and re-ordering in its search to find them a meaning. But it also acts as a liberator by its protest against the idea that anything can be meaningless. . . ."[6] This involves exponentially more complex transformations than merely subsuming myths in a functional explanation of the social order.]

The abstract system distinguishing human from ape society was the web from which all future webs were spun out. Its first strands were there before the beginning. Its alphabet was "thought" itself. Its first words were "flits" and "blurs" becoming "stars" and "birds." We continue to think these strands, though we also have come to think such bigger and more cosmic things *with* them that we have forgotten their mere existence. The first doctors were barely yet apes, and their healing said that. Our healing (as our astronomy) will contain their healing (their celestial magic likewise) embryonically.

Near the end of *The Savage Mind,* Lévi-Strauss adds:

> … what [man] lives so completely and intensely is a myth—which
> will appear as such to men of a future century, and perhaps to him-
> self a few years hence, and will no longer appear at all to men of a
> future millennium. All meaning is answerable to a lesser meaning,
> which gives it its highest meaning. . . .[7]

Here prehistoric totemism meets zen at the point at which both
replicate the computer and the DNA chain. Each lofty thought and
seemingly cosmic object rests upon frogs shooting bows and arrows
and macaws releasing diseases into the world by farting. "[The] *meaning is never the right one:* superstructures are *faulty acts* which have 'made
it' socially."[8] All systems of medicine are, of course, included therein.

WE TEND TO LOOK at groups like the Bushmen solely from the
outside, where we are. From there we see a simple grid of families bound into local groups, autonomous nexuses allied in a society.
We see raw primitivity. From within, though, the members form a
kaleidoscopic shifting field requiring all the wit and deviousness of
similitude, transformational logic, and ritual symbolism to hold it
together. As units move, change, fuse, and split, the symbols also fission and flex. They take on new meanings from beyond conscious
thought. Ideas change even as dialects of speech do. From this maelstrom all systems of thought, including formal science, were spawned.

Wherever agriculture was developed, a more complicated tribal level
of organization emerged along with it. With farms comes dramatically
increased population density; people organize their domains in different ways. Now, occasionally, descent is traced through a female line of
males to protect a domestic continuity of gardeners. Economic, political, and religious institutions continue to expand and, although there
are still no corporate entities outside the framework of kin, the roles of
doctor, priest, smith, war chief, etc., begin to differentiate. Social anthropologists consider it crucial that everyone is still "equal" in terms of

access to critical goods and judicial rights, but what have emerged amidst peers are titled offices, hereditary societies, and elected councils.

In Western civilization, economics is by now a game in which the players, the citizens, compete for limited desirable goods. Economic survival is the original activity of which ritualized gambling itself is an imitative game. Tribal society, however, is too vulnerable for life to be left to contest. Cooperation and exchange are crucial to group as well as individual survival. Winners require losers, and losers do not maintain peaceful communities.

Gift giving is a most ancient and serious custom. The giver expects an equal or better gift in return, but it is not a self-serving strategy, and it does not hoard great wealth. Since trading always involves incommensurate items (there are no controlled markets), it is by definition unequal; native society ignores the inequality and puts the emphasis on the sheer flow of goods.

We should not be surprised when, during a Kwakiutl potlatch, a "gift-giver" destroys a valuable copper at sea and his trading partner boastfully reciprocates by destroying an even more valuable one. This exchange is a "war," a war of competing generosities. The value of these coppers is almost inestimable. The worth of one fathom-and-a-half-long copper was described by the following priceless utterance of totemic oratory masking as currency:

> ... There was nothing that was not paid for it. It made the house empty. Twenty canoes was its price; and twenty slaves was its price and also ten coppers tied to the end was its price, and twenty lynx skins, and twenty marmot skins, and twenty sewed blankets was its price; and twenty mink blankets was its price; and one hundred boards was its price; and forty wide planks was its price; and twenty boxes of dried berries added to it; and twenty boxes of clover, and also ten boxes of hemlock-bark, was its price; and forty boxes of grease was its price; and one hundred painted boxes was its price; and dried salmon not to be counted was its price; and two hundred dishes was its price.[9]

The Cultural Basis of the Cure

This valuable object existed only in order to be given away. As one Koskimo song put it:

> Of olden times the Kwakiutl ill treated my forefathers and fought them so that blood ran over the ground. Now we fight with button blankets and other kinds of property, smiling at each other. Oh, how good is the new time!
>
> We used to fight with bows and arrows, with spears and guns. We robbed each other's blood. But now we fight with this here *[pointing at the copper which he was holding in his hand],* and if we have no coppers, we fight with canoes and blankets.[10]

At a secret meeting a Kwakiutl elder exhorted his tribesmen: ". . . the Koskimo are likely to beat us in our war with property. Therefore I ask you not to be asleep, else the Koskimo will surely walk right over us, friends!"[11]

Another speaker added: "Let me ask you chiefs and new chiefs of my tribe, do you wish to be laughed at by our rivals? We are almost beaten by the Koskimo. We are only one potlatch ahead of them. After this pile has been distributed, we shall only be two potlatches ahead of them, instead of four, as our fathers used to be."[12]

The logic of such "gift wars" underlies our later discussions of the syntax of medicine in the same groups. However, we will discuss the "barter" aspect of them in its own terms here.

Ongoing exchange stimulates kinship ties and softens tribal boundaries. It keeps goods moving between regions of differential resources and seasonal harvests. Irregular abundance is automatically traded off or shared. What seems to be a primitive economics and sublimated warfare is also an unconscious system of transfer nested in a social

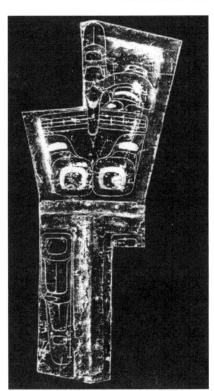

"Killer Whale" copper with broken sections from potlatch activity

ceremony. Much frantic-seeming activity—feather props, drums, dancing, etc.—goes into the delivery of ostensibly tiny gifts, but the invisible component of these exchanges includes a benefaction so large that
we no longer have the means to give it. Listen to the honorific names
of some valuable Kwakiutl coppers: "it glides out of one's hands like a
steel-head salmon," "making the house empty of blankets," "too great
a whale," "all other coppers are ashamed to look at it."[13] Our inflated
philanthropy is a meager replacement for the true object of power our
ancestors possessed.

The new holistic health movement is nostalgic for just this ancient
network with its nexus of power. But original holism had a thoroughness we lack, short of re-creating primal communities from scratch,
each one identical, from within, to the universe. And it is impossible
to do that now, knowing what we do. Our efforts to return to tribal-
ism and nature take us on a journey elsewhere; they will always (always!)
be some other thing. Our only hope for regaining power is to forge it
out of our own web—a possibility I will come back to in the Epilogue
in Volume Two. We simply can't do the potlatch anymore—or anything like it—without conning ourselves. But we can still invent the
"potlatch" from raw materials anew.

I T IS NO WONDER that Indians, Africans, and other Aborigines, insofar as they maintain any of their traditional world-views, do not show
the enthusiasm for harmony and holism one finds in the Western counterculture. They do not know any other world.

There are, of course, also deficiencies in primitive holistic medicine.
Its "doctor" cannot transplant hearts; he cannot intervene successfully
where serious infection has set in. Many curable illnesses are terminal
in his society. The Western doctor inherits tools with which to prolong
life and escape such crises, tools which could have come from nowhere
else but the Pleistocene and early farming communities and which
emerged from the symbolic web along with man and woman as a species.
He has lost their original context and meaning, hence, their spirit.

The Original Medical Ideology

THE ARCHETYPAL NATIVE medicine man prolongs life in the act of restoring balance; his skill is in the dynamics of actual cure. He takes each patient out of dysfunction back into harmony, but he exacts a sacrifice, which is no more than the price the gods levy for health and reintegration. In our culture, patients pay larger medical bills, but with abstract, inflated currency. They still get to drive their cars to work and watch TV at night; in fact they are encouraged to do so. The edge is taken off their uncomfortable symptoms, but the real disease may in fact be a lifestyle, of which they will die in the end anyway. Even such a death is not as serious a condemnation of this hygiene as the fact that they will live it until they die of it; they will not get a chance to explore what they might otherwise be.

It took the universe working all the time until our births to produce us, each of us in our uniqueness. Native medicine does not think in this way, but medicine men and women act with an equivalent sense of the cosmos. It takes the universe working all the time until our disease to bring it into being too; such a disease cannot be dismissed without an acknowledgment of this web. Life can never be made the same as it was before. It must be recast from unintegrated elements. The same totemic currency that established the meaning of the potlatch underwrites native medicine. What is a "copper" in one is a raven mask in the other.

In a Navaho ceremony we see the overall mind of the culture and the reifications of the landscape joining in a *metadrama* through which pollution, infection, guilt, grief, excitation, and mortality are purged. The same purgation, named otherwise, is the goal in contemporary hospitals: allopathy is also ceremonial.

Western medicine exists in its technological mode because Western society as a whole is in a technological phase, and individuals respond to a medicine that embodies their own cultural myth.

In light of this, it is important to look again at the Western export of a universal health system. In areas where infectious diseases thrive and the infant mortality rate is high, the new method makes a miraculous debut—like gunpowder. Just as the master of martial arts—with his tools from a samurai lineage—can be done in by a cheap pistol, so can the shaman be embarrassed, in individual instances, by antibiotics. But <u>technologies are tricks</u>, and once the tricks are familiar and everyone has learned them, the persistent problems of the society resurface, and the gods and their mediators are gone. Penicillin and baby formula may save lives, but, administered as mass social welfare, they cause irreparable alienation.

INTEGRATED SHAMANIC MEDICINE is not medicine at all by scientific standards. It is a method of dispelling disease through a pre-scientific (though not *un*scientific) process of totemic conversion, a process that is also pre-political and pre-economic. This disease was never an isolated condition from which the sick person could be extricated. It was his lot, personally and socially. It was also his opportunity. New holistic medicines are beginning to recover some of this ceremony, albeit in a communityless facsimile of such a culture.

What's missing in the West is an understanding of the consequences of an individual human life, to say nothing of entire communities and societies or of the species and life itself. Native medicine stakes its reputation on curing people who must return to spiritual battle, and this means all people, not just priests. Western medicine is based on healing people to go back to jobs and niches. The decay of the cities and the alienation of modern man, the ubiquity of crime and the mass production of meaningless junk: all of these, to the medicine man, are disease, a vast unchecked plague.

In much of the disappearing aboriginal world, spiritual development and ancestral responsibility, not personal attainment, are the reasons for living. This is not "spiritual" in the civilized sense; it is not "religious" or "mystical." It is "spiritual" as in "power"—power by the agency of cosmic nature. Accumulating power is as common an activ-

ity in indigenous society as shopping is in the United States. Agriculture is power; war is power; destroying a priceless copper is power; marriage mediates the power of clans; transactions are exchanges of the accoutrements of power. That is, each of these things has an invisible component that is dangerous and harnessable.

And we must not forget: the native Californian Pomo and Miwok called them "doctors"—those who dressed up in bear and panther costumes and hid out in the woods, ambushing and killing people.

Doctors?

Yes. Because of their power. Because they got so good they could mimic even minor details of the behavior of the animals they "were." The bear doctor in the wild was virtually inseparable from the wild bear, and his claws left equivalent marks in his victim.[14]

We see brutality and sadism—ritualized and unnecessary. They see epic spiritual accomplishment.

Among the Plains Indians, war and thievery may have been indistinguishable from the practice of medicine. After all, a devious and deadly enemy requires skills of a shamanic order. This enemy, no matter how poorly treated, was never institutionally objectified and dehumanized. The web was never snapped, as it has been in twentieth-century holocausts.

The excruciating torture of war captives, described with righteous horror by early European observers, is identical in many of its aspects to the training of Indian physicians. Those who survived or escaped merited great medicines for their travails. They became doctors, or, if not doctors, adjudicators of rain and wind, or enchanters—for all these powers derive from the same sources.

Notes

1. Claude Lévi-Strauss, *The Savage Mind* (Chicago: University of Chicago Press, 1966), p. 95.

2. Ibid., p. 227.

3. Terence McKenna, *The Archaic Revival: Speculations on Psychedelic*

Pomo bear doctor's suit

Mushrooms, the Amazon, Virtual Reality, Evolution, Shamanism, the Rebellion of the Goddess, and the End of History (San Francisco: Harper-Collins, 1993).

4. Lévi-Strauss, *The Raw and the Cooked: Introduction to a Science of Mythology, I,* translated from the French by John and Doreen Weightman (New York: Harper and Row, 1969), p. 83.

5. Ibid.

6. Lévi-Strauss, *The Savage Mind,* p. 22.

7. Ibid., p. 255.

8. Ibid., pp. 253–54.

9. Helen Codere, *Fighting with Property: A Study of Kwakiutl Potlatching and Warfare,* 1792–1930, Monographs of the American Ethnological Society, Vol. XVIII (New York: J. J. Augustin, 1950); reprinted in Tom McFeat (ed.), *Indians of the Northwest Coast* (Seattle: University of Washington Press, 1966), p. 99.

10. Ibid., p. 93.

11. Ibid., p. 94.

12. Ibid.

13. Franz Boas, *The Social Organization and Secret Societies of the Kwakiutl Indians,* Reports of the United States National Museum (Washington, D. C., 1895), reprinted in McFeat, *Indians of the Northwest Coast,* pp. 76–77.

14. S. A. Barrett, *Pomo Bear Doctors,* University of California Publications in American Archaeology and Ethnology, Vol. 12, No. 11, July 11, 1917 (Berkeley: University of California Press).

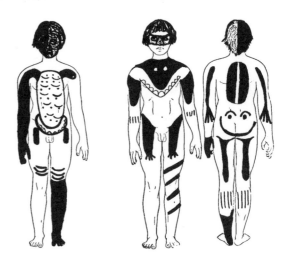

CHAPTER FOUR

The Origin of Medicine

Rudiments and Variations

SELF-TREATMENT IS INSTINCTUAL; rudimentary forms of it exist even among the animals: the cat chews grass and then vomits, the deer licks the dew from flowers.* When a limb is injured, a dog holds its paw aloft. "A snake which gets wounded heals itself," writes Paracelsus. "If now this is done by the snake, do not be astonished for you are the snake's son. Your father does it, and you inherit his capacity, and therefore you, in a brutish sense, are also a doctor."[1] We were "doctors" before we were beings. Our cells knew; at our conception, they began doing the impossible from matter. They continue their holographic craftsmanship our whole lives.

Many techniques are so basic that they have arisen independently virtually everywhere. Certainly, pharmacy is a concomitant of the simplest human systems of empirical observation and an early by-product of food gathering. Lévi-Strauss has proposed that fish poisoning (for instance, in jungle pools in South America) may be the missing Mesolithic link between plant gathering and agriculture: *timbó,* the popular

---

*Fresh dew from different herbs and grasses is still prized as an elixir. It was the inspiration for Edward Bach's early twentieth-century remedies made from blossoms in Wales. (See Chapter Seven.)

vegetable fish poison, remains mythologically homologous to both watermelons, a product of cultivation, and honey, a product of insect husbandry. *Timbó* is not actually medicine, but it is certainly pharmacy—pharmacy as an adjunct to hunting and in transition to domestic botany.[2] (The water must not be polluted nor the fish spoiled.) Arrow poisons may provide the same bridge elsewhere. To be poisoned (but not fatally) is one modality of being cured. Hence, to learn how to poison is to learn one of the rudiments of healing. In this regard Eurasia, Africa, and the Americas likely share either very old pre-dispersal customs or equivalent etiologies of invention. In the initiation of tribal doctors, it is as though totemic "bees," "snakes," and "shellfish" signify parallel hierarchies of codes. (See "Regional Ethnobotany" in the next chapter.)

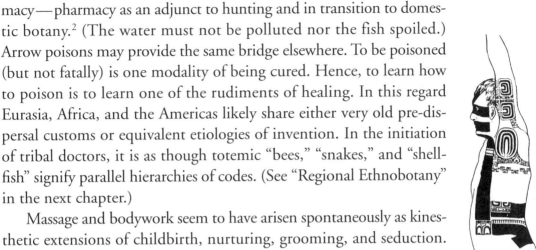

Massage and bodywork seem to have arisen spontaneously as kinesthetic extensions of childbirth, nurturing, grooming, and seduction. Complex variations of these activities were likely developed and ritualized by the first somatic therapists and bonesetters. Styles of making incisions in flesh, including various modes of inserting needles, scarring, scratching grooves in skin, scraping tissue, cutting off parts of the anatomy, are universally known, though particularly common in native Australia and Asia and a part of the vision quest in North America. We will explore the variety of these techniques later.

Tattooing is another parallel technology that is not actually a medicine. Images can be imprinted onto flesh in contexts ranging from therapeutic and empowering to mutilating and hexing, depending upon the intent of the parties. Tattoos are visualizations lodged in anatomy, so they change a person's relationship to his body: how he uses it, how he internalizes it, and how he heals it. Indigenous peoples are masters at incorporating the shadow into daily life (and the disease into the act of healing). Insofar as scars are the remnants of diseases, and stains (as those in rocks and on animal skins) are remnants of natural processes, tattoos are both replicas of and antidotes to the forces that bring on and defeat diseases. They are also representations of clan totems and, as such, the most effective means of impressing newcomers (captives, for instance) into a group by changing symbolically but permanently their "race." Tattoos function both positively and negatively in relation to pathologizing and curative modalities, respectively.

Contemporary tribal peoples describe the origin of their medicine quite differently. Somehow, once, they say, we were in touch with a great instructional power.

What was that?

Supernatural beings?

Ourselves in primal forms?

Our spirit selves before we were women and men or the beavers were beavers, the hawks hawks?

The Carrier Indians of British Columbia told the anthropologist Diamond Jenness:

> We know what the animals do, what are the needs of the beaver, the bear, the salmon, and other creatures, because long ago men married them and acquired this knowledge from their animal wives. Today the priests say we lie, but we know better. The white man has been only a short time in this country and knows very little about the animals; we have lived here thousands of years and were taught long ago by the animals themselves. The white man writes everything down in a book so that it will not be forgotten; but our ancestors married the animals, learned all their ways, and passed on the knowledge from one generation to another.[3]

The literal truth of this matter is unimportant, for there is no literal truth. Esoteric wisdoms develop their own expressions. The insistence of so many Indian groups that they were originally animals or married to animals must reveal more than it fictionalizes. Certainly it implies an intimacy and experiential wisdom to which we have almost entirely lost access. It says, "We know what we know in a permanent and internal way." A look at the Egyptian collection in any museum will confirm the intuition that animals and human beings esoterically share polymorphic bodies. These ibis-headed humanoids and hippopotamus demi-gods gradually mutated and blended into the hieroglyphics of aboriginal speech. Their prior condition of beast-blending was honored as a lost state of grace and enlightenment.

Long before we came, in our popular culture, to the curious assumption that the newer is always better and the more progressive is the more authentic, we held the opposite view: that ancient things were empowered and true in ways that could never be again. Primitive knowledge was firsthand knowledge of creation. The way in which things were originally made (and still hold together) was the best account we had of their agency and origin, the most unerring clue for partial recovery. And what could be a more primordial source of medicine than the pure handiwork of nature: stars, animals, flowers, diseases? Lacking access to their skills, we are robot doctors attempting to ply petals and threads of light.

Paracelsus again: "[Do] not be astonished that the snake knows medicine. She has had it for a longer time than you, and you have it from her; for you are made of the matter of brutish nature, and therefore both of you are equal."[4]

We may heartily agree, but two unexamined prejudices stand in the way of our acknowledging the seminal importance and immense scope of native medicine: our ethnic chauvinism (or Eurocentrism) and our temporal chauvinism (or progressivism and futurism).

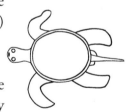

I F WE TAKE, roughly, five million years as the length of time for the human species (and even that figure will probably be conservative by the time most people read this), that makes the last three thousand years, the years to which we relate as comprising most of known historical time, less than one tenth of one percent of human history. Five million years is 50,000 centuries; it is 200,000 generations. Although all of those centuries were "stagnant" in comparison to even the last hundred years, they were still centuries of philosophy, economic transactions, healing,

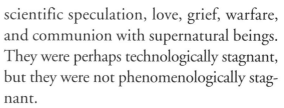

scientific speculation, love, grief, warfare, and communion with supernatural beings. They were perhaps technologically stagnant, but they were not phenomenologically stagnant.

Full-blown medicine was practiced in each of these generations distinctively by all of the cultures throughout the planet; however, we pick up the fragments of these lineages in only the last few of the thousands of ancient worlds leading to our single modern epoch. By then it is too late for us to talk about origins, so instead we reconstitute the last dregs of ancient and classical medical thought in textbooks and museums and extrapolate the rest from primitive cultures still in existence. For most uses, this is an acceptable reconstruction and, even if it were not, it could hardly be improved upon except by hypothetical surmises.

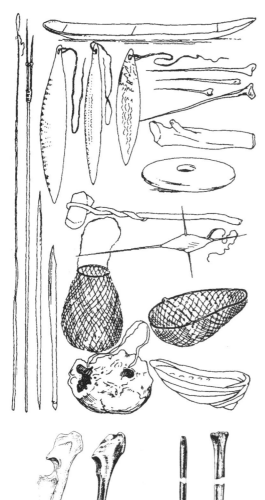

A LL THINGS BEGAN in the timeless past. For all practical purposes, the origin of language is as remote from us as the origin of the universe itself. In our efforts to re-create such a past, we run into two fundamental difficulties: (1) we have no first-hand account of events—no one presently alive was alive at the dawn of time; and (2) the very nature of our present understanding is totally different from the way in which things happened—so that even should a marvelous event suddenly place one or more

ORIGINS

of us at the dawn of matter itself or even of our species, we would not know what we were seeing and we would have no way of communicating it. Of course, the second difficulty may pertain in the present also and is really the dilemma of understanding anything in context. Members of the same family do not see eye to eye, so what possible insight could we have into the mind of prehistoric man?

While all this may appear obvious, it is important to understand that our removal from original things is not just a removal by vast amounts of simple time, millions and millions, or billions and billions, of years. The epochs of nature contain different phenomena and, though universal physical laws hold from one end of creation to another, those universal physical laws are fundamentally unknown. Newton, Darwin, Einstein, Heisenberg, etc., simply offer interpretations of them in the context of one particular culture's view of nature. Their theories are not themselves the "universal physical laws." (See pages 19–21 in Chapter One.)

Thus it is worthwhile to imagine the realms of early medicine, but it is a mistake to trivialize or caricature them. For the persons living in prehistoric times the displays of ancient pharmacists and shamans were as radiant as the dawn sun and as explosive as thunder—not once in some Biblical sense or like a July Fourth parade, but again and again and again, like the seasons, decade after decade, everywhere from the Arctic to the Equator and each time and place in radically different forms—with snakes and frog masks and firelight dances; with roots and blossoms and awls of caribou teeth; with pigments of sand, feather headdresses, and circles of drummers.

We must not be misled by the primitivity of native medicine. Wisdom is there; experiment is there; only the awakened objectifying mind is not. And the universal value of that mind is hardly beyond dispute.

The Origin of Medicine

Vision Quest

MODERN WESTERN RESEARCH is carried out in a laboratory setting where the scientist, anchored in his trained analytic mind, makes a connection between society and his experiment. He establishes relevance and applicability of results through a process of objective reasoning. He does not necessarily concentrate fully, for he may have other things "on his mind." He may be unconsciously alienated from the experiment, his devotion to science notwithstanding. Alienation need not be some monstrous exercise of distance; it can also be a subtle abstraction. A medical researcher may think, "This experiment isn't me; it's chemicals, it's rats; I don't care whether they live or die; I don't even have this disease."

The sense that he may be working toward a cure that will someday be used on him or someone he knows engenders no somatic urgency. It may engage him intellectually, but the *actual* quality of his charge is not harnessed to the research. His body is irrelevant, except as another laboratory tool, the proprioceptor turning phenomena into data. Rats or guinea pigs may replace it insofar as "bodies" are needed. And his relationship to these intermediary animals is neither intimate nor benevolent. Objectivity *requires* his aloofness.

The scientist is a late-comer. Far and away the most common source of medicinal knowledge on this planet is dream and vision. Early human experimenters had as their goal to get back inside nature so they could hear her original medical voice. They  diagnosed and cured illnesses through subjective links between themselves and nature, and then between their patients and nature (in the form of an ikon or a remedy). They were mediums not money-changers. They presented their own bodies, and they healed by the actual health emanating from their being. Training was literally death, rebirth, empowerment, as we shall see.

"I had a powerful dream," says the Delaware Indian doctor. "It was a clear day, a beautiful day. The sky was bluer than I have ever seen it. There were white birds flying directly at me. Then I awoke."[5]

This is the initiating event in an opposite type of medical research. The dream suggests a direction worth following. The doctor can either wait for the next such dreaming or test this one right away. Unless he responds seriously, the dream will be forgotten, merely an exotic visitor during a busy week. If he ignores it, perhaps it will return, slightly changed; then he will have the same decision to make. But if the day is good, he may drop his plans and go immediately to the wilderness: "Office hours canceled. I'm doing a week of research out of town."

He must now get inside nature. He seeks the *place*—where the sky is bluest and clearest and the birds are flying *at* him.

There could be no clearer statement of different cultural relevances. We postpone the dream until past our lifetimes. We do not perceive the white birds as the bearers of medical knowledge. We are busy at other things, always. The native doctor conversely must postpone objective scientific thought until beyond his lifetime (the lifetime of his culture).

The Indian assumes that a dream's choice of him indicates an authentic lineage and that his research will succeed along strands of his own inner nature. The research scientist has no use for such a dream, or any like divination. His responsibility is to clear his mind of just such affinities and to pick up the thread of cause and effect in an externalized and predetermined grid. The significant connection he seeks already exists in physical laws and has nothing to do with him; he must only wrest it from the labyrinth of nature. But he is not a unique receptor. If he doesn't find the serum, someone else will.

There *are* documented cases of Western scientists making discoveries in dreams (a priest holding tablets with the translation of unknown Babylonian) or visions (Friedrich Kekulé imagining the chemical bonds of benzene ring arising as a serpent bites its tail in the fireplace, James Watson getting insight into the DNA helix from transposed images of "Hedy Lamarr's romps in the nude" in the movie *Ecstasy*[6]). These are treated as exceptions, curiosities—at best, kinds of mnemonic devices. We do not honor exogenous information.

THE NATIVE PHYSICIAN is neither a dilettante nor a scoundrel. The outcome of his quest is not a matter of luck and trickery. Medical knowledge from visions is a treacherous business; there is a proper way to do things.

We may question: what do birds know about healing? And even if they knew something, what could they possibly say? And how would we understand it? And who's to say what's good for them is good for us? But we have little experience in the matter. We do not play the game, and the opinion of the Western savant for centuries has been that it is a game not worth playing.

The anthropological literature only begins to convey a sense of the vision quest's beauty and power as well as its peril. Among the Jívaro Indians of the Ecuadorian Amazon Basin, a boy may begin to seek his soul as early as the age of six. He does not get one simply by being born, and he must, at all costs, avoid dying without one. Although this is not strictly a medical quest, it is a quest for those powers of which healing is one. According to Michael Harner:

> If the *arutam* (soul) seeker is fortunate, he will waken at about midnight to find the stars gone from the sky, the earth trembling, and a great wind felling the trees of the forest amid thunder and lightning. To keep from being blown down, he grasps a tree trunk and awaits the *arutam*. Shortly the *arutam* appears from the depths of the forest, often in the form of a pair of large creatures. The particular animal forms can vary considerably, but some of the most common *arutam* include a pair of giant jaguars fighting one another as they roll over and over towards the vision seeker, or two anacondas doing the same. Often the vision may simply be a single huge disembodied human head or a ball of fire drifting through the forest towards the *arutam* seeker. When the apparition arrives to within twenty or thirty feet, the Jívaro must run forward and touch it, either with a small stick or his hand ... It instantly explodes like dynamite and disappears.[7]

This is the moment, unknown to most Western scientists, when the seeker merges with his search.

> After nightfall, the soul of the same *arutam* he touched comes to him as he dreams. His dream visitor is in the form of an old Jívaro man who says to him, "I am your ancestor. Just as I have lived a long time, so will you. Just as I have killed many times, so will you." Without another word the old man disappears and immediately the *arutam* soul of this unknown ancestor enters the body of the dreamer, where it is lodged in his chest.[8]

The Crow doctor of the Great Plains prepares for *his* vision quest with various baths.[9] He scrubs his flesh, then smokes his pores and brain with pine needles. Thus purified, he does not consume again until the vision quest is complete.

He chooses a special place. It might be atop a knoll. Or on the windy prairie. Wearing a buffalo robe smeared with clay, he builds a mound of rocks three feet high, oriented east and west, and he lies on it. In order to entice a vision, or if a vision does not come during the first couple of days, he may mutilate himself—dig lines into his arms or chest, cut off a fingertip. He is not sick, but he is suffering. This act is a testament to the seriousness of the occasion and the value of what can be obtained. We all have an intuition of its formula: the greater the sacrifice (i.e., the deeper into one's self it goes), the more powerful the medicine.

The quester lies there, hungry, exposed, in pain, meditating and praying to the supernatural beings of the world "Without Fires." Here the personal charge and the experiment meet. Research is conducted inside phenomena, at the nondualistic source of mind and matter.

The vision quester remains calm and alert. His whole life and career hang in the balance, and his attention by now is rigorous. He grasps the essential relationship among symbols and events. These grow more detailed and clearer with time. At a moment of insight, all nature, as it were, falls from its visible aspect and shows a feature of hidden artistry. The medicine man does not reenact the event as such. His powers derive purely from having experienced it. By his life as a Crow and his training in mythology, he has come prepared. An animal appears, in creature or human form (if human, with animal robes indicating species); it speaks. Perhaps in words. Perhaps by actions and signs . . .

> A chicken hawk flew at me, landed as a man, and then did a dance. His enemies surrounded him but they could not touch him. Then he became a hawk and took off back into the sky.[10]

> I was lying there for three days when a jackrabbit came toward me. I looked again and it changed into a man. He was wearing a wolf's skin on his shoulders. The wolf's head was red and shone in the sunlight. The wolf's body was painted with yellow stripes, and its tail was a bunch of grouse feathers with a jackrabbit tail. It sang two songs in succession, ending each with a wolf howl. Then it showed me how to make a suit like that.[11]

After five days, I saw an elk in the water. But it walked up to me and changed into a man wearing an elkskin robe and carrying a bone whistle. He turned in all the directions, first to the north, blowing his whistle so that lightning seemed to shoot out of it, singing songs. Each time hundreds of animals, all the females of the different species, walked toward him from the direction to which he was blowing. He said: "I am the medicine man of the wilderness. Go home and make such a robe. Sing these songs and whistle as I have. The girl you love cannot refuse you." Then he sang another song, and a thunderstorm brewed right up. Lightning sprang into the sky, and I was soaked with rain.[12]

From the first two visions, war powers were bestowed. From the third, a love charm was invented and a man was conferred with powers of making rain. He was middle-aged and had been spurned recently by a young woman, so he went to a nearby sacred mountain, fasted, received the elk vision, then successfully wooed her, and lived to the age of one hundred as a rainmaker. Out of this so-called mid-life crisis arose a new career that benefitted the people.

Slippery Eyes's healing medicine was presented in a reptile vision. After fasting unrewarded for three days, he was about to give up the quest. But he had suffered smallpox and his face was so horribly pitted that people had difficulty looking at him. His desperation alone kept him on his vigil.

On the fourth night a voice called him to the spring. The water turned into a tipi and he entered to find snakes living there. The largest was a male, a gigantic eye in the center of its head and a horn. One of the others told Slippery Eyes that this snake was the doctor and had taken pity on him. They all changed into humans, and a real human was carried in on a buffalo-hide stretcher. He was very sick, but the snakes cured him, teaching Slippery Eyes their techniques. Afterwards the chief led him to another tipi, which was his own house (also previously a spring). It was a magnificent dwelling, shingled with furs and jewels.

The snakes administered to him there, removing most of the pockmarks.

After this episode, Slippery Eyes became a successful doctor, and he continued his relationship with the snakes; they often sought him, and he would pet and hold them and coax new secrets.[13]

VISION QUEST IS the primary source of medical and magical knowledge on this planet. I repeat: *vision quest is the primary source of medical and magical knowledge,* but its information is not self-evident or literal as given. It manifests under esoteric circumstances and must be transliterated into daily life. Because it does not speak in any native tongue, shamans are forced to interpret their observations by divination and totemism. The iconography then compounds itself in a self-generating but endlessly redecipherable code.

Some features may be explicit: make a medicine from this plant; prepare a robe like mine; sing this song over this sick person, I will teach you the words and melody. Yet the supplicant must still remember precisely what he sees and hears. Often what makes a medicine effective is a seemingly minute or throwaway gesture, an unacknowledged pause, a nonsense half-syllable disguised as a slight lisp. These are the lynchpins between dimensions.

No matter how pagan and exotic its source, the code gradually becomes civilized and vernacular. Its series of decipherments is not "written down" (these are preliterate peoples); they are preserved, instead, in a far more indelible language, in ceremony and in a medicine bundle. All relevant symbolic and mythological cues come to reside in the materials of the bundle. It is not a souvenir or relic but an active device. Any future medicine man or woman can add details of visions to it; they can record actual doctoring experiences; and they can pass it on as a formulated medicine to someone who did not have the original visions. Several generations after its assemblage, the medicine bundle becomes an objective technique of sorts, a functional totem. It has songs, herbs, charms, stories, all keyed to an original revelation and annotated by those who have used the medicine.

William Wildschut writes:

The contents of the medicine bundles comprised symbolic representations of the supernatural beings and forces seen in the owner's
dream or vision. Together with the owner they formed a clan. The
chief of this clan, the principal supernatural responsible for the vision,
is represented in each bundle. With it are included its helpers or servants who assist in guarding the life of the owner. The vision may
also have been seen wearing distinctive facial or body painting. If so,
different paints were included in the bundle. If a certain kind of
necklace was worn by a supernatural visitant, a close copy of it was
made and placed in the bundle.[14]

A bundle might include feathers, beads, skeletons of animals, a snake-
skin, a wolf pelt, stones, shells, dried plants, etc. Since its elements are

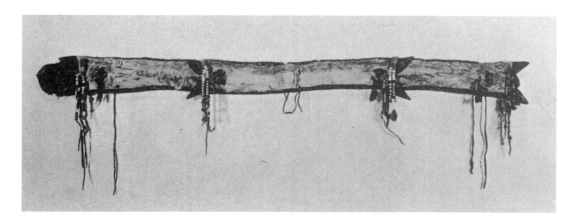

"words" and lack intrinsic potency in and of themselves, there is no reason why anything might not be in a bundle. The contents correlate relationships of power at a given eternal moment. As mythology changes, a bundle can be creatively revised. Later Crow medicine codes include rusty guns, matches, lanterns, and other European "junk." The white man's contempt for an Indian who attached so much meaning to a trinket or feather that he might trade half a dozen good horses for it ignores the obvious comparison with our annals of rare books or the priceless trinkets and rare metals of the laboratory, which would be valueless to the Crow. A Crow's precious experience precedes the trinket; its real value is finally immaterial. The value of the microscope, after all, is that it is the source of new experience. The Crow has already had the experience and seeks its refulgent touchstone. While we wander through mysterious ratios of scale from microcosm to microcosm, he seeks the key to a palpable transformation among utterly discontinuous scales of unknown dimensions. He seeks it because he knows how to make medicine from it.

*Elk
Headdress
from Long
Tail's Love
Medicine
Bundle*

Native Science

A COMPENDIUM OF KNOWLEDGE has been assembled by indigenous practitioners like Slippery Eyes from the beginning of time, in songs, myths, and practical instructions and in the various codes of sand paintings, medicine bundles, garden designs, plant species, and even, it appears, astrological botanies and zoologies of bone, parchment, and stone from deep into the Ice Age.[15] At least 99.99 percent of the concrete features of these have been lost, along with most of the species of plants and animals to which they referred and the tribes whose systems gave them meaning. But for all we have lost, we have not yet lost everything. We seek now to rekindle the syntax of sacred space so as to remake a world almost depleted of spirit.

Our task in spiritual totemics is more difficult than any imaginary problem in cosmological field theory, for we must invent the equivalents of galaxies, the laws of gravity, and molecular recombinants each time anew. The principles of assembling a medicine bundle or conceptualizing the choreography of a healing ceremony are as complex in their own way as the most sublime mathematics. They may lack tables of detailed quantified information, proof of microstructures, and a technology of information retrieval, but none of this affects the accuracy and precision of experience behind these ceremonial integers and their compilation into working systems.

"Native classifications," writes Lévi-Strauss, "are not only methodical and based on carefully built up theoretical knowledge. They are also at times comparable, from a formal point of view, to those still in use in zoology and botany."[16]

When he called the intelligence behind these taxonomies "the savage mind" (in the title of his book), he meant, in effect, to include our mind as well—the human mind in all of its cultural states. He meant: "the mind itself is savage"—not "the mind of the savage."

La pensée sauvage possesses a wild, gashed-open syntax with its own requirements of rectitude. "The exceptional features of this mind which we call savage . . . relate principally to the extensive nature of the ends it assigns itself. It claims at once to analyze and synthesize, to go to its furthest limits in both directions, while at the same time remaining capable of mediating between the two poles."[17] Every curative herb has a totemic and metalinguistic identity inseparable from its medicinal qualities. Every healing ceremony occurs within a prior, etiological ceremony. A medicine of prayersticks and sand paintings and chanting is

both coterminous with and ancestral to a medicine of antibiotics and serums—and maintains hierarchical priority over it. That is, magic and vision remain the principal sources of new information. The rest is writing between the lines—gathering fruit after the tree is ripe. The tree planted in the Mesolithic epoch is now fully bearing.

Scientific institutionalization has changed the outward reality of medicine, the problems to which it addresses itself and the solutions it offers, but it has not touched the core of generative symbols from which primal cures emerged (and still emerge).

Prehistoric peoples kept vast gardens, bred subspecies of plants and animals, hunted creatures ranging from insects to mastodons, and invented the Stone Age micro- and macro-"techn ologies" we inherit, from agriculture and metallurgy to wedlock and the family. With our present dependencies on custom and conceptual limitations, we could not reinvent these things. And we do not have to reinvent them. Primitive man (and woman) have already given them to us, and they will always be fundamental, as s/he is.

Who else could have taken a tropical grass from the jungles of South America with no particular distinguishing characteristics and nursed from it countless varieties of corn—ornamental and popping, grain, medicinal, magical—and adapted these to virtually every climate short of polar in North and South America? Gardens of tamed grass, cultivated locus by locus without a microscope, covering pre-Columbian Mexico and extending clear over the Penobscot River and the Gulf of St. Lawrence to Nova Scotia, equally west and north across the Mississippi and the Sierras.

Once we accept native science's success in a world we no longer privilege, we can understand its vitality. We may doubt that the Indians actually had animal wives, but the durations they spent noticing plants, animals,

The Origin of Medicine

land and sky formations, spirits, and their associations were a form of matrimony. Even in the late twentieth century, field scientists all over the world continue to learn regional taxonomies from natives that include items far exceeding the official repertoire of species reported or even suspected.

The Pinatubo Negritos of the Philippines distinguish something in the neighborhood of 15 species of bats according to living habits— for instance, one that inhabits the dry palm leaves, another that lives on the underside of the leaves of the wild banana tree, another in bamboo clumps, another in dark thickets, etc. This same people classifies 450 species of plants, 75 species of birds, and even 20 species of ants. The Negritos also have more than 50 different types of arrows and can identify, from childhood, the kind and "sex" of a tree from the smell, hardness, and appearance of a small fragment of wood. They are also thoroughly acquainted with the behavior and sexual differences of a variety of fish and shellfish.[18]

Despite this abundance of knowledge, there is a tendency to equate prehistoric medicine with the remnants of contemporary tribal medicine and, at the same time, to condemn practices on the supposed evidence of sociological observation, as marginal first aid mixed with pathetic magic. One historian, fairly typically, claims that in primitive societies, a sick person was deserted "as a menace to the community . . . and left to die; or to recover on his own, if he was lucky."[19] This kind of semi-fictive narrative carries an aura of detached plausibility, but it is possible that the deserted victim was either a single undocumented episode that the author has generalized into a custom or an out-of-context fragment of a larger system with an entirely different meaning. What is at first convincing becomes suspicious the moment one questions its facile cliché. It actually sounds like something from a Tarzan movie. It says absolutely nothing about indigenous medicine.

Victor Turner's writings on African religion, especially among the Ndembu Lunda of Zambia, are much admired in liberal academic circles. He is considered one of the more sympathetic observers. Generally,

he is, but not in matters of medicine, i.e., of practical ethnoscience. He concludes that "medicine is given to humor rather than to cure" and that "a rich and elaborate system of ritual and magical beliefs and practices provides a set of explanations for sickness and death and gives people a false sense of confidence that they have the means of coping with disease." Why do such beliefs persist? he wonders. And his answer is that "they are part of a religious system which itself constitutes an explanation of the universe and guarantees the norms and values on which orderly social arrangements rest."[20] In other words, these people are stuck with their medicine because they are stuck with the symbols which back it up and which their social and economic survival has come to require. Forget the vision quest and the ancient art of healing!

The author goes on to prescribe a big dose of Western pharmacy and an extension of Western-type hospital facilities, likely the very things that depleted the system he is belittling.

So much for African medicine. There's nothing happening but hocus-pocus, delusion, and placebo. And this from a person who knows more about the subject than all but one or two of his readers (including the author of this book). Knowledge, it appears, doesn't make the difference. Not when observation is blinded by bias.

We must do away with our illusion of diseased and miserable native society, which is correct to no greater or lesser degree (though in a totally different way) than our illusion of diseased and miserable industrial society. The longevity we value, which our medicine has seemingly won for us, is a false one, especially since it is a longevity in an industrial society which steals years of life by labor alone. Our medicine has given us a statistical longevity only, which our machines and bureaucracies have relentlessly taken back in units of experientiality. The primitive mortality rate is only a statistical mortality rate; it says nothing of the real lives or possibilities of individuals. Furthermore, diseased native society is at least in part a result of colonial invasion, which brought not only new diseases but also destroyed much of the existential fabric of cultural life.

We are talking about 200,000 generations of medicines, during which tens of thousands of different medicines may have been practiced. If medicine were only the progressive development of more systematized coda, then we might be justified in bunching all these generations of doctors together, reducing their repertoires to a few tricks and traits, and dealing briefly with native medicine as a single defective line. But <u>if medicine is the art of healing, then there is no single lineage or universal fallacy</u>. In fact, each of these other traditions is comparable to ours. In homogenizing and trivializing them we are spurning a cornucopia of healing techniques. Unless we accept, from the beginning, that these were mostly successful, complex, empirically based medicines, we cannot regain an integrity of individual practice or the legacy of the art of healing. That there were corrupt and superstitious native systems also—indeed, corrupt and superstitious elements in all cultures—is obvious; to emphasize them would be to harp on the abuses at the expense of the richness of often-ingenious practices. We do not reduce science to its frauds and missteps. Contradictions and insoluble riddles work their way into any system—since no system is perfect or permanent— and these duly represent, as illness itself in the body, the movement of life through a changing universe.

The man wrongly killed by poison in an African witchcraft trial is an innocent victim of imperfect science. So is the factory worker who comes down with environmental cancer, or the political prisoners of totalitarian states, or the soldiers killed in the wars of their times.

We so value quantitative data we forget that each individual culture, including ours, can have only *one* existential reality. Information itself may be limitless, but it is sterile. When a culture builds machines to ferret out substructure after substructure, it does not thereby correct or enlarge reality. Reality goes as deep as the cosmos goes, and as deep as human beings go for living in such a cosmos. The Navaho and Australian Aborigine have the same amount of *real* information as we do; they go as far into meaning, but not on the basis of industrial achievements, data banks, or star counts, and certainly not on the basis of number of members. They are as deep and real as we are on the basis of their singular and discrete profundity, their living phenomenology, and their ability to hold the loyalty of one participant—even one—in a way that is fundamental. Reality requires neither universities and think tanks, nor world exploration, nor knowledge regarding cell growth. It requires presence among the facts of existence and the ability to experience life's exquisitely complex textures as an integrated whole. From that standpoint a dance is as much a statement of "I am here and know what it is like to be here" as a research paper on DNA. The native totemic reality is as real as the Western orthodox reality. The trained anthropologist and historian simply invent and reinvent the myth of the dominant culture's comprehensive world-view. For all their seeming access to dozens of different cultures, they do not have any more access to reality than any one inhabitant of any one of these cultures.

Stone Age Medicine

T HE EARLY ANTHROPOLOGISTS, James Frazer and Bronislaw Malinowski prominent among them, saw tribal man and woman as primitive and childlike. *La pensée sauvage* was a sentence, condemning them to the preconscious jungles of human thought. African and Melanesian societies had a rough, cannibal look to them, and these anthropologists were not inclined to query beyond their initial judgments, though they reported a great variety of exotic customs. In a sense, ethnological bias about indigenous peoples was established over centuries of European self-congratulation for getting out of their own Dark Ages and the specters of sorcery.

In the last fifty years that prejudice has all but turned around. Social science, in keeping with a fashion of being politically and ethnically "correct," has discovered, or rediscovered, the institutions of tribal society that challenge those of civilization. These range, as noted, from practical skills of hunting, toolmaking, cooking, etc., to exquisitely homeostatic systems of resource exchange, peaceable marriage between small groups, and epic cosmologies. In the last fifty years, some anthropologists (notably in the tradition arising from Leslie White and including Marshall Sahlins and Elman Service) have developed a working distinction between technological evolution, in which increasingly larger amounts of energy are harnessed by a society, and cultural coherence and stability, which have no intercausal relationship to increasing amounts of accessible energy. The consumption scale is always a fast-rising linear curve. Agricultural societies release and use more energy than hunting bands, and industrial societies convert exponentially more energy than large agrarian civilizations. The precision and refinement of craft or quality of life within these cultures and their capacity to enact social justice have little to do with such extrinsic development.

Sahlins' subsequent work on the economics of technologically primitive peoples provides a model for reevaluating the native physician too. Malnutrition is the condition most often assigned, along with disease, by those like Turner to indigenous societies. Ceaseless backbreaking labor is said to be the lot of most humans unfortunate enough to have been born before or outside modern civilization. Sahlins offers catch phrases of average anthropological opinion concerning primitive societies: "'Mere subsistence economy,' 'limited leisure save in exceptional circumstances,' 'incessant quest for food,' 'meagre and relatively unreliable natural resources,' 'absence of an economic surplus,' 'maximum energy from a maximum number of people.'"[21]

The Origin of Medicine

Ethnography rarely confirms these generalizations. It turns out that such opinions, like "the menace to the community," are mostly mixtures of exaggeration and misinformation. Primitives work relatively short hours, live in a limited abundance of resources whose cycles of replenishment they rarely exceed, and share easily without the distraction of formal institutions for maximizing wealth.

No doubt, many anthropologists were "culture-shocked" by the absolute material poverty of natives and deduced from that an unhappiness and suffering that were probably more their projection than their true observations. Primitive peoples may have a low standard of living, but as Sahlins put it, "*they are not poor.* Poverty is not a certain small amount of goods, nor is it just a relation between means and ends; above all it is a relation between people. Poverty is a social status. As such it is the invention of civilization."[22]

An invention, it turns out, that is more our birthright than theirs!

We are the ones who live in a market-industrial economy that institutes false scarcity "in a manner completely unparalleled and to a degree nowhere else approximated."[23] It is our world in which "every acquisition is simultaneously a deprivation . . . a foregoing of something else, in general only marginally less desirable, and in some particulars more desirable, that could have been had instead."[24] Now is the time when almost half the population of the planet lacks subsistence nourishment—"this is the era of hunger unprecedented."[25]

We have actually projected the wolf who is at our own door onto a fiction of indigenous peoples. We refuse to believe they could have existed in more peaceful, stable, and better-fed societies. Says Sahlins: "That sentence of 'life at hard labor' was passed uniquely upon us . . . And it is precisely from this anxious vantage that we look back upon hunters . . . If modern man, with all his technological advantages, still hasn't got the wherewithal, what chance has this naked savage with his puny bow and arrow? Having equipped the hunter with bourgeois impulses and paleolithic tools, we judge his situation hopeless in advance."[26]

Sahlins' *Stone Age Economics* echoes Lévi-Strauss's *The Savage Mind.* It also suggests *"Stone Age Medicine."* Either one, Stone Age Economics or Stone Age Medicine, is what we, at best, point toward in our future—post-Marxist, post-capitalist—a renaissance of small, cooperative, ecologically sound communities.

But it is also something we have left behind. We have improved our means of production and freed our species from absolute environmental control, but we have laid waste the diversities of regional agriculture, the arts of healing, the elegant networks of exchange. We have, in Sahlins' terms, "enriched" ourselves while "impoverishing" ourselves. We have increased anxiety and poverty to exactly the degree we have increased information and wealth, without deepening the profundity of our awareness or our individual capacities to survive. We have reached a point where even the servants of our industrial wizardry are aghast at our social and humanitarian barbarism. Are we, in fact, healthier and wealthier than Pithecanthropus? Do we understand what we have given up compared to what we have gained?

The Shamanic Controversy

PERHAPS THE SINGLE most shocking event on this planet during the last five hundred years has been our decimation of its diversity of species and human cultures. Because the remnants of native technology are still available for tourist viewing and scientific exploitation, and because there remain a few practitioners of the old arts (and because our very fragmentary literature on these subjects is itself vast and unman-

ageable in a lifetime), we retain the illusion of an accessible primitive world. In fact, most anthropology, even that of the nineteenth and early twentieth centuries and certainly that of these later decades, has come far too late. Perhaps it was already too late from the beginning. Western civilization was a blundering, overarmed child when it stumbled upon the New World. Spain sent her criminals to the Americas to meet with philosophers, medicine sages, and statesmen. The scientists that followed were concerned more with confirming the superiority of their sciences than initiating a dialogue with equals.

It is for this reason that Carlos Castaneda's account of his training with the Yaqui shaman Don Juan Matus in Mexico had such a stunning effect, especially outside of anthropological circles.[27] Castaneda gave his readers what they had been looking to anthropology for, with disappointment, for generations: an account of the shaman's experience of his own realm. Despite the general impression that he discovered a whole range of practices previously unknown in the West, we see, upon closer consideration, that his real discovery was more existential than ethnographic. There is no technique described in his books that was not already documented in the existing literature. In fact, all of it had already appeared in the annals of North America alone.

Vision quest: we've gone over that earlier in this chapter.

Talking to animals: one could fill a library with accounts.

Drugs: a regular feature of native American society, especially Latin America (some observers claim there is no nonhallucinogenic pharmacy in South America).

Appearing and disappearing: shamans the world over cultivate other planes.

Waking one's self within dream: the Crow and Iroquois, among others, specialize in this.

Magical war: did Indians ever fight a nonmagical war?

Castaneda reports nothing outstanding or shocking. Yet there is something shocking about his account, less in what it says than what it portends about the other accounts.

He finds, to his astonishment, that from within, the system is far vaster and more powerful than it seems from without. Notably it is more intricately alive, not only more than it would appear from previous accounts but also (in its access to the internal realm of mind as creator) more alive than the whole of Western philosophy and science.

Remember the Pomo Bear Shamans. Don Juan is such a doctor. He is a practitioner of universal shamanism, thus of medicine, which is one of its branches.

Carlos comes to Don Juan in order to be trained lightly in his Yaqui Indian system of occult knowledge, trained enough to write a traditional, descriptive account of it. All of his initial questions and activities are consonant with his professional goal. He speaks to Don Juan as though they are both reasonable intelligent people, as though Juan accepts that he himself is practicing mere totemism. Carlos presumes he will go on being an anthropologist, Juan will go on being a shaman, and neither will think less of the other for his culturally determined preference.

Don Juan does not accept these terms. He is seeking a disciple and intends to teach the real thing. When Carlos offers him money as an informant, Juan says that he requires only Carlos' time. Half-comedian, half-warrior, he proceeds by degrees to initiate him. He does not explain what is happening, at least not in the polite language of cause and effect, so Carlos finds himself suddenly in a world (or perhaps a whole cosmos) that is miraculous and terrifying. He speaks to lizards, moths, cacti; he meets personable spirits; not only do they disappear and reappear, but he does too, along with them. This is not Jenness' mythology of animal partners lodged in legend and rumor of prehistory. This is not peyote happy hour or *Fantasia*. Carlos says: I talked to the lizards, they talked to me; I was a crow, I flew.

Yet he continuously questions Don Juan: Are these things real? Did they happen? Or are they only in my mind? He asks: Would my friends have seen me flying like a crow?

Don Juan answers: If they knew how to look.

Tricks alone would not be enough to hold Carlos' (or our) interest, but then tricks alone would not have been worth the trouble of inventing. The purpose behind this show is that, without it, Indians as well as Anglos live in a meaningless world. Carlos is less awestruck by the visions and appearances than he is devastated by the shallowness of his prior world. So, as a social scientist, he reports on not the poverty and misery of this primitive society, but the richness and beauty of life lived within its magic. *He* is deprived, naive, and cosmically insignificant. Don Juan towers above him in a tradition that seems so much more worth incarnating. The science, the rationale that Carlos clings to, primarily to keep from losing his identity and sanity altogether, is a useless hedge in Don Juan's world. Only a small fraction of things are explained by reason, the Yaqui teaches. Even the rock in the desert is a rock by convention only; that is not its most interesting or even useful attribute. The physical body is not a firm substance at all, but a bundle of fluid, luminous fibers. In this body a talented shaman can make a joke of the machine-suited astronauts. In this body Buddha perceived the binary flashing of all reality millennia before electron microscopes and cyclotrons. The wonder is that Carlos became this. That is why his account is radiant and dangerous, and earlier accounts were merely outsiders' reports of weird behavior and social extensions of totemism.

At first Carlos sets his sense of propriety against Don Juan's world of unpredictability and outrage. Don Juan never deigns to debate at this level. Instead, he asks Carlos what he gains from his rigid continuity: Does he possess power? Is he even happy? Does he have anything more than a bag of trinkets and a rigid sense of personal history?

Carlos is stunned because Don Juan has proven to him the emptiness of his own life. The experiments are important not so much because they work as because they are "real" in some totally other way; they are clues to a world in which Carlos' life might regain meaning. This is the critical criterion of healing and will remain so throughout this book.

The ostensible diseases and their symptomatic cures are not the key to a science of planet medicine. True medicine offers freedom, power, and happiness. It downplays disease as object. The advanced native doctor works on the overall framework of a person's life and identity, the collection of events and lore locating that person in his or her milieu among artifacts of creation. All crises and necessities come together in one symbolic context, condensed by myth and symbols, summarized in a disease. Hence, Don Juan as healer ignores Carlos' objections; they are simply symptoms of his disease. Life is important, not its explanations. Phenomena exist as we interact with them, but they have no abstract significance otherwise as data. Don Juan tells Carlos:

> For you the world is weird because if you're not bored with it you're at odds with it. For me the world is weird because it is stupendous, awesome, mysterious, unfathomable; my interest has been to convince you that you must assume responsibility for being here, in this marvelous world, in this marvelous desert, in this marvelous time. I wanted to convince you that you must learn to make every act count, since you are going to be here for only a short while, in fact, too short for witnessing all the marvels of it.[28]

From the Western scientific point of view, this is an outrageous claim. Some sociologists can admit side benefits from herbal medicine, massage, or ritual, but they do not endorse the savage premise.

Medicines from dreams, somatic resurrection, psychic vision into the disease body, voices from clouds and cacti, magical darts, articulate reptiles, "planetary systems" inside parts of plants, supernatural visitations—all of these are described, in essence, with faint heart and withheld enthusiasm by even the most sympathetic observers. One gets the sense that our ethnographic witnesses always feel they have been told something childish, something mad. Their scientific responsibility is to report and explain it neutrally, but their language betrays them. They credit the savage mind often with a dazzling trickery for its naive constituency, sometimes a psychedelic transcendence of ordinary reality. But they stand in the comfort of their own cosmology. For instance,

Lévi-Strauss grants the complexity of the savage mind, but at the expense of biological and ontological accuracy. Native peoples are at best brilliant "psychologists" and plant "geneticists," but not spirit healers.

Castaneda's work is a breakthrough, for it reveals the inner ceremony. He comes late in history to an almost vanished people, but he reports what was almost totally missed for centuries.

W E HAVE LOST something big. We have ceded a huge luminous planet for a bowl of toxic porridge.

We must approach the native medicine that anthropology pretends to give us from beneath its accountable surface. It is our own culture's distorted version of the external features of another event. Almost from the beginning, previous accounts of native medicine set the sole boundaries and terms for later investigators. Later investigators were almost always true to anthropological tradition rather than to the observed events. Of each ceremony and healing we now have only the outlines; we do not know what happened inside. And the thin outlines and descriptions themselves were culled at a time when the source culture existed in an extreme, almost terminal doubt as to its own validity and the validity of its traditions. Even individual informants who cling stubbornly to the old and traditional are already born into a world of invaders that must be explained and integrated into their cosmology—invaders who have power, unimaginable power, even though they deny and violate the deities and the sacred law. Each cargo cult and ghost dance is a generic release of that outrage.

In 1523 the Aztec priest replied to the emissaries of Pope Hadrian VI and Emperor Charles V, as translated in verse: "You say/that we don't know/the Omneity, of heaven and earth/you say that our gods are not original/That's news to us/and it drives us crazy/it's a shock and a scandal/for our ancestors came to earth/and they spoke quite differently/they gave the law to us/and they believed/they served and they taught/honor among gods/they taught the whole service."[29]

We must certainly do away with the fantasy that we have access to a true native medicine tradition. As with trade of goods and statistical markets, our illusion of fullness dooms us to find only hunger and disease where there is another kind of fullness. Our "purchase" lies in kind with the famous joke about Manhattan being bought from the Indians by the Dutch for sixty guilders, when "in the eyes of these same Delawares the currency was the symbol not the value equivalent of the relinquishment of their hereditary rights to the land as well as its products . . . a symbol over which they transferred their good-will and spiritual power over forces dormant in the land."[30] And look what else we got in the bargain!

Later archetypal psychologists now see, in the debris of African and American Indian religions, in European alchemy, and in Oriental philosophy, a reflection of a totem and spirit force. They understand that "primitive" peoples lived closer to the meaning of unconscious and primal symbols. Much of the popular literature on mythology, ancient cosmology, and native lore is written on the assumption that we understand them and we "are" them, but we have betrayed them. Our vanity is to presume that we can sell this *apologia* to the gods too and receive back shamanic powers. But "meaning" and "symbol" are Western concepts, and accounts of non-Western modes of initiation have become excuses for psychohistorians, like Mircea Eliade and Joseph Campbell, to carve out marketable new intellectual territory—territory which expresses the ambition of the West more than the life drama of the native. It is an ambition to get back to something authentic, to heal ourselves, to reclaim the internal sense of things.

It is much like the fabled return to nature. Surely we *are* nature. What we go to in the wilderness is our own trained minds. They are a trap and a birthright and cannot be honorably renounced. Likewise, what we find in Amerindia—"we" as mythographers and Marxist

Priest of the Hopi Snake and Antelope Fraternities

*The Origin
of Medicine*

romanticizers this time instead of "we" as authorities of the church and social anthropology—is simply Western symbolic process, a confirmation of Jungian imagery, a treasury of personal images of ecological tranquility and cosmic harmony. This is who *we* are, not what *they* are.

We must be careful not to seem to steal their religion as we have stolen their land or to claim that we can go back to primary symbolic processes in the same way we have pretended to go back to the land. If our visualizations and symbols are to work, they must contain within them exactly those things that are indigenous to us and for which we are responsible. We can always make prettier sand paintings than this, but they won't quack.

Not only must we do away with the illusion of access to native medicine, but with it, we must do away with the illusion that recovery of lost traditions is our main hope. Recovery is no longer possible. These alien systems are hidden by esotericism and time, and their final obscurity is their seeming to stand in clear, understandable English (or some other Western language) which makes them even less accessible by bringing them superficially near. We are members of a scientific Western society, and that is what we must live out; our greed and hunger will not give us back what we have already forfeited. In the terms of our scientific society and its modes of inquiry, we can now begin to move toward new native traditions and new discrete regional varieties of craft and knowledge. It is that revival that can be informed by the last relics of a dying order. Having lost Creek and Australian Aboriginal medicines, we must reinvent them, from "memory," as something else.

Reinvention takes into account who we are, the reality of our own circumstance rather than a misleading neutrality of reconstruction. We, as people, as a culture, are in our own spiritual crisis and face true paradoxes and perils Stone Age men and women could not have imagined. To pretend that our aim now should be to set up a museum of extinct practices and peoples is as dishonest as it would be wasteful if it were possible. We do not have either the time or the resources. We face the end of history-as-we-know-it as surely as the Apache once did. The fact that, by our presence here, we are the true descendants of Miles Standish and Hernando Cortez will not allow us to be innocent keepers of archives, but it also does not prevent us from going ahead into our own history. For many Africans, American Indians, Australian Aborigines, the situation is the same; their ancient wisdom is inaccessible and they struggle, along with Europeans, to make something that will sustain them.

There is a further paradox in the Castaneda lore. Anthropologists have come, more and more, to suspect that the tales of Don Juan are fiction. At this point, a substantial proportion of the scientific community refuses to admit them as ethnography. They cannot be cited, even as I have cited them here, as academic evidence of anything.

This verdict only seemingly restores law and order to shamanism. In fact, once the anthropological judges admit they have been fooled by a fiction posing as ethnographic description, they have opened Pandora's box, for how can any report of another culture be verified? It has no more been proven that the works of Castaneda are fiction than it was previously demonstrated that they were fact. It is not impossible that they are a mythologized or esoteric account of an initiation. It is also possible that the narrator entered a realm in which he himself was unable to distinguish between hallucination and objective experience. There is no explicit way for any subsequent anthropologist to "find" Don Juan Matus and confirm or refute the events.

Anthropology cannot "go back on" Castaneda without opening the whole field to a fundamental crisis of meaning. In fact, it is already open to that, and the haggling over Castaneda's fieldwork has brought it to the forefront. Different systems of meaning co-occupy space. Don Juan cannot be disproven, though, for some in committee, he may be postponed. If he is not the shaman to show the West the disparity of meaning and reality on this planet, another will take his place. Castaneda either *had* the experience (and is no longer interested in convincing us of that because the "fieldwork" became more of an initiation than the academic defense it originally served) or he had an intuition of what that experience is like and has given it to us in a sort of parable. For our purposes, in raising questions of meaning in cross-cultural contexts, either resolution, or even another more "quantum" one, is acceptable.

THIS BOOK BEGINS by establishing the rightful position of "old" medicines, but it is about "the new medicine." The apparent contradiction masks a unity which modern culture, obsessed with progress, has tried to dualize. In fact, so-called "new age" seers, Castaneda among them, are at the same time "recoverers," reinventors of ancient wisdom.

The poet and lay physician Theodore Enslin translates this dilemma into a medical axiom for our present opportunity: "Things are what they are, and no amount of worry over 'primal causes' will change what they are at the moment of perception. There is a direct link here between a consideration of the totality of symptoms at a given moment, and treating *them,* rather than an unreal idea of disease. . . . "[31]

The true doctor seeks more than a sick person's account; he demands a present redynamization of the disease on the assumption that its causes are still actively locked in the person's system, although not in the way they were at the time of his becoming sick.

We can imitate this process in making a book about it. Along with our reconstruction of the origins of medicine and our proclivity for mythological and quasi-historical sequences, we can recreate, in a dynamic manner that suits this present moment in history, the sources of medicine on this planet. The intention toward recovery of the lost medicine men and women of our species can become a journey into our collective state of illness. As Owen Barfield writes, *"the moment at which [the mind] first began to entertain the idea of transformation should also be the moment at which it was itself in the act of becoming the transforming agent!"*[32] The record of that moment will be passed along as our case to some other "doctor," a time capsule of the "incurable" condition we lived.

It will also be an account, paradoxically, of the beginning of our attempt to get well. As long as the book follows the mystery, not pretending to resolve it, it will suggest the unknown cures toward which we are struggling, at least insofar as such seeds exist. The alternative would be an objectified summary of the healing going on, and an attempt to name our disease and dilemma and place their blame disingenuously on us. We would be working under the assumption that publishing, anthropology, holism, and Manhattan Island were more important than the silent occasion of healing in the world.

Notes

1. A. E. Waite, trans., *The Hermetic and Alchemical Writings of Paracelsus the Great* (London: James Elliott, 1894).

2. Claude Lévi-Strauss, *From Honey to Ashes,* trans. from the French by John and Doreen Weightman (New York: Harper & Row, 1973), pp. 57–58.

3. D. Jenness, "The Carrier Indians of the Bulkley River," Bulletin No. 133 (Washington, DC: Bureau of American Ethnology, 1943). Quoted in Claude Lévi-Strauss, *The Savage Mind* (Chicago: University of Chicago Press, 1966), p. 37.

4. Waite, *The Hermetic and Alchemical Writings of Paracelsus.*

5. The information behind this "story" comes from Frank G. Speck, *A Study of the Delaware Indian Big House Ceremony,* Vol. II (Harrisburg, Pennsylvania: Publications of the Pennsylvania Historical Commission, 1931).

6. James Watson, *The Double Helix* (New York: Atheneum, 1968), pp. 114–18.

7. Michael J. Harner, *The Jívaro* (Garden City, New York: Doubleday/Natural History Press, 1972), p. 138.

8. Ibid., pp. 138–39.

9. The information behind this and the succeeding stories comes from William Wildschut, *Crow Indian Medicine Bundles,* John C. Ewers (ed.), Museum of the American Indian (New York: Heye Foundation, 1975).

10. Ibid.

11. Ibid.

12. Ibid.

13. Ibid.

14. Ibid., pp. 9–10.

15. Alexander Marshack, *The Roots of Civilization* (New York: McGraw-Hill, 1972).

16. Claude Lévi-Strauss, *The Savage Mind* (Chicago: University of Chicago Press, 1966), p. 43.

17. Ibid., p. 219.

18. R. B. Fox, "The Pinatubo Negritos: Their Useful Plants and Material Culture," *The Philippine Journal of Science,* Vol. 81, Nos. 3–4, 1953; quoted in Lévi-Strauss, *The Savage Mind,* pp. 4–5.

19. Brian Inglis, *A History of Medicine* (Cleveland: World Publishing Co., 1965), p. 6.

20. Victor W. Turner, *Lunda Medicine and the Treatment of Disease,* Occasional Papers of the Rhodes-Livingstone Museum, No. 15, Livingstone, Northern Rhodesia [Zambia], 1964, pp. 61–62.

21. Marshall Sahlins, *Stone Age Economics* (Chicago: Aldine-Atherton, 1972), p. 2.

22. Ibid., p. 37.

23. Ibid., p. 4.

24. Ibid.

25. Ibid., p. 36.

26. Ibid., p. 4.

27. The discussion on this and the following pages deals with the writings of Carlos Castaneda, primarily *The Teachings of Don Juan: A Yaqui Way of Knowledge* (Berkeley: University of California Press, 1969); *A Separate Reality* (New York: Simon and Schuster, 1971); *Journey to Ixtlan* (New York: Simon and Schuster, 1972); and *Tales of Power* (New York: Simon and Schuster, 1974).

28. Carlos Castaneda, *Journey to Ixtlan,* p. 107.

29. Edward Dorn and Gordon Brotherstone (trans.), "The Aztec Priest's Reply," *New World Journal,* Vol. 1, Nos. 2/3 (1977), p. 52.

30. Frank G. Speck, *A Study of the Delaware Indian Big House Ceremony* (see footnote 5 above), p. 65.

31. Theodore Enslin, "Journal Note," quoted in Grossinger (ed.), *Alchemy: Pre-Egyptian Legacy, Millennial Promise* (North Atlantic Books, 1979).

32. Owen Barfield, *Unancestral Voice* (Middletown, Connecticut: Wesleyan University Press, 1965), p. 71.

CHAPTER FIVE

Practical Ethnomedicine: The Ancient Skills

Science and Healing (an overview)

The previous chapters embrace an idealization of "planet medicine." They give a model for understanding the potential sophistication of Stone Age healing, but they do not account for either the
actual variety of peoples and environments or the essential primitivity
that must go hand in hand with even the most magnificent cosmological refinements. Any ethnomedicine is both an elegant and comprehensive integration of social and ecological resources and a patchwork
of pragmatic solutions to an ongoing crisis of health, totemism, and
survival. That is why there are such wondrous and exotic systems.
Because each disease is an exigency, it must be mediated by the tools
and paradigms at hand.

All systems are technologically limited. Even our own computer-
ized medicines will be judged mechanically primitive by such twenty-
first century scientists as may follow us.

The first and most obvious dichotomy is between secular and
spiritual medicine (as distinct guilds if not separable cosmologies).
The present schism between technological medicine and the art of healing begins in a likely initial occupational distinction between herbalists, wound-dressers, and midwives on the one hand, and shamans,
medicine men, and voodoo chiefs on the other. Progressive medical

craft, as a grass-roots tradition, has developed only more refined and elaborate tools for diagnosis, drugs, and surgery, not a new strategy; likewise, on some level, the lineage of pure healing remains unbroken from the first shamans to Leonard Orr and Randolph Stone.

There have also been many scientist-healers throughout history—individuals who have cured inspirationally and charismatically and who have contributed at the same time to the practical knowledge of pharmacy and anatomy. Paracelsus, for one, was immersed simultaneously in an ancient priesthood and the nascent experimental sciences of his time. Homeopathy is an alchemical science developed in an eighteenth-century German laboratory by a doctor, Samuel Hahnemann. The contemporary American osteopath John Upledger has combined intuitive energy work with surgical precision and research anatomy in his development of the craniosacral system of healing. All of these foreshadow a "planet medicine."

Pharmaceutical Ethnomedicine

B Y ONE SET OF CLASSIFICATIONS, there are conceptually three orders of pragmatic medicines practiced by primitive peoples, and the third of these (shamanic voodoo) forms a bridge to spiritual medicine. The other two might be called pharmaceutical and mechanical.

Pharmaceutical medicine, with its central herbal component, is a universally practiced empirical science. Natural remedies are available to peoples in all habitats. Their sources include: plants, animals (including fish, insects, and reptiles), rocks and minerals, waters (salt and fresh, surface and subterranean, still and moving), earth and sands, fossils, and occasionally, manufactured items. These are administered either as simple substances, as compound substances, or as specially prepared totem formulas. Much of modern pharmacy originates from these traditional remedies (and continues to evolve from new drug-company research in the Amazon, Africa, and elsewhere), though the original ingredients have usually been disguised under trade names and synthetic adaptations. Whether or not the Western drug industry uses its materials efficiently (in their compounded and synthesized forms) or whether it has weakened them from lack of traditional knowledge and original contexts, these remedies were its starting point and are still its staples. Some modern remedies were transmitted directly through the Western tradition from prehistoric European and Middle Eastern sources; others were picked up from centuries of later European contacts with Asian, African, American, Pacific, and Australian peoples.

It was only during the early twentieth century that the forerunners of today's pharmaceutical executives began seriously to compete with herbalists and botanical doctors to develop their own patents. Before that, herbal medicine flourished. The drug industry has been a seventy- or eighty-year exotic elaboration on a multimillion-year tradition of planet pharmacy. Insofar as we inherit the recent victory of the synthesizers, we are misled both as to the percentage of indigenous remedies in modern pharmacy and the length of time since manufactured medicines "replaced" them. Much of our present diversified pharmacy comes not so much from recent breakthroughs of science as the planetwide repertoire of indigenous herbal formulas. Modernity mainly reflects the conspiracy of the pharmaceutical industry to establish itself as the exclusive source of legal drugs and the individual ambitions of companies to outdo their competitors. The origins of remedies are purposely concealed, but many of our most basic ones come from native doctors, from as long ago as the Ice Age or as recently as the active botany collected in the Amazon by Manuel Córdova-Rios under the auspices of the Astoria Company (Compania Astoria Peruana)[1] and the diversity of recipes brought from the Australian outback by Warwick Nieass on his many sacred journeys with Aborigines.[2]

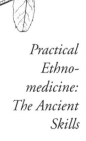

Wild Grape

Practical Ethno-medicine: The Ancient Skills

Erwin Ackerknecht writes: "It is amazing what an enormous number of effective drugs is known to the primitives. From twenty-five to fifty percent of their pharmacopoeia is often found to be objectively active. Our knowledge of opium, hashish, hemp, coca, cinchona, eucalyptus, sarsaparilla, acacia, kousso, copaibo, guaiac, jalap, podophyllin, quassia, and many others is a heritage from the primitive."[3]

In fact, up to the twentieth century there was a very vital tradition in the New World (the so-called Eclectic School) based entirely on the adaptation of the North American Indian pharmacy to general public use. Supporting this was the common belief that remedies native to a locale are most suitable for the individuals living in that locale.

The universal academic scorn for the Eclectic tradition was perhaps best summed up by the following statement from Benjamin Rush, an early and prominent American doctor: "We have no discoveries in the materia medica to hope for from the Indians in North America. It would be a reproach to our schools of physic if modern physicians were not more successful than the Indians, even in the treatment of their own diseases."[4]

Mountain Mahogany

Time did not bear him out, and among just the North American Indian pharmaceuticals adapted by modern medicine were Mayapple (as a laxative), Yellow Jessamine (for tetanus, gonorrhea, headaches, and fevers), Iris, Blue Cohosh, Yellow Dock, Bayberry, Indian Hemp, Wahoo, Black Cohosh, Indian Tobacco, Golden Seal, Wild Indigo, Bloodroot, and Spotted Evergreen.[5] To this fraction of northern New World ethnobotany, we could add remedies from African, South American, East and Southeast Asian, Australian, Polynesian, Siberian, Eskimo, Arabic sources, etc. The current last-ditch (post-Rio Conference) advocacy for the diversity of species and traditions rests in part upon the presumption that unobserved nature with its exquisitely selected molecular syntaxes and mutations is a more sophisticated pharmaceutical laboratory than any biotech firm. It is a blithe illusion that we can gene-splice anything at all into being, for we are consciousness-obsessed and do not appreciate the unconscious basis of structure and morphology. Most fundamental properties of medicines take thousands if not millions of years to originate in the latticework of chromosome permutations and random background radiation.

Although there is now general grudging consensus about the efficacy of many native pharmaceuticals, and the value to our species in preserving rain forests, marshes, ocean-bottom, etc., there remains far less sympathy for regional ethnosciences. The usual explanation for the striking "chemical" knowledge of "backward" peoples is that, during generations of trying out native materials, groups gradually separated workable medicines from inert substances and poisons, some of the latter of which were used for homicides, warfare, and fish kills. That is, even if the primitives had no *other* means of discernment, chance cures (and fatal toxins) were inevitable. Needless to say, the toxins were rapidly removed from any conventional herbal short list. But chance cures discovered over thousands of years in locales should be considered on at least the same level as prior molecular "chance" inventions of biologically active substances. There is no substitute for careful observation and experience over generations, especially by comparison to our rushed experiments and fly-by-night scavenger hunts. Native pharmacopoeias should not be disparaged automatically. Nor should we ever presume blind, random testing. Indigenous doctors used tools of intuition vis-à-vis plants to which we no longer have access. As the anthropologist George Harley puts it in his discussion of African medicine: "In spite of [the] possible admixture of the magical element, there is no doubt that most remedies ... have therapeutic value—a value learned, not in laboratories, but by the process of trial and error, in which the successful remedies have been handed down from father to son, or from the midwife to the daughters of the tribe—and continue in use because they are known to work."[6] There is nothing intrinsically wrong with trial and error. Modern laboratory science employs just as much. Intuition and sacred knowledge played major roles in the origin of physics even as they did in the evolution of ethnopharmacy.

We must be suspicious also of Ackerknecht's claim of only "twenty-five to fifty percent" and understand that he means those substances which later "tested out" in modern laboratories. If a substance does not appear objectively efficacious, there are many possible explanations. Perhaps the transmission of information about it was inaccurate and incomplete, and some aspect of the composition or preparation was left out. Perhaps a particularly crucial stage of preparation was omitted because it was prejudged merely superstitious. After all, pharmacists regularly assume that mythological language or chemically absurd instructions are functionally useless without ever trying to translate them or seek their medicinal purpose. Early Renaissance chemists discounted references to the "king" and "queen" and "mercurial seed" in the alchemical literature without considering that these terms might denote unique qualities of gold, silver, and antimony not covered in their own dispensatories (qualities perhaps related to those appearing now in cold-fusion experiments). (See "The Roots of Alternative Medicine" in Chapter Eight.)

Even the full biochemical effects of medicines cannot be extrapolated from conventional formulas and tests. Cultural context determines the range of assimilation of substances, especially substances whose uses have religious or social ramifications. Mythological language may predispose people psychosomatically in ways that make certain substances active rather than inert, beneficial rather than harmful.

Administration of medicine can occur in situations ranging from domestic calm to large, adrenalized public gatherings. A substance can be ingested in isolation or in concert with other substances or other activities, such as chanting, dancing, fasting, vomiting, etc.

Because all of these phases involve delicate interrelationships, it is impossible to dissociate medicines from their manner of preparation and ingestion. It is therefore impossible to evaluate the different herbal treatments simply by an external pharmacological standard. Some medicines work *only* in the context of a long and complicated ceremony. So the herb requires the ceremony as much as the ceremony requires the herb. Without the ceremony, in fact, the herb might not be a medicine.

Once we consider additionally the *possible* alchemical, vital, microdose, paraphysical, and parapsychological characteristics of pharmaceuticals in the context of chants, musical instruments like the Australian didgeridoo, vibrations, rhythms, and sequences of preparation, we have entered a whole universe of metabotanical medicine. There are also likely native potentization systems (not so named of course) that are functionally equivalent to the decimal and centesimal successions of homeopathy (see page 248). Taking all these into account, it is not idealistic to assume that a great amount of practical information is subsumed in "mythological" references. Ceremony is the original human computer, and myth is a mnemonic device for storing totemic data.

Parts of a plant considered active may be roots, bark, sap, leaves, shoots, flowers, buds, fruit juice, stems, pulp, fruit meat, seeds, even the whole plant or the whole plant only when combined in potions with other plants. Medicinal varieties may be cultivated in gardens near houses or collected wild, on the outskirts of settlements or in the distant mountains, etc.

The hard seeds, roots, bark, or leaves, etc., may be pulverized, soaked, pounded, crushed, ground in a metate, toasted, sun-dried, or compounded. They can be mixed with other ingredients in different orders. Indigenous peoples were intuitive bakers, pharmacists, and alchemists.

Materials also can be collected under a multitude of sanctions: "only in the morning," "from the shady side," "not the first plant, not the second, but the third," "not the lower bark, the upper bark," "only the petals in the third week of blooming," "under a full moon," and so on. Magical though many of these sound, any of them might have practical ramifications. On cellular and molecular levels living substances—and even minerals—maintain exquisitely calibrated cyclical clocks. Though astrology may be suspect in the modern world, astrological botany includes a whole range of biological timing mechanisms set to gravitational influences both near and far (and not just to massive celestial objects). Cells and molecules engage in their own microastrologies. After all, embryonic development requires strict multi-levelled coordinations of substances in pathways and orbits. Ethnopharmacists likely tracked their timing "through a glass darkly."

Shamanic Ethnobotany

THE BOTANICAL PREPARATION ayahuasca has received new attention not only as a direct healing agent but a tool in shamanic diagnosis of disease. It was a feat for an ancient trans-Amazonian culture to invent this brew at all, since, in order to be active, it requires two distinct agents, the stem of a jungle vine which is cooked together with the leaves of one or another plant (depending on the region). Aboriginally developed in the Upper Amazon, the Orinoco Plains, and the Pacific coast of Colombia and Ecuador, the brew has now spread through urban areas of Brazil, Colombia, and Peru to the cities of North America.

Ayahuasca is the main ingredient in an antiparasitic, antimalarial herbal mix. More crucially, its ingestion leads to visions which reveal the properties and uses of other medicines through the internally perceived forms of plant, animal, and celestial spirits.[7] It is sought by shamans for insight into methods of curing. In fact, one anthropologist (Luis Eduardo Luna) reports that ayahuasca has entrusted shamans with the ability to hear the pain of the whole Amazon crying out, as well

Section of a painting from Ayahuasca Visions: The Religious Iconography of a Peruvian Shaman *by Luis Eduardo Luna and Pablo Amaringo (Berkeley: North Atlantic Books, 1991), p. 115. Details show several acts of shamanic healing of people harmed by malevolent spirits or sorcerers. Overseeing the events is a cosmic journeying prince (Quekaltec) and a golden snake that serves as his vehicle.*

as the individual spirits of plants and animals. If this is so, then we might hearken not only to the voices of responsible scientists warning us about the destruction of the rain forest but the jungle itself in epigrammatic molecules rushing through its species. In a universe of transcendent and disembodied intelligence, surely stars and vines and even molecules of water "speak" too.

During a recent speech to a homeopathic conference, Edward Whitmont remarked, "All of the illness and growth potentials of man, the microcosm, are also to be found in the macrocosmic information of the body of our mother, the Earth. We are like aspects, microcosmic replications of a vast cosmic form process.

"Perhaps it is not too far-fetched then to consider whether our attitudes, and illnesses, may not also be forms of communion with the Earth planet, particularly as we resort to the help of external medicinal substance fields. Perhaps, in some way which we still do not understand, some form of consciousness development occurs and is of use to the planetary process rather than only to ourselves. I leave it to you to ponder what this may mean in terms of the ways in which our chemical and drug technology currently pollutes and poisons the Earth as well as our own organisms."[8]

Yes, planet doctors apparently yet linger in the Australian deserts and the remaining wilderness of Africa, Asia, and the Americas, but collectively at this moment we have as much chance of hearing them as of hearing a conversation on Neptune. We are trenchantly tuned to other channels.

Luna's main informant, the shaman Pablo Amaringo, recently pointed to the center of a photograph of a galaxy I was showing him and spoke a cosmology I render from his own rough English as: "There is where I have gone. It looks like this on the outside; but inside, in the mind, it is a series of waves undulating eternally from the bark on the outside of the cosmos, bark like a tree. Those waves are dynamic and have terrible dark places in them, voids so great I thought I was going to die." He went on to explain that these waves pass through plants and the etheric levels of animals even as they simultaneously penetrate us through the unconscious aspects of our minds and impart a lore. Such a cosmology in itself guarantees a metabotany transcending even the most assiduous ethnopharmacies.

In this context, botanical medicine is millennially far vaster than the contents of single regional systems. However, without details, we are lost in psychedelic fantasy. The deep and voluminous textures of regional systems offer a first step into a cosmology as concrete and subtle as it is vast. Although I do not expect readers to try out any of these repertories, I hope they will at least imagine their smells and flavors, feel the water running through them, visualize their bright and subtle colorings, and also try to picture both indoor and outdoor vignettes of medicine men and women treating their clientele.

Regional Ethnobotany:
Subtleties of Preparation and Administration

THE SERIES OF EXAMPLES that follows loosely runs from nature toward culture (or from medical craft toward totemism and abstract science).

Peru[9]

"The Capanahua Indians of the upper Río Tapiche use [macote] to kill fish. They gather several bushels of the vine and chop it up. Then they choose a lake and scatter the chopped vine over the surface at night. The water turns black, and within twenty-four hours the effect of this poison brings everything living in the lake to the surface dead, including alligators, boas, etc. The Indians, from this abundance of dead animals, choose only what they prefer for food. . . .

"The [Sangre de Grado] tree grows around the flanks of hills and near the headwaters of small creeks flowing from the highlands. It occurs in groups. It is called by this name because the sap looks like blood. The sap is difficult to gather because it drops very slowly from cuts in the bark.

"Use: The resin is used to stop bleeding from cuts and hemorrhages and also for uterine illnesses. . . . In the case of wounds and resulting hemorrhages, put the liquid sap of this tree on cotton or soft cloth and apply directly to the affected part, and leave until bleeding stops. In the case of uterine difficulties, dilute the sap in water and give it to the patient to drink. . . .

"[Vaca Nahui] is a climbing plant that is found in abundance in both the uplands and the lowlands of the Rio Tapiche and the small streams and also on the banks of the Amazon. The local people call it *curarina*.

"This plant produces a seed that looks like a bull's or cow's eye, hence its name . . . The fruits or seeds of this plant appear in abundance in January. The people that live along the rivers never go without having with them several of these seeds to be used in the case of snakebite.

"Preparation: Take several of these seeds and extract the nut from inside the shell, grate in warm water and drink a glassful if bitten by a poisonous snake. Also put warm gratings on the area of the bite, after making the bite bleed by an incision."

Hawaii[10]

"The pharmacopoeia is very extensive, including mineral, vegetable, and animal elements.

"Some dozen mineral elements, other than fresh and salt water, are used. Salt *(paakai)*, particularly Hawaiian red salt, which is colored with dust from red clay strong in ferrous oxide, is made from sea water and hence is rich in iodine. It enters into enemas, purges, and other remedies taken internally, and serves as well as the base for astringents, prophylactics, and counterirritants applied externally.

"Next in importance is a certain red clay *(lepo alaea)* found in only a few pockets or veins on each of the islands and very highly valued by Hawaiians, who will guard the smallest piece with greatest care. It is strong in ferrous oxide and has a rather chalky taste. This red clay, mixed with water and generally compounded with vegetable juices, is drunk to allay all kinds of internal hemorrhages, from the lungs, bowels, or uterus. . . .

"Animal elements to the number of 29 (as counted to date of writing) entered into Hawaiian prescriptions. A few, like spiders' eggs, may represent borrowings from Chinese practice. But others, like sea urchin, lobster, and marine snail are certainly indigenous. The use of the sea urchin in compounds to be taken as tonic for debility is interesting, for this creature's flesh is strong in vitamins. Ashes of human hair and of tortoise shell are used.

"Up to the time of writing this paper, 317 botanical varieties furnishing constituents in remedies have been counted. These include seaweeds and mosses, lichens and moss, water weeds, ferns, grasses, herbs, vines, bushes, and trees. Roots, bulbs, tubers, corms, barks, leaf buds and flower buds, leaves, flowers, fruits and seeds, saps, gums, and resins are used. . . .

"*Popolo (Solanum nodiflorum)* is sometimes referred to as 'the foundation of Hawaiian pharmacy.' The raw juice of leaves and ripe berries of the *popolo* is used alone and in compounds for all disorders of the respiratory tract, for skin eruptions, and, when mixed with salt, as a prophylactic and healing agent for cuts and wounds. . . .

"The leaves of the *noni (Morinda citrifolia)* are used for sweating when there is fever; crushed or singed, they are applied to bruises, boils, sores, and wounds. The bark of the stem is said to be good for cuts, and the juice of the roots for skin eruptions. The seeds are also mashed and used on cuts. Tiny *noni* fruits, crushed with *popolo* leaves, form a remedy taken internally for womb trouble. . . .

Hawaiian Tree-Shells

Practical Ethno-medicine: The Ancient Skills

"The oily nut of the *kukui (Aleurites moluccana)* eaten raw has a strong cathartic effect. The juice of the bark is used in compound for asthma. The blossoms and seedlets are also taken raw as cathartics … The fresh leaves serve for poultices on swellings, deep bruises, or other ailments where local concentration of heat and sweating are desired. The oil from the roasted kernel of the nut has many uses: it softens the skin of the pregnant mother's abdomen and of the infant and serves the masseuse as an external lubricant; it becomes an internal lubricant when taken as a laxative or injected (with salt water) as an enema … The *kukui* with long narrow leaves is one of the 'bodies' of Kamapuaa, the legendary lover of Pele.

"Another of the 'bodies' of the hog god, Kamapuaa, is the grass called *kukae puaa* (hog's excrement; *Syntherisma pruriens*). The leaves chewed and swallowed, or juice extracted and compounded with other ingredients, are recommended for stomach and intestinal disorders. Tender shoots are used in a remedy for cataract of the eye…."

Amaranth

Bali[11]

"The violent rainy seasons bring epidemics of tropical fevers, and malaria takes many lives, especially of children. The Balinese attempt to cure the fevers with concoctions of *dadap* leaves, onions, anise, salt, and coal from the hearth, which, after straining, is given to the patient to drink, and he is put to sleep. It is also effective to rub the sides with a paste of mashed *dadap* leaves, onions, anise, and *tinké*, a sort of nutmeg, and to rub the back with coconut oil with scrapings of *dadap* bark…. The Balinese love a clear skin and they are disturbed by the prevalent skin disease, from the ugly but harmless *kurab*, a skin discoloration produced by a parasitic fungus, to itches, framboesia, and tenacious tropical ulcers. The *kurab*

(called *bulenan* when in small patches) appears as whitish spots on the brown skin and spreads all over if not checked. It is cured by rubbing the affected areas with *lalang* grass, but it has been discovered that it disappears quickly with salicylic alcohol from the Chinese druggists. Itches are cured with lemon juice, coconut oil, and frequent baths in hot water in which *legundi* and *ketawali* leaves are macerated....

"Headaches are cured by massage, but it helps to spray the forehead with a mixture of crushed ginger and mashed bedbugs. For stomach-ache they drink the red infusion of *medarah* bark from Java. A cough is relieved by drinking an infusion of *blimbing buluh* flowers mixed with parched, grated coconut, also sprayed externally on the throat...."

Dutch Guiana[12]

"The Bush Negroes possess an extensive system of primitive medicine. Various roots, herbs, and nuts are gathered in the jungle, and their use is mingled with various superstitions. The witch doctor or medicine man who prepares infusions from these herbs holds no excelled position in the esteem of the villagers; he is simply following a particular profession to which no special prestige is attached....

"He prepares several kinds of medicine, among them the *snakee-kutti,* or snake-bite cure. It cures the bites of all reptiles and makes the person immune from future attack. *Snakee-kutti* is made in this way: a venomous snake is killed and the head and the tail-end are cut from the body; the tail is placed in the mouth of the snake and the whole is roasted over a slow fire, along with certain herbs. Incantations accompany the business. After the materials are thoroughly charred they are reduced to a homogeneous powder, which is administered in two ways: first, internally, and second, by making a small incision in the arm and rubbing some of the powder into the wound....

"Minor cuts and wounds may be treated with the bark of the *apro-conyo* tree. This is ground up and mixed with the brew prepared from the leaves known as *pekein fol caca* (little rooster)."

Gros Ventre[13]

"A plant called häyaaⁿtᵃ is used both as a perfume and as a medicine. Pieces of it tied by a string to the shoulder of the shirt give a pleasant smell. It is also laid in warm water without being boiled, and the water is then used as medicine for sore eyes.

"The green stems of a plant containing a white juice are used for women who have no milk. The Arapaho use the same plant for similar purpose and call it milk liquid.

"A root called bäetset ('hand,' on account of the peculiar conformation of the roots) is laid in very small quantity into cold water, which is drunk by women to insure easy child-birth.

"The flowers of a composita called nihaⁿnäänou ('yellow-head'), or tjitjixtäⁿsibyiisöö, are put on coals for a woman who has given birth. She stands above the fire to incense herself.

"Another plant called nihaⁿnäänou ('yellow-head'), which grows close to the water, is boiled, and drunk for pain in the back or in the body.

"A root called niitasou ('sharp') is pulverized, and then applied to sores in the mouth and on the tongue.

"A rock lichen called benaatsün is chewed for a sore mouth.

"The root of tyätyäniçä is obtained from swampy land far to the north of the Gros Ventre habitat. The roots are soaked in water and the black portions removed. Then they are grated, mixed with water, and applied to the neck for sores.

"A root called kouhⁱyaⁿ is chewed until a sticky paste results, which is applied to sores.

"A fungus called tsäädjinaⁿ is set on fire, and when glowing is applied to wounds or sores. It is also pulverized, and put on the gums of children when they are teething. It is said to grow on birch-trees, near the root.

"The roots of iniitsöö are boiled and the water used to wash the part of the body which has been burned by the application of the glowing fungus tsäädjinaⁿ."

THESE FEW HERBAL EXAMPLES speak for the rest of the planet much as single poems of Geoffrey Chaucer, William Blake, and Emily Dickinson might give a taste of all of English literature.

Mechanical Ethnomedicine

THE SECOND CATEGORY of functional ethnomedicine is the one I have called mechanical; it encompasses an astonishing diversity of techniques. Some of them, such as trephining, scarification, bonesetting, stamping, and cupping, are extraordinarily ancient and multicultural. More sophisticated somatic applications such as acupuncture, bloodletting, cranial adjustment, and deep-tissue massage may have had their origin, generations later, in such primitive manipulation. (We will discuss some of the more energetically based systems in the three chapters following this one.)

Crude surgical methods must have arisen heuristically from basic exploratory anatomy, in emergency situations, or whenever gross physical distress or unpleasant maladies proved the mother of invention. Injuries and fractures fashioned bandages and splints. Boils and swollen wounds provided straightforward occasions for lancing. Rashes and skin ailments designed their own poultices. Arrowhead-removal was no doubt a Paleolithic necessity carried out for millennia with bone awls and the like. Midwifery was one of the first surgeries; from the mechanics of helping a baby out of its mother's body may have come a general science of incision and massage. If overlooked otherwise, massage was clearly taught by mammals in their rubbing and scratching and primates in their caressing.

Modeled by nature itself, manipulation is one of the oldest therapies: "The sun, the air, water, exercises, and manipulation have been Medicine's handmaidens since earliest times."[14] Oftentimes stiff necks and backs have been cured by merely a stumble or dodge. A painful fall leads to sudden relief from a longstanding sciatica or lumbago. Over time, practitioners develop more scientific means of producing the same effects and pass on their trade secrets to apprentices. According to a contemporary orthopedic surgeon:

"Manipulation . . . consists of different sorts of passive movement performed by the hands in a definite manner for a prescribed [therapeutic] purpose. Its use does not involve the operator in any particular belief in the causes and treatment of *all* disease; he is merely treating the patient with a mechanical disorder in what he believes is the best way. Fractures and dislocations often require manipulation for the reduction of the displacement, and the same applies when a loose fragment of cartilage has become displaced within a joint, blocking movement."[15]

The author betrays an orthodox medical prejudice that manipulation is useful only for mechanical disorders. This is likely not the case. Medical complexes with manipulation at their core arose in the Pacific, Africa, Australia, the Americas, and India, if not in fact everywhere, and they probably developed visceral and fascial healing concomitant to their attention on cartilage and bone. However, such systems have been described as if only mechanical, their organic aspect not fully recognized or understood in a Western context until their reinvention within chiropractic and osteopathy at the turn of the nineteenth century. We cannot know the full range of such indigenous and prehistoric treatments as described throughout this chapter because their ethnographic witnesses were limited by this prejudice.

Bone-setting is a generic term for pre-chiropractic forms of clicking or snapping cartilage in order to return skeletal elements to their so-called natural positions. It does not mean reducing dislocations and fractures (as it might today); it means manipulating and adjusting small bony displacements. Modern scientists, using X-ray technology, deny that bones are actually "put back." But then these same scientists do not view bone-setting as implementing a general theory of disease. According to them, bone-setters "merely manipulate to the best of their ability those who come visit them."[16] They do credit them with success in such treatments as restoring displacements from the rupture of a meniscus and improving mobility in cases of tendinitis and bursitis.

Bone-setters dissipate nonfunctional adhesions that have grown from disuse and stimulate areas of capsule shrinkage brought about by stiffness and pain. However, notions such as the impingement of the spinal cord, the impedance of blood and cerebrospinal flows and nerve activity, and the translation of pathology to contingent organs through impaired autonomic function are regarded as mere fantasy and quackery outside of chiropractic and osteopathic circles. Yet these are in fact the traditional epistemology of bone-setting.

Most non-Western and early Eurasian manipulation methods were adjuncts to massage and almost indistinguishable from it in practice. However, throughout Africa, the Middle East, and traditional Europe, popular folk versions of manipulation were performed by direct blows to parts of the body, particularly the back. "Weapons" used in these activities included brooms, shovels, hammers, and steelyards. In one contemporary African tribe, "the medicine man uses an instrument shaped like a hammer to bring the vertebrae back into position."[17] Similar techniques were also described in early Rome by Avicenna as means of repositioning a vertebral luxation.[18]

Not all manipulation is hands-on. In the "lifting cure" of Norway, "the patient leans against the projecting edge of a 'stabbur' (a storehouse on pillars), pressing his back against it, trying to 'lift' the house."[19] Exotic treatments throughout the world involve equivalent isometrics and displacement. In the Orient, steel balls are rotated along the plane of one hand therapeutically. Ritual statues, pitchforks, and stones have also served as subtle fulcra by which a practitioner instructs a patient in a set of curative movements.

A form of manipulation midway between the "lifting cure" and hands-on massage is known as "weighing salt" in Sweden where it is used as a cure for lumbar and thoracic pain. "A healthy person of the opposite sex stands back-to-back with the patient, takes hold of his arm, lifts him up and shakes him three times."[20] This kind of technique recurs throughout Breema, a Kurdish bodywork system described in Volume Two, Chapter Five.

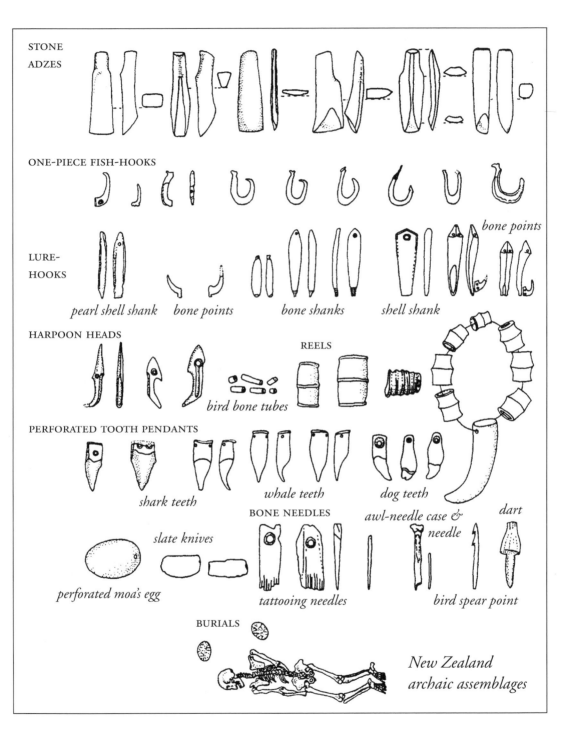

STONE ADZES

ONE-PIECE FISH-HOOKS

LURE-HOOKS

bone points

pearl shell shank   *bone points*   *bone shanks*   *shell shank*

HARPOON HEADS

REELS

bird bone tubes

PERFORATED TOOTH PENDANTS

shark teeth   *whale teeth*   *dog teeth*

awl-needle case & needle   *dart*

BONE NEEDLES

slate knives

perforated moa's egg   *tattooing needles*   *bird spear point*

BURIALS

New Zealand archaic assemblages

Other more esoteric forms of bodywork and movement were modeled in animal actions and behavior. We might note how many martial and internal energetic techniques retain animal names ("wild horse parts mane," "snake extends tongue," "ape offers fruit," "rhinoceros shoots at moon," "stork cools wings," "frog lies below surface of water," "bear scratches tree bark," etc.). These mean what they say—that preconscious animal postures and motions are intrinsically medicinal and empowering. The coda implies: we can acquire equivalent powers by imitating them with our own bodies. (See the illustration on page 368.)

T HE MOST IMPORTANT distinction I would make among mechanical procedures involves their degrees of subtlety from gross surgery to light stimulation.

As primarily an emergency intervention, surgery emphasizes physiological results regardless of how the operation *feels* to the patient. With anesthesia, the goal is for the patient not to feel at all.

Yet aside from explicit reconstructive goals of surgery, the great majority of mechanical healing methods are directed toward either stimulation, relaxation (of an overactive organ), or pulsation (altering the basic rhythm of the muscular and/or nervous systems). Stimulation cures through generating feeling, or feeling-like waves, in the nervous system. Even where there is a mechanical goal, as there is in many forms of massage and manipulation, the sensations of the treatment are crucial because the patient is responding to his or her system's sensitivity as much as to any concrete physical adjustments. The secondary (or self-generated) long-term response is often more the actual goal of the treatment than the direct effect of contact.

There is likely a continuum, such that even the most invasive surgery has a secondary stimulating (or, more likely, deadening) effect on the nervous system (and thus overall health). Gall bladder surgery, for instance, even if initially efficacious, may be psychosomatically disastrous months or years later for reasons having nothing to do with the Western conception of the gall bladder. Conversely, even the most gentle stimulation has an ultimately structural effect on the body. For the latter to be true, in such methods as acupuncture and massage, it is necessary to posit <u>some sort of electrical or neural field unknown as yet to science</u>. For instance, it is generally believed, among traditional acupuncturists, that subtle changes caused in this "field" by needles ultimately transpose the actual organs of the body and that the field is so discretely responsive that a skillful physician can alter the internal relationships and contingencies of organs in profound ways without ever touching them. Insofar as herbs, needles, fingers, and even chants affect harmonic balances in the psychosomatic field, they might produce organic changes—ripple effects—more substantial and lasting than those that a surgeon can. After all, as noted earlier, even the finest scalpels and lasers work on a gross level compared to the resonance that joins cells. (See also "Internalizing and Externalizing Medicines" in Volume Two, Chapter Eight.)

Paul Pitchford, an American trained in native Chinese medicine, has discussed the possibility of a wider anatomical field in lectures:

> All medicine is making changes in the body. We try to make small changes now so that big changes later will not be necessary. The longer we wait, the bigger the change we have to make. American medicine is involved mainly in big changes, so it waits a long time until drastic action is necessary. The doctor doesn't recognize the need for change until it is almost too late.
>
> Acupuncture makes very tiny holes in the body. Sometimes needles aren't necessary—pressure is enough. Sometimes even a massage without touching is enough. Surgeons make large holes. They move the organs like stones. But we mustn't think that is any different than acupuncture. We make small holes and move the organs slight distances without disturbing their rhythms. We cause them to move by changing their fields. Surgeons make large holes and move the organs a great distance directly, but this is sometimes too much for the system to absorb.[21]

To sell subtle manipulative systems short because they don't get at

organs is to forget that most genetic and biological-field messages are also subterranean and profound in their origin and subtle and multi-levelled in their transmission and expression. This is why the causes of disease and healing are often difficult to pin down.

Regional Mechanical Ethnomedicine

Iᴺᴅɪɢᴇɴᴏᴜs ᴍᴇᴄʜᴀɴɪᴄᴀʟ ᴛᴇᴄʜɴɪǫᴜᴇs are diverse and ingenious. Insofar as any activity can be internalized, likely any activity can be medicinalized by a skilled teacher or physician. The true "planet medicine" is a ceaseless magic show rather than a prime-time hospital set. George Harley's ethnomedical survey for just one group (the Mano of West Africa) includes: enema with a long-necked gourd, powder blown up the nose, infusions into the urethra with a long reed, mild juices in the eyes, mud baths, sweat baths, hot medicated baths, splints, fumes, tourniquets, leaves as bandages, incisions over wounds, lying on hot leaves, bloodletting, poultices, chewing without swallowing, and licking small amounts of medicine daily from the finger, plus a basic herbal complement including effective worming medicines, treatments for skin diseases, relief of cough, gas, and constipation, a preventive pharmacy based on swallowing small amounts of poison, and a rudimentary system of vaccination learned from neighbors under Moslem influence.[22]

The following are among the more common mechanical techniques described in the ethnographic literature, beginning with the milder and moving toward the more roughly manipulative. The scale itself is meant to be suggestive only. In fact, though, some procedures are mild and subtle in different ways from others (for instance, acupuncture is mild with only a minute point of physical contact, but it is also deep and organ-penetrating on the level of the meridians). Techniques are presented here in relative isolation from the contexts which give them meaning. There is obviously an almost unlimited number of additional techniques, especially when we consider the combinations that make up actual systems of therapeutics,

Doctor's charm, Gros Ventre

purification, massage, etc. In fact, I would guess that in a true compilation of manipulative, palpating, and sensory-motor techniques from all ages and regions of the Earth, the following would represent a mere fraction. I would not be surprised if they were less than one percent. However, they were what I could glean from the ethnographic literature.[23]

Also, many of these techniques have shamanic components to be explored in the next chapter.

Bathing

Bathing as medicine is common in all areas of the world: salt-water bathing in the ocean, hot-springs bathing, and stimulation by stream water.

Sweat-Bathing

The usual method is to make a special hut beneath which steam or smoke is generated. The patient is bathed in a vapor, sometimes mixed with medicine.

Crow Indian: "He prepared a sweat-bath and ... then he purified his body again in the smoke of pine needles."[24]

Delaware Indian: "After the fire has burned down sufficiently to

form a bed of coals, more logs are added and the rocks, usually limestone, brought in. Twelve stones of medium size are placed in the fire. For handling them, a branch of hickory or any hard wood, about five feet long, is split at one end for use as a fork. After the rocks have been thoroughly heated, water is poured over them to produce steam."[25]

Hawaiian: "... a little hut made with *hau* branches arched over at the top, presumably erected over a long

oven of heated stones ... A common practice in treating piles and sometimes in treating a woman who has suffered perineal injury in delivery
is to have the patient sit over a vessel containing a steaming decoction
of prescribed herbs."[26]

Sweating

Dry heat to remove toxins is an ancient medicine. Sometimes a patient
with a fever is wrapped in leaves.[27] Varieties of ritual sweat lodges
abound, but this is a subject too extensive to cover here.

Touch

"Centipede *(Alia)* Bites: the bitten area is rubbed with the bark of the
tutuku plant. If the bite is very painful, someone who has had such a
bite and who did not suffer great pain is called upon. This person then
touches the bite and it is thought that his experience of painlessness
will be transferred to the person suffering pain from the bite."[28]

Brushing

"Medicine-men cured the sick by sucking the body and by brushing
it. As is customary among Indians, they were believed to suck through
the skin without biting, cutting, or puncturing it. They might suck
blood, pebbles, cloth, human finger-nails, bunches of hair, and many
other things. If they sucked out old pus, it was evidence that the disease was of long standing. If they brushed or rubbed the patient, they
used owl-feathers, skunk-skin, prairie-dog fur, or similar parts of animals. Some used bells as rattles, some whistles, and some drums; and
all sang, each doctor having his own songs."[29]

Spitting

"The spitting treatment makes use of tobacco, rue, sage, and artemisia,
of which the first is the most important. The curer chews one or several of these and spits his saliva all over the body of his patient, blowing or spraying it with a hissing sound through his teeth. The patient

is spit on from head to foot, especially on the face, and in serious cases the curer spits the form of a cross on the body, running from the head to the crotch, and from shoulder to shoulder. This is usually done four times and is repeated after a lapse of eight days if the patient does not improve."[30]

Stamping

"The most primitive cure for lumbago was named the 'stamping' or 'trampling' cure. It has been practiced in many countries from Hippocrates' time until today. A woman stood with both feet on the invalid's back and trampled up and down. Or she might walk across—or up and down—his back. . . .

"Among the Huzuls in Austria, it was customary for the priest to trample on the invalid's back during mass, or even let a tame bear do so. (!) A similar practice was reported in Rumania. Kuzela tells [us] from the Ukraine that when his father was stricken by acute backache, the first-born child pressed on his back with hands or feet. In Finnish folklore, Forsblom states that 'a woman who has given birth to twins stamps on the back with both feet and stays there for as long as it takes her to count backwards from 9 to 3 three times. . . .'

"Patients have been trampled upon by women chosen on sexual grounds (virgins, mothers of seven children, etc.); birth by presentation of the foot has been regarded as giving magical powers to the stamper."[31]

"An Arab camel-driver in the desert is exhausted and unable to proceed. He rolls himself in the hot sand. One of his fellows comes up and tramples on him, or beats him. He jumps up ready to resume his journey. . . .

"A Tartar, having an hour to rest, prefers a bath to sleep. He enters as if drugged with opium, and leaves it, his senses cleared and his strength restored. . . . This is not attributed to the moisture alone but to the shampooing, which in such cases is of an extraordinary nature. The Tartar sits down and doubles himself up; the shampooer (and he selects the most powerful man) then springs with his feet on his shoulders, cracking the vertebrae; with all his force and weight he pummels the whole back, and then turning him on his back and face, aided by a second shampooer, tramples on his body and limbs; the Tartar then lays himself down for half an hour and perhaps sleeps."[32]

"It is a custom in Berwickshire, among women-workers in the fields, when their backs become very tired by stooping while hoeing turnips with short-handled hoes, to lie down with their faces to the ground, and to allow others to step across the lower part of their backs, on the lumbar region, with one foot, several times, until the fatigue is removed. Burton, in his 'First Footsteps in East Africa,' narrates a very similar custom amongst females who led camels; who, on feeling fatigued, lie down at full length, face downward, and stand on each other's backs, trampling and kneading with their toes, until they rise like giants refreshed."[33]

Massage

This mode of treatment is cultivated universally, originating independently with almost every imaginable variation of technique along a hypothetical spectrum from light sensual contact to neutral adjustment to painful deep-tissue transposition. Rhythm of contact, intensity and duration of touch, and sequence of body-parts and/or working tools of the therapist also vary to a remarkable degree. The intention of the contact may be primarily energetic and inwardly directed or purely mechanical and external.

Guatemalan: "The massagers are usually men who are supposed to be versed in human anatomy and are employed to relieve pains which cannot be cured by medicines. The massager cures only natural ailments, since, like the herbalist, he usually uses no prayers and does not have the *sahurin* in his leg. His work consists of massaging the body for the purpose of forcing out the ailments through an extremity. The patient is laid on the bed in the sleeping-house, and the massager rubs the pain area with both hands and sometimes beats the spot with his fists. He rubs toward the nearest extremity, the purpose being to force

the fright or *aigre* out through that extremity. For example, if the *aigre* is thought to be in the arm, he rubs toward the hands until the *aigre* is forced out through the fingers. An *aigre* in the leg is forced out through the toes, and one in the lower back, out through the penis or leg. He pulls an *aigre* out also by drawing his hands through the air in a pulling motion directly above the patient's body and toward the extremities. If done properly, this imitative magic is said to be more effective than the rubbing.

"The massagers often pinch the patient's flesh violently, pulling it out from the body as far as possible and letting it snap back. This causes a loud, popping noise and is said by the massagers to be the breaking-loose, or 'unfastening,' of the *aigre* from the body. The massager calls upon the *aigre* or other sickness to break loose or unfasten itself. An important sickness treated by the massagers is sour stomach, or dyspepsia. The patient is covered with warm hog grease and massaged in the abdominal and dorsal regions in the manner described above. Much suggestion is used, until finally the stomach *aigre* 'unfastens' itself. (The massager says, '*Aigre* of a snake, *Aigre* of a bull, Fright of thunder, make yourself crack, unfasten yourself,' etc.) For nine days thereafter the patient drinks a boiled tea made of the *hierba del toro* plant."[34]

Burmese: "A professional has a most wonderful knowledge of all the tendons and muscles in the human body, and follows them up with a light pressure of the fingers that affords a relief...."[35]

Negrito: "When a child gets fever, a ceremony called *luya-luya* is executed and the roots of the ginger are obtained immediately. The *babaylan* pounds the roots. The pounded roots are held by his two hands. He then blows the roots for some minutes and wraps them with a piece of cloth. He massages the sick child with the wrapped ginger from the tip of the toes, up to the legs, abdomen, breast, through the arms, the tip of the fingers, and then towards the face and head. When he reaches the forehead, the *babaylan* makes a cross. Then he proceeds to massage the head. On top of the head, he lets the ginger stay for some minutes then blows it so that the air penetrates into the scalp."[36]

Tahitian (James Cook, 1777): "I returned on board with Otoo's mother, his three sisters and eight more women. At first I thought they came into my boat with no other view than to get a passage ... but when they got to the ship they told me they were come ... to cure me of the disorder that I complained of, which was a sort of rheumatic pain in one side from my hip to the foot. This kind offer I excepted of ... and submitted myself to their direction. I was desired to lay down in the midst of them, then as many as could get round me began to squeeze me with both hands from head to foot, but more especially the parts where the pain was, till they made my bones crack and a perfect mummy of my flesh—in short after being under their hands about a quarter of an hour I was glad to get away from them. However I found immediate relief from the operation. They gave me another rubbing down before I went to bed and I found my self pretty easy all the night after. They repeated the operation the next morning before they went ashore, and again in the evening when they came on board, after which I found the pains entirely removed. ... This they call *Romy,* an operation which in my opinion far exceeds the flesh brush, or anything we make use of of the kind. It is universally practiced among them. ..."[37]

Hawaiian: "The exact procedure in Hawaiian massage should probably not be defined more definitely than by saying it consists in both gentle and hard rubbing and stroking, in gentle and vigorous kneading, and in such heroic measures when occasion demands as treading on the backbone of the prone patient with one or both feet."[38]

Called *Lomi,* after the Hawaiian word for "knead," the massage was often done with *lomi-lomi* sticks—"curved implements of wood with long straight handles and lower ends crooked at an angle of about 45 degrees and flattened. The handle is held with both hands in front over the chest so that the implement curves over one shoulder and the flattened lower end may be pressed and drawn up and down on the upper muscles of the back; or the lower back muscles are massaged by holding the stick so that its crook curves around one or the other side of the body."[39]

"*Lomi-lomi* is an ancient Hawaiian version of massage. Its main feature is that the masseur walks on the patient's back, and while he walks, he kneads the flesh while regulating his weight by holding on a bar above the massage table."[40]

The *lomi-lomi* method of kneading and walking on the patient's back is apparently part of a larger trans-Pacific medicine guild (contacted first by a surprised Captain Cook in the eighteenth century). It is a very old tradition with a variety of techniques and regional forms ranging from Japan to Hawaii to Polynesia:

Pacific Islands: "The *omi-omi* of [the Pacific] islands, and the *lomi-lomi* of the Hawaiians, all have a relation to the *momi-ryogi,* practiced by tens of thousands of whistling blind itinerants throughout Japan. I had a remarkable illustration of the curative merits of *omi-omi* when, having bruised my back in sliding down a giant waterfall, [first I] was given a steam-bath for about ten minutes in a tiny penthouse with a wooden trencher of water in which white hot stones were dropped. Then I submitted myself to the ministrations of Juno and Vanquished Often ... They handled me as if they understood the location of each muscle and nerve. They pinched and pulled, pressed and hammered, and otherwise took hold of and struck me, but all with a most remarkable skill and seeming exact knowledge of their methods and results."[41]

The name *"Lomi"* is appropriately preserved in a California academy of bodywork and spiritual exercise, Lomi School in Santa Rosa (see the section on "Breath" in Volume Two, Chapter Four; the section on "Somatic Philosophy" in Volume Two, Chapter Six; and the Resource Guide at the end of Volume Two).

Cranial Adjustment

"In India today, families of bonesetters still specialize in cranial bone manipulation, a skill handed down from father to son. These bonesetters practice their art with a nimble dexterity which would shame many western chiropractors and osteopaths. There is a little fellow who sits on a burlap bag outside Poona railway station who, for the equivalent

158

of about ten cents, will adjust all of your cranial bones. He works sitting cross-legged: one sits down opposite him and he makes deft, quick, chiropractic-like adjustments to all of your head bones, including the palatines and the nasals. It takes about five minutes. Ask him where he learnt and he will tell you 'father.' Ask him where his father learnt, and he will say 'his father'...."[42]

Manipulation

"It is thus hardly surprising that experiences like these [a young woman who was suddenly relieved of lumbago when she was twisted round by a huge wave while swimming] have led to the emergence of jerks intended 'to put the spine back in place.' In Central Europe there have been gipsies who, one generation after another, have possessed the ability to cure 'Hexenschuss' (shot of a witch, i.e., acute lumbago). Travellers returning from Tibet relate that some people there had developed a fine technique, and in Japan 'distortion of the spinal column' resulting from jiu-jitsu and judo injuries to the neck is cured by special manipulations. ...The Indians in Mexico used spinal treatments [likened] to manipulation; in due course, these methods were adopted by their white conquerors and are still employed today, e.g., 'the shepherd's hug' or 'the farmer's push.'"[43]

Egypt: "The bather soon starts to sweat profusely owing to the damp heat. He now sits down on the 'leewan.' The attendant starts to work, eliciting clicks from his neck and back. The limbs are then apparently violently twisted, but so dexterously that it never hurts and is without danger. He then goes on to massage the muscles."[44]

Acupuncture

Chinese acupuncture is itself a prehistoric medicine. However, there have probably been many other diverse independent discoveries of the therapeutic value of needles and thorns.

Sri Lanka: "In spite of the seeming lack of interest in Chinese acupuncture among Buddhists in India there appears to have existed in Sri Lanka an indigenous form of acupuncture. Even today in present-day Sri Lanka there are reports of acupuncture being used by traditional healers in cases such as snake bite, and the use of acupressure with elephants. Dr. A. Jayasuria suggests that this unique system of acupuncture was a branch of Deshiya Vedakamae, an ancient medical system practiced on that island well before the arrival of Ayurvedic medicine during the middle of the 3rd century B.C. This does not, however, exclude the possibility of Chinese acupuncture having initiated or influenced the development of this healing science in Sri Lanka, since contact between these two lands did exist as far back as the 2nd century B.C.

"In Sri Lanka the utilization of acupuncture in veterinary medicine seems to have been greater than in China, and ancient charts have been found illustrating the points for use in treating, among others, elephants, water buffalo, tigers and pigs."[45]

South America: "Dr. Javier Cabrera Darquea writes in his book *The Message of the Engraved Stones of Ica* [self-published, 1988; Lima, Peru] about the ancient use of acupuncture that is illustrated on the engraved stones found along the Ica River in southern Peru. These stones are of unknown date, but definitely were engraved long before the Inca empire by an unknown people; they show acupuncture being performed on various humans, including a pregnant woman . . . I have heard also from local experts in Chile that the Mapuche Indians had a tradition of acupuncture, using sharp thorns of bushes as their needles. Apparently they (and it seems only women healers did this form of therapy) utilized a variety of points for numerous diseases, but they did not have a meridian concept (as exists in China). The Mapuches had no written history or drawings to record their past, and unfortunately there were no living practitioners that I could interview. It seems that this form of treatment with thorns died out with the last few generations."[46]

Cupping

Very hot suction is applied to the body to bring blood to the surface.[47]

Emetics

Vomiting is forced, usually by a poison. During the Creek "bush ceremony," the Indians drink a strong hot tea called *assee* made from cassina leaves out of a conch shell. There is a special round of drinking for the warriors toward the end of the ceremony, with each participant grunting aloud in a different key after swallowing his portion. This stirs up a deep regurgitation and simultaneously clears the head and the stomach.[48]

The African poison ritual, while not literally a medicine, is one of the most famous emetic rites in the world. A man or woman accused of voodoo murder is tried by poison. The defense and the prosecution both have lawyers; the accused's lawyer addresses the poison, asking it to declare the innocence of his client; the prosecution demands of the poison that it do justice and kill the murderer. The prisoner drinks the preparation, after which the lawyers continue to argue and the members of the community press around the defendant for the verdict. It is now in *his* hands. If he can somehow neutralize the poison or vomit it up, he is innocent; he is also alive. On the surface, this appears a very unfair trial, at least from a Western judicial standpoint, but, as in all such affairs, we must look twice.

There are various versions of the poison trial in Africa. Harley describes the sasswood ordeal among the Mano. The poison is a dark orange broth made from the bark of the sasswood tree, and the trial is held on a scaffold built beneath the same tree. Harley quotes the head man, who addresses the tree while collecting the poison:

"We are here. We came to call you to settle a dispute. You are a tree that never lies, a tree full of power. You give justice to all alike."[49]

There are countless points at which a bribe can fix the strength of the poison, and even if a direct bribe did not fix it, the unconscious flow of public opinion could sway the brewers. Furthermore, an unsympathetic audience in the court could make the defendant tense enough that he or she would be unable to vomit up the poison.

Practical Ethno-medicine: The Ancient Skills

All of this, however, also suggests that the trial is not fixed. Deep psychophysiological currents underlie the seeming divination. Vomiting the poison is a spontaneous skill. It may well be, as with a lie detector, that it is difficult to fake innocence. If they involve different vascular rhythms, the physiology of lying would work against the physiology of vomiting. Then vomiting becomes truth-telling.

It is also possible that "handling" poison internally requires medical and martial training. That theme was brought into popular vogue by Frank Herbert in the science-fiction novel *Dune.* The native "Dune Planet" peoples passed on, from generation to generation in secret societies, a technique of using their own guts to convert the poisonous secretions of giant worms into a visionary serum.[50]

A trial by poison is extreme, but it suggests a universal attitude: all illnesses are such trials, and the doctor is there as lawyer, to help the sick person marshal his or her forces against the illness.

Harley mentions a notable Mano case. "An old woman anxious to show her innocence once drank all twelve cupfuls at one time and vomited it immediately on climbing the scaffold."[51]

What a personal triumph!

Burning

Hot irons are used to burn diseases out. In Bali and elsewhere, fire walking itself is a healing exercise. The fire is said not to burn when its teeth are taken away by a mantra or prayer.[52] This practice is currently being revived as a form of Western consciousness training by such organizations as Tolly Burkan's Firewalking Institute in the Sierra Nevada of California.

Incision

The incision may be a very thin scratch or a deep, painful groove. It may also be a permanent scarification of the body. In some systems, the position and angle of the line on the body is crucial. In Vietnamese medicine, there are over a thousand vital points, each one related to months, days and hours by the lunar calendar.[53] This system is no doubt related to Chinese acupuncture in which needles are inserted without pain or cutting. The precise map may have evolved from an earlier practice of incision or trephining joined to a set of astronomical and seasonal correspondences and perhaps an internal geomancy in which vital nodes of the body were located internally by meditation.

Creek Indian: The Creeks make four deep scratches before drinking herbal medicine during the busk.[54]

Fiji Islands: A short, four-thorned reed is used in the Fiji Islands to cure muscle aches.[55]

Africa: "Throughout the African territories medicine men are well versed in the art of scarification. Fine linear incisions about half an inch long are made in the skin, usually in pairs on the site of pain. Neither medicine man nor patient realizes that, with this treatment and that of cupping, the blood supply to the affected part is increased and so in some instances the remedy is efficacious. Certainly with the incisions into which powdered roots are rubbed the benefit derived is ascribed to the medicines."[56]

Australia: "In south-western New South Wales, other medicine-men, or a cult-hero, performed the central rite in the 'making.' An incision was not made in the postulant's body, but in spite of that, an assistant totem or familiar and magical substances such as quartz crystals and mysterious cord, were pressed or rubbed and 'sung' into him. . . .

". . . in Eastern Australia, magical substances and 'agents' were inserted into the postulant either through an abdominal incision, or were rubbed or pressed, and 'sung' into his body and limbs; or the quartz might be inserted in a hole made through his head."[57] We examine this practice again in different contexts in Chapter Six, and in Chapter Two, Volume Two.

Bloodletting

What is enigmatic about this treatment is the assumption that letting blood out of the body releases more of the bad blood and the pressure caused by the disease than it does of the good blood and necessary visceral tension. An ancient Tibetan medical document gives a possible explanation for its own version:

"Bloodletting should not be performed before separating the pure from the impure blood; this is done by giving the patient the medicine called *Hbras-bu-gsum-than* which separates good from bad blood, and then bloodletting can be performed."[58]

Trephining (Surgery)

Trephination involves using a saw to cut disks of bone out of the skull, or sometimes other parts of the skeleton. No doubt ancient surgeons developed a wide range of other skills and techniques, but we shall discuss those in more detail in Chapter Eight and Volume Two.

"That prehistoric humans, using the most rudimentary surgical instruments, were able to bore open a human skull—and that the patient survived—is an incredible medical achievement ... Skulls from the Mesolithic cultural period have been found to have round depressions suggestive of primitive trephination efforts, which would date the initial efforts at trephination at 10,000 to 5000 B.C. ...

"The simplest but crudest method would have been simply to scrape a hole in the cranium, using a sharpened rock or shell. A second method would have required a circular cut in the bone with a flint or obsidian knife. Boring a series of holes in a circular or oval pattern and later cutting through the separating partitions to join the holes would have been another possible scheme. Finally, a crude hammer and chisel could have been used to create four grooves in a cross shape so that the square piece of center bone could then be lifted out. This button of bone, also called a rondelle, was frequently worn as an amulet or used in magic or religious ceremonies to ward off evil spirits.

"Trephination appears to have been conducted for different reasons in different locales. The South American Incas performed trephination primarily for spiritual, magical, and religious reasons. In Europe, trephination appears to have been practiced most frequently in areas where weapons that produced skull fractures were used. Such injuries have been associated with patient distress or bizarre behavior. For traumatic injuries, it has been estimated, little more than 30 minutes would have been required to complete a trephination. Empirical evidence eventually must have shown the prehistoric surgeon that removal of depressed bone fragments and wounded tissue could possibly restore an individual's health."[59]

As the oldest medical technique for which there is archaeological evidence, trephination confirms that the surgical branch of ethnomedicine—a forerunner of allopathy—was a Stone Age science. The Sumerians and Egyptians continued to refine what was already a millennia-long art. Additionally, the surgical branch of medicine developed its own heritage quite separate from shamanism and herbalism. According to the above historian, "... early in the development of medicine and surgery, society made the distinction between the learned physician who worked with books and theories to prescribe remedies and the usually illiterate but highly practical surgeon who worked with his hands. Perceived as craftsmen or technicians rather than men of learning, surgeons were viewed prejudicially as an inferior caste."[60]

Practical Shamanism and Psychoanalysis

M Y THIRD SCHOOL of ethnomedicine is a forerunner of psychoanalysis and psychosomatic medicine. It might be called "psychophysiological healing." What I am describing is basically a universal method in which a shaman combines narrative recapitulation of a disease with the sucking out of a supposed disease entity. Whether or not the patient suspects trickery (and clearly he does in many cases), he participates in the drama of symbolically extracting a concrete object.

In a typical version of such mythodrama, the doctor summons the friends and relatives of the sick person. He then invokes traumatic moments from the life—violations of taboos, worldly griefs, ancestral

Practical Ethno-medicine: The Ancient Skills

clan tragedies—and everyone acknowledges them. Using a plausible medley of astute perceptions, psychic intuitions, graphic personifications of marginal data, and characterizations of actual events, he draws the patient into a picture of his illness.

"He gazes at him silently, after drawing attention to his presence by showing him the feathers—a sign of magical power. He speaks to the spirits and so creates atmosphere, and then gets the patient to gaze through the feathers at his, the doctor's, body, and to see only the latter's 'spiritman'."[61]

Power and suffering are conveyed both to and from the doctor, as *his* energetic body replaces the ailing one.

For decades various ilk of behavioral scientists have speculated on the mechanism behind the astonishing power of shamanic projection. Walter B. Cannon's 1942 article "Voodoo Death" has served as a baseline for inquiry into psycho-transference.[62]

Cannon begins by pointing out that death from sorcery is common in an area stretching from Africa to South America and the islands of the Pacific. A variety of remarkable cases have been reported throughout Australia. In documented instances, a victim entered a hospital in good health, i.e., showing no pathological signs even upon examination. The only complaint was that the shaman's bone had been pointed at him. "A spell has been put on me," the Aborigine would say. "I have come here only to die. There is nothing you people, with all your medicine, can do to save me." In the ensuing days, he would grow weaker and weaker. Finally, after death, an unedifying autopsy would be performed. Cause of death: unknown.

Cannon accepts these reports at face value and so commits himself to figuring out how, in fact, an attack by voodoo could be fatal. His method is to reason through such episodes without resort to magic as the explanation.

For instance, initial shock from the awareness of the attack could act like a physical blow, especially when combined with later, increasing

terror of social condemnation. The emotional impact would be greatest for those in small groups outside whose borders survival was not
possible. The shattering would then branch out through the sympa-
thicoadrenal system, with a drop in blood pressure leading to a starvation of oxygen in key organs. "In these circumstances," writes Cannon,
"they might well die from a true state of shock, in the surgical sense—
a shock induced by prolonged and intense emotion."[63]

Parapsychologists usually prefer a faster-than-light telepathic delivery of the message, since, in many instances, the victim need not even
know of the attack in order to be affected by it. But either way, voodoo
works. The physical explanation Cannon gives is the only one he can
imagine: psychosomatic death from social ostracism and the projected
charisma of a powerful wizard. He at least confers sociological dignity
on a phenomenon that was previously dismissed as gullibility and naive
observation. "The suggestion which I offer," Cannon affirms at the

*Practical
Ethno-
medicine:
The Ancient
Skills*

end of his essay, "... is that voodoo death may be real, and that it may be explained as due to shocking emotional stress — to obvious or repressed terror."[64] For decades afterwards, anthropologists have referred back to the reductionist Cannon hypothesis for insight into repeated similar instances of a truly puzzling sequence of events.

Lévi-Strauss's 1949 essay, translated into English as "The Sorcerer and His Magic," begins by acknowledging the reality of "voodoo death" and summarizing the Cannon proposition.[65] But the structural anthropologist is more interested in the "psycho-" half of the psychophysical formula: how is belief established in a magical system — belief not only by the victim and community in the power of a magician, but of the magician in his own power?

He retells a theretofore overlooked story from Franz Boas' account of the religion of the Kwakiutl Indians of Vancouver Island. We can summarize the tale from its original source with somewhat different emphases:

A young Indian, who is later to take the shaman name Quesalid, does not believe in the medicine men's ability to cure illness. He not only suspects they are connivers and charlatans but intends to prove this and debunk them publicly. First, he hangs out with the local adepts until they finally take notice and invite him to join their society. Once on the inside, he finds his worst suspicions confirmed: the "doctors" theatrically perform traumas and reveal ostensible violated taboos in skillful episodes constructed (i.e., fabricated) from their own observations of the sick person spiced with secrets purchased from spies. Most notably, Quesalid discovers how, when the shaman sucks the disease out of an organ, he actually conceals a tuft of down in the corner of his mouth which, at the height of the healing crisis, he vomits up, covered with blood from his biting his tongue. This hoax is passed off as the extradition of the pathology.

Quesalid is now in a position to betray the profession but, in a fateful moment of reticence, he decides first to learn more. Before he has a chance to make his revelation public, he is interfered with by a seemingly minor event. In traditional fashion a sick woman, learning of his apprenticeship, summons him for help. Etiquette requires his attendance. As her chosen physician, he has no choice but to treat her according to his training. To his surprise and chagrin, he "succeeds," at least to the satisfaction of this first client; soon thereafter, he becomes widely known as a healer and hired, patient by patient, to treat other diseases. In fact, he becomes the best—the top medicine man of his generation. He is so successful and popular he never seems to find the opportune moment for his exposé. Although somewhat disturbed by the unlikely turn of events, he remains a muckraker at heart, holding to his original cynicism, passing off his success as the belief of his patients in him.

Yet on another level, he gains a strange confidence and bravado. He transcends his lack of true methodology and strides around as a healer-at-large. Though he has no saving explanation, somehow he regards the world differently. He sees his power as something authentic, something he has earned. It is a strange system indeed in which the most successful practitioner is the one with the least commitment and enthusiasm!

Eventually, Quesalid comes to explore the healing system of the neighboring Koskimo tribe. When he finds out that their doctors do not even produce a bloody down but instead spit into their hands, he is astonished and more than a bit scandalized. This is a true fraud! And a less attractive one at that.

For Quesalid this is also a wonderful turn of events. He can now expose the shamans of other tribes as shoddy performers and confer at least a shred of honor on his Kwakiutl brethren. Once again, though, he is trapped by circumstance. Princess Woman-Made-to-Invite of the Koskimo learns of his presence. None of her native doctors have been able to cure her, and she calls upon Quesalid to be her physician. This royal invitation leads ultimately to his engaging in a dramatic contest with the Koskimo shamans before the princess. Quesalid arrives in a boastful and superior mood, anxious to try out his stagecraft:

169

Now I took the water in the cup and rinsed my mouth. After I had rinsed my mouth, I spat the water on the floor near the fire in the middle of the house. Now the four shamans came who had been taking out the sickness of the woman and sat down on each side of me. Also the four praying women came and sat down where they had been sitting before. After I had rinsed my mouth I bent down my head on the back of the sick woman and I did not act roughly when I first sucked, but finally I sucked strongly and I nearly lifted my head. Now I tasted the blood when it came and filled my mouth, coming out of my gums. Now the four women were praying together. Then I lifted my head and I put the blood from my mouth into my hand, among it the down, the pretended sickness. Now I just held the blood in my right hand ... When all the blood had come out, I passed it from one hand to the other like a worm with a long round body, the down in my hands being covered with blood. Now this was seen by all the Koskimo and by the sick woman. While it stuck on my hand I was singing my sacred song.[66]

By this dramatic performance Woman-Made-to-Invite is cured. She says: "You alone will be my shaman, Quesalid, for you have brought me back to life, although I had already been given up by the shamans of the Koskimo."[67]

The Koskimo shamans, embarrassed at the now-obvious "falsity" of their own magic, are also profoundly troubled by this seemingly more authentic extraction. They argue theory with Quesalid, protesting that the disease is spiritual and can have no physical source, so how could he extract an object? Quesalid is mum, despite his historical opportunity to clear matters up, despite their attempts to lure him into further discussion and even the seductive offers of their daughters. He has become a shaman.

He must next answer the challenge of a doctor in his own tribe but of a different clan. The outcome by now is familiar. Once again he is able to heal the incurable cases of his rival, who begs for the secret, also assuming that Quesalid has found some valid disease object. Quesalid holds out for an explanation of *his* system, which he gets. It too is sleight

of hand and deception. He then refuses to confess his own method, and the disgraced doctor goes into exile, returns mad, and dies soon after.

Decades pass. Now an old man, chief of the guild of shamans, Quesalid is narrating his story to Boas. Told matter-of-factly, it is a remarkable confession. Quesalid retains a cynical attitude toward the bloody down, defending it only as a step in the direction toward reification, but the sage in him admits that something is happening on a whole different level. The killer whale and the toad, he tells Boas, are the real shaman makers; ultimate rectitude rests solely with them.[68]

His Kwakiutl patients know the killer whale, the toad, and other totem powers in their own way. Outside of an objective material equation seeking a literal disease object, these express a truth about curative intelligence and the relation of mind and body, if not about the role of the Linnaean toad and whale. The bloody down is just the first symbol in a chain of symbols.

Interestingly, Filipino psychic surgeons also extract seeming diseases, in their case by putting their hands straight through flesh into the organs. While their reputation among paraphysicists is of actually opening up tissue, reaching into the body, and sealing their incisions, they too may slip in extraneous artifacts. When caught on film making a substitution of a chicken part for an organ, one such healer acknowledged the deception but said that it was far healthier not to penetrate the actual body. A true disease extraction, of which he claimed also to be capable, would have been far less effective and would have suppressed rather than invoked the patient's natural healing powers. Drawing out a merely symbolic disease startled the sick person into healing himself.[69]

The relationship between authenticity and chicanery is clearly not congruent to the relationship between effectiveness and ineffectiveness in such systems.

A. P. Elkin is explicit on creative "chicanery" among the Australian Aborigines:

A number of writers refer to the native doctor as an "impostor," "the greatest scamp of the tribe," or "as a rule the most cunning man in the tribe and a great humbug." These opinions are, however, based on superficial observation. When a native doctor sucks a magical bone out of a sick person's abdomen, and shows it to those around and to the patient, he is not a mere charlatan, bluffing his fellows because he introduced and produced the bone at the psychological moment by sleight of hand. Nor is he just play-acting for effect when, having rubbed the affected part of his patient in the "corrected" manner, he gathers an invisible something in his hands, and solemnly walking a few steps away, casts "it" into the air with a very decided jerk of the arms and opening of the hands. These are two of a number of traditional methods which he has learnt, and in which he and all believe—methods for extracting the ill from the patient, and so giving the latter assurance (often visible) of his cure. . . .

We should remember that if a medicine-man himself becomes ill, he, too, calls a fellow practitioner to treat him in one of the accepted ways, although he knows all the professional methods (which we might call tricks). But *he* also desires earnestly, like all other sick persons, assurance that the cause of this pain or illness has been extracted and cast away, or that his wandering soul (if that be the diagnosis) has been caught and restored. The actions and chantings and production of "bones" and "stones" are but the outward expression and means of the doctor's personal victory over one or both of two factors: first, the malevolent activities of some person practicing sorcery on the sick man or woman; and second, the patient's willingness to remain ill or even die.[70]

Clearly we are dealing with a complex system that contradicts itself by working on more than one level at the same time. Shamanism operates through a ritual of archetypal transformation reaching down under the "concrete" disease and its symptomatic complex. The depth needed to enact a cure often requires epic abreaction from mass community participation. Note the following account from another Northwest Coast tribe:

By far the principal function of Tenino shamans was the practice of magical therapy. When a person fell ill and did not respond to lay treatment, his family summoned the shaman, who immediately proceeded to his bedside. In the house were assembled the relatives and friends of the patient, lending him social support and enhancing his faith in the therapeutic procedures and his will to recover. On hand were the necessary accessories, including especially a coiled basket full of water. During the performance the audience sang and beat time on a dry log with short sticks, and the shaman accentuated the drama of the occasion by singing his spirit songs, uttering explosive sounds, making biting motions, and pantomiming the struggle of the spirits.[71]

So begins a medical procedure as profound and desperate as open-heart surgery—the symbolic projection of space into time and the conjury of invisible forces toward the restitution of body-mind wholeness.

The necessary first step in the cure was diagnosis. After washing his hands, smoking, blowing on the basket of water, and sprinkling the patient, the shaman summoned his diagnostic spirit and projected it into the patient's body, usually through a tube. After an interval of time for its exploration of the interior of the body, the spirit returned to the mouth of the shaman and informed him of the identity of the intrusive spirit (or, alternatively, of the absence of the soul). If the shaman had no guardian spirit with ascendancy over the intrusive one—if, for example, the latter was the grizzly bear and he did not control a rattlesnake spirit—he resigned immediately from the case and recommended another shaman to take over. Otherwise he would have lost his life when his spirit was overcome by the intrusive one in the ensuing struggle.

If however, the shaman's roster of supernatural helpers included one with ascendance over the intrusive spirit, he summoned it and meanwhile called upon two strong men to assist him. They stood on either side of him, grasping his arms, while he blew his spirit helper into the patient's body. When the latter encountered the intrusive spirit, a violent conflict ensued between them, during which the patient writhed helplessly. When a moment of calm intervened, the shaman sucked the intrusive spirit into his mouth. Then began a titanic and dramatic struggle—this time between the vanquished spirit and the shaman—in which the shaman's body tensed, was thrown into contortions, and then became inert as he lost consciousness. His two assistants exerted themselves valiantly to keep him erect, for had he fallen he would have lost his life. Ultimately ...ubsided, and the shaman spat the intrusive spirit ...hands, thereby initiating a new struggle in which ... the help of his assistants, with great effort gradu... ...ands into the basket of water. This finally subdued

...der again whether the "voodoo force" is more con... ...imagined and whether it might include a para... ...an actual demon from an exorcism or the impact ... UFO.

...withdrew his hands from the water and exhibited ...irit to the audience on the palm of his hand. Only ...nt, of course, could actually see it, but perhaps the ...erested in a shaman's description of an extracted ...o John Quinn, such a spirit, regardless of the ani... ..., was approximately the size and shape of a ciga... ...grayish in color, and had a colloidal or mucus-like ...e viewing, the shaman, with a puff of breath, sent ...ts proper place in nature. He then retrieved and ...d his own guardian spirit.[73]

...ts out the more than superficial similarity between extractive shamanism and psychoanalysis. In both systems, the origin of a disease is relived and, through an emotional participation, pathology is overcome. But the strategies are opposites: In psychoanalysis, the patient retells an event while the psychiatrist listens; in shamanism, the doctor narrates an event and the patient listens. In addition, Lévi-Strauss reminds us, the psychiatrist must undergo, in his training, the same abreaction he requires of a patient in healing.[74] Shamanism and psychoanalysis thus share an initiation: for the shaman it is a dream vision experienced during a vision quest; for the psychiatrist it is his own psychoanalysis by another doctor. These initiations are the

Practical Ethno-medicine: The Ancient Skills

literal empowerment and entitlement in either system. The shaman also foreshadows the psychoanalyst by engaging in astute, semi-fictional character analysis while building up to his sleight of hand. Conversely, the psychoanalyst's recreation of the past is no less imaginal (the real past is always different from what is elicited or remembered), and his sleight of hand is a semantic one (through puns and free associations).

Though neither therapist produces the true disease as a substance extracted (or even a spoken truth), each locates it in a fake concrete event, an object or trauma, to which the patient responds instantaneously. The response itself is what is crucial, even if the method is a sham. Westerners are aroused by stuff at least as unlikely as the bloody down. Healing and emotional change can come from a basketball or soccer game, a revival meeting, a new car, or a timely telephone call. The body is pagan and multicultural. At the moment of decision, it simply responds.

A Kwakiutl patient will react more sensitively and intelligently to a portrayal of events within a mythology and sociology with which he is

familiar than he will to a supposed Western "biography" of his life, which would omit supernatural and ancestral interconnections and community taboos and obligations, and focus instead on his childhood. He would *rather* hear about toad and killer whale than his parents' treatment of him during his formative years. So apparently would his illness.

Although many holistic medicines abjure concrete etiology of disease, they are very much interested in the way the sick person conceives of the advent of the disease. "How I came to be sick," whether or not the real story, is itself part of the illness.

People are trapped by their own cultural prejudices when they presume automatically that their psychohistories, inner children, and suppressed memories of abuse are more true than Indian mythohistories. Either way, we take the past—the profound, unknowable, esoteric past—and recreate it episodically and ritually. But the past is inert except as it lives in the present body and mind, so whatever we give life to we become—the traumatized child is reclaimed as either (in twelve-step parlance) a neurotic victim or (shamanically) an initiate at the beginning of a vision quest.

The danger of an over-reified "inner child" or co-dependency addiction is that, even "cured," a person accepting this mythology can never be more than an ego reaction to a negative state, which is not itself necessarily potentiated. The patient of the shaman no doubt also has an "inner child," but that child is experienced as a raven or wild bear and thus liberated to transmute, finally, into something larger than the neurosis. The so-called neurosis may have been no more than the unborn "shaman" within, careening toward its voice. No real growth can happen as long as the victim state requires either comforting or revenge. In fact the more deeply wounded the victim, the more powerful must be his or her potentiation in order to overcome the wound. A woman viciously raped and then discarded for dead in a garbage can by her attacker devoted herself tirelessly (after her long spell in the hospital) to becoming a warrior and a healer, not out of some sense of rage or self-protection but as the only way of healing herself, of literally mutating what had been done to her. It was so intense and powerful it could only be healed by her adopting its power.[75]

Ackerknecht writes:

> In a certain sense, the primitive psychotherapist uses more and stronger weapons than the modern psychotherapist. He works not only with the strength of his own personality. His rite is part of the common faith of the whole community which not seldom assists *in corpore* at his healing act or even participates in singing and dancing. The whole weight of the tribe's religion, myths, history, and

community spirit enters into the treatment. Inside and outside the patient he can mobilize strong psychic energies no longer available in modern society.[76]

Public trances, drumming, sacred songs, etc., add to the conviction of a powerful seance in which things not ordinarily seen and heard present themselves. We will examine this aspect of shamanic healing in the next chapter. For now, it is sufficient to see that one face of shamanism is psychoanalysis, or perhaps psychoanalysis is intellectual shamanism rediscovered. At very best, contemporary forms of psychoanalysis and ritual healing struggle toward such cathartic, transformative power. Sometimes, as in the case of the rape victim described above, an exceptionally strong person can start a new tradition all by herself.

THE GAP BETWEEN, on the one hand, aboriginal shamanism and medicine voodoo and, on the other, contemporary shamanism is absolute and unbridgeable. Indigenous medicine does not resolve the mind/body split, or at least our mind/body split, because it operates under other definitions. When psychoanalytic theory apparently restores to Western theory the missing psychosomatic element, it does so in a tradition already bracketed by classical, rational philosophy. Even as we were given an intimation of primordial unconscious powers by the early Freudians, we were given a normative clinical framework in which to apply them. The Freudian "unconscious" includes the things we are and do not know, but, by summarizing them symbolically in a single context, psychiatry also in a sense continues, even as it liberates them, to keep those things out. This is the reason Reichian and Jungian metaphors transformed the Freudian system so early: these exact elements had been lost in the millennia of retreat from the shamanic hearth. But, even in archetypal and somatic psychology, the symbol is not toad or killer whale reborn; it is at best a mediating archetype or somaticized trauma. The bloody down still has not regained its primal role.

When we speak of the prehistoric "replacement" of as-yet-uninvented psychoanalysis by ritual, we mean that a ceremony provides an arena for the reenactment of trauma and rituals for collective abreaction. Civilization lost this method of catharsis and transformation and then regained a version of it, through the work of Freud, in a ritualization of language and dream. But this symbolic recovery of psychosomatic and archetypal modes is not the same as the ontological experience of them. The aboriginal initiation is not merely a by-product of life. It is real, perhaps more real (because more condensed and focused) than the events it represents. The educated psychoanalyst unravels the charges and structures behind life events, but the shaman carries the whole tribe or clan *through* them into a new cosmology. Contemporary psychoanalytic shamans and renegade therapists attempt to restore this process through imitations of Australian and American Indian rituals, etc., in the context of depth therapy and various confrontative gestalt techniques. However, the same evolutionary destiny that did not allow early man and woman to reflect on the symbolic aspects of their "symbols" does not allow modern men and women to experience the unreflected entirety of the ceremony. We are condemned to prove our shamanic authenticity by writing books like this to seek the lost key to charismatic systems of thought that are accessible to us now only through ethnography and textualization. At least this path trains us to recognize our own ceremonial magic when it arises fresh in unexpected places, for instance, aikido, rebirthing, Reiki, revamped Huichol ceremonies, or the somato-emotional release of craniosacral therapy.

IN A 1972 INTERVIEW with the parapsychologist Jule Eisenbud, I asked him why, if mankind once had powers of telepathy, precognition, and voodoo death, they were not more evident or accessible now: "Did we lose them or have we never really had them collectively?"

"I have no idea," he replied. "It's beyond me. But you see my own feeling is that we have a lot of false development, in some way, to backtrack on, in much the way ... most people have a lot of backtracking to do to get over hang-ups, bad development in childhood, the accidents of the way they happened to develop, and I think that mankind has a lot of backtracking to do too, to get rid of its ways of looking at things, its ways of feeling and *not feeling* things, its peculiar denial of complicity in each other's lives."[77] Here Eisenbud approached the voodoo issue thirty difficult years later than Cannon. A lot had happened in those thirty years for him to go on to say:

> ... thoughts alone can kill; bare, naked thoughts; isn't all this armor of war, this machinery, these bombs, aren't they all grotesque exaggerations? We don't even need them. ...
>
> To put it schematically, and simplistically, and almost absurdly, because we don't wish to realize that we can just kill with our minds, we go through this whole enormous play of killing with such—, of overkilling with such overimplementation; it gets greater and greater and greater as if ... it's a caricature of saying: how can I do it with my mind; I need tanks; I need B-52 bombers; I need napalm, and so on, and so on ... I have examples of people who died this way. Not that I could see them do it but if I put together the jigsaw, it looks as though this one was responsible for that event.[78]

At this point I mentioned Cannon's "Voodoo Death," but Eisenbud was markedly impatient with that:

> Yes, of course, of course. But the whole point is that there a man deliberately said, "I'm going to kill you." We mask it. It goes on unobtrusively. Which doesn't make a damn bit of difference. What's the difference whether I do it or streptococci do it. We have cover stories, you see. All science has produced cover stories for the deaths we create; it's streptococci; it's accidents, and so on. But, what I'm trying to say is, there must be, I feel, a relationship between this truth, which we will not see, and this absurd burlesque of aggression that goes on all around us, as if we're trying to deny that the other is possible.[79]

The implication could not be more serious: All science has produced cover stories for the deaths we create. The shaman, who has disappeared from his calling in the West, is in fact everywhere, unconsciously projected as both healer and killer through the shards of our fragmented personalities.

But what can kill can also cure, and all these weapons are the allies of healing under other circumstances.

Notes

1. F. Bruce Lamb, *Rio Tigre and Beyond: The Amazon Jungle Medicine of Manuel Córdova-Rios* (Berkeley, California: North Atlantic Books, 1985).

2. Warwick Nieass, lecture and slide show, Berkeley, California, 1984.

3. Erwin H. Ackerknecht, "Problems of Primitive Medicine," *Bulletin of the History of Medicine* XI (1942), Johns Hopkins Institute of the History of Medicine, Baltimore, Maryland; quoted in William A. Lessa and Evon Z. Vogt (eds.), *Reader in Comparative Religion* (New York: Harper & Row, 1958), p. 399.

4. Benjamin Rush, *Medical Inquiries and Observations,* Vol. I (Philadelphia: Pritchard and Hall, 1789), p. 29; quoted in Harris Livermore Coulter, *Divided Legacy, Vol. III: The Conflict Between Homoeopathy and the American Medical Association* (Berkeley, California: North Atlantic Books, 1982), p. 40.

5. Harris L. Coulter, *Divided Legacy, Vol. III,* pp. 262–63.

6. George Way Harley, *Native African Medicine* (Cambridge, Massachusetts: Harvard University Press, 1941), p. 85.

7. Luis Eduardo Luna and Pablo Amaringo, *Ayahuasca Visions: The Religious Iconography of a Peruvian Shaman* (Berkeley, California: North Atlantic Books, 1991).

8. From a tape of a lecture; material appears in rewritten form in several places in Edward Whitmont, *The Alchemy of Healing: Psyche and Soma* (Berkeley, California: North Atlantic Books, 1993).

9. Lamb, *Rio Tigre and Beyond,* pp. 190, 192, 194.

10. E. S. Craighill Handy, Mary Kawena Pukui, and Katherine Livermore, *Outline of Hawaiian Physical Therapeutics,* Bernice P. Bishop Museum, Bulletin 126, Honolulu (1934), pp. 17–19.

11. Miguel Covarrubias, *Island of Bali* (New York: Alfred A. Knopf, 1938), pp. 352–53.

12. Morton C. Kahn, *Djuka: The Bush Negroes of Dutch Guiana* (New York: Viking Press, 1931), pp. 154–55.

13. A. L. Kroeber, *Ethnology of the Gros Ventre,* Anthropological Papers of the American Museum of Natural History, Vol. I, Part IV, New York (1908), p. 225.

14. Lord Herder, quoted in Eiler H. Schiötz and James Cyriax, *Manipulation Past and Present* (London: William Heinemann Medical Books, Ltd., 1975), p. 15.

15. Schiötz and Cyriax, *Manipulation Past and Present,* p. 85.

16. Ibid., p. 165.

17. Ibid., p. 23.

18. Ibid.

19. Ibid., pp. 22–23.

20. Ibid., p. 23.

21. Paul Pitchford, in a lecture given in Berkeley, California, August 1976.

22. Harley, *Native African Medicine,* p. 38.

23. I would like to thank anthropology librarian Dorothy Koenig and anthropology graduate student Amy Champ for their help in compiling this section.

24. William Wildschut, *Crow Indian Medicine Bundles,* John C. Ewers (ed.), Museum of the American Indian, Heye Foundation, New York (1975), p. 7.

25. Gladys Tantaquidgeon, *Folk Medicine of the Delaware and Related Algonkian Indians* (Harrisburg: Pennsylvania Historical and Museum Commission, 1972), pp. 22–23.

26. Handy, Pukui, and Livermore, *Outline of Hawaiian Physical Therapeutics,* p. 14.

27. Ibid.

28. Karl Böhm, *The Life of Some Island People of New Guinea: A Missionary's Observations of the Volcanic Islands of Manam, Boesa, Biem, and Ubrub* (Berlin: Dietrich Reimer Verlag, 1983), p. 112.

29. Kroeber, *Ethnology of the Gros Ventre,* p. 189.

30. Charles Wisdom, *The Chorti Indians of Guatemala* (Chicago: University of Chicago Press, 1940), p. 349.

31. Schiötz and Cyriax, *Manipulation Past and Present,* pp. 16, 19, 63.

32. David Urquhart, *Manual of the Turkish Bath,* edited by Sir John Fife, M. D. (London: Churchill, 1865), pp. 27, 189.

33. Quoted in Schiötz and Cyriax, *Manipulation Past and Present,* p. 22.

34. Wisdom, *The Chorti Indians of Guatemala,* pp. 355–56.

35. Shway Yoe, *The Burman* (London: Macmillan, 1910), p. 421.

36. Timoteo S. Oracion, "The Bais Forest Preserve Negritos: Some Notes on Their Rituals and Ceremonies," in Mario D. Zamora (ed.), *Studies in Philippine Anthropology* (Quezon City, Philippines: Alemar-Phoenix, 1967), pp. 426–27.

37. James Cook, *The Journals of James Cook: The Voyage 1776–1780,* Vol. I (London: Hakluyt Society, Extra Series, No. 36, 1967), pp. 214–15.

38. Handy, Pukui, and Livermore, *Outline of Hawaiian Physical Therapeutics,* p. 13.

39. Ibid.

40. Schiötz and Cyriax, *Manipulation Past and Present,* p. 21.

41. Frederick O'Brien, paraphrased in Schiötz and Cyriax, p. 21.

42. Hugh Milne, *The Heart of Listening: A Visionary Approach to Craniosacral Work,* unpublished manuscript at the time of publication (Berkeley, California: North Atlantic Books, 1995).

43. Schiötz and Cyriax, *Manipulation Past and Present,* p. 16.

44. E. W. Lane, quoted in Schiötz and Cyriax, p. 25.

45. A. Lade and R. Svoboda, *Tao & Dharma — A Comparison of Ayurveda and Chinese Medicine,* unpublished manuscript at the time of publication.

46. Arnie Lade, personal communication in a letter dated October 29, 1993.

47. Michael Gelfand, *Medicine and Custom in Africa* (Edinburgh: Livingstone, 1964).

48. John R. Swanton, *Religious Beliefs and Medical Practices of the Creek Indians,* 42nd Annual Report to the Bureau of American Ethnology, Smithsonian Institution, 1924–25.

49. Harley, *Native African Medicine,* p. 156.

50. Frank Herbert, *Dune* (New York: Berkley, 1965).

51. Harley, *Native African Medicine,* p. 157.

52. Covarrubias, *Island of Bali,* p. 353.

53. Gerald Cannon Hickey, *Village in Vietnam* (New Haven: Yale University Press, 1964), p. 81.

54. Swanton, *Religious Beliefs and Medical Practices of the Creek Indians.*

55. Dorothy M. Spencer, *Disease, Religion and Society in the Fiji Islands* (New York: Augustin, 1941).

56. Gelfand, *Medicine and Custom in Africa,* pp. 56–57.

57. A. P. Elkin, *Aboriginal Men of High Degree* (Sydney: Australasian Publishing Company, 1944), pp. 29–30.

58. Ven. Rinpoche Jampal Kunzang Rechung, *Tibetan Medicine* (Berkeley: University of California Press, 1973), p. 89.

59. Ira M. Rutkow, *Surgery: An Illustrated History* (St. Louis: Mosby-Year Book, 1993), pp. 1–3.

60. Ibid., p. 7.

61. A. P. Elkin, *Aboriginal Men of High Degree,* p. 50.

62. Walter B. Cannon, "'Voodoo' Death," *American Anthropologist* XLIV (1942); republished in Lessa and Vogt (eds.), *Reader in Comparative Religion,* pp. 321–27.

63. Ibid., p. 326.

64. Ibid., p. 327.

65. Claude Lévi-Strauss, "The Sorcerer and His Magic," in *Structural Anthropology,* translated from the French by Claire Jacobson and Brooke Grundfest Schoepf (Garden City, New York: Doubleday/Anchor, 1967).

66. Franz Boas, *The Religion of the Kwakiutl Indians,* Part II: *Translations* (New York: Columbia University Press, 1930), pp. 17–18.

67. Ibid., p. 19.

68. Ibid.

69. John Upledger, personal communication regarding the work of Elmer Green, 1994.

70. A. P. Elkin, *Aboriginal Men of High Degree,* pp. 15–16.

71. George Peter Murdock, "Tenino Shamanism," in George Peter Murdock (ed.), *Culture and Society: Twenty-Four Essays* (Pittsburgh: University of Pittsburgh Press, 1965), p. 257.

72. Ibid., pp. 257–58.

73. Ibid., p. 258.

74. Claude Lévi-Strauss, "The Sorcerer and His Magic."

75. Randy Cherner, case history given during a lecture, Corte Madera, California, 1992.

76. Ackerknecht, "Problems of Primitive Medicine," p. 400.

77. Jule Eisenbud, interview conducted by Richard Grossinger, January 8, 1972, in Grossinger (ed.), *Ecology and Consciousness: Traditional Wisdom on the Environment* (Berkeley, California: North Atlantic Books, 1992), p. 158.

78. Ibid., pp. 158–59.

79. Ibid., p. 159.

CHAPTER SIX

Spiritual Ethnomedicine

Intelligence and Spirit

SPIRITUAL MEDICINE ASSUMES the priority of the spiritual origin of diseases and so attempts to cure them on a paraphysical plane. Native doctors (as a class) examine lethal wounds, dissect corpses, and learn as much physiology firsthand as most contemporary physicians, but almost all of them regard the physicalization of pathology as a secondary effect of the *real* supernatural intrusion. African and Andaman doctors may even locate the seat of a tumor in a corpse and remove it, probably to bury it separately, but only because it can corrupt the soul or inflict further damage on the village.[1] It bears spiritual danger through a physical malignancy. Even this statement does not fully characterize the world-view, for, to the African doctor, the spiritual and physical work in such complicity that the physical is simply the spiritual manifested bodily and in matter. He does not think: "Here spirit enters into matter." He assumes spirit is always in matter, *is* matter—not only during the disease but from the moment of embodiment. The Australian medicine man mediates power in a dimension transcending the separation between life and death:

> In Aboriginal terms, at death one leaves the *yuti,* the perceivable world in which mind and matter are separate and delineated, and enters the shimmering realm of the Dreaming, where bodies in their vibratory forms merge and correspond through a structural resonance

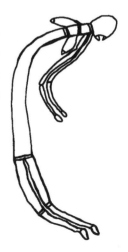

that is the innate meaning of things. The personal unconscious, like the vibratory atomic world, is the level of awareness where animals exist most of the time.... Animals live, for the most part, in the Dreaming.[2]

This is why animals are incomparable spirit guides. They teach the vibratory level on which power is transacted.

The movement into death is similar to the process of moving into sleep or trance, the difference being that the center of being or awareness shifts through the personal unconscious to the energetic realm of vibratory appearances to the boundless activity of the quantum continuum, otherwise called the collective unconscious or the Ancestral Realm. *Death, in the Aboriginal view, is not a termination or a dislocation from this world to another; rather, it is a shift of the center of one's consciousness to invisible, subjective layers that are substrate to, and involved within, the natural world of mind and matter.*

For the Aborigines the highest goal of initiation is to create a condition in which, for a time after death, the spirit can move at will between all three realms. This spiritual integration after death is possible for the Aborigines because during life, the mind, body, and spirit are cultivated to remain integrated, that is, all in one piece and in one place, *ngurra.* Through life the power of empathy is intensely cultivated so that the Aboriginal psyche, while centered in place, is permeable by the psyche and being of all nature's forms and creatures.[3]

Phenomena reach us in mind and body, and no doubt in other ways too, but we have no name for them since we consider mind and body a duality comprising a complete system. We would tend to assign those other modes to mind and body also. But even our biggest archetypal mind is not the Apache "mind" by which their whole world and the domain of Earth and Sky was overridden. It is not even Buddhist nondualistic "mind." It is the romanticized mind of the ego attempting to trace its own epistemology.

In order to understand spiritual and native medicine in the context of the traditional Western dichotomy between what is physical, concrete, and revealed, and what is disembodied, psychic, and merely epiphenomenal, I will propose here a different "Mind-Body" or "Spirit-Matter" split.

Intelligence is that thing (or name) I will assign to the stuff which embodies all being and through which other entities pass, which most resembles the mind, and which includes many of the components of Western mind. *Spirit* (surprisingly) will be its physical counterpart. If both names sound nonphysical, we must remember that they are inherently nonmental too. For coming from our language, they are heir to our Mind/Body prejudice, suggesting that we assign to mind (to fantasy and delusion) most of those things whose concrete existence is imperceptible to us.

Although all native medicines have components which translate into our versions of purely physical or purely mental categories, these same polar aspects are more properly integrated in a system resembling a dichotomy of Intelligence and Spirit.

Intelligence is the pure idea or shape of things. It is creation, it is the impulse behind the hunt, the vision quest; it informs a plant of the plane and manner of its own existence, also a stone; it is why atoms and genes seem to be letters in a hidden language, why the embryo grows harmoniously, why plants, animals, and stars are arranged in a "philosophy" older than life or man and woman. It does not require Mind in order to be Intelligence. It might also be called "existence," but this word is too neutral, coming as it does from the Latin for "stands," and taking on the sense of a portrait or finished action. Intelligence moves and changes, and that thing which directs its change, however seemingly neutral and accidental and natural, is perhaps its Mind—the primary componential Mind, which is also Nature.

The poet Edward Dorn states this in terms of an Apache creation myth: "He is the Sky

Man/the agency of the metaphor/the One who lives above.//He wakes as from a long sleep./He rubs his face and eyes/with both hands, and where/his eyes light, light appears/Everywhere//Above and below/a sea of light."[4]

Spirit is the physical manifestation of all things—the present shape of unconscious impulses and intentions. It includes phantom animals and physical animals, voodoo darts and the arrowlike potency of medicines, ghosts and bones, ancestors and relatives, supernatural entities and rivers and mountains and fields. It is where the world most resembles Body, but it is thoroughly endowed with Mind.

Spirit/Intelligence is another false duality. Just as we develop psychosomatic medicines to activate the suspected Mind/Body unity, native healing and philosophy work toward a unity of something like Intelligence and Spirit. We regard these indigenous systems as if they were skillfully joining Mind and Body, for they do that too, and so we twist them into our own myths of holism and psychosomatic unity. Our failure to gauge their true depth is symptomatic of a prideful myopia by which we neglect to see that even an idealized unity of Mind and Body is superficial, hence irrelevant, to a unity of Intelligence and Spirit. We credit the Indians and Africans, et al., with solving our special problem, and that is truly to damn them with faint praise. They are not interested in our problem, and they perhaps understand us better than we understand them. Intelligence and Spirit (or what these words of mine imply about native polarities) are notions totally unfamiliar to us, so we translate them into Mind and, at best, in rare cases, into Mind/Body. Even if at times we think about native categories, we do not think *in* them. We translate Cherokee and Balinese words into American, but the people do not think of themselves as Xhosa. They are simply "the people." Their world is "the world." Their medicines are whatever such people in such a world have come to call the act of healing.

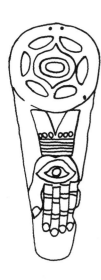

A medicine of Spirit and Intelligence is a medicine of the dynamic process of embodiment and world making, of Mind becoming nature, of Spirit entering matter. It exists in reference to the ultimate unity that lies behind any true unity of Mind and Body. This is not of course the final statement on the situation; it is primarily a suggestion to look more discerningly at a semantic dichotomy which influences much of our schematizing of healing systems.

Healing Is a Dialogue with Spirit

In ONE SENSE, spiritual ethnomedicine is not a different system from practical ethnomedicine; it is merely a different way of interpreting natural and supernatural relationships. Both systems are spiritual, and both systems are practical and physical. The distinction makes sense when we distinguish voodoo shamans and faith healers from trephiners and herbalists. However, incisions and herbs can also be interpreted spiritually, and voodoo can be viewed as mere focalization of an energy already present in nature. (See the next chapter.)

We begin our discussion of spiritual ethnomedicine at the point we left off our discussion of practical ethnomedicine. At the moment a medicine man manifests and extracts the disease entity, a curative bolt (like the wounding shock of voodoo) strikes the psychosomatic (Spirit-Intelligence) plane . . . even if the precise object elicited is a "fake." There is a paraphysical impact either in addition to or distinct from the psychological abreaction. The following Jívaro example is quite graphic:

> When a curing shaman is called in to treat a patient, his first task is to see if the illness is due to witchcraft. The usual diagnosis and treatment begin with the curing shaman drinking *natemä,* tobacco water, and *pirípiri* in the later afternoon and early evening. These drugs permit him to see into the body of the patient as though it were glass. If the illness is due to sorcery, the curing shaman will see the intruding object within the patient's body clearly enough to determine whether or not he can cure the sickness.
>
> A shaman sucks magical darts from a patient's body only at night, and in a dark area of the house, for it is only in the dark that he can

perceive the drug-induced visions that are the supernatural reality. . . .

When he is ready to suck, the shaman regurgitates two *tsentsak* into the sides of his throat and mouth. These must be identical to the ones he has seen in the patient's body. He holds one of these in front of the mouth and the other in the rear. They are expected to catch the supernatural aspect of the magical dart that the shaman sucks out of the patient's body. . . . He then "vomits" out this object and displays it to the patient and his family, saying, "Now I have sucked it out. Here it is."

The non-shamans think that the material object itself is what has been sucked out, and the shaman does not disillusion them. At the same time, he is not lying, because he knows that the only important thing about a *tsentsak* is its supernatural aspect, or essence, which he sincerely believes he has removed from the patient's body.[5]

This is the other plane of disease extraction—Eisenbud's plane. Remember the Pomo bear doctors, Slippery Eyes' snakes, etc. On one level of perception, diseases are full-fledged wild animals, binding creatures who entrap and capture people. They have their own unique qualities, their own hungers, and when a human has been caught by one of them, their alien aspects show clearly through the sick person's personality.

In Vietnam such diseases travel as ghosts, embodied in dogs, pigs, cats, oxen, and buffalo: "Villagers believe they swarm over the fields after sunset, often getting tangled in the legs of those who tarry too long on the paths."[6]

In Bali these ghosts *(leyaks)*

appear as dancing flames flitting from grave to grave in cemeteries, feeding on newly buried corpses, or as balls of fire and living shadowlike white cloths, but also in the shapes of weird animals: pigs, dogs, monkeys, or tigers. Witches often assume the form of beautiful mute girls who make obscene advances to young men on lonely roads at night. *Leyaks* are, however, progressive and now they are said to prefer more modern shapes for their transformations; motorcars and bicycles that run in and out of temples without drivers and whose tires pulsate as if breathing. There are even *leyak* airplanes sweeping over the roof-tops after midnight. Children cry during the night because they see *leyaks* that become invisible on approaching to gnaw at their entrails. . . .

The ever unwilling patients of the modern hospital in Den Pasar claim to have seen strange shadows under doors and flocks of monkeys that grimace at them through the windows; the congregation of sick, magically weakened people naturally attracts legions of *leyaks* and for this reason they fear having to go to the hospital.[7]

In his ethnobotany of the Hopi Indians, Alfred Whiting cites this equation from its other side:

All the animals, birds, insects, and every living creature, including trees and plants, in the forms in which we ordinarily see them, appear only in masquerade, for, as the Hopi say, all these creatures that share the spark of life with us humans, surely have other homes where they live in human form.[8]

In the Fiji Islands, a man described to Dorothy Spencer how his disease approached as a young girl sitting on a fallen log, smoking. She let her *sulu* drop, showing him her genitals. "While they were smoking, he looked at her closely; he saw that she was not a human girl, because her eyes were not quite like those of mortals, her speech was very rapid, and she used archaic words and expressions in talking."[9]

Don Juan warned Carlos about just such people. They exist everywhere, even in cities, but we no longer recognize them in the crowds. How could we? This Fijian "disease" seduced her victim, and, after making love to her, he took ill and almost died.

Man's (and woman's) coming into life and death is a bargain with spirits all the way—spirits who finally let go of his soul, spirits who give her breath, spirits who battle him and make him sick, spirits who kill her and feed off her remains. The spirits of animals do not forget their hunters. The Norwegian anthropologist Knud Rasmussen was

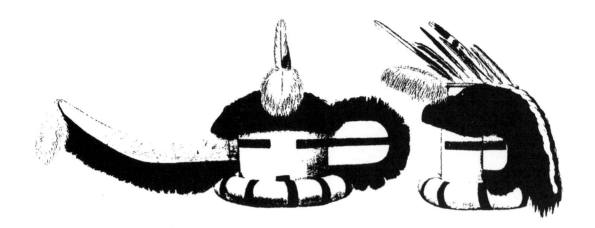

taught that priceless piece of Pleistocene wisdom by his Eskimo friend Ivaluardjuk:

> All the creatures that we have to kill and eat, all those that we have to strike down and destroy to make clothes for ourselves, have souls, like we have, souls that do not perish with the body, and which must therefore be propitiated lest they should revenge themselves on us for taking away their bodies.[10]

Insofar as disease is the primary weapon of the spirit world, the human species' first primitive tool was neither fire nor hand-axe, but medicine. Beasts wearing the dried faces and horns of transmogrified creatures, invoking the unseen hallucinations behind their manifestation—such was the crucible of defense and counterattack. To put on bloody masks demonstrates the severity of the crisis. Medicine is spirit supplication, spirit discourse individuating the ritual makers from the great rolling bellows of creation. Aboriginal man and woman read the world in this context and so began the medicine lineage. *If you have to kill in order to eat, then you have to be able to banish ghosts.* From this old shaman magic came all other powers. The code George Harley cites for Africa is confirmed everywhere:

Nye is man controlling nature....[11]

To the Mano man the medical and religious elements of *nye* are never completely separated, and a certain degree of magic runs through it all....[12]

Man bolsters and protects himself from evil human spirits by using *nye,* which is usually the substance and spirit of trees, etc. If a man's soul were so very different from other spirits, the spirit of a tree would have no power over it. Nor would a man seek to strengthen himself by contact with a strong tree such as *wai ba yidi* which is considered invulnerable because its smooth branny bark cannot be climbed by monkeys, and because lightning has never been observed to strike it.
    Nye [is] spirit substance, or power under control....[13]

Nye actually does more than fight disease in the interest of the individual; it also fights tribal calamity in the interest of the community as a whole. Just as *nye,* consisting of the substance and power of plants and other things, is used in the control of disease and defense against *wi,* or witchcraft, so *nye,* consisting of human substance and power, is used in control and aversion of tribal misfortune and the placation of the spirits of the ancestor.[14]

In Fiji the various diseases are manifestations of *vu;* yet the power that cures them is *vuniwai.* "Terminologically, magic and medicine are synonymous."[15]

The spirits can ruin the harvest or give bounteous crops; they can stir up thunder and lightning or bring soft rain; they can wreck marriages or bless families; they can come from the north or the east (as the White Man did) and devastate the land. Shamanic training is essentially training in how to conduct a dialogue with spirits, how to interest them in using their powers benevolently and sharing them with men and women.

In this context, primitive pharmacy must be viewed as not only both an herbal and an energy medicine, but as a spirit medicine too, an adjunct to sorcery. Often we have no idea anyway where the thread of cause and effect originates and which is the active factor. A true healer—botanical or shamanic—masters remedies by making allies of the spirits who control the plants, animals, stones, and springs from which tonics are blended. In nature these spirits are free and their power is a moiré in the vastness of nature. A trained shaman can awaken their specific virtues and direct these toward a disease. This process is potentially one mysterious basis of pharmaceutical potency. Medicines in fact may be purely chemical, chemical and alchemical, some combination of these and spiritual, or substantially spiritual (with a physical component). Remember, even allopathic drugs must have a totemic component.

This hierarchy becomes axiomatic: Just about all indigenous medicine is either spiritual medicine, potentially spiritual medicine, or spiritual medicine tamed. We are claiming nothing for medicine we would not claim for boat-building or any other craft of power. However, in medicine, the spiritual exercise dominates the technology in a way it cannot in boat-building or fish poisoning. The herb doctor, the masseuse, and the surgeon are eternally apprentices to the shaman, the witch doctor, and the master of voodoo.

At least the working fisherman and hunter construct the shells of physical boats and weapons and track down and kill the outward carapace of their game. They may require the blessings and protection of the shaman, but they mostly run their own shows. The naval craftsman cannot send his people off sailing without a boat, at least not in waters of three dimensions. But the shaman can summon a higher authority and override botanical substance.

We may recall that Herman Melville's adventures among native peoples of the Pacific preceded his writing of *Moby Dick:* after deserting his ship with a friend, he was captured by cannibals and almost tattooed into conscription as a permanent member of the tribe. The subsequent novel can be read as the symbolic account of a supernatural event. A powerful, perhaps malevolent being hides behind the mask of the White Whale. Western man intuits this, but, without an

ongoing dialogue with the supernatural, he is unable to address it. He behaves, from Don Juan's point of view, as a petulant child.

"... I see in him outrageous strength, with an inscrutable malice sinewing it," says Ahab, says Melville.[16] But for the native, all of nature is so inhabited, and if it is malice, it is also opportunity. It is neither wicked nor incorrigible. It is intelligence of another order going about its business contiguous with the human world. "Man," writes Melville elsewhere, "seems to have had as little to do with it as nature."[17]

Melville, though he is rarely acknowledged as such, was one of the first American anthropologists to return from the "bush" a believer. He had lived among natives long enough to understand the true "savage mind." Through Ahab, he seems to berate and blaspheme the Church of New England. But he is also the Church's agent returned, to warn "atheistic" civilization about the extent of our spiritual isolation on this planet. While its ministers preach so confidently and invulnerably, they are essentially unprepared and unarmed (science equally so).

We take it for granted that our problems are physical and mechanical and that they can be solved by a refinement of industrial and other

*Spiritual
Ethno-
medicine*

Enlightenment techniques. We continue to propose environmental protection agencies and energy departments and arms control treaties, welfare reform programs and military conversions. The "natives" continue, out somewhere in the eternal past-present of the planet, to wage a spiritual battle. To this day, the Hopis are attempting to send messages about the spiritual crisis in the world to the United Nations, meaning the crisis of real "power"—power transcending nuclear bombs and industrial complexes and plagues and manifesting through them.

"'Vengeance on a dumb brute!'" cried Starbuck, 'that simply smote thee from blindest instinct! Madness! To be enraged with a dumb thing, Captain Ahab, seems blasphemous.'"[18]

To which Ahab responds: "All visible objects, man, are but as pasteboard masks. . . . some unknown but still reasoning thing puts forth the mouldings of its features from behind the unreasoning mask. If man will strike, strike through the mask!"[19]

The medicine of the shaman is different because his definition of life is different. The medicine man works on the personified spirit of the patient; the Western doctor works on his physical body. When Carlos Castaneda is told by Don Juan to kill a rabbit that he has caught in his trap, he refuses. He balks in classical Western fashion, out of reverence and pity for the singular life of the rabbit and the essentially happenstance event of its becoming snared in *his* trap. Don Juan points out that Carlos has killed many animals in his life.

> . . . not with my bare hands.[20]

Don Juan sees through the physical rabbit. He scoffs at the pity and restraint seemingly offered in the rabbit's behalf. The concern for the rabbit's body shows no respect for its soul. To spare it is to belittle it, to deny it its greater journey in space and time.

> He yelled at me that the rabbit had to die. He said that its roaming in the beautiful desert had come to an end. I had no business stalling,

because the power or the spirit that guides rabbits had led that particular one into my trap, right at the edge of twilight....

I felt nauseated. He very patiently talked to me as if he were talking to a child. He said that the powers that guided men or animals had led that particular rabbit to me, in the same way they will lead me to my own death. He said the rabbit's death had been a gift for me in exactly the same way my own death will be a gift for something or someone else.[21]

Would not the medicine man, archetypally, have the same message for the medical doctor? Heal if you can, with respect—but do not tamper wastefully with a person's destiny. The ostensible result of symptomatic cures will be living corpses, individuals who no longer have access to spiritual power because they have bought off a serious encounter with their souls.

We are not obvious prey for visible predators, but that does not mean (remember Eisenbud's warning) the invisible can't mask itself in accidents or tumors. Though we are not primitives or warriors, we still have destinies to live out.

IN MATTERS OF DISEASE (and healing) we are almost always dealing with *at least* a transpersonal aspect of one's being—the doctor's as well as the patient's, the shaman's as well as the sick person's. Even garden-variety ailments activate cosmic elements of individuals, creating complexes in which familiar and conventional symptoms combine physiological disturbances, unintegrated emotional contents, and archetypal conflicts. The symptom "argues" its case within the body, and the body accepts it, for whatever reason of partial development or personal crisis. If the body prefers the disease to its health, then nothing can intervene, or no heroic intervention will have lasting effect.

Like diseases, medicines develop distinct qualities in the layers of personality (physical and psychic alike), interacting with diseases on the levels of inner hunger where they first occur. Anyone can talk to or prescribe for a sick person, but a medicine man alone, through his cosmic resonance, can directly address a disease. Whether he chants in unknown tongues or paints in sand, cuts incisions or prepares tonics, he works, ultimately, to establish communication with the disease spirit in its own terms. Shamans intercept messages between agencies of a superior order, messages humans must intercept anyway, by the fine materiality and tuning of their bodies. Ceremonial medicine and magic thus speak to the unconscious body, to the Intelligence—not to the Mind. They argue their case, and raw somatic Intelligence accepts it or not, regardless of what the person "thinks." The "shaman without" reaches to the "shaman within":

> The wild naked figure in all its contortions, with head thrown back and half-closed glazed eyes, flowing locks encircled in a cloud of down, the patient, the shadows cast by the fitful burning logs, the confusion of sounds, the atmosphere of smoke-dried salmon and human bodies, the tense expectancy of the crowd, all served to keep alive the belief in the unknown and in this juggler of life. When we consider that from childhood the Tlingit were reared in this atmosphere, is it any wonder that after a rudimentary education they should still revert to the past?[22]

When we consider that from humanity's childhood a dialogue with spirits was real, is it any wonder that the ceremony burns with an original radiance?

Materialistic medicine treats visible manifestations by opposing their effects. But as long as disease is literally non-integration, integration alone can catalyze cure. The healing process must begin on a cosmic level at the same time as on a mundane pharmaceutical or surgical one; genuine transformation will not follow either unless a large enough psychosomatic territory is activated.

Divination

ONE OF THE PRIMARY nuts-and-bolts tools of diagnosis in ethnomedicine is divination, an ancient method of using ritual objects and processes to infiltrate seemingly acausal chains. Divination is familiar to the West in one form as horoscope astrology, in another as translations of the Chinese *I Ching*. A hybrid of practical and psychic processes, divination combines intuition, mathematical games, and con-artistry. It is closest to telepathy when it works and gambling when it doesn't. Like a master of card tricks, a diviner reaches out into the void and pulls in a card he could not possibly have. Stated otherwise, diviners shuffle the bottomless deck and somehow draw exactly the correct diagnosis. Lévi-Strauss, among others, has pointed out that true divination—that is, the forms of it closest to totemism—contain in their componential logic a "through a glass darkly" inference of principles behind also quantum theory, modern genetics, information theory, and statistics: "The savage mind is logical in the same sense and the same fashion as ours, though as our own is only when applied to knowledge of a universe in which it recognizes physical and semantic properties simultaneously."[23] In divination God *does* play physical-semantic dice with the universe.

On the surface, chance operations would seem to be entirely vapid, for they elevate arbitrary fortune above rational intelligence. They are unique, however, in directing attention into avenues that would otherwise be overlooked. Divination is an admission that even all our information is not enough and that we must receive new data from obscure sources. A shaman may go straight to gods and spirits, as discussed, or he may petition nature randomly, nondiscursively. In some cultures he may do both simultaneously.

The divinatory deck differs from culture to culture. Its cards, like those of the tarot, are sequences of totemic symbols. These are sorted in some formally prescribed fashion. The Burmese medical diviner "keeps writing down numbers and characters on his parabaik tablets and rubbing them out, chanting to himself all the time. Sometimes he shakes cowries and seeds together, and when they fall out, decides from their position which of the pictures or rhymes [including a wild figure galloping on a horse, a monkey mounted on a goat, a crow breaking a vessel full of money with its beak] is to be consulted. Each of these gives its own answer, but they are not always as definite in their character as is desirable."[24]

The Navaho system, according to Gladys Reichard, combines divination and vision quest:

There are three ways of determining an illness—gazing at sun, moon, or star, listening, and trembling. Listening is nearly, if not quite, extinct; 'motion-in-the-hand' indicates trembling induced by proper ritualistic circumstances. The diviner is seized with shaking, beginning usually with gentle tremors of arms or legs and gradually spreading until the whole body shakes violently. While in a trembling state, the seer loses himself. Guided by his power, he sees a symbol of the ceremony purporting to cure the person for whom he is divining. Gazing may be accompanied by trembling; usually the diviner sees the chant symbol as an after-image of the heavenly body on which he is concentrating.[25]

Many systems, like the Hawaiian *iliili,* use a replica:

The kahuna laid out pebbles so arranged as to represent the human body and the points on the abdomen that the pupil must be able to feel with his fingers in order to detect the symptoms of various illnesses. When the student's touch had become thoroughly familiarized with pathological abnormalities as represented by the pebbles arranged by the kahuna, he was allowed to perfect his technique by practicing on the sick....

In learning this method of diagnosing disease, a pupil was trained by working his fingers over 480 pebbles that we laid down in the shape of a man. And on this pebble shape, he practiced how to feel out with his fingers the different diseases found in man. It was said that by this method of diagnosing, 280 diseases could be found....

There were three kinds of pebbles used in learning the art of diagnosing by feeling with the fingers, white, red, and black pebbles. These pebbles were kept in a long gourd called an *olo.*[26]

This might be divination, or it might be a kind of intuitive telekinesis through an anatomical map.

The Method of the Egg, practiced in rural Laos, is closer to pure divination:

The egg must first be rolled lightly and slowly over the body of the patient, insisting particularly over the aching spot. After a few minutes of this treatment, efforts are made in order to stand the egg on a horizontal board. The operation is repeated until the egg stands somewhat unstably on its appropriate end. At this moment, the operator slightly taps on the board; if the egg topples over the operation has to be repeated.

If it stands up to the test, the shell of the egg is broken on a clean plate, taking care not to spoil the yolk. . . .

1. If it is free of any foreign matter, the illness is due to a pathological cause and therefore is of the resort of the quack.

2. If the yolk is abnormally developed, the illness is due to an evil spirit, and the magician has to be called.

3. If, however, the yolk is found to contain some impurities, no doubt then that the sick person is under the spell of a sorcerer. In this case, the disease can only be cured with the help of a more skillful sorcerer (witch-doctor).[27]

More commonly the innards of small animals are the medium for medical divination. After holding its squealing body over the sick person, a sorcerer will break a guinea pig's back and turn it inside out in an instant, probing diligently for signs of the ailment in the *guinea pig's* organs. (I remember my then nine-year-old son watching an ethnographic film that showed this process graphically. As the narrator remarked on this solemn attempt to find the cause of the sick woman's disease, my son whispered in outrage: "The woman! What about the poor guinea pig?")[28]

THE BENEFITS OF pure divination are explored in Omar Khayyam Moore's classic analysis of a prehistoric form of hunting augury called "scapulimancy." In this system, still prevalent in the Canadian Arctic, the severed shoulder blade of the caribou is used to track animal herds. Prealigned by a traditional method with a visualization of the hunting territory, the bone is held over a fire as if it were a map, with cracks occurring as trails where the caribou themselves are ostensibly moving just then.

Because of the longevity of this custom in many areas of the world, one assumes some sort of empirical efficacy. But what could a disembodied scapula reveal as fire threads random images over it? Moore argues that the light-show eliminates confusion about where to hunt and brings the group together in a suspenseful lottery, and that it also randomizes the forays into the territory so that the hunters will not repeat strategies to which the caribou may have become unconsciously sensitized.[29]

Moore's guess is just a beginning, but it is helpful because it shows that our hasty assumptions about what constitutes useful and strategically promising behavior on even a simple practical level are not always sound. Roy Rappaport, following Gregory Bateson, has pointed out that purposeful behavior itself is often counterproductive. In seeking immediate goals (food, energy, wealth), men and women generate unending secondary effects in the natural system of which they are part, a system which is far more complex and subtle than their information about it. It is not so much that any one activity or set of goals is in itself disruptive and self-defeating. "Conscious purpose, which aims toward the achievement of specific goals, does not usually take into account the circular structure of cause and effect which characterizes the universe, and this cognitive failure leads to disruption." Rappaport goes on to show that true wisdom may "reside as much in the nondiscursive aesthetic sensibility as it does in knowledge."[30]

Divination, totemism, and forms of augury pick up things that simple observation misses. In the web of mind and nature, nonsense and meaning are intermixed, and signs and associations replace causal chains. The augurer may pay a price in short-term goals, missing the obvious and explicit, but he participates in a larger system of concealed knowledge. He gets to invent new meanings.

We need only examine the herbals of Europe to see that the choice of remedy, as recently as three hundred years ago, was made on the basis of mainly nondiscursive clues. We find in William Coles that walnuts are good for curing head ailments because they

> have the perfect Signatures of the Head: The outer husk or green Covering represents the pericranium, or outward skin of the skull, whereon the hair groweth, and therefore salt made of these husks or barks are exceeding good for wounds in the head. The inner shell hath the Signature of the Skull, and the yellow skin, or Peel, that covereth the Kernel, of the hard Meninga & Pia Mater, which are the thin scarfes that envelope the brain. The Kernel hath the very figure of the Brain, and therefor it is very profitable for the brain.... For if the Kernel be bruised, and moystned with the quintessence of Wine, and laid upon the Crown of the Head, it comforts the brain and head mightily.... The little holes whereof the leaves of Saint Johns wort are full, doe resemble all the pores of the skin, and therefore it is profitable for all hurts and wounds that can happen thereunto.[31]

This method of determining pharmaceutical value is known historically as the "Doctrine of Signatures." The meaning assigned to a given characteristic may well not be accurate, especially without a microscope to examine the activity of molecules. The "correctness" of the native system must be in its unique classification, simultaneously, of cognitive and formal qualities, qualities which also intersect in the system of "thought" in which a disease arises. It is also possible that morphological resemblances are merely cues for other characteristics discovered empirically, or even, as Edward Whitmont argues, that botanical morphology archetypally replicates aspects of anatomy and personality.[32]

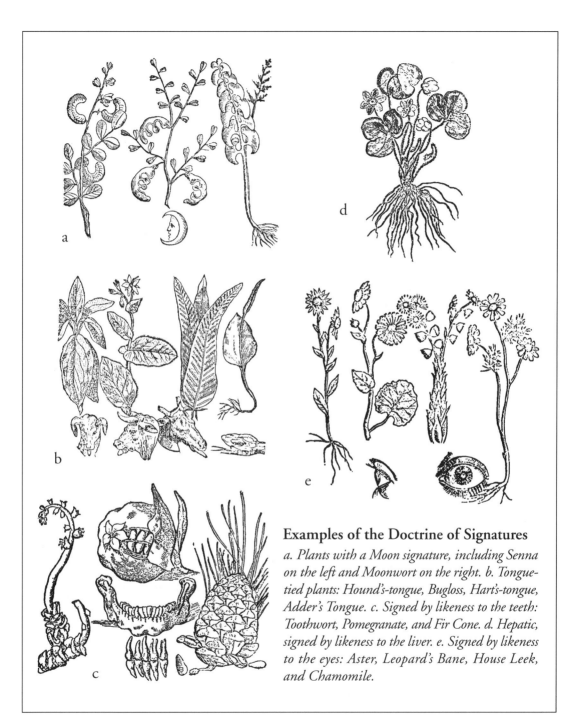

Examples of the Doctrine of Signatures

a. Plants with a Moon signature, including Senna on the left and Moonwort on the right. b. Tongue-tied plants: Hound's-tongue, Bugloss, Hart's-tongue, Adder's Tongue. c. Signed by likeness to the teeth: Toothwort, Pomegranate, and Fir Cone. d. Hepatic, signed by likeness to the liver. e. Signed by likeness to the eyes: Aster, Leopard's Bane, House Leek, and Chamomile.

The Crow Indians recognize a rock "medicine" they periodically find. Their most famous such rock was uncanny in gambling. It "led" successful war parties and kept its possessors alive into their eighties and nineties. It also inspired visions, years early, of the coming of cattle and the dwellings of the European. The description of its discovery is a matter of Crow history:

> This rock medicine was found by One-Child-Woman, wife of Sees-the-Living-Bull, mother of Medicine Crow, and stepmother of Little Nest. Sees-the-Living-Bull, when still a young man, was married to two women. One of them, One-Child-Woman, he neglected, and she finally became so desperate that she decided to leave him.
>
> Taking her robe and leading her favorite horse, she left camp and went toward the mountains. When some distance from camp she turned her horse loose, saying to it, "I am going to die on this prairie, but you may roam wherever you wish."
>
> She traveled on foot along what is now called Fishtail Creek. Finally she reached the top of a hill where she rested for a while. Suddenly she noticed a glittering object not far away, and she walked to it. Coming close she noticed that it was a remarkable rock with several faces marked upon it. Yet she knew that no Indian had made it. One of these faces resembled her husband, so she thought. Another face was that of a buffalo, a third the face of an eagle, and the fourth resembled a horse. The human face pointed east and the stone was lying in a small depression, surrounded by small stones.
>
> One-Child-Woman realized she had found a remarkable rock which was undoubtedly a powerful medicine. She sat down near the rock and cried. Then she picked it up, and upon closer examination found that it carried marks of horse and buffalo tracks. Carrying the rock with her she descended the hill. There she found a buffalo wallow and a quantity of buffalo wool. She picked up the wool, wrapped the stone in it and fastened it under her dress against her chest.[33]

We might compare her "geosophical" emotion to the power the Moon rocks have for Western man. The differences in sacred stones suggest fundamental differences in cultures and realms of knowledge. Both rocks are arbitrary geological formations; both mark historic occasions. Western science, as we noted in our discussion of the vision quest, gains its power from seeming to transcend previous boundaries (the invention of rockets took generations), while native science achieves its power by filling in equally limitless internal space. For One-Child-Woman the rock medicine had some of the impact that the tomb of Philip of Macedon did for the Greek archaeologist who uncovered it. For both, it was an act of touching the roots of the system of time and history in which they existed and from which their lives derived meaning.

In a world in which the obvious is not always obvious, the abstruse and disjunctive have incredible power. Just by coming from outside the rigid logic of the system, they reveal and elucidate its hidden chinks.

Shamanic Initiation and Transference

THE TRAINING OF DOCTORS, in most primitive societies, is as grueling and thorough as in Western medical schools. In the desert of South Australia, where the doctor is also a rainmaker and voodoo master, a young initiate is taken from his home by the clan of doctors (at which time his family mourns him as if he had died); he is blindfolded and fed to a mythological lei-line snake, in the seclusion of whose belly he meditates for many days. The body of the snake, Wonambi, encompasses, at this present time of history anyway, the Djabudi water hole. Later in the ceremony, the doctors lead him into the bush and cover him with red ocher. Fires are lit. He lies full length before them on his back. According to A.P. Elkin's description, the head doctor then "breaks" his neck and wrists and dislocates his joints at the elbows, the upper thighs, the knees and ankles. It seems improbable that they are actually broken. More likely he is wounded by the charmstone of black australite used in this ceremony, and a *maban* shell is placed in each wound, plus additional ones in his ears and the angle of his jaw "so that he can respectively hear [understand], and speak to, everything—spirits, strangers, and birds, and animals."

Then a shell is placed in his forehead to give him divine and x-ray vision; one is cut into his neck "so that it may be turned in all directions." A number of them are placed in his stomach to protect him from attack. During this *daramara* rite he is limp; then he is revived by the singing over him of the doctors.[34]

Healing begins in a conscious or self-inflicted wound. As we discussed in the previous chapter, only the scarred can heal others. Edward Whitmont proposes a general initiatory chain:

> The healing force impersonated and mediated by the healer and his initiator inflicts illness and death and, paradoxically . . . itself suffers

illness and death, in the service of consciousness and transformation. Prometheus and his Christian counterparts, Lucifer the bringer of light in the shape of the serpent of paradise, and Adam, the symbolic first man, all suffer for the sake of consciousness. The illness-healing progression thus includes the striving for consciousness, the suffering of sickness, and the capacity to wound as well as the potential to cure....[35]

We saw this process in Pomo shamanism and will see it again in all manner of alternative medicines and faith-healing.

IN THE MANO "Society for the Treatment of Snakebite" the initiates are taught the correct plants to pick and the proper preparation and application of snake medicine. They learn how to find and catch snakes, i.e., which snakes to grab by the tail, which by the neck, and how to paralyze them by tapping or spitting on them. The student also masters a whole rite not connected in the usual sense with the handling of snakes—for instance, how to behave in the cult house, passwords, the use of quartz crystal in sending messages, and a variety of other obviously related skills and disciplines.[36]

Writes Harley:

Health of body and of mind are so related that although the so-called medicine-man may be deficient in physical science, his function as a soul-doctor has to be treated as on the whole salutary, given the psychological condition of his patients. His sincerity is attested by the strictness of his training, the severest taboos being judged necessary to preserve his power over the forces of evil.[37]

The medicine man is god, warrior, thief, musician, and doctor. He is the stage master of the healing ceremony. But the initiation goes far deeper, into a realm where polarities vanish and identities are transformed. The healer must train until he becomes a suitable vehicle for the disease to recognize itself and depart the sick person. Whitmont adds:

His or her own wounds [a psychotherapist's in this case] resonate with the client's in the course of the mutually inductive effects of the therapeutic relationship. In a similar deliberate identification with his patient's state, to the exclusion of his own ego bias, a genuine physical healer can tune into his patient's therapeutic needs. Thereby healers put their own flames, their own life energies, at their patient's disposal. In all likelihood, this vicarious offering up of life energy by the healer may be as important a factor as the healer's technical knowledge and skill.[38]

We will return to this theme in Volume Two, Chapter Two.

Healing Ceremonies

IN MOST INDIGENOUS SOCIETIES, healing is a community event in which large numbers of kin and members of ritual sodalities collaborate. In its fullest form, this includes: an invoking of gods, spirits, ancestors, and totems; a large, participatory support network; and a public unwinding of the symbolic elements of a disease such that the society and the sick person are healed together. We certainly still hold such ceremonies, but they have become privatized and fragmented into prayer meetings, rock concerts, Rainbow Family gatherings, and the like; in native societies they were nondenominational and mainstream.

A full healing ceremony serves as psychic inoculation for the larger community as well as a specific intercession with spirit powers on behalf of the victim. Whatever their practical therapeutic results, ceremonies are internalized at a different level by the participants than are more neutral acts of herb dispensing or manipulation and surgery. The variations of this internalization include the most profound modalities of healing.

One of the topics of this book is the forced medicalization of Western culture such that all systems purporting to heal must either adapt to a scientistic paradigm (which means dropping most of their spiritual and energetic aspects); hide behind a church; or default their right to present themselves as a medical agency. Christian Science, osteopathy,

and homeopathy all lost major parts of their identities by trying to operate in the climate of enforced medical orthodoxy newly dominant in the United States after the Flexner Report during the 1920s and 1930s. For systems that heal through internalization and psychic energies, this guarantees depletion and marginalization.

THE CENTRAL ELEMENT in a traditional Navaho healing ceremony is its sand painting. This painting represents, simultaneously, the spiritual and physical landscape in which the patient and his or her illness exist, the etiology of the disease, and the mythological narrative that has been chosen for its cure. Representations of stones, plants, and sacred objects play discrete roles inside the painting. Their mythological relationships are iconicized by shapes of colored sand. The figures may

Spiritual Ethno-medicine

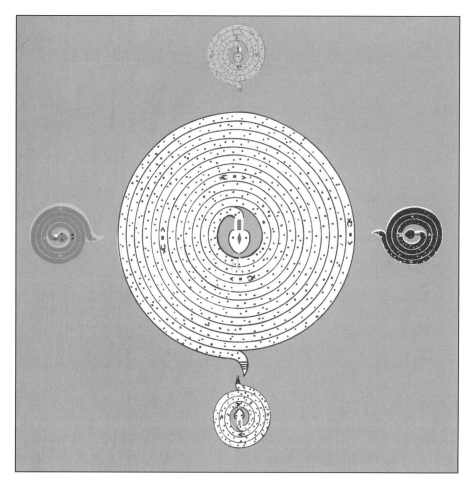

include stylizations of clouds or turtles or whatever is needed to track the path of the disease through collective ritual space.

Gladys Reichard writes: "[Things] predominantly evil, such as snake, lightning, thunder, coyote may even be invoked. If they have been the cause of misfortune or illness, they alone can correct it."[39] Ursula Le Guin provides a fairy-tale version of this axiom in her story of Ged, the young magician who seeks to undo the curse he has unleashed on the world through an act of magical hubris *(A Wizard of Earthsea)*. In this instance, as so many, the cause of the illness is the sick person himself, in another, externally projected form:

Aloud and clearly, breaking that old silence, Ged spoke the shadow's name and in the same moment the shadow spoke without lips or tongue, saying the same word: "Ged." And the two voices were one voice.

Ged reached out his hands, dropping his staff, and took hold of his shadow, of the black self that reached out to him. Light and darkness met, and joined, and were one.[40]

Only by invoking the cause of a malaise at its precise similitude and resonance can a healer reverse its course of destruction.

"... look, it is done. It is over." He laughed. "The wound is healed," he said, "I am whole, I am free."[41]

The ceremony is a primal mandala. Before we were granted narratives of personhood, science-fiction stories of our own, our ancestors lived collective archetypal lives. Thus, they were responsive (i.e., susceptible) to internalized totemization of even the most physical diseases—then, subsequently, to the totemic healing of them.

A Navaho ceremony, whatever it may be called, is a combination of many elements—ritualistic items such as the medicine bundle with its sacred contents; prayer-sticks, made of carefully selected wood and feathers, precious stones, tobacco, water collected from sacred places, a tiny piece of cotton string; song, with its lyrical and musical complexities; sandpaintings, with intricate color, directional and impressionistic symbols; prayer, with stress on order and rhythmic unity; plants, with supernatural qualities defined and personified; body and figure painting; sweating and emetic, with purifactory functions; vigil, with emphasis on concentration and summary.[42]

The chanting and vigil bring disperse elements together. The patient suddenly sees her sickness and her life together, joined in the cosmos, everyone she knows and cares about singing and praying for her. There is a reason for her to want to get well, and there is all the support she could imagine. "The chant is a recapitulation of scenes in the myth drama.... Events of the lower world are remembered and certain episodes are acted out or represented in symbols to preserve the time-lessness of power."[43]

> The patient, wearing a piece of unbleached muslin over her shoulders and holding as many as possible of her valued possessions, sat within the corn-meal circle in the hogan, waiting until everything was ready. Then the chanter led the procession to the place of the bundle layout; the patient followed him and the audience followed her—all blanketed and carrying the things they valued most: clothes, small grips, even a baby. At the far end of the hoop arrangement the patient pulled the unbleached muslin over her head, and placed her feet on the bear tracks, then bent over and passed through the hoops; the chanter stood beside the hoop farthest from the hogan. As the patient passed through the black hoop, the chanter pulled the muslin off her head; when she went through the blue hoop, he pulled if off as far as her neck; as she came under the yellow hoop, the muslin was pulled below her shoulders; when she passed through the white hoop, it fell to her waist; and, as she went through the thorny hoop, it fell off completely.[44]

The ceremony may have the sick person in its center, but then every participant in his or her unique state is drawn into the stream. "Since power is to the Navaho like a wave in a pool, always effective though becoming weaker the farther it radiates from chanter and patient, each person in attendance derives benefit from what is done in proportion to his proximity to the ritual."[45] The ceremony *is* literally a fire, a core of symbols at critical mass.

Because of the collective cleansing, there is tremendous community enthusiasm for these ceremonies. Reichard describes how a young Navaho man will ride fifty miles to bring back a single herb that a chanter needs. The event itself, especially the vigil, may seem long and monotonous, but no one is bored.

A FULL NAVAHO ceremony is composed of thousands of discrete events that flow one into another, sometimes over days. Reichard

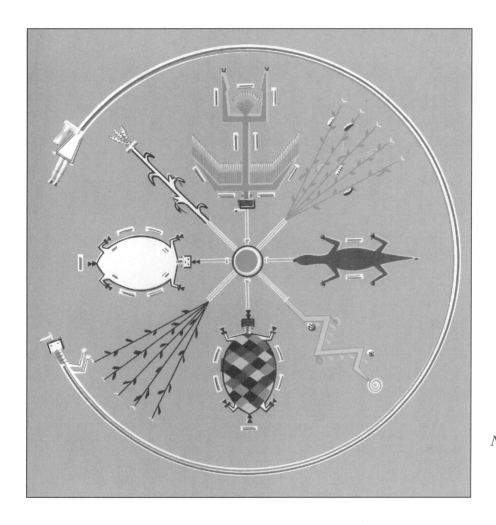

has described, with extraordinary thoroughness (800 pages), a single such ceremony. We can sample one of its mosaics:

> *Thunders and Water Monsters* painting: at the center a blue glass bowl was placed; water was poured into it from the four directions and from above; it was covered with chant lotion herbs, black sand, and four rainbows; then it was sunk into the floor, surrounded by white and yellow outlines, and sprinkled with pollen. The double-tiered clouds at the center correspond in color with the major figures. The Maltese cross is composed of black squash, blue tobacco, blue corn, blue bean.

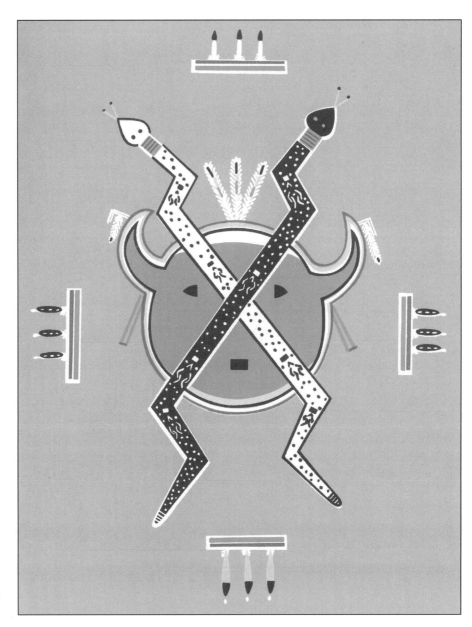

Sand
Painting at
Dropped-out
Mountain

The figures are: Black Thunder at the east, Blue Thunder at the
west, Pink Water Horse at the south, and Yellow Water Monster at
the north. The Thunders' black tails have no rain symbols; they are

outlined in white-yellow-blue-red-brown; Yellow Water Monster's tail is outlined in white-blue-black-red. The trail from Water Horse's feet to the center is white.[46]

Such images extend their domain, in part, through visualization. This general method of transdimensional projection is mainly familiar to the West in Tibetan practices of death preparation. Visualization of mandalas with their distinctive color fields and deities trains the soul for passage through equivalent *bardo* realms. Each symbolic journey helps to internalize and make real an actual esoteric journey.

The Navaho patient likewise must concentrate on the specifics of the sand painting to internalize its healing aspect; otherwise, it is just an art collector's relic. Throughout rural Asia, in a milder ritual, people hang sacred images on the walls of sick people's rooms for either passive or active meditation, for instance, peacocks and hares for headaches.[47]

In a current instance of Western adaptation of this custom, cancer patients imagine their own malignant cells, the way they form and grow, and the relation of that process to themselves and their being sick, and, finally, they try to initiate a cure from within by visualizing, in whatever personal or biological imagery they can come up with, a marshalling of their deepest strengths and a redirection of the process.

In each case, though, success depends on a belief in the activity, a trusting of imaginal as real. Only if the internalization is actualized will the path of images deepen and transform.

It is a major undertaking to alter soma through psyche, one that may not be possible (from a scientific viewpoint) but which still happens. We do not understand the mechanism, but we can't pretend it is alien to us; most people carry out limited versions of this all the time in wishes and fantasies. Formal magic through formal visualization (for both good and evil) has long been part of the European occult tradition. Compare, for instance, a segment of instruction from Aleister Crowley, a European magus of the early twentieth century:

Two and twenty times shall he figure to himself that he is bitten by a serpent, feeling even in his body the poison thereof. And let each bite be healed by an eagle or hawk, spreading its wings over his head, and dropping thereon a healing dew. But let the last bite be so terrible a pang at the nape of the neck that he seemeth to die, and let the healing dew be of such virtue that he leapeth to his feet.[48]

If the patient complains, to the Navaho shaman as well as to the visualization practitioner, that the illness is more real than the imagination, the answer would have to be that the illness exists also in the imagination (the Intelligence). It may in fact respond more directly to a symbolic entreaty than a stubborn physical jolt.

Certainly cancer is as severe a disease as a Western pragmatist could submit to the test of a seemingly immaterial technique. If the disease is real and its cells are real, he might ask, why would they respond to the imagination, which is "imaginary"? The answer, Navaho and Western, is that the imagination is the Mind of the body as well as of the Mind and has access to the same level of DNA somaticization as the disease.

The widespread presumed futility of this method in Western society is really prior to any experiment. Experiments in internalization don't work very well unless images are truly internalized and not just vaguely directed inward. Skepticism, on a deep subliminal level, can be a self-fulfilling prophecy, and even when a patient is newly enthusiastic, he can undermine the process by never *really* believing in it. Not believing in the ceremony is functionally equivalent to accepting the finality of the disease. Hoping is far weaker than believing, and passively observing images is different from penetrating through visions to their center. Visualization need not be a lazy way out; it provides an opportunity for commitment, faith, and sustained attention. So-called miracles are often little more than intention transduced into form, i.e., living tissue. (For an Oriental method of visualization in *Chi Gung*, see Chapter Nine.)

Nothing is more misleading than to think that the gods come from afar like star dwellers or Olympian strangers. The gods are incarnate. That is why they heal. The ceremony is a collective invitation to curative forces to manifest themselves in the personalities of human beings. In our culture, we dress doctors and nurses in neutral costumes and forbid them to enter the crisis of possession. The possibility of zombiism frightens us and threatens the foundation of our social being more than the dreadest pathologies. Better to be dead dead than living dead! In societies that accept curative possession, it is exactly this profound and disorienting power of the gods that inspires people to call them, to give up their individuality to them. Louis Mars graphically describes the state of possession in a Dahomean voodoo ritual preserved in Haiti:

> And how do the gods manifest themselves?
>
> They become incarnate in the body of their servants. They eat, drink, speak, and dance in the person of their medium. They are gods who become men throughout the day. Nothing is more common than to meet a spirit at one of these gatherings, and a single individual can experience several successive incarnations during the same meeting. The leader of the ceremony can summon the spirits or send them away. The drummer, because of his talent in beating the drum, can invite the gods to come down from Olympus. . . .
>
> In the middle of all this confusion of possessed ones and normal dancers, the drums maintain the cadence of the steps under the watchful eye of the priest, who keeps watch over the progression of the ceremony, calling on some to calm their ardor, and bolstering the physical strength of the singers when they begin to falter. . . .[49]

At the point at which the gods become dancing men, religion also becomes medicine.

> How condescending these gods are to the men in whom they incarnate themselves, for they borrow men's organic foundation, leaving them with beating hearts gnawed by anxiety, and with the oppression of chests panting in fear.[50]

Yet some gods require men and women to be happy. They must make men and women healthy if they are to have health themselves. So, often despite themselves, they cure.

Notes

1. A. R. Radcliffe-Brown, *The Andaman Islanders* (Glencoe, Illinois: Free Press, 1948).

2. Robert Lawlor, *Voices of the First Day: Awakening in the Aboriginal Dreamtime* (Rochester, Vermont: Inner Traditions, 1971), p. 360.

3. Ibid.

4. Edward Dorn, *Recollections of Gran Apacheria* (Berkeley, California: Turtle Island, 1974), unnumbered pages.

5. Michael J. Harner, *The Jívaro* (Garden City, New York: Double-day/Natural History Press, 1972), pp. 161–63.

6. Gerald Cannon Hickey, *Village in Vietnam* (New Haven: Yale University Press, 1964), p. 76.

7. Miguel Covarrubias, *Island of Bali* (New York: Alfred A. Knopf, 1938), pp. 324–25.

8. Alfred F. Whiting, *Ethnobotany of the Hopi,* Northern Arizona Society of Science and Art, Museum of Northern Arizona, Bulletin 15, Flagstaff, 1939.

9. Dorothy M. Spencer, *Disease, Religion and Society in the Fiji Islands* (New York: Augustin, 1941).

10. Knud Rasmussen, *Intellectual Culture of the Iglulik Eskimos: Report of the Fifth Thule Expedition to Arctic North America* (Copenhagen: Gyldendalske Boghandel, Nordisk Forlag, 1929), p. 56.

11. George Way Harley, *Native African Medicine* (Cambridge, Massachusetts: Harvard University Press, 1941), p. 14.

12. Ibid.

13. Ibid., pp. 17–18.

14. Ibid., p. 137.

15. Spencer, *Disease, Religion and Society in the Fiji Islands.*

16. Herman Melville, *Moby Dick* (originally 1851) (Berkeley: University of California Press, 1981), p. 168.

17. Selection from the journals of Herman Melville. The full entry with further discussion appears in Richard Grossinger, "Melville's Whale: A Brief Guide to the Text," in Grossinger (ed.), *An Olson-Melville Sourcebook, Volume I:*

The New Found Land, North Atlantic Books/*Io* #22, 1976, pp. 104–105.

18. Melville, *Moby Dick,* p. 167.

19. Ibid., p. 168.

20. Carlos Castaneda, *Journey to Ixtlan* (New York: Simon and Schuster, 1972), p. 114.

21. Ibid., pp. 114–15.

22. George Thornton Emmons, *The Tlingit Indians* (Seattle: University of Washington Press, 1991), p. 385.

23. Claude Lévi-Strauss, *The Savage Mind* (Chicago: University of Chicago Press, 1966), p. 268.

24. Shway Yoe, *The Burman* (London: Macmillan, 1910), pp. 425–26.

25. Gladys A. Reichard, *Navaho Religion,* Bollingen Foundation (New York: Pantheon Books, 1950), pp. 99–100.

26. E. S. Craighill Handy, Mary Kawena Pukui, and Katherine Livermore, *Outline of Hawaiian Physical Therapeutics,* Bernice P. Bishop Museum, Bulletin 126, Honolulu (1934).

27. Omar Khayyam Moore, "Divination—A New Perspective," *American Anthropologist* LIX (1957), pp. 69–74. Republished in William A. Lessa and Evon Z. Vogt (eds.), *Reader in Comparative Religion* (New York: Harper & Row, 1958), p. 302.

28. Richard Cowan and Douglas Sharon, *Eduardo the Healer* (Oakland, California: Serious Business Company, 1978).

29. Moore, "Divination—A New Perspective," in Lessa and Vogt (eds.), *Reader in Comparative Religion.*

30. Roy A. Rappaport, "Sanctity and Adaptation," in Grossinger (ed.), *Ecology and Consciousness: Traditional Wisdom on the Environment* (Berkeley, California: North Atlantic Books, 1992), pp. 105–106.

31. William Coles, "Adam in Eden, or The Paradise of Plants," republished in Grossinger (ed.), *Doctrine of Signatures* (Ann Arbor: North Atlantic Books/*Io* #5, 1968), pp. 39–45.

32. Edward C. Whitmont, *Psyche and Substance: Essays on Homeopathy in the Light of Jungian Psychology* (Berkeley, California: North Atlantic Books, 1980, 1991).

33. William Wildschut, *Crow Indian Medicine Bundles,* John C. Ewers (ed.), Museum of the American Indian, Heye Foundation, New York (1975), pp. 105–106.

34. A. P. Elkin, *Aboriginal Men of High Degree* (Sydney: Australasian Publishing, 1944), p. 113.

35. Edward C. Whitmont, *The Alchemy of Healing: Psyche and Soma* (Berkeley, California: North Atlantic Books, 1993), p. 192.

36. Harley, *Native African Medicine.*

37. Ibid., p. 202.

38. Whitmont, *The Alchemy of Healing,* p. 152.

39. Reichard, *Navaho Religion,* p. 5.

40. Ursula K. Le Guin, *A Wizard of Earthsea* (New York: Bantam Books, 1975), p. 179.

41. Ibid., p. 180.

42. Reichard, *Navaho Religion,* p. xxxiv.

43. Ibid., p. 116.

44. Ibid., pp. 652–53.

45. Ibid., p. xxxvii.

46. Ibid., p. 707.

47. Réné de Berval, *Kingdom of Laos* (Saigon: France-Asie, 1956), p. 423.

48. Aleister Crowley, *The Confessions of Aleister Crowley,* John Symonds and Kenneth Grant (eds.) (New York: Hill and Wang, 1969).

49. Louis Mars, *The Crisis of Possession in Voodoo,* trans. from the French by Kathleen Collins (Berkeley, California: Reed, Cannon & Johnson, 1977), p. 20.

50. Ibid., p. 21.

PART II

GUILDS

CHAPTER SEVEN

Vitalist Science and Energy Medicine

Vitalism: A Definition

W<small>E HAVE VIEWED</small> indigenous sciences in terms of their own belief systems and validations of internal realities. However, such validations have no standing in contemporary Western thought, and the belief systems they represent are generally assigned to a group of historically rejected modes of naturalistic explanation collectively known as vitalism. Actually, vitalism is the most generous assessment of their cogency; the more common alternative is to consider them animistic, hence totally heedless of cause and effect and based solely on wishful thinking and projection.

Of course, no native system of thought proposes either vitalism or animism as such. These names arise when historians and philosophers treat indigenous systems as if they adhered to formal codes of proto-scientific paradigms. Even though shamans do not try to legitimize their practices by anything resembling Kantian philosophy, vitalism becomes either our idealization of or our apology for not only shamanism but all energy practices. For the last two centuries we have avoided dealing with the complexity of the relationship between spirit (animation) and matter (substance) by inventing an ethereal, undifferentiated force and assigning it as an homogenous agency to this whole unknowable realm.

Palaeolithic herbalists surely did not split hairs between the herbal

signature of a plant as tincture and its vital message as deific force, nor would they have distinguished messages passing within nature from the phenomena of nature as transmissions themselves. The pure spirit of a plant is identical to the vital energy of the plant and the plant's position within a sacred geometry of stars, seeds, and morphological affinities. Only with the modern attempt to ascribe all effects to a chemical basis does vitalism enter the picture, cast as a *deus ex machina.*

Vitalism offers a mechanical language for transcendental functions. Thus, vitalists can explain any inexplicable physical events as being the effects of either presently unknown or ontologically unknowable realms. Information transmitting itself without a material trace, moving faster than light or outside the grid of space-time, may be proposed to exist in the form of transdimensional waves, quantum particles, vibrations, chreodes, synchronicities, spirits, or ancestors, depending on the originating culture and ideology. The shaman and faith healer are fully covered. When we examine contemporary sciences which depend secondarily on vitalistic explanations, we enter a surrealistic landscape in which spirits and quantum particles nimbly change places with each other, auras radiate from plants and stones, and metaphor replaces explanation. Located outside a prior unity of physical and spiritual realms, we find ourselves with no rational yardstick by which to separate actual effects and their possible unknown causes from pure stage magic or delusion. From UFOs to spoon-bending, from pyramid power to healing at a distance, this is where we are today and making little headway.

Medicine is perennially on the cutting edge of this paradox, for a remedy succeeds only when the patient is improved, not when the treatment has revealed the locus of the disease, which may never happen. Thus, mystery medicines will always appear and eventually be assigned to vitalism. Unorthodox methods will receive a sympathetic audience from those who are cured in the context of their practice and dismissal or disinterest from those who protect the institutions of their scientific heritage and seek consistent explanations for results. Vitalism has become the maxim that allows these two groups to coexist without dialogue.

Vitalism states more or less that living systems possess properties transcendent of their physics and chemistry. In medicine, inanimate matter is assumed to embody a seed force that can be aroused by a suitable form of hermetic pharmacy or psychic invocation. In many vitalistic systems, sound alone is considered capable of changing molecular structure, mind of influencing matter, and disincarnate beings of interceding directly as healers. Over the remainder of both volumes of this book we will consider each of these processes in detail.

Vitalism does not deny the physico-chemical oneness of the universe, but it poses a second tier (or a hierarchy of superior tiers) of reality. On an astral or essential plane all things have inner bodies; those bodies are joined to one another according to affinities and associations, relationships which have no chemical basis (though manifested in chemical terms) and (in some systems) pay no heed to relative diameter of or distance between bodies. The Sun in its essence is the same size as Pluto or any other planet or moon or even bug or plant. The inner bodies of each of these open into whole congruent fields containing vast landscapes of paraphysical contour.

There are two versions of vitalism: biological vitalism in which life energy (the animation and sentience of living beings) is presumed to be a unique distinct force (or fusion of forces) preceding or emanating from molecules and cells, and spiritual vitalism in which unimaginably powerful entities exist on totally nonmaterial planes and are thus permanently irreducible to scientific definition as we presently know it.

Since biological and spiritual forces are often the same "energies" classified according to different traditions, it doesn't matter how we treat this demarcation except to note that biological vitalists perennially design experiments in hopes of locating the precise sources of vital energy and offer a wide range of models based on interpretations of the nervous system, the circulatory system, or other "electrical" or "magnetic" fields of the body.

Biological vitalism holds simply that the chemistry of life did not arise sheerly from inorganic chemistry. Life *is* a special condition and brings its own qualities into the stellar debris: direction, shape, freedom, consciousness, and intelligence. This life force is universal and omnipresent. In recent centuries, it has been identified, on the borders of biological science, with electricity, radiation, and general energy fields around organisms. Wilhelm Reich's later discovery of orgone recalls Luigi Galvani's life force, the mesmerism of Frank Mesmer, the odic force of Karl von Reichenbach, Prosper Blondlot's N-rays, Emile Boirac's nerve radioactivity, and innumerable other semielectric, semimagnetic vital energies.

Hermetic vitalism more specifically summarizes the millennia-long quest for a series of acausal relationships among objects—acausal, that is, by the principles of physics and chemistry. Whereas a biological vitalist may believe in the single life force and seek to define it as an unknown energy within science, the hermetic vitalist presumes an enormous variety of occult and psychospiritual linkages which he derives by esoteric study and personal meditation. Most important, he has his culture's oral and written records of such associations going back for generations. In the West he can begin his inquiry with the traditionally ascribed affinities of astrology, alchemy, and the Gnostic sciences. Some hermetics, in fact, become so bogged down by the weight and authority of lineage that they simply expound, superstitiously, famous connections and have little experience of energy. This leads these days to an obsession with gross aspects of sun-sign astrology, theosophical bibles, and ritual amulets. But hermetics also borrow images and paradigms from astronomy, genetics, biochemistry, geology, and botany, recognizing that science is an archetypal record of visualizations of the inside of matter and contains everpresent evolving phases of relationships between consciousness and nature. From this union, new versions of paraphysics, radionics, and other pseudo- or para-sciences (depending on your point of view) arise.

We are left finally with a vast realm of unidentified agencies, each of them different, each of them defined by peculiar historical and cultural circumstances. Voodoo (Africa), *chi* (China), *prana* (India), orgone

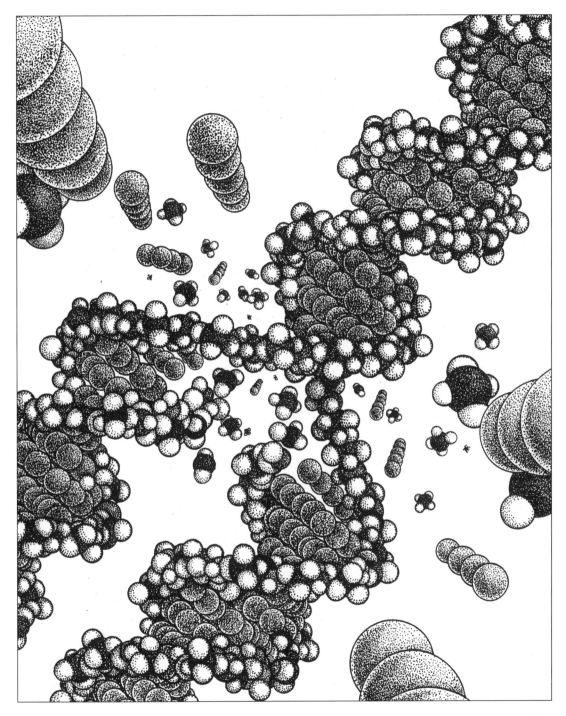

231

(Reich), *wakonda* (Dakota Sioux), the *astrum* (Gnostic Europe) need not, finally, be precisely the same things. The undiscovered energy spectrum, even if it is single, may be distinguished by the localism of its effects, its capacity to draw on internal cultural images and provide people with the semblance of distinct forces and spirits for their own indigenous systems. Despite tantalizing similarities, these forces have different heredities and should not automatically be translated into one another or into one universal current. Some healing energies may thus have vanished from the Earth forever with the tribes that practiced them.

There is perhaps no more succinct way to define vitalism than to say it is everything which modern science is not. In fact, formal vitalism (as opposed to the individual energy systems making it up) is a nineteenth-century catechism, archaic in both its language and the mechanisms that language contrived to represent—utterly ignored in most circles after the 1930s. The universal acceptance of Darwinism is what doomed vitalism and continues to. Nothing *marks* contemporary thought more completely than the Darwinist reduction—not necessarily the theories of Charles Darwin (1809–1882) himself, but the translation of those theories into foundation stones of science.

Darwinism and Vitalism

A BRIEF SUMMARY OF the Darwinian world-view goes as follows: The universe is composed only of inanimate matter. At some point in the history of this matter—when it was simple, uniform, and infinitesimally dense—it condensed still further and exploded, and has since been expanding, giving the space its multidimensional geography. The original universe had no intrinsic fire. Ignited from condensation, the stars are the only source of heat anywhere. All energy is stellar-based.

The planets are small, globular beads dripping off stars, hot from their relatively recent inclusion in suns and kept moderately warm by their continued proximity to them. On specific planets, comets, and asteroids, chance combinations of matter agglutinate, exist for the duration of their kinetics, and disappear by merging with other molecules. Events can never be distinguished from environments, for events *are* environments.

There is no real basis for our existence, but since we are here we must be explained within this system. In Darwinian theory, consciousness is said to originate solely from inanimate matter, molecular junk processed in the star cores of the ancient universe and passed in elemental assemblages onto the cooled planets of individual solar systems. On these random worlds, the elements become organized in discrete energy-conserving creatures self-assembling out of cells. For something so subtle to occur in this inimical circumstance is nothing short of incredible.

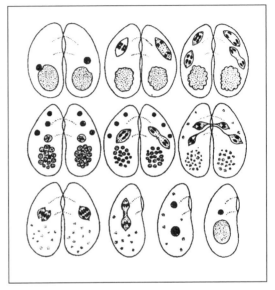

Paramecia in conjugation

It is an embarrassment to all those Darwinian scientists, who, themselves, must be a product too of this unlikely event. People are finally a ridiculous burden for a theory which could not have "evolved" without them. The conventional excuse for us is that, in an infinite amount of time, anything will happen, even beings with intelligence to know that such an unlikely infinite set is unfolding and to spin theories acknowledging that fact.

But has an infinite amount of time passed? There is an unacknowledged consensus among many biologists and mathematicians that it has not and that chance occurrence alone is not sufficient to explain the startling configuration of living structures on the Earth today. The physicist Werner Heisenberg tells the story of the mathematician John von Neumann's debate with a confirmed neo-Darwinist (Von Neumann is known mainly for the formulation of game theory):

[Von Neumann] led the biologist to the window of his study and said, "Can you see the beautiful white villa over there on the hill? It arose by pure chance. It took millions of years for the hill to be formed; trees grew, decayed, grew again, and then the wind covered the top of the hill with sand, stones were probably deposited on it by a volcanic process, and accident decreed that they should come to lie on top of one another. And so it went on. I know, of course, that accidental processes through the aeons generally produce quite different results. But on just this one occasion they led to the appearance of this country house, and people moved in and live there at this very moment."[1]

A vitalist might laugh and say: "This is the beautiful white villa, this living Earth of ours that the Darwinian mechanists have proposed."

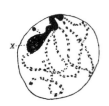

But such is the truth, for as unlikely as it is that the villa would be produced by chance, it is a bare step less unlikely that life, even the simplest worms, would arise fortuitously. The Russian astronomer I. S. Shklovskii, in his landmark book *Intelligent Life in the Universe* (the English version done with American astronomer Carl Sagan), calculates the basic odds in order to back up his own neo-Darwinism:

> Four and one half billion years ago the Earth was lifeless. Nowhere—not in the primitive atmosphere, not in the early oceans, nor in the newly forming crust—could even the simplest, most unassuming microorganism be found. Two billion years later, the Earth was fairly teeming with one-celled organisms of appreciable complexity . . . How? Was it a vastly improbable event which, to our good fortune, occurred by chance in this small corner of the universe, and not elsewhere? Or, starting from the physics and chemistry of the primitive terrestrial environment, was the origin of life a likely event, given only a billion years of random molecular interactions?
>
>
>
> . . . the probability of living systems arising, even over 10^9 years, would be $10^{-12} \times 10^9 = 10^{-3}$, a very small number. In this case, we would conclude that the origin of life was a highly improbable event in the time available in the early history of the Earth, and that life is here at all only though an extraordinary stroke of luck.[2]

That particular stroke of luck, later in the book, is considered to have been perhaps an accidental development of the ability, in some compounds, to distinguish between left-handed and right-handed rotation inside their boundaries. This might have happened, initially, as a spontaneous photochemical response to polarized light striking the deep waters of the primitive Earth. These compounds would then develop three-dimensional structures with left or right lock-and-key relationships to maintain their singular integrities. Later, as these sticky, wriggling lumps came into contact with a turbulent environment, the lock-and-key topology would distinguish them from the rest of the external world and provide a basis for them to duplicate themselves. Once they were able to reproduce, they could begin to dominate their immediate locale. So began the superhighway eulogized as "survival of the fittest." The first organism was no more than a chemical anomaly in the oceanic eternity; as the only such anomaly, however tiny, it would develop a special relationship with everything else with which it came into contact. If it was not absorbed back, it would eventually draw material out of its surroundings by chemical reaction to nourish and sustain itself—itself discrete, that is, from everything else. It would not change into the material, any more than we change into the foods we eat; it would convert all "digestible" material into it. Anything else would be rejected or would destroy it (as the first "toxins"). These interactions would lead to protean biochemical chains and enzyme systems.[3] Of course, this is not what happened. It is simply a model of how an accidental process might lead to life.

In Heisenberg's account, he next tells the "parable" of Von Neumann's villa to Niels Bohr, the Danish physicist. Bohr responds:

> Darwinian theory in its present form makes two independent assertions. On the one hand, it states that, through the process of heredity, nature tests ever new living forms, rejecting the great majority and preserving a few suitable ones. This seems to be empirically correct. But there is also the second assertion: that the new forms originate through purely accidental disturbances of the gene structure.

This claim is much more questionable, even though we can hardly conceive of an alternative. Von Neumann's argument was, of course, designed to show that, though almost anything can arise by chance in the long run, the probability of this happening in the time we know nature has taken to produce higher organisms is absurdly small. Physical and astrophysical studies tell us that no more than a few thousand million years have passed since the appearance of the most primitive living beings on earth. Now, whether or not accidental mutations and selection are sufficient to produce the most complicated and highly developed organisms during this interval will depend on the time needed to develop a new biological species.[4]

But Bohr knows (as Shklovskii knows but won't admit) that the time is too short, and pure chance is inadequate as an explanation. A little later, Bohr adds:

> We can admittedly find nothing in physics or chemistry that has even a remote bearing on consciousness. Yet all of us know that there is such a thing as consciousness, simply because we have it ourselves. Hence consciousness must be part of nature, or, more generally, of reality, which means that, quite apart from the laws of physics and chemistry, as laid down in quantum theory, we must also consider laws of quite a different kind.[5]

At this point, a possible alternative to an explanation of form as exclusively the result of variation from mutation is some version of vitalism. This option makes quite contrary assumptions right from the beginning. Vitalists propose that cohesive systems on worlds arise not by chance molecular accretion but are imparted by a nonstellar source or template originating outside of matter. In biological vitalism, this is often an energy contained in the Sun at spectral levels beyond our capacities to detect and measure. It is part of the planetary core and thus works its way into our lattice from the beginning. "... A certain mass of elementary consciousness was originally imprisoned in the matter of earth," wrote Jesuit palaeontologist Pierre Teilhard de Chardin. This was "... the psychic face of that portion of the stuff of the cosmos enclosed from the beginning of time within the narrow scope of the early earth."[6] Such a layer in some unknown way forged a path through the archetypal qualities of atomic and molecular substance and transmitted preexisting morphologies or morphological potentials onto emerging entities. Or, in other words, the emerging layer met the maelstrom of the physical landscape with a quantum realm of numerical, energetic, and geometric attributes.

But, in present-day science, there are no hidden conditions; what is not demonstrable simply requires better tools: electron microscopes, chromosome samples, further fractal analysis. Forces from outside nature by definition do not exist. Vitalists would agree, but only as long as the domain of nature is expanded to include everything anywhere in any form. Of course, what else could nature be?

Darwinism is not an intentionally harsh legacy, for much of enlightened humanitarian science has sprung from it. It is not even necessarily antivitalist. Darwin did not argue the secular and chemical basis of life from any profound atheism. He simply could not find any other influence, and he wanted to clear scientific inquiry of magical projections and authoritarian religious dogmas. The primitive forces that are in evidence, he said, are sufficient to bring this entire multiplicity of phenomena into being. A fish is a fish; a bird is a bird. These have their own integrities, for they have arisen naturally from other novel forms, all untainted by external design.

Nature was suddenly young and beautiful, freed of royal decree or God as its architect. That was Darwin's real contribution—not the law of natural selection, variants of which had been postulated many times already—but the statement that there was nothing *but* natural selection. Darwin said, simply, LIFE IS NO SPECIAL CONDITION.

Contemporary Darwinian schools of thought have found classical Darwinism far too simple to handle the complexities of living systems and thus have tended to complexify the formulas instead of heretically abandoning them. It is now generally accepted that living systems possess aggregate characteristics, emergent properties, that cannot be ascribed to any of their components, that such systems continue to coalesce into larger and more intricate systems, and that these higher-order synergistic systems generate the kinds of special behavior that seemed once (to vitalists) to require a metachemical explanation. These would include mobility, reproduction, sentience, intelligence, and civilization. The "self-organizing universe" is a somewhat unwieldy device, but it does provide natural selection with a dynamic hierarchy of complexifying lattices to test and build upon without discarding the Big Bang.

VITALISM AND SYSTEMS theory are competing metaphors or models for the riddles of nature. Many biologists believe they are congruent and that the development of systems theory has eliminated the

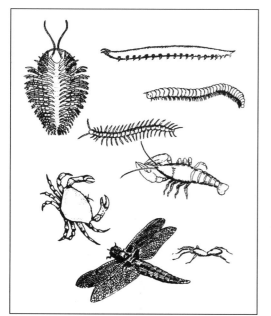

need for vitalism. It is seen as a more precise, elegant, and cybernetic solution of the same paradoxes. Yet as long as vitalism is noncybernetic, it cannot be completely isomorphic with even the most labyrinthine synergistic compromise.

During epochs when life was presumed to have discrete properties, it was possible to base whole sciences and medicines on the *a priori* existence of those properties. To paraphrase Thomas Aquinas, we might not have known what they were, but we knew *that* they were. Such notions do not find an audience in today's empirical colleges. Shklovskii's view is standard:

In primitive times, when very little was understood about the nature of living systems, the most routine biological activities, such as the germination of a seed or the flowering of a plant, were attributed to divine intervention. In the early years of the Industrial Revolution, when advances in celestial mechanics gave something close to a complete understanding of the positions and motions of the heavenly bodies, the concept arose that living systems may be nothing more than a particularly intricate kind of clockwork. But when early investigations failed to unveil the clockwork, a kind of ghostly mainspring was invented — the "vital force." The vital force was a rebellion from mechanistic biology, an explanation of all that mechanism could not explain, or for which mechanisms could not be found. It also appealed to those who felt debased by the implication that they were "nothing more" than a collection of atoms, that their urges and supposed free wills arose merely from the interaction of an enormously large number of molecules, in a way which, although too complex to use predictively, was, in principle, determined.

But today, we find no evidence for a vital force; indeed, the concept is very poorly defined, a kind of universal catch-all for anything we cannot explain. The opposite tack — that all living systems are made of atoms and nothing else — has proved a particularly useful idea. An entire, new science of molecular biology has made startling progress and achieved fundamental insights starting from this assumption. And there is nothing debasing in the thought that we are made of atoms alone. We are thereby related to the rest of the universe; and if we are made of the same stuff, more or less, as everything else, then elsewhere there may be things rather like us. We are a tribute to the subtlety of matter.[7]

This is the vision of life once needed for science to develop after millennia of magic and religious fundamentalism. It defines our origin in a pagan turbulence of matter. In fact, it honors our existence as an exquisitely precise thickening of a lifeless molecular pool.

The Alchemical Legacy

THE ALGEBRA BEHIND Darwinism led indirectly to machines and computers, but it was, ironically, the prior vitalistic model that gave birth to experimental science itself. The quest for magical energies in the West led to the very discoveries of chemical compounds, electricity, gravity, magnetism, etc., that lie at the basis of physics and academic medicine.

Early science, for which alchemy is a prototype, did not distinguish (because it lacked the necessary instruments) between simple mechanical changes of chemistry and ostensible vital changes of essence. This is because knowledge of molecular cause and effect is a relatively recent phenomenon. Thus, quintessence and numerology were real, the same as charge or any other physical characteristics. When purely mechanical changes were eventually isolated and given their own set of explanations by chemists and physicists, alchemy and related quintessential sciences were abandoned (historically by the many, that is) in favor of more rational molecular and atomic explanations. As inquiry into the mechanism of nature has continued successfully (and underwritten the design of instruments for further inquiry), mainstream scientists have been less and less willing to admit even the possible existence of unknown or unknowable energies. Everything so far has yielded to orthodoxy, and anything that hasn't is viewed with skepticism or disdain. Subatomic theory in particular has left us with the illusion that research into the infinitesimal will yield all missing relations of cause and effect. Meanwhile medicine has become the realm of microbe- or micro-hunters.

The seventeenth-century Rosicrucians were both magicians and scientists. They proposed a "solar" power that was concomitantly an angelic

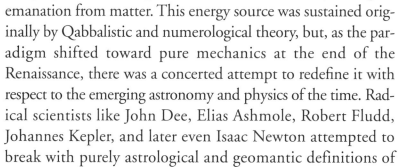

emanation from matter. This energy source was sustained originally by Qabbalistic and numerological theory, but, as the paradigm shifted toward pure mechanics at the end of the Renaissance, there was a concerted attempt to redefine it with respect to the emerging astronomy and physics of the time. Radical scientists like John Dee, Elias Ashmole, Robert Fludd, Johannes Kepler, and later even Isaac Newton attempted to break with purely astrological and geomantic definitions of energy and to apply mathematics to nature in a different, more componential way. Yet despite their substantial roles in the birth of physical mechanicism, to one degree or another all of these investigators tried to explain the existence of forms in the world by invoking aspects of their primary nature, such as color, rhythm, shape, affiliation, even as Uriel, Gabriel, and Saturn were invoked in ritual magic.

The properties the last wizard-scientists hoped to elicit were mostly the same utilitarian ones later manifested by physics: light, motion, transformation, hierarchy, increase, unity. Before vitalistic entities were discarded in favor of pure thermodynamics, squares, circles, pyramids, cones, etc., were thought to have intrinsic geometric power as energy sources, as were certain combinations of numbers and names and the movements associated with the zodiac. These hidden properties could then be tapped (nonthermodynamically) by an appropriate rearrangement of their constituent elements. If a city was built properly, it would light automatically without extrinsic sources; have perpetual fountains, inexhaustible wealth; and be impregnable.[8] We will return to a discussion of these and other vitalistic energies in Volume Two, Chapter One.

Discoveries arising from the astrological/alchemical tradition include, surprisingly, those of the mysterious inexhaustible force of gravity and the elliptical orbits of the planets—and even later, the elemental chart. Of course, they were discoveries made as hermeticism was turning into thermodynamics; they prove the twin meaning of the Rosicrucian science of this epoch. It was angelic and numerological, but it also was empirical and mathematical. When we, today, accept the laws of physics and chemistry as they come to us from then, we forget that we have since homogenized them and disowned their magical placenta.

It is pointless to dwell on whether the early astrophysicists really believed in astrology and vital energy or whether they were the unknowing victims of religious superstitions which their culture imposed on them. Historians of science choose to venerate their best work as having transcended the magic they ostensibly innocently inherited and could not escape. Yet it is exactly the millennial association of that magic with science that suggests a possibility

Vitalist Science and Energy Medicine

we now mainly look back to nostalgically or assign derisively to the New Age.[9]

One seventeenth-century science and philosophy was confirmed and exploited by the future; the other was lost. For the makers, though, there was only one science. When Newton and Kepler discovered the algebraic and trigonometric laws of nature, they interpreted them as part of a larger series of which our particular spatial and thermodynamic applications were one corollary (God was another, touching every domain of his creation down to the last spider and atom simultaneously with the finger of gravitation). Newton and Robert Boyle were inextricably allied with Philip Sidney and Giordano Bruno in the same profession—the same cosmic revelation. It is our prejudice, not theirs, to make a distinction between, for instance, orthodox Newtonian thought (physics) and the actual theosophical beliefs of Newton. From a hermetic point of view, we have refined one way to light a city and set vehicles in motion, but there are countless others still hidden in nature. Ours is linear and materialistic; another may be transdimensional and vitalistic. Having used up so much of the Earth's nonrenewable resources in just a century or so, we might at least consider now whether the devalued constructs of Newton and Kepler touch on the other puzzles of nature neither they nor we have resolved.

WHEN THE ROSICRUCIAN quest was severed from the march of technology, it did not die. Each generation since has produced its contenders to this mystery of science and magic. The New Alchemy Institute (1969–1992), which explored wind and solar energy, plant genetics, and fishpond ecosystems, among other things, was named that in express recognition of the Rosicrucian scientists of the seventeenth century. The members of the Institute were committed enough scientists to doubt that seventeenth-century cities could have been lit by pure squares and circles, but they caught intimations of another clockwork behind that veil. They didn't complete the search, but they turned over a few more clues—an extra quantum of energy here and there—to the next generation. If something like tetrahedronal energy or biological transmutation is ultimately found to be real, it will have also been real then—in the seventeenth century and, in fact, a million or two million years ago likewise—ready to be seized by asking the right question.

Of course, Stone Age man was not equipped for such research, but who is to say when our species began looking away from the crack in the door such that we now slip past it a thousand times daily, our attention elsewhere? For having lost the glimpse historically, we must labor mightily, a step at a time, against a massive megastructure, in the vague direction of magic, not sure if it exists or what ilk of thing it is. We do not know whether we inherit opportunity missed or an elusive mode of thought so remote from us that it will take an utterly different culture to uncover it.

Today, John Todd, the founder of the New Alchemy Institute, is the director of both Ocean Arks and Center for the Restoration of Waters. He is researching the intrinsic capacity of living systems to draw on unquantifiable sources to purify their highly toxic surroundings, i.e., introducing the right plants, animals, and microbes for a dead pond to interpolate and expand biology (microorganisms, algae, snails, fish, frogs, aquatic plants) throughout itself. This artificial version of the "primordial soup" develops its own intelligence whereby not only do individual species thrive but they contribute in mysterious ways to a revivification of the entire ecosystem. While each species transmutes its favorite food into raw materials favored by other species in the pond, the living entities also collaborate in transformations that are not measurable in any simple sense. Heavy metals "disappear" into plants, and even dioxins are converted by some plant or animal. Not only might microenvironmental alchemies lodge in this process at different levels, they might be the very agencies that sparked life in the Gaian oceans in the first place. They also might be the raw integers of homeopathy and other energy medicines.

By the same token, how do we explain the nonradioactive release of heat by deuterium in the context of a palladium rod in a Salt Lake City laboratory? Named "cold fusion" for lack of an alternative, this process may not be nuclear at all but alchemical or cosmological in the most basic fashion. It may be a "cold" version of the transmutative energy at the heart of the star machine.

VITALISM HAS FOUND a new place for itself on the fringes of orthodox science. In the last half century, psychology and statistics have collaborated on a research protocol of divination, telekinesis, future vision, synchronicity, and transdimensionality. Parapsychology (as a catch-all for these reported events) has explored energies which, if they exist at all, are at best intermittent and do not follow many of the basic laws of science. Insofar as they are not "universal" or duplicatable, they violate fundamental properties of time and space. That is, they are not laws for the science we have. If, as parapsychologists report in their journals, plants communicate with one another and people dream of future events and levitate objects by mental power, we are forced to acknowledge that the twentieth century still bears two realities, one revealed and one equally present but intangible.

The recent popularity of books about "psychic discoveries behind the Iron Curtain," "the secret life of plants," "the Kirlian aura," "biological transmutation," etc., heralds our renewed search for an explanation of paraphysical events. While vitalistic intrusions are not yet blatant enough to impinge on scientific doctrine, the increasing attention given them portends that problems have arisen that, at present, have no solution, hence are best treated by metaphor or denial. When renegade scientists (who have had the full course of university and graduate study and thus should know better) begin to discuss photography of the aura, fields of energy around plants and crystals, and the geological dowsing, it seems that alchemy, as the prototype science for the unsolved riddles of nature, still might have the greater claim on our future than chemistry (which would then turn out to be its solely material branch).

Quintessence

Hermetic pharmacies (such as homeopathy or Bach Flower Remedies) raise the age-old paradox of the "specific," that is, the medicine that works because of its essential relationship to the sick person and/or the disease. Paracelsus (1493–1541) was one of the West's original occult chemists, and in his writings, he denied that it was through *any* property of hot or cold, moist or dry, as was traditionally believed, that substances could cure. They acted from qualities having to do with their own fundamental place in nature. He says: "In the specifics there are many rare virtues which do not take their origin from the fact that they are hot or cold, but have an essence outside all of these...."[10] In another place he notes: "So the oil of cherries and acetum after their digestion produce a laxative, though neither of them in its own nature has a laxative property ... such specifics are produced out of their own nature by composition of elements...."[11]

In the work of Paracelsus, one finds reference not only to specifics but to a general elixir, which he calls "quintessence":

> The quintessence, then, is a certain matter extracted from all things which Nature has produced, and from everything which has life corporeally in itself, a matter most subtly purged of all impurities and mortality, and separated from all the elements. From this it is evident that the quintessence is, so to say, a nature, a force, a virtue, and a medicine, once, indeed, shut up within things, but now free from any domicile and from all outward incorporation....
>
> Now the fact that the quintessence cures all diseases does not arise from temperature, but from an innate property, namely, its great cleanliness and purity, by which, after a wonderful manner, it alters the body into its own purity, and entirely changes it.[12]

He adds that "each disease requires its own special quintessence," though there are some which can be used for any disease.[13] Needless to say, orthodox medicine does not recognize quintessence, though it has many remedies that "work" for no clear reason. Aspirin, for one,

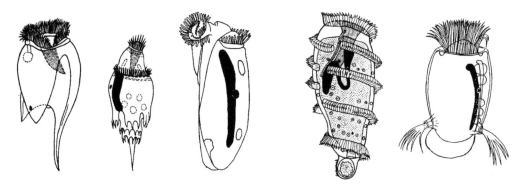

Oligotrichid ciliates

might have quintessential properties.

In pure energy medicine in which no perceptible physical substance is administered, treatment is by definition "specific" or on a quintessential, not a material plane. The cure is qualitative and whole, not quantitative and incremental. This is true whether the remedy is words, the sound of a didgeridoo, the directed touch of a healer, or a homeopathic potency. The physical aspect of the treatment is often the barest possible under the circumstances because it exists merely to invoke a paraphysical domain.

If a court case arose from ostensible murder with a homeopathic remedy, the "suspect" could not be incriminated by a forensic toxicologist. There would be no substance present in the Western legal and scientific sense (even though homeopaths have traditionally claimed their high potencies, like the bloody down, are powerful and dangerous). The same problem would exist in a murder by voodoo or any other psychokinesis. Vitalistic medicines are fundamentally nonmaterial. There is no way their thread can be picked up or reified by a later mechanistic physician, who, if he ever noted their strange "effects," would undoubtedly attribute them to something else. Thus, the shamanic/alchemical paradox has not been eliminated; it has been buried in the chaos of daily life.

ORIGINS

Homeopathy, Feng Shui, Bach Flower Remedies

HOMEOPATHY IS ONE of the most remarkable intact vitalistic medicines.[14] It arose in a unique historical context in the early nineteenth century (when experimental science was in a state of creative chaos and gave birth to vitalistic and mechanical theories side by side with no distinction between them); it was invented by one man (Samuel Hahnemann [1755–1843]) who creatively combined Hippocratic, Rosicrucian, and biological principles; and it survived because its methods "worked," that is, people were cured of chronic, acute, and even life-threatening illnesses after ingesting homeopathic microdoses. These microdoses retained nothing in them of the material—plant, animal, or mineral—used as the basis of their manufacture, nothing physical, that is. The medicine *Apis* (named for the bee) was made of crushed bees but diluted to such an extent that there was no bee residue left. Homeopathic salt was saltless. Homeopathic *Silica* was a chemically inert substance lacking sand. There is no reason to fear ingesting homeopathic rattlesnake poison, homeopathic mercury, or homeopathic dog's milk because the pills contain no traces of these substances—that is, they are suffused in a neutral medium and succussed (shaken) many times in sequence until there is none of the herb or mineral with which preparation of the medicine began.

Samuel Hahnemann, the founder and codifier of homeopathy, did not intend a vitalistic medicine using spiritual doses, but he did not have the advantage (or disadvantage) of living in an era when thorough laboratory analysis was routine. He used those dilutions that worked, and in the process he (and his successors, to this day) found that the greater the dilution (with succussion), the deeper the healing power, the more lasting the cure, and the fewer the side effects. Thus, he unknowingly continued diluting substances that were already nonmaterial with regard to their proposed active ingredients and, since he observed that the most dilute were the safest and most powerful, he based his metapharmacopoeia on them.

Whitmont marvels at homeopathic doses diluted and rediluted to such a degree that there is undoubtedly not a single molecule left of the tincture from which they began:

> Astonishingly [the chemical] characterizations [of dematerialized earth substances] do actually apply quite accurately to the ultra-molecular (above the thirtieth) potencies of the medicines used in classical homeopathy: They are imperishable, their functional efficacy transmits itself to—"infects" by contact—any material that comes into contact with them, viz. the inside walls of their container or any inert sugar granules mixed with them or used as refill when the container has been emptied; some extant preparations (also in the possession of this writer) thus perpetuated are more than a hundred years old and are still as effective as recent preparations. Their 'radiating' effect can be picked up by the organism and registers kinesiologically and by pupil reflex over thirty feet in distance; their effects include not only a removal of symptomatic disturbances but . . .are constitution-strengthening, hence, indeed "life-prolonging, strengthening and rejuvenating."[15]

These are not ordinary substances in a Darwinian universe! But by the same argument, neither they nor we ever were.

DRAWING ON THE ancient Greek Law of Similars, i.e., assuming that disease symptoms are the body/mind's attempt to heal itself of a deeply interiorized pathology (often hereditary in origin), a homeopath prescribes microdoses that encourage instead of suppress or dampen these catalytic symptoms which, to most doctors, are the malaises to be attacked and eliminated. The historical roots of these principles are discussed in the next chapter and again under "Occult and Esoteric Traditions" in Chapter Twelve.

The precisely congruent remedy, i.e., the one which in a material dose in a healthy person would engender symptoms most resembling the disease at its *essential* level, becomes, after homeopathic preparation, a vibration not a molecular compound. Think what kind of activity this might have caused in the primordial oceans of the Earth or still activates in John Todd's reinoculated Flax Pond on Cape Cod.

As Whitmont proposes, homeopathy is the ultimate nonmaterial medicine, the remedy for an utterly materialistic time:

> The symbolic "simillimum" in resonance with the critical pattern in need of integrative healing is itself a live spirit, whether on the level of psyche or soma. We have reached a threshold here where our accustomed separation of matter from psyche or spirit is no longer valid.[16]

The simillimum is hardly just a homeopathic issue. In fact, its aliases now permeate pop science and the New Age. In describing the mysterious power of mind in healing, the guru of quantum healing, Deepak Chopra, concludes rather facilely:

> We already know that intelligence can take the form of a thought or a molecule; . . . [as] having "mind" and "body." . . . The two are always matched to each other, even when they appear to be separate. To coordinate them, I have [proposed] a quantum level, called the "quantum mechanical body." This is not a physical artifact but a layer of intelligence, the layer where the body as a whole is organized and correlated. This is where the know-how comes from that makes molecules "smart" instead of inert.[17]

The incredibly complex process which takes place within us and was defined as spiritual or alchemical in earlier times (giving rise to homeopathy and vitalism) is now projected onto the relation of mind and molecule, at the level of depth of black holes, the relativity of time and space, and quantum mechanical events. "Quantum medicine" is an attempt simultaneously to gain legitimacy for vitalism by relocating it at the cutting edge of post-modern physics and to entice science into an exploration of the effects of disembodied Intelligence.

(It is of potential importance for healing that contemporary physics suggests convertibility of matter and energy, holographic unity, and reversal of space-time; likewise that experiments in paraphysics show seeming psychokinetic influence over substances and events — but how these incipient models themselves bear on actual healing systems remains substantially unknown. Quantum physics itself is not yet proof for or against spirit healing and vitalistic science.)

DESPITE THE MANY attempts of homeopathic sympathizers to invent a wave-particle model of microdose healing, this must remain a metaphor for the foreseeable future. Homeopathy cannot wait for proof. It has new patients in need of treatment every day, patients who accept its results as cures. There is every reason it should have died, at least as a clinical medicine, as another false trail from Rosicrucian science, if it were not for its astounding success in defiance of "mere" chemistry. Even as the mechanism of this success remains unknown, homeopathy continues to be successful and to expand. The roster of historical and statistical trials using homeopathy in competition with other clearly material medicines is astonishing. During nineteenth-century outbreaks of plagues and influenza epidemics, people flocked to homeopathic clinics and hospitals because of their well-publicized high percentages of cures by comparison with those at allopathic institutions. Was this placebo in the form of mass curative resonance, or an unknown vitalistic energy? To those cured, it didn't matter. In the days before the AMA, they didn't even know homeopathy wasn't supposed to be real medicine, its pills real pills!

MOST ENERGY REPERTORIES have developed similarly over generations of empirical testing. The ancient Chinese science of *feng shui* (from which lei lines perhaps originated) postulates a flow of *chi* through all of nature, landscapes as well as creature bodies. Circulating in patterns corresponding to the eight trigrams of the *I Ching* (Yin and Yang in all possible combinations of three positions), this energy can become either too strong or stagnant, hence needing either to be stimulated or dispersed. As one contemporary writer defines it:

> *Feng shui* is the application of these principles [of Yin and Yang] to physical space. *Feng* means "wind," or the active, moving, yang qualities of a situation. *Shui* is "water," the deep, still, yin qualities. How

250

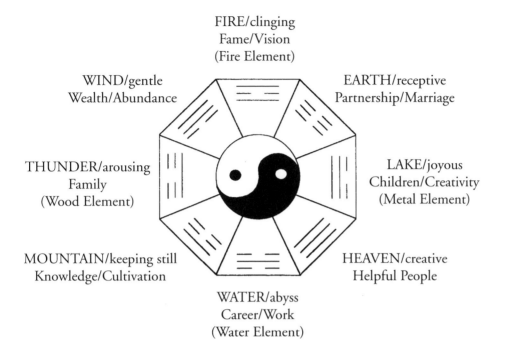

FIRE/clinging
Fame/Vision
(Fire Element)

WIND/gentle
Wealth/Abundance

EARTH/receptive
Partnership/Marriage

THUNDER/arousing
Family
(Wood Element)

LAKE/joyous
Children/Creativity
(Metal Element)

MOUNTAIN/keeping still
Knowledge/Cultivation

HEAVEN/creative
Helpful People

WATER/abyss
Career/Work
(Water Element)

Ba-gua *diagram showing eight* I Ching *categories and associations. In the ancient art of* feng shui, *the* ba-gua *is mapped onto a house or room with "Water/Abyss/Career" in the center of the main entrance wall.*

these occur and interact in any given place and moment will strongly affect our health and moods.

Just as the blood chemistry and fluid content of the body tissues affect the flow of natural electricity *(chi)* in the body, the flow of energy in a house or landscape is stimulated, channeled, obstructed, deflected, siphoned, etc., through the influence of hills, trees, water, paths, windows, mirrors, furniture, wiring, plumbing—even the actions and intentions of those who use the space. Making even minor adjustments can have a significant impact on the quality of life in that location.[18]

We will pick up the discussion of *chi* sciences in Chapters Eight and Nine.

Vitalist Science and Energy Medicine

For all intents and purposes the medicines developed in the 1930s from flower blooms by the British physician Edward Bach are also resonant and spiritual. They are not decreased to even a fraction of most homeopathic remedies, but they are clearly diluted past the herbal phase. Bach's original legacy was thirty-eight blooms, which turn spring water into medicine when floated on its surface in bright sunlight for three to four hours. Brandy is added to preserve the essence. Later the mother tincture is diluted a few drops to an ounce of water.

The remedies are administered only according to the emotional planes of ailments. From there, effects are presumably translated to the levels of corresponding physical disturbances which are understood as present simultaneously at the same vibration. That is, the whole disease is diagnosed and treated only on the emotional level, even if it includes infections or tumors.

Rock rose, mimulus, and aspen are prescribed for different kinds of fear, gentian and wild oat for qualities of uncertainty, honeysuckle for living in the past, mustard for susceptibility to gloom, heather for always seeking companionship and fear of being alone, chicory for being overcareful of children and relatives. In addition, Bach developed a thirty-ninth remedy, a composite of five blooms: star of Bethlehem (for shock), rock rose (for terror and panic), impatiens (for mental stress), cherry plum (for desperation), and clematis (for being bemused, far-away, and out-of-the-body); this he called the Rescue Remedy, and he describes using it mainly in crises for near-drowned seamen washed ashore, for victims of automobile accidents, for shock from injury, fright, dental surgery, and other crises—always with miraculous results.[19] As often is the case with vitalistic medicines, the exact bound-

*Fruit
and seed
formation of
the four fruits
related to
the rose*

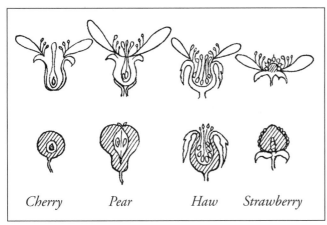

Cherry   Pear   Haw   Strawberry

aries of application are unclear. Bach devotees may use Rescue Remedy several times a day, for minor pain (rubbed on the skin), close calls in traffic, business disappointments, and other unpleasant incidents—much as primal screams are used to root out traumas before they settle in, or as a Muslim cleanses himself anew with a prayer at appointed hours. Where there are no overdoses and the microdose is a dynamo of "subnuclear" power, the patient himself must decide how he wishes to ritualize his arrangement with the vital force.

Current Bach practitioners distinguish between homeopathy and the flower remedies on the basis that a homeopathic microdose touches the astral and electromagnetic planes of the body whereas a Bach Flower Remedy "speaks" through the archetypal language of botany to emotional conditions, which *are* flowers on another plane of manifestation.

With only thirty-nine remedies and thumbnail sketches of these ethnocentrically derived, the Bach lexicon runs the risk of seeming reductive and simplistic. For that reason some have attempted, over the objections of purists, to expand the system. A group in California has developed its own system of native essences, and one could imagine equivalent systems from Australia, Madagascar, or Japan. There are millions of planetary flower essences, some of which seem to have no curative properties in this system. But why, if they are all fashioned by the same archetypal forces of nature? The answer of the purists is that the original Bach set is a "perfect state of the art"; Bach found the system whole. Since, like a piece of music, it works as a whole, to attempt to enlarge it is only to diminish it.[20]

MYTHOLOGICAL AND ENERGY medicines have always been gleaned by cultures from native environments and symbols in a direct attempt to cure sick people. They were maintained only when people were healed through or synchronous with them. For indigenous reasons they were once assigned to gods and, later, temples. Our own culture prefers formularies, hence homeopathy and the Bach. Yet, as implied in Chapter Five, homeopathic and flower-essential principles—insofar

as they exist at all—have probably always had effects within other categories of definition.

For vintage empirical medicine, the goal is not to explain nature, which may ultimately be an impossible task, but to relieve and reenergize the ailing. Indigenous cultures honored the totemic pantheon and received remedies as gifts. We hunt them down or extrapolate them from the algebra of possibility. Bach did not sentimentally ascribe spirit to flower blooms in sun upon water; Hahnemann did not propose increased power in microdoses because of belief in some atomistic principle. They simply parted veils until something moved on the other side.

Lost Sciences

Vitalistic and paraphysical modes of inquiry continue to expand toward imagined new energy sources. Current fashion is to try to link all energetic anomalies and seemingly acausal relationships to one another—the mysteriously forming crop circles, the putative "intelligence" of plants, UFOs, etc., with more ancient systems of bioplasmic

and astral bodies, the pyramids of Egypt and Mesoamerica, and other edifices and lei lines on the sacred-geometry grid as one field of cosmic energy. At this point, biological (or chemical) vitalism has come all the way around its circle to meet the ghosts and sigils of hermetic vitalism back at its Stone Age beginnings.

During the 1980s a group of astronomers, geologists, and computer scientists discovered on a pair of NASA photographs taken in 1976 a complex of "monuments" on Mars (highlighted by the aforementioned mesa resembling a human face) and subsequently "decoded" their shapes and relationships to "reveal" the existence of a physical force originating from tetrahedronal geometry and ostensibly responsible for sunspots, the red oval on Jupiter, similar cyclones on Saturn and Neptune, and the volcanoes of the Hawaiian Island chain—hence, able to provide almost unlimited energy.[21] The Martian "Sphinx" explicitly reinvokes the Eygptian Pyramids—and the question of how those mammoth blocks of stone got raised and set with such precision.

The so-called "lost science" is one of our favorite riddles. People attribute it to Atlanteans, visitors from outer space, and even ancient Mayans and Easter Islanders. In various versions, these magi are said to

Vitalist Science and Energy Medicine

255

be able to fly between star systems by going through suns and to hoist massive weights using intrinsic energy of the Earth and certain shapes (like pyramids) by a system we no longer have (hence, the late inclusion of Martian tetrahedrons in this tale). Doctors in the same tradition now supposedly dissolve tumors like sugar in water, and their fellow gardeners grow tomatoes as big as cantaloupes, both of them tapping power grids of the cosmos that pass through the Earth's field. These lei lines deliver energy that could not be corrupting or polluting the way we have corrupted and wasted our material fuels and sources of power.

This New Age legacy, like Castaneda's tale, is also a myth, neither true nor false, but carrying information of another order. Infallibly it says more about us than "them," for if such powers existed, we have certainly lost them, as well as our own sense of our place in time and history. If the powers did not exist, something else did, or might still, and we are equally cut off from that.

Even if one does not accept its historical validity, our transhistorical myth of Atlantean wisdom is a poignant metaphor for our dissociation from vital energies. The notion of a global Palaeolithic shamanic culture is its liberal humanitarian alternative. While the Atlanteans imply a galactic civilization and extraterrestrial visits to this planet, Stone Age science endows us with a Fourth World lineage evolving through the earliest human bands to the ancient peoples of prehistory. The former gives us almost infinitely knowledgeable non-human teachers; the latter places legendary wizards in our past. But neither are presently available upon summons, crop circles and channeled wisdom notwithstanding. We must still train our own doctors.

I will pick up this theme again in earnest in Volume Two, Chapter One.

Afterword on Vitalistic Medicine

Homeopathy, acupuncture, chiropractic, curing by sound and vision, faith healing, and their allies have certainly not been proven even mildly effectual by the mainstream scientific credentialing process. In fact, there have been innumerable assertions by quackbusters that all of these processes are now conclusively debunked. Proof or disproof of this genre changes nothing. We do not live long enough and are not objective enough to see the universe blink.

I believe we are energy bodies. That is, I believe we are more than tissue formed by cell growth and differentiation, or that tissue is imbued with a subtle *prana* current. But in our time this must be an expression of faith, not quantification. If you accept the existence of an energy body and have enough courage to set your star by it, then the above medicines are ultimately your true pharmacy (and true surgery). They are forerunners of an era (at least we might hope) in which men and women will aspire to be more than well-groomed machines.

But do not expect vitalism to replace technological medicine in this generation. Do not expect it even to engage professional allopathy in a substantial dialogue. Concede the present spoils to the AMA. Use vitalistic medicine only to treat actual disease. Cede the reign of quantity and proof to the neo-sophists and computer hacks.

The adherents of the scientific model of our existence are religiously fanatical in their dread of an unbounded universe of psyche and energy. For the weary scientist, far along in his professional life, death of spirit is his only hope, his only way out. So the two camps of a potential "planet medicine" remain substantially isolated. Vitalistic medicine operates without currency, and allopathy has become pure deficit spending. Some future generation will have to make the alchemical marriage.

(But, remember always, there are no guarantees in the world of spirit. There are at least limited guarantees in the search-and-destroy world. In the end one must make the bargain he or she can abide.)

Notes

1. Werner Heisenberg, "The Relationship Between Biology, Physics and Chemistry," in *Physics and Beyond,* trans. from the German by Arnold J. Pomerans (New York: Harper & Row, 1971), p. 113.

2. I. S. Shklovskii and Carl Sagan, *Intelligent Life in the Universe* (New York: Delta Books, 1967), p. 227.

3. Ibid., pp. 243–44.

4. Heisenberg, "The Relationship Between Biology, Physics and Chemistry," p. 114.

5. Ibid.

6. Pierre Teilhard de Chardin, *The Phenomenon of Man*, trans. from the French by Bernard Wall (New York: Harper and Row, 1959), p. 72.

7. Shklovskii and Sagan, *Intelligent Life in the Universe,* p. 184.

8. Frances A. Yates, *The Rosicrucian Enlightenment* (London: Routledge & Kegan Paul, 1972).

9. Frances A. Yates, *Giordano Bruno and the Hermetic Tradition* (Chicago: University of Chicago Press, 1964).

10. Paracelsus, quoted in Harris L. Coulter, *Divided Legacy: A History of the Schism in Medical Thought, Vol. I. The Patterns Emerge: Hippocrates to Paracelsus* (Washington, DC: Wehawken Book Company, 1975), p. 478.

11. A. E. Waite, trans., *The Hermetic and Alchemical Writings of Paracelsus the Great,* Vol. II (London: James Elliott, 1894), p. 59.

12. Ibid., pp. 22–23.

13. Ibid., p. 24.

14. For a full discussion of this topic, see Richard Grossinger, *Homeopathy: An Introduction for Skeptics and Beginners* (Berkeley, California: North Atlantic Books, 1993).

15. Edward C. Whitmont, *The Alchemy of Healing: Psyche and Soma* (Berkeley, California: North Atlantic Books, 1993), pp. 183–84.

16. Ibid., p. 184.

17. Deepak Chopra, *Quantum Healing: Exploring the Frontiers of Mind/Body Medicine* (New York: Bantam Books, 1989), p. 107.

18. Mary Buckley, "Feng Shui: The Art of Grace in Place," *New Dimensions Newsletter* (Spring, 1993), pp. 16–17.

19. Philip M. Chancellor, *Handbook of the Bach Flower Remedies* (London: C. W. Daniel Co., 1971).

20. From a conversation with Eric Love, Lela Center, Eureka, California (March 1982).

21. Richard C. Hoagland, *The Monuments of Mars: A City on the Edge of Forever* (Berkeley, California: North Atlantic Books, 1986).

CHAPTER EIGHT

Eurasian Medicine

Elements and Humors

THERE IS ANOTHER, far more ancient paradigm that resembles vitalism to such a degree that the two are regularly confused, but this science is based less on paraphysical energy than on the componential aspects of substance. Cross-culturally it has a variety of different names and versions; in its Western form these are usually summarized under elementalism.

Elemental philosophy proposes a lattice of morphological potential through which matter, life forms, mind, and spirit ceaselessly spawn and regenerate. "Elements" may describe either vital qualities of form, as they did in ancient Eurasia, or the structural-mechanical basis of matter, as they do in the periodic table of modern chemistry. Superficially, ancient elementalism seems like biological vitalism, but historically it lies at the basis of *both* vitalism and materialism (though it was of course itself preceded by uncountable forms of shamanism and other extinct medicines). The elements of contemporary science developed originally from the "elements" of prescientific philosophy.

The confusion is such that the famous (perhaps even infamous) biologist Jean Baptiste Lamarck is often misclassified as a vitalist because of his fire-based elementalism. Lamarck believed that living germ cells were informed not by vital energy but an elemental flame leading to life and "activity everywhere manifest":

In the fixed state, in coal, wood, or what will burn, fire is the principle of combustion. Conflagration is fire in its state of violent expansion, penetrating the pores of a burning body and ripping it to shreds.
Evaporation occurs when fire in a state of moderate expansion sur-
rounds molecules of water and bears them upward, so many tiny
molecular balloons, to rejoin the clouds where the specific gravity
of the water molecule encased in its light shell of fire balances that
of air.... And all the phenomena of light and heat, all the effects of
sun and atmosphere, are manifestations of fire in its different states,
forever striving to regain that which is natural.[1]

This is vintage elemental etiology.

The elemental principle is defined by its fusion of an intuition of the
mosaic basis of matter with the genesis of all phenomena from the
dynamic interplay of the mosaics. In that sense, modern physics and
chemistry represent a continuation of the search for more and more primal (if devitalized) mosaics with the aid of microscopes and computers.

As chemistry in the West became more sophisticated, many verifiable "vital" effects were reassigned (as properties) to compounds, and
later to molecules. Thus, traditional vitalistic aspects began to be translated into vectors of mere mechanical energy underlying biophysics.
The Periodic Chart reconfigured the repertoire of mosaics from four
or five integers to ninety-two, until gradually the ninety-two were themselves discovered to be combinations of more rudimentary particles,
which could be artificially altered to manufacture even more. All of the
original ninety-two (except the first two, hydrogen and helium, which
are star-born) assembled themselves from these more basic particles in
the cooling environment of the pre-Cambrian oceans. Our present
inquiry into their composition is governed by the technology of mag-
nification and belief systems based on quantitative reduction. The
ancient Eurasian elements, by contrast, were qualitative, energetic, and
philosophical, hence irreducible. They were also experiential and phenomenologically accessible, not the outcome of an exclusive tier of
experiments.

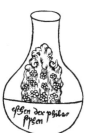

THE EASIEST MISUNDERSTANDING that one can have about the four original elements of Greek science is that they represented crude versions of earth, air, fire, and water—i.e., raw soil, gases, heat-light, and liquidity. Not only do true elemental forms exist prior to any manifestation, but even when manifested, they are never in absolute or pure form. Elements are always mixed with one another such that there is no substance that does not contain all four.

The earthen soil gives rise to a variety of plants, some of them a degree fiery, some of them cold and moist, some of them dense and clayey, some of them even airlike and ethereal. Elemental earth, air, fire, and water are then each expressed differentially in the roots, the branches, the flowers, the fruits, the tropisms, and again in the overall coherence of each plant and in the properties of medicines made from its parts.

In another example, we might note that while lightning is a warm and dry manifestation of fire, snow also has fire in it—cold and dry fire.

Even as we observe a cycle of hot light in the sky followed by mushrooms on damp bark, we feel these same elements circulating within us. The similarity between lightning and our nervous system, noted in Chapter Two, is a key factor in the selection of homeopathic phosphorus for treating neurological conditions (phosphorus contains an unusual amount of accessible elemental fire).

ELEMENTS EXPRESS THEMSELVES in human beings as humors. Just as it is a mistake to think of the Greek elements as merely forerunners of those in the Periodic Chart, it is an oversimplification to think of the humors as only the forerunners of a psychochemistry of the body. They portray fluidity, layering, melancholia, passion, sedateness, and so forth. They were phenomenologically discernible in prescientific times and they remain imaginal concepts today, particularly as expressions of personality traits and the psychosomatic relationships between negative emotions, such as anger and guilt, and chronic illnesses, such as ulcers and arthritis.

Metabolism is a function of the continuous homeostatic transformation of elements and humors into one another. Any excesses in lifestyle or diet will distort this process and cause a corresponding excess, of fluid or flesh, somewhere in the organism. Disease is first an elemental imbalance, afterwards a pathology. This paradigm does not recognize a distinction between neurosis and organic dysfunction. Environment, diet, constitution, and emotions all interact together.

The elements and humors are cosmic substantiating forces working on psychosomatic vectors. When they are simplified into animisms, they lose their multidimensional aspect and become mere metaphors.

One should also not misunderstand elemental terminology as primitive; it provides an elegant framework for understanding the interaction of factors that result in the genesis of human organisms, their constitutional differences, and the gradual etiology of imbalances leading to diseases. Likewise, it postulates cure on the basis of precise energetic diagnoses. Using observations of elemental gradients, the physician observes and analyzes the being as a kind of superconcentrated weather

"Water from Combustion" from Michael Faraday, The Chemical History of a Candle

system of impermanent substances rather than as either a linear sequence of mechanical responses with functional requirements or a pure psychospiritual manifestation. Gerrit Lansing writes (of the Ayurvedic humors):

> After learning to recognize them in one's own daily body experience the conditions they signify become verifiable without necessity to reduce their range of application by translation.[2]

Unlike many vitalists, elemental philosophers do not assume we can draw energy simply and spontaneously onto the physical plane. Acupuncture needles are metal or bone, and herbs have a basis in soil. All elemental medicines must contact hard substance, if only the original tincture from which an alchemical seed is derived or the flesh of a practitioner's or patient's body. The San Pedro cactus of Peru which, according to the shaman Eduardo Calderón, transfers its light and vibration to the patient and locks with his or her aura to drive all physical and mental aspects of alienation to the surface, originates in the physical properties of the desert.[3]

Even if herbal remedies activate vital forces, if needles and fingers summon energy to the *chakras,* a person must still integrate these processes on a physical plane. The elemental system is one of ongoing embodiment and transmutation; in fact, it literally depicts an incarnating process, from stars to lakes to life-forms. There are no short-cuts via spirit. Nothing is transcendent until something has been transcended. Yoga remains a valued healing technique within elemental medicine for just this reason.

Ancient Medicine

THE RESEARCH TECHNOLOGY of allopathy had its beginnings in many branches of practical ethnomedicine. Yet the Hippocratic Corpus, assigned by historians to the fifth and fourth centuries B.C., is the usual recognized starting point of Western medicine. This body

of literature is more accurately described as a library than a book. It
was certainly not written by one person, and it is likely that the historical Hippocrates did not write any of it. Its oldest extant sections
are vitalist and humoral, but it also carries the echo of divine medicine. The Greek gods, who were once Egyptian and pre-Egyptian gods
(who are still the *daemonic* intelligences in the West), are the closest
affiliation our medicine has, at the Greeks' already late date, with the
supernatural sources of more ancient peoples. In the words of an
unknown Mediterranean shaman-scientist: "The healing art involves
a weaving of a knowledge of the gods into the texture of the physician's
mind."[4]

The therapeutic systems and anatomical beliefs of older Mediterranean civilizations were, in essence, inherited by the Hippocratics as
a medley of blatantly contradictory formulae, which they adapted and
transformed with the ultimate goal of clarification and cohesion. What
the Corpus represents is the residue of formal medical knowledge at
its time, along with speculations on that knowledge by early philosophers and scientists. It stands in relation to medicine much as Homer's
Iliad and *Odyssey* stand in relation to mythohistory, marking boundaries outside of which we cannot go, no matter how many single islands
and planets we discover that were unknown to the Greeks. It frames
our axioms and proposes our basic dilemmas. It remains the reason
why truly alternative medicines receive scant attention.

The most primitive aspects of the Greek pantheon are vitalist and
humoral. The universe was said to be compounded of four elements
(Earth, Air, Fire, and Water); the attraction and repulsion of these led
to complex substances, including the four humors, each possessing its
own vital force:

> The human body contains blood [the hottest humor, also watery,
> and regarded by some as a combination of all the other humors],
> phlegm [the coldest, and watery], yellow bile [hot and dry], and
> black bile [cold and dry, and sometimes regarded as a toxin rather
> than a natural humor]: these constitute the nature of the body, and

through them a man suffers pain or enjoys health. A man enjoys the most perfect health when these elements are duly proportioned to one another in power, bulk, and manner of compounding, so that they are mingled as excellently as possible. Pain is felt when one of these elements is either deficient or excessive, or when it is isolated in the body without being compounded with the others.[5]

Humoral metabolism is a field of counterbalancing forces:

For when an element is isolated and stands by itself, not only must the place which it left become diseased, but the place where it stands in a flood must, because of the excess, cause pain and distress. In fact, when more of an element flows out of the body than is necessary to get rid of superfluity, the emptying causes pain. If, on the other hand, it be to an inward part that there takes place the emptying, the shifting and the separation from other elements, the man certainly must, according to what has been said, suffer from a double pain, one in the place left, and another in the place flooded.[6]

This is the same equation one finds in Taoist medicine based on meridians.

Man and woman, made of shifting humors, were immune to direct pathology; what they experienced was a change in elemental relationships activated by a disease tendency at their cores. The symptomatic characteristics of the individual diseases—often potent or even deadly—were still auxiliary phenomena caused by the reflex of the vital force in initiating cure. This etiology sets Hippocratic and homeopathic medicine clearly apart from allopathy.

When a humoral imbalance occurs, the vital force is naturally excited into action and begins transforming the excess humor, a process called "coction" (boiling) or "pepsis" in recognition of its similarity to both cooking heat and peptic excitation. This is the basis of all healing, including the migration of the gods to bodily functions. The disease is literally the message, i.e., the medicine. A physician can only stimulate or deflect this intrinsic process. He cannot provide the external agency for it. He observes and interprets the character of the coction and intercedes at the moment of crisis with a medicine sympathetic to the disease (i.e., healing) process. He selects its intensity as well as its type: too weak or too early a response might retard the accumulating current, and too strong a dose might snap the vital force *(physis)* and injure or kill the patient.

As the disease "cooks" (with its succession of prodromes), digestion (assimilation) improves and the pathology gradually dissipates. The physician's skill lies in interpreting the kind and degree of coction and picking a medicine similar to it, i.e., which provokes a symptomology *like* that of the disease. Homeopathic medicine is based on precisely this formula, using microdoses instead of herbal mixtures or mechanical treatments.

Generally speaking, if a doctor interceded on behalf of the vital force, then he prescribed hot baths for fever, laxatives for diarrhea, "cold" herbs for chills—in other words, encouraging a reaction which was trying to happen anyway. The implication was that symptoms bear no fixed relationships to diseases. A fever does not mean that a disease is hot; it also does not mean that it is *not* hot. The disease is unknowable. Its cause is a spiritual or cosmic wobble, a draft or a spook. *Pneuma* (breath or air) was but one primordially acknowledged source: "Outside it causes epidemic diseases, and when it enters the body with the food it causes diseases usually ascribed to regimen."[7]

The Hippocratic diagnostician tracked coction by its evacuations of raw humoral stuff:

> ... thick, thin, black, scanty urine ... watery, uncompounded, unconcocted, bilious, greasy, green frothy, crude, scanty, or copious stools. The sputum is also examined for signs of compounding. The urine is a very important source of knowledge about the interior of the organism. Not only can it be thick, scanty, unconcocted or concocted, but the physician can derive further information from observation of the sediment deposited....
>
> The vomit is most useful which is most thoroughly compounded

266

of phlegm and bile, and it must not be too thick nor brought up in too great quantity.

   The perspiration and menstrual blood are also examined for signs of coction.[8]

All of these methods of diagnosis have been retained in some form in modern medicine, though by the latter decades of the twentieth century, laboratory analysis had all but replaced experiential observation and the specialist had supplanted the family doctor. That's how long the system survived. As recently as the 1950s, most doctors in the Western world still visited their patients' homes, literally sat at bedsides, and examined the disease *in situ,* including its urine, stools, etc. They may not have been looking for coction by name, but they were discerning the progress of the disease and the healing force according to an ancient legacy and craft based on coction.

   Though the humoral basis of Western medicine was maintained for centuries, it was redefined again and again, first by early Greek philosophers, including Plato and Aristotle, in terms of "rational" constructs; these were adopted as such by the Cnidian and Alexandrian schools of medicine and their successors and ultimately converted into a materialist version of healing *sans* a vital force. On the one hand, in keeping with the oldest aspect of the Hippocratic heritage, an empirically based tradition of medicine continued to treat individuals as elemental wholes animated by a *physis* and healed through the physician's enhancement of coction; on the other hand, a rationalist, proto-scientific tradition developed similar, even identical medical techniques solely on the basis of a search for universally applicable and fixed disease categories.

   Empiricists were not necessarily vitalists. They studied indications of diseases and their cures regardless of whether their agencies were spiritual or physical. It is a mistake likewise to equate the Rationalist School with pure materialism. Early on, its members were simply functional categorizers, model-makers, and incipient academicians; this included many religious and Fundamentalist vitalists. While Empiricists kept medicine an art of timing and disease a mystery, Rationalists sought to break out of all primitivisms and old-fashioned restraints and to take control of nature by broad theories and models of action.

Rationalists from ancient times have invented each next post-modern stage of medicine. They continued to streamline, simplify, and probe, and, although they did not overlook the more functional discoveries of the Empiricists, they tended to co-opt these for their own advancing technology.

The Empiricists treated symptoms as signs of imperceptible, inherently unknowable disease processes; the keynote of their medicine (revived as a motto by homeopaths in the nineteenth century) was: *there are no diseases, only sick individuals.* Meanwhile, advocates of the Rationalist school have continued to dissect corpses, develop taxonomies of pathology, and seek ever more proximate disease etiologies. Viewing diseases and their symptoms in ever simpler loops, they came to interpret the humors as mere mixtures of the four elements—little more than picturesque character types. Their goal was to locate the ultimate source of health and disease in entities much like the atoms proposed by Democritus. They were micro-hunters from the beginning.

To summarize:

Rationalists throughout history have sought the basis of human functioning more and more in laws also governing lifeless matter. They developed principles of healing that, if not directly based on laws of physics, were at least compatible with a definition of life as merely sophisticated mechanical chemistry. Their human body was a mechanism, later a machinery; thus, it had to obey rigorous laws of mechanics. Rationalists have thus simplified medicine to memorizable formulas.

Empiricists, by contrast, have endowed life with a special capacity to react with its environment and to protect and expand itself by means not limited to simple applications of thermodynamics. As noted, this does not mean that Empiricists were always Vitalists. Many Empiricists believed simply that living systems are so complex that they are able to develop unique levels of organization and sensitivity. The living organism of the Empiricists consolidates multiple expressions of the drive to go on living, responds creatively to environmental challenges, and makes both instantaneous and long-term corrections (or adaptations). Hence, its principles of cure must be based on the actual reactions of human beings in the world. They may not be adaptations of mechanical laws.

In keeping with this philosophy, the Empiricists generally regarded symptoms as beneficial, adjuncts to a cleansing process. Not only were symptoms not suppressed or eradicated in Empirical medicine, in many instances they were stimulated and enhanced. For the Rationalists, symptoms *were* the diseases, hence were harmful and had to be quenched or eliminated so that the body could resume its normal operation. Homeopathy is an elegant case of the attempt to restore health by stimulating symptoms and fortifying the patient's natural powers. Allopathy is a contrasting example of the attempt to relieve the patient of a disease by knocking out the disease's symptomology.

Additionally, the Empiricists believed that each person's symptoms were unique and followed a path and process intrinsic to that individual alone. They could be interpreted only by a physician experienced in the art of pathology and cure. Empiricists were certainly aware of the resemblances of symptoms from case to case and person to person, especially during epidemics, but they focused on individual manifestations of even common symptoms in order to tailor a remedy for each person. Each new disease was, in a manner of speaking, the first appearance of that event in the universe—a creature never seen before, never to be seen again. The credo was always: no diseases, only sick people. Empiricists practiced an unusual phenomenology of viewing each illness as a single event subject only to its own intrinsic developmental pattern and not routinely comparable to any similar event.

The Rationalists tended to ignore individual symptoms and identify conditions only by common symptoms through which they could be assigned to recognized disease categories. Each individual case was merely a repetition of a category. The presumption was that the same precise diseases originated in everyone in more or less the same way, had comparable prognoses, and could be cured by identical means. The Rationalists opened the gates to mass-produced, industrial medicine and ultimately marginalized individual doctors relying on intuition and skill. The Empiricists kept alive the flame of natural and holistic medicine—cures based on treating and invigorating whole organisms.

The Rationalist lineage of Western physicians, while preserving a relic of elemental and spiritual medicine in their rhetoric of healing and medical ethics, obliterated its reality in an obsession of concretization. The observance of elements passed utterly into biochemistry, and the subsequent evolution of medicine attached itself to microbiology, where it adopted the drama of morbific agents and antibodies to replace the harmonics of humoral balance. This is our present religion.

The Empiricist lineage was initially overwhelmed by the momentum of allopathy and the liturgy of the industrial revolution. Its adherents were gradually identified only with the ranks of quackery. The apparent success of Rationalist disease categories has sometimes made it difficult to discriminate viable, scientifically empirical treatments from merely superstitious and inept doctoring. But with the recent development of alternative medical institutions, Empiricism is returning in legion. Medicines with long traditions of empirical cures are being refined and institutionalized in more accountable ways. Without knowledge of the traditional underpinnings of these treatments, many presume naively that they are inventions of the counterculture and the New Age. In fact, Empirical medicine is primeval and traditional; industrial medicine is an offshoot of current deterministic philosophy and a relative newcomer.

THE ALEXANDRIANS OF the fourth century B.C. were among the earliest European medical experimenters. Erasistratos of Julis not only described the structure of the brain and the valves of the heart, but "he performed vivisection on condemned criminals and is recorded as having carried out the first biological experiment, so to speak, *in vitro:* desirous of proving that part of the body's substance is exhaled with the *pneuma,* he placed a bird in a glass jar without feeding it; upon removal, the bird and its excrements were found to weigh less than the bird alone at the outset of the experiment."[9]

Erasistratos conceived the body as "a porous solid through which matter and air can flow freely in corpuscular forms. Thus the ambient air enters the lungs and passes from there to the arteries. It flows through the arteries and is then exhaled through the body's pores.... [Food] is not digested but is ground up mechanically by peristalsis and aided by the *pneuma.*"[10] This mechanical model floated around for over a millennium, throughout the entirety of the so-called "Dark Ages," half accepted yet always hybridized with different contradictory beliefs, until it was seized, isolated, developed to its logical conclusions, and converted into medical orthodoxy in relatively modern times. In truth, the skeleton of technological medicine was unveiled in extremely ancient times, but it waited for a whole civilization to pass before it achieved its destiny.

By the first century B.C., the Rationalists were in the driver's seat; they had turned humoral philosophy "into a rigidly determined mechanical theory of causation."[11]

> Asclepiades laid the groundwork for this doctrine (which was brought to its culmination by Thessalos) by reintroducing atomic theory into physiology.... In health the fluids flow at a normal rate through [Erasistratos'] solid. If the pores are too wide open, i.e., if the atoms are moving too fast in the solid parts of the body, the fluids will flow too freely. By the same token, when the atoms are not moving fast enough, but are too close together, the fluids do not move rapidly enough through the pores.[12]

This left two polar disease states, that of relaxation (or *fluxus*) and that of restriction. A third state alternated between *status laxus* and *status strictus.*

Galen, a second-century Roman physician, wrote the corpus that rests at the basis of Western medicine. He summarized all the medical doctrines of his time—Hippocratic, Aristotelian, Platonic, Alexandrian, etc. Experimental science was well underway by then, and he presumed, innocently enough, that the growing philosophical breach in medicine (between the art of healing and research) was superficial and temporary, and thus he solved it in a naive way. He modernized the elements and the vital force by fully materializing them. Anatomy, physiology, and logic became his cornerstones. With a solid doctrine of liturgical authority behind him, he expected doctors to work from theory to observation to new theory, adding techniques only in the context of existing paradigms. One was to infer the nature of the disease solely from what was already known of the body. No one could make radical new discoveries. The ancestors were the true physicians, and the weight of tradition was king.

Galen's writings succeeded, more by assumption than proof, in transferring the powers of the elements to organs. That is, the meaning of the vital force no longer existed except as it was expressed by the individual organs through the humors. As Deepak Chopra reminds us, "... the whole system of organs, tissues, and so on was set up intellectually to make the body easier to classify."[13] It was never meant to replace the body.

By Galen's principles each organ had its own behavior, its peculiar combination of qualities. Yet, when faced with the difficulty of explaining contradictory actions of some organs, Galen returned to the unity of the vital force. By going full circle, he came out nowhere. Ultimately, he recommended collecting more data, licensing physicians, and, in general, institutionalizing medical authority. Even though he did not propose a consistent general theory of medicine, his mere attempt to do so *was* the general theory, and its precedent was assumed ever after. He wrote some thirty volumes of medical folklore which became the "literature."

We need not take issue with the scholarly content of Galen's work, only with the author's assumption that medical sanction conferred the unique ability to cure sick people. Yet, so convincing was Galen's synthesis that it has survived and absorbed all attacks and given the profession its historical identity: Not that doctors today see things exactly as Galen did, but those organs he proposed as the locations and centers of bodily process remain our general images of the sites of metabolism and pathology. Their collective mechanism is what mainstream medicine has observed in place of the healing force, and in place of the cure, too.

European Medicine

THE GREEKS OF the Cnidian and Alexandrian schools, and later Galen and the Romans, gradually synthesized "laws" arising from notions of elemental and vital energy in the body with laws arising from their latest theories of chemical and mechanical relationships. Then the countries of the West, as they passed through feudalism, rural theocracy, mercantilism, and the birth of science, eventually adopted the Roman medical and legal orthodoxy and carried it to Africa, India, and America. Galen's medicine became global medicine.

By the eighteenth century the Rationalists had turned medicine into a branch of chemistry and come to view the organism as a solid endowed with nervous properties, the sources of which "lie concealed beyond the reach of the knife and the microscope."[14] They completed the loss of elementalism by identifying essence with qualities such as sensitivity, excitability, nervous energy, etc. This synthesis finally subsumed elemental energy in materiality. A vital force continued to exist as a philosophical construct, or as the piety of religion (the hand of God or Jesus) behind healing. Doctors observed it rhetorically rather than actually. Most doctors still think that they observe it actually (i.e., as the body's healing power) because the rhetorical observance has fully merged with the language of popular chemistry and physics. Even in the modern hospital, surgeons and specialists invoke Hippocrates and the body's healing power. But they do not practice them.

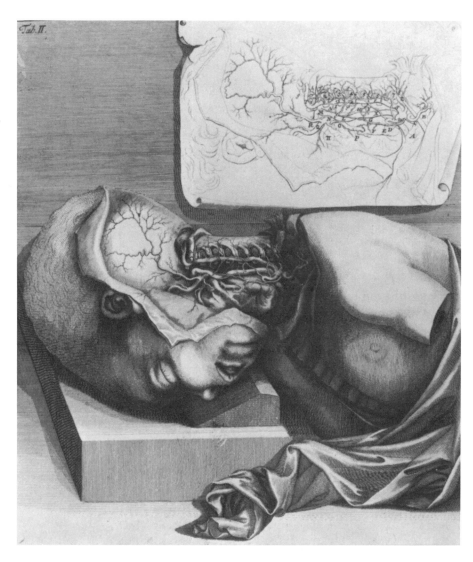

*Plate from
the* Icones
Anatomicae
*(1743–56) of
Albrecht von
Haller. See
also page 276.*

Meanwhile, all during the scientific revolution, the Empiricists continued to search for specifics by trial and error and to encourage "the fevers, evacuations, skin eruptions, etc. which occur in disease [as] part of [the] healing effort."[15] They were remarkably prescient in foreseeing the dead end toward which Rationalism was heading: "All that anatomy can do is only to show us the gross and sensible parts of the body, or the vapid and dead juices, all which, after the most diligent search, will be no more able to direct a physician how to cure a disease than how to make a man."[16] As they advanced beyond the humoral theories of the Hippocratics, they developed new elemental sciences based on derivations of the vital force (the *Archeus* of Jan Van Helmont and the *Anima* of Georg Ernst Stahl among these). They maintained the pagan apostasy that "the physician's intellect cannot penetrate inside the *physis* to cognize the sources of health and disease . . . [and] that the least and subtle texture of the solid and fluid parts of the living body is hidden from us and will ever remain hidden, not only from the senses but from the edge of the human mind,"[17]

> . . . though we cut into their inside, we see but the outside of things, and make but a new *superficies* for ourselves to stare at.[18]

The gap between medical paradigms was growing even as doctors continued to presume a single fraternity. By 1819 a German medical professor could write:

> We are now in a time when the most varied systems are blended and amalgamated. The mechanical and chemical views of the organism have joined and subordinated—or at least taken a position beside— the dynamico-vitalistic view. The humoral and solidist theories have joined together and been reduced to the idea of the reciprocity of the solid and liquid parts of the organism. The individual organs and functions are recognized both as integral parts of the organism and as manifestations of its life, and the seat and essence of the various diseases are sought in them. . . . The evacuating and irritating, the depleting and strengthening, as well as many other opposite methods of treatment stand peacefully side by side in general therapy and reciprocally restrict one another; our learned contemporaries make use of all these systems in the various diseases, although each one may have his own preference.[19]

The Rationalists then seized the discovery of the cell as their ultimate vehicle of triumph. Here was a new level of life seeming to claim

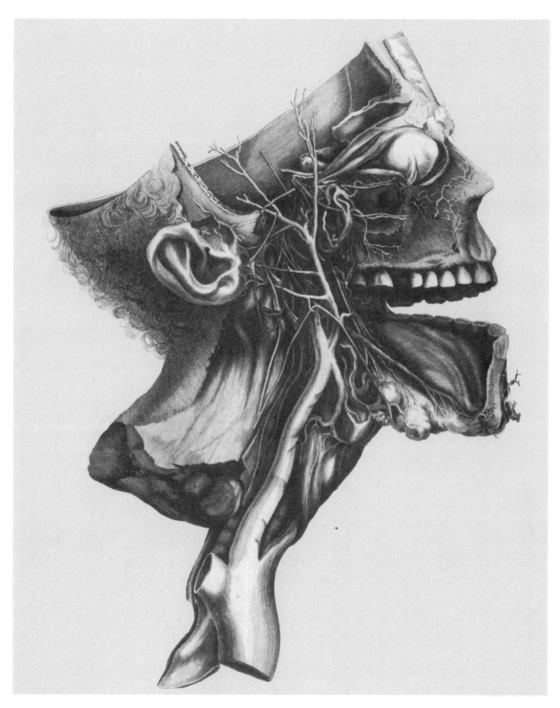

276

the last ghost of the vital force from the humors. Consisting conveniently of "both liquid and solid parts,"[20] an integral organized atomism of life, subject entirely to mechanical and chemical laws yet fluid and dynamic, the cell provided a self-contained, reproducing layer between the simple motions of the molecules and the complex chemistry of the organs. According to Rudolf Virchow (1821–1902), "Life activity is cell activity; its uniqueness is the uniqueness of the cell. . . . The cell is really the ultimate morphological unit in which there is any manifestation of life, and . . . we must not transfer the locus of intrinsic action to any point above the cell."[21] It is not far from here to bacteria, infections, enzymes, immune globulins, allergic responses, the photoactivity of compounds in the primitive oceans, and Francis Crick's attempt to reduce the soul to nerve action. Life became Darwin's thermodynamic accident. Pathology with its invading diseases and the immune system with its defenses became opposing forces in a morality play of darkness and chaos against civilization and progress. The rule of contraries utterly supplanted the stimulation of coction by similars (except in the renegade branch of medicine that found its eventual destiny in homeopathy, osteopathy, and the revival of Taoist medicine in the West). The allopath's perennial arguments were the acme of reasonableness and remain so today:

> If, for example, an artery is open, we clearly must not favor nature which makes the blood come out and leads to death. We must act in the opposite direction, stop the hemorrhage, and save a life. Just so, when a patient has an attack of septicemia, we must act against nature and stop the fever if we mean to cure our patient.[22]

Medicine in the West has reaped from this logic a destiny of dissection, vivisection, and experimental chemistry. Of course the outcome did not show itself immediately, but with each discovery—alkalis and acids, the circulation of blood, the mechanics of motor and sensory nerves, the biology of cells, bacteria, antibodies, viruses, penicillin, etc.— a momentum of wonderment and new success gathered, unimagined vistas opened, and technology became the indispensable oracle and handmaiden of healing. Our humors finally became proteins, nucleic acids, and nucleoproteins, themselves constructed of amino acids and nucleotides. Our diseases became complex living organisms capable of mutating to provide ever new varieties. Biology was understood variously in terms of antigenic, allergic, and other metabolic reactions. We perfected how to maintain life in the complex and toxic civilization we were concurrently creating.

Medicine is now headed at full speed toward not even chemistry but physics where we will become the *reductio ad absurdum* of quantum particle reactions. We have traveled, like fabled cinema voyagers, down the sea of blood and encountered the viscera, fibers, and cellular monsters that make us up. We have viewed the ultimate pandemonium of health and disease in its madcap microcosm and have given names of various vintages and proportions to its nightmarish battles—tuberculosis, cancer, lupus, chronic fatigue syndrome, AIDS. Yet there is no consistent therapeutic resolution on this level. We are now truly obsessed by the forces and effects of pathology and their proximate chemical traces rather than by the mysterious homeostasis that jells and curdles us from seed and restores us to health despite our layers of dissonance and fragmentation.

The tradition of energetic healing has never been defeated or disgraced in open battle. It is simply out of fashion. The modern bias toward visible demonstration and proof has grown into a cult. We have inherited the hunger of our forebears for this one kind of knowledge, and we have built a world in which to enjoy its ever and ever more dazzling fruits.

Karl Menninger describes the state of affairs just past the turn of the century:

> What I got out of medical school was the conviction that the world was full of healthy human beings, and that now and then a victim was struck down by a cruel blow from an unheeding Nature—an infestation, a lurking bacterium, a malignant cell. Now and then an

inexplicable perversity seized the liver or the pancreas or the bone marrow. As a result, a *"disease"* developed and a patient appeared on the doorstep of the physician.... Disease, as I viewed it, and I think I fairly accurately caught the spirit of my preceptors, was an entirely unwanted, useless, purposeless misfortune, acquired inadvertently through an unfortunate concatenation of forces emanating from the best of all possible worlds or from the defective architecture of a hereditary constitution.[23]

Homeopathy, psychiatry, acupuncture, and osteopathy have all confronted this monolith, but its attraction has been enough at times even to suck them in and convert them, by degrees, to itself.

The Roots of Alternative Medicine

As we saw in the last chapter, many European scientists of the Renaissance adopted the legend of the Greeks as missionaries of an older, hence possibly more authentic medicine. Again and again, in different Rosicrucian and alchemical guises, they tried (and now we try) to recover first rites, sometimes from Egyptians (or imaginations of them via Gnostic and other occult lore), sometimes from lingering Druid influences or contemporary witches, and eventually (in recent generations) from the more exotic magi of the East. Over time, cohesions of lineage and ancestry have become blurred. On the level of myth and magic, Roman and Celtic, Egyptian and Persian, Chinese and Arabic have become as if one occult body of work. Even now, Taoist and Gnostic sages seem collaborators in the remote past; their quite distinct legacies fuse.

The physician who stood historically at the crossroads of these esoteric traditions was Paracelsus, a Swiss hermetic scientist (1493–1541), originally Theophrastus Bombastus von Hohenheim (he took the name of his predecessor Celsus—a noted critic of Rationalism—and thereby placed himself squarely outside the Roman synthesis). Despite the ridicule sometimes heaped on him, Paracelsus was an early superstar—

charismatic, unruly, larger than life—one of those rare individuals who stands between shattered worlds and fuses them for a moment of time. He was a more accomplished medicine man than any of his known contemporaries not because of feats of magic but because his learning and experience encompassed a dimension of both scholarship and street knowledge lacking in scholastic circles. He embodied the logos of Western medical learning and inquiry plus everything else that was available from Arabic, Persian, Oriental, and proto-Indo-European sources. In truth, Islamic and Hindu culture had developed the scientific aspects of Greek medicine much farther than feudal Europe. So, in the role of an itinerant healer, Paracelsus explored Eastern Europe and the Mediterranean, seeking out scholars, peasants, sorcerers, and hermits alike, and considering everything, including local folk cures. Whatever he culled he later tested and practiced. Like a snowball, the further he traveled the more massive he became. He viewed so many different illnesses in different climates and at different levels of society and read so many obscure manuscripts that he became Europe's "barefoot healer."

Paracelsus considered the Romans and their heirs squanderers and despoilers of ancient medicine:

> I am Theophrastus, and greater than those to whom you liken me;
> I am Theophrastus, and in addition I am *monarchia medicorum,*
> monarch of physicians, and I can prove to you what you cannot
> prove.... Let me tell you this: every little hair on my neck knows

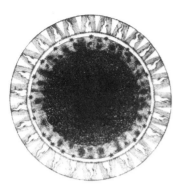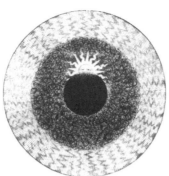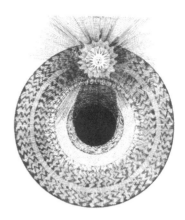

more than you and all your scribes, and my shoebuckles are more learned than your Galen and Avicenna, and my beard has more experience than all your high colleges.[24]

Paracelsus had the arrogance of one who walked the walk. He gathered enough hands-on experience to consider himself far above the isolated medical establishment. He not only summarized the mediaeval hermetic tradition; he taught himself diverse other traditions, and he gained access to both the Hippocratic and pre-Hippocratic corpus as it was honored and maintained outside the Graeco-Roman orbit:

> I went not only to the doctors, but also to barbers, bathkeepers, learned physicians, women, and magicians who pursue the art of healing; I went to alchemists, to monasteries, to nobles and common folk, to the experts and the simple.[25]

Paracelsus was an alchemist in the purest sense: he believed that all matter was alive, even minerals and stones; he accepted the possibility of the transmutation of substances into radically different substances. His universe was astral. The stars and planets travel in paths beyond the Earth, but that is only in their physical manifestations. Their inner harmonic progression radiates within the organ systems and among stones and herbs. The duty of the physician is to discover the hidden virtues of these things and to extract from them their astrally sown elixirs.

Eurasian Medicine

Paracelsus translated the Aristotelian version of the four elements into a system of three primal matrices: mercury, the raw material; sulphur, the luminous force perfected in gold; and salt, "the irreducible ash which remains when organic matter is tried by fire."[26] For him, the whole of macrocosm and microcosm were born of these three primordial substances; "thus man, too, is nothing but mercury, sulphur, and salt."[27] And, "basically there are only three kinds of medicine and three kinds of illness . . . each *medicus* will remember to give mercury to mercurial diseases, salt to saline disease, sulphur to sulphuric diseases."[28] Yet from just this triunity he developed a diverse armamentarium of medicines that passed muster among later pharmacists, including ones out of sulphur, calomel, copper, arsenic, and lead.

Paracelsus' scientific legacy can be confusing, for, while he is considered a father of chemistry, his alchemical experimentation contributed in equal measure to a guild of divination. When his record is viewed in retrospect, it would appear in fact that he attempted two quite different types of remedies, one we might call "conventional herbal," that is, mixtures of vegetable oils, ground plant parts, spices, liquors, etc., presented in his writings as ordinary recipes; and the other, astral and alchemical, based on the exotic extraction of vital qualities of metals like antimony and tin and then the long-term coction of

them under low-grade heat. The former summarized the traditional formulas of European and Arabic pharmacy and have a continuity with modern-day herbal prescriptions and drugs; the latter required the spiritualization of inorganic matter by activation of the vital force and provided one of Samuel Hahnemann's templates for the invention of homeopathy.

Certain common features define all vitalistic pharmacies: the liberation of medicinal potency from a quintessential, potentized form of original substance (which may not itself be therapeutic at all: compare raw metallic mercury to either alchemically or homeopathically prepared mercury); the conversion of matter into energy; the priority of quality over quantity; and the prescription of remedies according to astrological, geomantic, or constitutional systems of signs and signatures. Whether or not such a process is possible, Paracelsus marks the watershed of the vitalistic pharmacy known as alchemy. Using ovens, alembics, decanters, and the like, and following magical equations written in the language of the king and queen, and sun and moon, he isolated not just silver, but the "silver of silver," the "gold of gold," the "sulphur of sulphur," all of which were elemental substances. These are experiments still awaiting the Nobel Prize in chemistry, for virtually no one since has brought them to fruition, at least in a public context.

This genre of pharmacy was revived most fully not by Paracelsus' immediate followers (who tended to pursue merely the chemical half of his equations) or by Samuel Hahnemann, but in the early twentieth century by Rudolf Steiner in his preparation of anthroposophical potions using astrological correspondences, signatures of color and sound, and elemental principles of transmutation. There have also been a number of later attempts to prepare the metallic elixirs. Paralab, a

1970s laboratory in West Jordan, Utah, near Salt Lake City, founded by Frater Albertus (the so-called "alchemist of the Rocky Mountains") and named for Paracelsus, purportedly manufactured a variety of astral remedies during its heyday. I have heard many second-hand and mythologized rumors about replication of these experiments in New Mexico; Vancouver, British Columbia; and Portland, Oregon—always something like a conventional laboratory in the front room (ostensibly not attracting the attention of illicit-drug enforcers) and "spiritual" gold equal to the national debt stored in a basement or barn.

The practice of occult medicine can sometimes sponsor a dogmatic regime of sterile divine vapors or pellucid journeys through ethereal space. Paracelsus gives us the other side; he took on the role of the artist-baker-pharmacist who cultivates the slumbering seed in the heart of material and transforms it into a medicine so potent it is simultaneously fire and water, molten and vegetable, organic and stellar. Colors of burning metals ignite in their flasks; trees and flowers spring up individually from protean seeds. Paracelsus honored the wetness of water and the fieriness of fire, the feminine and masculine "semen" of the minerals, the elemental riot of blossoms in the spring, the golden luminosity of the Sun, the lunar phosphorescence of silver, and so on. He remarked that it was preferable to know one herb in the meadow absolutely, root and flower and seasons, than to gaze piously on the whole meadow.

He reclaimed for medicine its folk origins, and at the same time, he took it forward into the age of experimentation. He lived an ancient law perhaps more seminal than the Hippocratic Oath: "The art of medicine is rooted in the heart. If your heart is false, you will also be a false physician; if your heart is just, you will be a true physician."[29]

AFTER PARACELSUS' REMEDIES were reassigned to chemical reactions and the law of contraries, iatrochemistry took over medicine. A host of physicians [Jan Baptista Van Helmont (1578–1644), Thomas Sydenham (1624–1689), Giorgio Baglivi (1668–1707), Georg Ernst Stahl (1660–1734), and Theophile Bordeu (1722–1776)] preserved vitalist empiricism by modernizing (and at times Christianizing) it. They rescued elementalism from Platonism and neo-Platonic Rosicrucianism and delivered it alternately to God and Cartesian geometry in a variety of guises: biomagnetic forces, the spirituality of blood, fermentation as *concoctio,* the spleen as "sensitive soul," etc. Van Helmont, for instance, "accepted the *physis* as an agent of cure: 'truly the natures themselves have been known of old to be the physiciannesses of disease.' But the *physis* is part of the pagan dispensation and thus can no longer remain the sole instrument available to the body. So he hypothesized a second, Christian, vital force, which, although parallel to the *physis* and often indistinguishable from it, was nonetheless different."[30]

But Vitalism and Empiricism did not disappear. As their alchemical and Cartesian dialects became marginal, their essences were fused in a singular medicine so vast and radical we have not yet grasped its terms today. It was Samuel Hahnemann who proposed the next grand synthesis on the scale of Paracelsus: homeopathy was an occult medicine written in scientific terminology. By contrast with Paracelsus the hermetic alchemist, Hahnemann was a strict vitalistic pharmacist seeking a class of energy based on algebraic principles. Alchemical medicine had plumbed the astral roots of matter through chemistry; it was muddy, metallic, and volatile. Homeopathic medicine was a prism compared to a forge; it got rid of substance altogether in order to climb the invisible octaves of spirit in matter.

When Hahnemann initiated his therapeutics at the turn of the nineteenth century, the state of perplexity and inconsistency in the medical field was such that virtually no one realized the degree to which this "new science" was a full-fledged and formidable revival of coction, Empiricism, elementalism, and the doctrine of healing by similars. Hahnemann redefined each of these in the context of modern pathology, anatomy, and laboratory science. Few doctors understood the depth of the challenge. So homeopathy has been located in the twilight zone ever since, neither herbalism nor pharmacy nor part of any medical establishment. It represents a separate Hippocratic lineage.

Since Rationalist medicine could neither accept Hahnemann on the basis of scientific principle nor totally exclude him because of his major contributions to hygiene and his legendary clinical successes, homeopathy became the alternative medicine of the scientific revolution, so distinct in its etiology that today the entirety of AMA-sponsored medicine is called "allopathy" by contrast.

EARLY ON, WESTERN science put its hopes into scaring out disease and making cure visible, but it paid a price, both immediate and millennial, for its neglect of both mind and spirit. It would have paid a different price had it wrestled with them throughout and it certainly would not have spawned the modern secular universe as we know it. The shamanic and Paracelsan traditions have stumbled through the centuries, familiars to science yet vestigial witches whom science cannot purge. Despite all the crusades and proclamations to the contrary, ghosts have made the journey too, voodoo and vital force, quintessence and spiritualized quartz, elements and similars. They were never merely empty baggage or cast-off placenta. They are something we will keep coming back to, forever.

Pancultural Influences

TO ASSEMBLE A SINGLE historical, cross-cultural map of early "planet medicine" is a dizzying venture. We mix Hippocratic texts, Australian myths, Taoist philosophy, and techniques of mummification. We go from the Yellow Emperor to Avicenna to Quesalid to Galen, crossing boundaries intellectually that are experientially impassable. We naively tend to imagine a shamanic tribal medicine distinct from the first proto-Eurasian doctors, but there is no real gap between late prehistoric medicine and the medicines of ancient civilizations. Even though the earliest Western medical codices—Egyptian, Persian, and Greek—suggest a formalization of theory and practice quite different from anything we find in present-day native cultures or the archaeology of preliterate Western peoples, this is partly because we lack descriptions of the intervening systems and partly because the act of textualization has provided its own closed continuity of biological and chemical speculation from generation to generation. This speculation must have begun very early as an overlay onto the surviving branches of tribal medicine in Africa and the Near East.

Medical systems have emerged and reemerged from the same basic fragments and dialectics since the dawn of history. While we retain historical records of only a few ancient medicines from the major Eurasian hearths, we have enough information about local cultures to fill in the gradients between them. For instance, seasonal and astrological correspondences were fully built into classical Indian and Chinese medical corpora on a semi-scientific basis, yet fragments of such systems persist the world over. The desert Arabs of Oman, for instance, attribute cholera to a yellow wind blowing during an unfavorable stretch of the Moon and stars.[31] Likewise, the formulas of Indian medicine seem like much more sophisticated versions of recipes preserved in a few Sumerian tablets.[32]

It is possible, even likely, that the humor-based medical philosophy that arose in the West, and, along different lines, in the East, stemmed from one original Eurasian system developed during tens of thousands of years of migration back and forth between European and Asian poles of the ancient world. After all, the distinction between Occidental and Oriental cultures is a relatively recent event. Marco Polo's journey to China in the thirteenth century symbolized the breakdown of barriers of a few thousand years before which waves of Asian tribes colonized Europe and a smaller number of European groups migrated to Asia. Even such diverse language groups as Uto-Aztecan, Sino-Tibetan, and Indo-European appear to share some basic root words (as *"pur"* or *"feu"* for "fire"), hence, a possible ancestral culture somewhere in the boundary zone of Europe and Asia.[33]

The underlying elemental and astrological themes of Europe, India, and Asia also seem to represent what was once a single system. Lunar mansions of sky-divination stretch from Babylonia to China with roughly 50 percent correspondence of star groupings, a Gaian ikon long before there were photographs, from some other "outer space," of a Whole Earth. Alchemy is a coda that spans the entire Old World. The internal alchemy of the Taoist sages and the external alchemy of the early chemists are variations on a theme. In the East, the mercurial *chi* "seed" was planted internally, the rainbow changes observed therein;

in the West, it was transposed outwardly into alembics and decanters and realized in metals. Likewise, acupuncture and homeopathy suggest each other, but only on the deepest level of the interpretation of disease and the micro-encoding of cure; their techniques are singularly different.

THE HEALING SYSTEMS of the Middle East combine aspects of Greek and Roman medicine with regional native pharmacies, rituals for antidoting the "evil eye," borrowings from Oriental medicine, and an Egyptian substratum. When Herodotus visited Egypt in the fifth century B.C., he found that one of the most popular forms of medicine was bowel cleansing through enemas, emetics, or cathartics. From what is likely a legacy of preparing the dead for transit to other dimensions, Egyptian doctors discovered that putrefaction began in the large intestine, hence extrapolated that "nutriment not absorbed into the body"[34] reached the other organs through the bloodstream. A contemporary historian observes that:

> ... an ancient Egyptian surgeon had working knowledge of human anatomy because the practice of mummification was prevalent. Embalmers were skilled in opening the body and removing the viscera, with the exception of the heart and its close appendages. They were also experts in bandaging and often taught surgeons this art. A type of adhesive tape made by impregnating gums, honey and myrrh into linen strips was used to pull gaping wounds together. ...
>
> Specialization was carried to absurd lengths. For instance, around certain pharaohs and their courts virtually every organ or sickness acquired its own specialist. One royal personage had one physician for his right eye and another for his left eye. In the Old Kingdom there was Iry, who was "keeper of the king's rectum," and Hesi-Re, a tooth specialist. ...
>
> In studying Egyptian surgery, special attention should be paid to circumcision, an ancient operation that appears to have originated in that country. ...[35]

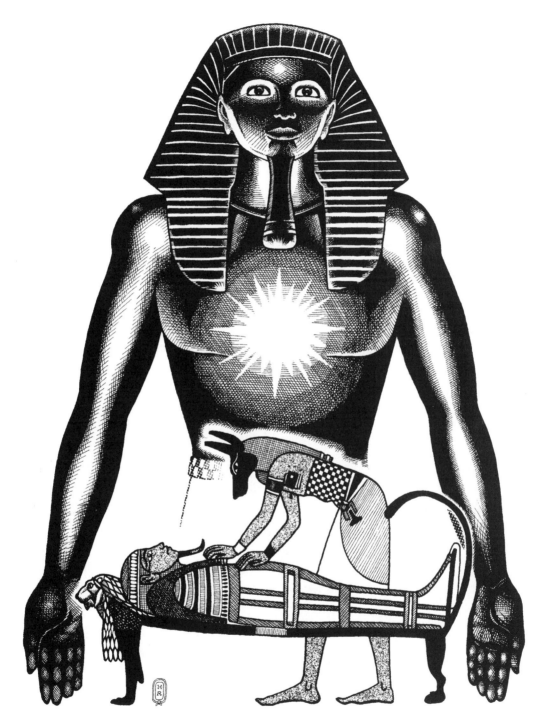

In general, historical documentation of ancient Occidental medicine is extremely sparse, revealing practices more on the level of the professional medicine men of Neolithic tribes than of the complete psychospiritual/anatomical systems of India and Asia. We have limited records of therapeutic ointments (oil, wine, and balsams) and proto-surgical techniques, for instance, in cuneiform tablets, the Old Testament, and the Code of Hammurabi. One Babylonian tablet bears the oldest known prescription; another shows the shield of a surgeon, Urlugaledin (2300 B.C.) in the pattern of two knives, gods, and herbs.[36]

> The Talmud discusses various surgical procedures, including how to suture wounds and clean traumatized edges, methods for dealing with imperforate anus, how to determine whether bleeding emanates from the uterus or only the vagina, the advantages of lessening pain during a surgical procedure, reduction of dislocations, amputations, and the use of wooden prostheses, attempts to repair defects by replacing or restoring the cranial bones, cesarean section, excision of the spleen, and detailed instructions concerning the use of artificial teeth constructed of hard wood or metal, especially gold. A veterinary surgeon is also mentioned. . . .[37]

Accounting for the passage of several millennia, this could describe Fifth Avenue in New York City or Main Street, Ohio. If anything like Ayurvedic or Taoist medicine was practiced in Babylonia or Egypt, its artifacts have been completely lost.

To a notable degree, orthodox Western medicine originated as much in the Middle East as in Europe, first by the indigenous development of surgery and allopathic pharmacy in Semitic, Babylonian, Egyptian, and Persian civilizations, and second via mediaeval elaborations and refinements of Hippocratic medicine by Islamic cultures. Both early European and Middle Eastern scientists appear to have preferred material and surgical over energetic medicine, attacking the disease as a demon or invasion. Their contribution to Judaeo-Christian definitions and epistemologies of health and sickness are deep-seated. Babylonian medical astrologers and priests driving off spirits and cosmic demons (as the sole purveyors of disease) foreshadow the separated domains of God and Satan, then therapy and pathology, antibiotics and microbes, etc. Disease was established as an externally originating and malefic agency to be purged. It was tantamount to possession or damnation. It still is.

The Zoroastrian civilization was one of the first to practice institutional medicine. Like the Arabic, Egyptian, Assyrian, Babylonian, and Hebrew systems, ancient Persian medicine seems to have been simultaneously surgical-pharmaceutical and shamanic-spiritual. There were traditionally two types of doctors in Persia, the *durustpat,* whose job was to eliminate the causes of disease, and the *tanbeshabak,* the healer of the body. The latter was not permitted to practice on Zoroastrians until he had successfully cured three non-Zoroastrians. Techniques

يَا غَلَنْمِشْ يَنْمُوْ اوْدِ سِنْ نَاكُمْ حُيْ دُشَه اَنْدَنْ صُكْرَ مِرْهَلَه مُعَالَجَه اَيْدَ سِنْ نَاكَمْ اوْ كُلَه

صُوَرَ طَبِيْبْ

وَ تَشَكُلِ آلَتْ

وَ صُوَرَة عَلِيْلْ

بُوْ نَمَرْ دُدْ

يَكْرِمِ اجْنَبِى قَصْ لَا وَلِّ لِعَ يَانِكْ

آوَ اَزْ بُوْغُلَاعِكْ وَ نَفَسْ طَارْلِنِكْ دَاغِنْكُ طَرِيقَه سِنْ يِلْدِ دُدْ

بِلْكِلِ اِيطَالِبْ كَمْ آوَازْ طِلْمُوَ وَ نَفَسْ طَارْ اوْلَمَقْ اَيكَنْكُ قَصَبَه سِنْدَ رُطُوبَة

Cauterization of swollen lymph nodes. From the Sharaf-ad-din-ibn-Ali manuscript (1465)

included use of fire, herbs, a fully array of surgical instruments, acids, and fumigation.[38]

The ancient Persians practiced a strikingly modern hygienic code. As well as requiring bathing and street cleaning, the *durustpat* specifically recommended removing the dirt and dung of poultry and cattle from homes. The Persian hospital and medical school Jondi Shapur at Ahvaz, completed in 271 A.D., became the model for later Islamic hospitals.[39] In many areas of present-day Afghanistan, doctors still rely on Persian and Arabic medical books that are centuries old, and sick people consult the mullas for verses from the *Koran* and incantations.[40]

ORIGINS

292

ARABIC MEDICINE OF the eighth century was a potpourri of Greek and Roman methods introduced by Syriac scholars, Persian medicine adapted by Jewish doctors, and spiritual medicine from the Egypto-Hellenistic School at Alexandria.[41] As noted, it was Muslim scientists who inherited the fruits of Greek science, abandoned during the European Middle Ages. The tenth-century physician Rhazes developed drugs that came back to the West as the forerunners of modern sulfonamides.[42]

> The caliph's personal physician and director of the largest hospital in Bagdad ... [Rhazes] is credited with writing 273 manuscripts, most of which are now lost. The clarity of his writings did much to bring Greek medicine, especially Hippocrates and Galen, to the Arabic world. His *Al-Hawi,* or *Continens,* is one of the greatest encyclopedias of ancient medicine....
>
> [Rhazes] provided the first authentic account of smallpox and measles. His ninth book was revised by Vesalius and remained the preeminent source of therapeutic knowledge until long after the Renaissance. Rhazes was known to perform surgical operations.... His seventh book is on surgery and is taken from Hippocrates, Paul of Agegina, Oribasius, and Aetius of Amida.
>
> Rhazes was a pioneer in the use of animal gut for sutures, and he introduced a number of remedies such as mercurial ointment. He described an operation for lacrimal fistula and cautioned against injuring the anterior branch of the ophthalmic nerve. It is known that Rhazes excised necrotic bone and wrote authoritatively on resection and removal of the whole tibia, the humerus, the radius, and the ulna. He extensively treated sciatica and spinal curvature and provided many details about bladder catheters. Considered an expert on gonorrhea, he was the first to consistently use urethral injections for its treatment.[43]

Western doctors often overlook the degree to which mainstream allopathy is primarily a borrowing and maturation of Persian and Islamic medicine. Our culture is more narcissistically enamored with the rebirth of science from purely European sources during the Renaissance.

To grasp the full scope of ancient medicine, we must turn to the East. Given the complexity and sophistication of traditional medicine in India and China, it is astonishing that it did not influence Western medicine earlier and more substantially. In truth, its greatest impact has waited until the late twentieth century. However, from a different perspective, we might view today's developing "planet medicine" as intersecting waves of systems originating over three thousand years ago and gradually combining Chinese, Islamic, Indian, European, and other indigenous sources. Also, if Western medicine were relatively immune to Eastern influences, the converse was not true. Persian and other Islamic medicines made their way into India, Tibet, and China at least throughout the Middle Ages; there is no reason this migration could not have begun dramatically earlier.

In their book *Tao & Dharma,* Lade and Svoboda give an overview of the historical significance of the major Oriental systems from the standpoint of their completely separate origination:

> Chinese and Indian medicine embody the two oldest continuously practiced traditions of medicine on the planet. These traditions are oceans of wisdom whose depth and breadth are almost incomprehensible to one who stands on their shores. Into these oceans of healing art tributaries of thought flow, and the two seas have at times mingled their waters together. Though the origins of these medical traditions have no fixed historical landmarks, they seem to have appeared at approximately the same time, yet independently, grown out of an understanding expounded by their sages and rishis. Centuries passed after Chinese and Indian medicine were founded before they first mingled to exchange ideas with each other. Why two great systems should appear simultaneously in two vastly different corners of the globe, each a unique expression yet possessing many similar characteristics, is a great mystery. Perhaps their fundamental vision and insights about life grew out of humanity's collective unconscious.[44]

The medical philosophies of China and India dominated Asia in much the way Rationalist allopathic medicine dominated the native traditions of the Western world. Chinese medicine had its strongest pure influence in Tibet and Vietnam, whereas a mixture of Hindu, Buddhist, Parsi, and Moslem medicines formed hybrid systems in South and Southeast Asia. Indian medicine has an enormous later impact on an underlying Sino-Tibetan system.

[In our search for original planetary healing systems we can also ask provocative "trans-Pacific migration" questions such as: Was there a Chinese influence in aboriginal Fiji, New Guinea, New Zealand, Australia, even indigenous North America? Does the Australian practice of incision share a Stone Age ancestor with the Chinese technique of acupuncture and moxibustion? Do the trance powers of the Bunaba and Yuin shamans sprout from the same ritual instructions as those of the Tibetan lamas? (Both sages gain their power from vision quests and from confronting spirits. Both learn to create palpable illusions, to vanish and reappear.) And what about the "science" of healing with quartz crystals, so prominent in both Africa and Australia? Did African mariners visit Australia, or is sentient quartz a basic element of some very early Old World healing complex that vanished in most regions but was retained in Africa, parts of North America, and Australia? Is there yet a cosmic or astral wild card?]

The possible Palaeolithic connection of Asia and North America was dramatized in the 1970s by the visit of the exiled Tibetan karmapa to the Hopi village of Hotevilla. The Buddhist spiritual leader was welcomed by the Indians as a kinsman, also as an ancestor. He and several other Tibetans joined the Hopis in their kiva, the underground religious sanctum, to chant together for rain. It had been dry for many, many months, and the Hopi rain dance had failed to produce moisture.

Superficially, the most remarkable event was the burst of rain that followed. However, the simple participation of ancient separated priests is what radiates over time. Hopis and Tibetans "understood" each other in their chants. The Hopis claimed later that they discovered they had lost certain primary elements of their own rain chant during the long diaspora, and that the Tibetan priests were able to guide them back into the rhythm and efficacies of their own ceremony.[45] If substantial technical elements have persisted for a hundred thousand years or more—and there is no reason why they could not have—we are confirmed in our intuition that healing and artistic and spiritual systems of high integrity have survived and continue to exist outside the framework of history and science. Traditions of curing, chanting, evoking, etc., go back to the oldest times and so, like the radio noise of the galactic explosion, are distributed most widely throughout our universe.

As noted earlier in this section, the traditional healers of the Orient (China, Tibet, Japan, Korea, India, etc.) internalized elemental theory and applied it directly to modify energy flow, either by external techniques (acupuncture, moxibustion, cupping, *shiatsu*) or internal remedies (herbs, *Chi Gung,* yoga). On the other hand, the Occident ultimately objectified elemental theory and used it for the development of analytical science and medicine. In the grossest sense, the former led to meditations based on breath and internalized motion and to spiritual medicines, the latter to systems of energy based on external wiring and electricity and to medicines based on dissection and surgery.

The separate evolutions of medicine in Europe and Asia quite clearly mark the difference between, on the one hand, Atlantic and Mediterranean cultures involved in secular science, hence delving into the purely physical properties of elements, and, on the other, Indian and Pacific cultures honoring the transcendental aspects of creation, thus developing science only in keeping with the reincarnational cycle of spirits. Lade and Svoboda characterize the Asian cosmology underlying medicine:

In ancient China . . . traditional beliefs such as Confucianism which encourage ancestor worship were hostile to anyone who disturbed the remains of the departed, for they believed that dissection might interfere with the Yin soul's (Po) return to the earth. Such a soul might then become a wayward ghost, unable to complete its journey after death. Pieces of jade were placed upon the orifices of the deceased bodies of the rich and famous so that the Yin soul would not escape, thus ensuring its return into the earth with the dissolution of the physical elements.

Similar prohibitions were in force in classical India, where rituals are performed after death to ensure that the deceased will enjoy healthy, undeformed limbs and organs in his or her next birth, and any damage to the corpse before its cremation is considered likely to show up on the succeeding body. Also, for a high-caste Hindu to touch a corpse was and is considered to be a profound defilement, one which could be counteracted only through intensive and complex purifications. There was also the ever-present awareness of the danger that the dissector might choose to use some of the dissected body parts in black magic rituals. In spite of all these impediments, dissection seems to have been practiced, though probably mainly on the sly, and students augmented their skills by practicing surgery on dummies, melons, dead animals, and lotus stems.[46]

We may intuit some of the gaps between late tribal medicine and early historical medicine here. Spiritual ethnomedicine stood squarely in the way of the advancement of science, providing not only sanctions but fearsome curses.

There is, however, a cadaver in the closet of the East. China's "allopathic" medical technology was likely the first on the planet. A medley of admittedly unreliable reports claims heart transplants and other surgical wonders from as long ago as second-century-B.C. China.

In rural Tibet, archaeologists have recovered substantial evidence for an ancient and sophisticated medical complex: bottle-shaped tools with nipples and holes for diagnosing anal disorders and trumpet-shaped tools for sending medicine through the anus. Saws, hooks for removing tumors and stones, plus a variety of pincers and scalpels (the former shaped like a lion's head, a crane's or crow's beak, etc., and the latter like the feather of a sparrow or a sickle) and three kinds of spoons (shaped, respectively, like a bird's beak, a frog's head, and a grain of barley, for removing pus, water, and tumors from surficial and internal cavities) all made up the tool kit of these Neolithic surgeons.[47] However, since surgery and experimental anatomy were not ultimately supported by the pan-Asian world-view, a historically much later and slower Europe established the global system of medical technology now in ascension. It took the Greeks to invent formal vitalistic and homeopathic medicines and the Indians, Tibetans, and Chinese to codify great elemental systems, each of which is a complete science of embryology, anatomy, diagnosis, and treatment. It took most of recorded history for these finally to meet and begin to fuse.

O F THE TRADITIONAL medical texts available in the West, the most fundamental is perhaps the Ilza Veith translation appearing under the title *The Yellow Emperor's Classic of Internal Medicine.*[48] Although operating according to a system of signs unfamiliar to most Westerners, and put into an unfortunate English, *The Yellow Emperor* survives surprisingly intact. It surmounts obstacles of time, space, and language to propose a clear, incisive, and often terrifying doctrine of the human condition and the absolute basis for life on this planet. It is not a medical book in our sense of the term. It is a philosophy of nature and cosmology. It is a medical book because it treats the subject of how man and woman come into being and perish.

The premise of *The Yellow Emperor,* familiar from other elemental systems, is that nature originates from the interplay of eternal cosmic forces. We never see them, but everything we see, including our act of seeing, is their effect.

The Chinese text itself is maybe four thousand years old, and the constructs it describes are obviously much older. It is no exaggeration to think of its surviving principles as our main guides to late Palaeolithic medicine. Like other possible Stone Age wisdom we inherit through Egyptian, Scandinavian, and even New World sources, these principles present a world of unceasing creation, cataclysm, and the subjection of all to a hierarchy of divine law.

We arrive at such systems quite unprepared to deal with their dietary and seasonal rigor, readily consuming oranges from Florida, pineapples from Hawaii, potatoes from Idaho, grain from Iowa, etc. We periodically transport ourselves from hemisphere to hemisphere and climate to climate in petroleum-powered machines. We sit now in a late American autumn trying to adapt to texts that formed over hundreds of generations of masters without technology or global ambitions, who barely moved, who simply observed, recorded, and healed. Their real teaching and mode of healing are as remote as clouds forming and dissolving impalpably in the sky.

Notes

1. Charles Coulston Gillispie, "Lamarck and Darwin in the History of Science," in Bentley Glass, Owsei Temkin, and William L. Straus, Jr. (eds.), *Forerunners of Darwin, 1745–1859* (Baltimore: The Johns Hopkins Press, 1959), p. 274.

2. Gerrit Lansing, "Fundamentals of Indian Medical Theory," from *Notes on Structure and Sign in Ayurveda,* unpublished manuscript, 1981.

3. Eduardo Calderón, Richard Cowan, Douglas Sharon, F. Kaye Sharon, *Eduardo el Curandero: The Words of a Peruvian Healer* (Berkeley, California: North Atlantic Books, 1982).

4. Philip Wheelwright (ed.), *The Presocratics* (Indianapolis: Odyssey Press, 1966), p. 272.

5. Ibid., p. 268.

6. Harris L. Coulter, *Divided Legacy: A History of the Schism in Medical Thought, Vol. I. The Patterns Emerge: Hippocrates to Paracelsus* (Washington, DC: Wehawken Book Company, 1975), pp. 51–52.

7. Ibid., p. 55.

8. Ibid., pp. 12–13.

9. Ibid., p. 176.

10. Ibid.

11. Ibid., p. 297.

12. Ibid., pp. 291–92.

13. Deepak Chopra, *Quantum Healing: Exploring the Frontiers of Mind/Body Medicine* (New York: Bantam Books, 1989), p. 140.

14. Harris L. Coulter, *Divided Legacy: A History of the Schism in Medical Thought, Vol. II. The Origins of Modern Western Medicine: J. B. Van Helmont to Claude Bernard* (Washington, DC: Wehawken Book Company and Berkeley, California: North Atlantic Books, 1988), p. 282.

15. Ibid., p. 191.

16. Ibid., p. 187.

17. Ibid., p. 186.

18. Ibid., p. 187.

19. Ibid., pp. 304–305.

20. Ibid., p. 621.

21. Ibid.

22. Ibid., p. 644.

23. Harris L. Coulter, *Divided Legacy: A History of the Schism in Medical Thought, Vol. IV. Twentieth Century Medicine: The Bacteriological Era* (Berkeley, California: North Atlantic Books, 1994), pp. 181–182.

24. Coulter, *Divided Legacy, Vol. I,* p. 358.

25. Ibid., p. 359.

26. Ibid., p. 413.

27. Ibid.

28. Ibid.

29. Ibid., p. 354.

30. Coulter, *Divided Legacy, Vol. II*, p. 28.

31. Wendell Phillips, *Unknown Oman* (New York: David McKay Company, Inc., 1966).

32. Maneckji N. Dhalla, *Zoroastrian Civilization* (London: Oxford University Press, 1922).

33. Morris Swadesh, "Diffusional Cumulation and Archaic Residue as Historical Explanations," in Dell Hymes (ed.), *Language in Culture & Society: A Reader in Linguistics and Anthropology* (New York: Harper and Row, 1964), p. 634.

34. Coulter, *Divided Legacy, Vol. I,* p. 110.

35. Ira M. Rutkow, *Surgery: An Illustrated History* (St. Louis: Mosby-Year Book, 1993), pp. 16–17.

36. Ibid., p. 5.

37. Ibid., p. 10.

38. Dhalla, *Zoroastrian Civilization.*

39. Ibid.

40. Phillips, *Unknown Oman.*

41. Dhalla, *Zoroastrian Civilization.*

42. Harvey H. Smith, *Area Handbook for Iran*, United States Government Printing Office, Foreign Area Studies, American University, Washington, DC, 1971.

43. Rutkow, *Surgery,* p. 55.

44. A. Lade and R. Svoboda, *Tao & Dharma: A Comparison of Ayurveda and Chinese Medicine,* unpublished manuscript at the time of publication.

45. Personal communication from a participant, 1975.

46. Lade and Svoboda, *Tao & Dharma.*

47. Ven. Rinpoche Jampal Kunzang Rechung, *Tibetan Medicine* (Berkeley: University of California Press, 1973), pp. 82–84.

48. *Huang Ti Nei Ching Su Wên,* trans. by Ilza Veith as *The Yellow Emperor's Classic of Internal Medicine* (Berkeley: University of California Press, 1966).

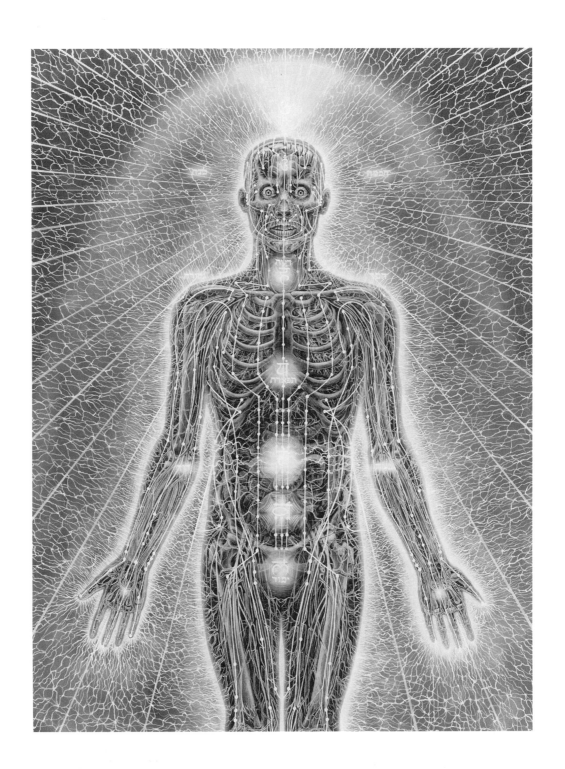

CHAPTER NINE

Ayurvedic and Taoist Medicines

Ayurvedic Medicine: A Brief History

ONE OF THE oldest and most elaborate systems of study on the Earth, Ayurveda (literally "life science") offers an exotic array of diagnostic techniques and treatments as well as explication of topics ranging from horticulture and metallurgy to sociology and ethics. In fact, classical Indian medicine seems like the relics of an advanced science from another planet. It is the medicine of a lost Indo-European kingdom.

For at least six thousand years Ayurveda has practiced pharmacy, horticulture, herbalism, color therapy, a version of alchemy (or mineral medicine), cookery, surgery, massage, sound healing, and meditation, while developing sciences of embryology, anatomy, and nutrition. Though Ayurveda has some similarities to European elemental medicine, its branches subsume a compendium of empirical research and ingenious methods substantially unknown in the West. Its foundation texts, the *Charaka Samhita* and its surgical counterpart, the *Sushruta Samhita,* were assembled, like the Hippocratic Corpus, from prior teachings, sometime around the tenth century B.C. Ancient Indian surgery included laparotomy and intestinal repair, cesarean section, vesical lithotomy, harelip repair, and cutting cataracts with a lancet while palpating the impurity in the eye.

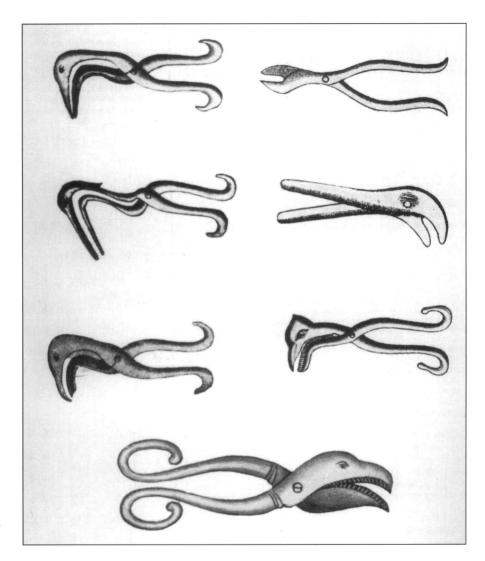

*Hindu
surgical
forceps as
described by
the* Sushruta
Samhita

Among the preeminent surgical operations pioneered by ancient
Indians were those of plastic and reconstructive surgery. The custom
of piercing an earlobe and then enlarging the opening to hold an
amulet that protected against evil powers was quite common. This
procedure often led to rips through the earlobe, or if infection was
present, the whole ear could be deformed. The Samhita contains fifteen methods for repairing such damage, many of which are essentially the same as in modern plastic surgery.[1]

In the early nineteenth century, Indian doctors from over a thousand years prior were still able to instruct Western doctors in techniques for the repair of ears and rhinoplasty (nasal reconstruction).

The *Charaka* was more elemental and etiological. A typical conceit advises, "A medicine is one which enters the body, balances the Doshas, does not disturb the healthy tissue, does not adhere to them and gets eliminated out through the urine, sweat and feces. It cures the disease, gives longevity to the bodily cells and has no side effects."[2]

Indian anatomical categories differ substantially from Western ones—a fact that underlies many of the unique aspects of Ayurveda. For instance, the *Charaka* recognizes 700 visible *siras* (vessels) and countless minute ones: "The siras by their contraction and expansion sustain and nourish the human being as canals and streamlets serve to keep a garden aqueous, moist, and fruitful."[3] The *Sushruta* classifies 107 *marmas,* Indian equivalents of the Chinese acupuncture points, "on the basis of the [underlying] structure involved (muscles, blood vessels, ligaments, nerves, bones, joints), regional location, dimension, and consequences of injury (swift death, death after some delay, death as soon as any foreign body is extracted from the wound, disability, or simply intense pain)."[4] The three most important *mahamarmas* are the head *marma* (between the eyebrows), the heart *marma,* and the *basti marma* in the lower pelvic area. These regulate discrimination, feeling, and the gross physical realm, respectively.

Ayurvedic medicine is famously and resourcefully sensual: Gandharva musicians play patterns of tones, including *ragas,* to transmit diurnal/nocturnal rhythms and increase or decrease the pulse rate; scents of basil, orange, rose geranium, sandalwood, mint and jasmine are expelled from bedside dispensers to treat aggravated *marmas;* and massages are enhanced with deep penetrating oils at whose touch the muscles melt.[5] Taste *(rasa)* is also a central element of Ayurveda, as we shall see. Among numerous methods described for stimulating and balancing *marmas* are: yoga, acupressure massage of points on the feet using sesame oil, aromatherapy, and a system of subtle medicated touch *(marma chikitsa)* involving special oils.

Later Ayurvedic texts (from the early centuries A.D.) include extensive botanical pharmacologies; formularies of metallic medicines; blends of oils, resins, and other ingredients into tonics and aroma essences; and manuals "on the treatment of trees, horses, and elephants [and] . . . such varied animals as cows, goats, sheep, donkeys, camels, and hawks."[6] By comparison, the homeopathic repertory—and even the diagnostic manuals of allopathy—are empirical neophytes.

Ayurveda is not simply a practice or set of techniques. It is a complete medical training embodying a curriculum of courses and specializations. Its traditional eight "limbs" are: "internal medicine, surgery, eye-ear-nose, gynecology-obstetrics-pediatrics, psychology, toxicology, rejuvenation, and virilization."[7] A practitioner in the time of Buddha had to pass exams in *all* of these to be granted a medical license by the king. Three centuries before the birth of Christ, India supported numerous hospitals complete with surgical, obstetric, and mental wards. In subsequent generations, maternity homes, village medicinal gardens, regional physicians, and a constabulary squad searching out unlicensed practitioners were arms of a vast imperial medical system—at its apex several Buddhist universities drawing students from throughout Eurasia. The United States of the twentieth century, admittedly with a much larger and more diverse populace, does not approach this level of healthcare accountability. The subsequent demise of Ayurveda is sad proof that progress is followed by decline and, as the Hindus affirm, kingdoms come and kingdoms go—no problem.

This elegant medical network was shattered and destroyed by Muslim invaders during the tenth and eleventh centuries. Historians may eulogize the prior loss of the Hellenic library at Alexandria to religious fanatics in 415 A.D., but at least as great a body of learning disappeared throughout mediaeval India from the sacking of its universities and burning of its libraries. Much of Ayurveda now survives only in Tibetan translations.

The Muslims tried to replace Hindu and Buddhist medicine with Greek-influenced Arabic science, but even during centuries of dissolution and simplification, remnants of indigenous practices remained widespread. Ayurvedic institutions were subsequently challenged by both allopathic and homeopathic philosophies from Europe, and in 1835 the British declared it unsanctioned medicine. However, the *Charaka* and *Sushruta* have deeper roots in pan-Indian culture than any other formal system of treatment. Despite centuries of disuse, a revival began in the twentieth century, and today Ayurveda "is one of the six medical systems which are officially recognized by India's government, the others being allopathy, Unani, Siddha, homeopathy, and naturopathy."[8]

Much of the restoration and revivification of Ayurveda may be credited to Maharishi Mahesh Yogi, who is best known for developing Transcendental Meditation and, with the aid of the British rock group the Beatles, bringing it to the West in the 1960s. Assisted by scores of colleagues, he helped to locate the remaining pockets of Ayurveda in India, assembling and "pool[ing] their combined expertise into a systematized body of knowledge, easily accessible for Western minds. The result is Maharishi Ayur-Veda, which has attracted the interest of not only the lay public, but also a number of M.D.s and D.C.s in the Americas, Europe, and Japan."[9] It is also taught at the Maharishi's own university in Fairfield, Iowa. Maharishi Ayur-Veda may not represent Ayurveda in its full original sense, but compare it to ancient Persian, Egyptian, or Mayan medicine, of which we retain virtually nothing.

Ayurvedic Theory

IT IS IMPOSSIBLE to give a brief account of the labyrinthine blend of biochemistry, vitalistic chemistry, and esoteric anatomy proposed in Indian medicine. A journey into its mysteries is like a journey through the different languages and bioregions of India itself. Ayurveda is, on the one hand, a classic constitutional medicine, analyzing each organism according to the elemental aspects of its character type, then the componental aspects of those, then the microcomponental aspects of those, etc. On the other hand, it is a pure psychospiritual system, prescribing states of attention in meditation, visualization, yoga, healing by sound, and the general practice of restraint. Renowned endocrinologist Deepak Chopra, trained in Ayurveda in his native India, describes this latter aspect: "... each and every symptom of disease, from a minor neck pain to a full-blown cancer, is under the control of attention. However, between us and the symptoms lie barriers—the veils called Maya—that prevent us from exercising our attention in a therapeutic way. All mind-body medicine attempts to remove these obstacles so that healing can take place ... Ayurveda has made use of this principle for thousands of years. Indeed, since the basic premise of Vedic knowledge is that consciousness creates the body, it is only natural that techniques for focusing attention should have been discovered."[10]

Would that healing were that simple and accessible!

NATURE ITSELF ORIGINATES in an undifferentiated state that gives rise to the five elements: Water, Earth, Fire, Air, and Ether (a highly refined field from which both space and matter form). These five preorganic *bhutas* are subtle material potencies never found unmixed in nature: *jala* (which is heavy, dense, flowing, moist, and cold, and associated with water); *prithivi* (which is bulky, motionless, steady, and hard, and associated with earth); *agni* (which is light, hot, penetrative, digesting food through the organs, imparting a glow to the body, and associated with fire); *vayu* (which is light, transparent, cold, and dry, and the source of air); and *akasha* (which is porous, soft, smooth, light and transparent, rules the sound-matrix, and is associated with elemental Ether).[11]

In order to materialize at all, these elements must generate intermediate energetic modalities. The first of these, *prana,* is the subtle energy binding the different fields of mind, spirit, and body into one functioning unit. Oxygen is one form of *prana* (breathing draws *prana* into the body). *Tejas* is transmutational, fomentative fire. *Ojas* is the watery, agglutinating aspect of life. However, even these modalities are too subtle to take on gross human form, so in differential pairs they propagate three *doshas*. These *doshas* function as governing humors—simultaneously somatic and characterological.

Jala goes together with *prithivi* to metamorphose *kapha-dosha* (also called Mucus): a source of fixed and solid aspects, such as bone, which give the organism its support and shape. *Kapha-dosha* is a repository of the bodily fluids which lubricate the joints and viscera. Stored in the brain, joints, stomach, lungs, heart, kidneys, fat, etc., it synthesizes saliva, pericardial and cerebrospinal fluid, and stomach mucus; its foods are cold, heavy, smooth, and soft.

Jala goes with *agni* to make up *pitta-dosha* (also called Fire), providing the heat and digestive and transformative capacity of the interior, as well as the secretions of the skin and "bile." It congeals to glutinous matter like fat, as well as to bodily fluids, blood, mucus, semen, lymph, hormones, etc.; it is stored in the liver, spleen, gall bladder, glands, small intestine, blood, sweat, etc., and synthesizes into hemoglobin, digestive juices, and neurotransmitters. Its foods are hot, oily, and strong.

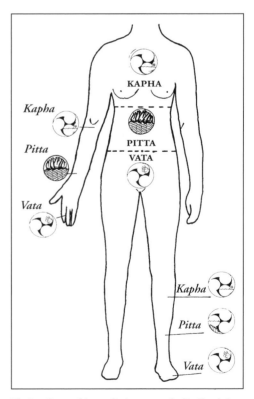

Vata (also called Wind) threads the nervous system, perceiving and animating, initiating motion, and drawing the various bodily elements together; it is a highly active *dosha* with more diseases ascribed to its imbalances than *pitta* and *kapha* together (the wind blows everywhere irregularly). *Vata* is made up of *vayu* and *akasha;* is stored in the nervous system, colon, bladder, pelvis, ears, bones, skin, etc.; and provides the geometry of the body's organization. Its foods are dry, rough, and unstable.

Reproduced with permission from *The Lost Secrets of Ayurvedic Acupuncture* by Dr. Frank Ros, Lotus Press, Box 325, Twin Lakes, WI 53181. © 1994. All Rights Reserved.

Seven *dhatus* (body-components) are dispersed embryonically by the vectors of the *bhutas*. *Srotas* are usually translated as "channels," including capillaries, fatty ducts, semen ducts, and intestines. They are expanding yet subtle morphologies projecting through the body from seed potential and manifesting as three-dimensional space. The substances they generate trickle and ooze through them and give somatic existence to the *dhatus*. *Srotas* that terminate at orifices (eyes, ears, breasts, genitals) are primary points of contact between the subtle roots of the organism and the external world. The *Sushruta* lists eleven *srotas,* including those carrying various proportions of blood, muscles, fat, water, food, urine, stools, semen, and even tumors. Correspondence of these to equivalents in Western hematology and endocrinology is only approximate. Indian anatomy not only originates independently and from different categories of physiology but seeks cosmological entities beyond simple body-parts. The *Sushruta* says, "There is not a single sira in the body which carries either the vayu or the pitta or the kapha alone. Hence each of the vessels should be treated as affording an opportunity for conveying all kinds of doshas of the body because as soon as they are deranged and aggravated they seem to flow through all the siras promiscuously...."[12]

Every *dosha* has five concrete aspects, some marking substances or activities clearly described by Western anatomy—*bodhaka kapha:* saliva; *pachaka pitta:* gastric juice; *ranjaka pitta:* hemoglobin; *prana vayu:* oxygen; *vyana vata:* the circulation of blood, etc. The five aspects of *vayu,* for instance, combine not only to sustain the body but keep the mind clear, generate speech, carry sensual information, and activate excretions.

The Wheel of Support (Alambra Chakra)

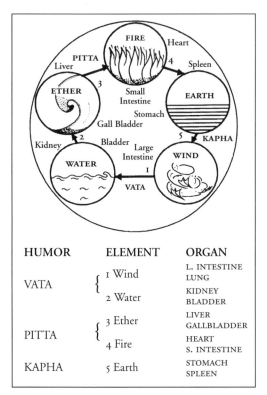

HUMOR	ELEMENT	ORGAN
VATA	{ 1 Wind	L. INTESTINE LUNG
	2 Water	KIDNEY BLADDER
PITTA	{ 3 Ether	LIVER GALLBLADDER
	4 Fire	HEART S. INTESTINE
KAPHA	5 Earth	STOMACH SPLEEN

If *apana vayu* is kept from moving downward, the passage of both urine and feces is stopped, so medicines which stimulate downward *apana vayu* are prescribed.

Foods abundant in qualities of each individual *dosha* increase the componential aspect of that *dosha* in the body. That is, too many moist foods lead to an overly wet system and *kapha* diseases, too many hot foods to an overly parched system and *vata* diseases. Likewise, thoughts and sense perceptions which represent the energies of a *dosha* are absorbed into the psychochemistry of that humor; thus, undigested sensations and emotions become the raw material of disease. Congestion of the *marmas* can come equally from unassimilated food or unassimilated emotions and images.

The transitions of seasons are critical points for aggravations of the *doshas: vata* diseases as summer turns into autumn, *kapha* illnesses as winter subsides into spring, and *pitta* malaises as spring matures into summer. This is because the body is in continuous homeostatic relationship with its environs and must adapt internally as climate changes. If one's basic constitution is unbalanced, an external imbalance often increases its disproportions.

The trinary cycle also governs assimilation. The elemental aspects of substances encounter corresponding aspects of the *tridoshas* in the mouth, intestines, and lymph cells. *Kapha* is activated when the food is in the body but undigested, *pitta* during digestion, and *vata* during assimilation. Likewise, *kapha* governs assimilation from sunrise to the middle of the morning, followed by *pitta* and *vata* in equal parts till sunset, when a three-part nocturnal cycle begins.

In an interactive system of sensory stimulation and nourishment, each of the *doshas*

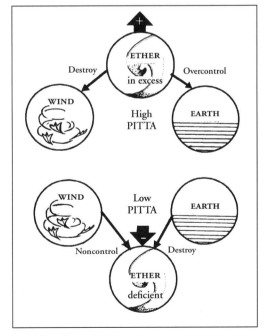

Reproduced with permission from *The Lost Secrets of Ayurvedic Acupuncture* by Dr. Frank Ros, Lotus Press, Box 325, Twin Lakes, WI 53181. © 1994. All Rights Reserved.

reacts idiosyncratically to the individual tastes of a food or medicine. A given taste tends to build up or nourish one *dosha* while drying out or burning others. Nourishment is not always beneficial nor is drying out necessarily unhealthy. For instance, *kapha* is aggravated by sweet foods (which swell the tissues) and soothed by bitter medicines (which dry out the tissues).

The six recognized tastes are sweet (like carrot juice or papaya), sour (like tamarind or hibiscus), salty (like sea salt or spirulina), pungent (like cardamom or cloves), bitter (like some squashes or quinoa), and astringent (like unripe mangos or persimmons). Most actual foods are combinations of tastes: banana is sweet and astringent (as well as cold and heavy), and mustard seed is bitter and pungent (as well as hot). Pomegranates can be either sweet, sweet and sour, or sour. These "tastes" represent elemental aspects of substances crucial to the nutritive and medicinal activity of all ingested foods and medicines.

Insofar as the six tastes reflect underlying potentialities, medicine relies not only on sound food selection from a nutritional standpoint but harmonious interaction on elemental and psychosomatic planes. Assimilation and desire (mind) are parallel and simultaneous hungers arising from the clarity of *vayu* and the primal fire of *pitta* within the colloidal substance of *kapha*. Westerners tend to think of flavor in the coarse sense of superficial stimulative qualities or hedonistic notions of pleasure and "dis"taste, but palatability originates deep within the molecularity of substance where the elements blend the formative characters of the *doshas*. Flavors are fundamental and profound aspects seeking

*The Organ
and Humor
Pulses*

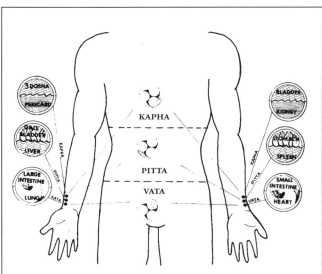

substantiating materials. Their diagnostic intelligence and natural healing functions are squandered when they are exploited only as attraction for sweets, meat, etc.—i.e., as compulsive luxuries. There is an entirely different taste system which calls upon the ability of the whole organism to savor substance as it is absorbed. This leads to a cuisine in which precise food combinations are prepared to satisfy tastes ordinarily given to hunger for excesses of single things, like meat or sweets. We and what we eat become the same potentiated field.

American Ayurvedic therapist John Douillard "prescribes periodic doses throughout the day of certain foods with concentrated, pure tastes. For example, if the pulse indicates a need for sweetness, then fennel seeds—not ice cream—is the taste of choice. Fennel is purely sweet and does not overload digestion or produce byproducts that are hard for the body to eliminate. Often the prescribed flavors satisfy cravings for less healthy foods, such as salty junk food, chocolate, coffee, and soft drinks."[13]

Chemical alchemy *is* ultimately both a culinary art and a yoga.

Tridoshas

THE MUCUS TYPE is compact, smooth, oily, with dark hair and pale complexion. Mucus is the raw matter of bodily structure, courage, and a capacity for calmness. An increase in Mucus leads to dullness, torpidity, and congestion. A lack of Mucus results in giddiness and trembling and a feeling of emptiness. Respiratory diseases are common. The disharmonic pulse of *kapha* swims like a swan.* For excess of Mucus: beans, hot spices, sharp vegetables (except radishes), and fruits with acid may be prescribed.

> When toxins are present, however, bitter should first be used to clear
> the channels and only then should pungent, to reawaken the diges-

---

*The late appearance of this mode of pulse diagnosis in Ayurveda suggests that it may have been added from Muslim medicine.

tive fire, and astringent, to expel excess "moisture," be employed. All medicines and foods should be hot, intense and dry. Aged wines and liqueurs in small doses, nights without sleep, frequent sexual intercourse, vigorous exercise like wrestling, running and jumping to cause copious sweating, fasting, smoking, rough dry warm clothes, and extremely hot baths all decrease *Kapha*.[14]

The Fire type is yellow and pink in color, with soft hair, often blonde, aggressive and tempery, with a tendency to age quickly. The pulse of its diseased states hops like a crow or frog. Fire supplies heat in the body, sparks vision, and manifests also as hunger and thirst. It is the elemental basis of joy and the catalyst for digestion. A lack of Fire increases inherent chilliness and hampers digestion. Excesses of Fire lead not only to unhealthy cravings disguised as hunger and thirst, and a sensation of burning, but also to excessive wakefulness and dimming of the sense organs. Sweet aromas, incense, and flowers (sandalwood, lotus, and rose) may be used to cool. Sweet milk, grains, beans, and bitter herbs may likewise be prescribed. Other treatments include:

> ... cool showers, moon bathing, pearl necklaces (especially chilled), white clothes, and residence in green gardens amid fountains ... to refrigerate the system ... [also] soothing music, meditations to keep the mind calm and cool, plenty of raw food, a job or hobby which requires plenty of problem-solving, and the like.[15]

The Wind type is classically brownish and small, talkative and fearful, with rough skin and hair. Elemental wind breathes and circulates fluids. As Wind increases, flatulence, lack of coordination, and general dryness follow. This is the ruling Humor of nervous diseases. A lack of Wind leads to depression and even loss of consciousness. The pulse of its disorders slides under the skin like a leech or snake. Wheat, milk, salty and acidic fruits, warm drinks, medicinal wines, and sweet vegetables heal excesses or deficiencies. Massage therapy is very often indicated.

In general, it is considered easier to treat a humoral deficiency through addressing one of the two nonconstitutional humors in any person. But triune systems develop dialectically, begetting ever new syntheses. Gerrit Lansing summarizes the heart of Ayurveda when he writes: "The three functional 'forces' in the human psychosomatic substance are considered to be ideally in an individual harmony or balance. Disease is finally an unbalance, not simply of two polar principles, but of three potentiating factors."[16]

Esoteric Anatomy

To understand Ayurvedic medicine in depth, one must take into consideration the realm of astral planes and subtle bodies. What our culture retains from shamanic times and what it has proposed anew in the guise of vitalistic science does not do justice to the esoteric Indo-European science of auras and energies. The Ayurvedic spiritual body is not only "real" but has been in existence and treated with spiritual medicines for thousands of years. It exists on an empirical therapeutic basis, not as speculation and not as the result of a specific vision quest or séance.

Subtle bodies have appeared in folklore and literature the world over as ghosts, spirits, plasma fields, etc., depending upon cultural interpretation. The full variety of distinct subtle bodies is unknown, for, as with vital energies, it is virtually impossible to tell what is a unique entity and what is simply one culture's version of a form known elsewhere under different names. Some traditions claim only a single astral body; many refer to a range of four, five, or six different energies; in a few systems there are as many as 9900 distinct forms of energy emanating from the human body. It is difficult enough to try to match plants, animals, and even social categories cross-culturally. It is all but impossible to classify genera of subtle bodies. One author gives a useful summary:

> The Astral Body may defined as the Double, or the ethereal counterpart of the physical body, which it resembles and with which it normally coincides. It is thought to be composed of some semi-fluidic

or subtle form of matter, invisible to the physical eye. It has, in the past, been spoken of as the etheric body, the mental body, the spiritual body, the desire body, the radiant body, the resurrection body, the double, the luminous body, the subtle body, the fluidic body, the shining double, the phantom, and by various other names.... for our present purposes we may ignore these distinctions and speak of the "Astral Body" as some more subtle form distinct from the organic structure known to Western science, and studied by our physiologists.

The broad, general teaching is that every human being "has" an astral body just as he has a heart, a brain and a liver. In fact, the astral body is more truly the Real Man than the physical body is, for the latter is merely a machine adapted to functioning upon the physical plane.[17]

Cultivation of subtle bodies is quite common in shamanism. Black witchcraft is often carried out by a malevolent shaman traveling in his or her subtle body and delivering a severe blow to the subtle body of a victim. One author describes "the flying by night of a sorcerer to attack a sleeping victim. The flying sorcerer can be seen as a moving light that is known as *sŭoŋmi,* that is, 'sorcerer-fire.' The belief that flying sorcerers emit a light was noted by Evans-Pritchard among the Azande, and it is also found among the Akan-speaking peoples."[18] Other shamans report entering the subtle bodies of plants and animals and gaining intelligence from these: remember Don Juan flying with Carlos Castaneda, both as crows. There are also legends of shamans throughout North and South America visiting other parts of the Western Hemisphere, i.e., a rain forest woman accurately depicting villages of the Crow, or an Iroquois doctor smoking weed with a Oaxacan seer.

For most people their own subtle body is an aspect of which they are unaware and which they relate to only by the metaphor of the soul after death. Hence, the preponderance of Western lore regarding subtle bodies addresses either ghosts—ostensible plasma fields of the recently dead still attached to the physical world and manifesting inter-

mittently (often with messages the delivery of which binds them to
this world, as the ghost of Hamlet's father in Shakespeare's play)—or
the related phenomenon of leaving the body in a near-death experience and then returning.

There is also an occult tradition in the West of traveling outside
the physical body:

> The Astral Body, belonging to every person, is an exact counterpart
> of the perfect physical body of the person. It is composed of fine
> ethereal matter, and is usually encased in the physical body. In ordi-
> nary cases, the detachment of the astral body from its physical coun-
> terpart is accomplished only with great difficulty, but in the case of
> dreams, great mental stress, and under certain conditions of occult
> development, the astral body may become detached and sent on long
> journeys, traveling at a rate of speed only less than that of light-
> waves.
>
> On these journeys it is always connected with the physical body
> by a long, filmy connecting link. If this link were to become bro-
> ken, the person would die instantly, but this is an almost unheard-
> of occurrence in the ordinary planes of action.
>
> The astral body exists a long time after the death of the physical
> body, but it disintegrates in time. It sometimes hovers around the
> resting-place of the physical corpse, and is mistaken for the spirit of
> the deceased person, although really it is merely a shell, or finer outer
> coating of the soul.[19]

The implications for healing are fundamental: if consciousness can
root itself in a vehicle other than the physical body and can maintain
continuity of ego-states, then the visible zone of the skeleton, viscera,
sense organs, and flesh is merely one layer of our actual being—one
layer for diseases to originate and lodge in and one layer in which to
initiate cures. Diseases can also arise in the subtle body (as proposed
by healers from Aboriginal Australia to ancient Greece) and can be
treated and cured there. Much ethnomedicine and energy healing
depends on some version of this cosmology.

Medicines of the subtle body are alluded to throughout this text. In fact, most systems of healing might be explained alternatively as medicines of the subtle body. In such a model, homeopathy and alchemy would be defined as pharmacies transferring the subtle bodies of plants and minerals (and other substances) to the subtle bodies of individuals; acupuncture would be stimulation of the energy sheaths of the subtle body; shamanic ceremonies would open a replica arena in which invisible entities transmit cures later manifested in viscera; and extremely light massages (notably those in which the hands do not even touch the body but palpate the "field" around it) would be massages not of the neuromusculature but of an energy field around the body. We pick up this theme in more detail in Volume Two, Chapter One.

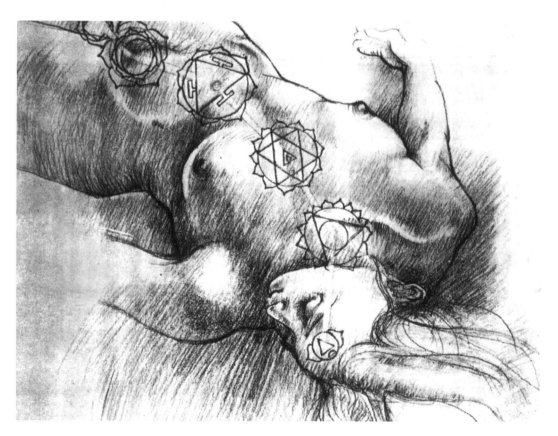

The subtle body is a full cosmological body, a product of the conception and birth of creatures in energy matrices. In one genre of astrological iconography, the human organism is represented as an orb which is also the axis of a zodiac through which miniature versions of the planets of the Solar System revolve in their annual cycles. This ikon depicts each one of us as a perfect Solar System. It suggests that, although electromagnetic emanations from physical planets may not orchestrate terrestrial events in the manner implied by horoscopes, cycles of cosmic astral bodies may govern the personality and destiny of creatures through their glands and energy centers, uncoiling in them sequentially as microcosmic springs. For instance, the Sun is said to rule the thymus gland and represent the heart at the center of the bloodstream, Uranus the sex glands, Neptune the pineal gland, the Moon the pancreas, etc. The interlacing ribbons of planetary orbits thus distribute bioelectric-like energy charged to differential tensions through the lymphatic, skeletal, fascial, visceral, nervous, arterial, and other liquid and electrical systems of the body.[20] Ayurvedic medicine provides us with a similar model of the sheaths of energy fields and subtle replicas around the physical body.

THE DEGREES AND types of subtle bodies described throughout the world may well represent series of ripples created by spirit descending into matter: at the outermost zone only the hint of a physical organism tints invisibility, then solider and solider sheaths congregate as spirit passes through denser and denser yet still subtle fields into the realm of mind, from there to the nerves and muscles, and finally into bodily fluids and tissues. Elemental medicine does not make a categorical distinction among these different levels of materialization; all are interwoven, their functions interdependent. What is blood at one level is a mixture of fire, water, light at another; spirit at another. In Hindu science the physical body is continuously refashioned of elemental components assimilated from food. The mental body is composed similarly of sensations, thoughts, images, emotions, and ideas—forms which

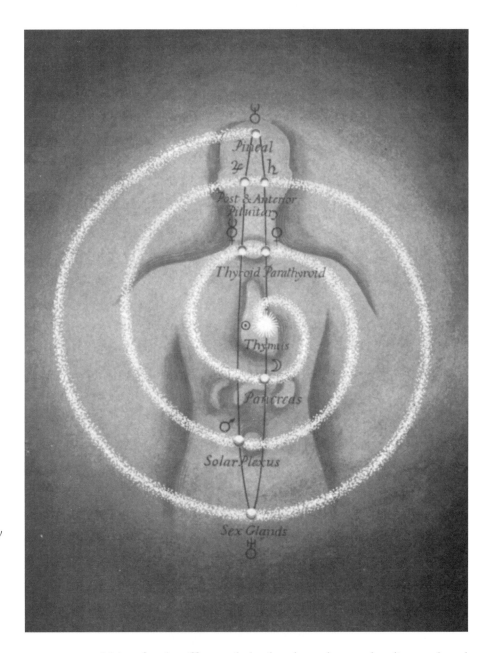

Man as Microcosm, from Rodney Collin, The Theory of Celestial Influence

are comparable to foodstuffs at subtler levels and must be digested and assimilated for healthy functioning (the astral body is considered an extension of the field of the mind, not a spiritual body *per se*). (See also the discussion of Gurdjieffian cosmology in "Esoteric Sources of Healing Paradigms" in Chapter Twelve.)

The *prana* body is closer to a pure spirit body. It draws energy directly from the air in the lungs and also stores the *pranic* aspect of food digested in the colon. Whereas corporeal substance moves through the channels, nerves, and arteries of the physical body and is assimilated into the flesh and thought, *prana* courses "through the ethereal channels called *nadis* and their plexuses *(chakras)*. The vital or *pranic* body exerts its effects by stimulating the physical channels which flow in synchrony with its *nadis*."[21] *Prana* is activated by nerves, fanned by deep, regular breathing, and dispersed through the skin and pores. When these channels become blocked and numbed, diseases originate. Illness can be cured directly by restoring the flow of *prana* through the practice of yoga and meditation. (See also "Rebirthing" in Volume Two, Chapter One.)

In Hindu science the *chakras* are the reservoirs and activating centers of *pranic* energy (in the West, as we shall discuss, they have become jargon for any and every form of energy plexus). The original Indian *chakras* are located at the base of the spine, in the sexual organs, beneath the solar plexus, within the heart, beneath the larynx, at the third-eye spot in the center of the forehead, and sometimes in the brain (these are also among the sites through which replicas of the astrological planets pass). Sometimes another energy center is proposed at the big toe, which is the point at which bodily sensation is said to awaken embryogenically and join to the central fissure of the brain (mythologically the river Ganges sprouting from the toe of the Creator).

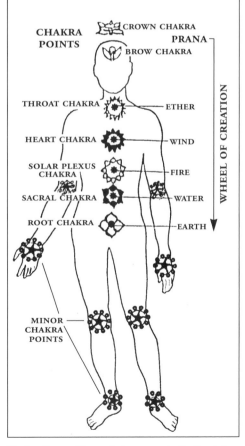

Reproduced with permission from *The Lost Secrets of Ayurvedic Acupuncture* by Dr. Frank Ros, Lotus Press, Box 325, Twin Lakes, WI 53181. © 1994. All Rights Reserved.

The actual movement of *prana* through the *nadis* is alone what creates *chakras;* otherwise, these are mere metaphors of energy centers. Even when they bloom in developed individuals, *chakras* are never conventionally perceptible. Different commentators report cones radiating beams of light, luminous arcs, spinning yarns of heat, spiralling vortices, whirlpools with rays of light traveling counterclockwise, carapaces lit like cities, etc. These radiances appear to emerge in the physical zones of the *chakras* and extend well beyond the body, from a range of twenty cm. to vast fields of incalculable size. An entire genre of immanent art is based on visions of such transcendentalia (for instance, religious iconography of China, Tibet, India, and even Mediaeval Europe, and, more recently, the "sacred mirrors" of American Alex Grey).[22] Paraphysical perceptions of the subtle energy of *chakras* may be visual, closed-eye after-images, sensations of heat, and tingling. Regardless of their mode of appearance or shape and activity, they may sometimes represent the *chakras* themselves and sometimes forms of energy in the corporeal aspects of organisms occupying the same spaces. Functionally it does not matter. Lade and Svoboda give one description of this system:

> The body's most important *nadi,* which is also the least used by the average individual, is called *Sushumna.* The *chakras* are arranged like flowers in a garland along the thread of *Sushumna,* which flows within the central sulcus of the spinal cord—or it would do so if it existed on the physical plane. More precisely *Sushumna* flows through the same space which on the physical level is taken up by the central sulcus of the spinal cord. Because these two structures exist on different levels of being they can occupy the same space simultaneously, an impulse in one often engendering an impulse in the other by resonance.[23]

A particularly potent form of *prana* described by Hindu practitioners is the *kundalini,* an energy represented as a serpent because of its powerful and potentially violent, cobralike uncoiling from the base of the spine where it is grounded. Dormant at birth, it provides a range of otherwise-inaccessible energies when activated by yogic practice.

The *kundalini* is experienced as extreme heat. The flesh tingles and vibrates. It is also described as colored lights and flashes, blue pearls, red curtains dancing, whistles, roars, chirps, hissing, and a sound like the playing of a flute. All of these represent the serpent rushing upward along the spine to its home in the brain. If aroused but not integrated, the snake itself becomes a source of disease and madness.

Each culture recognizing such an energy gives its own meaning to this event. For instance, the Bushmen of the !Kung bands of Northwest Botswana obviously do not know the Hindu serpent by the same name; yet they describe a fact:

> You dance, dance, dance, dance. Then n/um lifts you in your belly and lifts you in your back, and then you start to shiver. N/um makes you tremble; it's hot. Your eyes are open but you don't look around; you hold your eyes still and look straight ahead. But when you go into !kia, you're looking around because you see everything, because you see what's troubling everybody.... Rapid shallow breathing, that's what draws n/um up ... then n/um enters every part of your body, right to the tip of your feet and even your hair.
>
> In your backbone you feel a pointed something, and it works its way up. Then the base of your spine is tingling, tingling, tingling, tingling, tingling, tingling, tingling ... and then it makes your thoughts nothing in your head.[24]

Wilhelm Reich's apprehension that the curative power of sexuality would be tabooed out of public terror is worth examining in light of these cross-cultural experiences. How much more terrifying could it be than the *kundalini* and the "tingling, tingling, tingling"?

I N PRACTICES THAT are not solely and specifically medical, such as yoga, ritual dancing, meditation, esoteric transmission, and astral projection, zones corresponding to the *chakras* become key sites for personal transformation and direct healing. Different systems provide their own reifications of these sites. In some circles of Western holistic practice, the *chakras* oscillate between actual physiological zones and energetic aspects of the body. While still being called *"chakras"* (from their Hindu source), they are identified in number as anywhere from six to eight to fifteen to hundreds. The more there are, the more the majority remain undeveloped in most individuals. They are described as transmitting directly to the pineal gland and the central nervous system via a mode of magnetic or electromagnetic energy (sometimes organic magnetite in the cells). They function as receptors of information variously about the Earth's magnetic field; the psychic and energy fields of other organisms; weather changes; environmental heat, radiation, and toxins (including overhead power lines); also the individual's own organ systems and ongoing assimilation or rejection of food and medications. As such, they and their metaphors have been carried over into many disciplines of holistic health where they now serve as anatomical guides to regions of power for the development of a variety of energetic techniques. Imbalances within the organism leading to disease are often interpreted as imbalances within the *chakra* system originating directly from karma (esoteric causes). Thus, healing techniques are conducted to the flow of subtle energy on the deepest accessible level. Treating the organism through the *"chakras"* is one of the most promising areas for the development of new alternative medicines.

Holistically inclined engineers shine a weak form of coherent light on *chakra* points in order to stimulate their assimilation and movement of energy. Simple colors are applied to induce a homeopathic-like effect in releasing blockages.[25] In other techniques, the zones are massaged gently, or mere attention is conducted toward them. Sometimes, as noted, they are "treated" by hands moving above them. Polarity Therapy and Zero Balancing use a variety of methods of touch in different sequences to alleviate stress, alter energy flow, and balance the *chakras.* We will explore these techniques in Volume Two.

Ayurvedic Treatments

IN THE RANGE of cures it offers, Ayurvedic medicine is nonsectarian and resourceful to the extreme. It stocks enough bottles of different pharmaceuticals and herbals alone to fill the warehouses of all the American drug and beverage companies combined. "Ayurvedic medicines are made of a wide variety of substances derived from animal, vegetable and mineral sources made into medicated pills, powders, jams, wines, milks, ghees (clarified butter) and oils."[26] Other remedies include tinctures of plant-juice in self-generated alcohol, mixtures of syrups and jellies, decoctions reboiled with oil or ghee, distillations in honey, tooth powders, suppositories, mercury and sulphur purifications, etc. These are not merely represented as active drugs for single conditions; they are among the most complex and multifaceted medicines on the Earth. Each item is furnished in combination with other recipes and modes of treatment to create a continuously deflected vector to the core illness. Three typical drugs might be described as: 1) removing blockages, heaviness, and coldness and causing perspiration; 2) cooling and calming balanced *doshas;* or 3) driving aggravated *doshas* from the upper canal.

Any substance is a potential pharmaceutical, any form of mental activity or exercise a potential cleanser or restorer of balance. Dietary prescriptions, wines, herbs, exercises, and purifications (collectively known as *panchakarma*) are all modalities for altering elemental imbalances. Food, medicinal preparations, and even massage and yoga postures can be selected so as to supply humoral lacks and balance relationships. Colors, scents, and heated or cooled water are each prescribed medicinally.

> Metals such as gold, silver, copper, iron, tin, etc. are also used. Each metal is purified. . . . The metal is turned into thin leaves and very fine wires are produced. After making the wire very hot it is immersed in various plant uses. After such purification it is made into fine powder and mixed in juices of effective herbs. . . .

Ayurvedic and Taoist Medicines

325

Loha Bhasma or iron oxide is so minute and in such [a] fine form of iron that given internally it does not cause any gastric upset or disorder, is assimilated in blood very soon and increases the haemoglobin percentage very fast, whereas iron prepared according to modern pharmaceutical method and manner given internally causes gastric upset and disturbance in digestion.[27]

Multilevelled characterological diagnosis is central. A good physician is able to observe a patient and intuit which of the humors is at the base of his or her condition. Each person has an underlying constitutional type, the eight major ones corresponding to a pure *dosha*, two *doshas* predominating as a pair, all *doshas* imbalanced, or all in balance. With the infinitesimal degrees of subtlety in human makeup, there are actually hundreds of thousands if not limitless permutations of types. Thus, the physician must read not just the predominating humor but the actual dynamics of a complex energy state.

Wheel of Destruction (Vinasha Chakra)

HUMOR		ELEMENT
VATA	{ 1	Ether
	2	Wind
PITTA	{ 3	Fire
	4	Water
KAPHA	{ 5	Earth

Remedies must take into account both the humoral type of the person and the humoral excesses and deficiencies causing the particular disease. Ayurvedic medicine, with its goal of neutralization, seems to have developed in accordance with highly sophisticated versions of the law of contraries rather than by homeopathic principles of similars. Although Ayurvedic principles emphasize gentle, gradual changes, the actual qualities invoked at every level of treatment are almost always diametric contraries of the *dosha* in excess. Diseases are interpreted as conditions of too much or too little, of excess or lack. Thus, anything in life which can reduce superfluity or supply missing qualities is a valued treatment. If a *dosha* becomes aggravated or imbalanced, Ayurveda generally antidotes or relaxes it with foods, medicines, and activities of the *dosha* with the countering quality. However, since the *doshas* are thoroughly mixed in both constitutions and medicines, the selection of a remedy involves perspicacity vis-à-vis both the person and the medicine. The goal is to conduct the exact proportion of the excess *dosha* out of the viscera back to the organs which store it without disturbing the whole system by too impatient and linear an approach.

An adjunct to dietary change or direct medicinal doses is one of various *panchakarma,* such as fasting, therapeutic vomiting, purgation, enema, nasal medication, sweating by medicated oils, and bloodletting. For the old or unusually weak, palliation is considered a safer strategy than purification; this consists of "medicine to digest toxins, medicine to increase the digestive fire, appropriate diet and drinks, exercise, sunbathing, and windbathing."[28]

Although all the medicines are given on a physical level, the ultimate goal is to increase the flow of *prana* and thus to allow the *doshas* to rebalance at a point closer to their original harmony. Even though the *chakras* exist at too subtle a level for treatments to contact directly, the *pranic* field provides a medium for the energetic transfer of elemental energy in the activation of a cure.

In conclusion, Ayurveda is a medicine in the most absolute and pure sense—a medicine's medicine—precisely because it is not a medicine but a statement of the governance of the universe, hence the governance of man and woman. Ayurveda reads like a treatise of medicine as a political document, or as politics in medical language. If we governed our own kingdom of man and nature as much in terms of elemental balance and reciprocity as the Ayurvedic philosophers did, our society would not be in so much political and medical turmoil (which humorally are the same dilemma). Of course, that would no more protect us from invaders than it did the Indians. In fact, we live in the world formed by precisely the invasions of the tenth through sixteenth centuries A.D., and our medicines continue to radiate them.

Tibetan Medicine

AYURVEDA PROBABLY BEGAN to permeate Tibet during the sixth century A.D., an intimate of Buddhism, and later specifically through the adaptation of the Tibetan alphabet into Sanskrit. King Sron-btsan sGam-po formalized this process in the early part of the seventh century. In a remarkable event he invited three famous doctors to come to Tibet from their homelands and each to translate a major work of medicine into Tibetan. These included an Indian doctor (Bharadhaja), a Chinese doctor (Han-wang-Hang), and a Persian doctor (Galenos). The works translated were *Big and Small Louse Gravel* and *Preparation of New Butter* (Indian), *Treatise of Great and Small Scattered Chinese Surgery,* and *The Treatment for Cock, Peacock, and Parrot* (Persian). In addition the three collaborated on a new medical text, a synthesis of the three systems, and bequeathed it to the King under the title, *The Weapon of the Fearless One.* The other two doctors went home, but Galenos remained as the court physician.[29]

Tibetan medicine is thus to some degree an amalgam of Asian and Near Eastern medicines. However, it brought its own aboriginal qualities to these and implemented them in new ways. For instance, Ayurvedic diagnosis in a Tibetan context relies on a native system of urine examination for color, stream, and sediment. Urine diagnosis was highly developed in ancient Tibet and included minute variations of color (reddish, brownish, bluish, or a rainbow effect); density and size of bubbles; fineness or thickness of scum and its location *vis-à-vis* the edges of the container; offensiveness or rustiness of odor; relative warmth; and degree of settling or sprinkling of sediment—each one of these indicating the elemental source of a disease.[30]

In Tibetan cosmology, the five elements are Earth (the matricial base), Water (liquidity), Fire (stimulating expansion), Air (the kinetic

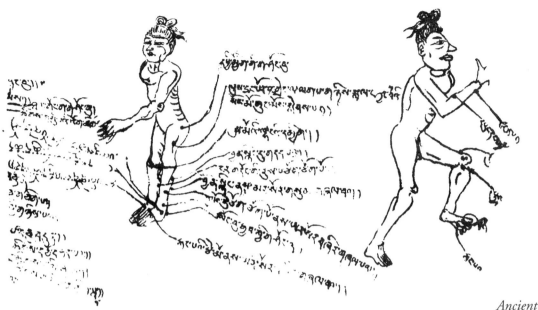

principle), and Sky (space). The three humors are Air, Bile, and Phlegm, as roughly translated into English terms. These humors represent, simultaneously, constitutional types, seasonal patterns, ailments, and medicinal properties. Their disease aspects accrete as imbalanced proportions: conditions of Air predominantly during the hot, dusty spring (and in hot-tempered people born in the spring), diseases of Bile and Phlegm correspondingly under the influences of summer and winter. Diseases of Air (giddiness, blue urine, hollow pulse, bitter tastes, stiff limbs) flourish in the heat and rain of summer and abate in the clear blue sky of autumn. Bile diseases (headaches, heat, hard pulse, reddish eyes, red-yellow urine) mature in autumn under the influence of strong winds and moisture and are dessicated by the wintry cold. Phlegm is frozen during the winter, so its diseases wait until the dampness of spring to thaw (loss of appetite, itches, swelling, slow pulse, whitish urine); they are absorbed into the heat of summer.

Air is not only the respiration of the lungs; it is the will to life, the spark of thought, and the coordination of nerves. Bile is the chemistry of digestion, but it is also the sharpness and focus of sight, ego and self-perception, vibrancy of the blood and brightness of the skin. Phlegm is a liquid and a flavor; it is also the kinesthesia of sensual reality, the source of somatic motion.

In what is likely an extension of Ayurveda embracing a more ancient North Asian medicine, foods, oils, types of water, etc., all have elemental predispositions toward both pathological and medicinal aspects. For instance, "peas are by nature sweet, bitter, cool and light. They cause diseases of phlegm combined with fever and constipation, stop diarrhoea, produce bloods, bile, and fat. . . . Sesame is by nature heavy and cold; it increases sperm and cures air diseases. . . . Rice diminishes phlegm, bile, and wind, increases sperm, and stops loose motion and nausea. . . . Oil derived from butter is by nature cool; it increases sperm, improves the complexion, creates energy and combats phlegm and fever diseases."[31]

The healing properties of plants are determined by their elemental biases as revealed in the five flavors (sweet, sour, bitter, acrid, and astringent): Earth herbs are heavy, pungent, and smooth, and administered to treat Air diseases. Water herbs are cool, oily, and soft, and used to combat Bile diseases. Fire herbs are sharp, hot, and tasteless, and effective against Phlegm diseases. Air herbs are whitish, unstable, and light, and prescribed in diseases combining Bile and Phlegm. Any of these herbs may have the hollow quality of Sky as well, in which case they are used as medicines for diseases of Bile, Phlegm, and Air. Like those in Ayurveda, the flavors of Tibetan medicine correspond to elements not on a one-to-one basis but as combinants in a complex system. The tongue serves as an ever-present physician, choosing those flavors propitious to the changing conditions of the organism.

THOUGH IT HAS five seats in the body, Air originates in the abdomen. The Air straight from the abdomen transforms food into nutrition. Brain Air aids in breathing and vision. Chest Air is turned into speech and memory. Heart Air enlivens the whole body. Intestinal Air passes into stool, urine, sperm, and menstrual blood, and also charges unrefined sperm with desire.

After the Air of the brain catalyzes the passage of food down the gullet to the stomach, the Bile there, aroused by abdominal Air, separates this food into sediment for the intestines and nourishment for the body. Abdominal Phlegm and liver Bile convert the nutrition into blood, some of which remains in the liver and some of which is passed to the different parts of the body as flesh. A portion of the sediment then continues into the urinary bladder, where it offers a diagnostic record of the process that formed it.

Bile from the heart is translated into self-awareness and wisdom. Bile also gazes through the eyes and forms the pigment of the skin.

Phlegm originates in the chest, assuaging thirst. Tongue Phlegm provides the flavor of food. Head Phlegm emerges in the orifices as the sense organs—the eyes, the nostrils, the ear sockets, the tongue, and the skin. Joint Phlegm makes movement at the junctures possible.

Refined flesh forms fat and bones, and unrefined flesh is secreted by the body. Refined fat crystallizes along the skeleton, the unrefined part of which becomes the precious oils of the body. The refined part becomes marrow. Refined marrow becomes sperm and egg. Refined sperm passes into the center of the heart, where it gestates the source of life itself. Unrefined bone forms the skeleton, teeth, nails, and hair. Unrefined marrow materializes into the flesh around the anus. Unrefined sperm is discharged during intercourse, along with unrefined ovarian seed.

Tibetan therapeutics integrate aspects of pre-Buddhist Bon shamanism and soul-retrieval with meditation, mantra-chanting, and visualization, i.e., "transforming yourself into a god, putting the god into the body and meditating on . . . the sixty-four principal gods . . . and

The mandala of the Medicine Buddha

[reciting] a mantra. . . ."[32] Meditational healers prescribe sacred syllables, movements, and internal visualization of colors, and conduct spirit guidance through internal states. The karmapa's successful visit to a Hopi kiva was not a cultural anomaly. Tibetan Buddhist doctors are shamans, lamas, and monks.

Traditional Tibetan medicine also incorporates the following: Chinese medicine, including acupuncture, moxibustion, and diagnosis both by pulse-taking and tongue analysis; Neolithic surgery (as discussed at the end of Chapter Seven) and other practical ethnomedicine, including cupping with copper bowls and bloodletting (as discussed in Chapter Five); a system of medicinal postures and movements (Kum Nye) resembling both the Chinese *Chi Gung* and certain Indian and Kurdish self-healing practices; and an ancient ethnopharmacy.

Lhasa sat at the center of its own medical hub, and students came to study at the university from rural Tibet, adjacent regions of China, Nepal, and Bhutan. The price of admission for Bhutanese was a collection of the various herbs and minerals in which their land was uniquely rich.[33]

The sophistication of Tibetan pharmacy is evident in the complexity and resourcefulness of its formulas. There are more than thirty different remedies alone mixing pomegranate juice or seeds with other ingredients. Other remedies use bones, rhinoceros horns, bear's bile, weathered human skulls, flesh, blood, herbs, copper dust, iron filings, millet wine, flowers ground with honey, yeast, buffalo milk, bark soaked in hot butter, secretion from bamboo joints, pine ash, and gold beaten as thin as a fly's wings. The following two recipes are among those still in use today:

> Glan-chen bcho-brgyad. Medicine with eighteen ingredients: yellow pigment taken from a concretion in an elephant's head or in the entrails of other animals, camphor, coriander seed, olive, black aloewood, bitter re-skon, red sandalwood, white sandalwood, blue water lily, aquatic insect, medicinal climber, costus speciosus, justicia ganderussa, gold flower, bitumen, chiretta, cloves. A different quantity of each ingredient is specific. When mixed, it helps against convulsions, choleric cramps, swellings and lupus. One teaspoonful should be mixed with boiling water and taken after meals.
>
> Srog-hdzin-bchu-dug, which has sixteen ingredients: cloves, black aloewood, nutmeg, a mineral drug called sho-sha, costus speciosus,

saffron, frankincense, sandalwood, lime, rush, yellow pigment, shan-dril, sha-chlen, salt, ginger, piper longum. It is used against nervous diseases and melancholia. To be taken in beer, or about one tea-spoonful of hot water.[34]

Tibetan medicine must also be considered in the context of Buddhism and reincarnation insofar as all births and deaths represent ongoing karmic cycles. Materialization cannot occur without desire at its core. Hence medicine is most purely practiced in the context of destiny, training a person to recognize underlying disease tendencies and awaken to his or her true nature—the ground luminosity that precedes incarnation in flesh. (See the section on "Buddhism" in Chapter Twelve.)

In Tibet, Buddhism contacted a regional tradition of divination, healing, and spiritual internalization. In that sense, Tibetan medicine, while replicating Ayurveda in many ways, is decidedly shamanic too from its implementation in the older Bon system. It is more oriented to reincarnational physics and breaking karmic cycles than to the Hindu delights of embodiment.

Chinese Medicine

THE EARLY CHINESE physicians and philosophers developed their own cosmology and methods of treatment. To a large degree, these resemble Ayurveda, though probably not because they share a common origin. Their likely last moment of connection was as branches of a basic Eurasian Stone-Age ethnomedicine of botanical lore, shamanic ceremonies, and elemental conceptions of matter. The original written texts of Indian medicine are five hundred years to a millennium older than the words of the Yellow Emperor. While some flow of migrants and traders between the two cultures probably occurred during this millennium (and afterwards), India and China were culturally and geographically too remote for it to have been significant. Yet we can still speculate: perhaps *prana* and *chi* are the same essential energies; perhaps two humoral pharmacies based on the law of contraries were once a single herbal formulary; perhaps *marmas* in another incarnation were primitive acupuncture points.

Traditional Chinese medicine and Ayurveda are also quite different. Despite obviously compatible principles, their actual etiologies do not match. *Marmas* notwithstanding, there is nothing in classical Ayurveda that resembles the fully developed Chinese system of meridians, nodal points, and energy redirection employed in acupuncture and *Chi Gung Tui Na.* Likewise, there is nothing in ancient China that replicates the comprehensive system of yoga and the subtly rendered relationships among tastes, scents, character types, and *prana* in India. It is difficult to make correspondences between the *doshas* and any equivalent humors in Chinese medicine, although clearly the same underlying elemental and energetic principles are at work in both. Thus, for all intents and purposes we are left with two almost congruent but distinct systems of traditional elementalism.

There are also some incidental differences. Hindu medicine has an esoteric aspect involving demons, possession, and voodoo that is not present in the more philosophically scientific Chinese model of healing. Hallucinogenic and medicinal uses of the psychotropic plant juice soma also originated in India. Rumor of its mystical virtues spread to the East, and the Chinese emperor Qin Shi sent out several unsuccessful expeditions in the third century B.C. to try to obtain samples of this plant.[35]

In conclusion, it is important to remember that each shamanic and elemental system is a whole cosmology, a full logos of the Earth or *imago mundi;* thus, individually they replicate one another in a pantheon of equals. They are not like separate academic disciplines, each with its own domain. They are each a science, with everything in their respective domains.

THERE IS ONE major current difference between Chinese medicine and Ayurveda. While Ayurveda has been adulterated and reconstructed from fragments and is a marginal holistic system today, Chinese medicine has grown from its roots into a powerful global system, rivaling orthodox Western medicine in some areas and in others integrated within it in hospital and clinical settings. Traditional Chinese medicine is presently reconstituted in the West to such a degree that academies with full curricula and degrees exist in many major cities throughout Europe and the United States. Although the template of this medicine is extremely old—the outcome of three thousand years of research—its present adaptation within the holistic-health movement is new, and the influence of an old template in an updated form is spreading exponentially. Whereas in the early 1980s, "Chinese medicine" in the West meant primarily acupuncture practiced by elder doctors from Taiwan and a selection of traditional herbalists and herbs available in Chinatowns in various cities, Chinese medicine in the mid-'90s means thousands of new young practitioners licensed every year, practitioners who often also have Western credentials in medicine, physical therapy, pharmacy, naturopathy, or psychotherapy. This roster continues to be enhanced by waves of Chinese doctors and *chi*-masters from the Mainland and the capitalism of companies importing and manufacturing Chinese herbs and herbal formulas and distributing them to the health-food market. As the number and variety of Taoist expatriates looking for students increased dramatically during the mid-'90s, *Chi Gung* classes were more and more being offered as physical education and/or movement therapy at universities in the United States and Europe.

The doctrine of the Yellow Emperor has been reborn and is expanding toward an unknown size and degree of influence. It may yet be that *Chi Gung* will become a primary therapeutic mode in the West, overshadowing all forms of exercise and aerobics, as well as replacing many traditional treatments for serious deteriorative diseases. This would not be terribly surprising. Taoist medicine seems remarkably adaptable to Western styles and flavors, so clothes itself easily in Euroamerican guises.

During the early 1990s Dr. Qingshan Liu, a practitioner with a medical degree (University of Beijing) as well as a Taoist background, began teaching *Chi Gung* to doctors and individuals throughout Germany while his mother continued to run a family school and clinic in Shanghai. He also fell in love on sight with the exotic motions of the mambo and tango, taught himself these from observation, and became the ballroom dancing instructor for classes of hundreds of students at the University of Munich. This endeavor led him to another rehabilitative "medicine"—wheelchair dancing. Ultimately he performed as the unimpaired member of a duo, won all the qualifying contests, and earned a berth in the international tournament in Holland, where he and his partner were crowned the wheelchair dancing champions of Europe. Whether or not this was a victory for *Chi Gung,* it was surely a statement of cultural flexibility and improvisation. Liu has recently invented a *Chi Gung* bicycle which he is trying to sell to American equipment manufacturers: the bike runs on mechanical power not *chi,* but the motions required to operate it develop *chi* in the body of the rider!

I N ORDER TO understand how Chinese medicine can propose something as exotic as the cure of internal pathologies with movement and breathing cycles, we must take into account a *chi* model of nature. Universal *chi* (either vital force, or bio-electric energy, depending on one's beliefs) flows through all of nature, sustaining life with its powerful current. *Chi* cannot be equated with any other substance or mode of circulation in the body. Though some Westerners claim that what the Chinese call "*chi* flow" is nothing more than the kinesthetic sensation of the flow of blood in the context of breathing, the Taoists, while agreeing that *chi* is associated with both blood circulation and breath, assert that *chi* comes into being prior to these substances at a subtler level and in fact provides their basis—literally activates them. Yet, in another sense, *chi* is more equivalent to gravity and electromagnetism than blood, for the Taoists say that anyone's *chi* is capable

337

of reaching to the end of the universe. Few people have such ambition, but the point is: it is hypothetically possible (given the inherent nature of *chi*) to extend one's personal quotient of it everywhere, in defiance of the laws of thermodynamics and the universal constant of the speed of light.

Whereas Western medicine uses for its diagnostic tests such things as chemical analyses, X-rays, MRIs, and CAT scans, etc., Chinese medicine seeks to measure the body's *chi* in order to tell whether it is strong or weak and whether it is flowing in balance. This means not only the *chi* of the body's fluids and organs but of its auras and energy fields. The Chinese herbalist or acupuncturist reads the *chi* by observation of eyes, tongue, physical movements, and speech. She may also instruct the patient to bring a urine sample. However, her main method of diagnosis is by feeling the thirty-six pulses of the body, each relating to a major energy function. The taking of the pulses is usually done at the wrists but may be attempted fruitfully at other parts of the body. The energies are interpreted not only *vis-à-vis* their own speed, strength, and regularity but in a total kinetic modulating pattern, each pulse relative to the other pulses. The separate pulses are different stations and interference patterns at varying depths along a single energy stream.

The internal organs, from I Tsung Pi Tu (1572)

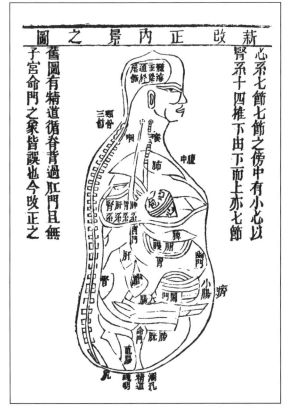

In three thousand years of empirical testing, *chi* practitioners have also palpated and identified between 4,000 and 5,000 secondary energy lines in the body. Masters of *Chi Gung Tui Na*—a bodywork system requiring years of training—can also feel *chi* directly in the body, especially at specific energy gates, and can sense its flow along complex secondary and tertiary pathways of the body and the aura.[36] How different this is from reading a lab report when the patient is no longer present!

One must remember that the most highly skilled Chinese practitioners begin by learning to feel the *chi* inside their own bodies before attempting the far more subtle feat of differentiating it in another's body. Practicing the art at this level is not a prerequisite for all Chinese medicine, but it is a requirement for the advanced *Chi Gung Tui Na* therapist.

PRIMAL ENERGY ARISES in the body in three ways: from the metabolic current established at conception (Original *Chi*), from eating and drinking (Grain *Chi*), and from breathing (Cosmic *Chi*). Once within the body chi segregates into Organ *Chi*, Meridian *Chi*, Nutritive *Chi* (blood), Protective *Chi* (affecting temperature and perspiration), and Ancestral *Chi* (affecting respiration, heartbeat, and circulation of fluids). Protective *Chi* forms an envelope around the body, roughly equivalent to the etheric sheath of the aura in the West; this layer shields the skin, viscera, and bones from external influences—weather, electrical and magnetic fields, and the effects of other creatures (including bacteria and viruses) beginning in their own etheric fields.

The organism is divided into four seas of energy which flow into the *chi*. The *chi* itself circulates through the meridians as the hours pass, from the lungs to the large intestine at 5 A.M., then to the stomach at 7 A.M., then to the spleen at 9 A.M., the heart at 11 A.M., and so on. Unrestricted circulation of *chi* through the meridians is considered necessary for health; where the circulation of *chi* is restricted, physical and mental imbalances arise, and the body-mind becomes sick or injured. Restoration of missing balance is ultimately a result of a modification of energy flow rather than concrete physical manipulation of an organ. Treatments may appear mechanical when physical devices and techniques are used, but the priority is always to regulate the flow of *chi*.

Bruce Kumar Frantzis is likely among the first Westerners to study in China long enough (ten years) to achieve a Taoist certificate of lineage; hence, his return to the United States to teach in 1987 was a major step in the acculturation of elemental medicine and the redefinition of medicine as a whole along global lines. While preparing this edition of *Planet Medicine,* I asked Frantzis for a list of the healing techniques of the Yellow Emperor's system, and he broke them down for me into sixteen basic components of *Chi Gung Tui Na,* indicating that, although some of these may seem to repeat others, the division among them is traditional—and crucial for training and purposes of attention:

- opening and closing all the physical body's tissues. That comprises joints, muscles, soft tissue, internal organs, glands, blood vessels, the brain, the cerebrospinal system. It also includes subtle energy fields and lines. Needless to say, these must be felt by the practitioner in order to be treated.

- directing energy up and down the body.

- measuring and shaping the external aura field around the body.

- initiating energy in circles and spirals at points inside the body.

- having the capacity to move *chi* at will to any part of the body, but especially the ability to conduct it with accuracy to such critical organs as the brain, the glands, and individual internal organs.

- being able to project energy from any part of one's own body.

- complementarily, being able to absorb energy originating elsewhere into any part of one's own body.

- mastery of the energies of the spine and their patterns.

- weaving the body into a unified field by connecting every part of the physical body energetically.

- stretching the body from the inside out.

- being able to differentiate and dissolve physical, emotional, and spiritual energies.

- feeling internal energies, moving them, and transmuting them.

- directing energy through the outer, secondary, and meridian channels of the body.

- being able to govern both the left and right energy channels of the body.

- being able to govern the central energy channel of the body.

- mastering the use of the three elixir fields or *tantien* of the body.[37]

A practitioner has to be able to do all these things in order not to deplete his own energy while treating a patient—specifically, to be able to pull his own energy back once he has transferred *chi* to the patient. He must be able to gauge the provision of his own energy reserves at all stages of the treatment and to have the skill and acuity to disperse from various levels of his field the negative projections and psychic influences of patients. Again, this facility marks the apex of mastery; it is not necessary to be able to perform all these deeds in order to practice acupuncture successfully. However, "physician, heal thyself!" is hardly a critique that one could direct at a doctor trained in this manner. Furthermore, "Historically in China doctors received fees from their patients on a regular basis and did not get paid if the patient became ill. In many cases the doctors paid the patients if they became ill for any reason besides accidents. They could do this because, at the level of *chi,* seeds do grow into trees, and it is the skill of the *chi* therapist to realize and compensate at the level of *chi* the way that *chi* will grow in the body and (subsequently) produce a corresponding level of wellness or health."[38]

T'ai chi teacher Benjamin Lo tells a story that illustrates the difference between medical expectations in the East and the West:

> The doctors in Palo Alto asked me to come and tell them how to have their patients relax. I thought that this was a good thing. When they're sick, people should relax. The doctors wanted me to show them *t'ai chi.* They wanted to teach it to their patients to help them relax. I came there, but they were so tense. How can those doctors

cure anyone ... tense themselves like that? I showed them the first moves, and they were unable to do them, they had too much tension. I said, "You can't go on, you must first learn to make the body soft, have less tension. Then you can teach your patients and be better doctors." But they said, "We don't have tension. You give us hard postures ... straining, awkward; they are not natural." But what did I ask them to do? Did I ask them to lift heavy weights? No. Did I ask them to lift even a piece of paper? No. I asked them to hold up the weight of their own bodies. And they could not do it. How can a doctor like that help his patients? If the old Chinese doctors were like that, no one would go to them.[39]

In the traditional East, overall health and vitality were credentials for the practice of medicine. In the West, doctors are by comparison academic bureaucrats.

Chinese Medical Cosmology

Cosmologically prior to the Five Elements, Yin and Yang underlie all Chinese cosmology:

Heaven was created by an accumulation of Yang, the element of light; Earth was created by an accumulation of Yin, the element of darkness....[40]

Yin stores up essence and prepares it to be used; Yang serves as protector against external danger and must therefore be strong. If Yin is not equal to Yang, then the pulse becomes weak and sickly and causes madness. If Yang is not equal to Yin, then the breaths which are contained in the five viscera will conflict with each other and the circulation ceases within the nine orifices. For this reason the sages caused Yin and Yang to be in harmony.[41]

In expression, Yin and Yang (like the elements) are integrated and thoroughly mixed.

If Yang rules the day, Yin enters with the night that meets it at dusk. Yang clears the air as Yin sprinkles fog. Spring and summer burst with ripening Yang; autumn and winter reclaim their fruits through Yin. Fire is dominated by Yang; water, night, and the Moon by Yin. But everything which is Yang is also becoming Yin. Everything which is Yin contains substantial Yang and is incorporating more of it, dissolving it in Yin.

Yang is the body surface, Yin its interior. The *chi* and the physical body exist in a Yin-Yang relationship, *chi* itself being Yin and the body being Yang. Yang rises; Yin sinks. Male is slightly more Yang; female, Yin. Yang accumulates, compresses, solidifies, thickens, integrates, fattens. The gravity that drives the hydrogen fire in the center of a star is the same Yang as holds the center to consciousness. Yin, on the other hand, distributes the light of stars and connects thought to nature and form. It blows out, puffs, softens, disperses. Because Yang is all the time hardening and materializing, Yin *must* disintegrate, lighten, loosen. There is finally only one cosmic force, with two poles of expression. As soon as a polar opposite manifests, its counter must come into simultaneous and equivalent being, hence, a ceaseless circle of cause and effect, effect and cause.

Paul Pitchford opens his book *Healing with Whole Foods* with a statement on the subtlety of Yin and Yang and their relationship to health and disease:

> Every object can be subdivided indefinitely, and each subdivision can be described in terms of *yin-yang* principles. Even in the case of a single carrot, unlimited *yin-yang* distinctions are possible. The carrot-top greens have less carbohydrate content than the starchy root, and are also of a different shape and color. If the top is removed, we can analyze the root alone, which has an outside, an inside, and also a top and bottom. It is more contracted toward the tip; the outside and bottom are more concentrated in mineral nutrients. Regardless of how one subdivides a carrot, there are still differences in every quality, including the quality of energy of each part. Even each cell has an orientation within the carrot and therefore a top and bottom, and an inside and outside.

With continuing subdivision (of any object), one eventually reaches the level of subatomic particles. On this level of continuous activity, the principle that all *yin-yang* relationships are in ceaseless transformation can be easily comprehended. Every object, when examined closely enough, demonstrates that all molecular and atomic patterns are either expanding or contracting, more energetic or less, or changing continuously in some other way. Therefore it is said that:

> *Yin* and *yang* are in continual transformation. Nothing is constant, even for a moment. A state of ultimate health occurs when the moment-by-moment transformations of the body and mind are harmonious. Disease is simply the state in which changes do not happen on time, or in the right way. They may be too much or too soon, too little or too late.[42]

Thus, as in Ayurveda, medicine must stimulate rebalancing rather than remove or kill symptomatic by-products. This is done, as noted already, by conducting energy along meridians.

The meridians, as channels of elemental *chi,* always take precedent over the physical organs. Western orthodox medicine is thus trapped in a fallacy of misplaced concreteness, which is why so many of its treatments merely redistribute diseases. We may think we experience solid skeleton and tissue, but at a deeper level we intuit the tides and pulses of our humoral composition passing along embryogenic pathways.

According to Chinese medicinal thought (and Taoist thought in general), the interrelationship of five elemental forces pervades nature, their cycles of mutual production and conquest reflecting the underlying basis of movement and change in the world. These original elements are Metal, Water, Wood, Fire, and Earth.

> The five primary substances of Qi *[chi],* Blood, Fluids, Essence and Spirit are energetic reflections of the Five Elements. The substances have no hierarchical structure: rather these substances are dependent upon and support each other. . . . The Five Elements play an energetic role in linking substances with specific tissues, organs and structures.[43]

The basis of *The Yellow Emperor's* diagnosis is assertedly elemental. In nature, *chi* flows harmoniously through the elemental cycle, and the degree to which the elements slip out of balance is the degree to which the world withers in spots. If the liver is inflamed, Wood is said to be on fire, and an acupuncture point must be chosen to douse that fire (i.e., to sedate flow). Diseases of the liver can also arise in the lungs, which are Metal, for decayed Metal (Air) stirs up Wood. Stimulation of Earth (stomach and spleen) creates fresh Metal.

A far-ranging system of correspondences and functional resonances provides further bases for diagnosis and healing. Colors, musical notes, planets, animals, aromas, emotions, etc., all have elemental designations. For instance, the Wood element is also blue-green, associated with the planet Mercury, Sourness, anger, wind, and the spring season.[44]

Weather is a primary factor in disease. Dampness or excessive heat enters the pores of the body through the skin and goes directly into the meridian channels. A physical wind dilates the pores and brings on the elemental Yang-Penetrating Wind, which breeds headaches and slows the pulse. This is because it penetrates inside the outer layer of protective *chi*. The dryness of autumn may conceal a deeper dryness, which parches, cracks, and convulses the interior of the body and psyche. Healthy circulation of *chi* provides a homeostat which continually protects the organism against these invasions. But *chi* is not only present (or not) from the genetic luck of the draw or as a result of arduous exercise. As in Ayurveda, one's ongoing emotional state and dietary practices are major aspects of the harmonious passage of *chi;* thus, maturation of the disruptive emotions of youth into calmer wisdom is crucial to the individual's quest for "long life, good health." In the straightforward parlance of the *Emperor:*

> Joy injures the heart, anger injures the liver, over-concentration injures the spleen, anxiety injures the lungs, fear injures the kidneys.[45]

This is a subtle process almost totally overlooked in Western medicine, or consigned on an imprecise, unscientific basis to the domain of

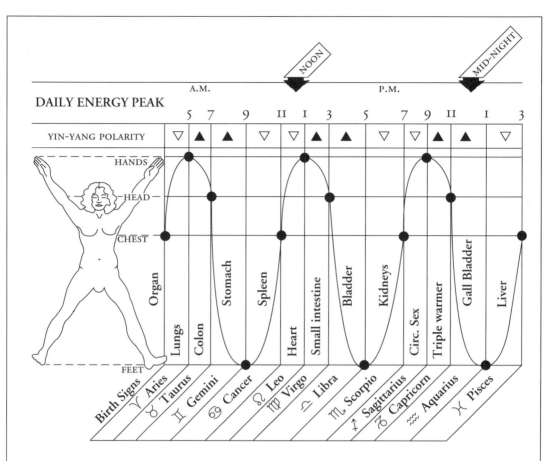

Traditional Oriental Medicine explains that there is one two-hour period in each twenty-four-hour day when the high wave of Ki energy makes each meridian in turn more receptive to corrective action: sedation or stimulation.

A person's birth sign is a clue to which organ tends to be weak and therefore in need of special attention and "energy care" during that portion of the day/night cycle.

From Jacques De Langres, Dō-in 2: The Ancient Art of Rejuvenation Through Self-Massage

psychology and counselling. In place of verbal therapy, Chinese medicine offers the more fundamental process of building *chi* through diet, exercise, meditation, chanting, prayer, and internal practices like *Chi Gung.* The premise is that everything we do and feel is connected to the basic energy reservoir on which we draw for survival and mobility.

ORIGINS

Our thoughts are as real as our tissues. If our *chi* is strong, then those thoughts will be clear and their emotions appropriate. If our *chi* is weak, then even radical changes of mind with psychotherapeutic insights will find no substance in which to take root and thus will blow away like straw. By comparison with our own system of mental, willed transformation, this is a noncognitive, unconscious process.

Taoist Embryology

IN MOST ORIENTAL systems embryology provides the operational diagram for healing. The formation of the organism in the womb endows all the elemental cycles with their initial bearings, morphology, vectors, and projective motions. Insofar as people are embryogenic fabrications maintained in an external environment, healing always reasserts a prenatal perspective: how systems like blood, bones, and fascia got formed and integrated in the first place; in what kinds of tissues they differentiated; along what course they migrated during embryonic development; and in what manner they maintain intrinsic visceral movements. There is nothing whimsical about treating meridians rather than organs: the meridians are preferable to the organs not only because they are more purely energetic but because they are prior to the organs embryologically and contain their developmental and sustaining currents. The organs must form around where the meridians have gone, trailing their energy of getting there. This is as basic a premise to osteopathy and homeopathy as it is to acupuncture.

As LIFE BEGINS, the human organism is divided into three channels: right, left, and central. All subsequent form arises as dichotomizations (yin and yang in cycles) from this trinary morphology. When the fetus is still shaped like a fish, the vein of life begins to sprout between its chest and navel. Branching second-by-second through the curd of semen and blood upward along the middle artery of the body, it forms the vertebrae and lays a plexus of tender veins at the right of the sixteenth vertebra of the back and, later, the first vertebra of the neck. From them it rises like a snake to the crown of the head, leaving a plexus track and the faint beginnings of sight. Another plexus forms at the heart, one at the navel, and another at the sexual organs. These ultimately fuse into consciousness.[46]

During the second and third months, the arms and hips and orifices form. The organs become outlined: heart, lungs, liver, spleen, and kidneys; after these, gall bladder, stomach, intestines, urinary bladder, and uterus or spermatic vessels. In the fourth month, the arms are threaded out, and the legs and palms emerge, ten fingers and ten toes form little beads. Fat, flesh, glands, sinews differentiate from the remaining curd.

During the twenty-first week, the system of internal air becomes sealed and a fine film forms on the top of the body, which becomes the skin. In the sixth month the sense organs are completed, so feelings and emotions begin to gurgle. The mind becomes extraordinarily clear, and the previous life is experienced in full. The being sees that it was "under the illusion there was rain and cold and thunderstorms" and that "people drove it [here]" to "seek shelter in the mother's womb as if it was entering a leafy hut or an earth hole or a cave or a clearing in the jungle."[47] This vista is familiar as Tibetan reincarnational cosmology. Actual birth will erase much of its clarity.

The raw tissue is relatively undifferentiated in the womb. There are outlines of heart, spinal cord, and gut. These are later imprinted and then carved out by the movement of humors along the veins and nerve grids that sprout as they form. Vital connections, such as that between the kidney and the uterus and testicles, or between the throat, esophagus, and stomach, are firmly established at this stage. As the body unwraps from its central core, its river systems trace the boundaries of morphology, embracing arms and legs to heart and lungs, brain to stomach and spleen, eyes to hands, etc. With this much nerve impregnation and the creation of guts and internal geography, it is no wonder that any lingering memories of possible past lives are obliterated.

They are subsumed in the sheer lightning and blood spurts of new embodiment. What could the ghost of a past life mean when one is being made again in the forge?

The body comes into being as the concrescence of embryological branchways; conversely, the meridian system is an ancient and original connecting network of energetic affinities. Our contemporary existence appears static and finished, but meridians are its archaeodynamic currents and channels. They maintain prenatal pathways among the organs in terms of structural anatomy and functional unity. Some historians believe that the development of canal systems and hydraulic agriculture in prehistoric China provided a model for both *feng shui* and the meridian system; however, I would imagine intuition of internal meridians is far older and gave rise to both geomancy and hydrology.

INDIVIDUAL ORGANS ARE joined to one another along meridians in paired cycles dominated by Yin or Yang at different levels. For instance, under Sunlight Yang, the stomach meridian runs along the leg and joins the large intestine meridian on the arm. Under Absolute Yin, the liver meridian runs from the leg into the pericardium meridian on the arm.

Then each of the meridians has an elemental predominance, half under Yin and half under Yang. Fire under Yin influences the heart and under Yang the small intestine. Wood under Yin influences the liver and under Yang the gall bladder. Earth respectively influences the spleen and stomach, Metal the lungs and large intestine, and Water the kidneys and bladder. These associations provide the clues for later application of needles and herbs. The doctor's goal is to subject elemental qualities (such as moisture and dryness, heat and coolness) to mutual tonifying or sedating at stations (points) along energetic pathways marked by the branches of meridians.

AS THE ORGANISM continues to develop, one series of meridians flows from the chest over the abdomen, down the insides of the

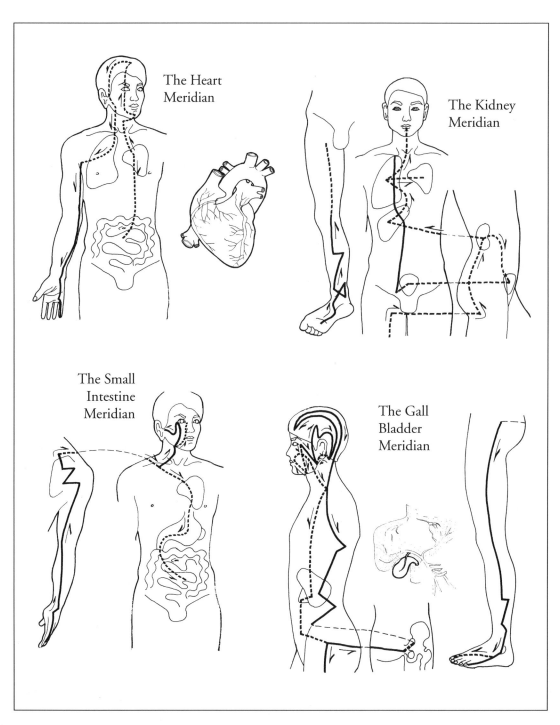

The Heart
Meridian

The Kidney
Meridian

The Small
Intestine
Meridian

The Gall
Bladder
Meridian

legs to the toes, and down the insides of the arms to the fingers. This Yin set includes pericardium (which is the membranous sac around the heart), heart, and lungs; in the lower half of the body: spleen, kidney, and liver. The Yang meridians go from the head and face down the surfaces of the arms and legs to the fingertips and toes; they include the upper meridians of small and large intestines and the so-called triple-warmer meridian which regulates metabolic functions (see below) and the lower meridians of stomach, bladder, and gall bladder.

It is important to remember (again) that these are meridians, not organs; as channels they are each given the name of one of the ports they connect (with its attendant elemental implications). The heart meridian is involved in harmonizing functions associated with the heart in the West (circulation of blood) but also with providing clarity in thought. The stomach meridian, as well as digesting substances ingested, catalyzes the flow of *chi* to the large and small intestine meridians. The spleen meridian, as well as receiving the stomach's products for assimilation, expands *chi* upward into the lungs and heart. The kidney meridian not only recycles liquids but stores *chi*.

That meridians are not organs is an axiom with corollaries at every level. A stomach ailment may be cured on the lung meridian passing through the arm because the ailment rightly belongs on that channel even though it is perceived as stomach-based and though it may be dominated by stomach pathology. As all of these points and lines are aboriginally connected, they pass into and out of specific organs that have solidified from humoral fluid. Thus the formative anatomy of an organ often takes precedent over its subsequent fixed position, and this is the basis for treatment. The distances among single organs, or at least our versions of organs, may well be overridden by ancient meridianal associations. Likewise, space not absolutely lying within the boundaries of an organ may still remain in its overall sphere of influence. The patient's sensation, with its accompanying attention to a site, may not always be an accurate guide to where the current is blocked (and certainly not to where activity must be directed to relieve it). The pain may be felt intestinally, but the crisis, or entry, may be in a point on the toe. The triple warmer, sometimes also called "three-burning spaces," which does not suggest any specific Western organ, presents thus a more accurate image of what a meridian is than one that *seems* to correspond to a known organ. In some writings this meridian is said not to have a form at all, whereas other writings describe it as fatty tissue. It is variously identified as rhythm, breath, temperature, metabolism, flushing toxins, and a link between man and the universe.

The twelve major meridians may be conceptualized as a series of three connected cycles. The first starts with the lung on the chest and goes down the outside front of the arms to the thumbs; there the large intestine picks it up at the tip of the index finger and proceeds along the outside back of the arm to the nose. The stomach meridian relays the cycle from just beneath each eye along the edges of the cheeks, across the throat, down the chest and outside of the front of the legs, ending at the second toes. The spleen meridian begins at the big toes, which have been twisted from their prenatal exteriorized position to the inside of the feet, and goes up the front of the abdomen and chest, ending just inside where the lung part of the cycle begins. In this, as well as the other two cycles, there are various branches, plus partial meridians, that spread like creases from the main flow, carrying impulses between meridians and distributing them to the most divergent parts of the body. For instance, the spleen meridian branches into the heart channel, and the kidney and bladder channels co-circulate at some points along their routes. Although the meridians have disparate connecting points, watersheds, and far-reaching influences across the body, their triunity suggests complicated

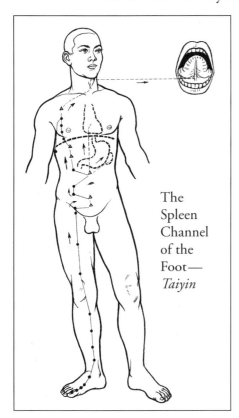

The
Spleen
Channel
of the
Foot—
Taiyin

352

unfoldments of the body in three layers, three interlocked creatures, each continuing to channel a prenatal stream through the organs that lie in its course. We may subtly intuit this partition in our wholeness as an interlocking of three overlapping lobes.

The second cycle begins with the heart on the anterior surface of the chest; it runs down the inside front of the arm to end at the little finger, where the small intestine begins. It proceeds up the other way, on the inside back of the arm, across the shoulder, to the cheek. The bladder line begins at the nose, goes past the eye, up over the forehead, down the center of the back in two main branches, down the back inside of the leg, to end at the inside of the embryo, which has been twisted outward into the little toe. The kidney starts on the soles of the feet and runs up the inside of the fronts of the legs, the abdomen, and the chest, to end near the heart.

The third cycle begins with the pericardium, continuing through the middle of the front of the arm between the heart and lung lines, draining and beginning again at the middle finger. The triple warmer originates on the fourth fingertip and passes up the middle back of the arm between the large and small intestines, draining at the ear. The gall bladder exits beside the ear and runs down the back between the stomach and bladder to the fourth toetip. The liver culminates on the side of the adjacent big toe; it travels up the middle of the leg, the abdomen, and the chest, between spleen and kidney, and ends near the lung on the chest.

There are also two additional meridians: The governing vessel originates between the tip of the coccyx and the

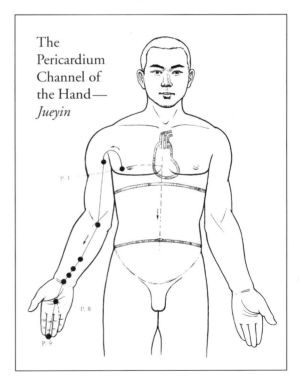

The Pericardium Channel of the Hand — *Jueyin*

anus and runs directly up along the vertebrae and the center of the
back to its twentieth point at the tip of the head. It has seven additional points continuing down the forehead to the tip of the nose and
ending at the upper gum. The conception vessel, the fourteenth meridian, begins at a point between the anus and the scrotum or labia and
continues up through the center of the body, with additional points
on the navel, at the middle of the abdomen where the diaphragm
attaches, and in the center of the lower gum.

Eight minor channels regulate the flow of energy and fluid through
these major fourteen, including one around the waist, which joins all
channels together.

From *Ling*
Su Wen
Chieh Yao

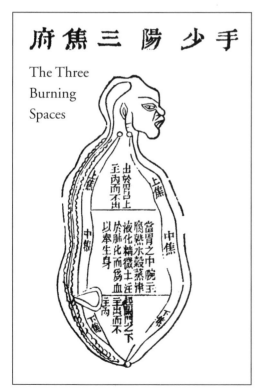

The Three
Burning
Spaces

THE FINE NEEDLES of acupuncture which seem to penetrate the
meridians are not so much mechanical intercessions, or even purely
exciters or sedaters, as they are "telegraph
keys" by means of which messages are sent
through the embryological channels from
"stations" called "points." The needles are of
different lengths, diameters, shapes, and
materials; they can be inserted quickly and
removed or left in and twisted or vibrated,
the latter by rapid lifting and lowering. After
application, the virtually invisible hole is
"closed" by slight pressure and massage. In
certain diseases a cone of herbs is burnt over
the point; ginger and garlic are most often
used. This is called "moxibustion." Cupping
with small jars is another method of directing flow; a vacuum is produced in a jar by
heat, and then the suction is attached to the
skin. In Japanese *shiatsu,* finger and especially
thumb pressure is used on acupuncture
points; the advantages include the direct

354

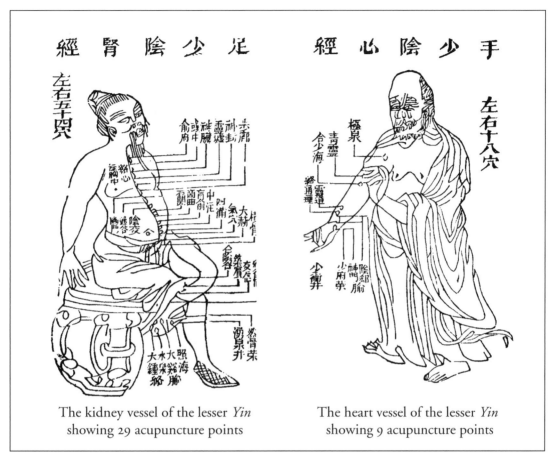

經腎陰少足　　經心陰少手

The kidney vessel of the lesser *Yin*
showing 29 acupuncture points

The heart vessel of the lesser *Yin*
showing 9 acupuncture points

From Ling
Su Wen
Chieh Yao

physical contact between doctor and patient and the incorporation of massage with corresponding effects on the nerves and muscles.

A 1975 Chinese government English-language publication describes the points as

> ... spots on the body surface through which the vital functions of the viscera and channels are transferred to the superficial parts of the body. They communicate with the viscera, sense organs and tissues through the channels. By applying acupuncture or moxibustion at these points, the channels may perform their function in evoking the intrinsic body resistance by regulating the vital energy of the viscera, the circulation of qi (chi) and blood, and so cure disease.[48]

*Ayurvedic
and Taoist
Medicines*

355

Acupuncture redynamizes and balances qualities of *chi* flow through bodily channels. As we noted earlier, while surgery moves the organs themselves and sometimes even removes them, acupuncture alters only the passage of energy through them; and since the meridians encompass the whole mind/body, it operates strictly on the level of holism. Chinese herbology is likewise a system of tapping into embryogenic potentials and distributing energy through the meridians. A particular formula may tonify or sedate the kidney, the heart, etc.

There exists no beneficent or harmful substance as such. Anything in excess is dangerous. Sickness occurs precisely when and where the underlying forces—Wood, Fire, Earth, Metal, and Water—are imbalanced in some fashion. But sickness is not itself the imbalance; it is the resistance that basic energy must dissipate en route to restoring its own equilibrium. After all, Yin and Yang are responsibly engaged in maintaining the universe, not in making life easier for creatures on worlds. They extend no charitable dispensations. If an organism resists, the flow cannot waste a second before it begins to restore the balance. It regulates harmony not justice; it seeks continuity not resolution. Otherwise, at any moment, in any galaxy, an imbalance might develop and spread by contagion to the rest of creation.

There is no "bad" energy; energy is simply in the wrong place. Perhaps the mind has stolen from the heart and lungs through the nervous system; the stomach has bloated itself with energy from the intestines; the kidney is overactive, the triple heater lethargic.

The same is true of the planet as a whole, and in *feng shui,* acupuncture of the Earth redirects energy in relationship to streams, seas, ponds, hills, mounds, animal trails, buildings, temples, graveyards, etc. Geomancy correspondingly provides information for where to locate structures, where to bury the dead, and how to avoid malefic forces.

Moving from a rough external map of meridian geography to the complex internal topology is a major transition for any healer. Points are not topographical *per se.* Each has a variety of influences and, though it lies on one meridian, may, of course, be stimulated or dulled to affect points, secondarily, on other meridians. There are also single points of exceptional power which lie on more than one meridian, and points which work in concert to amplify or to reach more deeply into the interior of the organism. When several lines pass through a region, as at the back and gums, it takes very subtle judgment to know which channel to ascribe a complaint to. An acupuncturist credentialled by a two-week workshop and bearing his kit of expensive needles and wall-charts is as much a hack as any quick-to-cut surgeon. Through misconception many Americans study the meridians and their points as if memorizing a color-chart anatomy of the frog. Yet the internalized experience of the system supersedes any geography, and a healer with good intuition but no knowledge of the charts can achieve better results than someone following a list of disease indications and a map.

(An incident with Paul Pitchford illustrates this point of view somewhat whimsically. As I was sitting in the backyard involved in discussion with him, I felt a sting on the inside edge of my middle finger and pulled my hand out of the grass with an "Ow!"

"Perfect," he proclaimed as I felt for my wound. "That was a point on which you needed work. See, Richard, the bee took care of your acupuncture. Now I don't have to do it.")

Chi Gung

THE TAOIST AND Buddhist system of energy accumulation and self-healing through physical and subtle breath, focused attention, and movement is known in the West as *Chi Gung* and has as its goal to connect the *chi* of every part of the body into a unified and unbroken whole called *Tong*. Any breaks in the *chi* will manifest as weakness, reduced vitality, pain, stiffness, pathology, neurosis, susceptibility to stress, an inability to carry out one's natural creative impulses, and a general sense of something being wrong. *Chi Gung* improves health both from immediate stimulation of the meridian grid and long-term restoration of the core supply of energy. There are thousands of named forms of *Chi Gung* (Cloud Hands, Dragon and Tiger, White Crane, Old Man Climbs the Stairs, Plum Blossom, etc.), but no matter the particularities, each genre originated as a set of exercises for training internal awareness and propagating and storing primal *chi*.

Frantzis describes being utterly baffled at first by the variety of schools and methods, all distinct and each claiming the most effective techniques. He now estimates that there are some four hundred separate lineages of *Chi Gung* in China, each of these with dozens of denominations. "The word *'Chi Gung'* is wrong anyway," he says (see the end of this section below); "plus, it is no more descriptive than 'car.' What we call *'Chi Gung'* is all over China and is part of early education and daily life. There are simple forms of *Chi Gung* that just about everybody knows, and then there are much more complicated forms that are jealously guarded secrets. It's like computer programs. There are some that are available to everyone and some that you need special authorization to learn."[49]

A skilled *Chi Gung Tui Na* therapist can literally affect the *chi* of a client's body by direct hands-on contact. Remember the sixteen components of training that sound like the trials of a Jedi warrior. More commonly these days in the West, *Chi Gung* is taught as an accessible series of exercises for general health or as a specific sequence of postures and breathing techniques designed by a therapist for a patient and intended to be practiced standing, moving, sitting, or even lying down (the most difficult posture). The patient is taught how to move his own *chi* within his body to heal a given ailment or to build up strength where weakness may later lead to disease. It doesn't matter whether the disease is tension or cancer—as least as far as the viability of using *Chi Gung* goes.

It is crucial to remember that *Chi Gung* is not exercise. It is an activation of the internal energy basis of the physical body, using external bodily mechanics primarily as aids—props for accessing subtler energy. If one is moving, one is often more alert, attuned to more subtle sen-

359

sations, and in approximate resonance with a *chi* layer. The *Chi Gung* exercises are meant to facilitate *chi* activation, but they are not themselves the heart of *Chi Gung*. *Chi Gung* is a hierarchy of internal kinesthetic and energetic techniques for moving *chi,* shifting it from areas of excess to areas of depletion. If this can be done with no physical motion at all, it is just as effective and sometimes more effective.

Students develop techniques for conducting *chi* and directing its flow through their meridians. They begin learning this skill by cultivating their capacity to feel their own bodies. At the simplest level, this means locating sensations, becoming more sensitive to them, and gradually comprehending their origin and range. *Chi* is a particularly fine realm of experience, but fortunately it overlaps with all sensations. Thus, the beginning of the differentiation of *chi* is the particularization of sensation itself. Westerners have difficulty with this initial step because, from their childhood, they are usually taught to suppress feelings and sensations. The topography of the body has come to register in their minds as a big blur permeated with bands of tension, spots of vague, inexplicable discomfort, and large zones of numbness or pure nullity. Frantzis describes a moment early in his study when he was asked by his teacher to move his liver. " 'My what?' " he recalls exclaiming. After the teacher made this same request again and then offered moving his kidney as an easier substitute, Frantzis had to acknowledge that he didn't even know how to feel let alone move these organs. "He looked at me without contempt, more with sympathy. Then he said, 'To whom did you sell your body? I hope you got a good price.' "[50]

A student cannot do *Chi Gung* until he learns first how to discriminate both gross and subtle sensations in his own body and how to specify these and send his mind to their locations. Gradually, after his perception of his body becomes more reliable and less intermittent, he begins to distinguish the actuality of energy currents passing through it (and later, through his more subtle emotional and psychic sheaths). Finally he becomes able to enhance those currents and to direct them to specific organs, glands, and brain centers.

As heroic as this sounds, it does not involve extraordinary feats. According to Frantzis,

> [This] is accomplished through internal concentration and motions that are externally small, but internally large, meaning that—from the point of view of someone watching—the practitioner's body may seem to be making small, meaningless motions. Internally, however, dramatic (or "large") events are happening: tissues are expanding and contracting, there is greater control over joint movements, nerve flow is increased, internal organs are pressurized and massaged, conscious awareness of internal body functions is markedly increased—even the fluids that make your body work can be felt and their pumping action increased.[51]

Chi Gung irrigates feeling in muscles that have been contracted or numb, eases stress patterns, and allows deadened emotions to melt in the overall flow.

Frantzis states simply: "The physical breath is used to forge a link between the mind and the *chi* or subtle breath."[52] More precisely, the energetic relationships among such regions as the crown of the head, the backs of the eyes, the spine, the joints, and the solar plexus are gradually and successively scanned, perceived, activated, and connected. As the internal map becomes real and differentiated, a practitioner can conduct special attention to certain power points, or energy gates (the third eye, the center of the temples, the armpits, the wrist joints, the lower *tantien* [at the center of the body two inches below the navel], etc.). As with the acupuncture points, there is no consistent external location for energy gates; they fluctuate in size in response to *chi*.

Chi Gung is also not just a visualization technique, though it may use images (like movements) as guides; it is the actual practice of energy cultivation and is based on meticulous principles requiring not only discipline but a willingness to accommodate sometimes unpleasant sensations and emotions. Visualization must move and transmute through actual sensations. Many New Age seekers tend to prefer systems which teach energy transfer through pure images, touch, prayer,

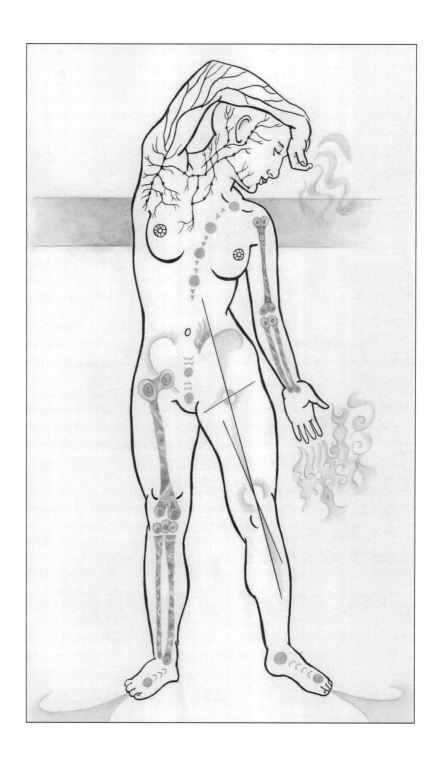

belief systems, etc.—that is, miracle or visionary breakthroughs of external power. Practicing *Chi Gung* is more like doing yoga or building a house than serving as a trance medium or studying philosophy. It is literally building an energy house by creating its materials and shape within the flesh. Frantzis reminds beginners:

> In doing your internal review, you may not have directly felt your body but merely visualized it, which is an infinitely easier task. You may not like some of the things you *did* feel, but these places will not go away if they are buried or ignored—they must be worked through. You need to *allow yourself* to feel the actual state of your insides. You will, over time, gain the power to release your internal blockages.[53]

Instead of releasing emotional energy in catharsis or abreaction (which can be draining and addictive), *Chi Gung* redirects it through the body/mind so that it can complete itself. Thus, *Chi Gung* is an Oriental version of psychoanalysis—or more properly, psychomutation—without interpersonal transference. At the same time, in keeping with elemental theory, it is as much a physical medicine as any surgery, for it flushes and charges the energy body. What we have here is quite possibly a primary system of internal medicine to which allopathy and psychoanalysis should be the adjuncts.

Yet it is difficult for most Westerners to accept that *Chi Gung* is even a real treatment. Accustomed as they are to aerobics, stretching, and jogging to increase strength and flexibility, i.e., muscular power, they may even have trouble accepting it as a form of health-generating exercise. From engineering to sports, conscious "efforting" is a dominant cultural theme in the West. *Chi,* on the other hand, requires receptivity. It is not a repetitive drill. It is alert and responsive to subtle change. *Chi Gung* achieves mobility precisely from looseness and its consequent effortless power.

We must remember that elemental medicine is neither literal nor quantitative in ways that we are used to thinking about, especially in regard to the physiology and milieu of the body. The elusiveness of *chi*

is reminiscent of the alchemical mystery of the philosopher's stone and the transmutation of metals. *T'ai chi* teacher Ron Sieh unintentionally summarizes this dilemma when he says: "I don't know what *chi* is. It is an abstraction. I experience sensation; it is real. We don't feel *chi*; we feel, period."[54]

To this, Frantzis adds, "Quite right. But we also feel *chi*."[55] That is, we feel many sensations but do not know which ones are *chi*. Until we learn to feel ourselves at all, we cannot feel *chi*. In our anesthetized state *chi* is simply a word, an abstraction. Thus we should learn to feel, period (Sieh). Once we do, then we can differentiate our *chi* (Frantzis).

Frantzis also emphasizes the importance of moving away from all levels of abstraction. "Westerners tend to read the *Tao Teh Ching* and say they're Taoists. They assume that Taoism is a system of mystical philosophy, but it's not. It's a concrete set of practices. It's something that is lived. The Taoists were the original book-burners. They felt if it couldn't be lived, it wasn't worth the paper it was written on."[56]

> *Chi Gung* is not some sort of spiritual visualization. It is physical, scientific, and replicable, as long as there are bodies. It has to do with the electrical wiring of the 'chi' body. This is not even the most subtle aspect of the human energy field. It's just one octave up from the physical body. The physical body is how dense, how compressed, matter gets on this planet. On a larger planet, it probably gets denser. The 'chi' body is just as real, just as physical, but at a slightly faster rate of vibration. There is nothing hypothetical about it. It's immediately accessible, and its grid is as reliable as that of any computer, in fact far more so. But you need the keyboard in order to access it.[57]

During the latter years of Mao, revolutionary China faced an epic medical crisis: the population doubled to 800 million while both Western and traditional doctors dwindled to half their former number, the outcome of executions, self-imposed exiles, or physicians going underground.

What the government did was this: they told the top Tai Chi teachers that they must design Tai Chi and Chi Gung programs for the health of the general population. Many of these masters wanted to keep their secrets to themselves, so their families could retain their "patents." It has been said that the government insisted that they make their secrets public, or face the extermination of their families down to the last child or relative.[58]

So, though a forced participant, *Chi Gung* became the first system of elemental or internal energy to succeed with a mass population in this crowded twentieth century. Ten of thousands of patients were directed from hospitals to local *Chi Gung* masters and required (through identification cards stamped by their instructors) to keep up their practices of this unlikely medicine. Now, a generation later, hundreds of such instructors have fled China and are showing up in the United States and Europe with longstanding traditions to offer and a statistically aging population as their potential clientele.

During the 1980s (and continuing), other highly publicized teachers with quite different agendas have been offering specialized and even notorious *Chi Gung* trainings, the goals of which vary from the cultivation of sexual potency, wealth, and power to martial prowess (arenas considered dangerous by experienced masters, perhaps even more so in the United States where they would be most superficially attractive). Needless to say, a certain confusion has developed in the West as to what the practice of *Chi Gung* actually is. The tendency to use it more for achievement than health is unfortunate in a time of widespread chronic disease and a beauty/prestige tyranny. In the words of Frantzis, "As *Chi Gung* becomes more public rather than being kept to a highly supervised elite, some students are being hurt by improperly practiced *Chi Gung* and by stupid practices."[59] It often takes an herbalist, acupuncturist, or *Chi Gung* therapist to reverse these negative effects.

Chi Gung is somewhat of a neologism anyway, having become a generic Anglicized term for a variety of *chi*-development exercises. Frantzis reminds his readers that *Nei Gung*, which embodies a diversity of forms for developing vital energy, is actually the parent Taoist system.[60] Chi Gung is its subsystem for energizing meridians and peripheral channels first, as in acupuncture, but has become the popular usage for both forms. *T'ai chi* arises from the antecedent system of *Chi Gung,* not vice versa, even though Westerners perceive the former as prior because it crossed the ocean and captured their imagination first.

We might consider that the homeopathic and osteopathic sciences (i.e., specifically the potentization of substance and the alteration of craniosacral rhythms) are Western counterparts to Taoist internal techniques, albeit from a quite different phenomenology and a more exteriorized relationship to nature. Underlying this dichotomy is a hope that someday we can combine Eastern and Western energy sciences, reinvent "alchemy" more ecologically, and derive technology from it anew in an elemental manner.

We return to *Chi Gung* in the general context of somatics in Volume Two, Chapter Five.

Internal Martial Arts

*C*hi Gung trains internal attention and alertness. The Taoist martial arts direct this outward. Using the awareness and power that come from the ability to move *chi* internally, martial artists have synthesized a triad of fighting sets from *Nei Gung* and *Chi Gung: hsing-i ch'uan, t'ai chi ch'uan,* and *pa kua (ba gua) ch'ang.* These are also self-healing modalities when trained without an opponent. Frantzis says simply,

> In the internal martial arts, all movement begins from deep inside the body and works outward toward the skin. The object is to completely fuse the inside and outside. External martial arts work the outside of the body, i.e., the muscles and reflexes, but eventually they can work their way to the inside if they incorporate Chi Gung. As a general rule, the internal arts of China work on general internal awareness, to feel the deepest subsystems in the body. External martial arts

are essentially concerned with moving the muscles and the outer frame of the body. Even if an external art has a movement that is exactly the same as one in an internal art, it will normally never penetrate below the outer layers of the body. For example, there are currently many Wu Shu people who are really only doing external Chinese martial arts with Ba Gua movements. To the trained eye, a T'ai Chi master and a ballerina doing the exact same movements would not look even remotely similar.... How the movements are done internally is the critical issue. The *Nei Gung* system is the difference.[61]

The basic sequences of internal movements (of which there are many different styles depending on historical origin from diverging lineages) go back to the Shaolin temple, which is also the legendary source of *kung fu* and Bruce Lee's *jeet kune do*. More accurately, the internal martial arts represent a fusion between Taoist *Nei Gung* internalizing techniques, which are far older, and the Shaolin fighting sets.

Hsing-i views the body as a microcosm of nature and assigns each of five vital organs to one of the elemental forces. The cycle of generating *chi* travels from Metal to Water to Wood to Fire to Earth; in the organs this is equivalent to a path from lungs to kidneys to liver to heart to spleen. If, for instance, there is too much *chi* (water) in the kidneys, then, reciprocally, heart *chi* is dampened and weakened; if there is not enough *chi* in the kidneys, then the heart burns too intensely and impedes lung *chi*. In *hsing-i* each of the five movements of striking corresponds to one of the elements and its corresponding organ. In this way when the cycle of movements is performed, the martial artist balances *chi* for the simultaneous purposes of improving his or her health and generating power.[62]

The splitting fist of *Pi Ch'uan*, much like a deep-springed slap-push (or literally "cutting"), is Metal. *Tsuan Ch'uan* (drilling fist) represents Water as it shoots upward in a tight spiral. The straight piercing fist of *Peng Ch'uan* introduces the element Wood. *Pao Ch'uan*, the sudden exploding fist that materializes outward above the forehead, is Fire. And *Heng Ch'uan* (crossing fist) is Earth as its baffling corkscrew punch

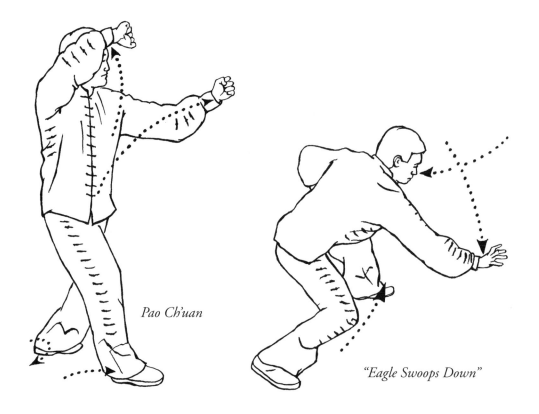

Pao Ch'uan

"Eagle Swoops Down"

appears on one side, twists under the opposing arm, and arrives from the unexpected direction. Complex combinations of these shapes are practiced as the movements of twelve animals including the twisting snake, the flapping dove, the swooping hawk, the leaping monkey, the clawing turtle, etc. The motions and postures forming each of these shapes are intended to nourish and stimulate a meridian passing through one or more vital organs, but also collectively to enhance the overall harmony of the body. As the shapes are performed, the flow of *chi* is facilitated and the fighter trains. The simultaneity of these two events is only now being understood in the West as a single unifying action.

The stronger the *chi,* the more effective the punch or elusive the dodge, also the more irrigated the meridians and the healthier the person. The external exchange is merely a replica of internal condensa-

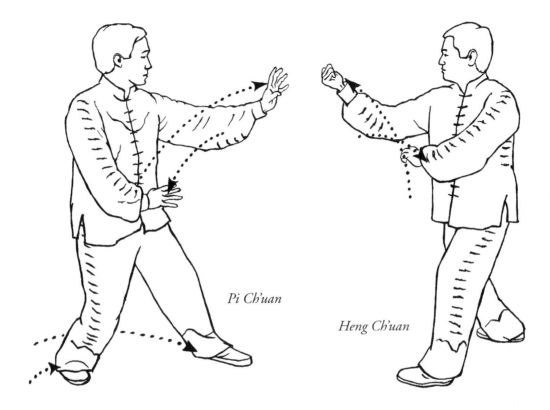

Pi Ch'uan

Heng Ch'uan

tion. As in *Chi Gung* the movements of *hsing-i ch'uan* should never be done merely mechanically; an external choreography is committed to memory only to imprint an internal sequence of those movements that have greatest leverage, compression from the earth, and angular momentum and lead naturally into one another. The transition from *Chi Gung* to *hsing-i* is crucial to correct martial practice.

The presently more famous *t'ai chi ch'uan* is a specific set of exercises linked in a regular sequence for addressing simultaneously the internal gravity of the body and the external field of the Earth; it is also a *chi*-generating form. The waist initiates a series of movements in which the body changes as a whole. The practitioner makes a ball of energy between his hands by alternately letting the lower hand and then the upper move with the waist. As he steps to the circumference

Ayurvedic and Taoist Medicines

of a circle to carry out subsequent moves, the ball is distributed and then recomposed, though never by moving the hands independently. In "single whip," the upper hand becomes a bird's beak and is shot outward by drilling the near foot into the ground. As the waist turns, the bird's beak is automatically a strike. In "stork cools wings," the leading waist twists the upper arm to one side and the lower to the other in a single motion forming two outward blocks. In "fair maiden works the shuttles," both hands follow the waist upward out of the ball. The lead hand rotates and curls one way to form a block; the following hand receives the full torque from the earth and rotates a quarter turn the other way underneath the upper hand's protection and delivers a strike. Each move is always itself while becoming the next move. There are thus no breaks and no separate moves, only a shifting sequence of Yin and Yang, one filling, the other emptying. As in nature, weight and substantiality exchange with emptiness and yielding and release back into them. One's self is a target for the opponent, then one is gone; then one strikes—all in harmony.

The *t'ai chi* master uses gravity and *chi* in a way that allows the body to move effortlessly without opposing any force it encounters (internal or external), thus gaining access to its own intrinsic resource of effortless power. That is, *t'ai chi ch'uan* teaches *chi* cultivation through yielding and flexibility of movement. Even as the person doing the set creates, builds, and moves the *chi* ball of energy, she practices precise footwork, dissolves muscular rigidity by sensing herself at every moment, and activates her *tantien*. All motion is generated from her core. The soft, willowy appearance of *t'ai chi ch'uan* is the outward manifestation of *chi* itself in a context of supple receptivity. The practitioner seems like water. *Chi* is a fluid.

The English translation of the *T'ai Chi Classics* puts the matter succinctly:

> Let the postures be without breaks or holes, hollows or projections, or discontinuities and continuities of form. The motion should be

rooted in the feet, released through the legs, controlled by the waist, and manifested through the fingers.... In motion all parts of the body must be light, nimble, and strung together.[63]

Then:

The *hsin* (mind) mobilizes the *ch'i* (breath). Make the *ch'i* sink softly; then it gathers and permeates the bones. The *ch'i* mobilizes the body. Make it move smoothly, then it easily follows (the direction of) the *hsin*.[64]

Those who mistake *t'ai chi* as just the position and torque of the body vis à vis a real or imagined opponent miss how the form includes the internal organs in their viscosity and contiguity, how the skeleton and muscles initially crowd the organs or give them space, how energy flows through the meridians. Even paralyzed people have been known to learn a form of *t'ai chi* from observation and to replicate it inside their body/mind without visible external motion. In a mode virtually identical to *Chi Gung,* the external power of the *t'ai chi* practitioner arises directly out of raising and dispersing internal vital force from the energy gate of the *tantien* through the governing and conception vessels, the nervous and circulatory systems, and the meridian branches. The script moves seamlessly from medicinal to martial: "Be mindful of insubstantial and substantial changes; the *ch'i* spreads throughout without hindrance. Being still, when attacked by the opponent, be tranquil and move in stillness; (My) changes caused by the opponent fill him with wonder."[65] They are caused by him because—in the sticky, closed energy cycle between two people—"my moves" mirror and neutralize his less internalized attempts to strike and retreat. In most people this potential for yielding and mirroring is impeded by imbalanced posture, restricted pliability, ambivalent movement, and unclear thoughts. Not only does rigidity make an ineffective fighter, but its distortion is transmitted through the organs in the form of latent diseases.

The martial result of *t'ai chi* is an almost incidental effect of correct posture and attention. Sieh writes:

When fist meets target we remain relaxed, aligned, and bottomed out. We actually displace their weight, their space, with our fist, and with relaxed alignment we put our weight into our fist. We hit, or simply move, with our whole body; everything is involved. They bounce off us.[66]

Even his description may represent a more mechanical form of *t'ai chi ch'uan* than that practiced by the most advanced masters. Ultimately they move internally without any discernible outward form. Their *t'ai chi ch'uan* seems ghostlike, psychokinetic. Old men repel young boxers who rush at them; without lifting a finger (or lifting a mere finger), they send them reeling uncontrollably backward, sometimes for a hundred feet or more. Contemporary master Cheng Man-ch'ing told his students: "The body is like a floating cloud. In push-hands the hands are not needed. The whole body is a hand and the hand is not a hand."[67]

More strenuous and exacting than most forms of medical *Chi Gung,* the *t'ai chi* exercises work on correcting internal distortions, effecting a gradual realignment through repetition day after day, year after year. *Pa kua ch'ang,* with its complex stepping techniques and multicircular patterns, generates a three-dimensional grid of emerging spirals which, if mastered, translate the circles of *t'ai chi ch'uan* into spheres. With each step the angle of the foot changes and the palms reflect the rotation of the *tantien. Pa kua ch'ang* is considered to be a direct experience of the energies of the *I Ching* trigrams and hexagrams—how they manifest in the human realm and how they change as the individual moves in fighting postures and concurrently through the positions of Taoist internal alchemy, whether sitting, moving or lying down. The seemingly simple act of walking a circle has such a plethora of ever subtler internal movements practiced and internalized simultaneously at so many levels that practitioners traditionally did their *pa kua* sets three and four hours a day.[68]

The role of the teacher in any of these arts is to correct the student over and over and to make the increasingly more minute adjustments that lead to an accurate alignment and more subtle manifestations and changes. The process is based on increasing self-awareness, not accomplishing gymnastic proficiency. In Benjamin Lo's description of *t'ai chi ch'uan:*

> First you do the move incorrectly and don't know it. How can you know? Then you learn the form and know you make an error but what is the error? How can you know? Then you know what is the error, but, even though you know, you cannot correct it. Finally you correct it. This is how we study.[69]

This is also how we internalize our attention and discover *chi.*

As sensation builds and movements are internalized, the meridians are flushed and infinitesimally but uninterruptedly the circulation of medicinal *chi* guides the spine to straighten and the organs to soften. It may take ten years of practice to achieve the slightest change of a fraction of a degree in the angle of the bones and the motility of the viscera, but this change, so minute from an external perspective, reflects an enormous shift for organs contained in the small spaces of the body cavity.

Notes

1. Ira M. Rutkow, *Surgery: An Illustrated History* (St. Louis: Mosby-Year Book, 1993), p. 68.

2. Quoted in A. Lade and R. Svoboda, *Tao & Dharma: A Comparison of Ayurveda and Chinese Medicine,* unpublished manuscript at the time of publication.

3. Quoted in Chandrashekhar G. Thakkur, *Ayurveda: The Indian Art & Science of Medicine* (New York: ASI Publishers, Inc., 1974), p. 34.

4. Lade and Svoboda, *Tao & Dharma.*

5. Eva M. Herriot, "Ayurvedic Sense Therapy," *Yoga Journal* (January/February 1992), pp. 28–29.

6. Lade and Svoboda, *Tao & Dharma.*

7. Ibid.

8. Ibid.

9. Herriot, "Ayurvedic Sense Therapy," p. 20.

10. Deepak Chopra, *Quantum Healing: Exploring the Frontiers of Mind/Body Medicine* (New York: Bantam Books, 1989), p. 237.

11. The information in this section comes from both Lade and Svoboda, *Tao & Dharma,* and Thakkur, *Ayurveda: The Indian Art & Science of Medicine.*

12. Quoted in Thakkur, *Ayurveda: The Indian Art & Science of Medicine,* p. 34.

13. Herriot, "Ayurvedic Sense Therapy," pp. 30–31.

14. Lade and Svoboda, *Tao & Dharma.*

15. Ibid.

16. Gerrit Lansing, "Fundamentals of Indian Medical Theory," from *Notes on Structure and Sign in Ayurveda,* unpublished manuscript, 1981.

17. Sylvan Muldoon and Hereward Carrington, *The Projection of the Astral Body* (New York: Samuel Weiser, Inc., 1970), p. 15.

18. David Tait, "Konkomba Sorcery," in John Middleton (ed.), *Magic, Witchcraft, and Curing* (New York: The Natural History Press, 1967), p. 156.

19. Muldoon and Carrington, *The Projection of the Astral Body,* p. 47.

20. Rodney Collin, *The Theory of Celestial Influence* (London: Stuart and Watkins, Ltd., 1954), p. 138 et seq.

21. Lade and Svoboda, *Tao & Dharma.*

22. Alex Grey, *Sacred Mirrors* (Rochester, Vermont: Inner Traditions, 1990).

23. Lade and Svoboda, *Tao & Dharma.*

24. Lee Sannella, *Kundalini—Psychosis or Transcendence* (San Francisco: Dakin, 1976), p. 14.

25. William Croft, C. S. T., "Light Energy Practices (Yoga/Qigong/Aikido) and *Working with Light*—a Synergy," flyer, 1993.

26. Lade and Svoboda, *Tao & Dharma.*

27. Ibid.

28. Ibid.

29. Ven. Rinpoche Jampal Kunzang Rechung, *Tibetan Medicine* (Berkeley: University of California Press, 1973), p. 15.

30. Ibid. (as a source for this and succeeding paragraphs)

31. Ibid., pp. 59–60.

32. Ibid., p. 267.

33. Personal communication from Steven Goodman upon his return from a visit to Bhutan in 1994.

34. Rechung Rinpoche, *Tibetan Medicine*, p. 27.

35. Lade and Svoboda, *Tao & Dharma*.

36. I am indebted to Bruce Kumar Frantzis for providing me with much of the information in this chapter. I have learned from him by taking his classes, interviewing him, and reading his drafts for a future book. Because this book is not yet published, I refer to it by its working title: *The Tao in Action: The Personal Practice of the I Ching and Taoism in Daily Life* (tentatively North Atlantic Books, 1996). I quote from Frantzis' already-published book separately.

37. See previous note. Material quoted may appear in Frantzis' book in a different form.

38. Ibid.

39. Benjamin Lo, verbal comments during a *t'ai chi* class in San Francisco, 1978.

40. *Huang Ti Nei Ching Su Wên,* translated by Ilza Veith as *The Yellow Emperor's Classic of Internal Medicine* (Berkeley: University of California Press, 1966), p. 15.

41. Ibid., p. 108.

42. Paul Pitchford, *Healing with Whole Foods: Oriental Traditions and Modern Nutrition* (Berkeley, California: North Atlantic Books, 1993), pp. 12–13.

43. Lade and Svoboda, *Tao & Dharma*.

44. *The Yellow Emperor's Classic of Internal Medicine* (see footnote 40 above).

45. Ibid., p. 117.

46. This and succeeding paragraphs are drawn from information in *The Yellow Emperor's Classic of Internal Medicine*.

47. Rechung Rinpoche, *Tibetan Medicine,* p. 32.

48. The Academy of Traditional Chinese Medicine, *An Outline of Chinese Acupuncture* (Peking: Foreign Languages Press, 1975), pp. 69–70.

49. B. K. Frantzis, statement during a class, Fairfax, California, 1994.

50. Ibid.

51. B. K. Frantzis, *Opening the Energy Gates of Your Body* (Berkeley, California: North Atlantic Books, 1993), p. 35.

52. Ibid., p. 29.

53. Ibid., p. 55.

54. Ron Sieh, *T'ai Chi Ch'uan: The Internal Tradition* (Berkeley, California: North Atlantic Books, 1993), p. 25.

55. Frantzis, comment on text of *Planet Medicine,* 1994.

56. Frantzis, personal communication, Fairfax, California, 1994.

57. Ibid.

58. Frantzis, *Opening the Energy Gates of Your Body,* pp. 9–10.

59. Frantzis, *The Tao in Action* (see footnote 36 above).

60. Frantzis, *Opening the Energy Gates of Your Body,* p. 27.

61. Ibid.

62. I am indebted to my *hsing-i* teacher David Tircuit for teaching me this formal conceit, continued also in the next paragraph.

63. Benjamin Pang Jeng Lo, Martin Inn, Robert Amacker, and Susan Foe (translators), *The Essence of T'ai Chi Ch'uan: The Literary Tradition* (Berkeley, California: North Atlantic Books, 1979), pp. 20–21.

64. Ibid., p. 43.

65. Ibid., p. 63.

66. Sieh, *T'ai Chi Ch'uan: The Internal Tradition,* p. 25.

67. Lo et al., *The Essence of T'ai Chi Ch'uan: The Literary Tradition,* p. 95.

68. Frantzis, personal communication, 1994.

69. Benjamin Pang Jeng Lo, comments during a *t'ai chi ch'uan* class, San Francisco, 1978.

CHAPTER TEN

Sigmund Freud and the Origin of Psychotherapeutic Healing

The Role of Psychological Medicine

THUS FAR IN *Planet Medicine* I have traced and mapped historical healing systems with the goal of understanding them in contemporary terms. In the remainder of this volume and throughout the second volume (subtitled "Modalities") I will focus on newer alternative healing systems plus individual modalities separate from their systems. I will also explore methods that have departed from their historic forms. From there I will work back toward a global synthesis. Though "planet medicine" was originally presented in terms of indigenous modalities, I will seek it anew in the collectivity of all systems—the latent features they share, the meanings they strive to establish, the commodizations they suffer, the manners in which they continue both to diverge and fuse, and the possible future of medicine itself.

I will begin with psychoanalysis because it is the single most unifying thread of contemporary alternative medicine. Although not all holistic medicines acknowledge or even admire psychoanalysis, they all to some degree or another share metaphors it provides, and they communicate with one another in its now universal language. While psychoanalytic healing is so flawed conceptually that its ultimate therapeutic impact may turn out to be almost nil, psychosymbolic analysis has itself become a code whereby many nonpsychological holistic systems influence and become influenced by one another. *Chi Gung,* shamanism, Buddhist meditation, Reiki, craniosacral therapy, etc., all owe a debt to psychology as the price of operating in contemporary Western society. Even when the currency of that debt is their explicit critique of psychoanalytic process as an effective mode of therapy, the price is exacted by their having to arrive at that critique—whether they realize it or not—in terms of some combination of ego definition, sublimation, projection, trauma, cathexis, and the unconscious mind. Stated differently, holistic practices use psychology as a compass to locate the degrees by which their own methods embrace or counteract its epistemology (i.e., the psychological origin and unconscious encryption and transfusion of disease states).

Psychoanalysis is also as far as orthodox medicine has been willing to come to meet the soul—or at least a metaphor of it (i.e., the psyche as an ego state outside of time). This does not make allopathic psychiatry either shamanic or vitalistic, for addressing cognitive processes is quite different from reifying spirits or disembodied energies. The "soul" is a person, so psychology is soul science not spiritual science.

Psychoanalysis emerged from pre-Freudian intimations regarding dreams, hysteria, and the like, developed through Freud's systemization of these, and then evolved into territories beyond his imagination. On the side of healing, psychiatry invented new roles for the shaman and "word doctor" so that at least some of their personae could join the Western physician as colleagues. But, on the side of science, it extended the mechanistic model to include language and psyche and thus further ostracized the true spiritual healer as a nonprofessional. Although Freud provided a framework of explanation for imaginal and psychic things, he maintained the Western bias by making them subsets and sublimations of concrete things. Back on the healing side, psychiatry obliterated the basis for a solely anatomical organism and thereby forced scientific medicine to abandon some of its core, including materialistic territory it had seized from the shaman and the spiritualist over the centuries. In that sense, it laid the groundwork for a return to "native" medicine, but, as we intimated earlier in this book, by setting the terms for that return in psychosomatic and symbolic language, it made it into an utterly new and privatized event.

O F THE FORERUNNERS of institutionalized alternative medicine, psychoanalysis was the one that provided the most ready-made niche within the professional mainstream; it is the "holistic godfather" in that sense. It offered Western thought the first inkling of solutions to problems that had previously been poorly conceived and thus insoluble (namely, the source of dreams, irrational acts, madness, and symbolism itself). Once the scope of the unconscious was evident, it was only a matter of time before all other formal philosophy was displaced and reformulated to provide it a space.

By "psychoanalysis" I mean a diverse network of traditions arising from the work of Sigmund Freud (1856–1939), not exclusively the ones he sanctioned but a broad transformation he catalyzed. In the birth of psychological medicine the assignment of Freud's absolute paternity is perhaps challengeable, but there is no other single pretender. Freud passed his scepter on to a clinical orthodoxy, its farthest extension now a series of behaviorist and psychotropic schools that pay little homage to their founder.

The Unconscious

F IRST AND FOREMOST, Freud disclosed unconscious process. Or more accurately, he opened the door of Western rationalism to the hidden nature of its own thought process during the height of its attempt to reify the entirety of the physical world. In this way, Freud both furthered and undermined materialism and logical positivism. Scientists were still delighting in the new levels of organization they had discovered through physics, chemistry, and biology when Freud added mental phenomena to the repertoire. By making thought formally part of nature, he enlarged both the categories of reality and the understanding of human existence.

Unconsciousness had adopted many prior personae and for millennia danced in different mysterious costumes in the West. Shamans, magicians, clowns, poets, and philosophers had embraced heterogenous shadow realms and unleashed some of their powers. But Western orthodoxy did not view these performers in their true dangerous and multidimensional regalia. It had come to divide the kingdom of reality between concrete scientific types of things whose existence was experienced directly and, to all intents and purposes, could be proven, and other phantasmagoria which were ceded to a realm of vestigial and primitive humanity—to the Dark Ages so recently past. The two *de facto* exceptions were those flights of imagination allowed to artists and the disease of insanity reserved for madmen. But neither was "real" in the sense of legal accountability or physical science; neither was held fully accountable to the laws of nature. They existed solely in a lacuna that was remarkable for the simultaneous blatancy of its presence and absence of any acknowledgment of that. Psychic phenomena may still be scientifically hypothetical, and artistic and spiritual life—the imaginal worlds of music, poetry, expressionist painting, and cosmic vision—have no scientific status at all and are usually identified with ethnocentric hierarchies of taste. The only way this whole latter territory could be salvaged for science was by being proven to be "true," i.e., to exist in the same way all things exist, by the same natural laws. This is the feat Freud accomplished. He gave unconsciousness shape and location.

He uncovered laws by which the worlds of fantasy, madness, and nonsense were directly connected to the world of concrete phenomena. These were finally the same world. The zaniest dream was as much part of nature as a boulder in a field or frogs about a pond.

Once Freud exposed the energetic basis of mind, nothing, no matter how bizarre or extravagant, could transgress its laws—no dream, no perversion, no attack on innocent civilians, no state of delirium, no slip of the tongue. Freud saddled Western civilization with its unconscious for the duration, and perhaps he did it just in time, before the illusion of grandeur and progress had gotten totally out of hand. There was no longer any way to pretend that the shadow realms could be purged forever by a golden age of reason.

Yet the ideal of transcendent progress was so strong that it continues to dominate our modern world at least as much as Freud's correction (and despite massive evidence to the contrary). With our ongoing expansion of knowledge, all things are presumed to be in the process of being brought under benign control; of course, this requires that all things first become conscious. Those things that cannot be made conscious are ostracized as illusory or fictive, unrelated to the advancement of science and the spread of prosperity. The world is presumed to be under control, although our enemy continues to strike from where we least expect him—in fact, from where we presume there is nothing at all.

Simple premeditated actions were once intended to solve the scourges of the past: tyranny by laws; poverty, disease, and famine by technology; and human quarrelsomeness, at last, by collective recognition of the common good. Two world wars, atomic weapons, and a host of ecological disasters may have done away with much of the sheen on that vision, but not the basic stuff of which it is made. Now computers and other algorithms have replaced progressive rationalism as ostensible "bringers to light" of all causes and effects down to a subatomic level. If a computer can consider a hundred thousand possible chess moves in a matter of milliseconds—and then advance to its next consideration, it should certainly be able to checkmate unconsciousness. Yet such is a blithe delusion of those who plan to invent artificial intelligence and then apply it retroactively to us. To their surprise they may have to wait long enough to build a computer as big as the universe, or perhaps one a little bit bigger, as one mathematician mused, "in order to nail the son of a bitch."[1]

We live during a transition of power. Our cities and industries, our very civilization and planet, stand under continuous threat of collapse from the proud forces they contain. Progressive nineteenth-century science, which drew the blueprint for this civilization, tried to make it eternally conscious. That seems doomed to failure, cataclysmic failure.

Freud gives back to the unconscious its clear deed to those same cities and industries. Or, we might say, the unconscious expropriated it anyway, but Freud named and predicted it at a moment when it was manifesting but had no name. He showed that it was unimaginably powerful, that it could not be suppressed or defeated, but he gave us a more distant hope that is sometimes forgotten: it is not the enemy—it is who we "really" are. The "other" threatens us only because we deny its existence. The fact that it already *is* propels it to claim, by law, its destiny, which must be our destiny.

We have suffered this haunting not only through the "golden age" of Freud but Hitler, Hiroshima, urban gang warfare, boat people, slaughter of Ibos, genocidal chaos in Bosnia, serial murderers, etc. It now no longer seems as deadly, even though it is far deadlier, because we have survived it for the better part of a century—through a series of encounters with our human nature that suggest the problem may have become so great exactly because we have ignored its essentiality for so long. It is no longer a surprise and a shock, and perhaps we need not feel shame or disappointment at our performance or even at our venal fascination with the minds of those who kill and maim for pleasure. We are more than curious, for our lives and the planet itself are at stake. In truth, the disclosure of the vast realms of unconscious activity and its imperatives is a millennial undertaking barely begun.

By identifying the unconscious, Freud established its priority. Once we acknowledge that living organisms carry the full potential of what they are and can ultimately suppress nothing, the weight and persistent upsurge of that underworld are reckoned to overwhelm the small amount that can ever become conscious. Most of our actions are thus driven by imperatives we neither know nor understand.

According to Freud, the events that go into forging ego structure are assimilated and reinforced throughout life—the earlier, more chaotic impressions always dominating the later reasonableness. The desires one is born with (and through), the instincts for survival and satisfaction, merge developmentally with the shaping of selfhood. In psychoanalytic theory, layers of personality form atop and within one another. An adult life of ease does not alleviate either primary desires or the original pain and embattledness of childhood. Unexperienced grief limits pleasure and freedom without the person even being aware of it. Meanwhile, our individual personal aspect (which Freud called the "ego") protects against our cosmic undifferentiated aspect (which Freud called the "id"). Illness is, at least in part, blocked emotional energy of the id. This is one of the dicta that calls all holistic systems—each in its own idiosyncratic way—home to the Freudian roost. Even vitalistic and *pranic* cures must break the logjam established by ego development.

No matter what a person's attitude or expressed moral position, his or her identity is rooted in instincts and actual behavior. Humanity at large is responsible for the conversion of these biological substrata into cultural institutions—responsible under the threat that whatever is not included will find a conduit of expression anyway. Ideological puritanism *vis-à-vis* sexual acting out, for instance, does not end the matter. The desire stays within the organism unconsciously and is expressed in other activities which compensate *exactly* even though the compensations may not have explicit sexual content.

Before Freud, doctors could innocently treat humoral conditions by contraries. Without getting to the bottom of the whirlpool, they could feign proficiency by skimming states of melancholia and rage from off its surface. Recurrences were viewed as aberrations. I have already argued that humoral medicines like *Chi Gung* may ultimately be more deeply curative than psychotherapy. However, for a society that has lost the energetic basis of the elements, *Chi Gung* is an impossibility. By the end of the nineteenth century the West needed Sigmund Freud, not the Yellow Emperor.

If *Chi Gung* heeds the preconscious Yin-Yang of universal forces, psychoanalysis warns that we must create safe modes of expression for the ruthless and primitive tantrums of the id, the raw energies manifesting as emotions. No doubt mankind requires both treatments. In fact, those who argue that only one is necessary are usually good candidates for the other. (Later we will discuss whether psychoanalytic treatment actually alters psychopathology, but for now we are merely proposing its model—as a rebirth of charismatic shamanism and mythodrama and a movement away from *all* forms of elemental and humoral medicine.)

The Energetic Basis for Mind

FREUD DEVELOPED A theory of energy for human thought processes. The mechanics themselves are implicitly Darwinian, but his was not a simple psychological metaphor out of biology. So far as I know, Freud did not even credit Darwin with contributing to his own paradigm. However, as we are heir to Freudian thought without acknowledgment, Freud was heir to Darwinian cosmology—i.e., life is not a special case. Nothing occurs unless there is energy behind it—physical force, electrical or magnetic force, biological force. Psyche, too, must be explained as kinesis in the natural world.

Once upon a time, mind was judged differently. After all, thought is apparently weightless and unruly, free to roam a limitless territory, ignoring laws everything else must obey. Thought must also obey, Freud declared—Freud the neurologist. Thought is another, perhaps topmost layer of biochemical activity. It is neither a simple flow of corpuscles nor an ethereal counterpart to personality. It is an epiphenomenal residue of biological process, reflecting the collective capacity and output of cells, organs, nerves, and muscles. Its content, like its physiology, is given in advance by the quanta that make it up.

The Darwinian laws of nature define the survival of the few—the "fittest," meaning only those creatures who, by chance adaptation to change, persist when every other one has succumbed. Just as animals cannot demand the longevity of their species on the basis of their own beauty, intelligence, or uniqueness, so thoughts cannot demand to exist by any property except their charge (defined by Freud as the moment-by-moment dynamic outcome of libidinal energy, death instinct [thanatos], and suppression by the ego and superego). Much as Darwin proposed the emergence of discrete species by natural selection, Freud proclaimed the relentless passage of thoughts from the unconscious into the conscious mind through a selective matrix of memory, resistance, and association. Crabs and algae in the pond, lions stalking zebras at the waterhole, dreams and insights—these (to quote Melville loosely) were obedient to the same volition.

In deriving his own physics of "quantitative distribution," Freud seems to have propagated a neurological version of "natural selection." Cognitive and emotional material runs solely on the nervous energy with which it was originally stored or cathected (charged); it can be reordered by experience, but its capacity does not change, and in any case, the new patterns become as indelible as the original distribution. Thus mental illness or trauma is a specific physical-emotional quantum which would require an equal and appropriate charge of energy to dislodge it. (As we saw earlier in this book, healing shamans propound this physics in quite different but complementary ways.)

From my viewpoint Darwin, Freud, and Lévi-Strauss "collaborated" on a mythic sequence in European thought, in which a law of quantitative distribution of energy was applied to phenomena ranging from species of animals to dreams to bodies of folklore and marriage systems, respectively. Darwin showed that the living were simply a special case of the nonliving and that no creature came into being except from the intrinsic properties of matter. Freud then revealed how dreams, neuroses, and fantasies were not only continuous with logical thought, but the base materials from which logical thought was formed. Lévi-Strauss subsequently explained the totemic customs of indigenous peoples as the actual source of all social and cognitive relations. He in fact opens his analysis of totemism with a description of Freud's work on hysteria:

The first lesson of Freud's critique of [Jean Martin] Charcot's theory of hysteria lay in convincing us that there is no essential difference between states of mental health and mental illness; that the passage from one to the other involves at most a modification in certain general operations which everyone may see in himself; and that consequently the mental patient is our brother, since he is distinguished from us in nothing more than by an involution—minor in nature, contingent in form, arbitrary in definition, and temporary— of a historical development which is fundamentally that of every individual existence. It was more reassuring to regard a mental patient as belonging to a rare and singular species, as the objective product of external or internal determinants such as heredity, alcoholism, or mental weakness.[2]

The notable thing about psychiatry, then—and what it transfers to the rest of medicine—is not that it deals with mental disease rather than physical disease, but that it deals with the energetic basis of all psychosomatic states, hence, the inevitability of disease. It demands, axiomatically, that every environmental and social influence be integrated as a corresponding charge within the organism. There is no way to destroy anything and there is no way to lose anything, Freud wrote, so man and woman are literally the accumulation and expression of their own biological existences. This is now a rule of holism. Traumatic events incubate physical diseases as absolutely as they do emotional ones:

> ... unconscious wishes are always active. They represent paths which are always practicable, whenever a quantum of excitation makes use of them. It is indeed an outstanding peculiarity of the unconscious process that they are indestructible. Nothing can be brought to an end in the unconscious; nothing is past or forgotten.[3]

This is a law of Navaho sand painting, acupuncture, and osteopathic adjustment as well.

In general, practitioners of radical forms of psychotherapy and systems of alternative medicine have accepted Freud's basic energetic dynamics while rejecting his clinical methodology and his explanations of resistance as an expression of the death instinct. Despite their differences from one another, they have consistently emphasized the regenerative capability of the human being. Nowadays this formula underwrites most energetic practices and psychic medicines, as well as diverse somatic therapies. In some humanist traditions, such as those associated with the Esalen Institute in Big Sur, California, it is precisely the ego-based, psychoanalytic elements which provide holism and restore energetic medicine to the expanding arena of humanistic practice. I would argue—as I did at the beginning of this chapter—that indigenous and vitalistic medicines were sufficiently holistic to begin with, but that psychoanalysis became their mode of discourse, breaking down their separate provincialities and opening the world to a "melting pot" transpersonal *lingua franca.*

Deconstructing Freud

F REUD'S PROPOSAL OF the unconscious, with its associative dynamics, was a watershed event. Since then, we have been trying to figure out what the unconscious includes and how it shapes each increment of conscious activity. Initially the unknown hemisphere of the mind was visualized as a kind of cellar of psychological memory, containing the entangled and fused events of a lifetime, along with assorted terrors, frustrated desires, and other ghosts. A classic cartoon of the era depicted it as a naked humanoid monster with fangs, claws, and a bulging, exposed brain, tethered by a rope to a stake yet holding a placid, smiling cutout mask in front of itself. It was also idealized as a woman with four faces and five eyes, her arms twisted in a pretzel around each other, her torso attached backwards, her right arm ending on her left side bearing a long, old-fashioned key, and keyholes everywhere while she stared in five or more directions at once.

But the unconscious is also merely the nerves and muscles and tissue in which emotional and psychic existence is recorded. The organs

Sigmund Freud and the Origin of Psychotherapeutic Healing

and their locations are intuited by us not as individual loci but as mind itself, whose contents then frame our memories. The external spatial quality of existence—our seeming location in space and with space around us—is an original experience of our own insides, their contour and depth of tissue projected outward onto the world. Materialists would have nothing lie beneath this layer except the ancient brain stem. They consider the tissues a neutral substratum and do not seek differentiated meanings beyond them. However, depth psychologists propose unconscious fields of energy and archetypes which are neither personal nor solely organic. We will explore these later in the chapter and in future chapters.

Whatever their attributed origin, pulses of information shoot out of unconsciousness, generating ever-new cognitive realities. Emerging syntaxes representing instinctual conflicts and ambivalences give rise to the styles and artifacts of daily existence. They make their own language. If they seem to speak in familiar dualities and clichés (desire and fear of its consequences is one such), that is because we already have adopted these clichés by the time we hear them. They control us; yet they are also the modes through which we express our intention of freedom and our very being.

Language, for instance, is a collectively arising unconscious system—whether one takes it from linguist Benjamin Lee Whorf (that our grammar shapes our morphology of the universe), or from cybernetician Noam Chomsky (that unconscious syntaxes interact dynamically with emergent thought processes to make ideas). One step removed from language are art, politics, economics, and religion—all once prized arenas of human independence and creativity and now dialects that tell people what they think even as people try to think *in* them. Physics and philosophy, the twin rulers who spurned the unconscious before Freud's time and then laughed at its fledgling attempts at reemergence, have now been forced to admit that they are opposed by a vast set of unknown vectors, right in the center of human thought and knowledge; that they themselves are mere fashions of language; and they must

acknowledge their origin and formation every step of the way toward objective reality if they are to have even a shred of it by the time they get there. Quantum physics and relativity theory are now as much psychologies as descriptions of nature.

The poor sister to queen philosophy—psychology—owns the West, and philosophers' current signpost gestures include rediscovering Freud himself more deeply in the process he unveiled and applying to his system the circular laws of which his system is made. A fashionable French school, for instance, has reconstituted Freud in terms of the history and set of cultural symbols that gave rise to him and those that he generated. One doesn't have to understand Jacques Derrida completely to feel the excavation of this collapsing series of ciphers against the history

Sigmund Freud and the Origin of Psycho-therapeutic Healing

of concrete rationalist thought. It is our contemporary dilemma. We don't need to name the unconscious anymore, for it names itself everywhere and by its Midas touch turns everything to nothing:

> Thus are perhaps augured, in the Freudian break-through, a beyond and a beneath of that enclosure we might term "Platonic." In that moment of world history "subsumed" by the name of Freud, traversing an unbelievable mythology, . . . a relation to self of the historico-transcendental scene of writing was spoken without being said, thought without being thought: written and simultaneously erased. . . .[4]

So, the Freudian system contained even the terms for its own erasure. Yet, by the same principle, it has been derived again and again through new modes of structuralism and linguistic philosophies. As that was happening, the excavation went beneath Freud's very existence and developed meanings that preceded and subsumed him. His intention, as it was written into the history of thought, disappears into the paradox he was portraying. By bracketing, for a moment, the affective emotional aspect of Freud and giving it a context (but not their explicit acceptance), the French "post-modern" philosophers transformed the old doctor into the spiffiest member of their own society. For them he had freed philosophy to consider itself, to consider its dreams, its unconscious, *its* philosophy in the making of true things. To all that would be spoken in the world, he gave the unspoken, an erasure, and a dream. But he also chained philosophy to a sterile regimen of interpreting every dream and folly, every babble and integer, in order to lay claim to the absolute.

The most common application of the unconscious was the one developed through conventional psychoanalysis and typified by the confident therapist who tells his neurotic patient: "You don't know what you are doing, but I do because I can intuit your thought process through your speech and behavior." Freud himself was usually this confident, and he defended a rational orthodoxy against his more improvisational followers.

Nihilistic Freud, though, was in awe of the power of the unconscious, and he diagnosed humanity's situation as hopeless because of it. The species, he predicted, would eventually be dragged down into its own creationary darkness, the thin veneer of civilization and consciousness crumbling around it. The confident therapist was lying through his teeth, buying time by tricking people into coping with their unbearable ambivalence and yearning.

Either way, the primacy of the unconscious was established. Yet Freud never resolved the level on which mankind was to be sentenced to darkness and whether it was to be eternal darkness or darkness through which a beacon could be shone. One side of him aided his patients on successful hypnotrance journeys through the Underworld; another side of him merged with mythic King Oedipus who blinded himself when the truth he saw was too terrible to behold. It was left for Freud's renegade disciples Carl Jung and Wilhelm Reich to mutate the unconscious in such radical ways that the sentence of shadows became an equally profound destiny of another order.

Sexuality and Libido

Freud's second major achievement was the development of a theory of sexuality. Before Freud, there was a general predilection to consider sexuality a defective and primitive series of usually scatological activities and to separate it ontologically from other behavior. In fact, there was a tendency to segregate modes of behavior in general and consider each realm of activity somehow self-explicit. Sexuality fell under this common assumption, with the extra burden that it carried enough charge to embarrass or distort most social inquiry into it. Sexuality was either trivialized or considered a threat to civilized discourse, or both. At best, it was condemned to a vestige of the animal kingdom.

Freud proposed an enlarged sphere of sexuality to encompass maternal breast-feeding, infantile desire for contact, and even toilet training. Instead of limiting sexuality to a single act and its foreplay, he differentiated its many aspects and offshoots, both personal and cultural, and extended them to cover a swath of human activities not previously considered sexual—a range from anal compulsions to feathered headdresses. In the process, he characterized a general ebb and flow of erotic energy in living systems, and he traced its complex role in the formation of primal personalities, neuroses, and psychosomatic disorders. He demonstrated that these could be described not only from the point of view of some abstract "phenomenology," but "from the point of view of their dynamics and economics [and] the quantitative distribution of the libido."[5]

Beneath the usual range of genital activity and erotic fantasy, Freud proposed a larger network of feelings, structures, and capacities for pleasure and pain which were reflected not only in genital behavior but all aspects of the organism's life. He said, in essence: "Genital being does not arise spontaneously with puberty, but is an aspect of the overall sexual orientation of the human animal." Thus, sexuality underlies much so-called nonsexual pathology.

"Why prioritize sexuality?" people asked. "Why not hunger? Why not money? Why not power?" Many considered Freud sex-obsessed because of the primacy he gave sexuality, though, of course, the objections expose more the obsessions of his critics than those of Freud himself, even if in a negative (i.e., a sex-phobic) way.

The criticism misses the point. Freud actually advanced a theory of the interrelationships of modes of behavior. All activities of the organism—not just sexuality—reflect its internal psychic components. Life is a process of translating discrete hungers and drives into social activities. The repertoire of "nonsexual things"—not only power, money, territory, and security, but also games, music, plans for cities, etc.—are equivalent expressions of this underlying dynamic drive. They all project symbolically and hierarchically through one another and generate a unified energetics.

Sexuality is singled out because it is a direct concomitant of the life force. That is, it expresses primary hungers relatively undiverted by cultural sublimations; it is an original component of the unconscious; and it is developmentally linked to the emergence and maturity of the ego. Oddly, we are creatures who grow and mature in direct relationship to our integration of sensations at our orifices. If this process is unimpeded, it may not carry a great deal of baggage. If impeded, it casts its shadow over everything else. Freud's emphasis on symbolic sexual masking was, implicitly, a cultural diagnosis. It is possible to imagine a culture in which primary emotional development would not leave a major residue of sublimated sexual symbology.

No doubt much of the erotic behavior reported by startled observers of the "primitive" world was sexy only by European standards, having other individual meanings in local customs and rites. Coming from a milieu of repressed sexuality, Freud may have projected the missing element too widely and without enough awareness of his own historical context, but his intent—remember—was to arrive at a theory of bodily drives. The sexual displacements of his patients compelled him to recognize such drives trapped and distorted in taboos of repressed sexuality. Freud's hierarchy of functions developed generically as he unravelled this network.

Just beneath the fabric of neurotic and psychotic activity he found a zone of abortive sexual imagery. He followed this by eliciting free association from patients. And the associations almost always led to sexual fantasies and events. Patients subsequently improved. They were happier, more functional. This defined Freud's goal for his own practice. He was, in essence, verbally de-layering biological rigidities. By enlarging a patient's notion of his own sexuality, he was inculcating a new framework of meaning, teaching him that he existed in a world not necessarily of epidemic sexual repressions but of symbolic layers reflecting a process of mutable energy. So, a neurotic was not trapped in a frozen patterning of his own self-images and personality grid. He could *act differently*. Sexual association energized this process and gave it emotional authenticity. The "talking cure" needn't have been sex-based, but Western history precluded any other alternative.

Phrased differently, we could say that Freud taught a new relationship between social etiquette and bodily intention. As the former attempts to establish universality, the latter maintains underground pressure, so the former clings more and more literally to its boundaries. Sexual repression becomes a symbolic mode for the repression of the *full* psychic contents of the unconscious. Thus, Freud could unveil the roots of behavior itself by tracing the etiology of sexuality.

THE FREUDIAN THEORY of the stages of the development of sexuality is revealing both as a description of how nonsexual behavior supplants sexual behavior without supplanting the sexual drive and as a model for the development of the social and symbolic capacities of the organism as a whole.

Freud called the basic drive, or pulse, "libido": this is the presexual or proto-sexual status of the sexual drive, or, more accurately, the life force itself which gets shaped into "Eros" through human anatomy. It appears first at the lips, as the desire for suckling but also as thumb-sucking and general lip and mouth contact with external things. Eventually, in the developmental process, this oral phase, without being overridden entirely, passes into an anal phase, in which the feelings that arise from excreting and withholding feces serve libidinal expression. With social and biological maturity, the oral and anal phases ripen into genital sexuality with oral and anal components. The adult personality lays claim to sexuality as its initiatory rite and even badge of honor. It is readily stylized to appear "ultra-mature" or sophisticated. Look at any fashion show or display of rock music album covers. The seducer and seductress forget their origins in oral and anal eroticisms, even as the man forgets the boy and the woman the girl. They become committed to merely the "adult" quality of their sexual expression. Freud cut through, as it were, these displays of sex and got to their substance. They are primary sensation contacting the world, seeking nutrition, satisfaction, and protection.

Freud emphasized that sexuality (i.e., libido) was a pure function for "obtaining pleasure from the zones of the body" and that it was "brought into the service of reproduction" only subsequently in the life of the organism.[6] There was an unexamined tendency even among intellectuals to assume that sexuality not in the service of reproduction was either nonfunctional or purposeless, even immoral. But Freud showed that it had a substantial role in maintaining health. Sexual atrophy or deviation led to a variety of mental and physical diseases. Conversely, restoration of sexual function led to an improvement in general health.

Of course, "libido" is just a word, and Freud used it to trace many developmental patterns of human behavior. It was his map of underlying energy. He did not mean libido to be synonymous with loving contact, despite its role in the formation of Eros. Libido was the primordial drive itself, which the organism expressed in whatever way was open to it. If libido encountered resistance or rejection of any sort, it could find expression as aggression, denial, or sadism. Freud described sadism as "an instinctual fusion of purely libidinal and purely destructive urges, a fusion which thenceforward persists uninterruptedly."[7] What might have become love is no longer perceived comfortably by the organism, but the ego gets some satisfaction from inflicting pain, so it does this from the same energetic source as it would to express love. The desire to hurt is, morphologically, the desire for contact.

Libido allowed Freud to propose the functional relatedness of ontologically distinct activities. Fetishism and other forms of sexual deviation might not be sexual in the usual sense, but they *are* libidinal. The oral and anal activities of the infant and child are not sexual in a genital mode but they are stages in a dynamic process which unfolds into adult sexuality at puberty.

Freud was the first to define libidinal healing so clearly. He advanced

395

a paradigm which now says, "Healing is, at least in part, always sexual healing." This is the case whether one considers redirecting psychopaths from their anti-social behavior or curing people of cancers presumed to have elements of emotional suppression in them.

Dreams

FREUD'S WORK ON dreams and dreaming was so fundamental that it has not been made even one iota obsolete by later studies on the subject. In fact, twentieth-century thought has merely honed its insights and developed an entire oneiric science from them. Yet *The Interpretation of Dreams* was one of Freud's earliest works, substantially completed before he was forty and published in 1899 (post-dated, prophetically, to 1900 as homage to the dawning century).

Dreams, to Freud, were remarkable relics of the subtle dynamics of the mind and nervous system. Insofar as they were partially exposed to view, perhaps more than any other part of the unconscious process, they were pathways into the basic structure of thought and mental illness—a "royal road to the unconscious."[8]

When the book first came out, Freud did not fully realize its import. His preface was modest and professional: he hoped that the study of dreams would provide clinical insight for other areas of psychology. In the ten years it took for a second edition to appear he began to understand the scope of his work and to regret its snubbing in clinical circles. He noted that the second edition was made necessary more by a general reading audience. Thereafter, though, acceptance increased and new editions came rapidly, all with extensive additions and footnotes, so that each edition was not only a reissuing of the original research on dreams but a decade-by-decade reevaluation of specific issues and an ongoing yearbook of new insights into the dream process. His preface to one edition, dated March 15, 1931, showed Freud's ultimate assessment of his original intuition of what became a paradigm for a psychological theory. Looking back, he wrote:

397

This book, with the new contribution to psychology which surprised the world when it was published (1900), remains essentially unaltered. It contains, even according to my present-day judgement, the most valuable of all the discoveries it has been my good fortune to make. Insight such as this falls to one's lot but once in a lifetime.[9]

Freud begins *The Interpretation of Dreams* by examining the state of dream theory in the late nineteenth century. The problem was that, in enlightened European circles, dreams were considered insignificant and arbitrary, more likely the effect of a bad meal than a meaningful layer of philosophy or emotional life. The notion that dreams were messages was disdained as archaic because educated people did not recognize the possibility of "biological messages." The diagnostic aspect of dreams was overlooked because they were regarded as either irrelevant incursions or superficial lapses. Whereas Freud was to rediscover dreams as brilliant condensations and encapsulations of psychic states, the custom then was to see them as dispersing of meaning.

None of Freud's predecessors persisted long enough to realize that the absurdities and paradoxes of dreams were the result not of paucity and shallowness but of the tremendous amount of information contained in their brief coda. To the general observer, they were unpleasant, unfinished, defective, primitive, and fragmentary; their bawdiness and unlikely associations further discouraged rationalists from looking more closely at what were already embarrassments to the mature people who dreamed them. Freud summarized the attitudes of some of his colleagues toward dreams in the early part of his own book:

> It is as though psychological activity had been transported from the brain of a reasonable man into that of a fool.[10]

> ... it seems impossible to detect any fixed laws in this crazy activity.[11]

> What laughable contradictions he is ready to accept in the laws of nature and society before, as we say, things get beyond a joke and the excessive strain of nonsense wakes him up. We calculate without a qualm that three times three make twenty; we are not in the

least surprised when a dog quotes a line of poetry, or when a dead man walks to his grave on his own legs, or when we see a rock floating on the water. . . .[12]

. . . an archaic world of vast emotions and imperfect thoughts. . . .[13]

Once Freud understood the importance of dreams in the psychic metabolism, he had to explain their peculiarly irrational form. His answer would elucidate the role of unconscious process in human life.

Between the psychic sources of the dreams in the nervous system and their representation as images in the mind of the dreamer is a vast network of quantitatively charged psychosomatic material that strives both to release the charge of its own neural process in dream states and to disguise by means of dreams the painful truths of its existence and contents.

Dreams, said Freud very early, are brief mental disorders (psychoses) that prevent more major disturbances of long duration. They are medicines, as we have since come to appreciate—in both the biochemistry of their original "being dreamed" and all later attempts to recall their dramaturgy and make coherent statements out of them. The individual not only dreams her energetic circumstance; she also experiences a progression of images and feelings arising from that dream by which to organize her waking state and contact the submerged requirements of her inner life.

The so-called deceptions and circumventions of a dream do not diminish its curative thrust; they *are* that thrust, for they define, by their existence, the contradictory elements of anyone's psychohistory. After all, by Freudian-Darwinian dynamics, a person in his dreams cannot be engaged in creative freelance deceit. Every dream (like every psychosis and neurosis) has a precursor in the quantitative distribution of psychic material, which can hardly be faked.

The paradoxes of a dream are the paradoxes of the life dreaming it which, if uncontacted, spill into diseases. The dream literally forms because another expression of the material would be more dangerous and destructive to the ego and psyche.

F REUD'S ANALYSIS OF "dreamwork" is seminal in the development of twentieth-century holistic healing, so we will summarize some of its aspects:

The meaning of a dream comes from latent material (submerged memories and unconscious charge) which endows the imagery of the mind with its contents. The state of sleep is what makes the formation of the dream possible, by breaking down ego resistance to unconscious material and forging a pathway between this profound material and the layers of ongoing mental static. These are the twin sources of dreaming. Without sleep, the psyche is held under unremitting censorship by the conscious mind, and its unconscious contents have no way to express themselves.

Dreaming assembles its semi-narrative trance by a combination of extreme compression, distortion, and replacement of information. The most latent material—that which is ancient but refuses to vacate the psyche because it is unresolved and has accumulated the deepest psychological charge—fuses itself with relatively superficial and recent gossip of the conscious mind to weave the oneiric language, which is marked by puns, rebuses, and associative logic. Freud writes: "If in the course of a single day we have two or more experiences suitable for provoking a dream, the dream will make a combined reference to them as a single whole; *it is under a necessity to combine them into a unity.*"[14] The necessity is enforced by the strength of the underlying psychic energy, not by any attraction of the peculiar imagery itself, which merely follows the path of least resistance: "The greatest intensity is shown by those elements of a dream on whose formation the greatest amount of condensation has been expended."[15] These are the segments charged with the most pain (or desire) and attached to the most traumatic moments. Their landscapes are often what is remembered as "the dream."

The psyche is not a waking-world linear creature and is under no obligation to keep its sources separate and whole or uncorrupted by random associations. Furthermore, it prefers to camouflage uncomfortable associations by devaluing them. This is done in a number of ways. One-time logical relations become illogical when they are combined and when, for instance, simultaneity in time is used to express what is actually association of meaning. Their emotional demands replace their social rationale. People and events are fused with each other, their inevitable contradictions resolved disjunctively but somehow within the demands of the narrative. One dream person may represent two or more people to varying degrees. A setting may merge elements from childhood, a movie, and a street visited on the day of the dream. Since the dream cannot choose between two proportionately charged streams, it must fulfill both of them instantaneously as they clash. The illogic of the dream is the logic, i.e., the logos, of the organism. The entanglement within the dream is simply a precise rendering of the tapestry of sensations innervating it, and, for being generic, it is far more organized than any intentional medley of its many and varied sources could be.

Our reality is precisely this jumbled and complex; that is, our infantile desires and unresolved conflicts erode the menial veneer of daily life. But the dream expression of this turmoil actually alleviates it. By dreaming and complexifying our instincts and emotions, we oddly simplify and transcend a layer of them. Dreams—even nightmares—are always healing experiences. One often awakens from a deep and disturbing dream feeling surprisingly and inexplicably better and even healthier with nothing that is identifiable having changed.

Dreams are voices of our own higher intelligence superseding our embroilment in our compulsions. They bring art and insight—even genius—to a *mêleé* we attempt to settle by mere will. We discuss "healing by dreams" in more detail in the section of that name in Volume Two, Chapter Eight.

A person, in the act of dreaming, has no choice but to express his truth. If the conscious mind is closed to certain psychically significant material, the material will associatively merge with some familiar and innocent event and insinuate itself into the dream without contradicting the narrative mechanics of the dream imagery (and so disturbing the dreaming), yet also without weakening its true impact by compromising its charge. The mental apparatus of dreaming even pulls external and present bodily stimuli into the trance, incorporating them in the same way it incorporates superficial events: it uses them to contact hidden material while keeping the person asleep. *"Dreams are the* GUARDIANS *of sleep and not its disturbers,"*[16] wrote Freud. Powerful guardians indeed, for they keep things out of the dream only by changing them into the dream.

A recent acquaintance is suddenly dreamed of with features and feelings about her that seem to belong to someone else forgotten from childhood. A house down the block is dreamed as having the eerie quality of another house in another place and time, or the dreamer finds a whole other floor of rooms beyond the attic. The *images* arise because they are current, but their weak charge is taken over by *ideas* which were intensely experienced but have been lost or suppressed and which now achieve enough strength to force themselves through the censorship (the extra rooms may represent roomlike entities of great importance in the dreamer's inner life). Paradoxically, the very conceits that might have had the greatest charge are often the ones most drained of intensity (i.e., camouflaged in glittering trivialities) by the dreaming, as though a master artist predisposed to irony and caricature were at work. The association of a high charge with an appropriate image might shock the dreamer into waking, or catalyze a mental illness. On the other hand, materials of low psychic valuation are suddenly overdetermined in a transference of psychic charge which, in itself, weaves the dream and fools the dreamer into accepting its converse. The bothersome and unlikely events which clutter the oneiric landscape are born of repeated instances of this mode of displacement.

There are no weak or innocent dreams, Freud insisted. Dreams are too important to be wasted on "trivialities and trifles."[17] They afford priceless opportunities for the organism to reveal its secrets to itself and briefly stabilize a psychic harmony. They are interludes in the lifelong wrangle between libidinal energy and censorship.

Dreams also do not discuss abstract or incidental matters. Everything represents the dreamer in some fashion or other. Relationships of personae or personality fragments of the dreamer to one another are translated, through the dream, into relationships between different individuals and things. Physiological components or conditions become dreamed scenery. For instance, the dreamer is walking in a flower garden, and the flowers become more and more colorful and aromatic. These blossoms may be the dreamer's erotic feelings which, as they penetrate consciousness, intensify the floral imagery. Even a gap in the dream sequence may represent a physiological fact which presents some problem to the dreamer and thus masks itself in amnesia. There is no break in imagery because the dream-flow reflects a present passage of energy—a pulse whose amplitude and texture may change but which never ceases. Thus, the gap means: Here is a darkness through which to cross, or here is a disjunction; experience it as a blank. Fall through it into something else. At one point Freud offers, despite his own reservations concerning literalism, an approximate dream code:

> The Emperor and Empress (or the King and Queen) as a rule really represent the dreamer's parents; and a Prince or Princess represent the dreamer himself or herself. . . . All elongated objects, such as sticks,

tree-trunks, and umbrellas (the opening of these last being comparable to an erection) may stand for the male organ. . . . Boxes, cases, chests, cupboards, and ovens represent the uterus. . . . Rooms in dreams are usually women. . . . Many landscapes in dreams, especially any containing bridges or wooded hills, may clearly be recognized as descriptions of the genitals. . . . Many of the beasts which are used as genital symbols in mythology and folklore play the same part in dreams: e.g., fishes, snails, cats, mice (on account of the pubic hair), and above all those most important symbols of the male organ—snakes.[18]

Every dream hides and expresses a latent wish. The wish is the dream's proximate source, its response to libidinal energy in the nervous system. The manifest scenery and plot are the secondary agency of the dream and the dreamer's defense against the full implication of that energy.

To deny something is also to express it, to give it form. Denial or excision in a dream is thus a common mode of resistance to emerging material, igniting the very axis of fear-desire on which most dreaming is sustained. For instance, a nightmare seems to be anything but a wish fulfillment; however, it may constitute the only acceptable mode for exploring tabooed and anxiety-provoking feelings. When one dreams of being unprepared for or failing an exam that was actually passed years ago, the reliving would seem to provide needless masochistic anxiety—hardly a wish. Not so, said Freud. The person is reminding himself that the fear of failing was groundless the first time, so it might be also in the future. Of one dream that seemed obviously not to be a wish fulfillment, Freud remarked that it fulfilled the secret wish of his friend who dreamed it to prove him wrong since he had been unsuccessfully competitive with Freud during their years together in school.

In a dramatic case reported by Freud, a father succumbs to sleep after the devastating death of his son while an old man sits watch by the body with a candle, praying. The father then dreams that the child is suddenly standing by his bed, catches him by the arm and says,

"Father, don't you see I'm burning?" The father awakens to a bright glare from the next room: the watchman has also fallen asleep and a lighted candle spilled onto the wrappings, setting the body on fire.

Freud points out that the glare is what disturbed sleep and awoke the dreamer, but why, he asks, at this crucial moment, did he remain entranced a moment longer to nurture a brief dream? Freud then explains:

> For the sake of the fulfillment of [a] wish the father prolonged his sleep by one moment. The dream was preferred to a waking reflection because it was able to show the child as once more alive. If the father had woken up first and then made the inference that led him to go into the next room, he would, as it were, have shortened his child's life by that moment of time.[19]

Another subtle wish involves one of Freud's own dreams. At a time when he had a painful boil the size of an apple at the base of his scrotum, he dreamed he was riding a horse. The answer to this anomaly, obscure at first, becomes obvious on closer scrutiny. Horseback riding was something he never did, but under these circumstances it was unimaginable. "It was," he wrote, "the most energetic denial of my illness that could possibly be imagined."[20] If the pain from the boil was threatening to disrupt the dream, the dream answered by having the dreamer engaged in an activity he could not possibly carry out with such a boil. Reassured, he continued to sleep.

Thus, dreams are episodes of self-directed healing and unconscious revelation, vision quests in which each person is his or her own spirit guide. More than half a century later, scientists have discovered that sleep deprivation, i.e., dream deprivation, leads to a hallucinatory breakdown in perception of reality itself and the capacity to act sanely in waking life. Only when the dream is a dream, it appears, can the world be the world.[21]

The Failure of Psychoanalysis as Holistic Medicine

Freud's primary act was the revelation of the unconscious mind by demonstration of its economic exchange with the organism. To everything that humanity had done or would do, he gave a different meaning; in fact, he gave a bottomless well of symbolisms, transformable through each other, none of them final. Because so much has been based on the Freudian unconscious and the theory of developmental sexuality, we tend to forget that, in and of themselves, these theories have no therapeutic value. Even dream interpretation is unproven as a core treatment producing lasting change. Freud's attempt to translate his theories into a consistent clinical methodology ultimately failed, though he was himself a successful therapist and began the lineage of psychoanalysis.

The central problem is that the system lacks a clear set of rules and indications—a replicatable technique—and it has no bloody down to compensate. In individual cases, of course, shaman-like doctors have been able to use Freud's healing style successfully and even to train others in it, but they are rare members of the guild of post-Freudians; the bulk of the rest practice merely the *form* of Freudian insight. Clever patients fool most therapists, unconsciously of course; a psyche which can make up whole dreams is more than a match for the average clinician. Nowadays relatively narrow sectors of wealthy patients attempt to reconstruct their illnesses out of the materials of dreams and free associations to gain insight into their dysfunctional behavior. This process is often protracted and without any attainable goal or consistent path.

Psychiatrists narrate (or suggest) to these patients an explanatory litany of the traumatic events of their past, their Oedipal relationship to their mothers or fathers, and the supposed psychohistorical sources of their present unhappiness. The worst of them sell these narratives as medicine but without a careful assay of what these things mean in terms of the quantitative distribution of libido.

Almost from the beginning, doctors were forgetting that Freud salvaged the Oedipal image as a temporary clue to a more remote form and that the image cannot be applied indiscriminately, and certainly not without some understanding of the thing he was groping toward as well as the thing he finally said. Superficially, the Oedipal complex suggested the erotic attachment of a child to the parent of the opposite sex, with corresponding feelings of jealousy and hostility toward the same-sex parental rival. Oedipus unknowingly slew his father, then wed a woman who turned out to be his mother, fulfilling the dreaded promise of an oracle. But Freud also was pointing toward how mythic structures embrace both individual developmental processes and the evolution of consciousness itself. In assigning Oedipus to every man and woman, he was assigning the evolution of consciousness to each individual ego and pronouncing that our desires are oracles hiding their forbidden designs in obscure narratives. In unveiling "Oedipus," he was naming this process. He certainly did not intend to have "Oedipus" become the story itself.

Freud initiated many of the controversies that succeeded him. He was quite anxious to institutionalize his findings and establish a profession, and this led him to simplify or palliate his actual insights. Even though he realized, in theory and by deep conviction, the priority of the unconscious biological process, the civilized doctor in him demanded that the rational mind attempt to control the beast. The system he elaborated suffered from the fact that he never actually believed in that possibility. He appraised civilization as the ultimate repression. Psychoanalysis compromised itself to become the medicine of that civilization, enabling the individual to mediate between his primal needs and the chains into which he was born. Society would always be in conflict with the individual's basic drives, leading either to the ultimate breakdown of order or the complete enslavement of the human animal. Either way it was a desperate trap. "Anatomy is destiny," he wrote, meaning *"No way out."*

"Do you see any joy for the human being?" the narrator of a documentary of Freud asked his British disciple and biographer Ernest Jones. Standing in front of a bust of his subject, Jones said solemnly:

"Life is not to be enjoyed. Life is to be endured."

Nothing could more fully express Freud's own pessimism.

IN PRACTICE, PSYCHOANALYSIS is based on the belief that if the unconscious "meaning" of a neurosis, character disorder, or even psychosis can be made conscious, the pathology will then be neutralized and no longer project its unfathomed charge into disruptive behavior. The patient is the only source of new meanings, since the distortion is contained uniquely in him. His diagnosable symptoms are his behavior, including his dreams and language patterns, both of which the doctor tries to "decode" by a system of "free association" whereby latent meaningful links between materials are supplied in place of obsessive logical ones. The doctor literally educates the patient in himself, gradually gaining his trust and breaking down his resistance and habit of denial, leading him to discover his pattern of distortion and self-abnegation. The hope is that he will gradually understand what he is doing and naturally resist self-destructive patterns.

This is not a "positive thinking" technique or a challenge to the stoutness of will. It is an actual training of new ways of thinking and feeling, transferred by the clinician to the patient in acts of mutual empathy. In this process of transference the therapist must stay clearly outside of the patient's life and not interfere directly. Otherwise, the patient's projections onto him (and vice versa) may reinforce and increase the pathology and even sometimes provoke a neurosis or psychosis in the therapist. In one famous case, Robert Lindner became so infatuated with a patient's imagined adventures among the "inhabited" galaxies that he entered into them as a willing participant, anxious for each session to get the next installment. Luckily this event shocked the patient into dropping the fantasy on his own. Lindner wrote at the time:

Sigmund Freud and the Origin of Psychotherapeutic Healing

Kirk was not able to appreciate the fact that when he abandoned his psychosis he had achieved my sole object for him; that to wean him from madness had been the conscious aim of my actions, and that this alone was important to me. As he saw and felt it, there had been a complete turnabout in our positions, a turnabout that confused and worried him, and one before which he remained helpless....[I]t was not because I was such an excellent actor that Kirk believed so thoroughly in the apparent reversal of roles: it was, rather, that he sensed how I had been attracted by the stupendous fantasy and felt, in myself, its magnetic pull....[22]

Few therapists today recognize the degree to which this is the danger of psychoanalytic transference. In fact, many New Age neo-Freudians pray for patients who will take them into outer space. They not only willingly join the patient in the labyrinth but rely on each patient to produce more and more interesting labyrinths.

Until Kirk Allen came into my life I had never doubted my own stability. The aberrations of mind, so I had always thought, were for others. Tolerant, somewhat amused, indulgent, I held to the myth of my own mental impregnability.[23]

This is the delusion anew of psychohypnotists who participate in their patients' "memories" of being abducted and abused by alien humanoids. Whether or not there is some literal truth to these memories is almost impossible to discern in a situation in which the incentive of the analyst has become to join in an apocalyptic UFO adventure.

THERE IS NO doubt that people are improved by traditional psychoanalysis, though the reasons may not be the ones Freud thought they were or related to psychoanalytic transference in a cause and effect manner. The shamanic aspects of the psychoanalytic episode, the charisma of the doctor himself, may—like the bloody down—supersede the ostensible concrete disease cause. Additionally, the improvement may fall well short of restoring functional behavior. But partial success of uncertain etiology was acceptable to Freud because he saw no cure-all for the vicissitudes of life. All the human animal could learn was how better to cope with his fate. Psychoanalysis has been maintained ever since as a middle-of-the-road therapy, neither scientific medicine nor charismatic healing, but uncourageously respectable.

Nothing distinguishes psychiatric therapeutics more than the unpredictable and inconsistent lengths of treatment, easily ten or fifteen years, commonly twenty-five, thirty, and longer. The patient becomes addicted to the psychoanalytic dialogue: the attention alone is an elixir in a society of alienated individuals. Both therapist and patient thus set out on a miniature journey mirroring both their lives, like a dream within a dream. Real cure is another matter. After all, a neurosis or psychological disorder is a defense which an organism has evolved in order to survive. The process of healing may reach an utter stalemate when the cause of the illness turns out to be the lifestyle itself, or some totally insoluble conflict. Most patients cannot change their family, job, habits, and marital situation without jeopardizing their overall sanity and sometimes the source of income for the therapy itself. This is not a tangential matter, since it speaks to the failure of the treatment to integrate itself into the social conditions in which it is trying to heal people.

The above represents the best of situations. In the Euro-American world, where this medicine is mostly practiced, patients are educated for and temperamentally suited to verbal analysis. They are the only ones on the planet who can afford such a long and sophisticated dialogue with a doctor. For the rest of the people, not only in the United States and Europe but much of the rest of the world, the Freudian legacy has degenerated into a kind of behavior modification backed by military and penal styles of group control. Drugs and simple authoritarian injunctions of various sorts have been found far more economical than protracted psychoanalysis. These do not treat any underlying disease, but then neither does psychoanalysis in the majority of cases.

Freud set the stage for the trivialization of the very process he invented by indicating that "coping" was the best that could be hoped for. From

*Sigmund
Freud and
the Origin
of Psycho-
therapeutic
Healing*

the position of beleaguered society, it was finally more efficient to bully and train people into submission and acceptable social behavior than to try to instill in them the possible sources of their freedom and humanity. And this, for the most part, is what mass psychiatry has become. The causes of behavior are considered incidental; and the focus is on how to generate the "correct" behavior. The only change from the Middle Ages—and even this may not have really changed—is that the emphasis has shifted from open confession and behavioral modification to unconscious confession and subliminal reprogramming.

Where Freud used subjective images for neuromuscular and mental processes, modern psychology has replaced them with neurons and hemispheres of the brain and the notion that men and women can be trained like rats and pigeons. Although Freud was headed in this direction anyway, the completeness of the dehumanization would have appalled him. He was a compassionate healer and his theories arose from his ability to treat illness. Those who came after him were all too often machinists and hacks.

However, there are schools of psychotherapy that, without adopting Freud's particular emphasis on purely libidinal aspects of development, emphasize the critical nature of very early internal splits, usually in the first years if not the first months of life. The reason why most therapies don't "solve" these splits is that they never get the patient to their level, so no actual reexperiencing occurs and no insight is gained at the degree of the depth at which the trauma is located. Only when an equivalent event occurs in adult life (such as the breakup of a relationship, the loss of a job, the death of a loved one, etc.) is the original sense of loss encountered again as it once was. Then the opportunity for actual treatment is suddenly present. Therapists can work to make the new experience a creative one that reactivates and heals the original split.

There are also schools of gestalt and transpersonal psychology using techniques of interaction and consciousness expansion to bring primary crisis into the present. These psychotherapies might have been almost as unappealing to the conservative Freud, but all masters have their unintended offspring, and the legacies of few would be as prone to such creative mischief as the very doctor who revealed the workings of unconsciousness.

While psychoanalysis may have waned as a viable medicine, its diagnosis of our condition has engulfed the entire world. So much has the psychoanalytic mode of thought permeated our culture and influenced our institutions, from labor relations to philosophy, that even, as noted at the beginning of this chapter, radical therapies that arise in direct defiance of the Freudian tradition partake in its basic design. Decades after Freud's death, Western science has been extending his model to include all human phenomena. In fact, "human" is an understatement. Animal "psychology" owes at least as much to Freudian influence: terms like "behavior," "instinct," "dominance," "learning," and their popular derivatives, have their roots in psychiatry. The stodgy domains of anthropology, ethology, ecology, and computer science inherit major parts of their structure from a system which began with the analysis and treatment of the mentally ill, i.e., the dysfunctional, the nonconforming. This in itself is an insight into how rigid and fragmented nineteenth-century Western civilization had become. Only madness and disorder could lead the way out of a banal and superficial paradigm for both medicine and social life. Psychology now lies at the center of modern aesthetic theory, linguistics, and art criticism—but equally physics, corporate management, criminology, and warfare.

We hear Freud's echo in Einstein, Derrida, and even Alfred North Whitehead. Military and aerospace sciences have inherited a Freudian component: the enemy operates from unconscious as well as conscious motives, and combat strategies are based on the "theory of instincts" and an "interpretation of dreams." Formal economic theory is a wish-fulfillment dream covering generations. Politics have become little more than a laboratory study in psychological manipulation. TV campaigns are pure Freud.

Of course, one man is not responsible for all of this. If it were going to come in such legion, it would have come anyway. But Freud was the one who recognized a burgeoning set of meanings and normalized it as a text. His synthesis stands, though its original clarity has been blurred by secondary issues, his own excesses, and sometimes the excesses of others claiming him. He is a feminist target because of his development of a psychology of women out of and subsidiary to a psychology of men. He is a political target because of his initiation of the privileged and exploitable role of the therapist. Modern social scientists exile him for his mystical theories of evolution and his "subjective" use of data. Humanists disown him for his cynicism and pessimism about human potential.

But Freud could hardly do everything, and he certainly could not transcend his own cultural biases. These mistakes, so-called, are minor and sectarian and do not negate his overall theory. So major and fundamental were his primary insights—in a sense the single insight—that they are without ideology and adaptable on a number of levels to a variety of different ends. No particular adaptations, including Freud's own, describe, let alone discredit, the essential discovery.

When he saw that his system did not, with any consistency, cure the mentally ill by insight alone, Freud proposed a specific death instinct impeding health, an instinct which must now balance libido in the psychosomatic economy, giving rise to the wars, suicides, and other destructive acts. As noted, he called this "thanatos," Greek for "death," and set its longing for self-destruction as the counterpart to the libidinal longing of contact. Thanatos resisted cure, resisted therapeutic work, and sought final cessation in lifelessness, where it began. It was mankind's destiny.

Death instinct was a primary basis of Freud's split with many of his disciples. Instead of revising his methodology on the basis of its own therapeutic flaws, he posited thanatos as a direct libidinal adversary. But not everyone was willing to accept his gloomy prognosis and, if they were willing to accept it philosophically, as a mythic judgment, they were not willing to accept it as a limitation of their curative prospects with individual patients. So they sought other definitions of the psychoanalytic proposition.

Freud in his later years tended to go farther and farther afield for explanations of the incurability of our species. He created a mythology of the pseudoanthropological origin of the Oedipal complex, suggesting that mankind somehow had implanted a self-destructive cycle in its biological base. His disciple Sandor Ferenczi took this to its logical conclusion in the germ plasm which, he argued, had been traumatized by the very arousal of life within its deadness.[24] Matter, he said, would have been happier staying inert forever.

For Ferenczi, civilization was certainly a psychological "catastrophe," as Freud had concluded, but it was preceded by prior calamities, of which life itself was the first, disturbing the eternal sleep of inorganic stone, forcing it to become protoplasm. In this sequence leading toward the Oedipal crisis of consciousness were the successive traumas of cell fission, emergence onto dry land, and the development of primacy in the genital zone, all of which we inherit and suffer ontogenetically. We cannot undo the damage, nor can we return to any of these primeval wombs within wombs. So when we experience our own depths, we are doomed to a passage of traumas, all leading back to the repose of a lifeless universe—the only cure, Ferenczi realized, for a condition as serious as birth. There is no bottom to this pessimistic regression, except perhaps that the men who formulated it themselves enjoyed fruitful lives.

Archetypal Psychology

Carl Jung (1875–1961), Freud's immediate disciple, did not share the innovator's gloom or circumscription of unconscious human thought forms to primitive creature instincts. Hence Jung added a cosmic and spiritual dimension to the basic unconscious, suggesting that not only chaos and fragmentation, but also creative and curative powers from beyond human ken were contained there. Freud himself perceived the healing function of dreams and other psychic material, but he placed a Victorian limit on what kind of information was stored in them—very little, he concluded, beside the already bottomless desires and terrors to which nightmare is our closest encounter. Jung's unconscious was collective and pre-embryological. He found in it the regularities of geometry and mathematics, the cosmic forms of gods and mythological heroes, and the blueprint for civilization itself—for temples and poems and cities, all of which bloomed from seeds in the human psyche. Freud interpreted civilization as merely the product of distorted instinct thrown up around himself by a frightened creature, but Jung insisted no, it is a realization of the boundless alchemical mind of nature too. In a psychoanalytic revival of the shamanic tradition of seeking

nonhuman intelligence in plants, animals, and gods, he proposed a healing psyche/soma as an aspect of the relationship between spirit and matter, and he gave humanity access to transpersonal healing forces through the portals of psychic space. We will explore his system in Chapter Twelve.

Jung also confirmed what Freud no doubt feared: that by opening a Pandora's box, he had let out everything. Derrida would later show him to have let out the nothing that everything is and so sent Western philosophy back to the totems and taboos of its beginnings. Freud discovered the inevitability of conflict and sorrow in instinct, but Jung showed Freud to have also rediscovered the hermetic arts and original sources of magic, not as mythological remnants, but reborn daily with the same living integrity as DNA and electrons possess. By the time holistic medicine inherited the psyche and the dreamwork, its shamanic element had been partially restored, and healers were once again prepared to face the shadow realm with confidence.

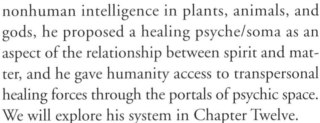

Freud had revealed, if only in rough semblance, the archaeology of a vast healing system, like an underground city inhabited by Navaho medicine men, Australian shamans, and African voodoo priests. As our sense of the unconscious has grown in the decades since then, it has burst out from the axioms that spawned it. Alternative medicines come to rely, post-psychiatrically, on the intuition that powerful primeval energies dwell inside us and that the forces which lead to our sickness and destruction are also the seeds of our revivification.

Notes

1. This quotation is approximately recalled from a *New Yorker* profile (March 2, 1992) of two Russian emigré mathematicians (David and Gregory Chudnosky) who turned the inside of their apartment in New York City into a computer in order to solve for pi. Though their wives worked fulltime to support this venture and their lives were otherwise in serious disrepair, the main concern the brothers expressed to the interviewer was that their computer might not be big enough and that their prey might thus elude them.

2. Claude Lévi-Strauss, *Totemism,* translated from the French by Rodney Needham (Boston: Beacon Press, 1963), pp. 1–2.

3. Sigmund Freud, *The Interpretation of Dreams,* translated from the German by James Strachey (New York: Basic Books, 1955).

4. Jacques Derrida, "Freud and the Scene of Writing," translated from the French by Jeffrey Mehlman, *Yale French Studies,* New Haven: Yale University Press, no date, p. 116. See also Derrida's *Of Grammatology,* translated from the French by Gayatri Chakravorty Spivak (Baltimore: Johns Hopkins University Press, 1976).

5. Sigmund Freud, *An Outline of Psychoanalysis,* translated from the German by James Strachey (New York: Norton, 1949), p. 13.

6. Ibid., p. 9.

7. Ibid., p. 11.

8. Freud, *The Interpretation of Dreams.*

9. Ibid., p. xxxii.

10. Ibid., p. 88.

11. Ibid.

12. Ibid.

13. Ibid., p. 92.

14. Ibid., p. 211.

15. Ibid., p. 366.

16. Ibid., p. 267.

17. Ibid., p. 215.

18. Ibid., pp. 389, 391, 392.

19. Ibid., p. 548.

20. Ibid., p. 264.

21. For a much more extensive discussion of dreams, see Richard Grossinger, "The Dream Work," in Richard A. Russo (ed.), *Dreams are Wiser Than Men* (Berkeley, California: North Atlantic Books, 1987), pp. 191–246.

22. Robert Lindner, *The Fifty-Minute Hour* (New York: Bantam Books, 1956), p. 206.

23. Ibid., p. 207.

24. Sandor Ferenczi, *Thalassa: A Theory of Genitality,* translated from the German by Henry Alden Bunker (New York: Norton, 1968), pp. 99–101.

CHAPTER ELEVEN

Wilhelm Reich: From Character Analysis to Cosmic Eros

Bodywork

THE CURATIVE ASPECT of physical contact between therapist and patient has been acknowledged and cultivated since the beginning of our species—from primate grooming to Pacific Island systems of massage to the Stone Age crafts of manipulation and bone-adjusting, which Americans Daniel David Palmer and Andrew Taylor Still refashioned from scratch during the nineteenth century. Hands-on healers and bone-setters have plied their skills in every tribe, village, and city on Earth. Contemporary modalities of postural realignment and somatics owe more to these lineages than to the bodywork tradition that Wilhelm Reich developed out of Freudian theory.

In fact, many pre-Freudian psychological modalities included substantial somatic work with clients. The renowned Berlin academies of breathing and subtle manipulation originated quite separate from Reich, more out of the legacies of naturopathy, physical therapy, and dance (see Chapter Twelve and Volume Two, Chapter Four). From the viewpoint that disease lay deeper than language or thought, psychologist Georg Groddeck (1866–1934) dismissed the possibility of reaching most of his mental patients on a conscious or linguistic level. He regularly bathed, massaged, and "adjusted" them and prescribed exercises. These methods, he thought, would speak to their "It" rather than to their persons.[1] He continued this method even after the advent of psychoanalysis:

The It influences fat formation, growth and character as if it were a rational being. It is the duty of the doctor to find out what meaning this uncomfortable obesity may have, with its attendant dangers of a stroke, heart trouble, or dropsy, what this leanness and tuberculosis may signify. The unconscious does not merely reveal itself in dreams, it reveals itself in every gesture, in the twitching of the forehead, the beating of the heart, yet also in the quiet warning of a uric-acid diathesis.[2]

From Groddeck's It, the thing which could not speak, Freud derived his term "id." Yet the founder of psychology diverted attention from the use of massage and bone adjustment in treatment of mental illness and redirected it exclusively toward unconscious dynamics. For newborn psychoanalysis the laws of unconscious process represented such a revolutionary insight that earlier mere physical therapies were abandoned as superficial and primitive.

When palpation and manipulation were picked up again (relatively recently) by the culture at large, they were already redefined in terms of Freudian dynamics of the unconscious mind and sexuality. "Gestalt" was the reigning prejudice in somatic and humanistic psychological circles through the 1960s and '70s into the 1980s. The different "cures" achieved by each nonpsychoanalytic method of somatics certainly had unique meanings in the lexicons of its practitioners, but, as discussed in the last chapter, with the exception of *Chi Gung* and other Eastern disciplines, these cures almost always came to include a psychoanalytic component, if only a simplistic, third-hand version of the Freudian dialogue. This was more a mark of the holistic synthesis of the late twentieth century than of any original thought process.

Thus Wilhelm Reich (1897–1957) could hardly be, as some propose, the inventor of bodywork. What Reich did was to establish a contemporary modality according to psychoanalytic theory of the unconscious mind and sexual sublimation. This prototype became a primary influence in the subsequent conversion of most Western systems of somatics to psychotherapy. But it was not the only influence. Research into the physiological components of effective mind/body states and relaxation initiated by American pragmatists of the Boston school in the late nineteenth century also played a role in the somaticization of psychology. Later elements came independently from the work of European phenomenologists.

Though Reich was not enamored of indigenous somatic therapies or medical systems of manipulation, he provided a major impetus for their revival. That is, while emphasizing but one link between somatics and the unconscious, he left behind unintended bridges by which others, outside the context of his orthodoxy, could follow. Many somatic therapists today either make deliberate use of some aspects of Reich's model (characterological or orgastic) or inherit them from the holistic consensus. Others may not even bear a scintilla of Reichian influence (or may intentionally contravene Reich in their practices), but they also exist in a milieu defined by Reichian formulas of character analysis and therapeutic somatology.

When I first wrote *Planet Medicine,* Reich was a major player. For European intellectuals of the post-war era, the renegade psychotherapist was a virtual ikon—an untamed twentieth-century cowboy philosopher. His blunt advocacy of sexual liberation and full orgastic expression as prerequisites to political revolution provided clinical ammunition for challenging longstanding mores and taboos of Judaeo-Christian tradition as well as the unexamined puritanism of an emerging left wing. At the same time, his critique of civilization was so fundamental and uncompromising (and proposed in such convincing biological terms) that after his death he became the darling of the neo-Marxists. Though a strident anti-Marxist for most of his life, Reich legitimized for others (who did not have to confront Stalinism so directly) their infatuation with socialist and communist alternatives to the capitalist plague. Herbert Marcuse's popular *Eros and Civilization* fit right into the lineage established by Freud and Reich. Whatever else he did or didn't do, Reich identified the immense power of cultural forces on the psyche and the inadequacy of psychoanalysis to counter these.

The nature of the public dialogue has changed dramatically in the last twenty years and, with the rise of both ecological and gender awareness and the decline of communism, the phalanx upholding Reich as a beacon of new humanity has been almost entirely supplanted. Even Reich's role as premier bodyworker and theoretician of somatics is now substantially under challenge. We are more concerned these days with developing new paradigms and understanding how things actually work than with grand theories and heroic men propounding manifestoes against the tide of history.

From this perspective, Reich's importance has been exaggerated quite out of scale with his actual role in the development of somatic therapies. First of all, it has become clear that even psychologically based bodywork and breathing techniques have arisen independently in Western culture a number of times in the last two centuries. In just about all instances, these methods have nothing to do with either Freud or Reich. In addition to Palmer and Still and the chiropractic and osteopathic lineages that have arisen from them, there have been many other non-Reichian models of somatics in North America alone. William James and Walter B. Cannon, among other experimental psychologists, explored neurophysiology, drugs, and mystical states. The Alexander Technique, Feldenkrais work, and Rolfing also developed substantially independently of Reich.

Secondly, the current bias in somatic psychology has been to move away from Reich's heavily ideological model and toward more undetermined and improvisational methods of hands-on palpation and natural movement. There also has been a new bias toward non-Western paradigms of physiology, elegance, and functional anatomy as well as treatment. (See also Volume Two, Chapter Four.)

Thus, various other lineages have been increasingly favored at the expense of either pure Reichian or Reichian-derived bioenergetic techniques. Nothing distinguishes popular bodywork of the 1980s and 1990s so much as its movement away from Reich's model of character armor and orgastic potency toward a multiple variety of circumstances of character resistance, armor, coordination, and intrinsic energy.

At the same time, Wilhelm Reich has become a favorite subject of biography and speculation, and the differing elements of his work continue to sustain both mainstream and marginal schools of therapeutic and vitalistic practices. These alone mark him as a notable figure in the history of alternative medicine.

As I mentioned in the introduction, this chapter has already been revised in publication several times. My initial choice was to leave it out of the present edition of *Planet Medicine* because it skewed the discussion of somatics toward one man's life and toward topics no longer meriting such priority. My decision to include it at the last moment was based on its illumination of a number of mysteries that remain at the core of not only healing but twentieth-century science. Reich dove right into the maelstrom of paradoxes that continue to haunt us and define our plight. In that sense, his career, even if not as seminal to the development of somatology as once proposed, is as dramatic a statement as we have of our continuing therapeutic dilemma. Reich may have ended up like Ahab going down with the ship, but no one could accuse him of accepting facile New Age solutions.

EARLY IN HIS CAREER, Reich was one of the first and most successful practitioners of the Freudian system. Progressively, as he came to recognize the seriousness of what he called "the emotional plague," he abandoned conventional psychoanalysis as unequipped and inadequate. Over the next thirty-five years he developed a new paradigm of psychology and physics, encompassing not only libidinal but cosmic energy. He went way beyond the series of clinical metaphors or literary symbols to which he condemned Freudian analysis. In fact, Reich gradually isolated and observed the "atoms" of his proposed energy in experiments and then pursued a technology of applying them medicinally as vital force.

His diagnosis of a collective ailment, like Freud's, was almost Biblical in its portent. He felt that the human species needed not only

Wilhelm Reich: From Character Analysis to Cosmic Eros

423

healing but a metamorphosis—a task requiring a physician in the largest sense of the term. His medicine ultimately embraced social, economic, and political arenas and fused the etiology of protoplasm, fascism, and galactic mass in a single science.

In order to map Reich, we need to examine the troubled seams in the Freudian logos. Later we may find that much of the Reichian cosmos has its separate origin in other pre-Freudian materials, like those of Groddeck, but that discovery takes on meaning only in the context of the subtleties of unconscious dynamics.

Freud and Reich

REICH MET FREUD in 1919 while still a student at the Medical School of the University of Vienna. As a disenchanted combatant in World War I interested in political change, Reich had originally entered the Faculty of Law but changed to medicine from the insight that pedantic legalism led nowhere. In the beginning he was committed to formal science, but he was also interested in human nature. Psychoanalysis presented him with the perfect blend of intuition and fact. Throughout his career Reich's orientation to the psyche and the emotions remained concrete and scientific, seeking quantifiable bases for behavior.

His talent in the new field surfaced quickly, and by the mid-1920s Freud considered him one of his most promising disciples. But Reich was troubled by the technical inadequacies of psychoanalysis, a criticism which, from the beginning, extended almost sacrilegiously to Freud's own clinical practice. From Reich's perspective, psychoanalysis had slipped out of real medicine. It was more like a specialized form of parental discussion. Doctor and patient were two philosophers engaged in a debate; neither of them could be wholly right or wholly wrong, and in any case the issues were irresolvable. Rather than admit defeat, therapists extended the period necessary for analysis or declared the patient cured, either one for arbitrary reasons. "A patient was usually considered 'cured,'" Reich wrote, "when he said that he felt better, or

424

when the individual symptom for which he had sought therapy disappeared. The psychoanalytic concept of cure had not been defined."[3]

But, he pointed out, when the patient declares himself cured, that does not mean he is cured; it means that he has chosen to end the treatment for whatever reason.

In this dilemma, psychoanalysts fell back on the semi-mystical dogma of "transference." Even though language in itself cannot cure, they admitted, the relationship between the doctor and the patient contains within it a shared identity, a moment when they are one and when the health and clarity of the doctor pass to the patient through the sanctum of mutual trust and assimilation of boundaries.

Transference is what transforms the dialogue into a medicine and provides the basis for internalization of the "verbal" cure.

Reich felt that a total reevaluation of this therapeutic process was necessary. He did not challenge transference itself, but he questioned the ability of therapists to recognize it and employ it, and he doubted its universal application as mere objectified language. He mentions his own "successful" treatment, early in his career, of a waiter who had been totally unable to have an erection. During the third year of analysis, patient and doctor were able to reconstruct a traumatic primal scene: the patient had witnessed the birth of a sibling, and "the impression of a large bloody hole" between his mother's legs had been imprinted on his mind. After this breakthrough, the treatment was soon terminated because the patient was cooperative, well behaved, and accepting of the role of this childhood trauma in his present condition. The only problem was that he was still impotent.[4]

At the time, several of Freud's major disciples in Germany held a seminar in psychoanalytic technique. When Reich presented this case to them, it was enthusiastically accepted and praised. Despite the patient's lingering functional problem, cure was said to be complete. Reich had followed standard methodology, established transference, and reconstructed a primal scene. By the rules of the system at that point, actual cure was not required.

Wilhelm Reich: From Character Analysis to Cosmic Eros

But why not, Reich wondered, consider the patient's very acceptance of an unacceptable situation the contemporary form of his resistance? Then he could remain sick, and the psychiatrist had no further avenue of treatment. By this perception, Reich cut right through the verbal bias of the Freudian movement. A patient's announcement of cure, in his own language, had always been considered a hopeful sign because it indicated a willingness to participate. But if verbal acquiescence was no more than another symptom, the civilized rationale of psychoanalysis breaks down. The therapist must now go against medical etiquette, denying the patient his right to a self-declared cure and keeping him in therapy.

To Reich, it was ludicrous that one could pretend to declare a truce with the unabated id on the level of a conscious exchange of albeit intimate material and a handshake. He assumed that Freud would go along with his objection and that psychoanalysis would reexamine its clinical tenets. When Freud rejected his ideas whole cloth, Reich did not retreat but instead assumed that the founder had become another victim of his own hypothetical death instinct. Since Freud never subsequently pursued a clinical solution to neurosis, he reasoned, psychoanalysis was maintained only as a middle-of-the-road therapy, neither scientific medicine nor energetic healing, but uncourageously respectable.

Because of his own professional failures, Freud had doomed mankind to misery, said Reich. He misread his own unhappiness. He settled on the death instinct in the 1920s, and after that, psychoanalysis stagnated, satisfied it could work no real cures, content to give palliative relief and help through his "too many pains, disappointments, and impossible tasks."[5]

Speaking of Freud late in his own life, Reich acknowledged this moment: "I know, today, that *he sensed something in the human organism which was deadly.*" But Freud called it an instinct. "'Death' was right," says Reich, but not death as an instinct. *Because it's not something the organism wants. It's something that happens to the organism.*"[6]

Character Analysis

R EICH'S INITIAL BREAK with Freud was over the death instinct, but once he had broken, he began to ask, "Why does the treatment take so long?" His answer, in essence, was: "It's because they're talking all the time." As he developed his own methodology, he decided to end the formal dialogue and treat *the full character* of the patient. Politeness and soft-spokenness were no longer virtues; if the person was sick, these were outgrowths of the ailment. The enthusiasm of the patient for free association and a willingness to provide juicy material from memory were also suspect, no matter how insightful the material. The patient's actual behavior was the only clue to the illness, for this was the thing he could not help, no matter what he said. Of the impotent waiter, Reich wrote:

> At that time, I incorrectly assessed the total personality of my patient. He was very quiet, well-mannered, and well-behaved, and did everything that was asked of him. He never got excited. In the course of three years of treatment, he never once became angry or exercised criticism.[7]

In the end, he accepted the failure of the analysis, even when described as success, with the same stoic equanimity with which he had acquiesced in everything else. "I was blind," Reich implied. "*That* was the disease!"

To Reich, dreams could no longer be the cornerstones of therapy, the one royal road. The manner in which the patient comes to the treatment, his politeness or recalcitrance, his mode of speech, his dress, the style and firmness of his handshake were all records of character. And this "character" is real; it embodies pathology; it can be isolated and treated. Reich directed attention to it and away from the complications and distractions of unconscious contents elicited by free association. He was inventing a new typology more in keeping with Groddeck than Freud.

Wilhelm Reich: From Character Analysis to Cosmic Eros

We will define "character" in Reichian terms in this chapter and in more universal and cross-cultural terms in Volume Two, Chapter Two.

Since the Freudian unconscious was composed of latent sensations and impulses in the body itself, Reich saw no predominant need to go back in time and memory to a traumatic moment and the origin of the condition. He wrote, *"The entire world of past experience [is] embodied in the present in the form of character attitudes. A person's character is the functional sum total of all past experiences."*[8]

This is as profound a description of holism as any. Historic memory becomes a present function, even when it fails to provide the traumatic moment, because memory is stored in the body and takes on an energetic form, usually as rigidity and resistance. Its very state of unconsciousness must be maintained somatically. Static charge becomes axiomatic to all energy medicines from shamanism to *Chi Gung:* Yes, a person's character *is* the functional sum total of all past experiences. Everything which has been continues to exist in some anatomical form somewhere. Just as chemists can track the vestiges of immune responses from forty years ago, so can somaticists pick up the present character traces of each formative event in the psyche.

The doctor does not need to reconstruct a critical moment; the moment persists in every breath the patient takes, in every gesture he or she makes. This is not to deny the importance of clinical history, but to place it in therapeutic context. Reconstructions of memory are instructive in mapping a disease, but they cannot alter the disease core. In fact, the collaboration of patient and doctor in recovering sources and implicitly sanctifying them is counterproductive in that it encourages the patient to focus on unhappy experiences and gives them an existential priority in explaining the rest of life. Initially discomfort may be eased by having a lineal cause for compulsion and anxiety, but ultimately the patient becomes so fascinated with his own history, he loses contact with his present somatic reality. The conscious mind becomes its own trap. In place of "psychology," Reich proposed "somatology"—but since mind and body are a unity, these are the same thing.

Reich perceived that an "actual neurosis," not a fright or a confusion, lay at the energetic core of symptomatic behavior and verbally expressed neurosis. This actual neurosis was not historical but present and alive as a new or reinvented thing.

In asking (rhetorically) what fueled the visible surface neurosis, Reich answered in classic Freudian terms: Compulsions, hysterias, and the like must derive from blocked sexual energy. By 1927 Reich had defined a *sine qua non* of psychoanalytic cure—it was not an imagined experience of ancient traumas but an actual capacity to express feelings of tenderness and sensuality in love-making. If not there, it had to be restored. Once restored, it dissolved neurosis without further psychoanalysis, much like *chi* flow. The traumatic moment need not ever be recalled as such. Although not all holistic systems agree that love-making is the *sine qua non,* all holistic systems share the notion of a singular energetic process that heals traumas without a need for psychoanalytic history.

Reich came to this insight only after a long odyssey of clinical exploration, and he considered it a correct application of orthodox Freudian theory, not the first axiom of a new system. He was not seeking a revolutionary replacement for psychoanalysis, only a way past the obstacle of sham cure.

However, despite his initial conservative intention, Reich had begun to redefine Freudianism in more explicit energetic terms, perhaps in keeping with Freud's original theories but definitely at odds with the psychoanalytic customs of the time. In that sense he had returned to the roots and become the most pure "Freudian" of all. But he was no longer a psychoanalyst.

Reich interpreted the human organism in terms of the characterological implications of its impeded reservoir of energy. Society was a mere artifact of this energy in a structured and ordered state (however ill-structured and disordered the state). Reich ultimately blamed such an outcome on the fashion of economic and business practices, though he never satisfactorily explained why, or what the evolutionary alternative might have been.

The function of analysis, he said, is somatic—to soften neuro-muscular blocks that have developed from suppression of natural energy. Verbal therapy does not accomplish this because language forms are already rigidly somaticized. They reflect levels of feeling, breathing, and orgastic potential that have been anesthetized, so their hyper-conscious play at insight can be only superficial. In that sense, he was as libidinal as Freud:

"Every increase of muscular tonus and rigidification is an indication that a vegetative excitation, anxiety, or sexual sensation has been blocked and bound."[9]

The collective effect of these bound responses is a wall of nerves and muscles built up by opposing forces. The wall prevents the organism from its singular expression of biological unity, the discharge of inner tensions. The forces within long for contact with other human beings, but the armor warns them of danger and seals them permanently in a consistent character the person comes to identify as himself or herself—a fake personality streamlined for the worlds of etiquette and business. Anything originating "outside" this character is a threat to the integrity of the organism, even if this happens to be the natural excitations of the organism itself. As Reich saw it, the basic somatic drive of human beings has been abnegated, on a planetwide basis, by a false social ambition. He identified the paranoia of psychotics exactly as their apperception of their own pulsations which have no identity within the structure of their personalities, so achieve their meaning as outside oppressors. Excitations seem like spirits, diseases, or even witchcraft, for they originate beyond accepted personal boundaries. To Reich, the work of great composers, painters, and poets comes from their remote apperception of the same pulses psychotics fear.

He emphasized functional sexuality to a degree that was appalling to Freudians (content with sexual metaphors and the secure—if repressive—management of real sex by the superego). This later became, as he feared, even a matter of contention among his own disciples. He stated his cure in exact words:

Psychic health depends upon orgastic potency, i.e., upon the degree to which one can surrender to and experience the climax of excitation in the natural sexual act.[10]

If insight is offered to a patient while armor is still present, she will automatically depreciate its meaning on a somatic level even while accepting it intellectually. That is, she will pretend quite honestly to agree while her body and unconscious mind remain alienated and aloof. Only when a healthy sexual function is restored can the patient make use of insights. Until then, she needs the therapist's direct hands-on aid in dissolving the armor. The reason why Freudian analysis failed, Reich stated with new confidence, was that it did not restore function. Words were not equal to the task; touch and movement were necessary components.

Somatic Psychotherapy

"Now, YOU KNOW that Freud began as a somaticist," Reich told his interviewer years later, "as a man who worked with the body. Then he discovered the unconscious. So he switched over into psychology. But he never forgot that he was a somaticist. *The greatest thing that ever happened in psychiatry was the discovery that the core of the neurosis was somatic, i.e., the stasis, the libido stasis, was somatic.*"[11]

If the core is somatic, then it must be diagnosed and treated somatically. This was not the case in psychoanalysis, which supported the status quo of body stances and etiquette. Reich did not have to look far for evidence of somaticized trauma. Every street and social gathering was a zoo of repressed bestiality. But everyone was pretending to be real and having fun. Everyone was involved in an unacknowledged collusion with everyone else, agreeing not to notice that no one was having a real experience, as long as they were not exposed either. The smiles thrown back and forth masked the underlying pain and the evasion of biological necessity, which then expressed itself in character disorders.

Wilhelm Reich: From Character Analysis to Cosmic Eros

People are dull. They are dull, dead, uninterested. And, then, they develop their pseudo-contacts, fake pleasures, fake intelligence, superficial things, the wars, and so on.[12]

Reich listed the various observable symptoms: "loud, obtrusive laughter; exaggeratedly firm handshake; unvarying, dull friendliness; conceited display of acquired knowledge; frequent repetition of empty astonishment, surprise, or delight, etc.; rigid adherence to definite views, plans, goals . . . ; obtrusive modesty in demeanor; grand gestures in speaking; childish wooing of people's favor; boastfulness in sexual matters; exaggerated display of sexual charm; promiscuous flirtation . . . ; pseudo-exuberant fellowship . . . ; bashfulness."[13]

His clinical strategy was to challenge these poses. Instead of talking to people *about* these habits, he talked to the habits in people. He encouraged the quirks and tried to draw them out. The stiff, polite gentleman was asked to exaggerate his stiffness. The ever-smiling woman was encouraged to expand her smile and fully experience the flippancy of her gestures. The superior knowledgeable lecturer was told to go on lecturing, but with attention to how he did it—his breathing and the grip of his muscles. If the patient produced provocative associations that seemed accurate but with a smile that depreciated them, Reich ignored the associations and asked the patient to bring out his irony, to increase his sarcasm. It was resistance Reich sought, not accounts or stories. These were simply words the patient chose with which to buy time. Resistance, the null space behind the words, was the true beast.

For instance, the patient may acknowledge that, of course, he has shown contempt for people in the past, that aloofness is one of his vices. The therapist may answer, "No, right now. You are being contemptuous right now. Even as you pretend to participate in this session, your expression says that you are merely indulging me, showing contempt for me." If the outraged and embarrassed patient denies this, the therapist can respond, "Feel your mouth. Your lips are frozen into a leer. You have no sensation of them anymore." Upon checking, the patient is astonished to realize this is true. Automatically he grins foolishly. One therapeutic method might then be to massage the lips in order to restore feeling. Another might be to have the patient stick out his tongue and pretend to attack with it. The painful stretching out of the lingual muscles breaks into the armoring of the face and jaw and undermines the intrinsic support for sarcasm.

Psychoanalysts had been too smart for their own good. While they were deciphering the conscious (and even the unconscious) minds of their patients in a labyrinth of symbols, the psychosomatic intelligence of the patients (as we saw in the last chapter) was leading them back through their own maze:

> The patients readily divined what the psychoanalyst expected in terms of theory, and they produced the appropriate "associations." In short, they produced material to oblige the analysts. If they were cunning individuals, they half-consciously led the analyst astray, e.g., produced extremely confusing dreams so that no one knew what was going on. It was precisely this continual confusion of the dreams, not their content, that was the crucial problem. Or they produced one symbol after another—the sexual meaning of which they readily divined—and in no time they were able to operate with concepts. They would speak about the "Oedipus complex" without any trace of affect. Inwardly, they did not believe in the interpretations of their associations, which the analysts usually took at face value.[14]

Reich mentioned trying unusual methods to shock a patient into awareness. With one person, he imitated for him his own sullenness and misery; he "lay on the floor and kicked and screamed."[15] The patient's initial response was astonishment, but then, according to Reich, he burst into full and spontaneous laughter which, in itself, was a major breakthrough.

The traditional analyst was content to have the patient recline on a couch, turned away from the doctor. This, thought Reich, heightened exactly those feelings of remoteness, lack of contact, and alienation that

Wilhelm Reich: From Character Analysis to Cosmic Eros

433

the analysis was supposed to dissolve. "This procedure did not eliminate but rather reinforced the patient's feeling that he had to deal with an 'invisible' unapproachable superhuman, i.e., in terms of the child's way of thinking, a sexless being."[16]

From this position, the detached and unreachable doctor reassures the patient and tells him she understands his problems. She encourages, even exhorts him, to produce material. If the patient is silent and remains silent, the analyst can only intensify her line of approach. She can tell the patient that he is resisting, interpret the silence as resistance, and hope to break it down by persuasion. But, argued Reich, the verbal pressure to produce material in fact intensifies the resistance. It arouses a "contemporary reason for being stubborn."[17] The alternative is to stun the patient with the precise character created by his own resistance. Then he can deal with a real and present event and is also relieved of the pressure for psychoanalytic performance.

Sexuality and Politics

REICH HAD CONSIDERED himself politically left wing, but his radicalism remained incipient until July 15, 1927, when he left a therapy session to get a firsthand look at a strike march. The police fired on the crowd, leaving eighty-nine dead in the street.[18]

This was a watershed experience for Reich, and it gave immediate expression to a number of unshaped intuitions. Some coalesced almost immediately; most formed gradually over the years. Soon after the event, Reich described the rigidity, the mechanicalness of both police and marchers—a depersonalized condition like that of warring soldiers, a collectivized pathology not even acknowledged in the narcissistic Freudian debate. How could scientists miss such blatant displays of disease?

Reich realized that the blocking of energy that lay at the core of individual neurosis was what led to mindless confrontation and destructiveness on a scale that dwarfed the single patient on the couch. When he joined the Communist Party in Germany, he was not satisfied with going to meetings and listening to speeches. These he regarded as further deadening activities, ineffective "therapy sessions." Instead he began to practice as a politically conscious physician, organizing like-minded doctors and traveling the streets in vans with sex-hygiene clinics (as he called them), giving out literature, holding counseling sessions for working-class youth, and in general trying to provide information about the sexual basis of true freedom.

This "sex-political" work was, to his new way of thinking, seminal to both community health and social change. As long as the masses were frozen in character defenses, they were not capable of using their energies to transform society, and they were particularly susceptible to the appeals of fascism, which at least provided an energetic charge and excited their suppressed sexuality. The workers had to be "healed" from the epidemic of social repression in order to be able to bring about an unneurotic new order.

Reich had integrated Freud and Marx—the psychological etiology with the economic dialectic.

He now took an active role in therapy, encouraging patients to break away from bad marriages, visiting their houses to observe the role of living conditions in sustaining neurosis. He openly denounced the psychoanalytic hierarchy (with its laboratory of office and couch, the patient pointed neutrally away from the doctor) as authoritarian, indulgent, and isolating itself protectively from the real causes of disease. Recognizing the importance of contacting patients somatically, he turned them around to face *him* and replaced dialogue with an aggressive encounter of their resistance; he instructed and observed them in physical exercises and touched them at their points of armoring (Freud immediately balked at this interventionist style—the replacement of free association with provocative confrontation).

Reich mentions going to the home of a woman living on the verge of starvation with three children, deserted by their father. She regularly had compulsions to push them into the water. As an orphan child she had been boarded with strangers, six or more people to a room, and raped by older men.

Not expecting her to make office visits, Reich went to her apartment. He was profoundly moved by her survival in a world of such misery. "I had to grapple not with the exalted question of the etiology of neuroses but with the question of how a human organism could put up with such conditions year in and year out. There was nothing, absolutely nothing, to bring light into this life. There was nothing but misery, loneliness, gossip of the neighbors, worries about the next meal—and, on top of it all, there were the criminal chicaneries of her landlord and employer."[19]

Reich put this case before the collective psychiatric profession at a local seminar and asked them to square it with their erudite theories of trauma and neurosis. He declared that it was impossible to have libidinal health under the existing social conditions (rushed intercourse often without the semblance of privacy). He argued that the Freudian movement had dealt only with the wealthier classes. Reich felt that its doctors were blinded by fake intellectualism and could not see the social conditions at the basis of psychopathologies. Their kind of therapy must be useless in the present social environment. They'd be better off forgetting practice until after "the revolution."

INITIALLY REICH WAS encouraged by Lenin's program of sexual reform, but when Stalinism followed, he quickly recanted. Over the years he moved further and further from his early left-wing position. The emotional plague ran deep, he reasoned. Fascism had corrupted even Communism. Mankind was too terrified of what lay within to advance sane political systems. People would always choose further symptomatic repression. Ultimately Reich attacked Communism as a fraud. The political radicals, he said simply, *promise happiness without really establishing the mental-hygiene requirements for it.*[20]

Reich's twin banishments from the German Communist Party and the International Psychoanalytic Association were a great achievement for their time; he exposed the limitation of both groups, one unable to handle sexuality except neurotically and the other unwilling to consider the societal underpinnings of neurosis. His critique remains as salient and unacknowledged today. Toward the end of his life he took an absolute position, without retribution and without amelioration: "There is no use in anything but infants. You have to go back to the unspoiled protoplasm."[21]

And elsewhere, about Freud:

> He gave up before he started. I came to the same conclusion, but only after much experience and failure. Nothing can be done with grownups.... Once a tree has grown crooked, you can't straighten it.... *He was disappointed, clearly disappointed. And he was right. Nothing can be done. Nothing can be done.*[22]

Long after Reich had been excommunicated from virtually every psychoanalytic and medical group, he still proclaimed his commitment to the initial insight of Freud: "I alone was true to the master," Reich said in effect. "Even the master was not true."

Orgasm Theory

Almost from the beginning, Reich was forced to disown misuses of his method. "Sympathetic" analysts jumped to the conclusion that sexual intercourse with ejaculation was all that was required. Reich pointed out that phrases like "I slept with my boyfriend" or "I made love every day last week" mask a variety of events, more different than similar. For doctors to conclude that patients are experiencing orgasm because they say they are proficient at the sexual act, or even worse, to encourage promiscuity, and, as the final sacrilege, to carry out the sexual act *with* their patients in order to "cure" them, was, by Reich's standards, criminally naive. He complained openly that the majority of practicing psychoanalysts were so dissatisfied sexually themselves that they were projecting their own deviant desires onto their patients. Reich explained pointedly what he meant by orgastic potency:

> Until 1923, the year orgasm theory was born, only ejaculative and erective potency were known to sexology and psychoanalysis. Without the inclusion of the functional, economic, and experiential components, the concept of sexual potency has no meaning. Erective and ejaculative potency are merely indispensable preconditions for orgastic potency. *Orgastic potency is the capacity to surrender to the flow of biological energy, free of any inhibitions; the capacity to discharge completely the dammed-up sexual excitation through involuntary, pleasurable convulsions of the body.* Not a single neurotic is orgastically potent, and the character structures of the overwhelming majority of men and women are neurotic.[23]

The involuntary submissive aspect of orgasm is key here. This is clearly not the sexual act as it is commonly understood in Western culture.

> The increase of the excitation can no longer be controlled; rather it grips the entire personality and causes an acceleration of pulse and deep exhalation.
>
> The physical excitation becomes more and more concentrated in the genital; there is a sweet sensation which can be best described as the flowing of excitation from the genital to the other parts of the body.[24]

This is the original natural medicine. The differentiation between male and female disappears beneath its unity. The organs may be sex-specific, but the same involuntary pulsing of energy passes through both (certainly Reich escaped the Freudian fallacy of deriving female sexuality from the male genital.) The organismic unity that each of them represents is joined to the single unity of both of them. The inner tension, from which disease might accrete, evaporates. Western man and woman, to Reich, had debased this intrinsic healing principle, this primal bliss, into a fake pleasure of flirtation, perversion, or conquest, on exactly the level of the fake lives they were already living.

Reich did not condone versions of forced and attentive excitation; he meant a unified pulse that passes through the body after the body is given up to the experience. This was his singular event for animal life on the Earth. To be able to do it maintains basic health. To be unable to do it leads to a variety of diseases, none or few of which are ordinarily ascribed to psychological or sexual causes. Reich explained most mental and physical pathologies as symptomatic consequences of the disruption of the life current. What produces psychic diseases like frigidity, neurosis, perversion, psychosis, and neurotic criminality at one level equally, bioenergetically, leads to cancer, heart disease, emphysema, epilepsy, and peptic ulcer.

Insofar as he was a moralist, Reich exposed Christian morality as mere moralism. He conceived the sexual function so profoundly he interpreted love-making as a sacred act akin to birth. Religious dogma had denigrated sexuality to a necessary evil in procreation, and that notion, even though it had not been taken literally in the secular realm, still had an unconscious and seminal role in all Western customs. Reich said, No—it is the life energy which endows the seed, not the seed which invents sexuality for its own transmission. From this we can extrapolate that it is only because of a powerful pulsing through the body, culminating in orgasm, that the sperm carries procreative potency. Living man and woman are functionally and energetically prior to responsibility for the continuation of the species. The egg and the sperm express the same tension in the "embrace" as the individuals do, and the orgastic "resolution" of that tension is the embryo.

Reich redefined therapeutic activity in libidinal terms, making dissolution of the body armor and release of the orgastic response the universal goal of somatic rituals, whatever their original intention. He thereby sustained the ethnocentrism of Freud, who also submitted non-Western cultures to analysis by Western symbolic methods. But that doesn't mean Reich was wrong; it just means that he objectified the libidinal aspect of all healing, so any somatic system derived from him adopts a sex-economic priority at some level (likewise, any bodywork system practiced by a Hopi shaman will be taken under Hopi mythology).

Bioenergetic Variations

ALTHOUGH THERE REMAINS an orthodox Reichian hierarchy, most post-Reichian bodywork forms now incorporate elements of Zen, yoga, kundalini, tantra, chiropractic, osteopathy, Alexander technique, Feldenkrais work, etc. Reichian therapy has been synthesized with skeletal adjustments, massages, herbal remedies, yoga, aikido, and karate.

Pure Reichians may lament dilution and bastardization, but orgasm may also not be the only method of health; in fact, it may not work as incontrovertibly as Reich proposed. Contemporary bodywork traditions have enlarged the framework of function and motility, allowing varied experiences of somatic freedom and self-awareness as a means of dissolving armor. After all, meditation, *Chi Gung,* and the martial arts embody thousands of years of empirical testing and address our somatic blocks from their own traditions of dissolving rigidity and freeing energy.

Interestingly, many bodyworkers have rejected Reichian dogma on precisely the basis that Reich first criticized Freud: the system doesn't have the clinical effect its ideology implies—it doesn't cure neurosis or dissolve somatic blocks; it merely reorganizes and displaces them. Karate and Zen *do* work; so does Reichian therapy of course, but within a less ambitious framework than Reich required: it does not appear to have a universal applicability.

Reich left behind a variety of therapeutic tools, but in the end he became methodologically fixed. Instead of remaining an intuitive healer, he came to prescribe a specific sequence of removing segments of armor (from the eyes down) and ignored contraindications. In fact, he even mentioned to Ola Rakness, his Norwegian disciple, that he left certain cases out of his writings because they seemed to improve without conforming to the rules.[25]

Although it diametrically contradicted his intention, Reich set a standard of absolute orgastic potency against which men and women had to measure their own shortcomings. Reich said, in effect: most people are ruined from early childhood and will never know "the real thing." This was a quintessential power play, and its consequence is a legacy of "feeling" elitists and promiscuous orgasm-seekers, all looking for the perfect wave and claiming to be his children.

The basic difference, for instance, between the Reichian orthodoxy and the offshoot bioenergetic tradition associated with Alexander Lowen and his disciples is that the emphasis on orgastic performance is replaced, in bioenergetics, by more attention to pure feeling. Feeling means subtlety, toleration, range. It means living somatically in the world as it is, experiencing all different sorts of emotions which are *also* energetically cleansing and curative. It means, as bioenergetic therapist Stanley Keleman puts it, "living your dying,"[26] that is, learning to "contain" and tolerate sensations as body, mind, and social exigencies change over a lifetime. Keleman writes:

> Life is a series of transitions through which a person has the opportunity to reshape himself, to reorganize his life. But many people do not or cannot make transitions well. These turning points require the learning of new living skills and the building of entire new body habits. Many folks get sick with these crises and changes because they do not have the necessary help, or a knowledge of somatic organization....
>
> Most of us are ill-prepared today to deal with transitions except to adopt the hero's stance or the victim's pose, because we do not have a language and a method to deal with somatic changes. The language of psychology has been the language of insight, but not the language of muscular and organic change....[27]

By this view, it is general neuromuscular stasis which propagates character armor and disease. Suppressed orgasm is merely one of its symptoms. Insofar as Reich prioritized the symbols and affects of sexual trauma and fashioned a highly charged arena for their reenactment and partial dissolution, his drama of high-profile villains and cosmic energies came to exist only by obedience to the absolute categories he proposed. The Reichian orthodoxy was a cult. That is why bioenergetic therapies provided the format in which character analysis and Reich's bodywork spread most widely. Not everyone who accepted the somatic premises wanted a role in the morality play.

In fact, most life activity takes place not in active crisis but on a vast undifferentiated landscape—a middle ground between events—where "nothing" may seem to be happening but when most of the impulses and decisions shaping somatic and social organization are habituated and reinforced. After all, it is not only orgasm in which men and women fail to have an authentic and spontaneous response; it is daily proprioception and breath. Becoming psychosomatically armored and developing gaps of functional incapacity are hazards of bare existence:

> People overeat, oversex, overwork, drink too much—all in an effort to relieve the tensions of middle ground, to deny the changes being felt, to drown out the messages from their interior. There is often the urge to be rid of the abundance of raw energy in middle ground, like children who act out every feeling and impulse. . . .[28]

While psychology tends to overanalyze and disperse this energy, pure Reichian work risks addicting the patient to its releases—outbursts which may themselves be affectations. Unnaturally instigated and provoked by the therapy itself, these expressions, in many instances, are their own dead ends. Meanwhile, the body continually provides other cues for completing and containing feeling and building to each next phase. Following these sequences combines somatic psychology with the ordinary world of human experience. Thus, bioenergetic therapists like Keleman work with shades of sensation, kinesthetic awareness, and visceral grounding in order to support a deepening experience of one's self in the world. Life is not a given but a constant unknown:

> It is important to develop a muscular pattern of readiness to respond to what is present. This stance of readiness to organize our behavior

is a most important attitude for going from middle ground into new form.... Deep and unseen connections are intensified or weakened. Life is immersed in mystery.

Middle ground is the great creative soup originating social form from creative chaos. It is the central moment of turning points, the space where something has ended and something may form. In middle ground bodily process becomes the educator, and those who are able to listen to and learn from themselves can participate in their own restructuring from the inside.[29]

Orgastic potency becomes less critical in a world of varied hopes and relationships and multiple pathways to core energy. In fact, all universal medicines become anachronistic. Because Reich adopted an idealist and religiously authoritarian position, his system has had difficulty preparing individuals for the bioenergetic "middle ground," that is, for sustaining a charge without having to erupt or explode—and for experiencing a wide, often uncomfortable range of ambivalent emotions. Living most of his life in a time of big ideas, world wars, and revolutionary change, Reich was unprepared for the subtle quanta and abstract expressionisms of the post-war era.

As a doctor, Reich was a prophet and apocalyptician; he wanted to transform humanity: without a planetary revolution, individual cure was meaningless to him. Nowadays, absolutist post-Reichian models of cure, like Arthur Janov's "primal scream," ostensibly produce "healthy" individuals who can make no peace with the "unhealthy" world around them. They must be vigilant, guarding against relapse, and there is virtually nothing for them to do in this scenario of unreal people and fake goals.*

---

*In the 1971 Yugoslav film *WR: Mysteries of the Organism*, directed by Dušan Makavejev, Robert Ollendorf, a Reichian physician, stands on the deck of an ocean liner, with Manhattan in the background, and states: "If any sane man or woman could be produced by a doctor suddenly, what would be the consequences? Well, this is very simple; he, very likely, would commit suicide!"

The feeling model avoids ideological postures and follows a Buddhist method: experience arising from situations and situations being changed by experience. There is no singular solution, likewise no negative prognosis for humanity. One simply lives out the individualized fact of his or her life. We will explore these issues more thoroughly in the next chapter.

Orgone

AFTER FLEEING NAZI GERMANY in 1933, Reich moved among Scandinavian countries, but his "sex-pol" mode of treatment and incendiary rhetoric led to his being maligned as a debaucher. He was subsequently investigated by authorities; his medical license fell under challenge.

Reich's utter rejection of the death instinct, an uncompromisable axiom of the Freudian logos, also led to his being spurned in all but the most radical psychoanalytical circles, and his resulting lack of professional backing exacerbated his civil difficulties. Eventually, in 1935, he settled in Oslo, where he had the most reliable support from a psychoanalytic community. It was during the Norwegian years that his investigations led him away from psychology (as it is traditionally understood) into experimental biology and toward vitalism.

Reich began his transition to biology with a series of bioelectric skin measurements—he was attempting to concretize and quantify the libidinal energy of sexual pleasure, and, at the same time, to prove that intercourse itself was no guarantee of orgasm or sexual potency (as most Freudians were satisfied to claim).

The roots of the orgastic response lie, Reich saw, in the metabolism of simple cells—there is a fundamental relationship between the pulsating of life and the structuring flow of cosmic energy through all of nature. Primordial organisms like protozoa generate bodywide pulses of breath and movement. These evolved over millions of years into the emotional and cognitive rhythms of the mammals.

444

Psychology had limited itself, he claimed, by looking only at man and woman. Pulsating head-to-tail motion was fundamental as well to wormlike creatures. If picked up, with resulting pressure against its sides from fingers, a worm exhibited exactly the twisting and blocked squirming of the torso of human character armor. Dropped, the worm regained its smooth and unified peristalsis. This was because the obstacle was external and superficial. But human armor comes from within and is earned through a lifetime. It cannot so easily be taken off.

Wilhelm Reich: From Character Analysis to Cosmic Eros

445

The somatic circumstance of the human is not, however, qualitatively different from that of the worm. When the worm is moving forward, with plasmatic waves of excitation, it is expressing itself as "wanting to," "saying yes to," to use Reich's words. After it is squeezed around the middle, the current is broken, and the animal twists and contorts itself, as if to say, "No, don't do that, I can't stand it." Likewise, people are frozen into permanent pain and discomfort by their armor. When it is dissolved, they express "yes" and "wanting to."[30]

In Freud, the id and libido were metaphors, intuitions that neurological currents flow through the personality. Instead of reinventing these metaphors, Reich was seeking their concrete somatic source. Sheer protoplasm, he observed, responds pleasurably by radiating outward to its periphery, in the human cell as in the amoeba. Painful stimulation causes it to contract from the periphery to the center.

> The central nerve apparatus of the jellyfish is located in the middle of the back, as is the solar plexus in vertebrates. When the jellyfish moves, the ends of the body approach and move away from one another in rhythmic interchange. This is the heuristic substance of our mental leap: *the expressive movements in the orgasm reflex are, viewed in terms of identity of function, the same as those of a living and swimming jellyfish.*[31]

These patterns are not only vestiges of past life forms, contained in our memory traces of early evolutionary stages; they are also the present vegetative basis for complicated emotional and intellectual structures, i.e., a functional sum total of experience. When the jellyfish pulses rhythmically, it not only suggests orgasm; ontogenetically it is orgasm, the same reflex which stimulates the animal to feed and swim. There is no difference between the energetic substratum of primitive grazing and motility and erotically induced pleasure. Likewise, a worm and a newt are contained embryonically in our nervous systems. Even the great armored deflection of civilization must be animal at its core, a ballooning, animalistic streaming. Man experiences cosmic dreams and oceanic fears, Reich said, not because he is in touch with a spiritual world but because his life force embodies the birth of the cosmos in waves of energy.

Freud had developed psychology from an understanding of the quantitative economy of the soma and its translation into mental function; this, according to Reich, was his singular discovery. Reich totally abandoned the rest of Freud's model (neurosis as a social and environmental dysfunction revealed in language) and replaced it with one of neurosis as a distortion of core energy manifested neuromuscularly. Freud may have been the first to understand that love and life are actual flows of current containing fixed quanta of electrical charge. Of course, Reich adds, "the libido which Freud talked about hypothetically and which he suggested might be chemical in nature is a concrete energy, something very concrete and physical."[32]

Furthermore, inorganic matter has the "same fundamental reactions of tension and relaxation, energy stasis and discharge, excitability, etc. . . . "[33] Bioenergy originates in atmospheric and cosmic energy. The "tension and relaxation" of the crystal or the cloud become the pleasure and fear of the frog which become the complex emotions and images of the mammals. All are protean "life" currents organized and differentiated in layers to make up real behavior.

Reich made this one point very emphatically: the difference between his universal energy and that of the alchemists or the anthroposophists was that his was physically discoverable. That required him to go one step further; he had to find it in nature. But reification of energy also moved him dangerously in the direction of organic mechanism albeit in the guise of a freelance biological vitalism. He forgot that the alchemists also "discovered" their universal energy physically.

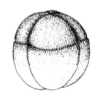

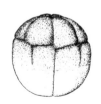

Since amoebae were primordial expressions of life energy, Reich interpreted their simple pulsatory motility as the historical substratum of the nerves and muscles of more complex animals. But, in an attempt to generate clusters of these protozoa from dead grass for experimental purposes, he came upon, to his astonishment, "amoebae-like" forms

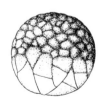

that had never been reported by scientists. These "bions," as he called them, were apparently vesicles that detached themselves from dead matter in solutions of sterilized organic materials. They resembled protozoa in their contractions and expansions, eventually gathering in clumps where they formed their own membranes. They could not be ordinary microbes, appearing as they did when parched grass or moss was placed in sterilized water or in solutions of incandescent coal dust, rust, and sand. Reich assumed he was observing the discrete pulsing of atomic "life energy." No mainstream scientist from the time of Darwin and Pasteur had proposed spontaneous life units; yet Reich was seeking the quantitative basis of life.

Further experimentation with bions seemed to reveal an energy of inexplicably unique properties, a form of radiation with optical properties (emitting a haze of fog and spreading in blue dots and lines). It escaped confinement and expanded everywhere, penetrating even concrete and steel. This "bionic" force appeared to paralyze cancer cells on contact and was also naturally present in human beings, more strongly in healthy people. Reich later named this fundamental energy "orgone" and began to explore its applicability in healing.

In his mind, Reich had now taken Freudianism to its natural conclusion. Orgone was proof of libido; it was its "visible, measurable, and applicable form."[34] Freud had grasped the essential pattern of psychosomatic disturbance, but had not gone far enough; he became stuck on the issue of "mind." "Are the 'electromagnetic waves' of Maxwell 'the same' as the 'electromagnetic waves' of Hertz?" Reich asked, comparing such terms as "id" and "libido" to an earlier intimation of the existence of an unknown energy. "Undoubtedly they are," he answered. "But with the latter one can send messages across the oceans while with the former one cannot."[35] The implication was that orgone was the concrete functional form of libidinal energy, hence the true psychological medicine.

By 1940 Reich had fled the critics of Europe and was living in New York, but the city was not a suitable place for his grail, either environmentally or professionally, so in 1945 he moved to a farm near the small Maine town of Rangeley. It was here that myths and facts became confused, and various extraordinary Reichian personae appeared one by one. To some, Reich transcended twentieth-century science and discovered and unleashed a force so powerful and far-reaching it went beyond the laws of Newton, Darwin, and even Einstein. To others, Reich lost his own sanity in the ancient quest for "vital energy" (the psychoanalytic establishment regarded him as a once-brilliant therapist lapsed into psychosis). In Rangeley, Reich experimented with a structure to contain and concentrate atmospheric orgone—an accumulator made of layers of alternating organic and inorganic material. The organic layers were to draw orgone out of the atmosphere, and the inorganic layers were to impel it into the core of the accumulator.

By general Reichian definition orgone is a primordial, omnipresent substance that differs from all other energies in that it does not obey ordinary thermodynamic laws but expands and contracts and is transmuted *sui generis* into the building blocks of matter and life. Orgone provides rhythmic, pulsating energy for blood and bones, for generation of cells, and for clouds and rain; cosmic orgone stores the original energy of the rotations of planets, stars, and star systems. Orgone is the ocean-aura in which Earth floats—the sparkle of the sky and the luminescence of galaxies. Though not electricity, magnetism, nor light, orgone can be converted into any of these under appropriate conditions. In human beings it is replenished from the atmosphere, its natural pulsations absorbed in cell generation, free neuromuscular functioning, and the waves of emotions. Reich propounds his new physics in these words:

> The "bions" are microscopic vesicles charged with orgone energy; they are developed from inorganic matter through heating and swelling. They propagate like bacteria. They also develop spontaneously in the earth or, as in cancer, from decayed organic matter.
>
> Orgone energy is also demonstrable visually, thermically, and electroscopically, in the soil, in the atmosphere, and in plant and

Wilhelm Reich: From Character Analysis to Cosmic Eros

animal organisms. The flickering of the sky, which some physicists ascribe to terrestrial magnetism, and the glimmering of stars on clear dry nights, are direct expressions of the movement of the atmospheric orgone....

The orgone contains three kinds of rays: blue-gray, foglike vapors; deep blue-violet expanding and contracting dots of light; and white-yellow, rapidly moving rays of dots and streaks. The blue color of the sky and the blue-gray of atmospheric haze on hot summer days are direct reflections of the atmospheric orgone. The blue-gray, cloud-like Northern lights, the so-called St. Elmo's fire, and the bluish formations recently observed in the sky by astronomers during increased sun-spot activity are also manifestations of orgone energy.

All cooked food consists of blue, orgone-containing vesicles or bions obtained through the heating and swelling of inorganic matter also containing orgone. Protozoa, cancer cells, etc., also consist of orgone-containing, blue energy vesicles. Orgone has a parasympatheticotonic effect and charges living tissue, particularly the red blood corpuscles. It kills cancer cells and many kinds of bacteria.[36]

Orgone Astrophysics

WILHELM REICH WAS not a single-theory radical. His life was a succession of radical departures from territories that were already perilously experimental. Denying the logic of his own line of development, he abandoned and even contradicted coherent sets of principles at each new stage.

Despite these enigmas Reichian science has had an enormous impact on a variety of therapeutic schools. Gestalt and other forms of "direct analysis" are Reichian in their interpretations of body language and character. As noted earlier, many diverse styles of somatic work draw on Reichian exercises and the Freudian psychology behind them. Even Reich's physics and biology do not seem as exotic in light of recent developments, including the discovery of organic molecules in space.

Yet, without firsthand experience of Reich's experiments in biology and physics, one is left with only the contradictory literature about them.

451

Those who believe in orgone cannot provide verifiable proof or translate their experiments into mainstream science, and those who don't either ignore it or refer to it only as one of the more flagrant delusions of the century. It is difficult to be accurate and consistent when discussing descriptions of energies and entities that are outside of scientific discourse and were discovered under inexplicable or at least paradoxical circumstances. While homeopathy and acupuncture are widely practiced, there are relatively few orgonomists.

A meeting with Albert Einstein in January, 1941, marked the end of Reich's attempt to merge his own science with existing physics. After Einstein responded to a provocative inquiry with an invitation, Reich prepared a series of experiments, then drove to Princeton, and for five intense hours presented his discoveries. Einstein expressed amazement at the flickering of orgone and wondered if it were not a subjective impression; he acknowledged that an inexplicable temperature difference Reich had discovered above his accumulators was a potential "bombshell." Reich then brought him a small accumulator. Soon afterwards Einstein reported that an assistant had discovered the critical anomaly was a result of simple heat convection from the ceiling. But Reich had also recorded the same temperature difference outdoors, and he reminded Einstein of that. Einstein never answered any of Reich's letters nor discussed the matter thereafter. At this point Reich concluded that he would be a pariah for the rest of his life. If the radical and open-minded author of relativity theory could not hear him, no one could.

It was as an "astrophysicist" and cosmic doctor that Reich came to his grand synthesis: eros, matter, plants and animals, starstuff were all formed within the same universal wave. Nature could not be an empty vacuum speckled with occasional stars and dust. This would deny its functional unity and integrity. Nature was a whorl of dynamic relationships, a cohesive field of primordial orgone. The universe we inherit from these theories is interpenetrated at all points with energetic streaming, differentiated in each zone by the interaction of shapes arising from this flow. We are autonomic self-healing "stars." According to Reich:

What is important is that a functional relationship has been found between the movements of primordial orgone energy and matter that, for the first time in the history of astrophysics, makes comprehensible the fact that heavenly bodies move in a spinning manner. Furthermore, it makes comprehensible the fact that our sun and our planets move in the same plane and in the same direction, held together in space as a cohesive group of spinning bodies.[37]

Now Reich had a primal explanation and definition for the charge in sexual intercourse and human procreation: it is concurrence of the macrocosmic and microcosmic orgone streams. The living membrane traps the free energy of nature, historically and contemporaneously, and forces it to cohere.

> The orgone, pressing forward and concentrated in the genital organ, cannot escape from the membrane. *There is only ONE possibility of flowing out in the intended direction—fusion with a second organism, in such a way that the direction of the excitation of the second organism becomes identical with the direction of the orgone waves in the first.* . . . With the superimposition of the two orgonomes and with the interpenetration of the genitals, the pressed and therefore 'frustrated' tail end can allow its orgonotic waves of excitation to flow in the natural direction, without having to force them back sharply. . . .[38]

Two structureless orgone streams approach, penetrate each other, and superimpose their "tissue," translating their excess energy into a unified galactic system. Spiral nebulae arise, their limbs flung out in an embrace which lasts for eternity (at least of our time). Within their "arms" the microcosm forms. Our sun with its planets was generated from two enormous streams of orgone energy which marked their center by the star and spewed out the planets like an animal birthing its young. Our own love-making repeats this rhythm, even as the cells within us fuse, exchange, and divide. The functional unity of the cosmos is an orgasm cycle: tension, charge, discharge, relaxation. Human beings are simply ripples, individuations in a cosmic orgone ocean.

Wilhelm Reich: From Character Analysis to Cosmic Eros

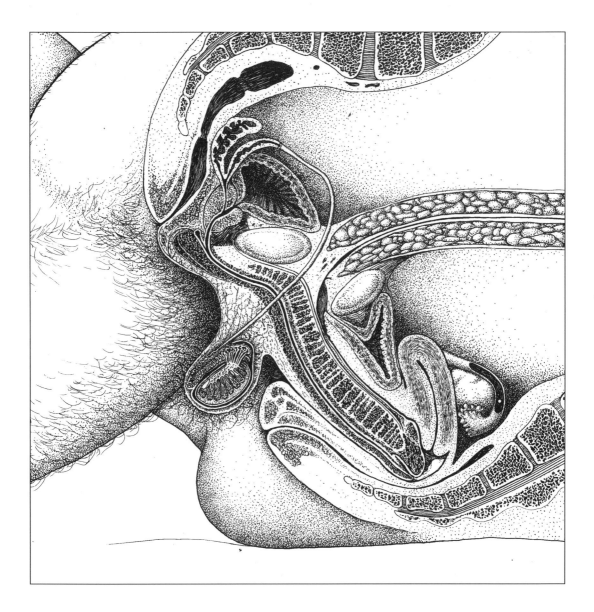

This is either psychoanalysis writ large or nature itself viewed as a psychic entity.

From Freud's intuition of the dreamworld and the cavernous unconscious, through the frozen smiles and sunken chests of Reich's patients, to the worms and jellyfish of northern Europe, to the ocean-charged sands of Maine containing a blue life force, dissolving armor before his eyes, the gnostic "Reich" represents the whole universe as a qabbalistic or anthroposophic drama. The galaxies themselves are huge "beasts," engaging in copulation billions of years long, extended through the very fabric of time and space, separated from us by a mere peristaltic membrane that also connects us to them.

The social and political objections to sexual freedom now become not only ludicrous but blasphemous. Sexuality is not an "invention" of human biology, eroticized in the "mind" of the instincts. It is the driving force of the sun and other stars, a gravitational import trillions and trillions of times the size of any one organism; nature itself is sustained from end to end by attraction. Eros is the abundant visible starstuff we call "light" or "gravity." This is also, despite all intentions to the contrary, a modern shamanic and Ayurvedic vision.

Humanity imagines itself locked in antiseptic empty space on an isolated planet, but Reich diagnoses this "old" cosmology as a symptom of the alienation felt by neurotic scientists (and clergy) and distorted into a theory of nature. Scientific man has denied the objective fact of the universe; religious man has slandered divine energy in the name of God. Reich writes:

> On the human stage, it is forbidden by law under punishment of fine or imprisonment or both to show or even discuss the embrace between two children of the opposite sex at the age of three or five. Somewhere in the audience sits a human being, broken in his emotional security, full of perverse longings and hatred against what he has lost or never known, who is ready to run to the district attorney with the accusation that children are being misused sexually and that public morals are being undermined. Outside, on the meadow, however, the genital embrace of two children is a source of beauty and wonder. What drives two organisms together with such force? No procreation is involved as yet, and no regard for the family. Somehow this drive to unite with another organism comes with the newborn when it passes from the meadow onto the stage. There it is immediately squelched and smolders under cover, developing smoke and fog.

Wilhelm Reich: From Character Analysis to Cosmic Eros

Inside, on the stage, the embrace between two children or two adolescents or two grownups would appear dirty, something totally unbearable to look upon.

Outside, under the glimmering stars, no such reaction to the sight of the embrace of two organisms would ever occur in sane minds. We do not shudder at the sight of two toads or fish or animals of other kinds in embrace. We may be awed by it, shaken emotionally, but we do not have any dirty or moralistic sentiments. This is how nature works, and somehow the embrace fits the scene of silent nights and broad meadows with infinity above....

Outside, a child is a child, an infant is an infant, and a mother is a mother, no matter whether in the form of a deer, or a bear, or a human being.... Outside, to know the stars is to know God, and to meditate about God is to meditate about the heavens. Inside, somehow, if you believe in God, you do not understand or you refuse to understand the stars.[39]

With statements like these, Reich became one of the true radical mystics and millennial scientists of his generation. It is no longer Freud but the echoes of both William Blake and Giordano Bruno.

DURING HIS CAREER as an orgonomist Reich moved further and further from conventional modes of psychoanalysis, even from energetic exercises. These were wastes of time, trifles in an epidemic of pathology. Mankind, in his interpretation, had become so diseased its very protoplasm was deadened. The best he could do was to heal with orgone itself, drawing on refined life energy from the ocean and sky to treat physical and mental disorders—cancer and schizophrenia alike (a modern philosopher's stone). Using different methods of orgone vitalization, he was able initially to prolong the lives of cancer patients; however, after reductions in their tumors, the draining of systemic "poisons" and emotional disturbances apparently led to malignant reappearances (even as they were their economic cause initially). This confirmed Reich's pessimism. He did not blame the quixotic orgone.

By adopting a vitalistic current that transcended psychoanalysis, Reich implicitly abandoned character analysis. Yes, he still recognized the need to work psychosomatically with patients after orgone treatment, but he made orgone a requirement of healing. Today, so-called "orgone" is a ghost substance of crypto-physics. Character analysis, on the other hand, has become a mainstay of psychoanalytic practice, while Reichian bodywork has its own professional standing and is the foundation of the popular bioenergetic modalities. Orgone therapists have nothing to do with either character analysis or somatics. They share more with faith healers and parapsychologists.

In 1949, Reich began to test a new use of orgone as an antidote to radiation. His experiments released a powerful "radioactive-like" cloud, a contamination which permeated the laboratory and surrounding buildings. Many collaborators quickly abandoned Reich out of fear they had raised a jinni they were not equipped to handle. However, after extensive investigation, he concluded that only the initial "response" of orgone to radiation is a kind of toxin (not unlike the reaction of a neurotic to a penetration of his resistance). After this pathological excitation the radiation is successfully antidoted. Ultimately, Reich named three basic forms of orgone energy—orgone, oranur, and dor. According to his co-worker Lois Wyvell:

> Clean, sparkling, soft orgone energy is free-flowing, beneficent and life-positive. When it is irritated by nuclear radiation (as Reich found in the Oranur Experiment and as has been evident from the effects of nuclear bomb tests), orgone is aroused, "angered" as Reich put it, and turns into a highly excited, hard pushing energy he called "oranur." This over-charge, over-expansion, of the atmospheric orgone leads to a contraction of the energy (just as over-expansion does in the biological realm), and the energy becomes "stuck," stagnant, and definitely life-negative (again, as in the biological realm). This condition Reich called "dor" for *deadly orgone* energy. The effect of over-charge is more difficult to assess, but it upsets the beneficent natural life-energy rhythms and can be deadly.

To repeat: Oranur is an energy expansion that can't be discharged in the normal way and thus becomes immobilized and turns into dor. Our own natural orgone energy is free-flowing and clean, but when it can't be discharged fully and naturally (in the sexual embrace, for instance), it may become dammed up, "stuck," and we become despondent, dull, depressed, and bored. The biological energy stagnates just as does the atmospheric energy, and when it does, it tends to become putrid, like a stagnant pond that has no outlet.

The difference between dor and oranur is distinct in most respects, since they are in fact diametrically opposite; one being the stagnant energy synonymous with death by aging, by undercharge and loss of movement, and the other by over-charge, pushing movement and hyped-up emotions and actions. It seems to me, however, that there is still considerable confusion in some orgonomic writings. Some authors lump the evidence of both under "dor," and others lump them under "oranur." Reich called his experiment that brought nuclear energy and concentrated orgone into contact the "Oranur Experiment," not the "Dor Experiment," perhaps because he tended always to emphasize the positive, but most probably because the initial reaction of orgone to nuclear radiation was irritation and swelling anger.

Dor and oranur are opposite in color, too. Dor is a dirty yellowish grey or brownish yellow, while oranur is usually purplish—complementary colors. Oranur can be reddish, too, but the red combines with the orgone blue to give it a purplish cast. Orgone, of course, is blue, the blue of the clean sky and the clear horizon. Most typically, it is indigo. On sunny orgone days, shadows and horizons are indigo blue.

On sunny dor days, the shadows and distances are devoid of blue and the air looks dirty, while the horizons are a dirty yellowish brown or yellowish grey. Have you observed the day through a very dirty window? That is the way dor looks. It smudges the sky. On dor days when you look at the dancing points of light in the sky, you will also see what looks like pepper sprinkled throughout the sparkles. Reich found that dor is not sheer, unalloyed radiation, but a transition between pure energy and matter....

The glaring white haze that covers the sky after an atomic test ... is another indication of oranur.[40]

Reich extrapolated that deadly orgone in the atmosphere was a cause of droughts and ultimately, deserts, so he devised a "machine," called a cloudbuster, for drawing dor out of clouds and dissipating it in healthy orgone from running water. The device consisted of several twelve-foot-long metal tubes concentrically mounted on a sort of tripod and connected with hollow coaxial cable to a source of running water. Stagnant dor is drawn from the atmosphere through the tubes into the flowing water. The effect is to stimulate the atmosphere in much the same way that an acupuncture needle stimulates the body. On several documented occasions Reich brought sudden showers to drought-stricken areas. In one instance, two blueberry farmers invited him to the Bangor area to help save their crops, and after the cloudbuster was employed, a fine drizzle began, followed by a strong steady rain. This recalls the ancient profession of the shaman who was both healer and rainmaker.

Like all of Reich's experiments, the "rainmaking" lies outside of orthodox science. Few have tested his cloudbuster because the concept is so outrageous. An institutional scientist would jeopardize his reputation by requesting funding for such research. Reich himself wondered why, with so many people looking through microscopes, no one saw the bions—with so many telescopes and astronomers, no one reported the sparkling of orgone among the stars; he could only conclude: "Because no one is looking for such a thing."

After a lull of over two decades, there was a surge of new interest in Reich's work in the late '70s. Robert Harman, M.D., replicated Reich's discovery of the bions. Using sterile solutions, he was able to "create" entities showing the lifelike characteristics of movement and pulsation. Courtney Baker, M.D., et al., performed a classic study using mice in which they demonstrated over several years how orgone energy can be used to facilitate the healing of wounds. Erecting their own cloudbuster, James DeMeo, et al., achieved some rather dramatic results in alleviating localized droughts, notably in the southeastern United States during 1986. Jutta Espanca, in a series of experiments spanning a decade, exposed both seeds and seedling plants to concentrated fields of orgone energy and measured their growth against untreated plants. She achieved an improvement in the number of tomatoes and in the weight and size of individual tomatoes grown from seeds that were kept for a period of time in an orgone accumulator. Jesse Schwartz, using an orgone seed sprouter, demonstrated similar differences in the growth of corn and soybean sprouts.[41] In an entirely separate context, Marcel Vogel, a highly respected IBM researcher, claimed repeatedly during the 1980s to have successfully replicated the entire spectrum of Reichian experiments and to have verified the properties of orgone precisely as described by Reich.[42] Although orgonomy continues in the '90s as a cryptoscience with its own journals and conferences, formal inquiry into its claims has not yet been integrated even into the general protocols of parapsychology or the physics of anomalous phenomena. The kingdom of orgone maintains its own proud legacy in hope of a future millennium, guarding its boundaries against the infidels.

It is a testimony to Reich's vision and also his blindness that so much of his methodology replicates Taoist medicine without his having been aware of it. His general view of mysticism was tainted by his contempt for the German theosophists and anthroposophists who, to his mind, took a mythological rather than empirical view of nature. Denying life as the final reality, they sought meaning in spirit, outside of psychology and biology. Reich considered this so-called philosophy mere mystification and armoring, but his own revelation of blue divine energy, living streams of starstuff, and UFOs strafing the atmosphere with deadly orgone (as we shall see) has delighted mystics ever since. Reich gave us an illuminated Darwinian/Freudian version of Gnostic and Zoroastrian hermeneutics.

Looking back from our perspective, we can say, rather blasphemously, that it is not orgasm which Reich most significantly defined, but objective soma, i.e., the organs, nerves, and muscles, of which we are unaware except collectively and kinesthetically. He defined it not as unconscious dream states arising through images but as sensations from tissue. By dealing directly with our resistance to unlocking our own habitual patterns and somatic blocks, Reich made possible a discovery of and connection to our core selves. How these core selves are defined cosmologically is another issue.

Cosmic War

DURING THE YEARS in Maine, Reich was under repeated and varied attack. The old innuendoes about sex machines, orgies, and the mad scientist creating life in the test-tube ran into new ones about cancer-quackery boxes, rainmakers, and mail-order miracle cures. Reich's fiery personality and lack of patience with anything outside his research contributed to a popular caricature. After a series of scurrilous and inaccurate articles on him, he became the victim of a protracted Food and Drug Administration investigation.

Since both the FDA and the scientists it hired shared an assumption that Reich's propositions were ridiculous, the conclusions of their tests were preordained (any positive reports or results were of course ignored). The idea that such a simple "box" could trap a "cosmic energy" seemed the height of chicanery. Reich had again presented the scientific and medical bureaucracy with an epistemological riddle they had no interest in assessing let alone resolving.

As FDA agents continued to visit his lab and interview doctors and patients who had contact with him, Reich became more bitter and isolated, and at the same time more fanatical about the urgency of his work. He saw himself as a key contributor to the struggle against the Russian inheritors of Stalinism. He fantasized enlisting President Dwight Eisenhower as a secret ally; he wrote to the Atomic Energy Commission offering to lend his assistance in countering the pathological effects of radiation. He interpreted jets flying over his laboratory alternately as government protectors and as enemy spies. He perceived also that UFOs were a sort of alien craft either intentionally or unintentionally polluting our atmosphere with dor. In curious resemblance to G. I.

Gurdjieff and Immanuel Velikovsky, he came to blame the human
scourge, the whole planetary plague, on an external space disaster. Once
awakened to the threat, he alone sought to repel the invader. It is a
strange landscape as his son Peter describes it from memory of when
he was eleven years old:

> When I got back upstairs, Daddy was looking through the telescope.
> "Here, look through. See if you can see. I can make out a thin cigar
> shape with little windows."
>
> I looked though the telescope and focused it. It was bright, bright
> blue and glowing, but I couldn't see the windows.
>
> "Do you see it?"
>
> Yeah, but I can't see the windows.
>
> "Well, they are there. Run to the cloudbuster and make ready.
> Unplug all the pipes and pull them out to full length. I'll be right
> there."
>
> My boots pounded against the dry dirt. My jacket was open, and
> each time my arms went back the sides of the jacket flapped against
> me and the fringes sounded like rain. As soon as I got to the cloud-
> buster I jumped on the platform and started unplugging. The pipes
> were like an old-fashioned telescope and had two more sections inside
> that pulled out. Bill and Eva [Reich's son-in-law and daughter] drove
> up just as I pulled out the last pipe. They parked near the truck.
>
> Bill pulled his binoculars out of the case and put the strap over
> his neck. "Where is it?" he asked.
>
> I pointed to it and Bill raised the glasses. He whistled.
>
> "Boy, it sure is something," he said, handing the glasses to Eva.
>
> She looked for a while and said, "I knew it would come. I felt
> bad all day and said to Bill that I thought there was something in
> the atmosphere."

Later, after Peter himself succeeds in driving off the invaders when
the others have failed, his father puts his arm around his shoulder and
says:

> "Yes, we are really engaged in a cosmic war. Peeps, you must be very
> brave and very proud, for we are the first human beings to engage

in battle to the death with spaceships. We know now that they are destroying our atmosphere, perhaps by drawing off Orgone Energy as fuel, or by emitting DOR as exhaust. Either way, we are the only ones who understand what they are doing to the atmosphere and we can fight them on their own ground. The Air Force can only issue misleading reports about the flying saucers and chase after them helplessly, while we are dealing with them functionally, with Orgone Energy. . . . We are dealing with the knowledge of the future. . . . And you, Peeps, may be the first of that generation of children of the future. Here at the age of eleven you have already disabled a flying saucer using cosmic Orgone Energy. Quite a feat."[43]

Reich had now reached the top of the mountain. There was no place to go. An avatar and magus, he had changed the face of the Earth forever. To such a one the FDA investigation was ludicrous. Here was a millennial scientist being challenged as a perpetrator of petty fraud. He ignored an injunction to appear in court in Portland on the grounds that the document was not properly signed (though he wrote the judge he was available at a moment's notice). This halfway measure did not work. When the court, in the absence of an active defense, found in favor of the FDA, Reich was in essence enjoined from further accumulator sales. However, he felt the legal system was in no position to fathom his work—to decide whether or not the universe contained orgone—so his associates continued to deliver the devices across state lines. Reich subsequently was summoned, appeared, and was found guilty—not of medical fraud but failure to obey the original order. He was imprisoned in 1956 and died in the Federal Penitentiary at Lewisburg, Pennsylvania, in 1957.

Even today, in retrospect, the FDA's behavior seems shocking and extreme. Their representative mocked Reich in court and pushed not only for conviction, but the harshest sentence possible. After the ruling, Reich and his associates returned to Rangeley to destroy their laboratory and its equipment as ordered. They carried out the task in brutal masque, using axes, as FDA agents looked on to ensure compliance.

Wilhelm Reich: From Character Analysis to Cosmic Eros

Reich's books and papers—not only those dealing with orgone but all of them—were burned en masse in four different public incinerators in Boston and New York. Six tons of material were turned into ashes in one New York incineration alone, perhaps the most massive book burning in American history.

How can we explain such a violent reaction? Reich believed that the human need to suppress biological energy was so deeply ingrained that the authorities, in the name of the masses, would turn against anyone who revealed its true nature and the extent of our sickness. Late in his life he wrote *The Murder of Christ* in which he presented Jesus as a biologically free, unarmored person crucified by those who could not bear the force of his love. Christ's murderers were now the Stalinists, the fascists, and the Higs (Hoodlums in Government, as he called the FDA and other officials).[44]

The extremity of the FDA reaction suggests that Reich had indeed released an unknown energy, had unlocked the power of rain and the sun, had neutralized radiation, had found the one universal medicine. We need not imagine a conspiracy to steal this discovery from him to suspect an unconscious impulse to drive the jinni back into the bottle.

But what was that jinni: The vital force? Alien cosmic energy? Love itself?

Pure Reichian science still cannot be practiced or defined. Even now we do not have a name for it. And so Reich's life stands as an allegory in judgment of our time.

> Your honor:
> We have lost, *technically only,* to an incomprehensible procedure treadmill. I and my fellow workers, have, however, won our case in the true historical sense. We may be physically destroyed tomorrow; we shall live in human memory as long as this planet is afloat in the endless Cosmic Energy Ocean, as the Fathers of the cosmic, technological age.[45]

Notes

1. Georg Groddeck, *The Book of the It,* translated from the German by V. M. E. Collins (New York: Funk & Wagnalls, 1950).

2. Georg Groddeck, "Psychic Conditioning and the Psychoanalytic Treatment of Organic Disorders," in M. Masud R. Khan (ed.), *The Meaning of Illness* (London: The Hogarth Press, 1977), p. 116.

3. Wilhelm Reich, *The Function of the Orgasm,* translated from the German by Vincent R. Carfagno (New York: Farrar, Straus and Giroux, 1973), p. 62.

4. Ibid., p. 85.

5. Ibid., p. 210.

6. Mary Higgins and Chester M. Raphael (eds.), *Reich Speaks of Freud* (New York: Farrar, Straus and Giroux, 1967), p. 90. Interview occurred in 1952.

7. Reich, *The Function of the Orgasm,* p. 85.

8. Ibid., p. 145.

9. Wilhelm Reich, *Character Analysis* (Third Edition), translated from the German by Vincent R. Carfagno (New York: Farrar, Straus and Giroux, 1972), p. 340.

10. Reich, *The Function of the Orgasm,* p. 6.

11. Higgins and Raphael, *Reich Speaks of Freud,* p. 69.

12. Ibid., p. 31.

13. Reich, *Character Analysis,* p. 325.

14. Reich, *The Function of the Orgasm,* p. 120.

15. Reich, *Character Analysis,* p. 244.

16. Reich, *The Function of the Orgasm,* p. 173.

17. Reich, *Character Analysis,* p. 319.

18. For specific biographical information in this paragraph and much of the rest of the chapter I have relied on Myron Sharaf, *Fury on Earth: A Biography of Wilhelm Reich* (New York: St. Martin's Press, 1983).

19. Reich, *The Function of the Orgasm,* pp. 77–78.

20. Higgins and Raphael, *Reich Speaks of Freud,* p. 85.

21. Ibid., p. 47.

22. Ibid., p. 70.

23. Reich, *The Function of the Orgasm,* p. 6.

24. Ibid., pp. 105–106.

25. Stanley Keleman, personal communication, 1978.

26. Stanley Keleman, *Living Your Dying* (New York: Random House, 1974).

27. Stanley Keleman, *Somatic Reality* (Berkeley, California: Center Press, 1979), pp. 61–62.

28. Ibid., p. 80.

29. Ibid., p. 81.

30. Reich, *Character Analysis,* p. 381.

31. Ibid., p. 396.

32. Higgins and Raphael, *Reich Speaks of Freud,* p. 123.

33. Reich, *Character Analysis,* p. 353.

34. Higgins and Raphael, *Reich Speaks of Freud,* p. 127 (footnote).

35. Ibid.

36. Reich, *The Function of the Orgasm,* pp. 383–85.

37. Ibid., p. 187.

38. Wilhelm Reich, *Cosmic Superimposition,* translated from the German by Therese Pol (New York: Farrar, Straus and Giroux, 1973), pp. 220–21.

39. Ibid., pp. 167–70.

40. Lois Wyvell, "Orgone and You," *Living Tree Journal* (1986), pp. 7–8.

41. James DeMeo, Richard Blasband, Robert Morris, "Breaking the 1986 Drought in the Eastern United States," *The Journal of Orgonomy,* Vol. 21, pp. 14–41; Robert Harman, "Current Research with SAPA Bions," ibid., pp. 42–52; Courtney Baker, Robert Dew, Michael Ganz, Louisa Lance, "Wound Healing in Mice (Part I)," *Annual of the Institute of Orgonomic Science,* Vol. I, No. I (Sept. 1984), pp. 12–32; Jutta Espanca, "The Effect of Orgone on Plant Life (Part 7)," *Offshoots of Orgonomy,* No. 12 (Spring 1986), pp. 45–50; Jesse Schwartz, "Some Experiments with Seed Sprouts and Energetic Fields," *Living Tree Journal* (1986), pp. 34–39.

42. Judyth Weaver, personal communication, Berkeley, California, 1995.

43. Peter Reich, *A Book of Dreams* (New York: Harper & Row, 1973), pp. 23–27.

44. Wilhelm Reich, *The Emotional Plague of Mankind: Vol. I, The Murder of Christ* (Rangeley, Maine: Orgone Institute Press, 1953).

45. Sharaf, *Fury on Earth,* p. 454 (see footnote 18).

CHAPTER TWELVE

Alternative Medicine

The "New Medicine" Counterculture

THE CURRENT ALTERNATIVE-MEDICINE movement in the United States appears to have arisen in the late 1960s and to have expanded during the ensuing decades. There *was* a revival and even a revolution during the '60s, but there have always been "other" medicines in the West, some of them involving significantly higher percentages of the population. Borderline vitalistic and shamanic medicines have been with our species since the Stone Age. Sophisticated elemental medicines in Asia have rivaled European medical traditions for the last three thousand years. Other prominent branches of healing were bequeathed from the dying generation of osteopathic, naturopathic, and homeopathic practitioners who flourished in North America during the nineteenth century.

The publicized emergence of alternative methods was more accurately a shift in emphasis and perspective. As different constituencies rediscovered ancient and vernacular healing modes, a fresh therapeutic paradigm emerged out of their convergent elements. At the same time, teachers and practitioners of non-Western healing arts began training students in the West or, in some instances, adapting their own traditions to Western uses. Together, these coalesced into a "new medicine" revival.

The trend toward technological monoculture has tended to obscure not only important nontechnological modes of healing (as we have seen) but the historical basis of medicine itself. Mainstream Western orthodoxy has tried to co-opt every imaginable territory, first by the corrective regimens of science, then by the equally disenfranchizing "standards" of ethnographic relativism. As a result, we have become disoriented to the degree that we are now dependent on ever accelerating "advances" and novelties (in alternative culture as well) to sustain our sense that we have a core and a meaning. That so many practitioners of holistic health think of their work as "new" is itself a symptom of a provincialism that threatens to turn their practices into a fad. In truth, even as we move toward a hypothetical futuristic synthesis, we keep inheriting fragments and vestiges of an original "planet medicine."

A MULTIPLICITY OF HEALING STYLES rather than a commonality of theme distinguished the sectarian medical community during the nineteenth into the early twentieth century. American Indian pharmacy was, of course, discovered in place by early settlers, and it subsequently gave rise to numerous different naturopathic schools, each based on idiosyncratic recipes of roots, barks, and herbs. Followers of New Hampshire farmer Samuel Thomson established "their own infirmaries, drug-stores, and drug wholesale houses—boycotting the firms which sold allopathic drugs."[1] Popular during the 1820s and 1830s, the Thomsonians favored steam baths and formulas containing lobelia root but also developed some sixty-five individual herbal remedies.

Other indigenous medicines—including fragments of not only Chinese, Ayurvedic, Irish, Norwegian, Russian, and Middle Eastern medicines but African, Southeast Asian, Latin American, and Pacific Island healing complexes—arrived with immigrants. Anthropologist Faith Mitchell describes a system of African herbal and "hoodoo" (hex) medicine practiced on the Sea Islands of South Carolina in virtually its indigenous form by the descendants of slaves.[2] In much the same manner, countless other Creole, Mexican, Hawaiian, and folk European systems were transplanted in cuttings to the New World.

Homeopathy was grafted from Germany (by way of Denmark and

Switzerland). American homeopaths established their own universities, the first being the Nordamerikanische Academy der Homoeopathischen Heilkunst in 1835 in Allentown, Pennsylvania. The founders, Drs. Henry Detwiller and Constantine Hering, taught only in German. Thirteen years later Hering replaced this school with the Homoeopathic Medical College of Pennsylvania, in Philadelphia. Homeopathy remained an important American medicine, gathering popularity through the Civil War into the twentieth century with dozens of medical schools until, following the highly critical Flexner Report on medical education in 1910, the American Medical Association succeeded in branding it with a stigma of quackery and undermined its professional infrastructure (for a complete account, see Grossinger, *Homeopathy: An Introduction for Skeptics and Beginners*). Homeopathy is not the only medicine to lose a trade war to the AMA.

There were many other "new" American medicines prior to the twentieth century, medicines that may not have been absolutely original but which had a distinct New World quality. The Christian Science of Phineas Quimby and Mary Baker Eddy originated as a course of prayer, self-hypnosis, and animal magnetism during the 1860s in Maine and New Hampshire. By a procedure similar to some already discussed in this book, the Scientists used images in their minds to tap divine energy and transmute it into medicine. Their branch of spirit-healing functioned as a mode of ritualized telepathy, drawing its energy ostensibly from "paraphysical radiations informed by love."[3]

Andrew Taylor Still (1828–1917) was a country doctor in Missouri when he "invented" osteopathy as a technique for restoring health through adjusting neuromuscular lesions affecting visceral function. Still had no formal medical training and based his therapeutic authority on a brief lecture course at the Kansas City School of Physicians and Surgeons. After losing three of his children to cerebrospinal meningitis, he took a strong religious stand against doctors as meddlers and against drugs as violations of God's way. He attributed to a divine revelation his cornerstone premise that the displacement of one vertebra on another compressed the attendant spinal artery and impeded blood supply to organs, causing most disease. We will examine osteopathy from a different perspective and in greater depth throughout the second volume.

Daniel David Palmer (1845–1913) was a grocer and lay spiritualist in eastern Iowa when he diagnosed subtle dislocations of spinal vertebrae (subluxations) impairing energy flow throughout the body. The origin of chiropractic is usually placed in 1895 when Palmer successfully adjusted the neck of a patient to cure his deafness. Claiming a privileged line of transmission from the Hippocratic and Roman methods of manipulating backs, Palmer was also clearly influenced by the bone-setting traditions of European immigrants whose methods he revived and amalgamated into a whole medicine. In another interpretation, though, chiropractic is primarily one man's entrepreneurial "reinvention" of osteopathy and differs from it only insofar as the systems diverged in their application of common themes over decades. In truth, Palmer had studied formal osteopathy and was considered a marginal member of the osteopathic community at least two decades before announcing his discovery of his own system. We will discuss some distinguishing characteristics of chiropractic Volume Two, Chapter Three.

Both of these traditions had origins in ancient customs of manipulation; both struggled to translate bone-setting paradigms into full systems of therapeutics in competition with allopathy; both were marginalized and aborted by the AMA. Yet they ultimately survived as unique naturopathic modalities integrating hands-on treatment of spinal structure and viscera, cranial manipulation, diet, and enhancement of overall nerve-muscle synchrony. By the 1960s kinesiologists were practicing a version of chiropractic synthesized with Asian interpretations of anatomy and a healing method based on connective-tissue responsiveness and "ensalivating" (allergically testing) herbal and nutritional materials. (See also Volume Two, Chapter Three.)

What tends to be overlooked is that osteopathy and chiropractic

each contain the nucleus of a whole medical system—separately as well as in overlap with general naturopathy. Allopathy itself possessed little more than that during the nineteenth century. All three of them had their versions of disease etiologies, family doctors, drugs, surgical techniques, and definitions of functional cure. It is not so much that modern science subsequently banished osteopathy, chiropractic, homeopathy, and the like to the scrapheap of history as that allopathy claimed exclusively for its own an emerging scientific hegemony and developed a medical trade monopoly on the basis of that claim (i.e., that it alone conformed to this new science; the rest was quackery). It would have been quite possible for osteopathy to have done the same thing, in which case we would *not* have osteopathy instead of modern medicine; we would have a modern medicine (surgery, X-rays, antibiotics, and the like) with an osteopathic rather than an allopathic core. Surgery done with an osteopathic orientation would be much lighter, moving viscera more gradually, and resorting to the scalpel and laser only when all other means failed.

Chinese and Ayurvedic medicine also provide full medical models for corporate science. Although they never became equal citizens in the West, they were the medical branches of their own scientific systems in Asia. Their present-day practitioners are more receptive to Western scientific authority, more eager for its sanction, and more readily accepted (at least provisionally) by the AMA than their purely vitalistic counterparts. An Ayurvedic endocrinologist like Deepak Chopra can attain recognition in the Western medical community (and mythical status among the general populace). Likewise, acupuncturists can give papers at medical conferences and practice in hospitals.

What we should remember from the opening arguments of this book is that it is not the *technology* of modern medicine that is at odds with alternative medicine; it is the philosophy behind the development and exploitation of that technology. The allopathic premise of confronting and excising disease co-opted scientific medicine prior to its full maturation, thus distorted its evolution. Pure technology could equally have been informed by vitalistic or osteopathic principles.

Yes, science fits allopathy like a glove, but that is because it emerged in cahoots with allopathy—sworn enemies of vitalism. Science needed allopathy as its "doctor" in order to build a solely materialistic philosophy and mechanistic empire. It is because osteopathy and homeopathy were vitalistic that allopathy overwhelmed them so swiftly and thoroughly. We still have not seen a "golden age" laser-and-electron-microscope/miracle-drug medicine at its full potential, unhampered by any political agenda or scientist ideology. At this rate we never will.

Although the term "naturopathy" (combining "homeopathy" with "nature cure") was not coined until 1902 (by water-cure advocate Benedict Lust, a German immigrant to the United States), formal natural medicine (a combination of herbalism, hydrotherapy, homeopathy, and manipulation) is older than even Hippocrates. The ancient Greeks, Egyptians, and Persians built temples by mineral or thermal springs where priest physicians conducted regimens of "internal" and external baths, massages, manipulations, and special meals punctuated with fasts. Their intention was to stimulate nature directly through the vital force. This folkway likely had its origin in a pan-Mesolithic hunting and fishing culture that stretched from the Baltic and the Aegean to the Atlantic and cherished hot springs and geysers (earthworks and stone sanctuaries still yield its possible medicinal pots and urns). Its lore was inherited by the Romans and revived by northern Europeans in the form of spas at Bath, Carlsbad, Evian, and elsewhere.

Present-day alcoholic clinics such as the Betty Ford Center in Southern California and live-in dietary hospitals like the ones at Duke University in North Carolina and St. Helena in Sonoma County, California, though highly scientized and allopathic, hearken back to these prehistoric ritual treatment centers. Until science and technology lured it with new methods, naturopathy was in fact one of allopathy's oldest and most stable methods of treatment. Osteopathy, chiropractic, and homeopathy can be viewed alternatively as branches of historical naturopathy, which would explain why they have been reintegrated into the revived naturopathic medical-school curriculum.

Early American naturopathy, while retaining its European roots enhanced by American Indian medicine, was dominated in the public eye by a medley of hucksterism, quackery, and charismatic healing, its traveling salesmen unflatteringly portrayed in many a Hollywood western (remember Clint Eastwood as Josey Wales squirting tobacco juice on a particularly unctuous bearer of a brown cure-all bottle?). "The prototype of the naturopath in the United States was that remarkable character Bernard Macfadden, 'a diminutive muscleman ...who parlayed physical culture, vegetables and sex into a multimillion-dollar enterprise.' He featured a kind of traveling circus act to demonstrate the value of good health, and his magazines, chiefly concerned with dietetics, sold extensively.... [He] managed 'to father nine children by four wives, jump from a plane with a parachute on his birthday when an octogenarian, and make America health conscious.'"[4] Corporate prototypes of the 1990s rely on best-selling how-to books, pseudoscientific vitamin lore, and cable TV. They have venture capitalists and lobbyists.

There were twelve schools of naturopathy operating in the United States by the 1920s, but few survived the advent of the American Medical Association and the Depression. By 1956, when the National College of Naturopathic Medicine was established in Portland, Oregon, formal naturopathy had all but ceased to exist in North America. The John Bastyr College of Natural Health Sciences began operation in Seattle in 1978, accepting also the students of another new institution, the Pacific College of Naturopathic Medicine (in San Rafael, California), which went out of business quickly. John Bastyr College now has full regional accreditation to teach and certify health-care professionals. There are also (internationally) the Ontario College of Naturopathic Medicine in Toronto, the Institut Naturopathique in Montreal, and the British College of Naturopathy and Osteopathy in London.[5] These trade schools offering degrees in naturopathy also teach chiropractic, homeopathy, Ayurveda, acupuncture, and a wide variety of

other techniques, including even elements of allopathy, such as testing
and evaluating blood and urine samples.

Naturopathic healing now runs the gamut from classic sanitoriums
featuring hydrotherapy, osteopathy, and massage to luxury resorts with
moderately healthy meals, no smoking or alcohol, gyms, and tennis
courts. Natural medicine—once a universal sectarian college of
ethnopharmacy—has gradually merged with unaffiliated holism.

Holistic Health

NATUROPATHY IS NOT synonymous with holistic health. "Holistic
health"—as a historic watershed—may be defined as a loose network of techniques and beliefs including:

- an acceptance of vital and elemental energies as healing sources;
- a field theory of "whole body" responsiveness translated either by
  meridian-like pathways, *chakras,* or fascial networks;
- doctors who respond to the clear presence of an illness (even a
  severe or so-called terminal disease) not by naming the pathology and alarming the patient but by addressing the underlying
  imbalance and prescribing a remedy that activates the intrinsic
  systemic forces that restore balance along that particular spectrum
  of distortion, no matter the degree of its severity;
- a belief that more dramatic and exteriorized healing modalities
  cure only the visible surface of the disease, often rendering the
  actual disease more intractable in the process;
- an appreciation for disease itself as a healing mode;
- a tolerance for pain and discomfort as a useful part of the healing process;
- a tendency toward lighter applications of invasive techniques and
  drugs;
- respect for as well as a direct relationship to the spiritual dimension of healing;

474

- the tendency to view death as a natural phase of life;

- a paradigm in which all disease occurs simultaneously on physical, emotional, psychic, and spiritual levels and can be treated by attention to any one of these from the standpoint that such a cure will spread to the other levels.

- a goal of treating disease not by targeting a specific organ, type of tissue, or pathologizing agent (as in allopathy) but by applying a remedy to the entire field of the body/mind. [This is the modus operandi in a wide variety of holistic systems (homeopathy, Reiki, and Navaho sand painting among them) in which the healing vector arises almost *sui generis* in a field of its own and without any demonstrable or tangible path connecting it to a given pathology. Since there is no way to explain homeopathic "pharmaceutical" action except by reference to whole fields of both medicine and disease, homeopathy is by default holistic. One could always propose that someday a physical vector will be discovered for any or all of these systems, thereby "reducing" homeopathy, Reiki, etc., to modalities targeting specific organs or cellular nexuses on an energy or quantum basis, but I assume that such an outcome would have required a prior shift of our whole world-view in a more holistic direction.]

Of course, much of the above could equally be said of Hippocratic, Ayurvedic, Taoist, and other elemental systems, so we must look to additional cultural and ideological factors to explain the advent of holism in the modern Western world.

Recognized holistic systems (to greater and lesser degrees) have tended to converge on features they did not all have originally — the ones that most support their informal holistic field theory. They have also tended to drop many of the more exotic, sectarian, and isolationist aspects of their own orthodoxies where these are culturally anachronistic.

Whether there has been an actual fusion of disciplines or a fad of compatible enthusiasms, the "holistic health" trade alliance persists to enough of a degree that widely diverse modalities are now successfully marketed together. After all, the present syncretism has forged an unlikely but dynamic federation among such disparate and sundry healers as herbalists, preachers, chiropractors, cranial osteopaths, homeopaths, Bach flower-remedy prescribers, adepts of *t'ai chi ch'uan* and *aikido*, Reichian therapists, bodyworkers of divergent traditions, *Chi Gung* masters, vegetarians, trainers of yoga and breathing, urban shamans, psychic healers, psychic surgeons, iridologists, etc. On one level the synthesis has been enthusiastic and intentional, reflecting a developing ideology; on another it continues to emerge naively (and perhaps archetypally).

To understand any of these alternative forms in their present use—whether they are of North American, European, or Asian lineage, or of other heritage—it does not always help us to know the older medicines that were their forerunners. New "holistic" meanings of traditional treatments have been reinvented from deep structures and meanings that underlie the various subtexts of the holistic theme from time immemorial. And this theme itself continues to be the product not only of medicinal concerns but—as implied above—of a number of different philosophical and political movements that interacted creatively during the mid-1960s and early 1970s.

Bodywork

Throughout the twentieth century a plethora of new systems of bodywork has emerged in the West, some as single acts of genius by individuals (F. Matthias Alexander, Moshe Feldenkrais, Ida Rolf, Milton Trager), others by disciples substantially altering traditional forms such as cranial osteopathy, chiropractic, and yoga. The evolution of bodywork was a result simultaneously of an increased interest in anatomy, a concern with enhancing athletic and theatrical performance, research into treatments for patients with serious neurological disorders (especially stroke victims), and a return to the notion of palpation itself as stimulative, noninvasive, and based on mechanical-energetic adjustments. At the outset of the holistic-health movement the trademark methods were still specialties with relatively small constituencies; yet they provided a template for therapeutic somatics, which emerged (more generally) from a combination of spa-oriented calisthenics, breathing exercises, Reichian bodywork, dance therapy, manipulation, and *chi*-based energetic systems.

What Reich did—as we have seen—was to integrate massage, skeletal manipulation, and breathing within a psychoanalytic model and thereby provide a template for the reinterpretation of other, primarily pre-psychoanalytic traditions of bodywork. Although Reich had little use for these traditional therapies, it was partially in the context of his system that the collective bodywork wisdom of the West was metamorphosed into a varied, character-based range of therapies. Additionally, Reich provided a key energy model by which others bridged the relationship between Eastern elemental systems and Western modes of skeletal manipulation. If before Reich bodywork was viewed as low-level exercise, a palliative massage—or a kind of primitive, amateur surgery—after Reich (or at least contemporaneous with his somaticization of psychoanalysis) it graduated into a holistic psychosomatic modality.

A growing recognition of the tendency of emotional conditions and somatic disorders to lodge in each other has tended to validate systems tracking the physical components of psychological and spiritual traumas. While pre-psychiatric bodywork traditions provided techniques for diagnosing physiological disorders and treating neuromuscular and skeletal diseases, the new psychotherapeutic paradigm added an emotional-affective basis. A practitioner could now interpret and manipulate both the etiology of deep-seated somatic blocks and the energy-release from the change effected by his touch. Release of emotional energy from guided physical contact enabled chiropractors and massage therapists to take on the role of healers of psychological wounds.

Bodywork became, in a sense, not just "body"work but the touchstone for mind/body holism. It provided a strategy for grabbing the disease by the tail and following it in—the tail being anything that wagged at the moment of interaction.

For instance, in its historical version, chiropractic was marked by a linearly mapped releasing of the bones and a general uneducatedness about anything affective including the subtleties of the psychosomatic origin of diseases. As a holistic modality, chiropractic became less mechanical, more energetic, and "understood" the subluxations of bones as the residues of mind/body traumas. This evolution afforded provisional credibility to chiropractic claims of being able to cure serious organic diseases. Its method literally was that of the "hand" of the chiropractor and the "mind" of the psychiatrist working together.

It would not be fair to mention Reich in this context without reminding the reader of the substantial and growing school of thought that believes the integration of bodywork and psychotherapy proceeded directly from Freud and without any major debt to Reichian epistemology or methods (see the previous chapter). I will not take sides on this point. When I first wrote this book, Reichian somatics with its offshoot of bioenergetics was a king in the world of holistic health, especially in the context of radical psychotherapies. Neo-Reichians attended the major conferences and expos and spoke with authority about de-armoring and the one orgastic path to functionality. They often mimicked Reich's short temper and bombastic style.

Twenty years later this mode is tangential at best. The present reigning somatic systems (i.e., osteopathy, chiropractic, *shiatsu, dō-in, Chi Gung, t'ai chi ch'uan,* etc.) virtually all existed prior to 1950 and in many cases prior to Reich. Hence, there is no question about who came first. There is only a question about how the influences of different ideologies and techniques fell upon later psyche-based somatology. Those who question Reich's influence would put such practitioners as Still, William G. Sutherland, Alexander, Feldenkrais, Rolf, Ilse Middendorf, and Marion Rosen in his place as the innovators.

THE CONTRIBUTION OF SOMATICS to holistic health goes well beyond purely clinical applications. It also includes dance-based therapies, performance arts, and Contact Improvisation; diverse rituals of movement, such as workouts, self-training regimens, and martial arts; and a wide variety of systems of enhanced breathing—in short, the entire range of teaching movement, posture, and performance.

Though their medicinal aspect is usually overlooked, traditional dance forms already include modes of curative improvisation and movements as therapy. They express somatic structure and function in a repertoire of individual gestures and creative movements liberating character shapes and patterns of energy. Insofar as they are "theater," they are unavoidably "ceremony" as well. Community dances replicate indigenous tribal medicines. In their simple, unexamined expression of fun and fellowship, square dancing, African and Zydeco dancing, and even rock and disco express medicinal aspects of the curative quanta of individual moving bodies (see "Art" in Volume Two, Chapter Nine). Though these dance forms stretch across communities and ideologies, it is primarily in the counterculture that their political, multicultural, and communal benefits have been observed and intentionally expanded. From evenings of square dancing at local New England and California food co-ops emerged experiments in Contact Improvisation and Sufi healing circles.

Formal choreography may be more involved with high art, but in the shifting paradigm, many avant-garde dances and other movement arts function directly as medicines. They evoke the "feeling" body and inspire the flow of blood and passage of breath and fluids to the organs. Experimental dancers such as Anna Halpern, Nancy Stark Smith, Ruth Zaporah, Alan Ptashek, Emilie Conrad-Da'oud, and Bonnie Bainbridge Cohen have assembled psychosomatic rituals out of "Effort-Shape" symbologies, subchoreographic micro-gestures, and personal styles of movement. In their dances and improvisations (which they teach to groups), organs and viscera are evoked, reified in "personalities," and invited to participate in larger shapes that, in essence, allow them to express their deeper selves, give off tensions and toxins, and define new orbits (see "Body-Mind Centering" in Volume Two, Chapter Six). These "dances" take place sometimes as open-ended Contact sessions in which people move about a room or stage, bump into (or otherwise intersect) one another, and abstractly alter one another's patterns of motion and courses. Dance forms become ritualized instances of bioenergetic work and Gestalt transference. Ceremonial somatic theater becomes group therapy.

Ptashek has adapted such rituals into the men's movement to evoke the particularly male aspects of organs and meridians, sometimes initiating ceremonies and drumming sessions that become sharing circles. He has also developed a somatic program for disabled people based on Contact Improvisation ("The Moving Body Class"). Of this experiment he writes:

> We live in a culture that holds strict definitions and value judgments about what it sees as moving and not moving. With so much of daily motion and perception dictated by task, function, and particular examples of productivity, movements at deeper levels than external appearances are less valued, ignored, and, at worst, unperceived. How we are being seen by others influences our self-image, presence and movements in the world. In our classes, I feel we were creating new layers of a collective story, a body politic or body mythology. Myths take place in a ritualized space....
>
> Having each student move with eyes closed, 'witnessed' by the group, was a beautiful and evocative ritual space. We were able to appreciate the most subtly articulated movements of each person, sensing and referring to our own bodies for the depth of response we gave one another....
>
> The focus on physicality and sensation established a ground for the stimulation and discussion of personal, social and political issues that became immediately relevant and integral to The Moving Body. This course is one that feeds into areas that are societal, clinical, biomedical, theoretical, educative, psychological, artistic, performance-oriented, and, largely, improvisational.[6]

That is, simply by expanding our range of social interaction in the context of "dance" and Contact Improvisation, we change the health-and-sickness patterns underlying daily life.

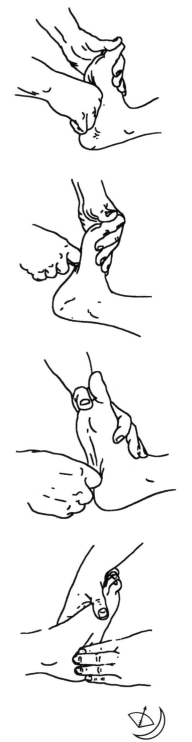

The translation of many Oriental bodywork systems into Western forms during the 1970s was another major factor in the development of holistic medicine. Modalities like *shiatsu* and reflexology, often under the catchall title of "Oriental massage," set the groundwork for lay somatic practice and the renaissance and fusion of other somatic systems in the late 1980s and 1990s.

The emphasis is on "lay practice," for many of these therapeutic modes can be learned (at least rudimentarily) in a weekend course or from one-night-a-week classes for four months. Thus, otherwise non-medical men and women took responsibility for a level of their own well-being and that of their friends and relatives. A sense of confidence and personal expertise grew. The spread of this simple activity did more to launch a new therapeutic paradigm than all the "tao of medicine" and "quantum healing" exegeses to the tenth power combined.

Reflexology involves applying brief shots of pressure to points on the feet that correspond on the meridians to particular organs, glands, and other tissues where there might be blockages. The practitioner's thumb is bent 90 degrees at each point and then released by straightening it. The practitioner moves rhythmically, point by point from the toes to the heel, from the outer to the inner edge of the foot, and from the left foot to the right, the thumbtip always pointing in the direction of blood flow. The assumption is that excess calcium and uric acid collect in crystalline deposits around the roughly 72,000 nerve endings in the feet. Massage crushes them and returns their elements to the bloodstream, activating the organs and stimulating flow through the lymphatic ducts. "Reflex" means that each organ responds instantaneously on a ganglionic level (outside the spinal cord and the brain) to stimuli from correctly positioned palpation.[7]

Shiatsu is a Japanese art, literally "finger pressure treatment" derived from the more ancient Chinese form of *dō-in*. The practitioner bases her physiography on the meridian map, releasing energy by pressing on points *(Tsubos)* but more globally using her fingers, palms, whole hands, elbows, knees, and feet, as well as various stretching postures and arrangement of the body in kinetic positions naturally without pushing, pulling, or jerking. Weekly *shiatsu* therapy is still common in Japan, and family members often treat one another.[8]

Shiatsu is a partner to acupuncture and moxibustion, using direct contact to affect *chi* flow and the autonomic nervous system. The Japanese Ministry of Health defines it as "manipulation ...without the use of any instrument, mechanical or otherwise, to apply pressure to the human skin, correct internal malfunctioning, promote and maintain health and treat specific diseases."[9] Acupressure is a somewhat more generalized variant of *shiatsu,* although it is sometimes just an Anglicized name for the latter.

In a latter-day holistic context, *shiatsu* has also become a spiritual discipline, an adjunct to sitting zazen, and an outward expression of grounding, renewal, and warmth, practiced while moving about in daily life.[10]

Other general Oriental bodywork forms include *tui na,* a system similar to *shiatsu* but emphasizing massage techniques and nerve reflexes (not to be confused with *Chi Gung Tui Na,* which uses a *tui na* base and *Chi Gung* techniques), and *anma,* a Japanese adaptation for relieving back and shoulder tension by stimulating blood circulation.

The enlargement and redefinition of manipulation and exercise to include energetic, psychological, and spiritual components gradually gave birth to its own therapeutic model. Growing awareness of the interlocking dynamics of movement, community, and touch contributed social elements to the emerging paradigm and synergized with pure bodywork to hatch even more innovative and radical techniques for healing. Discussion of this topic will continue in Volume Two.

Ecological and Political Influences

THE BIRTH OF the present environmental movement is sometimes set in the early '60s with the publication of Rachel Carson's *Silent Spring*—an attempt to awaken our distracted civilization to the effects of its agricultural pesticides. At the time, *Silent Spring* was praised, but its ominous prognosis was not openly acknowledged. By the end of the decade, however, there was a common if not universal recognition of interlocking problems of overpopulation, food contamination, radiation from atomic tests, pollution of the atmosphere, erosion of farmlands, etc., as well as a growing appreciation of the role of homeostatic regulating factors in population shifts of animals and a new interest in solar energy, wind power, and other self-sustaining technologies. The first astronaut-broadcast image of a luminous planet in the vacuum of space reinforced a sense of one world of ceaselessly recycling oceans and weather systems. We saw both our vulnerability and our cosmic isolation. The emblem of the Whole Earth provided environmentalists with an image as fresh and poignant as organs in a sea of blood.

But the planetary body is also the human body, and a medical crisis parallels an ecological one: short-sighted, goal-oriented, and materialistic responses to intricate and subtle organic processes lead to iatrogenic diseases, a degraded biosphere, and, of course, addiction to more of the same in increasingly simplified loops of diagnosis and treatment. The gap between the illusion of health and real health becomes more profound and elusive as we seek to make up for what is lacking with a panoply of clever imitations.

The healing crisis facing our species is deep-seated; yet allopathy has tended to promote miracle cures, vaccines, and community hygiene while decentralizing only on superficial levels and paying virtually no heed to the naturopathic tradition. It keeps treating diseases on fragmentary and symptomatic bases, ignoring the requirement of a major change at the roots. The same dilemma of fragmentation and abstraction not only characterizes both environmental and medical crises but joins them in the same crisis, along with the failures of education, criminal rehabilitation, and international drug control.

Despite all that has happened in the last three decades of the century, the catalysts of real revolution have floated mostly at the periphery of Western culture, often segregated not only from one another but from any political or social context. Philosopher Murray Bookchin grasped this dilemma at its beginnings among the false optimisms that followed the defeat of Germany and Japan in World War II. In retrospect, he wrote:

> As I published [my revolutionary ecological] ideas over the years—especially in the decade between the early sixties and early seventies—what began to trouble me was the extent to which people tended to subvert their unity, coherence, and radical focus. Notions like decentralization and human scale, for example, were deftly adopted without reference to solar and wind techniques or bioagricultural practices

> that are their material underpinnings. Each segment was permitted to plummet off on its own, while the philosophy that unified them into an integrated whole was permitted to languish. Decentralization entered city planning as a mere stratagem for community design, while alternative technology became a narrow discipline, increasingly confined to the academy and to a new breed of technocrats. In turn, each notion became divorced from a critical theory of social ecology....
>
> That a society is decentralized, that it uses solar or wind energy, that it is farmed

organically, or that it reduces pollution, none of these measures by itself or even in limited combination with others makes an ecological society. Nor do piecemeal steps, however well-intended, even partially resolve problems that have reached a universal, global, and catastrophic character. If anything, partial "solutions" serve merely as cosmetics to conceal the deep-seated nature of the ecological crisis.[11]

The same was true for medicine insofar as particular innovative techniques and clinical outreach programs came to substitute for a complete reexamination of the principles and ethics behind institutional medicine and the biomedical drug industry. Considerations of food source and diet were utterly divorced from the actual treatment of disease, as though these had nothing to do with each other. Vegetarianism, opposition to fluoridation, challenges to universal vaccination, preference for non-pesticided foods, and criticism of the overuse of antibiotics in raising meat animals and treating human flus, etc., were all regarded as marginal fads and isolated ideologically from one another. It is no wonder that a holistic alternative medicine was slow to take root.

For the reasons Bookchin cites, the political-ecological alliance that might have emerged during the late 1960s did not even begin to take shape until the early 1970s. Battered by ideological conflicts and confusions of priorities from its inception, its camaraderie was forged by the Civil Rights movement and one concrete victory of American withdrawal from Vietnam (and the abdication of Lyndon Johnson). A nascent counterculture flourished here and there with last-chance communes, cooperative farms, domed houses, and windmills. Yet a highly mythologized campaign against capitalist imperialism always took precedence

over actual stewardship of species and environments. Agriculturally progressive Marxist regimes in China, Cuba, and Eastern Europe routinely ignored pollution and resource depletion to the point of myopia, so for the American radical movement these became historically non-issues, or mere elitist and ethnocentric concerns.

Certainly the energy crisis precipitated by the Arab oil embargo accelerated cognizance of civilization's (communism's as well as capitalism's) dependence on resources and the greater priority of preserving nature itself. In time, the New Left would realize that the medical establishment formed a perfect mirror to the military-industrial complex. In fact, in many ways the oil, drug, and timber industries and agribusiness are the same mega-cartel. The goals of sound minds in sound bodies, communities in balance with nature, and an unpolluted biosphere not only naturally reinforce one another but also collectively cry out for new methods of raising food and compounding drugs. In the 1980s, emerging from a twenty-day fast, the comedian Dick Gregory said: "They control us by the food we eat. We must stop eating it." Within a few years he had developed and marketed his own diet. One may not personally choose his meal-in-a-can, but the underlying critique is still salient.

Alternative sources of energy and alternatives to synthetic drugs reflect each other all the way from micro- to macroenvironments. The short-term exploitation of tropical rain forests and old-growth temperate and boreal woodlands foreshadows the abortion of entire ethnobotanies, ethnozoologies, and unknown pharmacies as well as a weakening of the atmosphere and with it the lungs and pulmonary systems of organisms and their will to build sound communities.

Not only are men and women part of the biosphere, they are its chief despoilers. To many (even today) this seems like a mere technical problem to be solved by computers, machines, and new laws. However, if pollution and ecocide are symptoms of a human malady projected outward, we are trapped in circular behavior which continues to make both us and the planet sicker.

During the early 1980s—just when some naively presumed we approached an epochal change in consciousness, the fabled Aquarian breakthrough—the culture veered back in the old direction. Suddenly it was as though we had never thought about limited resources and a threatened environment. The West was plunged into a Reaganomics, junk-bond, yuppie-cocaine binge that lasted well into the 1990s. Even as mainstream culture was enjoying this splurge of materialism, its infrastructure was eroding. Economically marginal residents of cities were pushed out of their homes; gangs of the dispossessed took over neighborhoods and roamed abroad. We found ourselves at the dawn of a post-apocalyptic world with armed children and war zones fed by drug economies. The post-Communist Soviet Union spawned its own "Blade Runner" gang-dominated habitats, showing just how permeating the planet's mega-culture has become.

It is clear by now that it is impossible to change the system. The system is not only vast beyond receptivity to individual action but is inside people's guts and cells. Confronting this is hardly a matter of ideology. Yet clear action is possible for moderately sane people. When Wilhelm Reich proposed an alliance of hygiene and politics before World War II, it was much too early. It was still too early in 1988.

DURING THE GENERALLY dismal yuppie era, a few modest experiments in alternative medicine, self-sustaining agriculture, and environmental preservation began. No longer fooled by the romantic promise of "the Revolution," many activists turned toward implementing such basic cohesive units as Bookchin proposed. Alternative healers and organic farmers formed small regional clinics and agrarian communities.

Clearly, one imperative of holistic medicine emerged from a general left-wing political revolution. Though this revolution did not come close to success in replacing the governments of the capitalist world, it did enfranchise alternative paradigms for many of its industries. The entire range of holistic medicines became attractive at the same time their decentralism, Third World character, and attack upon the privileges of allopathy were recognized. Not all of them were adopted simultaneously, but gradually they were uncovered, investigated, studied in depth, tested, and institutionalized to one degree or another. The holistic landscape of the mid-1990s is the result.

If the 1970s provided some of the mythological scenery of a new world, the 1980s provided tools and disciplines. The failure of so many of the '70s communes was exactly their failure then to develop healing and holistic disciplines, to internalize changes they were attempting to make ideologically, and to develop a second tier on which the Revolution could emerge communally out of their lives and families. The abstract quest for higher consciousness, plus justice in a classless society, overwhelmed the subtler requirements of daily life, which are difficult enough to nurture even with full attention. However strong people's ideology and dreams, they were co-opted, almost seamlessly, into the very hierarchies and structures of domination they were fighting. What had alienated them and pushed them to the outskirts of society, step by step they became.

Ideally, bodywork should merge with farming to make life less mechanical, more attuned to an awareness of both labor and the plants being grown (and animals being tended). This issue was almost entirely missed during the 1970s when ordinary being was confused with transcendence and millenary idealism. Authoritarian social and religious cults followed like clockwork. At Jonestown we learned (if we didn't already know) that ungrounded rhetoric and hierarchy can lead to anything, even the opposite of its stated goals.

Sometime during the 1980s, the culture of environmental awareness and holistic medicine became focused enough to define a politics beginning at one's own center. Healing ourselves *is* healing the world. Thus, the new social goal became one of purging the somato-psychic condition of having been born and raised in the belly of the dragon.

The rebellion of younger, more radical doctors in the late '80s and early '90s against the establishment may have initially targeted the social domination and profits of the establishment as well as the medical bureaucracy of schools, hospitals, insurance companies, HMOs, etc.; but its subtext quickly became the failure of industrial medicine to treat—or even acknowledge—chronic disease. Progressive and well-meaning on the surface, standard procedures of scientific proof had led to widespread fraud and sham experiments as well as abuses of laboratory animals and creation of homogenized healing technologies based on capitalist homilies of production. So powerful is the image of a bio-industry churning out miracle potions that, for lack of real breakthroughs under the demands of the marketplace, panaceas are regularly sold in place of truly effective drugs. While a pharmaceutical and hospital hierarchy generated profits for the upper classes it also helped spawn, it often palliated diseases, further disenfranchising its own patients, the very groups that might have justifiably rebelled. Antibiotics, tranquilizers, psychotropics, and pain pills secondarily numb activism and preserve the existing order for its beneficiaries.

The new medicine ideally spawns a lifestyle that empowers people, cures their diseases, and, at the same time, stands against the privileges and palliatives of modern material society. These features make it attractive to veterans of '70s left-wing politics, some of whom became the new doctors and healers. Osteopathy, chiropractic, Oriental massage, and naturopathy were gradually applied from a new political perspective. After all, these methods transferred the power of restoring health back to the people while challenging the privilege and authority of the doctors in the medical establishment. Translated into a socially progressive, even politically radical environment, such alternative practices were forced to abandon their own traditional conservatisms and authoritarian orthodoxies. More often, they branched off as holistic modalities, often separated from their original institutional contexts. These changes defined the birth of alternative medicine as an aspect of the counterculture.

From this perspective we can reinterpret the homeopathic revival in the United States, which began in the San Francisco Bay Area at the end of the '70s, as only partially the consequence of a new interest in homeopathic principles. It was equally a rallying point for an attack on the establishment. Homeopathy offered a completely professional alternative medicine. Instead of feigning its dues to social justice by offering mass-produced, technological health care, it proposed a different, more egalitarian solution for treatment itself. Thus, it represented a rebellion not just against the medical hierarchy as a class but the whole set of meanings establishing the hierarchy. Here Marxism met vitalism. And it was not too early: Western civilization was ready, almost.

Innovative alternative modalities did not necessarily have to prove their benefits to their adherents right away, at least in a scientifically replicable way, because "verifiability" deceitfully served the manipulative rhetoric of mainstream medicine. People who were actively seeking new paradigms were willing to risk long journeys down false trails. Many graduates of medical schools who adopted homeopathy during this period of enthusiasm in the late 1970s and early 1980s admitted, often defiantly, that they hadn't the slightest idea how homeopathic potencies work, but then, they claimed, no one *really* knows how standard pharmacy antidotes disease states either.[12]

Finally medicine was driven from its long-standing guise as a politically neutral do-gooder and forced to stand beside the other technocracies and consumption-driven industries. The doctor could no longer identify himself with the Red Cross on the battlefield and claim immunity; he was one of the combatants.

Occult and Esoteric Traditions

THE 1960s GROWTH of left-wing political activism coincided historically with a regenesis of occult disciplines. Although these occupied contiguous sectors of the counterculture (and were sometimes practiced by the same enthusiastic people), they usually found embarrassment in each other's company. It is notable that the lessons of Mahatma Gandhi were not graftable as such in a Western arena, that is, graftable in a way that preserved their political effectiveness as well as their spiritual base. Instead, one or the other was retained beside a shadow of its antipode. Americans at first preferred the political pole, i.e., the Civil Rights movement and the nonviolent disobedience taught by Martin Luther King, Jr. It was not until a fuller incorporation of Buddhist precepts into Western civilization in the late 1980s that politically committed spirituality provided a meeting ground for the two movements—a fusion that did not compromise either spirit or action.

HEALING HAS A prehistoric esoteric heritage. It likely originated with language itself and guided Stone Age peoples through the portals of history. Shamanic, vitalistic, elemental, and divine medicines have persisted even in depleted and hybridized forms into the present, and these have provided a wealth of resources for holistic medicine. The tradition of Biblical faith healing shares pre-Christian sources with alchemy and homeopathy, though it has dressed itself in Protestant or Mormon fundamentalism almost since the *Mayflower* landed. Mediumship and channeled healing are also ancient and universal forms.

An esoteric American Indian tradition also has had a major impact on alternative medicine. Western adaptation of the paraphernalia and choreography of shamanism was first popularized in the mainstream in the late 1970s by dropout New School anthropologist Michael Harner, who subsequently founded the Institute of Shamanic Studies in Connecticut. This ethnographer of the Jívaro switched careers from teaching the social science of Indian shamanism to teaching people how to practice an Americanized version of shamanism itself. He has been followed by both New Age simplifiers and blue-collar radicalizers. Advanced versions of vision questing *sans* any intellectual overlay, and involving peril and hardship, have been developed by (among others) Brant Secunda and his Dance of the Deer Center for Shamanic Studies in Soquel, California, out of the Huichol traditions taught by don Jose Matsuwa (who lived to the age of 110 in 1990) and his partner, doña

Josefa Medrano. Long periods of fasting; remaining in a circle in the hot sun amidst insects, dust, thirst, etc.; tracking one's way through the landscape psychically after long fasts; awakening within dreams; and hiking for many days to places of power all provide stages and opportunities for personal transformation. Westerners have learned how to experience a version of the vision quest directly and become initiated thereby as magicians and healers. They have also participated in trainings involving the use of herbs, medicinal tobacco, quartz, crystals, feathers, drums, and even sand paintings, all in the context of therapeutic rituals.

M OST OF THE esoteric influence on holistic health has originated from either the theosophical West or the Hindu and Buddhist East. Where emerging methods of alternative medicine seemed to correspond to occult traditions, whatever survived (or was imagined) of the olden form was incorporated into its new modality (often without a change of name). Thus, even as New Age shamanism took on the accouterments of indigenous shamanism, holistic medicine became one of the vehicles for the reclamation of traditionary wisdom as well as an aspect of its epochal expression.

Alchemical medicine, for one, quite likely began in remote pre-Egyptian times; underwent a "chymical" revision during the Paracelsan age; and was salvaged and made over again in a New Age context. Homeopathy (as we shall discuss again below) was an offspring of Hippocratic and Paracelsan medicine. Modern-day herbalism is a descendant of an alliance of diverse indigenous ethnopharmacies and astrological botanies, which have separate roots also in Indo-European cultures. Astrological chart-making has itself been subsumed in character analysis and life counselling, especially among Jungian practitioners.

What sprouted in some instances as decorative attraction to tarot images, tribal petroglyphs, and mandalas inspired later inquiry into how these and other symbolic modes actually worked. Gnostic Christian rituals and traditionary Western modes of prayer and affirmation, given new expression during Rosicrucian and pantheist revivals of earlier epochs, have been rejuvenated again not only in secular contexts but as threads of the faith healing of Phineas Quimby, Mary Baker Eddy and, currently, Oral Roberts, Rex Humbard, and the Course in Miracles.

Among occult traditions that had major impacts on the development of particular holistic modalities in the 1970s (with just a few of their offshoots in parentheses) were: archetypal imaging and mandalas (visualization, autogenic training, and self-healing), tarot and divination (healing by symbols, radionics, and color therapy), *chakra* theory (polarity, applied kinesiology), anthroposophy (Eurhythmy, cleansing of the aura, Waldorf Schools), alchemy (homeopathy, Jungian therapy, and a basic metaphor for internal change through external symbols), Sufi rituals (healing by mind and by sound), Gurdjieffian practices (gestalt therapy, bodywork), Christian mysticism and Gnosticism (faith healing and affirmation), shamanism (psychoanalysis and contemporary shamanic revivals), native ritual (psychosynthesis), vision quests (hallucinogenic medicines and rebirthing), goddess religions (natural birth control, natural childbirth, herbalism), hermetic botany (flower essences, aromatherapy), Oriental dietary philosophy (macrobiotics), Hindu spiritual practices (yoga, polarity, the popularization of Ayurvedic medicine by Deepak Chopra), kriya yoga (rebirthing), Native American sclerology [to diagnose by the tiny blood vessels in the whites of the eyes] (iridology), numerology (toning), and astrology (holism itself). This is a partial list in more ways than one. The categories—both ancient and contemporary—are vaguely defined and, in some instances, overlap. The adaptations I have chosen are also preferential. But a revival of each of these traditionary sciences led to their incorporation in at least one holistic medicine.

Homeopathy provides an accessible example of epochal transitional stages. This medicine probably originated in prehistoric applications of the Law of Similars and characterological herbology and, simultaneously, in the shamanic, energetic, and symbolic potentization of substances. In the subsequent adaptations of Celsus, Paracelsus, Van Helmont, and other empirical physicians of historical (but pre-scientific) times, the techniques were enhanced with Platonic, numerological, and alchemical layers and then fused into a new, semi-formal "science." It was this system that Samuel Hahnemann adapted, named, and reconstituted in a format that was at once vitalistic and biophysical. When microdose pharmacy and diagnosis by Similars were resurrected again in American holistic circles of the 1970s, they were already prepackaged as Hahnemannian professional medicine. Yet their further modernization required a post-Einsteinian, relativistic scientific language and the acceptance (even if unacknowledged) of Jung's theory of synchronicity. This introduced occult and psychotronic influences not previously associated with Similars, microdoses, and potentization, thus instigating a break between traditional Hahnemannian homeopathy and new holistic, "quantum homeopathy." Individual homeopathic provocateurs have administered remedies psychically, in bracelets, and through nonelectric devices made of wires and circuits—imitation machines generally subsumed under the paradigm of "radionics." This is still "homeopathy" insofar as no official boundaries for healing vitalistically by Similars have been defined, but it hardly satisfies the quasi-medical purists and Hahnemannian fundamentalists.

Radionics (psychotronic medicine) arises uniquely from vitalistic definitions of electricity and magnetism that attached themselves to the scientific revolution. It is usually practiced without the semblance of a theory of diagnosis or a materia medica. The "physician" prescribes symbols, emblems, and "unplugged wiring," to be "ingested" psychically as images or transmitted to a person's unconscious. One can purchase books of magical patterns to stare at in order to be healed of particular diseases—different patterns for different diseases—although recent FDA monitoring of such products makes them difficult to find. Whether modes of radionic and vibratory medicine share anything with traditional homeopathic and Paracelsan practices, it is likely that *both* they and homeopathy have origins in rituals too old to date or have emerged from identical "vital-substance" (Mercurial) archetypes which are recurring in post-scientific forms.

Jungian Psychology

CARL JUNG'S LEGACY to us is as much his books as his progeny of archetypal psychotherapists. These familiar black volumes in the original Bollingen library include: *Archetypes and the Collective Unconscious, Symbols of Transformation, Psychology and Alchemy, Alchemical Studies, Psychology and Religion, Civilization in Transition,* and more than a dozen more. They are among the bibles of alternative medicine.

Jung reified the holism of psyche, body, culture, and spirit. He redefined the unconscious mind of Freudian psychology to include a racial, planetary, and cosmic memory. Through this collective unconscious, men and women contain in some form or other every phase of their evolution—from raw matter to mind, from cells to animals, and from prehistoric tribes to one-time originators of civilization. Such a legacy legitimizes a full spectrum of healing modalities.

According to Jung, all forms in nature arise synchronistically (anachronistically too) from templates prior to form—the archetypes. These archetypes (parallel to the elements of the Ayurvedic doctor and Yellow Emperor) incorporate the most powerful healing energies available; they constellate life before its incarnation, thus bring unique psychosomatic wholes into being. The actual contents of these will never be named because they exist only as instantaneous coherences of mind, matter, and meaning transcending ordinary concepts of the difference between mind and matter or between matter and energy. From beyond time and consciousness they express themselves everywhere: in myths, cathedrals, fairy tales, etc., as well as in the geometry and crystalline structure of plants and animals, the symbols of forgotten civilizations, and even the intelligence of an order beyond humanity. How such transpersonal dimensions of existence came to merge with each individual organism and psyche is of course unknowable, but they provide

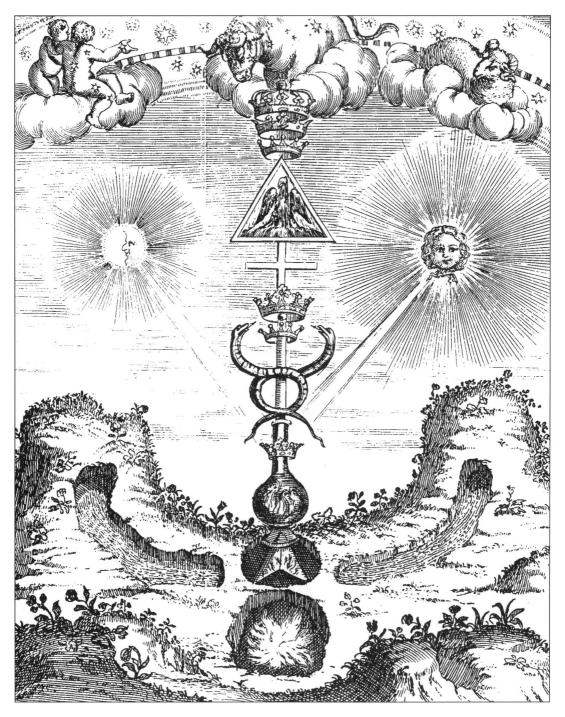

the templates for manufacturing and iconicizing archetypal medicines. In true holistic fashion, such cures must spread from the spiritual to the emotional to the physical dimensions of existence.

As defined by Freud, most of the vast unconscious realm can never be made conscious, but, according to Jung, the destiny of every living being is to incarnate some part of it creatively, an aspect which forms one's singular birth chart at the moment of inception. In fact, incarnating unconscious elements is a necessity, for unexpressed psychic contents, when ignored, give rise to long-term disease and interpersonal conflict.

Jung proposed that the whole pantheon of deities who dwelled once safely on Olympus, in Valhalla, etc., and then were consigned to the museums of myth, have become much more dangerously intimate with modern man and woman in the form of complexes, psychopathologies, and chronic diseases. Over the centuries we have abandoned the theogony, but it has not abandoned us. The potentiations of Mars start modern wars. The seeds of Pan become panic. Archetypal crabs turn into actual cancers. Yet the gods are pathogenic and rapacious only insofar as they are depreciated or suppressed, and that is because they are aspects of us as well as discrete forces reigning beyond us. Their demand on the personality is to deepen and encompass some tiny portion of them during a lifetime.

It is for medicine to find the gods again in diseases, and offer them expression. Standard medicine deals only with their vernacularization as symptoms—and do we ever have symptoms in abundance! We are symptom-ridden, driven into flimsy shelters by a deluge of psychosomatic and obsessive compulsive fixations that would do shame to mere thunderbolt-bearing Zeus and Hera. Archetypal medicine attempts to track beyond these symptoms to their cosmic sources. In Jungian therapy, as a patient becomes aware of a larger sphere around her personality, she begins to accommodate metacultural and archetypal images, and, at the intersection of her psyche and personality, disparate aspects are integrated, symptoms uprooted before they express themselves as serious diseases. From his intimation of synchronicity, Jung presumed that meaning itself (hence, cure) abides simultaneously in man/woman and in nature and the world at large, spawning ceaseless junctions that have in them potential for further meaning, like an endless, unfolding system of divination. It is from this largest field of wholes alone that individuals are healed.

On the other hand, when a disease is treated as anything but a god—i.e., as an unwelcome guest, an intruder, and a violation of the genetic code—its archetypal aspect is never healed, no matter the amount of medicine poured in and surgery successfully completed. The Egyptians' warnings about such practices speak to us today if we could hear them for what they actually are rather than for their overlay of archaic superstitions:

> When thou meetest a large tumor of the God Xensu in any part of the limb of a person, it is loathsome and suffers many pustules to come forth; something arises therein as though wind were in it, causing irritation. The tumor calls with a loud voice to thee: "Is it not like the most loathsome of pustules?" It mottles the skin and makes figures. All the limbs are like those which are affected. Then say thou: "It is a tumor of the God Xensu. Do nothing there against."[13]

It is the recognition of Xensu and succor in his temples and ceremonies that begins the long road to cure. In order to replace a lost archetypal modality, Jung developed a modern medicine to the same end.

Jungian therapy puts a person in touch with his or her psychosomatic destiny through patterns that emerge autonomically as images, feelings, experiences, relationships, visions, creative deeds, etc. These might originate anywhere, most obviously from one's own culture and religion, but also from the myths and symbols of remote cultures or from accidental ancient material stirred up by dreams and daily life.

The very formation of a human being with the potential for "making himself or herself" is heroic and mythic. "Even without artistic talent, even without the ego strength of great will, even without good fortune," writes contemporary Jungian James Hillman, "at least one form of the creative is continuously open for each of us: psychological creativity. Soul-making: we can engender soul. 'If you have nothing at all to create,'" he adds, quoting Jung, "'then perhaps you create your soul.'"[14] If you have nothing else to heal, you can always practice archetypal medicine on yourself.

Whereas native shamans experienced such a process as fact, Jung had to wrest its act of invocation into Western psychology. The raw materials of soul-making are sown everywhere throughout his work—as totems, as unredeemed psychoses, as pathologies and tumors, and in character analyses of transpersonal and deified entities. His methods thus provided a model for the adaptation of *all* non-Western therapies into a clinical context. They gave holism a common thread that was at once attractive, cohesive, and multicultural while being accessible to Western ideals.

The complex circles of symbols (mandalas) familiar to us in stained glass windows, Tibetan *tangka* paintings, petroglyphs, zodiacs, Persian rugs, alchemical codices, etc., Jung identified as projective images of the soul and cosmos. These offered passageways into the primal realm and zones for meeting the diseases originating there. (Many a mandala and alchemical figure now decorate a holistic waiting room or handbook on health in recognition of that.)

Not all artistic circles represent the collective unconscious and not all dreams are archetypal. Jung made a distinction between the more familiar aspects of the personality (identified by Freud) and his own new layer of cosmic symbolism. He treated familial and societal disorders much as Freud did (though always with an awareness of their potential transpersonal dimensions). However, he distinguished the archetypal realm as an arena for true personal growth (individuation). Insofar as this realm also contained the pathologies of stymied growth (which often took the form of serious, even fatal, diseases), Jung sought symbolic forms of medicines in the unconscious.

It little matters in that sense that archetypes are "mere images," for they are the actual spontaneous relics of the deepest aspects of the self.

*Mandalas
painted by a
patient of
C.J. Jung.
© The Estate
of C.J. Jung*

Medicine as symbol is fed to disease *as* symbol. On the symbolic level,
this might resolve in a myth, dream, or work of art; on the physical
level, though, the symptoms are alleviated, and ultimately the core disease. Such medicines are experienced autonomically in visions, as direct
dialogue in therapy, or even through the archetypal elements present
in a standard drug or other mode of medical treatment. Homeopathic
pills are Jungian archetypes temporalized. Herbs are simultaneously
chemical and archetypal. Some holistic medicines even adopt a parallel Jungian symbology for their treatments (as when invoking synchronicity or providing symbology for visualization).

Archetypal psychology provides a way to treat Westerners with non-
Western medicines. One doesn't have to be a Yoruba or Yuin to be healed
by an African or Australian icon in a dream or act of therapeutic transference. In fact, Jung even accepted spontaneous animal medicine. He
presumed that a real-life butterfly fluttering through the window during a session could synchronistically evoke its own archetypal ancestor

and thus transmit a spontaneous cure. An intruding gold beetle could likewise function as the *ka* of an Egyptian scarab.

The interchangeability of treatment modes running a gamut from psychic to surgical is Jungian and has become a mainstay of the holistic professional ethos. Jungian psychology furnishes the themes for a unification of all branches of therapeutics. At such a point, the holistic health movement itself becomes an archetypal medicine for the restoration of the gods and goddesses to nature.

The proposition that self-knowledge and self-deepening are curative is axiomatic to most of the new alternative medicines. It transcends the orthodoxy of any one modality and provides a rationale for holism. For instance, today bodywork may be done according to Reichian principles but with Jungian associations and meanings. A feeling of one's self as a rich-leafed tree, wind blowing in its branches, could suddenly emerge upon the freeing of a deeper layer of breathing. The archetypal tree of the nervous system unfolds, with meridians and axons for

Alternative Medicine

branches and buds, and skin and *chi*-breath for wind, but at the same time the tree might be Yggdrasill, the great Norse ash that connects Heaven, Earth, and the Underworld by its roots and branches; it is equally the craniosacral system, the Druid yew, the *chakras,* the path of the *kundalini,* and the Qabbalistic Tree of Life.

We may change physically in a measurable duration of body and mind, space and time. We also change archetypally, and that is equally instantaneous.

The medical implications of this cosmology are far-reaching. Physical and mental disease utterly converge. If symbols and their expressions can share a deep layer of interchangeability, then having them transformed into cellular messages and new tissue is hardly an infeasible undertaking. Every disease, in that sense, exists in the archetypes, has an archetypal counterpart, and, if cured, is cured archetypally.

Jung was explicit on the psychosomatic origin of diseases when he described:

... cases where the carcinoma broke out ... when a person comes
to a halt at some essential point in his individuation or cannot get
over an obstacle. Unhappily nobody can do it for him, and it cannot be forced. An inner process of growth must begin, and if this
spontaneous creative activity is not performed by nature herself, the
outcome can only be fatal. At any rate, there is a profound disability, i.e., the constitution is at the end of its resources. Ultimately we
all get stuck somewhere, for we all are mortal and remain but a part
of what we are as a whole. The wholeness we can reach is very relative.... Just as a carcinoma can develop for psychic reasons, it can
also disappear for psychic reasons. Such cases are well authenticated.[15]

Using the Mediaeval and Renaissance alchemists as examples, Jung
proposed that men and women labor (usually unconsciously) to transmute the substance of their beings. This was the goal of therapy, to
make ordinary life epic and provide an opportunity for individuation
and fulfillment of destiny. The popular illusion was that the alchemists

Alternative
Medicine

were neutrally sorting and combining substances in order to produce mere external compounds, even if vital ones. But they were simultaneously working with the ingredients of their own incarnations and effecting self-transformations akin to cures in the very activities of their art. We do the same in all our professions, even if most modern industry attempts to squelch archetypes. Unfortunately this leads to either depleted psychospiritual "immunity" or the actual incursion of pathological archetypes in the place of curative ones. Who could doubt this in the factories and offices of modern civilization?

By the same token, medicine archetypally plumbs the world of substance (including the substances of pharmaceuticals and surgical instruments) for the preconscious agents of cellular change. Technological medicine is an alchemical dream, pretending to cure seamlessly while in fact creating its own rugged hierarchy of complexes and pathologies (see the section on "The Pathogenic Healer" in Volume Two, Chapter Two). This is because science is not neutral either, and its invasion of nature gives rise to unwanted archetypes even prior to any individual experiment or treatment. Stated otherwise, healing itself (and the doctors that practice it) are archetypes; that is the sole way they transmit cures and the only way we are able to allow their healing attempts and respond to them. Even herbal remedies, chiropractic adjustments, Reichian exercises, and insights in psychotherapy are alchemical "transmutations." Edward Whitmont has stated this in the contemporary language of the new physics:

> Homeopathic provings and their therapeutic applications have demonstrated that all disturbed physical and psychological functional patterns, fixations, crises, etc., have macrocosmic substance likenesses "out there." That means our complexes are in functional correspondence not only with the code systems of our organs—our muscular body armor, acupuncture meridians and points—but also with the informational systems encoded in the various substance patterns and field systems of the outside world. They correspond to equivalent patterns encoded in cosmic planetary cycles and in our

various ways of responding or misresponding to stress in terms of organic or functional symptoms, or tensions of certain muscle groups. All of these, in their turn, have their equivalents in the codes of the proving patterns of the various external substances. Note that homeopaths speak of phosphor, sulfur or sepia (the ink of the cuttlefish) as personalities, or of aconite or belladonna states.[16]

Even the impersonal matter from which a pharmaceutical or vital medicine is synthesized has a component that could be considered "personal," or isomorphic to personality on an archetypal level.

To say that holistic medicine is all archetypal is an exaggeration, but holistic medicine *is* transcultural, transmutative, and open to butterflies and beetles of all nationalities when they appear. Jung is certainly the hierophant of the new medicine and also its ringmaster.

DESPITE THE DRAMATIC differences between the two men, Jung and Reich each made universal medicines out of the Freudian unconscious. Jungian spiritual dynamics are clearly homologous to Reichian biodynamics. In a book comparing their work, therapist John P. Conger writes:

> Both Jung and Reich reached that level where timely, cultural, and individual differences no longer distract us from the vast, inexhaustible life we share in common. Jung found language for this lifelong experience in the concept of the collective unconscious. Reich, by his commitment to the study of nature, through his attention to the natural uninhibited functions of the body, saw the body of man reconnected to the expansion and contraction of all living things. Reich felt rooted in nature as a part of the cosmic orgone ocean.[17]

An objective psyche is no more or less mystical than an objective soma. Both jell from the chrysalis of seed and egg, merging with the personality of childhood, maturing with the organism into its adult form. In Reich's reading, we are remnants of vast physical systems: galaxies and planets and orgone. In Jung's version, we are a lattice of archetypal psychic systems: equally galactic and originary. Reich spells out the consequences of ignoring soma in pathology and distorted function. Jung reminds us that hidden layers of psyche continue to exist and will fuse with us in sickness if we do not open a way to them as health.

Conger finds an epiphany in both men's work:

> Reich, in his later years, reflected upon the cosmic orgone ocean and man's function and place in nature. In *Cosmic Superimposition,* he wrote: "Thus in an ultimate sense, in self-awareness and in striving for the perfection of knowledge and full integration of one's bio-functions, *the cosmic orgone energy becomes aware of itself."*
>
> Jung described an experience he had in Africa that filled him with faith concerning man's evolution to a higher consciousness and confirmed for him the purpose of nature to know itself:
>
> "But why on earth," you may ask, "should it be necessary for man to achieve, by hook or by crook, a higher level of consciousness?" This is truly the crucial question, and I do not find the answer easy. Instead of a real answer, I can only make a confession of faith: I believe that, after thousands and millions of years, someone had to realize that this wonderful world of mountains and oceans, suns and moons, galaxies and nebulae, plants and animals, *exists.*"[18]

Esoteric Sources of Healing Paradigms

ULTIMATELY MEDICINE IS a branch of both cosmology and thanatology—the sciences of creation and death. The Egyptians and Tibetans both healed by preparing people for death. To the same degree, true priest physicians must address not only transient pathologies but our human place in a vast and unknowable universe. To what end one lives and dies determines what kind of medicine may be practiced.

If the forces of life and death are arbitrated directly and absolutely, then medicine becomes, as it was for Christ, resurrection. Whereas the West has tended to cede this power to God the Father, other cultures have granted it, *in absentia patris,* to yogis, avatars, and various magi.

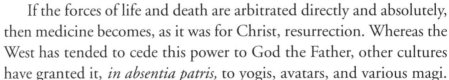

When Babaji restored a disciple who had broken every bone in his body jumping off a cliff to demonstrate his faith,[19] it set a new standard for occult medicine: Anything is curable! Medicine is ultimately a rearrangement of matter and energy in a field created by higher mind.

This is the conversion every aspiring healer longs to have, the moment of truth in which the universe as appearance melts into the game behind the game.

One contemporary healer describes his astonishment at being able to treat a serious burn with "thought energy":

> I stood there a long time looking at that, and something changed inside of me. . . . I knew. That was the first time I really understood that *it's just light and thoughts.* I got it!

He goes on to develop a standard New Age liturgy concerning such miracles (one can take the following at face value or accept it as a myth informing esoteric healing):

> I've seen so much since then I now know beyond any doubt that *absolutely anything whatsoever can be healed.* I don't care what it is. It doesn't matter what they say. It doesn't even matter if you're missing your arm—you can grow another one. . . .
>
>
>
> There was a young boy in New York, eleven years old I believe (and this is on video by the way) . . . who collected salamanders when he was little. And a salamander—if you pluck off a leg or pluck off a hand—just grows another one. And no one ever told him that humans couldn't do that. They forgot!
>
>
>
> And so when he was about eleven years old he lost his leg up to his hip or somewhere around there. . . . Of course, the doctor said, "Nah"; he said, "It's all over." But [the kid's] belief systems weren't tied into that, and he just grew another one. It took him almost a year . . . grew a leg, started growing a foot. Last time I heard he was growing those little toes on it.
>
> Then there's the story of Yogananda—you're familiar with that too? He lost his arm. He just stuck it back on.
>
>
>
> "Ah, better now!"
>
> But he was really good . . . a Kriya Yoga expert.[20]

We pick up this "Believe It or Not" discussion in the first chapter of the second volume with the immortality practices of Leonard Orr.

The world—the universe—is likely filled with telekinetic and alchemical medicines, most of them camouflaged or deflected in the cosmic mirror, billions of them likely practiced through the countless galaxies of time/space. If we could experience a sampling of the medicines from throughout the universe, the AMA would shrivel and vanish, not from an embarrassment of technological primitivity by comparison to the science of advanced civilizations but from the diversity of nontechnological principles that can be institutionalized and work. Alchemy, homeopathic microdoses, and elemental transmutation are the minutest tip of the iceberg. Just as cold fusion might turn water into a nonpolluting fuel by a principle that is neither nuclear nor chemical in the conventional senses of either, so might a medicine from another world provide an Australian shaman with the tools to enter any hospital in the world and apply the techniques his clan was in the mere infancy of perfecting. He would end up becoming every other doctor's teacher.

Aleister Crowley offered as a law: "Every force in the Universe is capable of being transformed into any other kind of force by using suitable means. There is thus an inexhaustible supply of any particular kind of force that we may need."[21] Healing is one of the beneficiaries of this grail.

THE ESOTERIC WING of the twentieth century has spawned Western innovations of many Near Eastern, ancient Egyptian, and East Indian occult, power-based practices, including musical healing, *chakra* balancing, a range of Hindu *kundalini* practices, and G. I. Gurdjieff's synthesis of Oriental and Islamic rituals. Much of this cosmology came straight from the pages of books. P. D. Ouspensky's account of Gurdjieff's pantheon *(In Search of the Miraculous),* Yogananda's instructional tales in *Autobiography of a Yogi,* Crowley's spells and rituals in *Magick in Theory and Practice,* Hazrat Inayat Khan's mantras and vibrations in his *Sufi Message,* Meher Baba's expression of cosmic joy in *God Speaks*—though none of them primarily instructing healing as a profession—all had dramatic impacts on how people thought about the nature of reality and what was possible. Add to these the innumerable descriptions of the Hebrew Qabbala, Sufi dances, kriya yoga, divinatory magic, and Babylonian and Zoroastrian numerology—all popular in the late 1960s. The readership created by these texts and others led to workshops, conferences, and intentional communities from Esalen Institute in Big Sur and Lama Foundation in San Cristobal, New Mexico, to the Holy Order of Mans in San Francisco, the Free Daist Communion in Clear Lake, California, The Self-Realization Fellowship in Los Angeles, and numerous other ashrams, weekly study groups, and spiritual communes. These, in turn, contributed to new definitions of spiritual healing.

G URDJIEFF'S SYSTEM COMBINED the "new science" of his day with traditional Sufi and Hindu teachings. The "unconditioned side of creation," defined as *"Trogoautoegocrat"* (built up from Greek roots meaning "I eat and so keep myself") prevented humans from breaking the trance of their embodiment and transmuting their stark situation. All disease and neurosis, he taught, derive from this hypnotizing cosmic force.[22] Humans are mere junk-producing machines headed for oblivion unless they learn to heal (transform) themselves to a higher level of creation.

Gurdjieff was referring to a cosmic event, but hypnosis is also a clinically inducible condition, employed curatively by Freud and others in memory regression. People under hypnosis recall past lives, abductions by aliens, possession by spirits, and satanic and ritual abuses. Did these things happen? To these people? Or are they part of some larger telepathic field?

From suggestions planted during a hypnotic trance, men and women can be instructed later on to do such things as hug a stranger when they hear a whistle or dance a jig when the hypnotist touches his nose.

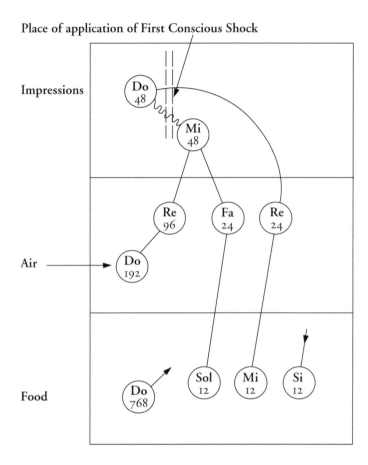

Place of application of First Conscious Shock

Impressions

Air

Food

If our wills are this pliable to unconscious suggestion, it is no wonder we are in semi-trances much of the time. Most of daily life hypnotizes us—its customs, jobs, vehicles, clocks, billboards, and other media all implant "post-hypnotic" messages while keeping individuals in zombi-like trances.

To Gurdjieff the basic trance state behind all the rest comes from interstellar vibrations and is reinforced by daily life. The hydrogen and nitrogen cycles were interpreted by him as the modern-day rediscovery of an ancient, universal cycle: the disintegration of stars and the decay of organic materials on planetary bodies from which all higher substances, including mind, are then generated. Thus, we are nodes in an upward flow of energies: matter rearranges itself into cells and higher life forms, and those give rise to creatures. Thought gradually mutates its way out of the hydrogen-nitrogen trap into a primal substance that ascends into the realm of the absolute, outside a world bounded by three dimensions and the speed of light . . . but only if it breaks the spell.[23]

We come into being as individual starlike centers capable of liberating raw elemental matter into consciousness. Our esoteric goal is to transform the food we eat and the air we breathe into higher and imperishable substances. We can accomplish this only through training awareness and conscious suffering. That is the purpose of the Earth and the lives of its inhabitants. Otherwise, life is disjunctive experiences of fragmentary ego states warring with one another for temporary dominance over an imaginary kingdom.

Gurdjieff preferred the most fundamental sorts of therapeutic exercises: regimens and round dances of repetitive actions, exhaustive and tedious, to break down the habitual sense people have of things. The Moon feeds off us, he warned; it eats the unfinished souls of men and women. Some are turned into light—"the souls of the damned"—by which the present living see the creation.[24]

It may sound like science fiction, but Gurdjieff meant it as physical law. He trained his disciples to spend their waking time working against habit to evade the gluttonous hungers of heavenly bodies millions of times their size. This teaching has an indigenous severity to it: Don Juan Matus also awakened Carlos Castaneda to spirit "eagles" and other vast beings eager to consume souls.

Today, while groups of committed practitioners enact Gurdjieff's exercises and dances (these include actors Deborah Winger, Bill Murray,* and John Cleese), others practice contemporary versions of Rosi-

---

*The movie *Groundhog Day* starring Bill Murray may be viewed as a spoof of Gurdjieff's vision of how repetitive and entrapping daily life actually is.

crucian and tarot ceremonies with less doctrinaire intentions. These do not follow Gurdjieff's strictly pessimistic view of the human situation, but they share his intention to use rituals to obliterate habitual patterns (unconscious rituals). The goal in all cases is to seek the guidance of an older and more sacred logos, perhaps broadcast throughout the cosmos at large, in breaking out of the trance of superficial modern consciousness. Health, in this context, is transmutation and immortality. It is regaining some control over the archetypes and the very somaticizing processes of incarnation.

It would be a mistake to assume that the Gurdjieffian system itself has played a major role in the evolution of alternative medicine. However, it and systems like it have contributed to a more galactic definition of healing and a more widespread notion of the importance of conscious practice (as opposed to mere exercise) in achieving higher states of being and developing natural healing capacities in oneself.

Paradoxically, the gaudy and ornate powers proposed by esoteric healing and the spareness of Buddhism balance each other within the holistic-health movement. Both are present, often simultaneously, creating a deeper truth from their dialectic.

Buddhism

I T IS HARD to believe that a system as vast, profound, and comprehensive as Buddhism could exist on the same planet as the various Judaeo-Christian traditions with their almost total ignorance of one another for millennia. The sheer scope of Buddhist thought is such that its gradual effect on all aspects of Western life (as cultural barriers have broken down) is fundamental and paradigmatic. The most basic issues of life, death, and resurrection; war and peace; relationships between humans and other living creatures; and the goals of civilization itself are radically altered by the impact of Buddhist epistemology. It could well be argued that the entire holistic-health movement is a reflection of the Buddhist lifestyle on the practice of medicine.

Buddhism, of course, is much more than a system of healing. It is a training for the passage between life and death. Thus, it deals with healing in terms of how we experience the whole of life and death. Its physicians *are* priests. At any given time, even before our birth and after our death, we are on the same path. The most important attribute of this path is not necessarily "to feel good," but to experience who we are and to spare other beings from suffering. We strive mainly to be well and pain-free, but the universe holds something far more substantial and wonderful for us. It means for us to grow and be transformed, ultimately out of this physical-mental shape entirely. But, unlike esoteric, transcendental, and magical healing practices, Buddhism intends to empower us by ridding us of false notions of ego and reducing us to a bare nucleus of pure mind. It generally does not encourage healing dramas and therapeutic inflation and phantasmagoria.

From the standpoint of Buddhism the entirety of technology and its remediations form a screen of illusions beside the true forces of the universe. Our obsession with this triviality leads both to our servitude and susceptibility to disease. We constantly try to invent pleasures and postpone discomfort. Medicine becomes a branch of the entertainment industry. We treat death as the ultimate endgame—banishment from the orgy of delight. But what if we were to forego this compulsion and return to our basic nature? In one of his famous talks on Zen mind Shunryu Suzuki said:

> You may think that when you die, you disappear, you no longer exist. But even though you vanish, something which is existent cannot be non-existent. That is the magic. We ourselves cannot put any magic spells on this world. The world is its own magic.... If someone is watching you, you can escape from him, but if no one is watching, you cannot escape from yourself.[25]

The level of ontological depth here dwarfs anything proposed even by quantum mechanics and superstring theory. It pinpoints our dilemma: wherever we go, our selves remain. We cannot kill our true selves. We cannot escape into something we are not. All our sophism and egoism to the contrary is mere sloganeering.

A statement attributed by Tibetans to Buddha throws into perspective this entire human condition: "I manifested in a dreamlike way to dreamlike beings and gave a dreamlike dharma, but in reality I never taught and never actually came."[26] Likewise, us . . . all of us.

BUDDHISM DID NOT so much arrive in North America at a specific time as it gradually percolated over a century and a half until it existed here as an actual practiced form. In one sense, Buddhism was probably always in America (its seed forms brought by Palaeolithic migrants), but its Colonial-through-Civil-War influence was sparse: a few immigrants from the Orient plus those who had traveled abroad and brought back smatterings, its principles otherwise transmitted indirectly through other spiritual and ethical systems. In the mid-nineteenth century Henry David Thoreau and Ralph Waldo Emerson, though neither having met a practicing Hindu or Buddhist, pored over the available translations and considered themselves kindred spirits. They popularized and poeticized (along with Walt Whitman) a transcendentalism ("out of the cradle endlessly rocking . . ." "when me they fly I am the wings") that served as passable vernacular versions of Buddhist sentiment.[27]

At roughly the same time (in the years following the 1848 Gold Rush in California), tens of thousands of Chinese teemed through the ports of the West Coast to serve as carpenters and railroad construction workers. These workers brought a folk amalgam of Taoism, Buddhism, and Confucianism invisible to the culture at large except as exotic temples and weird chants.

Japan was also a source of early American Buddhism. A group of influential professors from Harvard University visited the islands during the 1870s and were so overwhelmed with the sophistication of their art, philosophy, and Noh drama that they became enthusiastic Nipponophiles. Some even learned the tea ceremony and how to sing Noh.

Many of these travellers returned to Asia, among them Ernest Francisco Fenollosa, a political economist and philosopher, and his wife Mary. They visited Zen temples and adopted Buddhist ethics and devotional practices. Both wrote books upon their return to the United States, and Ernest became curator of the Boston Museum's Department of Far Eastern Art.

Fenollosa may not have turned into a full Zen monk, but he understood the bodhisattva vow, "as early as baptism to lead to the strenuous path of battling for the right, to consecrate one's career throughout any number of necessary incarnations to loving service."[28] Even to grasp the implications of this was a significant conversion for any Westerner at that time.

By 1905, Japanese Zen masters were making the journey across the Pacific. The first historically recorded such teacher was Soyen Shaku, who was invited personally to train an American family (the Russells of San Francisco) in meditation and daily practice. He later made these teachings public, emphasizing to all that Buddhist *dhyana* was not, as popularly reported, " 'trance or self-hypnotism,' nor was it 'a sort of intense meditation on some highly abstracted thoughts.' What it proposes to accomplish is to make our consciousness realize the inner reason of the universe which abides in our minds."[29] It took many decades before the full import of this lesson sank in, before educated Westerners realized the *dharma* was no Orientalized Kant or Hegel or even Schopenhauer but a moral proposition of an entirely different order. Soyen was followed by his disciple Nyogen Senzaki and then a second contingent headed by Sokatsu Shaku. Zendos were soon established in San Francisco and Los Angeles.

Over the next half century D. T. Suzuki (Soyen's main translator) inspired a number of people in the United States and Europe, including the British writer Alan Watts, who moved to New York and began teaching seminars on Buddhist philosophy. Later, Suzuki followed him there. He and Watts tried to present Buddhism less as a scholarly or philosophical investigation and more as a principle of daily activity.

Suzuki downplayed doctrines, styles, and pantheons of gods and goddesses in order to emphasize straightforward virtues and ordinary commitments. Zen, pronounced Suzuki, is not just Buddhism. It "is the ultimate fact of all philosophy."[30] The message by then was not only considered profound but chic.

The birth of popular contemporary Buddhism in America is mythically linked to poet Allen Ginsberg's 1953 visit to the First Zen Institute in New York, a center associated with Suzuki's teaching. About the same time, Jack Kerouac encountered a similar teaching accidentally by pulling a "life of Buddha" off the library shelf. After he and his good friend Ginsberg traveled separately to California, they joined up together and introduced themselves to Gary Snyder, a young poet about whom they had heard legendary tales. From Kerouac we inherit a fictionalized account of hitching freight trains West to meet Snyder while every step of the way intensifying his own shaky commitment to the *Diamond Sutra:*

Jumping off the train by Santa Barbara, he writes,

I cooked hot dogs on freshly cut and sharpened sticks over the coals of a big wood fire, and heated a can of beans and a can of cheese macaroni in the redhot hollows, and drank my newly bought wine, and exulted in one of the most pleasant nights of my life. I waded in the water and dunked a little and stood looking up at the splendorous night sky, Avalokitesvara's ten-wondered universe of dark and diamonds.[31]

This is an indelible image for the arrival of Buddhism in the American imagination. It made it not a foreign ritual but a hip way of being full-blooded American. Its clarity and wonder came to life "on the road" rather than among museum Orientalia. (Kerouac did not even note the moral contradiction of hot dogs with Avalokitesvara!)

Under the pseudonym Japhy Ryder, Snyder later became Kerouac's idealized American Buddhist savant. On an informal mountain-climbing expedition in the Sierra, Ryder tells the "Kerouac" character:

"Yeah man, you know to me a mountain is a Buddha. Think of the patience, hundreds of thousands of years just sittin there bein perfectly silent and like praying for all living creatures in that silence and just waitin for us to stop all our frettin and foolin." Japhy got out the tea, Chinese tea, and sprinkled some in a tin pot....[32]

After dinner they went to the edge of the promontory overlooking the valley, and Japhy took up a full lotus cross-legged posture and fingered his wooden juju prayerbeads. Kerouac sat as best as he could on a nearby rock:

The silence was an intense roar....
 "Rocks are space," I thought, "and space is illusion." I had a million thoughts. Japhy had his. I was amazed at the way he meditated with his eyes open. And I was mostly humanly amazed that this tremendous little guy who eagerly studied Oriental poetry and anthropology and ornithology ... should also suddenly whip out his pitiful beautiful wooden prayerbeads and solemnly pray there, like an oldfashioned saint of the deserts certainly, but so amazing to see it in America with its steel mills and airfields.[33]

THE WORK OF the Beat writers directed the attention of an emerging counterculture to the previously unfathomed landscape of temples and monasteries built by immigrants from China. However, mainstream America got this message initially as cool hipsters and beatniks, even goofy Maynard Krebs on TV sitcoms flaunting the American materialistic way of life in a caricature of jazz and jive. Meanwhile, new groups of practitioners continued to arrive from China, Japan, Korea, Vietnam, and other parts of Asia and establish their own schools and teachings out of native lineages.
 Only when Americans discovered Buddhism as a practice, not an exotic poetry or philosophy or an excuse to "drop out," did a true American Buddhist tradition emerge. Dogen Zenji, the patriarch of Soto Zen, had set the guidelines centuries ago in no uncertain terms: "According to the law of Buddha, body and mind are originally one; essence

and form are not two."[34] Buddhism was not an idea or set of cosmologies. To practice sitting meditation (zazen) *was* Buddhism.

Sitting zazen is the pure Zen form of medicine. It means simply achieving a cross-legged posture and breathing. The so-called "full lotus" position calls for the left foot resting on the right thigh, the right foot on the left thigh. The spine is straight but not rigid. Ears and shoulders are parallel; the chin is tucked in; the back of the head is drawn up toward the sky; the diaphragm is pressed toward the *tantien*. With shoulders suspended, hands fall naturally together in a lotus, left within right, middle joints in contact, thumbs barely touching. The medicine is not: what happens next. *This* is the medicine. Zen does not make a distinction between attaining this posture and a practice of meditation. The act of attaining the posture is the act of meditating.

A S THE CHINESE SWORD split the seed-pod of Tibet in the late 1950s, a whole new *dharma* was sown. Tibetan Buddhism—with its high drama, bright colors, ceremonial magic, cinema-like quests for reborn lamas, and warriorship through death itself—was well suited to Western tastes.

Kagyu lineage-holder Chögyam Trungpa, who, at the age of twenty, had heroically guided three hundred escapees from Chinese-overrun East Tibet, came to Barnet, Vermont, by way of England, in 1970 and founded Tail of the Tiger there. Later that year he moved to Boulder, Colorado, and set the groundwork for what was to become the first American Buddhist University, Naropa Institute. He has since been followed by the waves of the Tibetan diaspora, both in North America and Nepal (where Westerners study with a refugee generation of lamas).

Trungpa disdained countercultural Buddhism, and opposed it by stating precepts in pragmatic and phenomenological language. He abstained from religious philosophy and symbolism and developed a fresh terminology of immediate spiritual practicality. His goal was to recover our lost wholeness and sanity—sanity of body and mind together, sanity of being present rather than seeking other worlds. This form of Buddhism became an alternative to psychotherapeutic rituals and practices of spiritual affirmation.

The talks transcribed in Shunryu Suzuki's *Zen Mind, Beginner's Mind* and Trungpa's later *Cutting Through Spiritual Materialism* heralded the entry of spare Buddhist training into the counterculture. They said: the universe is as it is; you are as you are—ordinary, neurotic, out of control. There is no higher sphere or greater power to petition. There are no gods to cultivate or blame. The answer to the questions like "who am I?" and "where did I come from?" is: "Look at what you are now and you will see who you have been (literally, your cumulative karma)." The answer to the question "what will become of me (in future worlds as well)?" is: "How you act now is who you will become and what future worlds will be." So even if Buddhism's premises rest on belief in a chain of successive lives, they set the moment of truth always now. The emphasis is never on any prior or forthcoming life, neither of which is accessible, but on changing present activity so that future states will be freed of the habits and disease tendencies of the past. This does not mean immediate dramatic action; it means developing different mental and behavioral tendencies, usually by sitting meditation. When one is practicing zazen, the sound of frogs or even a dog barking and a motorcycle starting up become one's teachers. Trungpa stated this succinctly as: "Situations are the voice of my guru."[35]

As Buddhist practice spread, the need for a new medical paradigm became more evident. Invasive surgeries and psychotropic drugs tamper with destiny, reinforce a superficial hedonism and attachment to the ego, and undermine the lucidity necessary for right practice. Rather naturally, Naropa and other Buddhist centers provided many of the sites where Oriental medicine, *t'ai chi ch'uan,* improvisational somatic systems, *shiatsu,* and vegetarianism were first taught in depth.

Buddhism provides medical ethics for an incarnation in which all beings must get sick and die and no being can escape from itself or put a spell on the world. Healing becomes a way of *allowing* natural processes rather than trying to defeat or deny them. This is axiomatic in holistic health. At any moment that something seemingly crucial does not occur (i.e., a disease is not cured), something else is happening, and this "something else" goes *with* the symptoms and enlists one's natural life force. The holistic notion of healing pain and disease by encouraging symptomology and blending with it honors a core Buddhist tenet—a strategy for living in a condition of insubstantiality and change in which all one's material hopes (including those of everlasting well-being) are doomed.

Buddhist training makes direct use of pain, hence the attention honed by disease, as a focus of cure. In fact, it encourages one to go toward pain rather than to shy away from or suppress it. Pain sharpens the message of the intrinsic self and catalyzes the immune system.

If the Zen master is not a doctor, it is because he is the "anti-doctor." The anti-doctor does not seek suffering in and of itself; even though he brings his patients pain, he is a healer. Where discomfort arises physically during zazen is where difficulty resides, at least in the mind's rigidity, prior to manifestation. The patient experiences the difficulty of her own body-mind beforehand so that she has some standing with it when actual disease or suffering manifests—and so that she can initiate her own healing process from a conscious intention.

Meditation is a precise means of self-knowledge and self-healing that comes from emptying the mind of ego states and problem-solving thoughts and shifting attention to existence in the form of breathing.

This is no meager event. The mind is not emptied in the sense of becoming flaccid or a cipher; nor is it emptied to be filled with emotional drama as in a dream, or with ecstatic and joyous visions; it is emptied of the full battery of habitual thoughts and repetitions of its emotions.

Trungpa writes:

> In the practice of meditation all thoughts are the same: pious thoughts, very beautiful thoughts, religious thoughts, calm thoughts—they are still thoughts. You do not try to cultivate calm thoughts and suppress so-called neurotic thoughts.[36]

IN THE WORST of situations, e.g., in an instance where one's child is suffering from an incurable disease, the only viable mode is to go toward things as they are. This criterion recurs in all breath-based healing disciplines as a technique for channeling energy. Suzuki presents it in vintage Zen terms:

> Normally the most comfortable place for you would be a warm comfortable bed, but now because of your mental agony you cannot rest. You may walk up and down, in and out, but this does not help. Actually the best way to relieve your mental suffering is to sit in zazen, even in such a confused state of mind and bad posture.... No other activity will appease your suffering. In other restless positions you have no power to accept your difficulties, but in the zazen posture which you have acquired by long, hard practice, your mind and body have great power to accept things as they are, whether they are agreeable or disagreeable.[37]

Although meditation is meant to be undertaken without the ambition of accomplishment or the expectation of any benefit (one practices simply to achieve a basic dignity and to express a commitment to the truth of existence without bribery), it is intrinsically a health-inducing state. In an ideal world in fact it would be the sole medicine (in relation to which all our other medicines stand as contrivances and contraptions to antidote materialistic distractions and shallow breathing).

BUDDHISM HONORS THE Freudian energetic equation but from an entirely different ethos. The originator of psychology observed the ceaseless flow of mind-body data, and he traced its modulations in order to invent his own hierarchies of structure and meaning. Then he proposed a quasi-neurological treatment based on prioritization of certain symbolic nexuses themselves based on childhood developmental sequences (from the presumption that the older infantile experiences were the most formative and profound).

Buddhism draws attention away from hierarchy or prioritization and toward sheer inexplicable transition of form after form. Despite their differing relative charges, all forms that come into being are temporary and transitory.

In other words, early Buddhist practitioners understood the complexity of our psychosomatic projections, but they did not try to interpret them symbolically. They chose to live them in the present.

Yet Freud is not to be denigrated as coming millennia later and dealing with energy only judgmentally and superficially. In fact, he discovered quite unique psychosomatic patterns, and he fashioned an energetic basis for thought out of purely scientific materials. In the process he unintentionally provided Western Buddhists, as well as holistic practitioners, with a method for integrating the dynamics of culturally bound emotions and stages of ego development with acts of

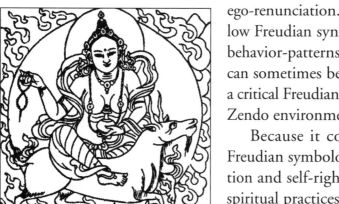

ego-renunciation. A holistic practitioner can follow Freudian syntax as a path through neurotic behavior-patterns to enlightened states. "Zazen" can sometimes be more effectively cultivated in a critical Freudian regime than in a self-conscious Zendo environment.

Because it constantly challenges the ego, Freudian symbology undercuts the sort of inflation and self-righteousness that may arise from spiritual practices that do not take into account the deviousness of ego-based goals (for instance, overly eager spiritual renunciation with its accompanying rigidity, or religiosity and authoritarian righteousness). Buddhism and Freudian psychology thus arrive at complementary realities and concordant healing tools.

IN SUMMARY, BUDDHISM proposes that all matter, substance, and mind arise in a profound originary state, a "ground luminosity" that shines through elemental dross to ignite the shards of our personality and flesh. At death, we return to those embers and reside back in the existentiality from whence we came. Such an ontology regards all diseases as taking seed as tendencies within the origination of consciousness. Hence disease is primordially curable by changing karmic patterns. In place of the magic tricks and power repertoires of other esoteric medicines, Buddhism teaches that healing arises almost solely from extending compassion and taking on the pain of the universe rather than, for instance, narcissistically, considering oneself a victim and trying to feel better. Personal spiritual transformations lessen the grip of karma and thereby heal at a deep level. In principle, if one is sick, he should embrace in his heart all the sick and dying and offer his own life as a vehicle for redeeming these sentient beings rather than himself. If one is in sorrow, she should try not to diminish her own anguish but to take on the collective suffering of those in greater sorrow, as though to say, "Come, give me all your burdens too. I can handle them." Such sincere acts of selfless compassion—usually achieved by a form of zazen—do in fact cut beneath the level of disease. However, to act with personal gain as an ulterior goal is not only a shoddy mode of practice but an ineffective one.

The legendary rainbow body manifested (even in the sky) by accomplished Tibetan lamas after death is a dramatic demonstration of the principle of ground luminosity transcending the familiar laws of nature. Holistic healing methods do not attempt such grandiose remissions, but they do draw on the same laws of karma, ground state, and rainbow bodies in their potentiation of people who have become ill. The question of whether "medicine" can operate on such an immaterial, existential level will be taken up throughout the second volume.

I N AN IDEAL SITUATION, a disease is experienced, through clarity of awareness, as what it is, and an endogenous adjustment is made. Death is the last available adjustment. Remember: the therapeutic emphasis in spiritual Buddhism is on cultivating attention and compassion rather than conscious healing. Intentional medicine is directed toward other sentient beings—literally projected from deep within to far without. All this begins with a shift in attention and a new perspective of mind and body. As Suzuki told an audience of students:

> It will take quite a long time before you find your calm, serene mind in your practice. Many sensations come, many thoughts or images arise, but they are just waves of your own mind. Nothing comes from outside your mind. Usually we think of our mind as receiving impressions and experiences from outside, but that is not a true understanding of our mind. The true understanding is that the mind includes everything; when you think something comes from outside it means only that something appears in your mind. Nothing outside yourself can cause any trouble. You yourself make the waves in your mind. If you leave your mind as it is, it will become calm. This mind is called big mind. . . .
> Big mind experiences everything within itself.[38]

A sick person may suffer terribly or even die before her time. But since most Eastern spiritual systems acknowledge karma and reincarnation, the information learned in this process will be invaluable in the passage of the core being into other manifestations. Perhaps disease in one incarnation will protect the future lives of that being against the tendency to become neurotic or sick. In the larger cosmic cycle, a sick body will ultimately give birth to a healthier one, for the lesson imbedded in a fatal illness (or mode of death) will be imprinted on the deathless aspect of the being—the luminosity. The mind that "survives" is big mind and has little to do with the ego's version of consciousness—or even the Freudian unconscious; it certainly does not carry secular memory. The hope is that innocent children who die young from severe and painful illnesses—in fact all who suffer—receive a great gift for their pain: the knowledge of who they are and the opportunity to become something larger and help save other beings from suffering. Disease is, in that sense, like a tiger preying on zebras, a rapid and cruel lesson, but an effective one. The spirit learns from it precisely how not to incarnate illness in the future.

T*he Tibetan Book of the Dead* is a script of lifelong preparation for death, our realm on Earth characterized as but one in the limitless sequence of bardos. Death is at the same time the work of Bile and Phlegm; Earth, Water, Fire, Air, and Sky. The stages of death are literally and elementally a reversing of the stages of incarnation. The elements disentangle and dissipate, and mind and ego dissipate with them in often excruciating episodes. Death occurs on an elemental level both physiologically and psychologically. It is through the cauldron of this lucid and reality-affirming process that the greatest possibility for karmic transformation exists. Sogyal Rinpoche spells this out in terms that cannot be dismissed as esoteric finery:

> The bardo teachings show us precisely what will happen if we prepare for death and what will happen if we do not. The choice could not be clearer. If we refuse to accept death now, while we are still alive, we will pay dearly throughout our lives, at the moment of death, and thereafter. The effects of this refusal will ravage this life and all the lives to come. We will not be able to live our lives fully; we will remain imprisoned in the very aspect of ourselves that has to die. This ignorance will rob us of the basis of the journey to enlightenment, and trap us endlessly in the realm of illusion, the uncontrolled

cycle of birth and death, that ocean of suffering that we Buddhists call *samsara*.[39]

It would be an exaggeration to suggest that most holistic medicines deal with the world at this level. Even secular Tibetan medicine does not fully attend this message. Yet there is a link between ordinary disease—fevers, poxes, tumors, and the like—and esoteric disease:

> Perhaps the deepest reason why we are afraid of death is because we do not know who we are. We believe in a personal, unique, and separate identity; but if we dare to examine it, we find that this identity depends entirely on an endless collection of things to prop it up: our name, our "biography," our partners, family home, job, friends, credit cards.... It is on their fragile and transient support that we rely for our security. So when they are all taken away, will we have any idea of who we really are?
>
> Without our familiar props, we are faced with just ourselves, a person we do not know, an unnerving stranger with whom we have been living all the time but we never really wanted to meet. Isn't that why we have tried to fill every moment of time with noise and activity, however boring or trivial, to ensure that we are never left in silence with this stranger on our own?[40]

Holistic medicines at least address this problem. They try to return us to ourselves, to that "stranger." They do not numb our pains, get our organs functioning according to a code of normality, and restore the chimera of security. From homeopathy to rebirthing, from shamanic transference to craniosacral adjustment, the intention is to make mind/body experience truthful. Then healing occurs naturally and fundamentally.

From a Zen standpoint, it hardly matters that the purported goal of holistic medicine is not bardo-consciousness or reincarnation because in this realm of existence one's activities *per se,* not their professed ideologies, determine their outcome. Studying massage and giving treatments to other people may be a form of zazen, a bodhisattva act. Practicing *Chi Gung* may be the functional equivalent of meditation and may lead to therapeutic changes in the world around the practitioner. In that sense, the goals of Buddhism and holistic medicine speak to the same acts of deepening, recovery, and healing the planet. In fact, as these two perspectives come together, we can see the integral connection between mind/body, core beliefs, and states of health. Sogyal Rinpoche writes:

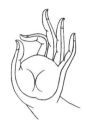

> I have heard of many . . . cases of people who were diagnosed as terminally ill and given only a few months to live. When they went into solitude, followed a spiritual practice, and truly faced themselves and the fact of death, they were healed. What is this telling us? That when we accept death, transform our attitude toward life, and discover the fundamental connection between life and death, a dramatic possibility for healing can occur.
>
> Tibetan Buddhists believe that illnesses like cancer can be a warning, to remind us that we have been neglecting deep aspects of our being, such as our spiritual needs. If we take this warning seriously and change fundamentally the direction of our lives, there is a very real hope for healing not only our bodies, but our whole being. . . .
>
> What a beautiful and what a healing mystery it is that from contemplating, continually and fearlessly, the truth of change and impermanence, we come slowly to find ourselves face to face, in gratitude and joy, with the truth of the changeless, with the truth of the deathless, unending nature of mind.[41]

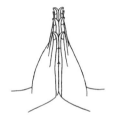

The New Paradigm

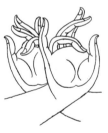

THE PRESENT CRISIS marks the decline of materialism and the first faint emergence of a radical new order of things. Materialism is as old as the animal kingdom and will die hard, spilling much blood. It has already consumed Christianity, Buddhism, the American Indian, the Australian Aborigine, and countless other peoples of the Dream Time. That is because their spiritualism lacked some key feature of matter-energy/mind-body transmutation, thus harbored substantial materialism in its core. Now all the chickens are hatched.

The new order must slice through the hard heart of greed and mechanism and touch the point where the universes of mind and matter meet and are interchangeable. This will perhaps be made of a substance resembling pure light, unlike anything our species on this planet has seen. It will clean the land and sky. But first it will behave like a wild beast. It will introduce itself to us in a form we will not recognize. Its medicines will be anything but medicinal.

Paradigm shifts are elusive, multidimensional phenomena. In their midst no one can guess how far they will go and what they will eclipse. I have posed here the medical aspects of a present paradigm shift, and I have garnered a number of related movements and ideologies to show the full political and psychospiritual scope of the event. Holistic health is finally a refraction of environmental awakening, political activism, and a synthesis of Eastern and Western epistemologies and ethics. It is not first and foremost a medical program.

The new paradigm represents a medical archetype for a larger shift of reality; it radiates a therapeutic metaphor throughout that shift. There are also political metaphors, spiritual ones, and cosmological ones. But the therapeutic one has become the dominant theme, no doubt because healing is what is most lacking globally and most likely needed. We imagine "holistic health" because we are ready for inner transformation.

A paradigm shift that interpolates such diverse elements as the Chinese invasion of Tibet, Jung's popularization of the Platonic archetypes, African dances, organic farms, homeopathic clinics, and bone adjustments is a massive shift indeed. It foreshadows epochal cosmological upheavals, many of which will not be as benign as the therapeutic one. We can expect the demons of pathology to challenge (and hopefully, over millennia, deepen) any true planetary medicine.

A change in cosmology is like a tilt in the axis of the zodiac. It is hardly confined to countercultural arenas or single metaphors. It goes right through the center of the Earth. Our new healers must also go straight through the center of the Earth; they must palpate the core of both bone and mind. The cultivation of this skill will take generations.

ONE CAN POINT to major segments of American culture seemingly unaffected by alternative medicine, for instance, the Christian Moral Majority, the scientific establishment, street gangs, and drug traffickers. However, in the larger sense, this is a misnomer, taking the metaphor for the reality. The rise of crime and violence is our immune response to an otherwise numbing pathology. The resurgence and politicization of Biblical fundamentalism is a fully parallel movement to holistic health. Like alternative medicine, it contains the seeds of faith healing and engenders a fierce resistance to scientific fragmentation and atheism.

Christian fundamentalism is a narrow and rigid holism, but it reflects a deep-seated desire for a merging of body, psyche, and spirit. In some future ideal circumstance (that at this moment seems particularly unlikely) it could join the holistic-health movement to promote a more global shift away from materialism. First, of course, it would have to abandon its own materialism, and second, it would have to accommodate and then synthesize other spiritual views.

The scientific establishment has its hands full with the new paradigm. Much of its present energy goes to defending its borders against encroachment (thus defining its own institutions and experiments in reaction against a competing model rather than investigating nature openly as during the eighteenth century). Additionally, in areas of physics and sociology in particular, scientists are more and more compelled to examine the subtexts of their theories and applications. The cosmological base of science is shifting, and the hardcore physical and biological disciplines will eventually either erode under the mass of their own contradictions or break through into a cybernetic infinitude.

Gangs, drugs, ethnic wars, and the like could not share less with healing circles, microdoses, and therapeutic touch. Yet they are their precise energetic shadow. They reflect the apogee of a disease process to which alternative medicines are the first tentative gropings for a response. I will discuss this issue in depth in the second volume.

A LTERNATIVE MEDICINE HAS originated simultaneously everywhere and nowhere. It most blatantly emerged as countercultural clinics, paintings of mandalas, herbal remedies, massage techniques, and treatment protocols. Yet it has expanded to welcome Tibetan lamas and *Chi Gung* masters and has allowed them and others both to critique and transform its paradigm. As the paradigm has grown, it has also embraced and mutated such stalwart sectarian programs as chiropractic, osteopathy, Alcoholics Anonymous, and laying on of hands.

What passes now as "holistic health" or "alternative medicine" is merely the faintest first glimmering of a new world. A new world will come anyway, as new worlds always have. This one, however, is millennial, not only because we approach the numerical millennium but because this is the historic moment at which progressive science and materialization of the planet have reached their physical limits. A new order *must* follow, so while we have yet the leisure and sanctuary of the old order, we express our faith—and some rhetoric—that the new order be healing as well as destroying.

Notes

1. Harris L. Coulter, *Divided Legacy: Science and Ethics in American Medicine 1800–1914, Vol. III. The Conflict Between Homeopathy and the American Medical Association* (Berkeley, California: North Atlantic Books, 1982), p. 92.

2. Faith Mitchell, *Hoodoo Medicine: Sea Island Herbal Remedies* (Berkeley, California: Reed, Cannon & Johnson, 1978).

3. Brian Inglis, *The Case for Unorthodox Medicine* (New York: Putnam, 1965), p. 231.

4. Ibid., pp. 69–70.

5. Harris L. Coulter, *Divided Legacy: A History of the Schism in Medical Thought, Vol. IV: Twentieth Century Medicine: The Bacteriological Era* (Berkeley, California: North Atlantic Books, 1994), p. 355.

6. Alan Ptashek, "The Moving Body: An Integrated Movement Course," in *Contact Quarterly* (Winter 1992), Northampton, Massachusetts, pp. 41–42.

7. Nevill Drury, *The Healing Power: A Handbook of Alternative Medicines and Natural Health* (London: Frederick Muller Ltd., 1981), pp. 171–73.

8. Barbara L. Schultz, "New Age Shiatsu," in Berkeley Holistic Health Center, *The Holistic Health Handbook* (Berkeley, California: And/Or Press, 1978), p. 195.

9. Drury, *The Healing Power,* p. 190.

10. Schultz, "New Age Shiatsu," p. 196.

11. Murray Bookchin, *The Ecology of Freedom: The Emergence and Dissolution of Hierarchy* (Palo Alto, California: Cheshire Books, 1982), pp. 2–3.

12. From interviews conducted during 1977–1981 with approximately thirty M.D.s practicing homeopathy.

13. Ira M. Rutkow, *Surgery: An Illustrated History* (St. Louis: Mosby–Year Book, 1993), p. 13.

14. James Hillman, *The Myth of Analysis* (Evanston, Illinois: Northwestern University Press, 1972), pp. 39–40.

15. Edward C. Whitmont, *The Alchemy of Healing: Psyche and Soma* (Berkeley, California: North Atlantic Books, 1993), p. 70.

16. Ibid., p. 215.

17. John P. Conger, *Jung & Reich: The Body as Shadow* (Berkeley, California: North Atlantic Books, 1988), p. 14.

18. Ibid., pp. 14–15.

19. Paramahansa Yogananda, *Autobiography of a Yogi* (Los Angeles: Self-Realization Fellowship, 1946).

20. Drunvalo Melchizedek, "Flower of Life Workshop," Dallas, Texas, February 14–17, 1992 (video recording).

21. Aleister Crowley, *Magick in Theory and Practice* (New York: Castle Books, no date), p. xvii.

22. P. D. Ouspensky, *In Search of the Miraculous: Fragments of an Unknown Teaching* (New York: Harcourt, Brace & World, 1949).

23. Ibid.

24. Ibid.

25. Shunryu Suzuki, *Zen Mind, Beginner's Mind* (New York: Weatherhill, 1970), p. 61.

26. Dodé Kalpa Zangpo, quoted by Sogyal Rinpoche in *Dzogchen and*

Padmasambhava, Rigpa Fellowship of California, 1990, p. 83.

27. As a source for material in this and subsequent paragraphs, I have used Rick Fields, *How the Swans Came to the Lake: A Narrative History of Buddhism in America* (Boulder, Colorado: Shambhala Publications, 1981), and I have also constructed a synopsis in conversation with him.

28. Ibid., p. 152.

29. Ibid., p. 174.

30. Ibid., p. 205.

31. Jack Kerouac, *The Dharma Bums* (New York: Viking Press, 1958), p. 7.

32. Ibid., p. 67.

33. Ibid., pp. 70–71.

34. Fields, *How the Swans Came to the Lake* (see footnote 27 above), p. 229.

35. Chögyam Trungpa, *Cutting Through Spiritual Materialism* (Berkeley, California: Shambhala Publications, 1973).

36. Ibid.

37. Suzuki, *Zen Mind, Beginner's Mind,* p. 40.

38. Ibid., pp. 34–35.

39. Sogyal Rinpoche, *The Tibetan Book of Living and Dying* (HarperSan Francisco, 1992), p. 14.

40. Ibid., p. 16.

41. Ibid., pp. 30–31, 40.

HOSPITAL
California

PATHOLOGY DEPARTMENT

Patient: **JOYCE**
Hosp. No.
        F: 57   Location: OP
                                       Date of Procedure: August 31, 1993
                                       Date Received: August 31, 1993
                                       Physicians:

PATHOLOGY CONSULTATION

SPECIMEN:
    RIGHT BREAST MASS

GROSS:
    Received and examined unfixed is a segment of breast tissue 3 x 3
    cm. The surface of the specimen is labelled with green dye prior
    to sectioning and upon sectioning a 1.1 cm. diameter sclerotic gray
    nodule is identified. From this tissue has been submitted for
    estrogen receptor studies.

MICROSCOPIC:
    Sections are comprised of breast tissue containing an invasive duct
    adenocarcinoma. Although there are abundant well-formed glands
    within the specimen, there are also foci of solid nests and cords
    of infiltrating tumor cells. This is given a histologic score of
    2, the nuclear score is 3 and the mitotic score is 1 for a
    cumulative score of 6, making this an intermediate grade tumor.
    Lymphatic space invasion is not identified and the lesion is
    demonstrated to reside on the dye-labeled margin of the specimen.

DIAGNOSIS:
    RIGHT BREAST BIOPSY: INFILTRATING DUCT ADENOCARCINOMA, 1.1 CM.,
    MODERATELY DIFFERENTIATED WITH EXTENSION TO MARGINS OF SPECIMEN.

    09/02/93
Report verified by pathologist.
** Report Electronically Signed Out **

JOYCE   SURGICAL PATHOLOGY

HOSPITAL
California
PATHOLOGY DEPARTMENT

Patient: **JOYCE**
Hosp. No.:
        F: 58   Location: OR
                                       Date of Procedure: September 30, 1993
                                       Date Received: September 30, 1993
                                       Physicians:

PATHOLOGY CONSULTATION

SPECIMEN:
    RIGHT BREAST AND AXILLARY NODES

GROSS:
    Submitted in formalin and labelled "right breast" is a right
    modified radical mastectomy. There is an overlying ellipse of skin
    measuring 17 cm. A healed scar is present above and lateral to the
    nipple. The scar measures 2.5 cm. in length. It is present 3.5
    cm. from the edge of the areola. Sections through the breast show
    fibrous breast tissue, with a biopsy site characterized by an area
    of fat necrosis. I do not see gross evidence of residual
    carcinoma. Sections from around the biopsy site and deep surgical
    margins are submitted as A-D. Sections taken at a distance from the
    biopsy site are submitted as E and F. Section of the nipple is
    submitted and labelled G. Section of the skin over the biopsy
    submitted and labelled H. Lymph nodes are dissected and submitted
    and labelled I,J,K,L,M,N,O,P.

MICROSCOPIC:
    The microscopic sections through the biopsy site show biopsy site
    changes including chronic inflammation, with infiltrating
    histiocytes and foreign body giant cells. There is fat necrosis.
    I do not see evidence of definite residual malignancy. The deep
    surgical margin is negative for malignancy. Sections taken at a
    distance from the biopsy site show benign breast tissue without
    evidence of malignancy. Section of the nipple is unremarkable.
    Section from the skin over the biopsy site shows reactive changes,
    without evidence of malignancy. The sections from lymph nodes show
    a total of 28 lymph nodes, all negative for metastatic carcinoma.

    JOYCE   SURGICAL PATHOLOGY

HOSPITAL
California

PATHOLOGY DEPARTMENT

Patient: **JOYCE**

DIAGNOSIS:

1. RIGHT BREAST, SHOWING FAT NECROSIS AND FOREIGN BODY GIANT CELL
REACTION, WITHOUT DEMONSTRABLE RESIDUAL MALIGNANCY (RIGHT MODIFIED
RADICAL MASTECTOMY).

2. TWENTY-EIGHT RIGHT AXILLARY LYMPH NODES, NEGATIVE FOR
MALIGNANCY.

10/04/93

Report verified by pathologist.

** Report Electronically Signed Out **

BIBLIOGRAPHY

The Academy of Traditional Chinese Medicine. *An Outline of Chinese Acupuncture.* Peking: Foreign Languages Press, 1975.

Ackerknecht, Erwin H. "Problems of Primitive Medicine," *Bulletin of the History of Medicine,* Volume XI, 1942.

Alexander, Gerda. *Eutony: The Holistic Discovery of the Total Person.* Great Neck, New York: Felix Morrow, 1985.

Alon, Ruthy. *Mindful Spontaneity: Lessons in the Feldenkrais Method.* Berkeley, California: North Atlantic Books, 1995.

Amaringo, Pablo, and Luis Eduardo Luna. *Ayahuasca Visions: The Religious Iconography of a Peruvian Shaman.* Berkeley, California: North Atlantic Books, 1991.

Aston, Judith. "Three Perceptions and One Compulsion," in *Bone, Breath, and Gesture: Practices of Embodiment.* Don Hanlon Johnson, ed. Berkeley, California: North Atlantic Books, 1995.

Bach, Edward. *Heal Thyself.* London: C. W. Daniel, 1931.

Baginski, Bodo J., and Shalila Sharamon. *Reiki: Universal Life Energy: A Holistic Method of Treatment for the Professional Practice/Absentee Healing and Self-Treatment of Mind, Body, and Soul.* Mendocino, California: Life Rhythm, 1988.

Baker, Courtney, Robert Dew, Michael Ganz, and Louisa Lance. "Wound Healing in Mice (Part I)," in *Annual of the Institute of Orgonomic Science,* Vol. 1, No. 1, September 1984.

Baker, Wyrth P., Allen C. Neiswander, and W. W. Young. *Introduction to Homeotherapeutics.* Washington, DC: American Institute of Homeopathy, 1974.

Barfield, Owen. *Unancestral Voice.* Middleton, Conneticut: Wesleyan University Press, 1965.

Barral, Jean-Pierre, and Pierre Mercier. *Visceral Manipulation.* Seattle, Washington: Eastland Press, 1988.

Barrett, S. A. *Pomo Bear Doctors,* University of California Publications in American Archaeology and Ethnology, Vol. 12, No. 11, July 11, 1917. Berkeley, California: University of California Press, 1917.

Bateson, Gregory. "Restructuring the Ecology of a Great City," *Io #14, Earth Geography Booklet No. 3, Imago Mundi,* Cape Elizabeth, Maine, 1972.

Bauman, Edward, Armand Ian Brint, Lorin Piper, and Pamela Amelia Wright, eds. *The Holistic Health Handbook.* Berkeley, California: And/Or Press, 1978.

Bennett, J. G. *Gurdjieff: Making a New World.* New York: Harper/Colophon, 1973.

Binik, Alexander. "The Polarity System," in *The Holistic Health Handbook.* Bauman, et al., eds. Berkeley, California: And/Or Press, 1978.

Boas, Franz. *The Religion of the Kwakiutl Indians, Part II: Translations.* New York: Columbia University Press, 1930.

Böhm, Karl. *The Life of Some Island People of New Guinea: A Missionary's Observations of the Volcanic Islands of Manam, Boesa, Biem, and Ubrub.* Berlin: Dietrich Reimer Verlag, 1983.

Bookchin, Murray. *The Ecology of Freedom: The Emergence and Dissolution of Hierarchy.* Palo Alto, California: Cheshire Books, 1982.

Bordeu, Théophile. *Oeuvres.* Paris: Caille & Ravier, 1818.

Brennan, Richard. *The Alexander Technique Workbook.* Rockport, Massachusetts: Element Books, Ltd., 1992.

Britton, Nathanial, Lord, and Hon. Addison Brown. *An Illustrated Flora of the Northern United States, Canada, and the British Possesions.* New York: Charles Scribner's Sons, 1913.

Buckley, Mary. "Feng Shui: The Art of Grace in Place," in *New Dimensions Journal,* Spring 1993.

Burger, Bruce. *Esoteric Anatomy.* Unpublished manuscript at the time of publication. Berkeley, California: North Atlantic Books, 1996.

Calderón, Eduardo, Richard Cowan, Douglas Sharon, and F. Kaye Sharon. *Eduardo el Curandero: The Words of a Peruvian Healer.* Berkeley, California, North Atlantic Books, 1982.

Cannon, Walter B. "'Voodoo' Death," in *American Anthropologist,* XLIV, 1942.

Carroll, Jon. "The Odd Saga of Marlo Morgan," *San Francisco Chronicle,* September 7, 1994, p. E8 and September 8, 1994, p. E10.

Castaneda, Carlos. *The Teachings of Don Juan: A Yaqui Way of Knowledge.* Berkeley, California: University of California Press, 1969.

——. *A Separate Reality.* New York: Simon & Schuster, 1971.

——. *Journey to Ixtlan.* New York: Simon & Schuster, 1972.

——. *Tales of Power.* New York: Simon & Schuster, 1974.

Caufield, Charles R., with Billi Goldberg. *The Anarchist AIDS Medical Formulary: A Guide to Guerrilla Immunology.* Berkeley, California: North Atlantic Books, 1994.

Celsus, Aulus Cornelius. *De Medicina.* Three Volumes. Translated by W. G. Spencer. Cambridge, Massachusetts: Loeb Classical Library, Harvard University Press.

Chancellor, Philip M. *Handbook of the Bach Flower Remedies.* London: C. W. Daniel Co., 1971.

Chopra, Deepak. *Quantum Healing: Exploring the Frontiers of Mind/Body Medicine.* New York: Bantam Books, 1989.

Codere, Helen. *Fighting with Property: A Study of Kwakiutl Potlatching and Warfare, 1792–1930.* Monographs of the American Ethnological Society, Volume XVIII. New York: J. J. Augustin, 1950. Reprinted in *Indians of the Northwest Coast.* Tom McFeat, ed. Seattle, Washington: University of Washington Press, 1966.

Cohen, Bonnie Bainbridge. "Research in the Field of Somatics," California Institute of Integral Studies, San Francisco, November 1992.

——. *Sensing, Feeling, and Action: The Experiental Anatomy of Body-Mind Centering.* Northampton, Massachusetts: Contact Editions, 1993.

Bibliography

Cohen, Don. *An Introduction to Craniosacral Therapy.* Berkeley, California: North Atlantic Books, 1995.

Coles, William. "Adam in Eden, or The Paradise of Plants," republished in *Io #5, Doctrine of Signatures,* Ann Arbor, Michigan, 1968.

Collin, Rodney. *The Theory of Celestial Influence.* London: Stuart & Watkins, Ltd., 1954.

Conger, John P. *The Body in Recovery: Somatic Psychotherapy and the Self.* Berkeley, California: Frog, Ltd., 1994.

——. *Jung & Reich: The Body as Shadow.* Berkeley, California: North Atlantic Books, 1988.

Cook, James. *The Journals of James Cook: The Voyage 1776–1780.* London: Hakluyt Society, Vol. I, No. 36, extra series.

Corbin, Henry. *Creative Imagination in the Sufism of Ibn 'Arabi.* Translated from the French by Ralph Manheim. Princeton, New Jersey: Bollingen Foundation, Princeton University Press, 1969.

Coulter, Harris Livermore. *Divided Legacy, A History of the Schism in Medical Thought, Vol. I: The Patterns Emerge: Hippocrates to Paracelsus.* Washington, DC: Weehawken Book Company, 1975.

——. *Divided Legacy, Vol. II: The Origins of Modern Western Medicine: J. B. Van Helmont to Claude Bernard.* Berkeley, California: North Atlantic Books, 1977.

——. *Divided Legacy, Vol. III: The Conflict Between Homeopathy and the American Medical Association: Science and Ethics in American Medicine 1800–1914.* Berkeley, California: North Atlantic Books, 1982.

——. *Divided Legacy, Vol. IV: Twentieth Century Medicine, The Bacteriological Era.* Berkeley, California: North Atlantic Books, 1994.

——. *Homeopathic Science and Modern Medicine: The Physics of Healing with Microdoses.* Berkeley, California: North Atlantic Books, 1981.

Cousins, Norman. "The Mysterious Placebo," in *Saturday Review,* October 1977.

Covarrubias, Miguel. *Island of Bali.* New York: Alfred Knopf, 1938.

Cowan, Richard, and Douglas Sharon. *Eduardo the Healer.* Oakland, California: Serious Business Company, 1978.

Crews, Frederick. "The Revenge of the Repressed, Part II," in *The New York Review of Books,* Vol. XLI, No. 20, December 1, 1994.

Croft, William, C. S. T. "Light Energy Practices (Yoga/Qi-gong/Aikido) and *Working with Light*—A Synergy," flyer, 1993.

Crowley, Aleister. *The Confessions of Aleister Crowley.* John Symonds and Kenneth Grant, eds. New York: Hill & Wang, 1969.

——. *Magick in Theory and Practice.* New York: Castle Books, n.d.

Das, Baba Hari, and Dharma Sara Satang. "Ayurveda: The Yoga of Health," in *The Holistic Health Handbook.* Bauman, et al., eds. Berkeley, California: And/Or Press, 1978.

de Berval, Réné. *Kingdom of Laos.* Saigon, Vietnam: France-Asie, 1956.

de Langre, Jacques. *Dō-In 2: The Ancient Art of Rejuvenation Through Self-Massage.* Magalia, California: Happiness Press, 1978.

DeMeo, James, Richard Blasband, and Robert Morris. "Breaking the 1986 Drought in the Eastern United States," in *The Journal of Orgonomy,* Vol. 21.

Derrida, Jacques. "Freud and the Scene of Writing." Translated from the French by Jeffery Mehlman. *Yale French Studies.* New Haven, Connecticut: Yale University Press, n.d.

——. *Of Grammatology.* Translated from the French by Gayatri Chakravorty Spivak. Baltimore, Maryland: Johns Hopkins University Press, 1976.

Dhalla, Maneckji N. *Zoroastrian Civilization.* Cambridge, England: Oxford University Press, 1922.

Diderot, Denis. *Encyclopedié ou Dictionnaire Raisoneé des Sciences des Arts et des Métiers.* Paris: Edition Garniere Frères, 1765.

Dodé Kalpa Zangpo, quoted by Sogyal Rinpoche in *Dzogchen and Padmasambhava.* Berkeley, California: Rigpa Fellowship of California, 1990.

Dorn, Edward. *Recollections of Gran Apachería.* Berkeley, California: Turtle Island, 1974.

Bibliography

541

Dorn, Edward, and Gordon Brotherstone, "The Aztec Priest's Reply," in *New World Journal,* Berkeley, California, Vol. I, Nos. 2/3, 1977.

Drury, Neville. *The Healing Power: A Handbook of Alternative Medicines and Natural Health.* London: Frederick Muller Ltd., 1981.

Duesberg, Peter. *Infectious AIDS: Stretching the Germ Theory Beyond Its Limits.* Berkeley, California: North Atlantic Books, 1995.

Eisenbud, Jule. Interview conducted by Richard Grossinger, January 8, 1972, originally published in *Io #14*, *Earth Geography Booklet #3, Imago Mundi.* Republished in *Ecology and Consciousness: Traditional Wisdom on the Environment.* Richard Grossinger, ed. Berkeley, California, 1978. Revised second edition, 1992.

——. *Paranormal Foreknowledge: Problems and Perplexities.* New York: Human Sciences Press, 1982.

Elkin, A. P. *Aboriginal Men of High Degree.* Sydney: Australasian Publishing, 1944.

Emmons, George Thornton. *The Tlingit Indians.* Seattle, Washington: University of Washington Press, 1991.

Enslin, Theodore. "Journal Note," in *The Alchemical Tradition in the Late Twentieth Century.* Richard Grossinger, ed. Berkeley, California: North Atlantic Books, 1979.

Espanca, Jutta. "The Effect of Orgone on Plant Life (Part 7)," in *Offshoots of Orgonomy,* No. 12, Spring 1986.

Faraday, Michael. *The Chemical History of a Candle: A course of lectures delivered before a juvenile audience at the Royal Institution.* New York: Viking Press, 1960.

Feldenkrais, Moshe. *The Case of Nora: Body Awareness as Healing Therapy.* 1977. Berkeley, California: Frog, Ltd., 1993.

——. *The Potent Self: A Guide to Spontaneity.* New York: Harper & Row, 1985.

Ferenczi, Sandor. *Thalassa: A Theory of Genitality.* Translated from the German by Henry Alden Bunker. New York: Norton, 1968.

Fields, Rick. *How the Swans Came to the Lake: A Narrative History of Buddhism in America.* Boulder, Colorado: Shambhala Publications, 1981.

Fiore, Edith. *The Unquiet Dead.* New York: Ballantine Books, 1988.

Flammonde, Paris. *The Mystic Healers.* New York: Stein & Day, 1974.

Foucault, Michel. *The Birth of the Clinic.* Translated from the French by A. M. Sheridan Smith. New York: Pantheon Books, 1973.

Fox, R. B. "The Pinatubo Negritos: Their Useful Plants and Material Culture," in *The Philippine Journal of Science,* Vol. 81, Nos. 3-4, 1953.

Frantzis, Bruce Kumar. *Opening the Energy Gates of Your Body.* Berkeley, California: North Atlantic Books, 1993.

——. *The Tao in Action: The Personal Practice of the I Ching and Taoism in Daily Life.* Unpublished manuscript at the time of publication. Berkeley, California: North Atlantic Books, 1996.

Freud, Sigmund. *An Outline of Psychoanalysis.* Translated from the German by James Strachey. New York: Norton, 1949.

——. *The Interpretation of Dreams.* Translated from the German by James Strachey. New York: Basic Books, 1955.

Frissell, Bob. *Nothing in This Book Is True, But It's Exactly How Things Are.* Berkeley, California: Frog, Ltd., 1994.

From Bindu to Ojas. San Cristobal, New Mexico: Lama Foundation, 1970.

Fulder, Stephen. *The Root of Being: Ginseng and the Pharmacology of Harmony.* London: Hutchison Publishing Group, 1980.

Fuller, John G. *Arigo: Surgeon of the Rusty Knife.* New York: Crowell, 1974; Pocket Books, 1975.

Gelfand, Michael. *Medicine and Custom in Africa.* Edinburgh: Livingstone, 1964.

Gillispie, Charles Coulston. "Lamarck and Darwin in the History of Science," in *Forerunners of Darwin, 1745–1859.* Bentley Glass, Owsei Temkin, and William L. Straus, Jr., eds. Baltimore: The Johns Hopkins University Press, 1959.

Ginzberg, Jeremy. "Pharmaco-Hell Calling," in *East Bay Express,* Berkeley, California, January 21, 1994.

Golden, Stephanie. "Body-Mind Centering," in *Yoga Journal,* Berkeley, California, September/October 1993.

Goodwin, Kathleen. "Alternative Medicine: A Note of Caution," in *City Miner,* Berkeley, California, Vol. 3, No. 3, 1978.

Grey, Alex. *Sacred Mirrors.* Rochester, Vermont: Inner Traditions, 1990.

Groddeck, Georg. *The Book of the It.* Translated from the German by V. M. E. Collins. New York: Funk & Wagnalls, 1950.

——. "Psychic Conditioning and the Psychoanalytic Treatment of Organic Disorders," in *The Meaning of Illness.* M. Masud R. Khan, ed. London: The Hogarth Press, 1977.

Grossinger, Richard. "Alchemy: Pre-Egyptian Legacy, Millennial Promise," in *The Alchemical Tradition in the Late Twentieth Century.* Richard Grossinger, ed. Berkeley, California: North Atlantic Books, 1979.

——. "Cross-Cultural and Historical Models of Energy in Healing," paper delivered at the conference *Conceptualizing Energy Medicine: An Emerging Model of Healing,* University Extension and School of Public Health, University of California, Berkeley, California, March 28, 1981.

——. "The Dream Work," in *Dreams are Wiser Than Men.* Richard A. Russo, ed. Berkeley, California: North Atlantic Books, 1987.

——. *Homeopathy: An Introduction for Skeptics and Beginners.* Berkeley, California: North Atlantic Books, 1993.

——, ed. *An Olson-Melville Sourcebook, Vol. I: North America. Vol. II: The Mediterranean.* Plainfield, Vermont: North Atlantic Books, 1976.

——, ed. *Ecology and Consciousness: Traditional Wisdom on the Environment.* Berkeley, California: North Atlantic Books, 1978. Revised second edition, 1992.

——, ed. *Io,* 1964–79. Amherst, Massachusetts; Ann Arbor, Michigan; Cape Elizabeth, Maine; Mount Desert, Maine; Oakland, California; Plainfield, Vermont; and Richmond, California.

Gurdjieff, G. I. *Views from the Real World: Early Talks.* New York: Dutton, 1975.

Haehl, Richard. *Samuel Hahnemann: His Life and Work,* Vol. I. London: Homeopathic Publishing Co., 1922.

Hahnemann, Samuel. *The Chronic Diseases, Their Peculiar Nature and Their Homeopathic Cure.* Translated by Louis H. Tale from the second enlarged German edition, 1835. Philadelphia: Boericke and Tafel, 1904.

———. *The Lesser Writings of Samuel Hahnemann.* Collected and translated by R. E. Dudgeon. New York: Radde, 1952.

———. *The Organon of Medicine,* Sixth Edition. Translated by William Boericke, M.D. Calcutta, India: Roysingh, 1962.

Handy, E. S. Craighill, Mary Kawena Pukui, and Katherine Livermore. *Outline of Hawaiian Physical Therapeutics.* Honolulu, Hawaii: Bernice P. Bishop Museum, Bulletin 126, 1934.

Harley, George Way. *Native African Medicine.* Cambridge, Massachusetts: Harvard University Press, 1941.

Harman, Robert. "Current Research with SAPA Bions," in *The Journal of Orgonomy,* Vol. 21.

Harner, Michael J. *The Jívaro.* Garden City, New Jersey: Doubleday/Natural History Press, 1972.

Harvey, Andrew. *Hidden Journey: A Spiritual Awakening.* New York: Henry Holt & Co., Inc., 1991.

Hauschka, Rudolf. *The Nature of Substance.* Translated from the German by Mary T. Richards and Marjorie Spock. London: Stuart & Watkins, 1966.

———. *Nutrition.* Translated from the German by Marjorie Spock and Mary T. Richards. London: Stuart & Watkins, 1967.

Heckler, Richard Strozzi. *In Search of the Warrior Spirit: Teaching Awareness Disciplines to the Green Berets.* Berkeley, California, North Atlantic Books, 1989.

Heisenberg, Werner. "The Relationship Between Biology, Physics, and Chemistry," in *Physics and Beyond.* Translated from the German by Arnold J. Pomerans. New York: Harper & Row, 1971.

Heller, Joseph, and William Henkin. *Bodywise: Introduction to Hellerwork.* Oakland, California: Wingbow Press, 1986.

Herbert, Frank. *Dune.* New York: Berkley, 1965.

Bibliography

———. *Whipping Star.* New York: Berkley, 1977.

Herriot, Eva M. "Ayurvedic Sense Therapy," in *Yoga Journal,* Berkeley, California, January/February 1992.

Hickey, Gerald Cannon. *Village in Vietnam.* New Haven, Connecticut: Yale University Press, 1964.

Higgins, Mary, and Chester M. Raphael, eds. *Reich Speaks of Freud.* New York: Farrar, Straus and Giroux, 1967.

Hillman, James. *The Myth of Analysis.* Evanston, Illinois: Northwestern University Press, 1972.

Hippocrates. *Medical Works.* Four Volumes. Translated by W. H. S. Jones. Cambridge, Massachusetts: Loeb Classical Library, Harvard University Press.

Hoagland, Richard C. *The Monuments of Mars: A City on the Edge of Forever.* Berkeley, California: North Atlantic Books, 1986.

Hodosi, Oskar. *Tantra Partnerschaft: Neue Dimensionen der Liebe Durch Eine Jahrtausendealte Kultur.* Munich: Mosaik Verlag, 1992.

Holbrook, Bruce. *The Stone Monkey: An Alternative Chinese-Scientific Reality.* New York: Morrow, 1981.

Hsu, Hong-Yen. *How to Heal Yourself with Chinese Herbs.* Los Angeles: Oriental Healing Arts Institute, 1980.

Inglis, Brian. *A History of Medicine.* Cleveland: World Publishing Company, 1965.

———. *The Case for Unorthodox Medicine.* New York: Putnam, 1965.

Jarrell, David G. *Reiki Plus: Professional Practitioner's Manual for Second Degree.* Celina, Tennessee: Hibernia West, 1992.

Jenness, D. "The Carrier Indians of the Bulkley River," in *Bulletin No. 133.* Washington, DC: Bureau of American Ethnology, 1943.

John, Bubba Free (Da Free John). *The Eating Gorilla Comes in Peace: The Transcendental Principle of Life Applied to Diet and the Regenerative Discipline of True Health.* Middletown, California: The Dawn Horse Press, 1979.

Johnson, Don Hanlon. *Body, Spirit and Democracy.* Berkeley, California: North Atlantic Books, 1993.

———. *The Protean Body.* New York: Harper & Row, 1977.

———. "The Way of the Flesh: A Brief History of the Somatics Movement," in *Bone, Breath, and Gesture: Practices of Embodiment.* Don Hanlon Johnson, ed. Berkeley, California: North Atlantic Books, 1995.

———, ed. *Bone, Breath, and Gesture: Practices of Embodiment.* Berkeley, California: North Atlantic Books, 1995.

Jung, Carl. *Archetypes of the Collective Unconscious.* Translated by R. F. C. Hull. Bollingen Series XX. New York: Pantheon Books, 1959.

———. *Psychological Reflections.* Jolande Jacobi, ed. New York: Harper & Row, 1953.

———. *Psychology and Alchemy.* Translated from the German by R. F. C. Hull. London: Routledge & Kegan Paul, 1953.

Kahn, Morton C. *Djuka: The Bush Negroes of Dutch Guiana.* New York: Viking Press, 1931.

Katz, R. "Education for Transcendence: Lessons from the !Kung Zhu Twasi," in *Journal of Transpersonal Psychology,* November 2, 1973.

Keleman, Stanley. *Living Your Dying.* New York: Random House, 1974.

———. "Professional Colloquium," in *Ecology and Consciousness: Traditional Wisdom on the Environment.* Richard Grossinger, ed. Berkeley, California: North Atlantic Books, 1978. Revised second edition, 1992.

Kent, James Tyler. *Lectures on Homeopathic Philosophy.* 1900. Berkeley, California: North Atlantic Books, 1979.

Kerouac, Jack. *The Dharma Bums.* New York: Viking Press, 1958.

Khan, M. Masud R., ed. *The Meaning of Illness.* London: The Hogarth Press, 1977.

Kroeber, A. L. *Ethnology of the Gros Ventre.* Anthropological Papers of the American Museum of Natural History, Vol. I, Part IV, New York, 1908.

Kushi, Michio. *The Book of Dō-In: Exercise for Physical and Spiritual Development.* Tokyo: Japan Publications, 1979.

Lade, A., and R. Svoboda. *Tao & Dharma—A Comparison of Ayurveda*

and Chinese Medicine. Unpublished manuscript at the time of publication.

Lamb, F. Bruce. *Rio Tigre and Beyond: The Amazon Jungle Medicine of Manuel Córdova-Rios.* Berkeley, California: North Atlantic Books, 1985.

Lansing, Gerrit. "Fundamentals of Indian Medical Theory," from *Notes on Structure and Sign in Ayurveda.* Unpublished manuscript, 1981.

Lawlor, Robert. *Voices of the First Day: Awakening in the Aboriginal Dreamtime.* Rochester, Vermont: Inner Traditions, 1991.

Le Guin, Ursula K. *A Wizard of Earthsea.* New York: Bantam Books, 1975.

Leigh, William S. *Bodytherapy.* Coquitlam, British Columbia: Water Margin Press, 1989.

Leri, Dennis. "Learning How to Learn," unpublished manuscript.

Lessa, William A., and Evon Z. Vogt. *Reader in Comparative Religion.* New York: Harper & Row, 1958.

Lévi-Strauss, Claude. *From Honey to Ashes.* Translated from the French by John and Doreen Weightman. New York: Harper & Row, 1973.

——. *The Raw and the Cooked.* Translated from the French by John and Doreen Weightman. New York: Harper & Row, 1969.

——. *The Savage Mind.* Chicago: University of Chicago Press, 1966.

——. "The Sorcerer and His Magic," in *Structural Anthropology.* Translated from the French by Claire Jacobson and Brooke Grundfest Schoepf. Garden City, New Jersey: Doubleday/Anchor, 1967.

——. *Totemism.* Translated from the French by Rodney Needham. Boston: Beacon Press, 1963.

Leviton, Richard. "The Healing Energies of Color," in *Yoga Journal,* Berkeley, California, January/February 1992

——. "Healing Vibrations," in *Yoga Journal,* Berkeley, California, January/February 1994.

Lewis, C. S. *The Magician's Nephew.* 1951. New York: Collier Books, 1970.

Lindner, Robert. *The Fifty-Minute Hour.* New York: Bantam Books, 1956.

Liu, Qingshan. *Qi Gong: Der chinesische Weg für ein gesundes langes Leben.* Munich: Hugendubel, 1992.

Lo, Pang Jeng, Martin Inn, Susan Foe, and Robert Amacker. *The Essence of T'ai Chi Ch'uan: The Literary Tradition.* Berkeley, California: North Atlantic Books, 1979.

Maitland, Jeffrey. *Spacious Body: Explorations in Somatic Ontology.* Berkeley, California: North Atlantic Books, 1995.

Makavejev, Dussan. *WR: Mysteries of the Organism.* New York: Avon Books, 1972.

Mann, Felix. *Acupuncture: The Ancient Chinese Art of Healing and How It Works Scientifically.* New York: Random House, 1973.

Mann, W. Edward. *Orgone, Reich and Eros: Wilhelm Reich's Theory of Life Energy.* New York: Simon & Schuster, 1973.

Mars, Louis. *The Crisis of Possession in Voodoo.* Translated from the French by Kathleen Collins. Berkeley, California: Reed, Cannon & Johnson Co., 1977.

Marshack, Alexander. *The Roots of Civilization.* New York: McGraw-Hill, 1972.

Max, Otto. Review of *Planet Medicine,* in *East West Journal,* Boston, Massachusetts, August 1981.

McKenna, Terence. *The Archaic Revival: Speculations on Psychedelic Mushrooms, the Amazon, Virtual Reality, Evolution, Shamanism, the Rebellion of the Goddess, and the End of History.* San Francisco: Harper-Collins, 1993.

Meek, George W. *Healers and the Healing Process.* Wheaton, Illinois: Theosophical Publishing House, 1977.

Melchizedek, Drunvalo. "Flower of Life Workshop," Dallas, February 14–17, 1992. Video recording.

Melville, Herman. *Moby Dick; or the Whale.* 1851. Berkeley, California: University of California Press, 1979.

Middendorf, Ilse. *The Perceptible Breath: A Breathing Science.* Paderborn, Germany: Junferman-Verlag, 1990.

Milne, Hugh. *The Heart of Listening: A Visionary Approach to Cranio-*

sacral Work. Unpublished manuscript at the time of publication. Berkeley, California: North Atlantic Books, 1995.

Mitchell, Faith. *Hoodoo Medicine: Sea Island Herbal Remedies.* Berkeley, California: Reed, Cannon & Johnson, 1978.

Moore, Omar Khayyam. "Divination—A New Perspective," in *American Anthropologist,* LIX, 1957.

Moss, Thelma. "Kirlian Photograph and the Aura," interview with Roy L. Walford, in *Io #19, Mind Memory Psyche,* Plainfield, Vermont, 1974.

Muldoon, Sylvan, and Hereward Carrington. *The Projection of the Astral Body.* New York: Samuel Weiser, Inc., 1970.

Müller, Brigitte, and Horst Günther. *A Complete Book of Reiki Healing.* Mendocino, California: Life Rhythm, 1995.

Murdock, George Peter. "Tenino Shamanism," in *Culture and Society: Twenty-Four Essays.* George Peter Murdock, ed. Pittsburgh, Pennsylvania: University of Pittsburgh Press, 1965.

Nicoll, Maurice. *Psychological Commentaries on the Teaching of Gurdjieff & Ouspensky.* London: Robinson & Watkins, 1952.

Olschak, Blanche Christine. *Mystic Art of Ancient Tibet.* Translated by George Allen. New York: McGraw-Hill, 1973.

Olsen, Stanley J. *Mammal Remains from Archaeological Sites, Part I: Southeastern and Southwestern United States.* Cambridge, Massachusetts: The Peabody Museum, 1964.

Olson, Charles. *The Maximus Poems.* 1950. Berkeley, California: University of California Press, 1979.

——. *Muthologos,* Vol. I. Bolinas, California: Four Seasons Foundation, 1978.

Oracion, Timoteo S. "The Bais Forest Preserve Negritos: Some Notes on Their Rituals and Ceremonies," in *Studies in Philippine Anthropology.* Mario D. Zamora, ed. Quezon City, Philippines: Alemar-Phoenix, 1967.

Orr, Leonard. *Bhartriji: Immortal Yogi of 2000 Years.* Chico, California: Inspiration University, 1992.

——. *Physical Immortality: The Science of Everlasting Life.* Sierraville, California: Inspiration University, 1980.

Ouspensky, P. D. *In Search of the Miraculous: Fragments of an Unknown Teaching.* New York: Harcourt, Brace, & World, 1949.

Oyle, Irving. *The New American Medicine Show.* Santa Cruz, California: Unity Press, 1979.

Palmer, Wendy. *The Intuitive Body: Aikido as a Clairsentient Practice.* Berkeley, California: North Atlantic Books, 1994.

Paracelsus. *The Hermetic and Alchemical Writings of Paracelsus the Great.* Translated by A. E. Waite. London: James Elliott, 1894.

Perlman, David. "Controversial AIDS Theories Debated at Forum in S.F.," *San Francisco Chronicle*, June 22, 1994.

Phillips, Wendell. *Unknown Oman.* New York: David McKay Company, Inc., 1966.

Pitchford, Paul. *Healing with Whole Foods: Oriental Traditions and Modern Nutrition.* Berkeley, California: North Atlantic Books, 1993.

Poncé, Charles. *The Archetype of the Unconscious and the Transfiguration of Therapy: Reflections on Jungian Psychology.* Berkeley, California: North Atlantic Books, 1990.

The Private Life of Chairman Mao: The Memories of Mao's Personal Physician, Dr. Li Zhisui. Translated by Tai Hung-chao. New York: Random House, 1994.

Ptashek, Alan. "The Moving Body: An Integrated Movement Course," in *Contact Quarterly,* Northampton, Massachusetts, Winter 1992.

Pujols, Lee, and Gary Richman. *Miracles & Other Realities.* San Francisco: Omega Press, 1990.

Quindlen, Anna. "Gulf War's Killing Legacy," *San Francisco Chronicle,* October 10, 1994.

Radcliffe-Brown, A. R. *The Andaman Islanders.* Glencoe, Illinois: Free Press, 1948.

Rappaport, Roy A. "Sanctity and Adaptation," in *Io #7, Oecology Issue,* 1970; reprinted in *Ecology and Consciousness: Traditional Wisdom on the Environment.* Richard Grossinger, ed. Berkeley, California: North

Atlantic Books, 1978. Revised second edition, 1992.

Rasmussen, Knud. *Intellectual Culture of the Iglulik Eskimos: Report of the Fifth Thule Expedition to Arctic North America.* Copenhagen, Denmark: Gyldendalske Boghandel, Nordisk Forlag, 1929.

Rechung, Ven. Rinpoche Jampal Kunzang. *Tibetan Medicine.* Berkeley, California: University of California Press, 1973.

Reese, Mark. "Moshe Feldenkrais' Verbal Approach to Somatic Education: Parallels to Milton Erickson's Use of Language," in *Somatics,* Novato, California, Autumn/Winter 1985–86.

Regardie, Israel. *The Eye in the Triangle.* Llewellyn Publications, St. Paul, Minnesota, 1970.

Reich, Peter. *A Book of Dreams.* New York: Harper & Row, 1973.

Reich, Wilhelm. *Character Analysis.* Third Edition. Translated from the German by Vincent R. Carfagno. New York: Farrar, Straus and Giroux, 1972.

———. *Cosmic Superimposition.* Translated from the German by Therese Pol. New York: Farrar, Straus and Giroux, 1973.

———. *The Emotional Plague of Mankind: Volume 1, The Murder of Christ.* Rangeley, Maine: Orgone Institute Press, 1953.

———. *Ether, God & Devil—Cosmic Superimposition.* Translated from the German by Therese Pol. New York: Farrar, Straus and Giroux, 1973.

———. *The Function of the Orgasm.* Translated from the German by Vincent R. Carfagno. New York: Farrar, Straus and Giroux, 1973.

Reichard, Gladys A. *Navaho Religion.* New York, Bollingen Foundation, Pantheon Books, 1950.

Reif, A. Veronica "Eurhythmy and Curative Eurhythmy," essay accompanying lecture at the Berkeley Anthroposophical Society, 1978.

Ros, Frank. *The Lost Secrets of Ayurvedic Acupuncture: An Ayurvedic Guide to Acupuncture.* Twin Lakes, Wisconsin: Lotus Press, 1994.

Roberts, Jane. *The Seth Material.* Englewood Cliffs, New Jersey: Prentice-Hall, 1970.

Rolf, Ida. *Ida Rolf Talks About Rolfing and Physical Reality.* New York: Harper & Row, 1978.

——. *Rolfing: The Integration of Human Structures.* New York: Harper & Row, 1977.

Rose, Jeanne. *The Aromatherapy Book: Applications & Inhalations.* Berkeley, California: North Atlantic Books, 1992.

Rubenfeld, Ilana. "Alexander: The Use of the Self," in *Wholistic Dimensions in Healing: A Resource Guide.* Leslie J. Kaslof, ed. New York: Doubleday & Company, Inc., 1978.

Rush, Benjamin. *Medical Inquiries and Observations.* Philadelphia: Pritchard and Hall, 1789.

Rutkow, Ira M. *Surgery: An Illustrated History.* St. Louis: Mosby-Year Book, 1993.

Sahlins, Marshall. *Stone Age Economics.* Chicago: Aldine-Atherton, 1972.

Sannella, Lee. *Kundalini—Psychosis or Transcendence?* San Francisco: Dakin, 1976.

Schaffer, Carolyn. "An Interview with Emilie Conrad-Da'oud," in *Yoga Journal,* Berkeley, California, No. 77, November/December 1987.

Schiotz, Eiler H., and James Cyriax. *Manipulation Past and Present.* London: William Heinemann Medical Books, Ltd., 1975.

Schreiber, Jon. *Touching the Mountain: The Self-Breema Handbook—Ancient Exercises for the Modern World.* Oakland, California: California Health Publications, 1989.

Schultz, Barbara L. "New Age Shiatsu," in *The Holistic Health Handbook.* Bauman, et al., eds. Berkeley, California: And/Or Press, 1978.

Schwartz, Jesse. "Some Experiments with Seed Sprouts and Energetic Fields," in *Living Tree Journal,* Bolinas, California, 1986.

——. "Science vs. Scientism," in *Brain Mind,* Vol. 18, No. 5.

Segal, Mia. Interview in *Somatics,* Novato, California, Autumn/Winter 1985–86.

"Sex Between Therapist and Patient," transcript of the June 21, 1976, meeting of the American Psychiatric Association, in *Psychiatry,* Vol. 5, No. 12.

Sharaf, Myron. *Fury on Earth: A Biography of Wilhelm Reich.* New York: St. Martin's Press, 1983.

Shklovskii, I. S., and Carl Sagan. *Intelligent Life in the Universe.* Translated from the Russian by Paula Fern. New York: Delta Books, 1967.

Siegel, Bernie. "Letter to the Editor," in *Common Boundary,* Bethesda, Maryland, September-October, 1994.

Sieh, Ron. *T'ai Chi Ch'uan: The Internal Tradition.* Berkeley, California: North Atlantic Books, 1993.

Smith, Harvey H. *Area Handbook for Iran.* Washington, DC: United States Government Printing Office, Foreign Area Studies, American University, 1971.

Sogyal Rinpoche. *The Tibetan Book of Living and Dying.* San Francisco: HarperSanFrancisco, 1992.

Speck, Frank G. *A Study of the Delaware Indian Big House Ceremony,* Vol. II. Harrisburg, Pennsylvania: Publications of the Pennsylvania Historical Commission, 1931.

Spencer, Dorothy M. *Disease, Religion and Society in the Fiji Islands.* New York: Augustin, 1941.

Stewart, Daniel Blair. *Akhunaton: The Extraterrestrial King.* Berkeley, California: Frog, Ltd., 1995.

Still, A. T. *Osteopathy: Research & Practice.* 1910. Seattle, Washington: Eastland Press, 1992.

Stone, Randolph. *Polarity Therapy,* Vol. I. Sebastopol, California: CRCS Publications, 1986.

———. *Polarity Therapy,* Vol. II. Sebastopol, California: CRCS Publications, 1987.

Suzuki, Shunryu. *Zen Mind, Beginner's Mind.* New York: Weatherhill, 1970.

Swadesh, Morris. "Diffusional Cumulation and Archaic Residue as Historical Explanations," in *Language in Culture & Society: A Reader in Linguistics and Anthropology.* Dell Hymes, ed. New York: Harper & Row, 1964.

Swanton, John R. *Religious Beliefs and Medical Practices of the Creek Indians,* 42nd Annual Report to the Bureau of American Ethnology, 1924-25. Washington, DC: Smithsonian Institution, 1928.

Tait, David. "Konkomba Sorcery," in *Magic, Witchcraft, and Curing.* John Middleton, ed. New York: The Natural History Press, 1967.

Tantaquidgeon, Gladys. *Folk Medicine of the Delaware and Related Algonkian Indians.* Harrisburg, Pennsylvania: Pennsylvania Historical and Museum Commission, 1972.

Teilhard de Chardin, Pierre. *The Phenomenon of Man.* Translated from the French by Bernard Wall. New York: Harper & Row, 1959.

Temple, Robert K. G. *The Sirius Mystery.* New York: St. Martin's Press, 1976.

Tenen, Stan. *Hebrew—First Hand.* San Anselmo, California: Meru Foundation, 1994.

——. *The Matrix of Meaning for Sacred Alphabets.* San Anselmo, California: Meru Foundation, 1991. Video recording.

Thakkur, Chandrashekhar G. *Ayurveda: The Indian Art & Science of Medicine.* New York: ASI Publishers, Inc., 1974.

Thera, Nyanaponika. *The Heart of Buddhist Meditation.* New York: Samuel Weiser, Inc., 1969.

Tierra, Michael. *The Way of Herbs.* New York: Simon & Schuster, 1994.

Tomlinson, Cybèle. "Breema Bodywork," in *Yoga Journal,* Berkeley, California, November/December 1994.

Tompkins, Peter, and Christopher Bird. *The Secret Life of Plants.* New York: Harper & Row, 1973.

Trungpa, Chögyam. *Cutting Through Spiritual Materialism.* Berkeley, California: Shambhala Publications, 1973.

Turner, Victor W. *Lunda Medicine and the Treatment of Disease.* Occasional Papers of the Rhodes-Livingstone Museum, No. 15. Northern Rhodesia, Zambia: Livingstone, 1964.

Tyler, M. L. *Homeopathic Drug Pictures.* Holsworthy, Devon, England: Health Science Press, 1942.

Upledger, John E. *CranioSacral Therapy II: Beyond the Dura.* Seattle, Washington: Eastland Press, 1987.

——. *SomatoEmotional Release and Beyond.* Palm Beach Gardens, Florida: UI Publishing, 1990.

Bibliography

Upledger, John E., and Jon D. Vredevoogd. *CranioSacral Therapy.* Seattle, Washington: Eastland Press, 1983.

Urquhart, David. *Manual of the Turkish Bath.* Sir John Fife, M.D., ed. London: Churchill, 1865.

Vallee, Jacques. *Forbidden Science.* Berkeley, California: North Atlantic Books, 1992.

Van Helmont, Jan Baptista. *Oriatrike, or Physick Refined.* London, 1662.

Vithoulkas, George. *The Science of Homeopathy: A Modern Textbook,* Vol. I. Athens, Greece: A.S.O.H.M., 1978.

Vlamis, Gregory. "Interview with Pierre Pannetier," in *Well-Being Magazine,* No. 28, 1978.

Waite, A. E. *See* Paracelsus, above.

Watson, James. *The Double Helix.* New York: Atheneum, 1968.

Westlake, Aubrey T. *The Pattern of Health.* Berkeley, California: Shambhala Publications, 1973.

Wheelwright, Philip, ed. *The Presocratics.* Indianapolis, Indiana: Odyssey Press, 1966.

Whicher, Olive. *Projective Geometry: Creative Polarities in Space and Time.* London: Rudolph Steiner Press, 1971.

Whitehead, Alfred North. *Process and Reality.* Toronto: Macmillan, 1929.

Whiting, Alfred F. *Ethnobotany of the Hopi.* Northern Arizona Society of Science and Art, Bulletin 15. Flagstaff, Arizona: Museum of Northern Arizona, 1939.

Whitmont, Edward. *The Alchemy of Healing: Psyche and Soma.* Berkeley, California: North Atlantic Books, 1993.

———. *Psyche and Substance: Essays on Homeopathy in the Light of Jungian Psychology.* Berkeley, California: North Atlantic Books, 1979.

Wildschut, William. *Crow Indian Medicine Bundles.* John C. Ewers, ed. New York: Museum of the American Indian, Heye Foundation, 1975.

Williams, William Carlos. *Pictures from Brueghel and Other Poems.* New York: New Directions, 1962.

Wilson, Robert Anton. *Cosmic Trigger.* Berkeley, California: And/Or Press, 1977.

Wisdom, Charles. *The Chorti Indians of Guatemala.* Chicago: University of Chicago Press, 1940.

Wyman, Leland C. *Beautyway: A Navaho Ceremonial.* Recorded and translated by Father Berard Haile. New York: Bollingen Foundation, Pantheon Books, 1957.

Wyvell, Lois. "Orgone and You," in *Living Tree Journal,* Bolinas, California, 1986.

Yates, Frances. *Giordano Bruno and the Hermetic Tradition.* Chicago: University of Chicago Press, 1964.

———. *The Rosicrucian Enlightenment.* London: Routledge & Kegan Paul, 1972.

The Yellow Emperor's Classic of Internal Medicine (Huang Ti Nei Ching Su Wên). Translated from the Chinese by Ilza Veith. Berkeley, California: University of California Press, 1966.

Yoe, Shway. *The Burman.* London: Macmillan, 1910.

Yogananda, Paramahansa. *Autobiography of a Yogi.* Los Angeles: Self-Realization Fellowship, 1946.

This is a cumulative index for *Planet Medicine: Origins* and *Planet Medicine: Modalities* or Volume 1 and Volume 2, respectively. Accordingly, the page references for each volume are identified as follows: Vol. 1 *(Origins)* page references are listed first in each entry, with a 1 preceding that list. Page references for Vol. 2 *(Modalities)* are listed second in each entry, with a 2 preceding that list. Where both Vol. 1 and Vol. 2 references appear, the lists are separated by a semicolon (;). For example:

planet medicine
    changes necessary for, 1.527–30; 2.8–10, 11, 450–53

entry Vol. 1 *(Origins)*   Vol. 2 *(Modalities)*

Page references in **bold** refer to illustrations or photographs. The term *passim* refers to a discontinuous discussion of a topic over several pages. The terms *above* and *below* refer to subentries within the main category. The letter "n" attached to a page reference refers to a note on that page.

Index

Index

Index

Index

Index

Index

and language, 2.66
as limited, 2.10
origins, 1.491, 492–93
practice of, 2.13, 20–22
Reiki as, 2.31
and shocks to system, 2.412
and vitalism, 1.228
see also spiritual healing
family
    concept origin of nuclear, 1.71
    kinship, 1.72–77
farming *see* agriculture
fascia, altering the, 2.271, 275, 276,
    329
fasting, 2.435
Faulkner, William, 2.472
fear
    of disease, 2.9–10, 193
    in healing, 2.150
    see also shocks, in healing
feeling *see* emotions; sensations
Feldenkrais Method
    Alexander Technique and,
        2.224–27
    and *Chi Gung,* 2.308, 309
    correction, mode of, 2.65–66, 199,
        219, 262–65
    as education, 2.212, 251–52, 253–54,
        266–67, 359
    energy basis of, 2.211, 212
    and internalizing medicine,
        2.409–10
    overview, 2.248–67, **255–63** *passim*
    Reich, independent of, 2.422
    resource for, 2.518
    and Rolfing, 2.271–72, 327
    and synthesis, 1.440; 2.207, 208
    vision, effect on, 2.243

Feldenkrais, Moshe, 1.476, 478; 2.93,
    173, 210, 212, 224–27, 248–67,
    333
feng shui, 1.250–51, **251,** 349, 356
Fenollosa, Ernest Francisco, 1.515
Ferenczi, Sandor, 1.415
fetishism, 1.395
Fiji Islands, medicine of, 1.163, 193,
    195, 295
Filipino medicine, 1.174
Finland, medicine of, 1.154
Fiore, Edith, 2.48
Firewalking Institute, 1.162
flavors *see* taste in medicine
Flexner Report, 1.213
Fludd, Robert, 1.240
Food and Drug Administration
    (FDA), 1.xxx, 461, 463–64
foods *see* diet
Foucault, Michel, 1.45–46
France and aromatherapy, 2.425
Frantzis, Bruce Kumar
    back injury of, 2.313
    and *Chi Gung*
        dissemination of, 1.366–67
        energy practice of, 2.88–89, 305,
          306–07, 312
        Feldenkrais Method,
          comparing, 2.251
        internal awareness, 1.360, 361,
          363
        physicality of, 1.364
        somatic systems, comparing,
          2.303–04
        as teacher of, 1.340–41; 2.196
    resource listing, 2.518
Frazer, James, 1.112
Free Daist Communion, 1.509

Index

cultural context, 1.51–52, 67,
    134–35, 136
and desire to be well, 2.392–98,
    471–74
destiny, context of, 1.334
distinction between, primary,
    2.9–10
dreams and *see* dreams and
    dreaming
energy fields and, 2.23
ethics *see* ethics
fear and *see* fear
grooming in origin of, 1.89, 145
healing and *see* healing
independently arising techniques
    of, 1.87–90, 146, 230–32
internalizing/externalizing
    spectrum, 2.401–04, **403**
irritants as, 2.394
life context of patient, 1.120, 126
long/short term, 2.374
as metaphor for change, 2.474
multiplicity of, 1.508; 2.7, 113–14,
    351
native *see* native medicine
origins
    in epochal time, 1.91–93,
        104–05, 107, 111, 491
    matrix of nature/culture,
        1.132–36; 2.509
paradigms, esoteric sources of,
    1.506–09
reform *see* reform of health care
rival modalities, 2.367–69
self-healing intrinsic to *see* self-
    healing
social structure, as necessary
    segment of, 1.73

spirit world and *see* spirit world
systems
    complementarity of, 1.30–31;
        2.367–69, 370–71, 373, 417
    cure as true critic of, 1.30, 52,
        247, 250; 2.16–17
    no single perfect, 1.43, 111,
        2.367–70
    opposite pole gravitation of,
        2.127–28, 145–46
    as technologically limited, 1.129
    see also individual systems
and transformation, 1.41–42; 2.82
    see also position
vitalism as explaining, 1.228
wellness model, 1.341
see also alternative medicine;
    disease; health
medicine bundles, 1.101–03, **102, 104,**
    105
Medicine Eagle, Brooke, 2.251
medicine men
    and Feldenkrais Method, 2.251
    initiation of, 1.163, 209–12; 2.74
    as internally guided, 1.94–95,
        133–34
    modern conditions as disease, 1.83
    sacrifice exacted by, 1.82
    spiritual origin of diseases and,
        1.187–88
    summoning higher authorities,
        1.196, 200–201
    training of, 1.84, 89, 94–105,
        209–12
    and vision quests *see under* visions
    West resulting from dreams of, 1.8,
        107; 2.458
    see also healers; shamanism

Index

as continuing source, 1.14–15,
16–17; 2.129
equated to contemporary tribal,
1.108–10
as future, 1.116
and native science, 1.104–07
science of, trephination as, 1.165
technology of, 1.107
Preparation of New Butter, 1.328
present, living in the, 1.518–19, 522;
2.84–85
primal scream therapy, 1.443; 2.65
primates and human society, 1.70–71,
77, 145
primitive societies *see* indigenous
societies
Principles of Light and Color (Babbitt),
2.430
Prison Integrated Health Program,
2.481–84, 523
prisons
Chi Gung taught in, 2.504–05
and culture, 2.105
and health care reform, 2.500, 503,
504–05
hospitals compared to, 1.68–69
somatics, use of in, 2.481–84
probability *see* chance
profitability, 1.28, 54–55
progressivism, 1.91, 379–82
projection of disease *see* pathology,
healers and doctors creating
proof
of alternative medicines, 1.250,
256–57, 490; 2.6
of cure, 2.6, 17–18, 28–29
prostitution as healing, 2.95–96
Prozac, 1.59

psyche *see* archetypes; body;
emotions; mind; mind/body
psychic surgery, 1.174; 2.16, 27–30
psychological medicine
addiction to, 2.389–92
allopathy, converted to, 1.279
behavior modification of, 1.409,
410, 411–12
character and *see* character
chemical reductionism of, 1.58–61,
411
Chinese practices and, 1.345–47,
363, 383–84
chiropractic/osteopathy and, 2.149,
161
craniosacral therapy and, 2.164,
180–82
definition of, 1.379, 409
failure of, 1.58–61, 407–15, 425–31
passim, 433–34; 2.82, 98
influence of *see under* Freud,
Sigmund
nonverbal therapies, compared,
2.154–55, 323
as outside patient's universe, 1.43
psychospiritual transformation vs.,
2.323
as remedy for somatic inflation,
2.180–82, 323
resistance *see* resistance
sanity, tests of legal, 1.69
schools of
additional, 1.412–13
Freudian *see* Freud, Sigmund
Gestalt, 1.412–13, 420, 450,
480; 2.190, 194, 280
pre-Freudian, 1.380, 383, 419–20
Jungian *see* Jung, Carl

Index

Index